Frontiers in the Economics
of Aging

A National Bureau
of Economic Research
Project Report

Frontiers in the Economics of Aging

Edited by David A. Wise

The University of Chicago Press

Chicago and London

DAVID A. WISE is the John F. Stambaugh Professor of Political Economy
at the John F. Kennedy School of Government, Harvard University, and
the director for Health and Retirement Programs at the National Bureau
of Economic Research.

The University of Chicago Press, Chicago 60637
The University of Chicago Press, Ltd., London
© 1998 by the National Bureau of Economic Research
All rights reserved. Published 1998
Printed in the United States of America
07 06 05 04 03 02 01 00 99 98   1 2 3 4 5
ISBN: 0-226-90304-4 (cloth)

Library of Congress Cataloging-in-Publication Data

Frontiers in the economics of aging / edited by David A. Wise.
        p.   cm. — (A National Bureau of Economic Research project
    report)
    Papers presented at a conference held at Carefree, Ariz. in April
1997.
    Includes bibliographical references and index.
    ISBN 0-226-90304-4 (cloth : alk. paper)
    1. Aged—United States—Economic conditions—Congresses.
2. Aging—Economic aspects—United States—Congresses.   3. Retirement—Economic aspects—United States—Congresses.   I. Wise,
David A.   II. Series.
HQ1064.U5F78 1998
305.26—dc21   98-11612
                                                               CIP

Relation of the Directors to the
Work and Publications of the
National Bureau of Economic Research

1. The object of the National Bureau of Economic Research is to ascertain and to present to the public important economic facts and their interpretation in a scientific and impartial manner. The Board of Directors is charged with the responsibility of ensuring that the work of the National Bureau is carried on in strict conformity with this object.

2. The President of the National Bureau shall submit to the Board of Directors, or to its Executive Committee, for their formal adoption all specific proposals for research to be instituted.

3. No research report shall be published by the National Bureau until the President has sent each member of the Board a notice that a manuscript is recommended for publication and that in the President's opinion it is suitable for publication in accordance with the principles of the National Bureau. Such notification will include an abstract or summary of the manuscript's content and a response form for use by those Directors who desire a copy of the manuscript for review. Each manuscript shall contain a summary drawing attention to the nature and treatment of the problem studied, the character of the data and their utilization in the report, and the main conclusions reached.

4. For each manuscript so submitted, a special committee of the Directors (including Directors Emeriti) shall be appointed by majority agreement of the President and Vice Presidents (or by the Executive Committee in case of inability to decide on the part of the President and Vice Presidents), consisting of three Directors selected as nearly as may be one from each general division of the Board. The names of the special manuscript committee shall be stated to each Director when notice of the proposed publication is submitted to him. It shall be the duty of each member of the special manuscript committee to read the manuscript. If each member of the manuscript committee signifies his approval within thirty days of the transmittal of the manuscript, the report may be published. If at the end of that period any member of the manuscript committee withholds his approval, the President shall then notify each member of the Board, requesting approval or disapproval of publication, and thirty days additional shall be granted for this purpose. The manuscript shall then not be published unless at least a majority of the entire Board who shall have voted on the proposal within the time fixed for the receipt of votes shall have approved.

5. No manuscript may be published, though approved by each member of the special manuscript committee, until forty-five days have elapsed from the transmittal of the report in manuscript form. The interval is allowed for the receipt of any memorandum of dissent or reservation, together with a brief statement of his reasons, that any member may wish to express; and such memorandum of dissent or reservation shall be published with the manuscript if he so desires. Publication does not, however, imply that each member of the Board has read the manuscript, or that either members of the Board in general or the special committee have passed on its validity in every detail.

6. Publications of the National Bureau issued for informational purposes concerning the work of the Bureau and its staff, or issued to inform the public of activities of Bureau staff, and volumes issued as a result of various conferences involving the National Bureau shall contain a specific disclaimer noting that such publication has not passed through the normal review procedures required in this resolution. The Executive Committee of the Board is charged with review of all such publications from time to time to ensure that they do not take on the character of formal research reports of the National Bureau, requiring formal Board approval.

7. Unless otherwise determined by the Board or exempted by the terms of paragraph 6, a copy of this resolution shall be printed in each National Bureau publication.

(Resolution adopted October 25, 1926, as revised through September 30, 1974)

Contents

III. METHODOLOGICAL INNOVATIONS

IV. VIEWS OF INEQUALITY

Preface

This volume consists of papers presented at a conference held at Carefree, Arizona, in April 1997. Most of the research was conducted as part of the Program on the Economics of Aging at the National Bureau of Economic Research. The majority of the work was sponsored by the U.S. Department of Health and Human Services, through National Institute on Aging grants P01-AG05842, and P20-AG12810 to the National Bureau of Economic Research. Any other funding sources are noted in individual papers.

Any opinions expressed in this volume are those of the respective authors and do not necessarily reflect the views of the National Bureau of Economic Research or the sponsoring organizations.

Introduction

David A. Wise

This is the seventh in a series of volumes on the economics of aging. The previous ones were *The Economics of Aging, Issues in the Economics of Aging, Topics in the Economics of Aging, Studies in the Economics of Aging, Advances in the Economics of Aging,* and *Inquiries in the Economics of Aging.* The papers in this volume discuss the implications of the rapid spread of personal retirement saving, discuss several aspects of health care, investigate important methodological advances in studying aging issues, and consider new aspects of inequality. The papers are summarized in this introduction, which draws heavily on the authors' own summaries.

Personal Retirement Plans

Three papers direct attention to important aspects of personal retirement saving plans: their effect on personal saving, the rapid increase in their use in recent years and future projected use, and the taxing of pension saving. In addition, using the analysis of the saving effect of individual retirement account (IRA) and 401(k) plans as a backdrop, there is an extended discussion of how personal retirement saving might be viewed from a behavioral perspective.

Their Effect on Saving

Contributions to personal retirement saving programs now exceed contributions to traditional employer-provided defined benefit and defined contributions plans. In "Personal Retirement Saving Programs and Asset Accumula-

David A. Wise is the John F. Stambaugh Professor of Political Economy at the John F. Kennedy School of Government, Harvard University, and the director for Health and Retirement Programs at the National Bureau of Economic Research.

tion: Reconciling the Evidence," James Poterba, Steven Venti, and I review the series of analyses on the saving effect of IRA and 401(k) plans that we have undertaken over the past several years and present additional results. We also give considerable attention to the analyses undertaken by others. We conclude that the weight of the evidence provides strong support for the view that contributions to these programs represent largely new saving.

A large fraction of American families reach retirement age with virtually no personal financial assets. The median level of all personal financial assets of families with heads aged 55–64 was only $8,300 in 1991; excluding IRA and 401(k) balances the median was only $3,000. Almost 20 percent of families had no financial assets at all. Other than social security and pension benefits, and illiquid housing wealth, the typical family has very limited resources to meet unforeseen expenses.

The IRA and 401(k) programs introduced in the early 1980s were intended to encourage individual saving. Although very small at the beginning of the decade, by 1989 contributions to all personal retirement saving plans exceeded contributions to traditional employer-provided pension plans. Whether these programs increase net saving can be of critical importance to future generations of older Americans and to the health of the economy in general. The issue remains an important question of economic debate. In a series of papers based on very different methods of analysis we have concluded that a large fraction of the contributions to these accounts represents new saving. Our previous research is summarized here, along with several new results.

As interest in the saving effect of these programs evolved, several other investigators also directed attention to the issue. In some instances, alternative analyses came to conclusions that differed dramatically from ours. Thus in describing our results we have tried to point out the differences between our methods and alternative approaches that have been used to address the same questions.

The key impediment to determining the saving effect of IRAs and 401(k)s is saver heterogeneity. Some people save and others do not, and the savers tend to save more in all forms. For example, families with IRAs also have more conventional savings than families without IRAs. Thus a continuing goal of our analyses has been to consider different methods of controlling for heterogeneity. The methods that could be used when each analysis was conducted were largely dependent on the available data. As new data became available we used alternative and possibly more robust methods to control for heterogeneity.

We first present our results, organized by the method used to control for heterogeneity. In each case the question is whether IRA and 401(k) contributions substitute for conventional financial asset saving. We also discuss closely related results reported by others. While early work in this area focused on the potential substitution between IRA assets and liquid financial assets, subsequent analyses considered the potential substitution between personal retirement saving plan assets and employer-provided pension assets and housing equity. Thus we also consider other margins of substitution, particularly the possibility that saving in these programs is financed by drawing down home equity. Finally, we address the divergence between our conclusions based on Survey of Consumer Finances data and the parametric analysis of the same data by Gale and Scholz (1994).

We emphasize that no single method can provide sure control for all forms of heterogeneity. Taken together, however, we believe that our analyses address the key complications presented by heterogeneity. In our view, the weight of the evidence, based on the many nonparametric approaches discussed here, provides strong support for the view that contributions to both IRA and 401(k) plans represent largely new saving. Some of the evidence is directed to the IRA program, other evidence to the 401(k) plan, and some of the evidence to both plans jointly. We believe that the evidence is strong in all cases. We have devoted particular effort to explaining why different approaches, sometimes based on the same data, have led to different conclusions. In some instances, we believe that the limitations of the methods used by others have undermined the reliability of their results.

Viewed from a Behavioral Perspective

Increasingly, economists are questioning standard analysis based on strong rationality and typical maximization assumptions. Many of the findings on IRA and 401(k) saving behavior and the saving effects of these plans are left unexplained by standard theories of saving. Thus there is considerable motivation to look more broadly for explanations of saving behavior. A realistic explanation of saving must recognize much broader economic and psychological determinants of individual saving decisions. Using the Poterba-Venti-Wise analysis as a backdrop, David Laibson in his comment considers the insights that behavioral economics bring to the discussion of personal retirement saving. He discusses four behavioral phenomena: bounded rationality, self-control problems, peer group sensitivities, and overoptimistic beliefs. He then discusses empirical strategies, suggested by the behavioral phenomena, that might be used to further our understanding of saving behavior. He finds that "most of the behavioral analysis that I have reviewed implies that tax-deferred retirement instruments will raise net national savings." After several cautionary notes, he goes on to conclude: "Nevertheless, the prospects for 401(k)s and similar tax-deferred retirement instruments seem bright. Social psychology research has identified a core set of features of successful behavioral interventions. The 401(k) seems to have been designed by someone who intuitively or formally understood those lessons."

Implications of Their Rapid Spread

About half of families now are eligible for a 401(k) plan, and the use of these plans is spreading rapidly. In "Implications of Rising Personal Retirement Saving" James Poterba, Steven Venti, and I consider the projected use of these plans and implications for the retirement saving of future retirees. We conclude that the cohort that reaches age 65 between 2025 and 2035 will have 401(k) assets that greatly exceed the personal financial assets of current retirees and that these assets are likely to exceed their social security assets, perhaps by a great deal.

Contributions to IRAs grew rapidly until 1986, when $38 billion was contributed to these accounts. The Tax Reform Act of 1986 curtailed this program, and by 1990 contributions had fallen to only $10 billion. They were only $8 billion in 1994. On the other hand, the 401(k) plan has grown unimpeded since 1982. Now contributions to the 401(k) plan alone are greater than contributions to traditional employer-provided defined benefit and defined contribution plans combined. In 1993, 401(k) plan contributions exceeded $69 billion. Approximately 45 to 50 percent of employees were eligible for 401(k) plans in that year, and over 70 percent of those who were eligible to contribute did in fact make contributions.

The increase in personal retirement saving can have important implications for the accumulation of retirement saving for future generations of retirees. Now, a large fraction of families approach retirement with virtually no personal financial asset saving. The median of personal financial assets of Health and Retirement Survey (HRS) families—whose heads were ages 51–61 in 1992—was approximately $7,000. This includes all financial assets held outside IRAs, 401(k)s, and related retirement saving accounts. Perhaps half of all families rely almost exclusively on social security benefits for support in retirement. The spread of 401(k) plans in particular could change this picture substantially. In this paper we simulate the 401(k) assets of future generations of retirees and compare these assets with the social security and other assets of the households who are approaching retirement now.

Our goal is to project 401(k) assets of households who will retire 35 or 40 years from now. We direct attention in particular to the cohort that was age 33 in 1993, and will be age 65 in 2025. We compare the projected 401(k) assets of this cohort to the assets of the HRS respondents. We first trace backward to obtain approximate lifetime earnings histories of the HRS respondents. Lifetime earnings are grouped into 10 deciles, assuming that over their careers household earnings were in the same decile. Contributions to 401(k) plans are projected for each lifetime earnings decile. Thus we are able to ask what level of 401(k) assets such families would have accumulated, in 1992 dollars, had they had the same earnings histories as the HRS respondents but different amounts of contributions to 401(k) plans. We base the projections on the past growth in 401(k) participation rates and on the fraction of earnings contributed to the plans. The growth in participation since their inception, however, has been enormous and simple projections—based on recent increases in participation—are not very meaningful. Therefore, we make what we believe to be plausible inferences about future participation.

We have projected the accumulation of 401(k) assets at retirement for the cohort that was age 25 in 1984 and the cohort that was age 15 in 1984. The cohort 25 projections are based on what we hope are plausible assumptions about future 401(k) participation rates. Indeed, our intention is that these projections be conservative and thus likely to underestimate realized contributions. The cohort 15 projections are further from historical rates but we hope are also based on plausible assumptions about potential future participation. For comparison, we have also made projections assuming universal 401(k) coverage.

In each case, the accumulation of 401(k) assets is large compared to current wealth at retirement. Because a large fraction of current retirees depend almost entirely on social security benefits for support in retirement, we have compared future 401(k) assets to social security wealth. Our cohort 25 projections suggest that when this cohort reaches retirement age—they will be age 65 in 2025—their average 401(k) assets are likely to exceed their average social security assets. But the projections also suggest that relative to social security wealth, 401(k) assets will vary a great deal with lifetime earnings. While this is surely true, we are uncertain about the exact magnitude of the variation by earnings decile. The projections suggest that the lowest earnings decile may have very little in 401(k) assets. But for families with lifetime earnings above the lowest two or three deciles, 401(k) assets are likely to be a substantial fraction of social security wealth. For families with lifetime earnings above the median, 401(k) assets could exceed social security wealth, and this would almost surely be true for families in the top four earnings deciles.

Universal 401(k) participation would likely yield 401(k) assets at retirement greater than social security wealth for all but the lowest lifetime earnings decile, and possibly for the lowest decile as well. The intermediate cohort 15 projections yield 401(k) accumulations that could represent a substantial fraction of social security wealth for lifetime earnings histories as low as the 2d decile.

Thus we believe that 401(k) assets will almost surely be an important component of the retirement wealth of future generations of retirees and could be the dominant component for a large fraction of them.

The Taxing of Retirement Saving

In "The Taxation of Pensions: A Shelter Can Become a Trap" John Shoven and I consider the greatly increased tax burden imposed on pension saving since 1982. In particular, we address the implications of the excess distribution and excess accumulation taxes that were introduced virtually unnoticed in 1986 legislation. We also consider the important implications of full estate tax imposed on pension assets, which before 1982 were not subject to estate taxes at all. We conclude that these taxes can severely limit the advantage of personal retirement saving and pension assets that pass through an estate can be virtually confiscated by tax rate that are often as high as 95 percent or more. Ironically, the excess distribution and the excess accumulation taxes were eliminated as part of the Tax Relief Act of July 1997, we believe in no small measure due to the attention that our analysis brought to this issue.

The recent legislation that raised the minimum wage was accompanied by the Small Business Job Protection Act of 1996, which, among other things, temporarily (for years 1997–99) suspends the 15 percent excise tax on "excess distributions" from qualified pension plans. Surely, few people know about the excise tax in the first place, let alone its suspension. In fact, while people are keenly aware that pensions allow them to save before-tax dollars and compound their investment returns without current taxation, it is our impression that very few people know how pension assets are taxed on withdrawal or on the death of the owner of the pension. In this paper we present a comprehensive examination of the taxation of pensions, with particular emphasis on large pension accumulations. The analysis answers a number of questions: (1) How do the excess distribution excise tax and its companion excess accumulation excise tax work? How do these taxes interact with the personal income tax systems and the estate tax? (2) Should only high-income individuals be concerned with these taxes or might they be imposed on people with relatively modest incomes? (3) Are pension plans still attractive saving vehicles once these excise taxes are applicable? For example, should someone whose base pension plan is likely to trigger either the excess distribution tax or the excess accumulation tax participate in a supplemental 401(k) plan? (4) Are pensions equally advantageous for stock investments and bond investments? If not, which assets should be held inside a pension plan and which should be held outside the plan? (5) Does it always make sense to delay distributions from pension plans as long as possible, thereby maximizing the tax deferral advantage that they offer? (6) How are pension accumulations treated when they are part of an estate? We focus on these microeconomic issues without discussing the social desirability of current tax policy. However, we should acknowledge at the outset that we see little economic merit in a penalty excise tax applying to people who save "too much" through the pension system. Most observers of the U.S. economy agree that the country's saving rate is too low. Since we know that savers only capture a fraction of the social return on their investments, it is unclear why the biggest savers in the economy should be penalized.

The Small Business Job Protection Act of 1996 is just the latest in a series of bills over the past 15 years that has changed the way pensions are taxed. To illustrate how radically the rules have changed, we consider four individuals with exactly the same wealth (and composition of wealth) at the time of their deaths, each of whom died at age 70. They differ only in the date of death—1982, 1984, 1988, or 1996. The estates, all valued at $1.9 million in 1996 dollars, are composed of $600,000 in nonpension assets including a house, $1.2 million in a defined contribution pension plan, and $100,000 in a supplemental plan such as an IRA or a Keogh plan. The estates of these individuals faced radically different tax laws. One important difference is that before 1983 pension accumulations were completely exempt from the estate tax. The result is that in 1982 the heir was able to consume more than 60 percent of the value of the inherited supplemental pension plan; the combined tax rate was less than 40 percent. In contrast, by 1996—because of the estate tax and the excess accumulation tax in particular—the heir could spend less than 15 percent of the value of the inherited supplemental plan. This case is far from extreme. We describe cases in which the total marginal tax rate on assets in qualified pension plans passing through an estate ranges from 92 to 96.5 percent. The highest such rate we have seen exceeds 99 percent. Thus we believe that any pension saving strategy adopted more than a few years ago needs to be reviewed, given how drastically the rules have changed. And, because large pension accumulations are taxed so heavily when they pass through an estate, withdrawing pension assets before death, if at all possible, needs to be considered.

The excess distribution tax and the excess accumulation tax were included in the Tax Reform Act of 1986 to prevent people from taking advantage of the favorable tax treatment of pensions to amass wealth beyond what is thought to be reasonably necessary for a comfortable retirement. We believe that the wisdom of this policy is open to question. People who increase saving because of the tax shelter opportunity offered by pension plans, or for other reasons like the payroll deduction feature of many pension plans, do not reduce the resources available to the rest of the population. In fact, individual savers reap only a portion of the social return of the incremental capital. If the extra pension saving results in extra capital for the economy, then this extra capital pays corporation income taxes and the pension saver ultimately pays personal income taxes, which improves the overall budget picture for everyone in the economy. The social return to the capital significantly exceeds the private return received by the pension saver.

Our analysis has led to several striking results:

- The tax rates faced by pensions deemed "too large" can be extraordinarily high. The marginal rate on distributions over $155,000 can be roughly 61.5 percent. The effective marginal tax rate faced by large pension accumulations passing through an estate can dwarf this rate, however, reaching 92 to 96.5 percent.

- These high tax rates, which include the excess distribution and the excess accumulation taxes, can be faced by savers who do not have extraordinarily high incomes. The "success tax" is not limited to the rich but rather primarily affects lifetime savers. For example, someone who works between ages 25 and 70, makes $40,000 at age 50, and contributes 10 percent to a pension plan invested in the S&P 500 will likely be penalized by the success tax for overusing the pension provisions.

- The advantage of pensions relative to conventional saving is greatly reduced and in many cases eliminated once accumulations exceed the amounts that will trigger the success tax. Even in cases where additional pension saving still provides more resources in retirement than conventional saving, when the plan owner dies, the heirs get less than they would have if the saving had been done outside of a pension plan.

- The advantage of pension saving is reduced by the availability of tax-advantaged investments outside of pension plans. Examples are tax-free municipal bonds and tax-efficient low-dividend stock portfolios.

- Not only is there little, if any, incentive to continue to save via pensions once the excess distribution and excess accumulation taxes become applicable, there is a strong incentive to withdraw money while living rather than risk the nearly confiscatory tax rates faced by pension assets transferred through estates. This means that there is an incentive to consume more in retirement than would otherwise be the case.

- Individuals can realize significant efficiency gains by allocating their investments appropriately between pension accounts and outside holdings. Simply locating assets in their most advantageous environment could improve the net proceeds of saving by almost 25 percent.

Now that it is recognized that pensions are the primary vehicle for personal saving in the economy, we emphasize that a careful reconsideration of the legislation of the early and mid-1980s is called for. Once the excess distribution and excess accumulation taxes are understood, we believe these taxes are likely to become quite effective at discouraging pension saving and hence will reduce economic welfare in an economy that surely has lower than optimal saving now.

Health: Spending Patterns and Implications and Effect on Work

A Forty-Year Perspective

The rising cost of health care has become an important public issue in almost all developed countries. In "The Medical Costs of the Young and Old: A Forty-Year Perspective" David Cutler and Ellen Meara investigate the nature of the rise in health care costs in the United States and the gains in health outcomes associated with this spending. They find that, just as medical spending at a point in time is concentrated among high-cost users, spending growth has also been concentrated among the high-cost users. They find further that the growth in expenditures for high-cost users has been accompanied by gains in health outcomes for these users.

It is widely known that medical costs have increased over time. In the United States, as in most of the developed world, medical spending growth has exceeded income growth by several percentage points per year for three decades or longer. In country after country, the cost of medical care has become a major public sector issue.

But much less is known about what medical spending is buying us. Is medical spending valuable or wasteful? Should we want to limit total spending or increase it? The answer to this question is by no means clear. On the one hand is voluminous evidence that medical spending conveys great value. Randomized clinical trials, for example, routinely document the benefits of new pharmaceuticals and medical devices. Cutler and Meara suggest that most people would prefer today's medical system to the medical system of 30 years ago, even given the much higher cost of medical care today. This suggests that people are on net better off because of the additional medical care spending than they would be without it.

On the other hand is a great sense that medical care often brings little in the way of health benefit. Nearly one-third of Medicare spending occurs in the last six months of life, which has been interpreted as evidence that a lot of medical care is wasted on those who will in any case not survive. Other studies such as the RAND Health Insurance Experiment show that putting people in less generous insurance policies reduces their spending on medical services but does not affect their health. And direct estimates of the value of medical care typically find that, at the margin, a substantial amount of medical care has little or no health benefit.

Cutler and Meara try to understand why medical care has become so expensive over time and what has been its value to society. They focus particularly on medical spending by age. Their analysis is based on periodic surveys of national health expenditures conducted in 1953, 1963, 1970, 1977, and 1987.

Their analysis of age-based spending documents two conclusions. First, there has been a dramatic change in the distribution of medical spending over time. While spending on medical care has increased for all people, it has increased disproportionately for the very young and the old. Over the 24-year period from 1963 through 1987, per person spending on infants increased by 10 percent per year, and per person spending on the elderly increased by 8 percent per year, compared to only 4.7 percent per year for the "middle-aged." The share of medical care spending for infants and the elderly doubled from 15 to over 30 percent.

The authors further show that essentially all of the disproportionate growth of spending for the very young and the old is accounted for by high-cost users within those groups. For infants, 90 percent of the excess spending increase over the middle-aged is accounted for by the top 10 percent of the spending distribution. For the elderly, the equivalent share is 70 percent. Thus, the authors emphasize, to understand the concentration of medical spending by age, we need to understand the concentration of spending among high-cost users.

Cutler and Meara also consider who the high-cost users of medical care are. They show that a substantial amount of high-cost medical use is associated with the increasing technological capability of medicine. Among infants, high-cost users are premature babies with substantial respiratory or other acute conditions. For the elderly, high-cost users are generally patients with severe cardiovascular problems or cancer. For both infants and the elderly, the capacity to devote many more resources to the most pressing cases has increased over time.

Finally, they consider how health outcomes for premature infants and the sick elderly have changed over time. They find substantial health improvements in most of the categories of high-cost medical care. Infant mortality among very low birth weight infants has fallen substantially at exactly the time when the cost of these infants has risen most rapidly. And mortality improvements among the elderly have been especially prominent in cardiovascular care, where spending increases have been most dramatic. The authors emphasize that their analysis is not causal: "We do not have any direct link between the technologies we discuss . . . and the outcomes we analyze." They conclude, however, that their results suggest such a link is plausible.

End-of-Life Expenditures

Perhaps a quarter of Medicare expenditures each year are for the care of recipients who die in that year. This has led some to conclude that much of end-of-life expenditure must be wasteful. But in their paper "Diagnosis and Medicare Expenditures at the End of Life" Alan Garber, Thomas MaCurdy, and Mark McClellan find that characteristics of high-cost users who die are very similar to those of like patients who live. Thus they conclude that it will be difficult to formulate policies that limit expenditures for persons who will die without at the same time limiting care for those who may live.

Expenditures for health care at the end of life have been the object of considerable policy interest. To many observers, aggressive health care administered shortly before death is wasteful, at least in retrospect, and there is no doubt that elderly Americans use health care heavily before they die. In 1990, the 6.6 percent of Medicare recipients who died accounted for 22 percent of program expenditures. Some question the benefits of such care, especially because severe morbidity and disability may compromise any years of life potentially gained from such treatments in the very old. The increasing use at advanced ages of costly and aggressive health interventions, whose impact on both the quality and length of life is often unknown, exacerbates these concerns. For example, the use of radical prostatectomy for invasive prostate cancer increased threefold between 1983 and 1989, and the rate at which both new and old major operations are performed in the elderly increased dramatically from 1972 to 1981 and from 1984 to 1991.

Nonetheless, the policy significance of end-of-life care is uncertain. Although they consume a large share of health dollars, patients nearing death are not the main source of large Medicare payments. Most high-cost elderly patients are survivors, not decedents. In 1990, for example, 8 percent of Medicare enrollees with over $10,000 in Medicare costs accounted for 65 percent of all Medicare expenditures. Even if every enrollee who died that year generated more than $10,000 in payments, they could have only been responsible for at most one-third of this total. In addition, some studies suggest that the elderly who are most likely to die are not responsible for the greatest expenditures.

An even more important limitation of an exclusive focus on end-of-life expenditures is its implicitly retrospective nature. If health care providers knew ex ante which patients would die despite their interventions, expenditures on dying patients could potentially be reduced. Yet often it is impossible, even with detailed clinical records, to predict *individual* patient mortality with sufficient specificity to influence medical decision making. Furthermore, specific policies designed to reduce end-of-life expenditures, such as advance directives and "do not resuscitate" orders, seem to have had only a modest impact on overall expenditures.

Although there is growing disenchantment with policies designed to identify and avert "futile care" at the individual patient level, the consequences of population-level policies merit further exploration. Little is known about the impact on the cost and outcomes of elderly populations with major illnesses of policies that would lead to a generally more parsimonious approach to health care delivery. Would efforts designed to limit major operations, aggressive diagnostic approaches, or care delivered in intensive care units lead to an increase in mortality rates, health complications, and other adverse outcomes in the populations with major illness? Would substantial cost savings result from associated reductions in technology use?

As a first step toward addressing these questions, Garber et al. explore the basic characteristics of Medicare recipients during the time approaching their deaths. What characteristics of patients are associated with high-cost care and high probability of death? Can these characteristics be used to identify individuals and populations with major illnesses prospectively, to guide policies on the use of intensive treatments? What is the distribution of costs and survival across high-risk illnesses, and across individuals with a given illness, and how are they correlated? They report the results of analyses of expenditures patterns for Medicare decedents and the associated Medicare expenditures.

Like previous investigators, the authors find that Medicare expenditures for decedents decline with advancing age. Overall, their results confirm that decedents have disproportionately high Medicare expenses. But a comparison with high-cost users suggests that many of the characteristics of decedents are similar to those of high-cost Medicare enrollees who do not die during a given period. The authors conclude that, at least based on the information available in Medicare claims files, it will be difficult to formulate policies to limit expenditures for individuals in the last year of life without simultaneously limiting health care delivered to sick Medicare recipients who have the potential to survive.

Correlation of Expenditures within Families

Work reported in the previous volume on the economics of aging concluded that the potential persistence over time in individual medical expenditures does not critically limit the feasibility of medical saving accounts, in conjunction with catastrophic health insurance, as a means of helping to control health care costs efficiently (Eichner, McClellan, and Wise 1998). The problem posed by persistence could, however, be worse to the extent that expenditures by family members are correlated, so that persistent expenditures by one member tend to be accompanied by persistent expenditures by other family members as well. In his paper "The Impact of Intrafamily Correlations on the Viability of Catastrophic Insurance" Matthew Eichner concludes that such correlation is not sufficient to importantly limit the feasibility of medical saving accounts.

This paper explores the relationship between health care expenditures of spouses. If expenditures are due largely to random shocks, the household's medical expenditures are smoothed by two or more family members each drawing from the distribution. On the other hand, if the shocks are positively correlated, the potential exists for negative wealth shocks that are greater than those that would be predicted based on studies of the persistence of individual medical expenditures over time. Under traditional systems of insurance, with relatively low coinsurance levels, the consequences of any putative positive correlation across family members in expenditures are relatively mild. But under the sort of high-deductible insurance that is currently attracting interest from the policy community, the wealth and utility effects may be appreciable. And under systems that include both high-deductible insurance and medical saving accounts, intrafamily correlations might dramatically change the accumulation of wealth in such accounts over a working lifetime.

Matthew Eichner seeks to determine the reasons for intrafamily correlations and then to determine where in the distribution of expenditures the correlations appear to be strongest. The empirical work in this paper—based on data from two Fortune 500 firms—suggests that, while correlation of expenditures among married partners is large at the low end of the expenditure distribution, the relation diminishes appreciably in the upper ranges. For example, Eichner estimates a correlation for positive expenditures of 0.41 for firm 1 and 0.69 for firm 2. But the correlations in expenditures above $4,000 are only 0.13 and 0.14, respectively. Thus the correlations are low in the ranges relevant for a discussion of catastrophic health insurance schemes. His analysis therefore suggests that intrafamily correlation in expenditures does not appreciably increase persistence in expenditures made toward a family insurance plan and thus does not appreciably affect the feasibility of medical saving account insurance schemes.

Health Shocks and Labor Supply

It has long been understood that persons in poor health are more likely than otherwise similar persons in better health to leave the labor force. The effect of specific health shocks, however, has not been analyzed. Mark McClellan, in "Health Events, Health Insurance, and Labor Supply: Evidence from the Health and Retirement Survey," analyzes the effect on labor supply of a variety of specific health events, many of which have very large consequences for labor supply.

The economic consequences of health problems are reported to be enormous. For example, many investigators have concluded that the cost to society of common health problems such as heart disease, diabetes, and cancer is many billions of dollars per year in terms of lost work productivity, intensive medical treatments, and additional supportive care. However, McClellan points out that estimates have several important limitations. Few data sets have incorporated detailed information on health problems and economic circumstances such as retirement. Consequently, most existing studies have had to combine data from different sources, possibly missing important correlations between variables such as insurance availability and the occurrence of health problems.

McClellan uses the first two waves of the HRS to provide insights into how changes in health status affect two issues of considerable policy interest: health insurance coverage and labor supply for middle-aged Americans. His analysis of new health events in older Americans in the HRS suggests several conclusions about the effects of health problems. First, new health events of all types are more prevalent in individuals with lower education, income, and wealth and are more prevalent in individuals with other prior health conditions as well. These relationships persist after adjusting for age. Second, health events may be quite heterogeneous in nature, and thus in their consequences for functional status and expectations about future functional status, consumption, and survival. Only a minority of new health events lead to substantial short-term functional impairments, even for major events such as heart attacks and strokes. Old health problems (or health problems for which information was not obtained in the HRS) are also important in explaining functional declines.

Third, different types of health events have quite different consequences for health insurance coverage and labor supply. Major health events have particularly large effects on retirement decisions, and these effects go well beyond the consequences of the events for functional status. For example, males with major events associated with major functional status declines leave the labor force at rates over 40 percentage points higher than males with major functional status declines in the absence of new health events. New chronic health problems have milder, though significant, effects on increasing rates of labor force exit beyond their association with functional declines alone. In contrast, health problems that are unlikely to have long-term consequences for health (accidents) are not associated with additional labor force departures. Though these health events have enormous significance for labor force departure rates, they have only modest impact on individuals' self-reported retirement status, especially for males in couples and single females. Examining the subsequent labor supply of individuals with these events is thus a question of considerable importance for understanding the long-term impact of health events.

In conjunction with their effects on labor supply, health events also have substantial effects on health insurance coverage, especially for males. Health events are associated with small increases in the probability of having health insurance, despite the fact that they tend to lead to reductions in private insurance coverage, particularly for males and for individuals without retiree insurance coverage. These reductions in private insurance coverage are offset by increased coverage through government insurance programs, primarily Medicare, as a result of qualification through the disability insurance system. These insurance changes are more related to the actual occurrence of disability than the labor supply changes, though major health events do lead to more switches to government insurance regardless of functional status change.

Methodological Innovations

Measuring Household Consumption and Saving

An important advance in the HRS is the use of bracketing methods to measure household assets, consumption, income, and other values. If when asked, for example, "How much money do you have in bank savings accounts?" the respondent gives a dollar value, the information is clear. But a large fraction of respondents—in some instances as many as 40 percent or more—give no answer or say they do not know. In the HRS, these respondents are pressed further by asking whether the amount is, for example, less than $5,000. If the response is no, the respondent is asked, for example, whether it is between $5,000 and $20,000. And so forth. The sequence is referred to as "unfolding brackets." Following a dollar value question with unfolding bracket questions very substantially reduces the nonresponse rate, perhaps reducing nonresponse from 40 percent to only a few percent in some instances. But the brackets also present a problem called "anchoring"—that is, to the interval at which the sequence of bracket questions starts. In "Consumption and Savings Balances of the Elderly: Experimental Evidence on Survey Response Bias," Michael Hurd, Daniel McFadden, Harish Chand, Li Gan, Angela Merrill, and Michael Roberts consider the effect of anchoring on estimated consumption and saving. They find that variation in bracket starting values can change estimated values enormously—in some examples by as much as 100 percent.

The authors emphasize that a prerequisite for understanding the economic behavior of the elderly, and the impacts of public policy on their health and well-being, is accurate data on key economic variables such as income, consumption, and assets, as well as on expectations regarding future economic and demographic events such as major health costs, disabilities, and death. Standard practice is to elicit such information in economic surveys, relying on respondents' statements regarding the variables in question. The authors emphasize, however, that economic studies are often too sanguine about the reliability of subjects' statements regarding objective economic data. They focus on biases induced by anchoring to prompts presented by questions on economic variables and show that anchoring bias is a significant issue in consumption and savings variables of key interest for study of the elderly.

Anchoring describes a family of effects observed in many psychological studies of beliefs about uncertain quantities. A psychological explanation for the phenomenon of anchoring is that a prompt creates in the subject's mind, at least temporarily, the possibility that the uncertain quantity could be either above or below the prompt. This could result from classical psychophysical discrimination errors, or from a cognitive process in which the subject treats the question as a problem-solving task and seeks an appropriate framework for "constructing" a correct solution, utilizing the prompt as a cue. Both formal and informal education train individuals to use problem-solving protocols in which responses to questions are based not only on substantive knowledge but also on contextual cues as to what a correct response might be. Consequently, it should be no surprise if subjects apply these protocols in forming survey responses.

In psychological experiments, anchoring is found even when the gate amount is explicitly random, suggesting that there is more to anchoring than "rational" problem solving. This could happen because subjects are subrational, making cognitive errors and processing information inconsistently, or because they are "superrational," going beyond the substantive question to "model" the mind of the questioner and form superstitious beliefs about the behavior of nature.

The study uses an experimental module in a panel of the survey of Asset and Health Dynamics among the oldest old to establish that anchoring can cause significant biases in unfolding bracket questions on quantitative economic variables. In the case of savings, variation in starting values for unfolding brackets from $5,000 to $200,000 induces a 100 percent difference in estimated median savings. The anchoring is even stronger for consumption: increasing the starting value for unfolding brackets from $500 to $5,000 induces nearly a doubling of estimated median consumption.

The authors find that a simple model in which each gate presented to the subject can induce discrimination errors is successful in explaining much of these anchoring effects. Thus variation in unfolding bracket gates, in tandem with the discrimination model or an alternative model of anchoring, promises to be effective in identifying the effects of anchoring and in undoing most of these effects. The authors recommend that survey researchers who wish to use unfolding bracket elicitations adopt experimental variations in their designs that permit identification and correction of anchoring biases and that they exercise caution in imputing economic variables based on stated brackets.

Accounting for Uncertainty in Social Security Forecasts

Social security forecasts of reserve fund balances typically provide median, high, and low forecasts. Most assessments of the financial status of the fund are based on the median forecasts and tend to ignore the high and low estimates. But even these high and low estimates provide a grossly inadequate picture of the true uncertainty faced by the system. In their paper "Stochastic Forecasts for Social Security" Ronald Lee and Shripad Tuljapurkar begin to develop a method that does provide a realistic picture of the uncertainty inherent in projections of fund reserves.

Population aging is projected to have a major impact on the federal budget in the next century, in part through its effects on health costs through Medicare and Medicaid, and in part through its effect on the retirement system. Despite the inevitability of the aging of the baby boom, and its dramatic effect on the old age dependency ratio, a great deal of uncertainty remains about the extent of future population aging. On the one hand, we do not know how rapidly mortality will decline and how long people will be living, and on the other hand, we do not know what fertility will be, and therefore we do not know how large the labor force will be in the future. Immigration adds another layer of uncertainty, but it is not considered in this paper. In addition to these demographic sources of uncertainty, there are economic variables with important effects on the future finances of the social security system, notably the rate of growth of productivity or real wages and the level of the real interest rate. Lee and Tuljapurkar emphasize that rational and foresightful planning for the next century must somehow take into account not just our best guesses about the future but also our best assessments of the degree of certainty about the future.

Currently, scenario-based forecasts are in virtually universal use. In these, the forecaster chooses, for each variable, a medium or best-guess trajectory, complemented by high and low trajectories. Then one trajectory for each variable is grouped with others in a scenario, or collection of trajectories. These scenarios may, in turn, be described as "high," "medium," or "low," or by other terms such as "optimistic" and "pessimistic." A high scenario would typically be based on a high trajectory for fertility and migration and a low trajectory for mortality; this combination would yield high population growth. Alternatively, a low-cost scenario for social security would bundle together high fertility and migration with high, rather than low, mortality; this scenario would generate the lowest old age dependency ratio. For the social security forecast, this low-cost demographic scenario would then be combined with high trajectories for productivity growth and (perhaps) for interest rates. The authors emphasize that this approach provides a very inadequate appreciation of the true uncertainty faced by the social security system.

In this paper, the authors build on earlier work to develop stochastic forecasts of the social security reserve fund. Their forecasts are based on stochastic models for fertility, mortality, productivity growth, and interest rates, which are fitted on historical data at the same time that they are constrained (except for mortality) to conform in long-run expected value to the middle assumptions of the Social Security Administration (SSA). The four factors the authors have modeled have the largest effect on the SSA forecast for 2070. Through analysis of the SSA projections, they find that the four variables they treat as stochastic account for 76 percent of the width of the SSA low-cost–high-cost range in 2070, and 63 and 70 percent in 2020 and 2045, respectively.

The authors emphasize that they are still at early stages of digesting their stochastic forecasts of the finances of the social security system and are still exploring new ways in which these forecasts and experiments might be useful and informative. Perhaps, they say, the most promising use is to test the consequences of a range of strategies for dealing with the uncertainty about the system's finances. Is it better to wait and see, adjusting policy continuously as we gain information? Or is it better to accumulate large reserves early on, to provide a buffer against unlikely but possible transitory insults to the system? Or should policy simply be set to deal reasonably with the mean trajectory, ignoring the uncertainty?

Views of Inequality

Health Inequality over the Life Cycle

In earlier work Angus Deaton and Christina Paxson documented that in several developed and developing countries inequality in income, consumption, and earnings increase with age. They now ask whether this phenomenon is true of other individual attributes as well. In "Health, Income, and Inequality over the Life Cycle" they begin to explore the relationship between age and inequality in health status. They find substantial evidence that, indeed, measures of health status become more widely dispersed within any given birth cohort as that cohort ages.

In their previous work, Deaton and Paxson used data from the United States, Great Britain, Taiwan, and Thailand to document that inequality increases within cohorts with age for consumption, income, and earnings. In this paper, they extend the analysis to two health-relevant measures, the body-mass index (BMI) and self-reported health status (SRHS). They use data on more than 500,000 adults in the United States to track birth cohorts over time and to document the evolution of the two measures with age, looking at both cohort means and within-cohort dispersion. They also consider the life cycle profile of dispersion in income and health jointly, presenting evidence separately for men and women, and for blacks and whites.

Their original work on consumption and income inequality was motivated by the prediction of the standard theory of intertemporal choice that within-cohort inequality in consumption and income should increase with cohort age, at least up to the date of retirement. Although the theory has no immediate extension to processes other than income and consumption, the authors point out that there are a number of reasons to extend the analysis to health status.

First, they wish to investigate the generality of the proposition that dispersion increases with age. For the four countries where they looked earlier, it is true of income, consumption, and earnings. They are now curious as to whether the proposition is true for other state variables, such as weight, BMI, SRHS, dexterity, intelligence, or ability to complete specified tasks.

Second, while health status is interesting as an example, it is also important in its own right. Inequalities in income and consumption are of concern because they are important components of welfare. But as we move from a narrow, economic measure of well-being toward broader definitions, health status has the most immediate claim on our attention. Nor is health status independent of economic status. Access to health care is expensive in the United States, so that health shocks can have a direct effect on wealth. Independent of this effect, there is a well-documented but poorly understood relationship linking socioeconomic status to a wide range of health outcomes. There is also a literature linking health status to relative deprivation, or to the income distribution. Third, it is plausible that the theoretical reasons that consumption, income, and earnings processes disperse also apply to health status.

Deaton and Paxson present evidence on life cycle patterns of BMI and SRHS, as well as on their relationship with income. They emphasize that it is important to explore differences between people in their health, even in the absence of an agreed methodology for thinking about inequality in health status, or even about health status itself. But by the same token, it is important to be cautious about attributing causality to any of their findings. Income and their measures of health status are linked in many different ways, through ability to pay for health, through education that is correlated with income, through lifestyle choices—such as whether to smoke and what to eat—that are conditioned by income, race, and sex.

From their findings, the authors highlight the following:

- There is ample evidence for the proposition with which they began, that their two measures of health status become more widely dispersed within any given birth cohort as that cohort ages. They view this as evidence in favor of a cumulative random model of health status.

- The rate of dispersion with age of BMI, but not of SRHS, is much more rapid for women than for men. BMI is more variable among women to start with. SRHS is more variable among young women than among young men, possibly reflecting pregnancy.

- Health status (positively measured) is positively correlated with income within cohort-year-sex cells. The correlation is lowest for the young, increases until age 50–60, and then diminishes. BMI is uncorrelated with incomes for men, but negatively correlated with incomes among women. This correlation is highest in middle age.

- The joint distribution of SRHS and income and the joint distribution of BMI and income "fan out" with age.

- Blacks consistently report lower health status than do whites. Some fraction—but not all—of this difference can be attributed to the lower income of blacks. Less of the difference is explained by income among women than among men, a result that is even more pronounced for BMI.

Pensions and Inequality

Quite a different view of inequality is investigated by Kathleen McGarry and Andrew Davenport. In their paper "Pensions and the Distribution of Wealth" they consider whether pensions increase or decrease inequality in the wealth of families approaching retirement. They find that pensions somewhat increase wealth inequality and find no evidence that pensions crowd out private savings.

Over the past few decades, the financial status of the elderly improved dramatically. Poverty rates for those age 65 or over fell from 25 percent in 1970 to 14 percent in 1994. These gains are attributed in large part to increases in the generosity of the social security program. Yet despite the inclusiveness of the social security system and the progressivity of the benefit schedule, some subgroups of the elderly continue to face disproportionately high risks of poverty. Unmarried women, for example, had a poverty rate of 22 percent in 1994, while the poverty rate for married women was 5 percent. Similarly, the poverty rate for elderly blacks is close to three times that for elderly whites (31 vs. 12 percent).

Social security is just one component of retirement income and given the structure of benefits, differences across individuals in the level of social security wealth are likely to be small in comparison to differences in the other components of total wealth. The large differences in economic well-being within the elderly population therefore stem from differences in the other modes of savings. Recently, much has been written about differences in net worth and savings behavior. Less well studied are differences in pension wealth and the interaction of pensions and individual wealth.

In this paper, McGarry and Davenport take advantage of the HRS to focus on differences in pension wealth for various subgroups of the retirement age population. They ask how pensions affect the distribution of wealth in the population. They compare the distribution of net worth to the distribution of private wealth (net worth plus pension wealth) and to the distribution of total wealth (net worth plus pensions wealth plus social security wealth).

They find evidence that pensions somewhat increase the inequality of wealth across the population. They demonstrate the relationship between total wealth and inequality directly and find that single women in particular fare much worse relative to single men and couples when pension wealth is included in the calculation of total wealth. The paucity of pension holdings among women suggests that their eventual well-being as widows will depend heavily on the resources left after the death of a spouse. Thus the issue of survivorship benefits for pensions will have important consequences for the eventual poverty rates of widows. While the results are purely descriptive, the authors fail to find evidence to support the notion that pensions crowd out private savings.

References

Eichner, Matthew, Mark McClellan, and David Wise. 1998. Insurance or self-insurance? Variation, persistence, and individual health accounts. In *Inquiries in the economics of aging,* ed. David Wise. Chicago: University of Chicago Press.
Gale, William G., and John Karl Scholz. 1994. IRAs and household saving. *American Economic Review* 84:1233–60.

I   Personal Retirement Plans

1   Personal Retirement Saving Programs and Asset Accumulation: Reconciling the Evidence

James M. Poterba, Steven F. Venti, and David A. Wise

A large fraction of American families reach retirement age with virtually no personal financial assets. The median level of all personal financial assets of families with heads aged 55–64 was only $8,300 in 1991; excluding individual retirement accounts (IRAs) and 401(k) balances the median was only $3,000. Mean values are substantially higher. Almost 20 percent of families had no financial assets at all. In 1991, the median value of the future social security benefits of retired families with heads aged 65–70 was about $100,000, the median value of housing was about $50,000, and the median value of future employer-provided pension benefits was about $16,000. But other than social security and pension benefits, and illiquid housing wealth, the typical family has very limited resources to meet unforeseen expenses.

Two saving programs introduced in the early 1980s were intended to encourage individual saving. IRAs rapidly became a very popular form of saving in the United States after they became available to all employees in 1982. Any employee could contribute $2,000 per year to an IRA and a nonworking spouse could contribute $250. The contribution was tax deductible. Annual contributions grew from about $5 billion in 1981 to about $38 billion in 1986, approximately 30 percent of total personal saving. Contributions declined precipi-

James M. Poterba is professor of economics at the Massachusetts Institute of Technology and director of the Public Economics Research Program at the National Bureau of Economic Research. Steven F. Venti is professor of economics at Dartmouth College and a research associate of the National Bureau of Economic Research. David A. Wise is the John F. Stambaugh Professor of Political Economy at the John F. Kennedy School of Government, Harvard University, and the director for Health and Retirement Programs at the National Bureau of Economic Research.

This research was supported primarily by a series of grants from the National Institute on Aging. The authors also acknowledge the support of the Hoover Institution (Wise), the National Science Foundation (Poterba), and the National Bureau of Economic Research. The authors are grateful to Bill Gale, Jon Gruber, Jon Skinner, and Richard Thaler for comments on an earlier draft of the paper.

tously after the Tax Reform Act of 1986, even though the legislation limited the tax deductibility of contributions only for families who had annual incomes over $40,000 and who were covered by an employer-provided pension plan. By 1994, only $7.7 billion was contributed to IRAs, and while over 15 percent of tax filers contributed in 1986, less than 4 percent contributed in 1994.

The other program, the 401(k) plan, grew continuously and almost unnoticed, with contributions increasing from virtually zero at the beginning of the decade to over $51 billion by 1991, when almost 25 percent of families contributed to a 401(k). Deposits in 401(k) accounts are also tax deductible, and the return on the contributions accrues tax free; taxes are paid upon withdrawal. But these plans are available only to employees of firms that offer such plans. Prior to 1987 the employee contribution limit was $30,000, but the Tax Reform Act of 1986 reduced the limit to $7,000 and indexed this limit for inflation in subsequent years. The contribution limit was $9,235 for both the 1994 and 1995 tax years.

Although very small at the beginning of the decade, by 1989 contributions to all personal retirement saving plans exceeded contributions to traditional employer-provided pension plans, as shown in figure 1.1. It seems evident that were it not for the Tax Reform Act of 1986, personal retirement plan saving would have been much larger. Whether these programs increase net saving can be of critical importance to future generations of older Americans and to the health of the economy in general. The issue remains an important question of economic debate. In a series of papers based on very different methods of analysis we have concluded that a large fraction of the contributions to these accounts represent new saving. Our previous research is summarized here, along with several new results.

As interest in the saving effect of these programs evolved, several other investigators also directed attention to the issue. In some instances, alternative analyses came to conclusions that differed dramatically from ours. Thus in describing our results we have tried to point out the differences between our methods and alternative approaches that have been used to address the same questions. We have not, however, attempted to comment on all analyses of the relationship between retirement plan saving and total personal saving.

The key impediment to determining the saving effect of IRAs and 401(k)s is saver heterogeneity. Some people save and others do not, and the savers tend to save more in all forms. For example, families with IRAs also have more conventional savings than families without IRAs. Thus a continuing goal of our analyses has been to consider different methods of controlling for heterogeneity. The methods that could be used when each analysis was conducted were largely dependent on the available data. As new data became available we used alternative and possibly more robust methods to control for heterogeneity.

The paper has several sections: Sections 1.1 through 1.5 present our results and are organized by the method used to control for heterogeneity. In each case the question is whether IRA and 401(k) contributions substitute for conven-

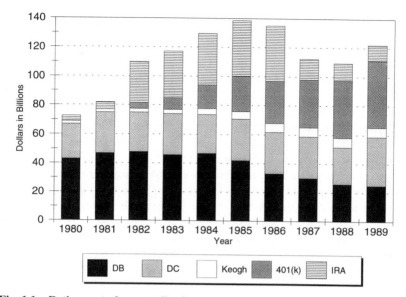

Fig. 1.1   Retirement plan contributions

tional financial asset saving. These sections also contain some discussion of closely related results reported by others. While early work in this area focused on the potential substitution between IRA assets and liquid financial assets, subsequent analyses considered the potential substitution between personal retirement saving plan assets and employer-provided pension assets and housing equity. Section 1.6 considers others margins of substitution, particularly the possibility that saving in these programs is financed by drawing down home equity. Section 1.7 addresses the divergence between our conclusions based on Survey of Consumer Finances 1983–86 summary data—introduced in section 1.2—and the parametric analysis of the same data by Gale and Scholz (1994). Conclusions are presented in section 1.8.

1.1   Early Parametric Analysis of Substitution at the Outset of the IRA Program

When Venti and Wise began work on the saving effect of IRAs in the mid-1980s, data on asset holdings were available for a limited time period. Assets could typically be measured at only two points in time, one year apart. To use these data, Venti and Wise developed an econometric model that could be used to estimate the relationship between IRA saving and other saving. Within a framework that allowed for any degree of substitution between IRA and non-IRA saving, the analysis asked whether persons who save more in IRAs in a particular year save less in other financial asset forms, controlling for age, income, other personal characteristics, and accumulated housing and financial assets. Given age and income, this approach used accumulated financial assets to control for "individual-specific" saving effects. The analysis accounted for the explicit limit on IRA contributions and placed substantial emphasis on the change in non-IRA saving after the IRA limit is reached.

The first results using this approach were based on data from the 1983 Survey of Consumer Finances (Venti and Wise 1986, 1987; Wise 1987). Subsequent analysis was based on the 1980–85 Consumer Expenditure Surveys (Venti and Wise 1990) and the 1984 panel of the Survey of Income and Program Participation (Venti and Wise 1991).[1]

The results suggested that the majority of IRA saving, even at the outset of the program, represented net new saving and was not accompanied by substantial reduction in other financial asset saving. These findings imply that increasing the IRA limit would lead to substantial increases in IRA saving and very little reduction in other saving. If the IRA limit were raised, one-half to two-thirds of the increase in IRA saving would be funded by a decrease in current consumption and about one-third by reduced taxes; only a very small proportion—at most 20 percent—would come from other saving.

The widely cited study by Gale and Scholz (1994), based on the 1983–86 Survey of Consumer Finances, was in some respects in the same spirit as these analyses, but their conclusions were radically different, suggesting that raising the IRA limit would have virtually no effect on total personal saving. A detailed analysis of the findings in this study is presented in section 1.7 of this paper.

Our subsequent analyses have taken a very different turn, using better data and more robust methods to control for heterogeneity. Our findings based on these approaches are discussed in the next four sections.

1.2   Following Individuals over Time at the Outset of the IRA Program

To frame the discussion in this and subsequent sections, we give a simple algebraic description of the key features of each method that we use to control for heterogeneity. We establish some notation and key ideas at the outset. Consider the flow of saving S_{it} of person i in year t. To capture saving heterogeneity among families, suppose that saving of person i depends on an unobserved individual-specific saving effect m_i. This effect is large for more committed savers and small for less eager savers. Saving may also depend on a program effect, which is denoted by p_{it}. For program participants, p_{it} is the component of saving that is due to the program; for nonparticipants, p_{it} is zero. If person i

1. In an earlier study, Hubbard (1984) found that the ratio of assets to income was higher for IRA participants, controlling for individual attributes and eligibility. He concluded that the results "provide strong evidence that contributions to IRAs and Keogh plans do increase individual saving." Feenberg and Skinner (1989) show that IRA participants save *more* than nonparticipants, controlling for initial wealth.

is a saving program participant and person j is a nonparticipant, $S_{it} = m_i + p_{it}$ and $S_{jt} = m_j$. The difference in saving between these individuals is

(1) $$S_{it} - S_{jt} = (m_i - m_j) + p_{it}.$$

This difference confounds the program effect with the difference in the taste for saving.

In this simple example the difference in saving rates between participants and nonparticipants does not provide an unbiased estimate of the program effect because the unobserved taste for saving is correlated with program participation. This form of heterogeneity is probably the most important source of potential bias, but there are others as well. In the following sections we present several methods to control for heterogeneity. Each method controls for important sources of heterogeneity, but no single method—other than a randomized controlled trial—can control for all possible sources. Each of the methods in this and the following sections is described in a consistent way, in an attempt to highlight both the way that heterogeneity is addressed as well as the potential types of heterogeneity that each method may not address. A specific form of heterogeneity that may confound an estimate obtained by one method may not present the same problem within the context of another method. Thus there is an important advantage to using several methods to address potential heterogeneity.

In practice, each estimate is a difference obtained in one of three ways: (1) by comparing the saving or assets of a "treatment" group in a later period with saving or assets of the same group in an earlier period, relying on *within*-group changes; (2) by comparing saving or assets of two different groups in the same period, relying on *between*-group comparisons; or (3) by comparing the assets at a given age of persons who attain that age in different calendar years, using "cohort analysis."

1.2.1 Change in Other Saving When IRA Status Changes

The Method

The most direct way to control for heterogeneity is to follow the same household over time, observing the change in S_{it} when program participation changes. Saving in periods t and $t+1$ for household i can be described by

$$S_{it} = m_i + p_{it},$$

$$S_{i,t+1} = m_i + p_{i,t+1}.$$

The "within-household" change in saving is therefore

(2) $$S_{i,t+1} - S_{it} = (m_i - m_i) + (p_{i,t+1} - p_{it}) = p_{i,t+1} - p_{it},$$

which yields an estimate of the program effect for households that participate in one period but not in the other (p_{it} is zero in the nonparticipating period). The unobserved individual-specific saving effects are "differenced" out.

If the heterogeneity is limited to differences in saving commitment among households, and the problem is simply that more committed savers are more likely to be program participants, then this within-household change in saving provides a clean estimate of the program effect. But this estimate can be confounded by another possible source of heterogeneity: differences in saving commitment over time within the same household. If individual saving commitment changes at the same time that participation status changes, this estimate will capture the effect of a change in the taste for saving as well as the participation effect. With this coincidence, the difference would be

$$(3) \qquad S_{i,t+1} - S_{it} = (m_{i,t+1} - m_{it}) + (p_{i,t+1} - p_{it}).$$

If the household began to participate in period $t+1$ at the same time that the unobserved propensity to save increased, the difference in saving would overestimate the program effect.

The Results

Venti and Wise (1995a) used this method in analyzing data from consecutive waves of the 1984 Survey of Income and Program Participation (SIPP). The SIPP panel data allow calculation of the change in non-IRA saving when IRA contributor status changes, although non-IRA saving must be inferred from asset income. They considered the change in non-IRA saving between 1984 and 1985 by IRA contributor status.[2] If non-IRA saving is reduced when IRA saving is increased, then when a household that was not contributing begins to contribute, that household should reduce its non-IRA saving. Likewise, when a household that was contributing stops contributing, non-IRA saving should increase. Venti and Wise find, however, that when the same families are tracked over time, there is little change in other financial asset saving when families begin to contribute to an IRA, or when they stop contributing. Illustrative results are shown in table 1.1.

These data reveal little substitution. The key information in this approach is the change in other financial assets when families began to contribute to an IRA. In particular, the non-IRA financial asset saving of families that did not contribute in 1984 but did contribute in 1985 declined by only $193 between 1984 and 1985.[3] This decline in other saving is only a small fraction of the increase in saving from the typical family IRA contribution, $2,300. These

---

2. Non-IRA saving is inferred from capitalized asset income at three points in time, measured in current-year dollars. Non-IRA assets include all interest-bearing financial assets including stocks and bonds.

3. If the underlying assets are measured in constant dollars, instead of current-year dollars, the change is $186.

Table 1.1   **Change in Non-IRA Saving When IRA Contributor Status Changed between 1984 and 1985**

	1985 Noncontributor	1985 Contributor
1984 Noncontributor	89.4	−193.5
	(102.1)	(413.6)
1984 Contributor	630.3	186.2
	(527.2)	(303.9)
	$F = 0.698$	

Source: Venti and Wise (1995a).
Note: Numbers in parentheses are standard errors.

data suggest that even near the outset of the IRA program there was only a small reduction in non-IRA saving when IRA contributions began.[4]

As emphasized above, this procedure does not correct for "within-individual" change in saving behavior. For example, suppose that the saving behavior of persons who began to contribute in 1985 changed between 1984 and 1985 and that this change happened to coincide with the newly available IRA option. If the IRA option had not been available, it could be argued, the person would have saved in the non-IRA form, but since it was available, the newly awakened saver stored assets in the more advantageous IRA instead. The alternative, of course, is that the IRA option induced the person to save in that form and that the new IRA contribution would not have been saved in another form. To us, the results seem more consistent with the conclusion that the two forms of saving are largely independent, with changes in IRA saving having little effect on other saving. It is clear that those who began to contribute in 1985 had not been saving $2,300 annually prior to 1984. Indeed, their estimated asset balance in 1984 was only $3,362. The same is true for persons who had contributed to an IRA in 1984 but quit contributing in 1985; their 1984 balance was $4,816.

It is nonetheless possible that individual behavior could have changed over time, and the method used here cannot formally correct for this. The cohort analysis discussed below, however, accounts for this possibility, and the results are consistent with the conclusions drawn here.

1.2.2   Attanasio and De Leire's Study of "Old" versus "New" Contributors

Attanasio and De Leire (1994; hereafter AD) analyze Consumer Expenditure Survey (CES) data to evaluate the substitution between IRA and other

4. The increase of $630.3 when contributions are curtailed also suggests some substitution as well, although the estimate is not significantly different from zero. Again, the amount is much less than the typical family IRA contribution. Asset balances are measured in May of each year because IRA contributions can be made through the 15 April tax-filing deadline.

financial assets. The CES data essentially provide a series of independent cross sections, but each cross section is in fact a short panel, providing asset balances at two points in time, one year apart. AD consider the difference between the annual non-IRA saving—measured by the change in asset balances—of "old" and "new" contributors. In a given year, old contributors are families that contributed in the previous year (and possibly earlier years as well); new contributors are those who did not contribute in the previous year. Within a regression framework, they find that old contributors save $1,740 more than new contributors.

At first blush, the results may appear to contradict the evidence just presented. On closer inspection, however, the method used by AD—the comparison of new contributors with old contributors—can say very little about the saving effect of the IRA program. Indeed, if taken at face value, the AD result suggests that in the *first year* that an IRA contribution is made, there is a drop in non-IRA financial assets, but in the next year and in future years when the household continues to contribute, other saving reverts to its pre-IRA level. So in the long run there is essentially *no offset* of IRA saving by a reduction in other saving.[5]

The key features of the AD method are shown in Figures 1.2A through 1.2C. These *illustrative* figures assume that old contributors start to make IRA contributions in the 1982–83 period and that new contributors start to contribute in the 1983–84 period, that both old and new contributors save $2,000 per year in the absence of the IRA, and that an IRA contribution is $2,000. The figures compare the other saving of old and new contributors in the 1983–84 period.

Figure 1.2A illustrates the situation when there is no substitution at all. Other saving remains at $2,000 when IRA contributions begin. When the new contributors begin to contribute, there is *no difference* in the other saving of old and new contributors. Figure 1.2B illustrates the situation when there is complete substitution. When the old contributors begin to contribute, their other saving falls from $2,000 to zero and remains at zero thereafter. When the new contributors begin to contribute one year later, their other saving also falls from $2,000 to zero. When the two groups are compared in 1983–84, saving is zero for both groups. Like the no substitution case, there is *no difference* in the other saving of new and old contributors. Thus the value computed by AD cannot distinguish between the two polar cases of no substitution and complete substitution.

Neither of the processes illustrated in figures 1.2A or 1.2B are consistent with the difference between the saving of old and new contributors that AD find. Figure 1.2C illustrates a process that is consistent with their finding. When old contributors first contribute, their other saving falls from $2,000 to zero. But in the next year other saving reverts to the previous level of $2,000. In this year, new contributors begin to contribute, and their other saving falls

---

5. A similar point is made by Hubbard and Skinner (1995).

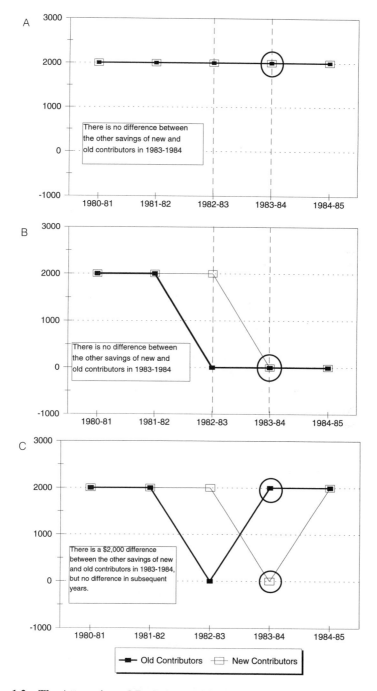

There is no difference between the other savings of new and old contributors in 1983-1984

There is no difference between the other savings of new and old contributors in 1983-1984

There is a $2,000 difference between the other savings of new and old contributors in 1983-1984, but no difference in subsequent years.

—■— Old Contributors   ⊟ New Contributors

Fig. 1.2   The Attanasio and De Leire method

Note: (*A*) No substitution at all. (*B*) Complete substitution. (*C*) One-year substitution.

Table 1.2   **Inferred Non-IRA Financial Asset Balances in 1984, 1985, and 1986, by Asset and by Change in IRA Contributor Status between 1984 and 1985 (in current dollars)**

	1985 IRA = 0			1985 IRA > 0		
	May 1984	May 1985	May 1986	May 1984	May 1985	May 1986
1984 IRA = 0	1,210	1,587	2,053	3,362	5,051	6,546
	(98)	(98)	(98)	(399)	(399)	(399)
1984 IRA > 0	4,816	5,896	7,606	7,457	9,659	12,048
	(509)	(509)	(509)	(293)	(293)	(293)
		$R^2 = 0.212$			$F = 434.60$	

Source: Venti and Wise (1995a).

Note: Numbers in parentheses are standard errors.

from $2,000 to zero. The difference between the other saving of old and new contributors is $2,000 in this year, approximately AD's finding. The next year, however, new contributors become old contributors, and their other saving reverts to its previous level of $2,000. There is a one-year reduction in other saving but no offset thereafter, and thus little substitution in the long run.

More detail on the non-IRA saving of households who do and do not change IRA status helps to show the limitations of the AD method. The asset data from which the numbers in table 1.1 were derived are shown in table 1.2.[6] For example, the change in the other saving of persons who began to contribute to an IRA in 1985 is derived from the three asset levels in the upper right corner of table 1.2 ((6,546 − 5,051) − (5,051 − 3,362) = −193.5). Two things are clear from these data: First, the assets of old contributors—in the lower right corner—are substantially greater than the assets of new contributors—in the upper right. Their annual saving is different as well—about $1,600 for new contributors, about $2,300 for old contributors. Second, there was little change in the other saving behavior of either group over the two-year period, −193.5 for new contributors and +186.2 for old contributors. Looking at these data, however, the method used by AD would show a difference between the non-IRA financial assets of old and new contributors of −$894 in 1985 ((6,546 − 5,051) − (12,048 − 9,659) = −894), which bears no particular relationship to substitution.

1.2.3   Joines and Manegold's Analysis of Saving Change When the IRA Limit Increases

Joines and Manegold (1995) use the "change" in IRA contribution limits determined by the Economic Recovery Tax Act (ERTA) of 1981 to estimate the

6. These asset levels are inferred from asset earnings reported in SIPP at three points in time, approximately one year apart. Inferred assets based on alternative methods are presented in Venti and Wise (1995a). Although the asset levels differ by method and the growth in assets differs as well, the basic difference-in-difference results, as in table 1.1, are very similar.

saving effect of the IRA program. Prior to ERTA, only wage earners without an employer-provided pension plan were eligible to contribute to an IRA. The contribution limit for wage earners in this group was $1,500. ERTA extended eligibility to all wage earners, beginning in 1982, and increased the limit for each wage earner to $2,000. In addition, nonworking spouses of wage earners could contribute $250.

Joines and Manegold consider the *change in the total annual financial asset saving* of *contributor* households between the 1979–81 and 1982–85 periods as a function of the *change in the IRA limit* between these time periods. Their analysis is based on a panel of individual tax returns. Saving in each period is determined by the change during the period in total financial assets, which are estimated by capitalizing reported asset income. Two groups of households are considered: "new" contributor households first contributed at some time in the later (1982–85) period, and "continuing" contributor households contributed in both the earlier and later periods. The "change" in the limit for new contributors was from zero to $2,000, $2,250, or $4,000 for single wage earner families, couples with a single wage earner, and two wage earner families, respectively. The limit change for continuing contributors was from $1,500 to $2,000 for single wage earners, from $1,500 to $2,250 for couples with a single wage earner, and from $3,000 to $4,000 for two wage earner couples.

Joines and Manegold estimate a relationship of the form

(4) $\text{Saving}_{82–85} - \text{Saving}_{79–81} = \beta(X) * (\text{Limit change}) + \gamma X,$

where the key parameter β is the relationship between the limit change and the change in saving. In some specifications β is estimated as a single parameter; in others it is a function of a vector of covariates X, describing primarily household tax status.[7] The covariates also enter separately, with coefficient γ. The parameter β is *not* the saving effect of IRA contributions. It does not represent the relationship between IRA contributions and saving but rather the relationship between saving and the change in the IRA limit. Thus it is not comparable to most other estimates discussed in this paper, which consider the proportion of contributions that represent new saving. For example, suppose that a single new contributor deposited $1,000 in an IRA. If the $1,000 were entirely new saving, β would be 0.50 (1,000/2,000), not 1.00. If the $1,000 were the only deposit of a single wage earner couple, β would be 0.44 (1,000/2,250). If the $1,000 were the only deposit of a two wage earner family, β would be 0.25 (1,000/4,000).[8]

7. The variables include a mortgage deduction indicator, number of exemptions, marital status, the first-dollar marginal tax rate, gender, and transitory income (measured by the mean deviation of income from average income over the 1979–86 period).

8. Although Joines and Manegold compare their estimates to those of Venti and Wise (1986, 1987, 1990, 1991) and Gale and Scholz (1994), their comparisons are inappropriate. Venti and Wise consider the proportion of IRA contributions that represent new saving, and to indicate the implications of the results, they simulate the proportion of the *increase in IRA contributions resulting from an increase in the limit* that would be new saving. Gale and Scholz direct their analysis to this proportion as well, as discussed in section 1.7 below.

When β is estimated as a single parameter, Joines and Manegold obtain values ranging from 0.17 to 0.73, depending on the method of estimation. The largest estimate is obtained by ordinary least squares and is very imprecise. Joines and Manegold favor robust least squares estimates, with β parameterized as a function of X. Their "best guess" estimate of β is 0.26. This implies that substantially more than 26 percent of the IRA contributions associated with an increase in the limit would represent new saving.

Joines and Manegold find that the median of estimated total financial assets of new contributors was only $4,396 in the 1979–81 period. The typical IRA contribution in the 1982–85 period was about $2,300. Since most contributors in this period were new contributors, the typical contribution of new contributors was clearly much greater than these new contributors had been accustomed to saving prior to the advent of the IRA program. Thus, although the analysis does not purport to estimate the net saving effect of IRA contributions, the Joines and Manegold summary data suggest that the saving effect is likely to have been substantial.

1.2.4 Analyzing the Change in the Assets of IRA Contributors

The Method

We now consider the change in non-IRA saving of IRA *contributors* as their IRA savings accumulate. The specification above relates saving in year t to an individual-specific taste effect m_i and a program effect p_i. Most surveys do not obtain direct measures of saving, however, but instead collect information on asset balances; saving must be estimated from changes in the balances. Since asset balances reflect the accumulation of past saving decisions, they also reflect individual-specific saving effects. Suppose an IRA contributor with individual-specific component m_i has been saving for s years and has participated in a retirement saving program for n of these years. Then the household's asset balance, after s years of saving and n years of program saving, is

$$(5) \quad A_{si}(n) = (1 + r)^s A_0 + m_i[(1 + r)^s - 1)]/r + p_i[(1 + r)^n - 1)]/r$$

$$= h(s) + m_i f(s) + p_i g(n),$$

where A_0 is the level of assets when saving began (possibly zero), r is the rate of return, and $h(\cdot)$, $f(\cdot)$, and $g(\cdot)$ are defined by context. This very stylized formulation need not be interpreted literally and indeed does not reflect saving behavior that might limit accumulation to some precautionary level, for example. Here the formulation simply serves to emphasize that the program effect as well as the individual saving effect are magnified by the number of years over which saving occurs. To illustrate the key features of this and other methods, we write the relationship in the simplified form, highlighting the key parameters in boldface.

Now assume that we observe *contributors* after n years of exposure and then

Table 1.3   **Survey of Consumer Finances Data Summary (in current dollars)**

	Year		Percentage Change
Contributor Status and Asset	1983	1986	
Contributors in 1986			
Non-IRA assets	**9,400**	13,500	43.6
IRA assets	1,000	7,000	600.0
Total assets	12,075	**24,000**	98.8
Noncontributors in 1986			
Total assets	729	1,000	37.2

again after $n+k$ years of exposure. After $n+k$ years of program saving, and $s+k$ years of nonprogram saving, the assets of participants will be

$$A_{si}(n+k) = h(s+k) + m_i f(s+k) + p_i g(n+k).$$

The change in assets over the k years is given by

$$A_{si}(n+k) - A_{si}(n) = h(s+k) - h(s) + m_i[f(s+k) - f(s)]$$
$$+ p_i[g(n+k) - g(n)].$$

If $A_0 = 0$, this expression becomes

(6) $A_{si}(n+k) - A_{si}(n) = m_i[f(s+k) - f(s)] + p_i[g(n+k) - g(n)].$

The change in assets reflects the program effect plus the saving that m_i type families would have done over k years in the absence of the program. To isolate the program effect, we use cross-sectional data at the earliest observation date to approximate $m_i[f(s+k) - f(s)]$, the expected change in saving over the next k years in the absence of the IRA program. We then compare this estimate with the actual change in assets for IRA contributors.

The Results

   Using 1983 and 1986 Survey of Consumer Finances (SCF) data it is possible to compare the asset balances of the same households over time. Venti and Wise (1992) considered how the assets of IRA contributors changed over this time period. The results are reported in table 1.3. Households that made IRA contributions over this period began the period with a median of $9,400 in other financial assets in 1983. Between 1983 and 1986, the IRA assets of these families increased from $1,000 to $7,000. Other financial assets increased from $9,400 to $13,500. These families ended the period with total financial assets, including IRAs, of $24,000, an increase of 100 percent over assets in 1983. Venti and Wise determined that an increase of this magnitude could not be accounted for by change in age, income, or rate of return between 1983 and

1986.[9] In particular, they find that the increase in other financial assets is no less than would have been expected in the absence of the IRA program. Thus they conclude that it is unlikely that the IRA contributions simply substituted for saving that would have occurred anyway.

Once again, however, it is possible that at least some IRA contributors experienced a shift in saving commitment that happened to coincide with the emergence of the IRA option and that the new commitment to saving was realized through contributions to an IRA instead of contributions to conventional saving accounts. But for the results to be explained by a within-household change in saving behavior would require that most IRA contributors over the 1983–86 period had not been committed savers prior to this period (to be consistent with the low 1983 asset balances) but became committed savers just as the IRA program became available and would have become committed savers in the absence of the program. This seems to us an unlikely coincidence of events.[10]

The numbers in table 1.3 come from the same data used by Gale and Scholz (1994) in their analysis of the saving effect of the IRA program. In section 1.7 below we return to consideration of their methodology and how the conclusions of their formal analysis could be so different from what we believe these simple data suggest.

1.3   Comparing the Assets of "Like" Saver Groups Over Time

1.3.1   Within-Group Comparisons

The Method

Each of the foregoing methods rests on comparing the same individuals over time, so that similar saving propensities can be "differenced out." Another way to eliminate the unobserved saving effect is to group households with similar saving propensities and then estimate the program effect by using the *within-*group difference in exposure to retirement saving programs. Poterba, Venti, and Wise (PVW 1994a, 1995) use saving program participation itself as a signal of taste for saving. "Like saver" groups are determined by observed saving behavior: families participating in an IRA only are one group, families who participate in both an IRA and a 401(k) are another, and so forth.

---

9. Prediction of the expected increase in non-IRA saving in the absence of the program is discussed in section 1.7 below.

10. The test reported in Venti and Wise (1990) provides more formal evidence against the coincidence hypothesis. Unlike the SCF data that pertain to the same households in 1983 and 1986, the CES data used in the Venti and Wise (1990) analysis is based on random samples of similar households for the period 1980–85. E.g., the 1980 survey respondents were about the same age as the 1985 respondents. If the saving behavior of contributors changed just as the IRA program was introduced, estimates of saving based on post-1982 data should predict pre-1982 saving poorly. But the formal model estimated on post-1982 data predicts well the pattern of saving by income in the pre-1982 period, prior to the advent of IRAs. If the saving behavior of contributors had changed dramatically over this time period, one would expect a poor match between actual and predicted pre-1982 saving.

We consider the *within*-group difference between the assets of a like group at two points in time, but we do not compare the *same* households in two periods. Rather the groups are obtained from random cross sections of households surveyed in different calendar years. Because the cross-sectional surveys are representative, the demographic attributes of the cross sections are approximately the same each year. The like saver groups will be the same if households that save in a given way in one year are like the households that save in that way in another year. The hope is that two randomly chosen cross sections from the same like group share the same unobserved saving propensities and thus would have the same asset balances, except for differential exposure to the special saving programs, which identifies the program effect. Families observed in 1984 had had about two years of exposure to the IRA and 401(k) programs, families observed in 1987 about five years of exposure, and families in 1991 about nine years.

Two factors may complicate this analysis of the effect of program exposure. First, although the IRA program expanded rapidly between 1982 and 1986, the Tax Reform Act of 1986 reduced the attraction of IRAs for households with incomes above $30,000 and led to a massive reduction in IRA participation by households at all income levels, even those who were unaffected by the legislation. There were few new contributors after 1986. Second, the 401(k) program grew rapidly throughout the 1980s, with more and more firms offering such plans. In both cases, but especially with respect to IRAs, the characteristics—and thus the saving commitment—of participants may have changed over time. In principle, there could also be year-specific macroeffects that might affect saving of both program participants and nonparticipants. (The results below show no effects for nonparticipants.)

Now consider explicitly the assets of a like saver group surveyed in two different randomly selected cross sections, conducted k years apart. The two random samples of a particular group have been saving in any form for approximately the same number of years s, but the sample surveyed in the earlier year has had n years of exposure to the program and the sample surveyed in the later year has had $n+k$ years of exposure. (It is not important that s be known, but only that s be the same for each random cross section.) Assume that m_i is the typical saving propensity of the sample surveyed at the later date and that $m_{i'}$ is the typical saving propensity of the sample surveyed at the earlier date. Then

$$A_{si}(n) = h(s) + m_{i'}f(s) + p_i g(n),$$

$$A_{si}(n + k) = h(s) + m_i f(s) + p_i g(n + k).$$

This implies

(7) $A_{si}(n + k) - A_{si}(n) = (m_i - m_{i'})f(s) + p_i[g(n + k) - g(n)].$

If $m_i = m_{i'}$, then the difference in assets of the two random samples represents the program effect. If $m_i \neq m_{i'}$, then the difference represents a combination of the program effect and the different saving propensities of the two samples.

If, as seems likely, less committed savers are drawn into the program as it matures, then $m_i < m_{i'}$, and the first term is negative. In this case, the direction of the "bias" is clear; the difference in assets underestimates the program effect.[11]

Results

PVW (1994a, 1995) used several saving choices to identify like saver groups. We grouped families in two ways: first, according to whether they contributed to an IRA, a 401(k), or both; and second, according to whether they were eligible for a 401(k) plan and whether they had an IRA. Altogether, we considered six different groups of "saver types," not counting those without IRA or 401(k) saving. We focused on the within-group change in the other saving of families in these groups using data from the SIPP for 1984, 1987, and 1991. Random samples of saver types are similar in each of these years, but the 1984 sample had had only about two years (1982–84) to accumulate 401(k) and IRA balances, the 1987 sample about five years, and the 1991 sample about nine years. The central question is whether longer exposure to these plans results in higher levels of saving by families who participate in the programs.

The key test for substitution is whether non–IRA-401(k) assets are lower for the random samples that had been exposed to the IRA and 401(k) programs for longer periods of time and that had accumulated more IRA and 401(k) assets. The answer is typically no. The data for six saver groups are shown in table 1.4 (abstracted from PVW 1995). The key finding is that, with one partial exception, within each saver group the level of other financial assets for the 1991 sample is not noticeably lower than the level of other financial assets for the 1987 and 1984 samples. Indeed, within each saver group, the level of total financial assets for the 1991 sample exceeds the level for the 1987 sample (the total is not available for 1984 because 401(k) assets were not obtained in that year). The only apparent aberration is a decline in the median of other financial assets of 401(k)-only savers between 1984 and 1987. For this group, there was a noticeable increase in total financial assets, but little change in non-401(k) assets, between 1987 and 1991. But there was a noticeable increase in the total assets of families who made IRA and 401(k) contributions or were eligible for a 401(k) (whether or not they had an IRA). Since there is no evidence of a reduction in other assets for any of these groups, we conclude that the increase in retirement plan assets was not funded by a reduction in other financial assets.

Consider, for example, families with an IRA only (group 2a). A comparison of the 1984 and 1991 samples reveals that the median total financial assets of such families increased from $19,068 to $23,892. But there was little change in other financial assets, which declined from $11,595 to $10,717. Or consider families with an IRA who were eligible for a 401(k) (group 5a). Because

---

11. This is what Bernheim (1994) refers to as the "dilution effect."

Table 1.4   **Conditional Median Assets by Saver Group, 1984, 1987, and 1991 (in 1987 dollars)**

Saver Group and Asset Category	1984	1987	1991
By IRA-401(k) Saver Group			
IRA and 401(k)			
1a. Families with IRA and 401(k)			
Total financial assets	–	42,655	45,724
Other than IRA or 401(k)	15,653	16,795	16,253
1b. Families with neither IRA nor 401(k)			
Total financial assets	1,060	972	939
IRA Only			
2a. Families with IRA only			
Total Financial Assets	19,068	20,969	23,892
Other than IRA	11,595	10,818	10,717
2b. Families without IRA			
Total financial assets	1,274	1,274	1,509
Other than 401(k)	1,180	1,091	1,089
401(k) Only			
3a. Families with 401(k) only			
Total financial assets	–	8,566	9,808
Other than 401(k)	3,723	2,587	2,498
3b. Families without 401(k)			
Total financial assets	3,570	3,602	3,312
Other than IRA	2,472	2,339	2,145
By 401(k) Eligibility and IRA Saver Group			
All Families			
4a. Eligible for a 401(k)			
Total financial assets	–	16,763	19,608
Other than IRA or 401(k)	6,924	6,796	7,037
4b. Not eligible for a 401(k)			
Total financial assets	4,516	4,607	4,573
Other than IRA or 401(k)	3,075	3,010	3,025
Families with an IRA			
5a. Eligible for a 401(k)			
Total financial assets	–	37,882	44,432
Other than IRA or 401(k)	16,881	16,032	17,212
5b. Not eligible for a 401(k)			
Total financial assets	20,686	23,537	27,094
Other than IRA or 401(k)	13,098	13,269	13,355
Families without an IRA			
6a. Eligible for 401(k)			
Total financial assets	–	5,748	7,013
Other than IRA or 401(k)	2,992	2,737	2,757
6b. Not eligible for a 401(k)			
Total financial assets	1,261	1,202	1,210

Source: Poterba, Venti, and Wise (1995).

Note: The estimates are conditional on age, income, education, and marital status. The medians are evaluated at the means of these variables.

401(k) asset balances were not reported in 1984, total financial assets are not available in that year, but between 1987 and 1991, total financial assets of this group increased from $37,882 to $44,432. Yet there was no decline in other financial assets, which increased slightly from $16,881 to $17,212.

Although the key comparison here is the within-group change over time in the other financial assets of persons who participated (or were eligible for) the IRA and 401(k) programs, we also show data for families that did not participate in one or both of these programs. In each of these groups, except 5b for which where was a slight increase, there was a decline in other financial assets between 1984 and 1991. For example, the median assets of persons with neither an IRA nor a 401(k) declined from $1,060 to $939. The assets of families without an IRA and who were not eligible for a 401(k) declined from $1,261 to $1,210. Because the assets of program participants and nonparticipants are typically very different, however, we avoid between-group comparisons of these very dissimilar saver groups. Because their saving propensities are apparently so different, there seems little reason to believe that they would experience similar changes in asset balances in the absence of the saving programs. We return to this issue below.

It is sometimes suggested that these programs may affect households with limited assets but have little effect on wealthier households. We have addressed this issue by comparing the distribution of assets in 1984 and 1991. Again we rely on the fact that households in the 1991 survey had had much more time than their counterparts in earlier years to contribute to the saving programs. As shown in PVW (1994b), the higher levels of total financial assets held by IRA and 401(k) participant families in 1991 was not limited to families with large or small asset balances. Rather the effect was evident across the entire distribution of households, from those with the least to those with the greatest assets. On the other hand, across the entire distribution, there was almost no change between 1984 and 1991 in the non–IRA-401(k) assets of contributors. At all points in the distribution there was a fall over time in the assets of noncontributors.

For these estimates to control for heterogeneity, it is important that the typical person within a like saver group not change substantially over time—that is, that the unobserved difference in saving propensity $m_i - m_{i'}$ be close to zero. To help to assure that this is true, we have controlled for age, income, education, and marital status in calculating all the numbers presented in table 1.4. Nonetheless, it is possible that there were changes not accounted for by these covariates.

1.3.2   Engen, Gale, and Scholz Between-Group Comparisons

The Method

The critical feature of the PVW like group comparison is the *within*-group change in other assets as the retirement assets of a group accumulate with increasing program exposure. This is the technique used to "difference out" the group-specific saving effect. Engen, Gale, and Scholz (1994; hereafter EGS) follow a very different *between*-group approach and present an alternative comparison as evidence of substitution between retirement saving program assets and other saving. EGS combine two of the PVW like groups, and they compare the assets of the combined group to the assets of another of the PVW like saver groups. Using a difference-in-difference approach, EGS compare the change in the assets of two very different saver groups. The first group—call it the "treatment" group—is composed of all 401(k) *participants*. This is a composite group, some of whom participate only in the 401(k) program and some of whom participate in both the 401(k) and the IRA programs. Assume that this composite program effect is cp_i and that members of this group have saving commitment m_i in the most recent year and $m_{i'}$ in the earlier year. The difference in the assets of two random samples of group i surveyed k years apart is given by

$$A_{si}(n+k) - A_{si}(n) = (m_i - m_{i'})f(s) + cp_i[g(n+k) - g(n)].$$

The EGS second group is composed of IRA participants not eligible for a 401(k) and is thus exposed only to the IRA program, with an IRA program effect denoted by b_j. Let m_j represent the saving commitment of the second group in the most recent period and $m_{j'}$ the saving commitment of this group in the earlier period. Then the difference in assets of two random samples of group j surveyed k years apart is

$$A_{sj}(n+k) - A_{sj}(n) = (m_j - m_{j'})f(s) + b_j[g(n+k) - g(n)].$$

The difference-in-difference estimate used by EGS is

(8) $[A_{si}(n+k) - A_{si}(n)] - [A_{sj}(n+k) - A_{sj}(n)]$

$$= [(m_i - m_{i'}) - (m_j - m_{j'})]f(s) + (cp_i - b_j)[g(n+k) - g(n)].$$

In principle, this method will estimate the program effect if $m_i = m_{i'}$ and $m_j = m_{j'}$, or if $m_i - m_{i'} = m_j - m_{j'}$, but there are several confounding effects. First, the estimate is the difference $(cp_i - b_j)$ between the composite group (IRA and 401(k)) program effect and the IRA program effect. Second, the program effect is assumed to be the same for both groups, but it is likely that the same program will have different effects on very dissimilar saver groups, even without a within-group change in saving propensity. Third, because IRA participants are a much more select group of savers than 401(k) participants, the between-group difference in the saving commitments of the composite group and the IRA group at a point in time $(m_i - m_j$ or $m_{i'} - m_{j'})$ may be very large.[12] Thus there is reason to question whether the within-group change in saving commitments will be the same for both groups.

In the EGS case, the within-group change in saving commitment $(m_i - m_{i'})$

---

12. The IRA participation rate never exceeded 16 percent; the 401(k) participation rate has been at least 60 percent among eligible households.

of the composite group is especially large. The two subgroups of the composite group have very different saving commitments. And the subgroup proportions in the composite group change over time. There is a substantially smaller proportion of committed savers and a larger proportion of less committed savers in the most recent year. Thus m_i is much less than $m_{i'}$.

Comparison of Results

Our reproduction of the central EGS results is reported in the top panel of table 1.5. EGS compare all participants in a 401(k) plan—combining PVW groups 1a and 3a in table 1.4—with IRA contributors who were not eligible for a 401(k)—PVW group 5b in table 1.4. EGS interpret the fall in the assets of 401(k) participants *compared* to the increase in the assets of the "control" group as evidence that 401(k) contributions did not lead to an increase in financial assets between 1987 and 1991.

The critical feature of our approach to controlling for heterogeneity is comparison of the within-group change in non–IRA-401(k) assets as IRA and or 401(k) assets grow, for each like saver group. Based on this reasoning, we find that the EGS comparison has two important shortcomings. First, the two groups EGS compare surely exhibited very different saving behavior before the advent of the IRA and 401(k) programs. In 1987, the non–IRA-401(k) assets of the EGS control group were almost twice as large as those of the treatment group of 401(k) participants ($11,823 vs. $6,635). From table 1.4, it can be seen that similar differences existed in 1984. Thus, in our view, the two groups should not be treated as like saver groups and the comparison *between* them is not meaningful.

Furthermore, the increase in the total financial assets of the control group is entirely due to the increase in the IRA assets of this group. There was virtually no change in the non-IRA assets of this group. This can also be seen in the PVW data for group 5b in table 1.4. The non-IRA assets of this group remained almost constant, increasing from $13,098 to $13,355 between 1984 and 1987. In arguing that IRA and 401(k) plans have no effect on personal saving, it seems awkward to use evidence that suggests a substantial effect of IRAs on saving to show that the 401(k) plan had no effect.

The second problem with the EGS comparison is also fundamental and leads to an incorrect interpretation of the fall in the assets of the composite 401(k) participant group. This group is in fact composed of two very different groups: 401(k) participants without an IRA and 401(k) participants with an IRA. The misleading interpretation created by combining these very different groups can be explained with reference to the bottom panel of table 1.5. The 1987 non–IRA-401(k) assets of the second group—401(k) participants with an IRA—are about 10 times as large as those of the first group—401(k) participants without an IRA.[13] It is clear that the past saving behavior of the two groups

---

13. The other financial assets of the "control" group are three or four times as large as the other assets of group 1 and only a third as large as the other assets of group 2. Thus the past saving

Table 1.5   **EGS Comparison and the Composition Fallacy (in 1991 dollars)**

Saver Group and Asset Category	1987	1991	Change	Percentage Change
EGS Comparison: All 401(k) Participants vs. "Control" Group— IRA Participants Not Eligible for a 401(k)				
1. All 401(k) participants[a]				
Total financial assets	20,630	19,300	−1,330	−6.4
Net total financial assets[b]	**17,710**	**15,999**	**−1,711**	**−9.7**
Other than IRA and 401(k)	6,635	4,747	−1,888	−28.5
Number	1,489	2,773		
Percentage of total	**100.0**	**100.0**		
2. "Control" group: IRA participants not eligible for a 401(k)				
Total financial assets	24,129	28,974	4,845	20.1
Net total financial assets	**21,052**	**26,100**	**5,048**	**24.0**
Other than IRA and 401(k)	11,823	11,000	−823	−7.0
Decomposition of EGS: All 401(k) Participant Group				
3a. 401(k) Participants **without** an IRA				
Total financial assets	8,686	10,000	1,314	15.1
Net total financial assets	**5,550**	**7,149**	**1,599**	**28.8**
Other than 401(k)	2,774	2,400	−374	−13.5
Number	780	1,744		
Percentage of total	**52.4**	**62.9**		
3b. 401(k) Participants **with** an IRA				
Total financial assets	44,638	50,275	5,637	12.6
Net total financial assets	**41,622**	**46,099**	**4,477**	**10.8**
Other than IRA or 401(k)	29,844	30,000	156	0.6
Number	709	850		
Percentage of total	**47.6**	**37.1**		

Source: Authors' tabulations from 1987 and 1991 SIPP.

[a]Group 1 is our reproduction of the EGS numbers. Although the match is not exact, it is very close and qualitative relationships are the same.

[b]Net of nonmortgage debt.

was very different. This confounds inferences made from changes in the assets of the combined group, particularly if the proportions of the two subgroups in the composite group change over time, as they do between 1987 and 1991. The proportion of the second (high saver) group declined from 47.6 percent to 37.1 percent of the total combined groups, leading to a fall in the assets of the com-

behavior of the EGS "control" group does not approximate the saving behavior of either of the component groups of the combined group.

posite group. The proportion of the low-saver group increased from 52.4 percent to 62.9 percent. Thus the non–IRA-401(k) assets of the composite group declined. In fact, the total assets of each group separately *increased*. Total financial assets of 401(k) participants without an IRA increased by $1,314, and total financial assets of 401(k) participants with an IRA increased by $5,637. In neither case was there an important change in non–IRA-401(k) assets. This is exactly the result shown by PVW for groups 3a and 1a in table 1.4. Thus the composition problem inherent in the EGS comparison creates the illusion of substitution when in fact the data do not show that.[14] The regressions run by EGS and reported in table 5 of their paper (1994) suffer from the same problem.

In all three of the groups used by EGS, there was an increase in total financial asset saving as IRA and or 401(k) assets grew. In none of the three groups was there a substantial change in non–IRA-401(k) financial assets. The increase in the financial assets of the EGS control group was due to an increase in IRA assets, which—when compared to the fall in the assets of the composite group—lead EGS to conclude that the 401(k) plan had no effect. But the fall in the assets of the composite group is an illusion created by the changing composition of the group.

1.4   The 401(k) Eligibility "Experiment"

Another approach relies on the "experiment" that is provided by the largely exogenous determination of 401(k) eligibility, *given income*. It considers whether eligibility is associated with higher levels of total saving, holding income and other demographic characteristics constant. In this case the key question is whether families who were eligible for a 401(k) in a given year had larger total financial asset balances than families who were not eligible, or, equivalently, did non-401(k) financial assets decline enough to offset the 401(k) contributions of eligible families? This approach is used in PVW (1994a, 1995).

1.4.1   The Method

Unlike the IRA program, only persons whose employers establish a 401(k) plan are eligible to contribute to such a plan. This creates a natural opportunity to compare the saving of eligible and noneligible households. In this case, we make a *between*-group comparison of assets at a point in time. The data set for each year represents a random cross section of respondents in that year. Thus

---

14. This composition fallacy is a classic error in empirical analysis made clear by Bickel, Hammel, and O'Connell (1975) in their analysis of graduate student admissions at the University of California, Berkeley. While grouping departments made it seem as though there was discrimination against women, looking at individual departments made it clear that in no single department was there discrimination. It was just that women were applying to departments where the admission rate was low and men to departments where the admission rate was high.

the random samples in different years have essentially the same demographic characteristics. But samples drawn in later years have had longer exposure to retirement saving plans. This means that s—the number of years of saving in any form—remains the same even though retirement program exposure is greater for more recent samples.

Suppose that the saving commitment of the typical eligible household in the most recent period is represented by m_i and the commitment of noneligible households by m_j. In an earlier period, the commitment of the typical eligible household is represented by $m_{i'}$ and the commitment of noneligible households by $m_{j'}$. After exposure to the program for n and $n+k$ years, respectively, the assets of eligible households are given by

$$A_{si}(n) = h(s) + m_{i'}f(s) + p_i g(n),$$

$$A_{si}(n+k) = h(s) + m_i f(s) + p_i g(n+k),$$

and the assets of noneligible households are given by

$$A_{sj}(n) = h(s) + m_{j'} f(s),$$

$$A_{sj}(n+k) = h(s) + m_j f(s).$$

To determine the program effect, p_i, we consider the between-group difference in the assets of eligible and noneligible households at a *point in time,* which after $n+k$ years of exposure is given by

(9) $A_{si}(n+k) - A_{sj}(n+k) = (m_i - m_j)f(s) + p_i g(n+k).$

If $m_i = m_j$, the difference represents the program effect. Thus a critical question is whether the saving propensities of the two groups are in fact equal. At the outset of the program, when $n = 0$, the assets of the two groups will differ only if $m_{i'}$ and $m_{j'}$ differ, with

$$A_{si}(0) - A_{sj}(0) = (m_{i'} - m_{j'})f(s).$$

Thus, if the two groups have equal assets at the outset of the program, the implication is that the saving commitments of the two groups are equal, and vice versa. We use this test to establish approximate equality of taste for saving near the outset of the program.

The estimate presented in equation (9), however, depends not on the equality of saving commitments at the outset of the program but on equality of saving commitments at a later point in time (1991 in our case). What would assure that this equality is maintained? Suppose that the two groups are composed of equally committed savers at the outset of the program, with $m_{i'} = m_{j'}$. Over time, more households became eligible for a 401(k). As long as newly eligible households are a representative sample of the former noneligible households, the two groups will continue to be composed of equally committed savers and the difference in assets at a point in time will represent the program effect.

Table 1.6   **Conditional Median Asset Balances by 401(k) Eligibility: Families with Income $40,000 to $50,000**

Asset Category and Eligibility Status	Results for 1991 (1991 $)	Results for 1984 (1984 $)
Total financial assets		
Eligible for a 401(k)	14,470*	–
Not eligible for a 401(k)	6,206	–
Non–IRA-401(k) assets		
Eligible for a 401(k)	4,724	5,027
Not eligible for a 401(k)	4,250	5,082

Source: Poterba, Venti, and Wise (1995).

Note: These are medians controlling for age, marital status, and education.

*Difference between eligibles and noneligibles is statistically significant at the 95 percent confidence level.

1.4.2   The Results

Inferences about the net saving effect of 401(k) contributions depend on the similarity of the saving behavior of families who are and are not eligible for a 401(k), m_i versus m_j, controlling for income. It is important, for example, that the eligible group not be composed disproportionately of savers. The data show little evidence of this type of difference in saving behavior. The most compelling evidence is for 1984. In that year eligibles and noneligibles had about the same level of other financial assets, controlling for income. Thus these data suggest that near the outset of the 401(k) program families that were newly eligible for a 401(k) exhibited about the same previous saving behavior as families that did not become eligible—m_i and m_j were about the same.

Data for families with incomes between $40,000 and $50,000, presented in table 1.6, illustrate the findings. In 1984, newly eligible and noneligible 401(k) families had almost identical non–401(k)-IRA assets—$5,027 and $5,082, respectively. By 1991, however, the median of total financial assets of eligible families was $14,470, compared to $6,206 for noneligible families. But in 1991, the *non–IRA-401(k) assets* of the two groups were still about the same, $4,724 for eligible and $4,250 for the noneligible group.[15] If families reduced saving in other forms when they became eligible for a 401(k) plan, the typical eligible family in 1991 would have accumulated less wealth in other financial assets than the typical noneligible family. This was not the case.

Similar comparisons are reported in appendix table 1C.1 for all income groups. In 1984, the ratio of median non–IRA-401(k) assets of eligibles to noneligibles, weighted by the number of observations within income intervals,

15. The apparent reduction in the non-401(k)-IRA assets of both groups between 1984 and 1991 is due largely to earnings growth. The income intervals are not indexed, and thus families in a given interval in 1984 will tend to have greater wealth than families in that same interval in 1991. Comparable calculations with the intervals indexed to 1987 dollars are discussed in section 1.6.2 and reported in tables 1.10 and 1.11 and in appendix tables 1C.3 and 1C.4.

was *exactly one*. The ratio of means was 0.87, indicating that the mean of non–IRA-401(k) assets of the eligible group was *lower* than the mean of non-eligibles. By 1987 the ratio of total financial assets of eligible to noneligible families was 1.62, and by 1991 this ratio was 2.22. This evidence suggests a sizable effect of 401(k) saving on the accumulation of financial assets and shows little if any substitution of 401(k) contributions for other financial asset saving.

Indeed, for all income groups, eligible households have greater total financial assets than noneligible households at virtually all points across the entire distribution of financial assets. But there is virtually no difference across the entire distribution of the other financial assets of eligible and noneligible households, as shown in PVW (1995).

For comparisons between eligible and noneligible households to shed light on the net saving effect of 401(k) plans, it is important that the saving behavior of the eligible and noneligible groups be comparable. As noted above, after controlling for income, the accumulated assets of the two groups were very close at the outset of the program. Nonetheless, there could have been some change in the composition of the two groups over time, even if eligibles and noneligibles were very similar in 1984. Data on measured household attributes, however, suggest that there was little composition change.

Many studies of saving behavior have shown that saving commitment is related to household demographic attributes, such as age and education. As appendix table 1C.5 shows, these characteristics did not change substantially over time. The average age of the head of eligible households was 41.8 in 1984 and 41.4 in 1991. The average years of education of the head of eligible households was 13.6 in 1984 and 13.7 in 1991. Within income interval, there was also very little change in the average age or education of eligible families. Similarly, there was little change in the age or education of noneligible households. The proportion of households with husband and wife present, which is typically found to be positively related to saving behavior, declined by 7 percentage points, on average, for both eligible and noneligible households. Much of saving commitment, however, cannot be explained by observed household attributes, and we rely on the cohort approach discussed below to provide a check on the eligibility experiment results. The cohort analysis is not confounded by the potential difference between the saving commitment of eligible and noneligible households.

EGS question the validity of our comparisons between 401(k) eligible and noneligible households. They argue that "401(k) eligible families save more in non-401(k) assets than observationally equivalent noneligible families, even after controlling for other factors." In our view, however, their numbers differ little from ours. They say, for example, that the two groups had different asset levels in 1984. But they estimate a (statistically insignificant) difference in *median* financial assets of only $173. They estimate a difference in median net financial assets of only $346. Given that our analysis controls for demographic characteristics and compares households within income intervals, while the EGS approach simply includes income as a single variable in a regression equation, their estimates seem hardly different from our findings.

EGS find a difference of $2,500 in 1984 in the net worth of eligible and noneligible households. The median for the entire sample is about $30,000 so the estimated difference represents a percentage difference of under 9 percent. In section 1.6 below, we repeat our analysis including housing equity, and controlling for income interval as above. We find essentially no difference in the housing equity of eligible and noneligible families in 1984.

EGS also find that eligible families are more likely than noneligible families to have a traditional defined benefit employer-provided pension plan. Whether this reflects a difference in saving propensity is questionable. That depends first on whether people choose jobs based on the pension plan. And, if they do, it is not at all clear that wanting a good pension plan means a stronger preference for saving. It could mean just the opposite. It may well be that choosing a job where the employer saves for you is a means of self-control. If a person is unlikely to save and would not do so were it not for the employer-guaranteed retirement income, then the people who choose jobs with pensions may be nonsavers, not savers.

Assuming further that persons with defined benefit pensions save less in other forms, Engen and Gale (1995) seem to argue that they should have lower financial assets in 1991 than noneligibles, if eligibility is *independent* of the taste for saving. In this case, according to their reasoning, a finding that eligible families have about the same, or even *more,* assets as noneligible households in 1991 confirms that they have a stronger commitment to save than noneligibles. Engen and Gale (1995) conclude that even a finding that eligible families save the same amount in non-401(k) assets as noneligible families can be interpreted as evidence that 401(k) eligibility is not exogenous, since eligibles should be saving less, if eligibility is exogenous with respect to saving. This reasoning seems to us self-fulfilling, assuming substitution to demonstrate substitution. It is a remarkable change from all earlier studies of IRAs, in which the central hypothesis was that IRA participants should have *less* non-IRA financial wealth than nonparticipants, if IRAs and other financial assets are substitutable. Here, the possibility that 401(k) eligibles may have *more* non-401(k) assets than noneligibles is used as evidence for substitution.

The weight of the evidence, however, is that persons with pensions do not reduce saving much, if at all, relative to persons without pensions. Gale (1995) argues that the methods that have been used by others to address this question are plagued by a series of biases that lead to an underestimate of the reduction in other saving for persons with employer-provided pensions. The key method that he proposes to avoid bias in his empirical analysis is a derived adjustment factor that multiplies pension wealth in regression equations relating other saving to pension wealth.

While Gale (1995) has pointed to a number of possible difficulties with prior estimates, his methodology, particularly his derived adjustment factor, raises new questions of interpretation. He derives the adjustment factor in a stylized life cycle model that assumes that a household's consumption and saving, even before retirement, are proportional to the present discounted value of lifetime wage and pension income. There are three difficulties with this approach. First, the model assumes that persons view pension wealth and other financial assets as perfect substitutes, that there is a "complete offset between pensions and other wealth" (Gale 1995, 16–17). Because the adjustment factor used in the empirical analysis is derived assuming complete substitution, the analysis cannot provide an unambiguous test of the extent of substitution. Much of the empirical research on saving, including the analysis of tax-deferred saving summarized here, suggests that the assumption is inappropriate. More conceptual "behavioral" explanations of saving behavior, in particular the work that emphasizes the "mental accounts" approach to saving, also bring into question this assumption. Second, the approach abstracts from the likely possibility that many households face liquidity constraints that make it difficult to consume out of pension wealth before retirement. Third, only a small fraction of persons who take a job with a pension early in the life cycle will retire from that job and acquire the rights to the defined pension benefit at age 65. Kotlikoff and Wise (1985, 1988, 1989) explain that a person who leaves a firm at age 40, for example, will have accrued only a small fraction of the age 65 pension. Such considerations imply that Gale's (1995) findings are subject to new biases that cloud interpretation of his results.

1.4.3   401(k) Eligibility and Other Pension Plans

Our analysis has focused on the substitution between 401(k) assets and other financial assets. Another potential trade-off is employer substitution of 401(k) plans for other employer-provided pension plans. The possibility of such substitution arises more directly with 401(k) plans than with IRAs because 401(k) plans are part of the workplace benefits package and their availability, like the availability of defined benefit or defined contribution pension plans, is subject to employer choice.

Although substitution between traditional pensions and 401(k) plans is a theoretical possibility, existing empirical evidence provides little support for such substitution in practice. As discussed above, EGS present evidence that workers who are eligible for 401(k) plans are *more* likely to be covered by a defined benefit pension plan than are workers without 401(k) eligibility. Although they interpret this as evidence of saver heterogeneity, it is prima facie evidence against the pension substitution hypothesis. Papke (1995) uses data from 1985 and 1991 IRS Form 5500 filings, and Papke, Petersen, and Poterba (1996) use data from a survey of 401(k) providers, to provide further evidence on this question. There is essentially no evidence that large firms offering 401(k) plans substituted these plans for other pension plans; the first 401(k)s were typically offered as "add-on" plans in large firms with preexisting defined benefit pension plans. Papke (1995) finds some evidence of substitution at smaller firms that have introduced 401(k) plans in recent years.

1.5   Cohorts and the Effects of Retirement Saving Programs

This method compares the assets of persons who are the same except that they reached a given age in different calendar years. Hence some cohorts had longer than others to contribute to special saving programs. For example, families that reached age 65 in 1984 had had only two years to contribute to an IRA or to a 401(k) plan, but families who attained age 65 in 1991 had had nine years to contribute. If these programs affect personal saving, they should lead to differences in asset accumulation by cohort.

1.5.1   The Cohort Method

Consider a random sample of *all* families, and assume for the moment that the typical family i has saving commitment m_i. Cohorts are distinguished by age (c) in 1984. We assume that cohort c has had s years to save. Suppose that in 1984 cohort c has had s years to save and during n of these s years was able to contribute to special retirement saving programs. We follow each cohort from 1984 to 1987 to 1991. For simplicity, we can assume that the cohort c *began* the period having saved for s years and ended the period having saved for $s+k$ years. By 1991, each cohort has had $n+k$ years to contribute to special retirement saving programs. (In 1984, n is about 2; in 1991, $n+k$ is about 9.) For cohort c, assets after n and $n+k$ years of exposure are given by

$$A_{ci}(n) = h(s) + m_i f(s) + p_i g(n),$$

$$A_{ci}(n+k) = h(s+k) + m_i f(s+k) + p_i g(n+k).$$

Consider now an older cohort $(c+k)$ that *began* the period having saved for $s+k$ years. For this cohort, assets after n and $n+k$ years of exposure are given by

$$A_{c+k,i}(n) = h(s+k) + m_i f(s+k) + p_i g(n),$$

$$A_{c+k,i}(n+k) = h(s+k+k) + m_i f(s+k+k) + p_i g(n+k).$$

This second cohort is k years older than the first cohort in the same calendar year. Thus the difference in the assets of the two cohorts when both have saved for $s+k$ years is given by

$$(10) \quad A_{ci}(n+k) - A_{c+k,i}(n)$$

$$= (m_i - m_i) f(s+k) + p_i [g(n+k) - g(n)] = p_i [g(n+k) - g(n)].$$

Thus the difference in the assets of families who reached the same age in calendar years n and $n+k$ is due to the program effect.

Table 1.7   **Summary of Cohort Effects at Ages 60–64 (in 1991 dollars)**

Asset	1984[a]	1991
Contributors and Noncontributors Combined		
Mean		
Personal retirement assets	5,118	14,156
Other personal financial assets	**37,132**	**36,263**
Total personal financial assets	42,250	50,419
Contributors		
Percentage of cohort	38	42
Median		
Personal retirement assets	8,171	22,148
Other personal financial assets	**22,983**	**21,528**
Total personal financial assets	34,975	50,182
Noncontributors		
Percentage of cohort	62	58
Median		
Total personal financial assets	2,687	2,134

Source: From Venti and Wise (1997), converted to 1991 dollars.

[a]The means and medians reported in this table are controlling for age, income, marital status, and education. The 1984 totals exclude 401(k) assets, which were small at that time. Thus the data for personal retirement and for total personal financial assets are affected to some degree by this omission. But the data on other personal financial assets are unaffected.

If the different cohorts had different saving commitments, however, the term $m_i - m_i$ in equation (10) would not be zero, and the difference would reflect this, as well as the program effect. Judgments about the likely importance of such differences may be based on several features of the analysis. Cohort effects are obtained for a succession of cohorts ranging in age from 42 to 70 in 1984. These cohort effects are obtained for several asset categories: special retirement saving program assets, total financial assets, and conventional financial assets. Differences in the cohort effects for different assets can be used to judge whether there was a systematic change in taste for saving over time. It is also possible to compare cohort effects for participants and nonparticipants in retirement saving programs.

1.5.2   The Results

The cohort method was used by Venti and Wise (1997). They find that households who attained a given age in 1991 had consistently larger total real financial assets than households who reached that age in 1984. The larger assets of the younger cohorts is accounted for almost entirely by more assets in IRA and 401(k) plans. There is on average no difference between the other financial assets of the older and younger cohorts. The results can by illustrated by comparing the assets of families who reached ages 60–64 in 1984 with the assets of families that attained those ages in 1991, as shown in table 1.7.

To control for heterogeneity, the data for all families—both contributors and noncontributors combined—are the most compelling. In this case it is the typical saving propensity m_i over all families that is important, and the possible effect of the changing composition of participant and nonparticipant families is avoided. (Because fewer than half of all families participate in these programs, the median of program assets for all families is zero and thus not informative.) The *mean* of total financial assets of all families that attained ages 60–64 in 1984 was $42,250; the mean of those who attained this age in 1991 was $50,419 (both values are in 1991 dollars and control for income, age, education, and marital status). The increase was accounted for almost entirely by personal retirement saving—$5,118 for the cohort that attained ages 60–64 in 1984 compared to $14,156 for the cohort that attained this age range in 1991. There was essentially no cohort difference in other financial assets ($37,132 for the older cohort and $36,263 for the younger cohort). Thus there is little evidence of substitution of personal retirement saving for other financial assets.

The data for families who participated in personal retirement saving plans provide a better measure of the potential of the plans to augment the financial assets of retirees. The *median* level of total personal financial assets of contributor families that attained ages 60–64 in 1984 was $34,975, compared with $50,182 for families who attained that age range in 1991. The median level of personal retirement plan assets of the families that reached this age range in 1984 was $8,171, compared with $22,148 for families who reached ages 60–64 in 1991. On the other hand, the other financial assets of these families were about the same in 1984 and 1991 ($22,983 and $21,528, respectively). Although not as compelling as the data for both groups combined, these data also provide little evidence of substitution. In contrast, the financial assets of families that attained ages 60–64 in 1991 and did not participate in personal retirement plans were somewhat lower than the assets of similar families who reached this age range in 1984.

The results for other age groups are summarized in figure 1.3. To understand the figure, consider age 66: The cohort that reached this age in 1984 had about $5,000 less in personal retirement assets *(heavy lines)* than the next younger cohort that reached that age about four years later. The difference in the total financial assets *(light lines)* of these two cohorts is also about $5,000. But there is very little difference in the other financial assets of these two cohorts.

Results of more formal estimation of cohort effects are shown in table 1.8. The estimates are obtained by fitting a cubic function in age to the cohort means, allowing for cohort shifts—the cohort effects—in the relationship between age and assets.[16] The estimate of the youngest cohort effect for personal

---

16. We fit the actual cohort means with a specification of the form

(11) $$A_{ic} = \alpha + \beta_c + \gamma_1(\text{Age}_i) + \gamma_2(\text{Age}_i)^2 + \gamma_3(\text{Age}_i)^3 + \varepsilon_{ic},$$

where A represents an asset category—personal retirement assets, other personal financial assets, total personal financial assets—c indexes cohort, and i denotes the ith cohort mean. The β_c are

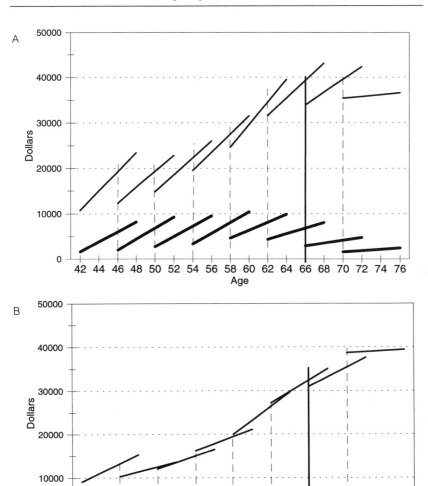

Fig. 1.3   Mean assets: total and retirement (A) and other (B), for contributors and noncontributors combined—indexed

Note: In panel *A*, light lines graph total assets, and heavy lines graph retirement assets.

cohort effects with $\Sigma\beta_c = 0$. Thus the individual estimates represent deviations from the mean effect, which is set to zero. The specification is intended to fit the age-asset accumulation pattern, allowing the differences in the levels of the assets between successive cohorts to be maintained and to cumulate as the cohorts age. It is assumed, e.g., that the estimated difference between the assets of the two youngest cohorts, C42 and C46, will be maintained as the cohorts age. It is likely that this assumption implies a conservative estimate of the projected cohort differences. Constant percentage differences as the cohorts age, e.g., imply much larger absolute differences at advanced ages than this model does.

Table 1.8   **Estimated Cohort Effects for Means by Asset: Both Contributors and Noncontributors (in 1984 dollars)**

Cohort	Personal Retirement Assets		Total Personal Financial Assets		Other Personal Financial Assets	
	Coefficient	t-Statistic	Coefficient	t-Statistic	Coefficient	t-Statistic
C42	14,076	19.0	16,002	8.2	1,927	1.0
C44	11,085	17.9	12,024	7.3	939	0.6
C46	9,997	17.3	9,568	6.3	−428	−0.3
C48	7,821	14.8	6,556	4.7	−1,264	−0.9
C50	5,759	11.9	4,132	3.2	−1,626	−1.3
C52	3,814	8.6	1,459	1.2	−2,354	−2.1
C54	1,944	4.7	452	0.4	−1,492	−1.4
C56	363	0.9	734	0.7	370	0.4
C58	−1,604	−3.9	−1,682	−1.6	−78	−0.1
C60	−3,815	−8.7	−5,165	−4.5	−1,349	−1.2
C62	−5,813	−12.1	−3,796	−3.0	2,017	1.7
C64	−8,130	−15.4	−5,234	−3.7	2,895	2.2
C66	−10,345	−18.0	−8,766	−5.8	1,578	1.1
C68	−12,049	−19.2	−12,203	−7.3	−154	−0.1
C70	−13,103	−17.8	−14,081	−6.1	−981	−0.4

Source: Venti and Wise (1997).

retirement assets is $14,076 *above* the mean while the estimate for the oldest cohort is $13,103 *below* the mean, a difference of $27,179. If there were no counterbalancing cohort effects with respect to other personal financial assets, the total personal financial asset cohort effects should approximately parallel the retirement asset cohort effects. The estimates show that the total personal financial asset cohort effect for the youngest cohort is $16,002 *above* the mean and the cohort effect for the oldest cohort is $14,081 *below* the mean, a difference of $30,083. The other personal financial asset cohort effects are typically small and not statistically different from zero. An *F*-test does not reject the hypothesis that all the cohort effects with respect to other personal financial assets are zero.

The analysis suggests that if current patterns persist families who reach retirement age 25 or 30 years from now will have much more in financial assets than families currently attaining retirement age, and the difference will be due solely to assets in personal retirement accounts.

We believe that the cohort approach provides the surest way of controlling for heterogeneity. When both contributors and noncontributors are considered jointly, the overall saving effects are not contaminated by potential changes in composition of the two groups. Nor are the cohort estimates confounded by the "coincidence" possibility that may affect the difference-in-difference estimates discussed in section 1.2. In principle, the cohort analysis compares families who differ only in the calendar year in which they reached a given age and therefore in their exposure to retirement saving programs.

A potential, although we believe unlikely, confounding influence would be an overall change in saving behavior, with each successively younger cohort wanting to save more than its older cohorts. The evidence suggests that such a systematic increasing taste for saving must have been realized only in contributions to the special retirement saving programs. We find this an unlikely possibility for two reasons. There are no cohort effects in other financial assets, as we would expect if there were an underlying change in taste for saving. Nor are there cohort effects for nonparticipants, as we would also expect if there were an overall change in the taste for saving. Therefore, we interpret the cohort results as supporting the results of the other methods of correcting for heterogeneity.

1.5.3   Further Results

Registered Retirement Saving Plans (RRSPs) were first introduced in Canada in 1957. As with the IRA in the United States, an individual can make contributions to an RRSP and deduct the contributions from income for tax purposes. Interest accrues tax free until withdrawal, when taxes are paid. The contribution limits were increased substantially in the early 1970s, and RRSPs were widely promoted. Since then, they have become a very prominent form of saving. Annual contributions grew from $225 million in 1970 to almost $3.7 billion in 1980 to $16 billion by 1992, when they accounted for about one-third of aggregate personal saving. In 1992 about 33 percent of families contributed, with an average contribution of $4,180. Now RRSP contributions exceed the total of employee and employer contributions to employer-provided pension plans.

Based largely on "cohort" analysis like the procedure described above, Venti and Wise (1995b) conclude that RRSPs have contributed substantially to personal saving in Canada. In virtually no case do the data suggest substitution of RRSP saving for other forms of retirement saving. In the two decades prior to the growth in RRSP popularity, the personal saving rate in Canada was typically below the U.S. personal saving rate. Since that time, the personal saving rate in Canada has become much higher than in the United States. Although it is difficult to make judgments about the RRSP saving effect based only on the trends in U.S. and Canadian aggregate saving rates, the cohort analysis suggests that a large fraction of the current difference can be accounted for by RRSP saving. Engelhardt (1996b) analyzes the similarly tax-advantaged Registered Home Ownership Saving Program (RHOSP), designed to encourage saving for home purchase. He finds that the RHOSP program also increased total personal saving.

1.6   Other Margins of Substitution: Home Equity

The foregoing discussion focuses on the substitution between contributions to special retirement saving plans and other financial assets. There are at least two other potential margins of substitution: employer-provided pension assets and home equity. As mentioned above, many analysts have considered the substitution between employer-provided pension assets and personal financial assets. The results are mixed, but the weight of the findings suggests little substitution.[17] Venti and Wise (1997) have also addressed this question, considering the assets of retired persons for whom pension assets are known, and using social security benefit percentiles to control for lifetime income. They conclude that there is essentially no relationship between employer-provided pension assets and either personal retirement saving plan assets or other financial assets. They considered the same question for retired persons in Canada, where the RRSP program has been widely used for several decades, again finding essentially no relationship between employer-provided pension assets and personal financial assets. We will not address that question further here.

We will, however, consider the potential substitution between housing equity and retirement saving plan assets. Our focus on the relationship between retirement saving assets and other financial assets neglects the possible interaction between these retirement plan assets and home equity, which is the largest asset of a large fraction of households. While many of the factors that are likely to determine whether to purchase a home, the value of the home, and how to finance a home purchase may be unrelated to the accumulation of retirement saving assets, it is possible that some of the buildup in these accounts has been financed through reduced accumulation of housing equity.

Several studies have considered the relationship between housing *prices* and financial assets. In his review article, Skinner (1994) finds little relationship between exogenous shocks to housing value and personal financial assets. Several other studies are based on the Panel Survey of Income Dynamics: Skinner (1996) finds a small relationship for younger households and no relationship for older households. Hoynes and McFadden (1994) find little relationship between exogenous changes in home values and changes in financial assets. Engelhardt (1996a) finds no decrease in financial asset saving among households with an increase in home values but finds a small increase among households with falling home values. Engen and Gale (1995) have considered the relationship between home equity and 401(k) assets based on SIPP data. While their results largely confirm our findings on the relationship between 401(k) and other financial assets, they conclude that the increase in the financial asset saving of 401(k) participants (or eligibles) between 1987 and 1991 was offset by a reduction in home equity.

We consider the relationship between retirement saving plan contributions and home equity using cohort analysis as in section 1.5 and comparison of 401(k) eligible and noneligible families as in section 1.4. The most important conclusion from the cohort analysis is that the timing of changes in mortgage debt and net home equity is inconsistent with a causal relationship between

---

17. Gale (1995) has summarized the results in table 1 of his paper.

personal retirement plan contributions and mortgage debt. With respect to 401(k) contributions in particular, we conclude from the eligibility comparison that there was no apparent offset to 401(k) contributions through a reduction in home equity. We consider briefly one possible reason for the difference between our results and those reported by Engen and Gale (1995).

1.6.1   Cohort Analysis

Cohort data make it easy to compare the trends in personal retirement saving and housing assets. As in the analysis above, we consider IRA and 401(k) participants and nonparticipants together.[18] The interpretation of financial asset versus housing equity trends must be tempered by at least two factors. First, market trends in housing values and financing practices that are unlikely to be induced by IRA and 401(k) contributions can have substantial effects on housing equity. There was probably little relationship between retirement saving plan contributions and the concerns that led to elimination of tax deductibility of nonmortgage interest as part of the Tax Reform Act of 1986. But this provision may have had a substantial effect on home mortgage debt.[19] Thus the home equity data may be subject to very important time effects.

Second, unlike other consumer debt, mortgage debt may, in the long run, increase future saving. Many financial planners tout mortgage debt repayment as the surest way for a household to commit to a long-term saving strategy. Regularly scheduled mortgage payments can thus be viewed as means of self-control as stressed by Thaler and Shefrin (1981), Shefrin and Thaler (1988), and Thaler (1990). While increased mortgage debt may appear as a reduction in wealth today, it may assure greater rather than reduced wealth at retirement. Similarly, a home equity loan that is repaid before retirement may not affect wealth at retirement.

The central results of the cohort analysis are presented in figure 1.4, which shows the relationships between contributions to personal retirement saving plans and housing market data. Like the results presented in section 1.5, the analysis here is based on 1984, 1987, and 1991 data for 15 cohorts: the youngest was age 42 and the oldest was age 70 in 1984.[20] The cohort data on housing value, mortgage debt, and home equity are shown in appendix tables 1C.2A through 1C.2C. Data for selected cohorts are graphed in figures 1.4A through 1.4D. Figure 1.4A shows data for mean personal retirement assets (including IRA, 401(k), and Keogh saving balances). Figure 1.4B pertains to home value, figure 1.4C to mortgage debt, and figure 1.4D to net home equity.

---

18. To maintain comparability with the cohort analysis discussed above, we have converted current dollar amounts to 1991 values using the Bureau of Labor Statistics earnings index. Using a price index instead has little effect on the trends.

19. Skinner and Feenberg (1990) find that each dollar of reduced consumer debt following the Tax Reform Act of 1986 was offset by a 67 cent increase in mortgage debt.

20. In principle, we would like to consider younger cohorts as well, but we wanted these data to be comparable to our earlier analysis of financial asset data that was directed to families approaching and entering retirement.

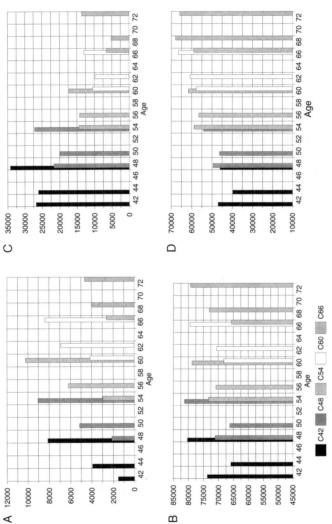
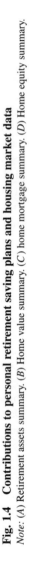

Fig. 1.4 Contributions to personal retirement saving plans and housing market data

Note: (*A*) Retirement assets summary. (*B*) Home value summary. (*C*) home mortgage summary. (*D*) Home equity summary.

All values are in 1991 dollars. The figures can be explained with reference to figure 1.4A. For each of the cohorts, mean retirement assets are shown for 1984, 1987, and 1991. For example, cohort C42 was age 42 in 1984, 44 in 1987,[21] and 48 in 1991. By 1991, this cohort had had nine years to contribute to the retirement saving program and had mean assets of $8,000 in these accounts at age 48. In contrast, cohort C48 had had only about two years to contribute to such accounts when first observed in 1984 and had only about $2,000 in these retirement assets at age 48. Similar comparisons can be made at ages 54, 60, and 66. The cohort that attained the given age later had much larger amounts in these retirement assets at that age. Figures 1.4B through 1.4D present housing data for the same cohorts, and the trends can be compared to the cohort trends for retirement assets.

Figure 1.4B shows a substantial fall in real home value between 1984 and 1987 for younger cohorts but an increase for older cohorts. For all cohorts, but especially for the younger cohorts, there was a large increase in home values between 1987 and 1991. Given that housing values were falling during the rapid rise in retirement saving plan assets—and only rising later on—these trends apparently reflect housing market effects that are unrelated to 401(k) and IRA contributions. It is clear, however, that at ages where direct comparisons can be made, the home values of younger cohorts are much greater than those of older cohorts. For example, the cohort that reached age 48 in 1991 had a real mean home value of about $80,000. The cohort that attained age 48 in 1984 had a mean home value at that age of about $72,000, in 1991 dollars.

Figure 1.4C shows a *fall* in mortgage debt between 1984 and 1987 for all cohorts. This pattern persists even for older cohorts that experienced an increase in home values between 1984 and 1987. Yet over this period there was a sharp *increase* in the IRA and 401(k) assets of these cohorts, as shown in figure 1.4A. Between the early 1980s and 1986 contributions to these programs grew from about $3 billion to almost $74 billion. Contributions to 401(k) plans almost doubled between 1984 and 1986. Yet it is clear that over this period when contributions to special retirement saving plans were growing dramatically there was no countervailing increase in home mortgage debt.

There was an enormous increase in home mortgage debt between 1987 and 1991 for all cohorts. Although assets in personal retirement saving plans continued to grow over this period, the increase was not as rapid as over the earlier period, when mortgage debt was declining. Indeed, new contributions to special retirement saving programs *declined* between 1986 and 1991. Because of the 1986 cutback in the IRA program, contributions to that program fell from almost $40 billion in 1986 to less than $10 billion by 1991. Contributions to all special retirement programs decreased from about $74 billion in 1986 to about $68 billion in 1991, a decline of about 9 percent. Thus when contribu-

---

21. The 1984 survey was administered between September and December 1984, and the 1987 survey between January and April of 1987, a difference of approximately 28 months.

tions to these programs were growing dramatically there was a fall in mortgage debt, and when contributions to the retirement saving programs were declining there was a dramatic increase in mortgage debt. This pattern does not appear to be consistent with substitution of IRA and 401(k) assets for housing equity.

The cohort data confirm that changes in mortgage debt, as well as changes in home value, were not induced by contributions to retirement saving plans. It seems likely that the increase in mortgage debt for all cohorts after 1987 was prompted by the provisions of the Tax Reform Act of 1986 that eliminated the tax deductibility of nonmortgage debt. We consider, though, whether there was a difference in the behavior of younger and older cohorts over this period.

Figure 1.4D summarizes the cohort data for home equity, which of course is the difference between housing value and mortgage debt. There is a change in the cohort relationships, starting with the cohort that attained age 54 in 1984. The youngest cohorts have lower home equity than successively older cohorts up to the age 54 cohort. For example, the younger cohorts that reached ages 48 and 54 in 1991 had lower mean values of home equity than the older cohorts that attained those ages in 1984. But for older cohorts, the reverse is true, younger cohorts have greater housing equity than successively older cohorts— at ages 60 and 66, for example. The cohort effects in home equity are very dissimilar from the cohort effects readily apparent in retirement saving assets and thus we judge were not prompted by contributions to special retirement saving programs.

The time effects in home value and mortgage debt complicate the identification of cohort effects (this issue is discussed further in appendix A). Nonetheless, to provide some indication of the housing equity of successively older cohorts, we have estimated cohort effects (as above) by fitting the cohort means with a function cubic in age. The results are shown in figure 1.5. The first series shows estimated home value cohort effects, the second series shows mortgage debt effects, and the third series shows home equity effects. The home value effects range from $+25,667$ for the youngest cohort to $-36,407$ for the oldest cohort, a difference of 62,074. The mean home value of each successively older cohort is lower than the mean for the immediately younger cohort. Interpreted literally, if there were no changes in the housing market, these data would suggest that when the current youngest cohort attains the age of the oldest cohort, the mean home value of the current youngest cohort will be $62,074 more than the mean of the oldest cohort.

The home mortgage cohort effects show a similar pattern, ranging from a high of $+26,180$ to a low of $-20,951$. Again, interpreted literally, these estimates would suggest that when the youngest cohort attains the age of the oldest cohort, that (future old) cohort will have $47,131 more in mortgage debt than the current old cohort. But here it becomes clear that the projections are likely to be exaggerated. Mortgage debt is likely to be paid down. If it were completely paid off by age 72, say, then the current young cohort would be wealthier than the current old cohort—by an amount given by the difference in their

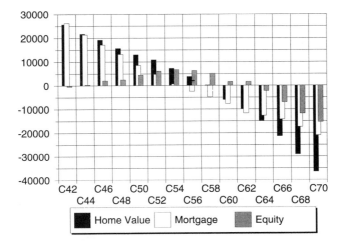

Fig. 1.5   Estimated cohort effects in home value, mortgage, and equity

home value cohort effects ($62,074). The key question, which is not addressed by these data, is how much the current mortgage debt of the younger cohorts will be paid down.

The home equity cohort effects mirror the pattern shown in figure 1.4*D*. The estimated effect for the youngest cohort is −513, while for the oldest cohort the effect is −15,456. If the home mortgage were not reduced, the difference of $14,943 indicates that when the youngest cohort attains the age of the oldest cohort, the youngest cohort would have $14,943 more in home equity than the current oldest cohort.[22] On balance, the home equity cohort effects *magnify* the financial asset cohort differences, showing successively greater financial assets with each younger cohort (see fig. 1.6). But if, as emphasized above, all mortgage debt is reduced with age and the trend in housing value persists, the difference in the assets of the younger and the older cohorts at retirement would be more closely indicated by the difference in home value. Since most retirement assets are likely to be accumulated until retirement, if mortgage debt is paid off by retirement age, wealth at that time will include retirement saving balances plus home value.

1.6.2   The 401(k) Eligible-Noneligible Comparison: Evidence on Housing Equity

An approach that is not complicated by a coincidental growth in retirement saving and mortgage debt is to compare the assets of 401(k) eligible and non-

22. The difference between the home equity cohort effects varies with age, however. The effects increase from the youngest cohort to the cohort that is age 54 in 1984. Thereafter, the cohort effects decline, with successively older cohorts having less home equity. The difference between the youngest and the C54 cohort is $7,193. The difference between the C42 and the oldest cohort is $22,136.

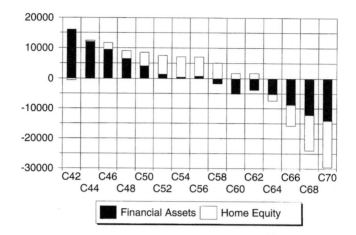

Fig. 1.6   Cohort effects in financial assets and home equity

eligible families in a given year, based on a random cross section of respondents of all ages. As described in section 1.4, for this comparison to be compelling, it is important that the eligible and noneligible households be similar with respect to saving propensity, controlling for income interval. As above, we use 1984 data, near the outset of the 401(k) program, to demonstrate the similarity of the saving propensities of eligible and noneligible families. We first discuss data on trends in the housing equity of eligible and noneligible households.

Trends in the Housing Equity of Eligible and Noneligible Households

The cohort data described above show changes in home mortgage debt and home values from 1984 to 1987 and from 1987 to 1991. Here we consider changes in home equity for families that are and are not eligible to contribute to a 401(k) plan. Table 1.9 shows that the trend was essentially *the same for both groups*. (These data show differences in the mean levels of home equity of eligible and noneligible households, *without* controlling for income interval. Within income interval, the differences are typically small, as discussed below.) There was very little change between 1984 and 1987 in mean home equity for eligible or for noneligible households. This is consistent with the cohort data, which shown a decrease for some cohorts and an increase for others. Between 1987 and 1991 there was a substantial decline in home equity for both eligible and noneligible households. The absolute decline is larger for eligible than for noneligible households, reflecting their larger absolute level of housing equity at the beginning of the period. The percentage declines were approximately the same for both groups, about 17 percent for noneligible families and about 19 percent for eligible families.[23] Given that the absolute effects

23. Home ownership declined 10 percent for noneligible and 4 percent for eligible families, and mean home value of home owners declined 12 percent for noneligible and 16 percent for eligible families.

Table 1.9   **Trends in Home Equity by 401(k) Eligibility, 1984, 1987, and 1991 (in 1991 dollars)**

	Year		
Measure	1984	1987	1991
Percentage own			
Eligible	0.78	0.75	0.75
Not eligible	0.63	0.60	0.57
Percentage own, relative to 1984			
Eligible	1.00	0.96	0.96
Not eligible	1.00	0.96	0.90
Mean home equity given own			
Eligible	70,723	71,189	59,880
Not eligible	61,197	61,688	54,629
Mean home equity given own— relative to 1984			
Eligible	1.00	1.01	.085
Not eligible	1.00	1.01	0.89
Mean home equity			
Eligible	49,747	47,685	40,425
Not eligible	34,073	33,088	28,273
Mean home equity, relative to 1984			
Eligible	1.00	0.96	0.81
Not eligible	1.00	0.97	0.83

of both market-determined housing price changes and availability of home equity loans are functions of initial housing equity, it is not surprising that the changes are roughly proportional to initial equity.

Although percentage changes in mean values were about the same for both groups, the proportionate decline in medians, and other quantiles, was much greater for noneligible than for eligible households. Quantile values (50th, 75th, and 90th) for eligible and noneligible households are shown in figure 1.7. Because a large fraction of households do not own a home, medians can be substantially affected by small changes in mean values. Like the means, the quantile changes between 1984 and 1987 were much smaller than the changes between 1987 and 1991. Between 1987 and 1991, median home equity for eligible households declined by 40 percent, the 75th percentile by 18 percent, and the 90th percentile by 5 percent; the declines for noneligible households were 71 percent, 25 percent, and 10 percent, respectively. These tabulations suggest that the forces that induced changes in home equity applied more or less equally to eligible and noneligible households during the 1987–91 period.

The Eligibility Comparison

We expanded our comparison of the assets of eligible and noneligible households at a point in time to include net housing equity. As emphasized above, the validity of this difference as an estimate of the eligibility effect depends on

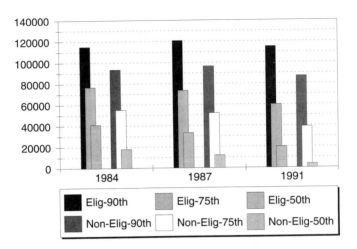

Fig. 1.7   Home equity quantiles by eligibility and year

the similarity of the underlying taste for saving of the two groups. Again, we rely on comparison of the assets of eligible and noneligible households near the outset of the program, in 1984, to establish the extent of similarity.

Median 1984 asset balances are shown in table 1.10, by income interval.[24] Within an income interval, the medians control for age, marital status, and education. The assets of eligible and noneligible families were roughly the same at the outset of the 401(k) program, whether the asset measure includes or excludes net housing equity.[25] There is, however, a noticeable difference for the $75,000+ income interval. There are only 83 families in the 401(k) eligible group in this interval. Because this top interval is open ended, the incomes of eligible and noneligible households in this interval may be quite different. For most families, net non–IRA-401(k) assets were negative or very small in 1984. Thus any significant contributions to a saving plan, from which assets are not withdrawn, would therefore represent a net increase in the financial asset saving of most families.

Median assets balances in 1991 are shown in table 1.11. Although at the outset of the program eligible and noneligible families had approximately the same level of net financial assets, by 1991 eligible families had substantially greater median levels of net total financial asset balances, and greater levels of financial asset plus home equity balances, than noneligible families.

The first two panels of table 1.11 show net total financial assets and net total

24. The estimates are evaluated at the median of sample values for age, marital status, and education. Thus they differ from similar calculations reported in PVW (1995), which are evaluated at the means of control variables.

25. Appendix table 1C.3 shows that eligibles and noneligibles had similar levels of other asset measures at the outset of the 401(k) program in 1984. We were unable to calculate conditional medians for home value and home mortgage.

Table 1.10   Conditional Median Asset Balances by 401(k) Eligibility and Income Interval, 1984 (in 1984 dollars)

Asset Category and Eligibility Status	Income Interval[a]							
	<10	10–20	20–30	30–40	40–50	50–75	75+	
Net non–IRA-401(k) financial assets								
Eligible	−1,288	−651	302	716	2,815	6,241	22,068	
Not eligible	−607	−348	130	775	2,080	5,208	17,802	
Difference	−681	−304	172	−60	735*	1,034*	4,267*	
Net non–IRA-401(k) financial assets plus home equity								
Eligible	11,594	16,616	21,371	28,136	38,799	53,060	104,748	
Not eligible	11,293	14,398	18,632	28,461	36,327	44,462	83,338	
Difference	301	2,218	2,739	−325	2,472	8,598*	21,410*	

Source: Authors' tabulations from the 1984 SIPP.

[a]Income intervals indexed to 1987 dollars.

*Statistically significant at the 5 percent level.

Table 1.11   **Conditional Median Asset Balances by 401(k) Eligibility and Income Interval, 1991 (in 1991 dollars)**

Asset Category and Eligibility Status	Income Interval[a]						
	<10	10–20	20–30	30–40	40–50	50–75	75+
Net total financial assets							
Eligible	1,102	1,073	2,464	7,554	17,022	34,726	67,878
Not eligible	−483	−57	370	2,307	3,652	11,597	39,218
Difference	1,585*	1,130*	2,094*	5,247*	13,370*	23,129*	28,660*
Net total financial assets plus housing equity							
Eligible	14,509	14,150	20,538	32,875	49,361	84,511	151,834
Not eligible	9,185	13,121	15,106	28,502	38,139	60,945	122,341
Difference	5,324	1,029	5,432*	4,373*	11,222*	23,566*	29,499*
Net non–IRA-401(k) financial assets							
Eligible	−491	−262	−95	1,089	3,094	8,838	18,925
Not eligible	−327	−142	116	907	1,968	5,667	26,909
Difference	−164	−120	−211	182	1,126*	3,171*	−7,984*
Net non–IRA-401(k) financial assets plus home equity							
Eligible	9,030	10,361	14,017	24,168	34,682	61,358	108,290
Not eligible	8,059	11,557	13,522	25,468	35,275	56,360	105,294
Difference	971	−1,196	495	−1,300	−593	4,998*	2366

Source: Authors' tabulations from the 1991 SIPP.

[a]Income intervals indexed to 1987 dollars.

*Statistically significant at the 5 percent level.

financial assets plus home equity, for eligible and noneligible households. For the most part, the difference between the assets of eligible and noneligible families remains about the same when home equity is added to net total financial assets. At the outset of the program, the financial assets and the home equity of eligible and noneligible families were about the same. They were also about the same in 1991 (more detail is shown in appendix table 1C.4). The difference between median levels of net non–IRA-401(k) financial assets plus housing equity of eligible and noneligible families is about the same as the difference in net non–IRA-401(k) financial assets. Thus these data suggest that the greater financial assets of 401(k) eligible families were not offset by a disproportionate reduction in the housing equity of eligible families. This is consistent with the data that show approximately equal proportional changes in the housing equity of eligible and noneligible families between 1984 and 1991.

1.6.3   The Engen and Gale Between-Group Results

Using a different approach, Engen and Gale (1995; hereafter EG) conclude that the increase in the financial assets of eligible families was offset by a reduction in home equity. We do not explore the differences between their results and ours in detail here, but we do describe the key elements of their method and provide some conjectures about possible reasons for the differences.

The Method

To study the relationship between 401(k) saving and home equity, EG use an approach similar to the one described in section 1.3.2 above. They consider several *between*-group comparisons, including 401(k) eligible versus noneligible families and 401(k) eligibles who have an IRA versus 401(k) noneligibles who have an IRA. For illustration, we consider first the former comparison, denoting the first group by i and the second group by j. We treat the Tax Reform Act of 1986 (TRA86) as a "program," with an effect on both groups. Using the same terminology as in equation (7), the "treatment" group (i) is subject to both the 401(k) and the TRA86 program effects, p_i and r_i, respectively, while the comparison group (j) is subject only to the TRA86 effect. The difference-in-difference estimate including both the saving program and the TRA86 effects would be

$$[A_{si}(n+k) - A_{si}(n)] - [A_{sj}(n+k) - A_{sj}(n)]$$

$$(12) \quad = [(m_i - m_{i'}) - (m_j - m_{j'})]f(s)$$

$$+ \{p_i[g(n+k) - g(n)] + (r_i - r_j)[q(u+k) - q(u)]\}.$$

To make clear that years of exposure to TRA86 may differ from exposure to the saving program, we let u indicate the number of years of exposure to TRA86 at the first observation (e.g., 1987) and $u+k$ the number of years of exposure to

TRA86 at the second observation (e.g., 1991). This method will estimate the 401(k) program effect p_i if two conditions are met: $m_i = m_{i'}$ and $m_j = m_{j'}$, or if $m_i - m_{i'} = m_j - m_{j'}$, as discussed above, and $r_i = r_j$. But if the two groups have very different levels of home equity at the outset, it is unlikely that the effects of TRA86, r_i and r_j, will be equal, at least in levels.

If the comparison is between 401(k) eligibles who have an IRA versus 401(k) noneligibles who have an IRA, the treatment group (i) is subject to three program effects: 401(k), IRA, and TRA86—p_i, b_i, and r_i, respectively. The comparison group (j) is subject to two program effects: IRA and TRA86—b_j and r_j. In this case, the difference-in-difference estimate is

$$[A_{si}(n+k) - A_{si}(n)] - [A_{sj}(n+k) - A_{sj}(n)]$$

$$(13) \quad = [(m_i - m_{i'}) - (m_j - m_{j'})]f(s) + [(p_i + b_i) - b_j][g(n+k) - g(n)]$$

$$+ (r_i - r_j)[q(u+k) - q(u)].$$

The program effect p_i will be isolated if three conditions are met: $m_i = m_{i'}$ and $m_j = m_{j'}$, or if $m_i - m_{i'} = m_j - m_{j'}$, $r_i = r_j$, and $b_i = b_j$. Again, whether these conditions are approximately met is likely to depend on the initial conditions of the two groups. As emphasized above, if the initial conditions of the two groups are very different it is more likely that the program effects on the two groups will differ as well. The effects of TRA86 are likely to depend on the initial home equity levels, and the potential effects of the saving programs may vary in nonsystematic ways with the initial financial assets of the two groups. Some committed *non*savers may be completely unaffected by the programs, for example. Thus it is problematic whether any differencing procedure will adequately account for differences in the potential program responses of very dissimilar saver groups.

Results versus Method: Some Illustrations

A complete understanding of why our results differ from those obtained by EG will have to await further analysis and discussion, but we believe one explanation is their use of dissimilar groups in computing a difference-in-difference estimator. Recall that PVW (1994a, 1995) emphasize *within*-group estimates in the like saver group comparisons discussed in section 1.3. EG use a *between*-group approach.[26]

The within-group approach that we used to evaluate the effect of the saving programs on financial asset saving may not extend satisfactorily to include housing equity. Although housing equity may be affected by 401(k) eligibility, it is also likely to have been affected by TRA86. A within-group estimator cannot distinguish the separate effects of the two programs. Thus it is natural to seek a saver group affected by TRA86 but not by the 401(k) plan, with which

---

26. EG cite PVW (1995) as the source for their method. This is a misunderstanding of our method.

the 401(k) group can be compared. This is what the between-group estimate that EG use is intended to do. But typically their comparisons are between dissimilar saver groups with very different saving behavior. The question then is how to obtain reliable estimates from between-group comparisons when the groups are so different. There may be no completely satisfactory way to do this—other than a randomized controlled trial—and we do not try to solve the problem.

We do, however, illustrate the issue using data for the saver groups defined by 401(k) eligibility and IRA participation status. These groups were considered by PVW in the like group analysis discussed in section 1.3. (The financial asset data for the groups are shown in the bottom panel of table 1.4.). In their within-like-group analysis, PVW emphasized that there was virtually no change between 1984 and 1991 in non–IRA-401(k) assets of 401(k) eligible households, 401(k) eligible households with an IRA, or 401(k) eligible households without an IRA (or in the non–IRA-401(k) assets of 401(k) noneligible households with an IRA). Yet for each of these saver groups there was a large increase in total financial assets. Based on between-group comparisons, EG argue that the increase in financial assets between 1987 and 1991 was offset by a reduction in home equity.

But this conclusion depends critically on whether the groups compared are similar or dissimilar, as the data in table 1.12 show. The question is whether there was a differential effect of TRA86 on the 401(k) eligible households, compared to the comparison households. Consider first 401(k) eligibles with an IRA compared to 401(k) noneligibles with an IRA. These two groups had similar housing assets in 1984 at the outset of the 401(k) program and experienced similar declines in housing equity (10.2 percent for the eligible and 10.6 percent for the noneligible group). In this case, the dollar declines were about the same as well. The decline for 401(k) eligible households was $379 greater than the decline for noneligible households. Were one to assume that this is the decline due to 401(k) eligibility—which we would not—this amount would offset very little of the increase in the total financial assets of 401(k) eligible households between 1987 and 1991.

When very dissimilar groups are compared, however, this approach can yield misleading results. For example, even though all 401(k) eligible and all 401(k) noneligible households experienced similar proportional declines in housing equity (15.7 vs. 13.7 percent), the *dollar* declines were very different ($4,513 vs. $2,254) because the two groups had very different levels of housing equity at the outset of the program. Thus it is misleading to ascribe the greater decline in the housing equity of the 401(k) eligible group to 401(k) eligibility per se, as the between-group comparison does. The greater decline for eligibles may simply reflect their larger initial housing equity. The groups also had very different levels of financial assets. This is why we emphasize within-group comparisons, and avoid inferences based on between-group comparisons, in our like group analysis.

One way to estimate the reduction in housing equity attributable to the

Table 1.12   Home Equity by Saver Group and Year, with Between-Group Estimates: Conditional Medians in 1987 Dollars

Saver Group	1984	1987	1991	Difference 1984 to 1991		Difference to 1987 to 1991	
				Percentage	Level	Percentage	Level
All families							
401(k) Eligible	32,658	28,743	24,230	−25.8	−8,428	−15.7	−4,513
401(k) Not eligible	18,699	16,469	14,215	−24.0	−4,484	−13.7	−2,254
Difference in difference				**−1.8**	**−3,944**	**−2.0**	**−2,259**
Equal percentage reduction[a]					−597		−579
Families with an IRA							
401(k) Eligible	52,621	48,451	43,531	−17.3	−9,090	−10.2	−4,920
401(k) Not eligible	46,385	42,913	38,372	−17.3	−8,013	−10.6	−4,541
Difference in difference				**0.0**	**−1,077**	**0.4**	**−379**
Equal percentage reduction[a]					**0**		**207**
Families without an IRA							
401(k) Eligible	22,905	19,704	15,578	−32.0	−7,327	−20.9	−4,126
401(k) Not eligible	12,399	10,575	8,696	−29.9	−3,703	−17.8	−1,879
Difference in difference				**−2.1**	**−3,624**	**−3.2**	**−2,247**
Equal percentage reduction[a]					−486		−625

[a]Difference between actual reduction of eligibles and the reduction had eligibles experienced the same percentage decline as noneligibles.

401(k) program would be as the difference between the actual reduction in home equity (28,743 − 24,230) and the reduction had the treatment group experienced the same *percentage* reduction as the noneligible group. This yields an estimate of $579, which is small compared to the increase in the financial assets of this group. This approach seems plausible in this case because programs that affect housing values and mortgages are likely to have effects proportional to initial housing values.

1.7   SCF: Summary Data and Gale and Scholz Parametric Analysis

In section 1.2.4 above, we discussed the change in the financial assets of IRA contributors between 1983 and 1986, as their IRA assets accumulated. We concluded that these data, from the Survey of Consumer Finances, showed no substitution of IRA contributions for other forms of saving, and that the IRA *contributions* between 1983 and 1986 represented largely new saving. Based on parametric analysis of the same data, Gale and Scholz (1994; hereafter GS) concluded that virtually none of the additional IRA saving resulting from an *IRA limit increase* would be new saving. This result has often been interpreted to imply that none of the IRA saving undertaken during the 1983–86 period represented new saving, although GS are careful to emphasize that their analysis pertains to a limit increase. They conclude that, of the increase in IRA contributions resulting from an increase in the limit, 31 percent would be financed by lower taxes, 2 percent would be funded by a decrease in consumption, and 67 percent would come from a reduction in other saving. Our conclusion and that of GS are not *necessarily* inconsistent, although it seems unlikely that they could both be true. Thus we now consider what lies behind our different conclusions.

We first discuss the data on which our results in section 1.2.4 and the GS results are based. We consider the deletion of observations that preceded the GS estimation, and we draw attention to the potentially important effect of sample selection on the GS results. Then we discuss more carefully the change in the non-IRA saving of contributors that would have been expected in the absence of the IRA program. We conclude that it is virtually impossible that IRA contributions between 1983 and 1986 came entirely from a reduction in other saving. We consider whether this conclusion could be consistent with the possibility that an increase in the IRA limit would result in no new saving. Finally, we explore the GS estimation procedure in detail and find that their results are not a robust reflection of the SCF data but rather are an artifact of their specification and estimation procedure.

1.7.1   The Data

The data and the GS estimation sample are described with reference to table 1.13. For background, several features of the SCF data are important: (1) Only households who were surveyed in both the 1983 and 1986 waves of the SCF

Table 1.13   **Observations in Matched 1983–86 Survey of Consumer Finances Sample, by IRA Contributor Status, Definition, and Observation Deletions**

	Using 1986 IRA Balance		Using GS Contributor Assignment		
	Without GS Savings Deletions	With GS Savings Deletions	Without GS Savings Deletions	With GS Savings Deletions	
				PVW Replication	GS Estimation Sample
IRA Status	(1)	(2)	(3)	(4)	(5)
All	1,670	1,486	1,670	1,486	1,483
Area probability	1,489	1,445	1,489	1,445	
High income	181	41	181	41	
Noncontributors	1,021	988	1,099	1,038	1,035
Area probability	996	982	1,042	1,025	
High income	25	6	57	13	
Contributors	649	498	571	448	448
Area probability	493	463	447	420	
High income	156	35	124	28	
Within limits			403	341	331
Area probability			340	324	
High income			63	17	
At limit			168	107	117
Area probability			107	95	
High income			61	11	

can be used in the analysis. (2) Some households are deleted because they did not meet the criteria for IRA participation or for other reasons were unlikely to contribute to an IRA. (3) The SCF data comprise of two samples: an "area probability" sample and a "high income" sample that oversampled high-income households. (4) Whether a family contributed to an IRA during the period is not reported in the SCF, so contributor status must be inferred. (5) Flow saving in other conventional forms must also be inferred from the reported levels of assets in 1983 and 1986. Although we have been unable to match exactly the GS estimation sample, we believe that the differences do not materially affect the conclusions that we draw below.

The 1983 SCF sample included 4,262 respondents, of whom 3,824 were in the area probability sample and 438 in the high-income sample. Of these, 2,791 were surveyed in 1986 as well.[27] Excluding families in which either the respondent or the spouse were self-employed, the age of the head was less than 25 in 1986, the age of the head was greater than 65 in 1983, or there was a change

27. The 1983 survey was conducted between February and August 1983, with the majority of interviews in March and April. Thus 1983 IRA balances represent 1982 contributions for the most part. The 1986 survey was conducted in June through September 1986, so 1986 IRA balances represent contributions through the 1985 tax year.

in marital status between 1983 and 1986 leaves a total of 1,670 households. Column (1) of table 1.13 gives a breakdown of this sample by area probability versus high-income sample status and by IRA contributor status.

Because the SCF reports IRA balances but not annual contributions, to determine whether a household contributed to an IRA between 1983 and 1986 requires assumptions about the return on assets, as well as other conventions. The GS assumptions are explained in appendix A to their paper. Column (1) in table 1.13 shows the number of observations using whether or not the family had an IRA balance in 1986 to indicate IRA contributor status. Of course some of these households could have contributed in 1982 but not thereafter and thus were not active contributors in the 1983–86 period. There were 1,021 households without an IRA balance in 1986 and 649 with a positive IRA balance. Of the households with an IRA balance in 1986, 24 percent of the respondents (156 of 649) were from the high-income sample. Appropriately weighted, only 4.5 percent of all contributors would be from households in this high-income group.

Column (3) shows the breakdown of "contributors" and "noncontributors" based on the GS contributor status assignment conventions. They use balances in 1983 and 1986 together with an assumed rate of return on 1983 balances to infer new contributions between the two years. These assignments yield fewer contributors than the number of households with a positive 1986 IRA balance (571 vs. 649), as expected. GS also use their assumptions to allocate households to limit contributor status (those with estimated three-year contributions greater than the estimated three-year limit) and nonlimit contributor status.

To estimate their model, GS eliminate a large number of additional observations, those with 1983–86 estimated saving less than −$100,000 or greater than +$100,000. The resulting sample is labeled "With GS Savings Deletions" in table 1.13. Their procedure removes 184 of 1,670 households, 61 noncontributors and 123 contributors. Of the 168 limit contributors, 61 are removed, including 82 percent (50 of 61) of the high-income sample limit contributors. Estimates based on the remaining 107 limit contributors determine the results of the GS estimation procedure. We were unable to replicate exactly the 117 observations used by GS. Column (5) shows the number of observations used in the GS estimation procedure, as reported in their paper.

These deletions have an enormous effect on the distribution of saving and assets in the estimation sample and on formal parameter estimates, as GS show. Mean and median estimated saving between 1983 and 1986 with and without these deletions, as well as non-IRA financial assets with and without the deletions, are shown in table 1.14. As the table shows, the sample deletions have enormous effects on the sample means. The GS estimation procedure is based on means, and their results are essentially determined by the few limit contributors in the sample, so sample deletions can have an enormous effect on the results. While in principle there is nothing wrong with "trimming" the data,

Table 1.14	**Change in Mean and Median Saving and 1983 Non-IRA Financial Assets with and without Sample Deletions**		
Measure and Deletion Choice		Mean	Median
Saving			
Without GS deletions		−13,303	1,132
With GS deletions		2,378	1,044
1983 Non-IRA financial assets			
Without GS deletions		217,668	5,700
With GS deletions		22,244	4,222

we show below that the key parameter estimate is extremely sensitive to exactly which observations are deleted, and the sample deletions that are made essentially determine the conclusions that GS report.

1.7.2 A Simple Reality Check

In section 1.2.2 above, we discussed summary data (table 1.3) based on these same SCF surveys. We return to a similar discussion here, based on data reported in table 1.15. As explained above, using the 1983 and 1986 waves of the SCF it is possible to compare the asset balances of the *same* households over time. We begin with respondents to the 1986 survey. We exclude households with self-employed members and households with a change in marital status between 1983 and 1986. There are two reasons why the values in table 1.15 may differ from "comparable" values reported by GS: First, we restrict the sample to all households between ages 25 and 65 in 1986. Because GS limit their sample to households with heads aged 65 and under in 1983, some heads are as old as age 68 in 1986. We believe that our sample is a better representation of the pool of potential contributors, that is, nonretirees. Second, we also use a narrower definition of financial assets, including only those assets that we believe are most likely to be substituted for IRAs. Our measure includes checking accounts and statement, passbook, share draft, and other saving accounts; stocks and mutual funds, saving bonds, and corporate, municipal, and all other bonds; and money market accounts and CDs. The GS measure includes in addition the cash value of life insurance, trusts, managed investment accounts, and notes and land contracts owed to the household.[28] In addition, the summary data reported by GS in their tables 1 to 3 are based on different age criteria than their estimation sample, including *all* households over age 25, even those over age 65.[29]

28. These additions change the magnitude but not the pattern of the data reported in table 1.15. Data based on the GS definitions are shown in table 1.17 below.

29. In addition, although the pattern revealed by the data is the same in both cases, the values reported here differ slightly from the numbers reported in table 1.3 for three reasons: (1) The 1986 SCF combines IRA and Keogh balances. GS present a method for inferring the 1986 IRA balance based on the 1983 response, and we use the GS method here. (2) We use the newer set of sample weights here. (3) We use the GS definition of a change in marital status here.

Table 1.15   **Survey of Consumer Finances Summary Data: Using GS Estimation Sample Definitions (in current dollars)**

Contributor Status and Asset	Year		Percentage Change
	1983	1986	
Medians			
Contributors in 1986			
Non-IRA assets	8,800	13,400	52.3
IRA assets	600	6,857	1043.0
Total financial assets	11,800	23,000	94.9
Noncontributors			
Total financial assets	750	1050	40.0
Median of Natural Logarithms[a]			
Contributors in 1986			
Non-IRA assets	9.083	9.503	42.0
IRA assets	6.397	8.833	243.6
Total financial assets	9.376	10.043	66.7
Noncontributors			
Total financial assets	6.620	6.957	33.7

Source: Authors' tabulations using the 1983 and the 1986 SCF.

[a]The percentage change is approximated by the difference in the logarithms.

Median IRA and non-IRA financial asset balances in 1983 and 1986, and the change in balances between these years, are shown in the first panel of table 1.15, by whether the respondent had a positive 1986 IRA balance. The table also shows total assets of contributors, including both IRA and non-IRA balances. (In anticipation of estimation results discussed below, the table also includes the median of the logarithm of assets.)[30] Several features of the data are important: (1) The median 1983 non-IRA asset balance of households with IRA accounts in 1986 was $8,800. Clearly, prior to 1983, this group had not been accumulating assets at the rate of the typical household IRA contribution, about $2,300 per year. (2) The $6,257 increase in IRA balances (from $600 in 1983 to $6,857 in 1986) clearly was not funded by transferring funds from the 1983 balance in non-IRA accounts, which was only $8,800 at the beginning of the period. (3) Indeed, the non-IRA assets of contributors did not decline at all as IRA assets increased between 1983 and 1986. On the contrary, they increased over 52 percent, from $8,800 to $13,400.

Without the IRA program, what increase in the 1983 non-IRA asset balance would have occurred over the next three years? The observed 52.3 percent increase was equivalent to an annual asset growth rate of 15 percent. If IRA contributions were funded either by withdrawing funds from non-IRA bal-

---

30. When logarithms are used, assets of zero are set to one and assigned a logarithm of zero.

ances or by reducing new saving in non-IRA assets, then the increase in non-IRA assets between 1983 and 1986 should have been much less than would have been expected in the absence of the IRA program. That is, the expected increase in non-IRA assets should have been much more than the observed increase—from $8,800 to $13,400. We consider a simple prediction of asset growth in the absence of IRAs.

Assets tend to increase with age and income. A simple way to estimate the expected increase in non-IRA assets between 1983 and 1986 is to predict the increase based on the 1983 relationship between age and income on the one hand and assets on the other, with some allowance for change in the rate of return on assets.

Even simple estimates of the income-asset profile are confounded by the nature of the data. There is enormous "residual" variance with respect to assets. For example, a linear regression of assets on age and income yields an R^2 value of about 0.06 with a residual standard deviation of $2,400,000. If the data are weighted by the appropriate sampling probabilities, the R^2 is about 0.07 and the residual standard deviation is about $540,000. (This portends the finding that sample deletions can have an enormous influence on the results.) In addition, the data exhibit enormous heteroscedasticity, which we attempt to correct for by using a semilog specification of the form

$$(14) \qquad \log A_{83} = a + b(\text{Income}_{83}) + c(\text{Age}_{83}) + e.$$

The predictions for 1986 are based on

$$(15) \qquad \log A_{86} = \log A_{83} + b(\text{Income}_{86} - \text{Income}_{83}) + c(\text{Age}_{86} - \text{Age}_{83}).$$

Thus the predictions account for the change in assets associated with an increase in age between 1983 and 1986 and for the change associated with the change in income.

Predictions based on equation (15) are shown in table 1.16. The predicted increase in median assets based on a weighted median regression is about 23 percent, which is less than the actual increase (based on the difference in logs) of about 45 percent. The predicted increase in mean assets is about 29 percent, compared to an actual increase of about 56 percent.

Thus we predict a 1986 non-IRA asset level that is *lower* than the observed level, not higher than the observed level as would be expected if IRA contributions simply substituted for saving that would have occurred anyway.

The 1983 cross-sectional regression implies a difference in the assets of families by age. We want to predict the increase for families who age three years and whose earnings change over these three years. The 1986 prediction based on the 1983 cross-sectional estimates accounts for the increase in age

Table 1.16   **Logarithm of 1983 Median and Mean Actual Assets and Predicted Median and Median 1986 Assets (in current dollars)**

		1986	
Measure	1983	Predicted	Actual
Weighted			
Median	9.048	9.280	9.503
Mean	8.786	9.072	9.344
Unweighted			
Median	9.598	9.817	9.957
Mean	9.594	9.839	10.555

between 1983 and 1986, and it accounts for the change in earnings by using in the prediction the 1986 earnings of the respondents. But the prediction does not account for any change due to the return on initial asset holding. Inherent in the 1983 regression estimates of the difference in assets of people differing in age by three years is also a rate of return, but for an earlier period. If the prior return differs from the 1983–86 return, the projected asset increase may not apply to this later period. The magnitude depends on the difference between the prior and ex post rates of return. Consider, for example, the AAA bond rate in 1980–82 versus 1983–85. The average during the first period was 13.30 and during the second period 12.04. So correction for the rate of return would *reduce* the estimated increase. The return on other assets may give a different sign; more detail on this issue is presented in appendix B.

1.7.3 The Saving Effect of Program Contributions versus the Saving Effect of a Limit Increase

The foregoing analysis suggests to us that it is very unlikely that the bulk of IRA contributions were financed at the expense of withdrawals from non-IRA accounts, or from a reduction in new saving in non-IRA accounts. Indeed, if anything, the data taken at face value suggest that other saving increased as IRA contributions increased. Thus from these data alone we would argue that the contributions under the existing program represented largely new saving. Yet GS conclude, and they say explicitly in their paper, that an increase in the IRA *limit* would not increase saving. Here we consider the summary data that GS highlight in foretelling their formal results. In particular, we consider how the inferences that GS draw from the summary data can be so different from our judgments based on the same data.

GS argue that limit contributors in particular, but nonlimit contributors as well, had substantial non-IRA financial assets in 1986. The implication is that if the limit were raised, these families could easily fund an IRA by transferring assets from non-IRA to IRA accounts without increasing net saving, and that because they could do that, they would. We emphasize the low level of non-IRA assets in 1983, at the outset of the program, and the increase in these non-IRA assets as IRA contributions were accumulating. We infer from these data that the IRA accumulation could not possibly have been funded by withdrawing funds from non-IRA balances and was unlikely to have been funded by reducing new non-IRA saving that otherwise would have occurred. We want to understand what accounts for the difference between the $8,800 level that we emphasize and the $41,269 for limit contributors emphasized by GS. Part of the difference is simply their emphasis on 1986 assets versus our emphasis on 1983 assets. Part of the difference is the definition of non-IRA financial assets. Part of the difference comes from differences in the meaning of limit contributor. We consider the last issue first and then turn to differences in financial asset definitions.

Limit Contributors versus All Contributors

We have framed our judgments in terms of the addition to net saving represented by the contributions of all contributors, both limit and nonlimit. But because such a large fraction of contributions were at the limit, we believe that a higher limit would have led to still greater net saving. Based on an analysis of 1983 tax returns, Burman, Cordes, and Ozanne (1990) find that 75.3 percent of all IRA contributions were at the family limit and that an additional 11.3 percent were at the limit for one spouse in households filing joint returns. EGS report that 63.3 percent of contributions were at the family limit over the period 1982–86. With such a large fraction of households at the limit, if all limit contributors funded IRA contributions by transferring funds or by reducing other saving, the summary data would show that. But they do not. We infer, therefore, that if the limit had been higher, we would have seen a greater increase in assets by 1986 than actually occurred.

In considering the effect of a higher limit, the number of *individual annual* contributions made at the limit is the relevant statistic. Presumably, each contribution at the limit would have been at least somewhat greater had the limit been higher. Thus we should have in mind that between 60 percent and 85 percent of contributions are by families in this category.

GS point to an entirely different measure, suggesting that only 22 percent of contributions are at the limit. The families that GS call "limit contributors" are those who are assigned limit status in each of *three consecutive years* (1983, 1984, and 1985) based on *their assignment* criteria. They report 21.8 percent at the limit based on these criteria. Thus the actual proportion of contributions at the limit is three or four times as large as the proportion assumed by GS. In considering whether persons at the limit would have contributed more, and saved more, had the limit been higher, recognizing that a much larger share of contributions are at the limit may well alter one's prior expectations about the saving effect of raising the limit.

Table 1.17   **Survey of Consumer Finances Summary Data: Using GS Definitions (in current dollars)**

Contributor Status and Asset	Year		Percentage Change
	1983	1986	
Contributors in 1986			
Non-IRA assets	13,085	19,000	45.2
IRA assets	600	6,857	1,043.0
Total financial assets	14,100	30,000	112.8
Noncontributors			
Total financial assets	1,200	2,269	89.1

Source: Authors' calculations based on the 1983 and 1986 SCF.

Assets of All Contributors and Limit Contributors

To understand the differences in the asset levels that we emphasize and those reported by GS, begin with the non-IRA financial asset values reported in table 1.15, which are $8,800 and $13,400 for 1983 and 1986, respectively. Following the presentation of the data in their table 3, GS would emphasize the 1986 balance, corresponding to $13,400. The 1986 balance reflects the *increase* in non-IRA assets during the time that IRA assets were accumulating.[31]

The GS asset definition also differs from ours. Based on the GS non-IRA financial asset definition—but still considering the assets of households with IRA balances in 1986, not the GS assignment procedure—we find the values reported in table 1.17, for households aged 25–65 in 1986.[32] The pattern is the same as that reported in the top panel of table 1.15. In particular, non-IRA assets by this definition are $13,085 and $19,000 in 1983 and 1986, respectively. But even including asset balances from which we believe IRA contributions are unlikely to be taken, the $13,085 balance in 1983 suggests that contributors had not previously been accumulating assets at the rate of $2,300 annually.

The asset balances reported by GS differ in still other respects from those in table 1.17. GS report 1986 non-IRA financial assets of $21,695 for households with *inferred* contributions between 1983 and 1986. In addition to the inferred contributor definition, this estimate incorporates a broader age range, including all persons over age 24, even those who are over age 65 and unlikely to make

---

31. Indeed, in the 1990 version of their paper, GS emphasized that the level of 1986 non-IRA assets of contributors was $13,500, very close to our measure of $13,400.

32. GS use an expanded definition of non-IRA financial assets that includes the cash value of life insurance, trusts, managed investment accounts, and note and land contracts owed to the household. This sample also includes all households over age 25 in 1986, including those over age 65.

IRA contributions. Because older households tend to have greater assets than younger households, expanding the upper age limit may significantly affect the results.

Based on the three-year inferred limit criterion, the more inclusive definition of financial assets, and the all-inclusive age range, GS report median financial assets of their "three-year limit" contributors of $41,269.[33] Because GS so severely underestimate the proportion of contributions at the annual limit, the assets of the much larger number of persons who actually contribute at the limit is probably lower than this. But there is no data-based value to compare with this figure, since the SCF does not report contributions between 1983 and 1986. Using the 1983 and 1986 CES, we calculate that the median non-IRA financial assets of limit contributors were $14,250 in 1983 and $19,500 in 1986.[34]

In our view, the summary data reported in table 1.15 suggest that most contributions between 1983 and 1986 represented a net addition to saving and, in addition, are inconsistent with the possibility that families who contributed at the IRA limit did not increase net saving. Since a large fraction of contributions are at the limit, most of the increase in non-IRA financial assets as IRA contributions were accumulating must be attributed to limit contributors. Thus it is implausible that if the limit had been higher, these limit contributors would not have increased total saving still more. GS emphasize large financial asset values for contributors by citing assets in 1986 instead of 1983, by using a broader definition of financial assets, and, in the case of limit contributors, by citing the assets of families at their "three-year limit" rather than at the annual limit.

1.7.4   The Gale and Scholz Model

GS present estimates of a formal model that they believe supports the view that limit contributors would not increase net saving if the limit were increased. We explain here why we believe that their conclusion is not supported by the data. We first describe their model and then present and discuss two-stage "consistent" estimates of it that may be easier to understand than the full maximum likelihood estimates. Finally, we explore directly the properties of the maximum likelihood specification used by GS. In each case, we decompose the specification to identify its critical features. The important features of the specification may be lost when looking at the whole, but they are easily discerned if the procedure and results are decomposed and built up step by step.

---

33. Based on our approximation to their sample, prior to their saving deletions, their estimation sample included approximately 168 persons at this limit. The number used to obtain this median asset balance will be somewhat larger than this because it included more older households.

34. The CES financial asset definition matches approximately the definition used in table 1.12 but is less inclusive than the definition used by GS.

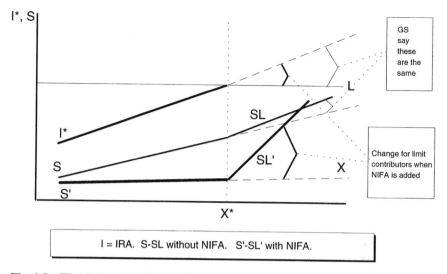

Fig. 1.8   The Gale and Scholz (GS) model
Note: NIFA = non-IRA financial assets.

We believe that the key GS results are an artifact of their model specification. The GS specification can be written as

(16) $I^* = X\beta + u,$

(17) $S = X\gamma_1 + \varepsilon_1$ if $I < 0,$

(18a) $S = X\gamma_2 + \varepsilon_2$ if $0 < I < L,$

$$S = X\gamma_2 + \eta(I^* - L) + \varepsilon_2$$
$$= X\gamma_2 + \eta(X\beta - L) + \eta u + \varepsilon_2$$
(18b)
$$= X\gamma_2 + \eta X\beta - \eta L + \eta u + \varepsilon_2$$
$$= X(\gamma_2 + \eta\beta) - \eta L + \eta u + \varepsilon_2, \quad \text{if } I > L$$

(19) $\eta = X\delta,$

where I^* represents desired IRA saving and S represents non-IRA financial assets saving. The variables X are a set of household attributes. The specification can be described with reference to figure 1.8. The line labeled I^* represents equation (16), which is desired IRA saving and is limited at L. Other financial asset saving of IRA contributors is represented by the line labeled S, and then S_L, and has two parts. Up to the kink point—associated with some X^*—it reflects equation (18a). We sometimes refer to this component as "underlying" saving. The change in slope after X^* reflects equation (18b) and in particular the value of η. After the kink, the steeper slope recognizes the possibility that desired IRA saving in excess of the limit may be made up by increasing other saving. If $\eta = 1$, the difference between desired IRA saving and the limit L is the same as the difference between S and S_L. Thus the key parameter is η.[35] Equation (17), which describes the other saving of noncontributors, is essentially irrelevant in this specification and is not represented in the figure. In fact, in the GS specification, the saving of non-IRA contributors provides no information about the substitution between IRA and non-IRA saving.

An identical figure was used by Venti and Wise to describe their specification (e.g., fig. 4.2 in Venti and Wise 1991). Thus in spirit the two specifications are very similar. But here the similarity ends. The method used to identify the change in the slope of S after the IRA limit is reached is very different in the two approaches.

How is η identified? We show below that in the GS model specification a downward bias in the "underlying" other saving function for limit contributors is balanced by an upward bias in η. One may conclude therefore that the estimation procedure does not identify an η, the key behavioral parameter. Before turning to this matter, however, we consider how η might in principle be identified and what the estimated value might mean.

Assume that β—the effect of X variables on IRA contributions—is identified from equation (16). Then η is identified by variation in L. Since most variation in L is due to marital status, η is determined in large part by marital status. If the limit for married couples is $2,000 higher than the limit for single persons, for example, and if $\eta = 1$, married limit contributors should save $2,000 less in other financial assets than single persons. If this is not the difference, in principle, η would change accordingly. Of the 107 limit contributors in our estimation sample, 80 are married and 27 are single. This does not provide much evidence on which to base an estimate of η. In addition, the specification assumes that marital status does not influence other financial asset saving, except through the lower IRA spillover effect. This raises a further confounding issue. Marital status is not allowed to affect other saving directly, nor to affect IRA saving. Thus it only enters the equation for limit contributors. If, as most prior research suggests, marital status should properly be an explanatory variable in the underlying other saving equation, then, for limit contributors, η will pick up this effect, in addition to any spillover effect.

Although marital status is critical in the identification of η, GS add to the

---

35. As GS point out, the difference in the tax treatment of IRA and conventional saving could lead to values of η greater than one. E.g., if households wanted to reach a given asset goal by retirement age, the amount saved in conventional forms would have to be greater than the amount saved in an IRA.

specification some complexity, which also influences the estimated value of η. They allow η to be a function of covariates X, with $\eta = X\delta$, but they do not allow a constant term in the relationship. (The absence of a constant is associated with an important error in the GS interpretation of the results, and this issue is taken up below.) Now the specification for limit contributors becomes

$$X\gamma_2 + (X\delta)(X\beta) - (X\delta)L = X[\gamma_2 + (X\delta)\beta] - (X\delta)L.$$

In this case, the effect of marital status is allowed to depend on other covariates.[36]

To demonstrate the critical features of the GS model we begin with a simplified version, using only income as an explanatory variable. Then we proceed to the full GS specification. We use both a two-stage procedure that provides consistent estimates under the GS assumptions and the maximum likelihood procedure used by GS. All of our estimates are based on our replication of the GS sample, described in table 1.13. We use all the GS variable definitions as well as their procedure to assign limit and nonlimit contributor status.

A Two-Step Procedure

Suppose that equation (16) is estimated independently using a Tobit specification to obtain estimates of the β coefficients. The other saving equation is

$$(20) \qquad S = X\gamma_2 + \eta(X\hat{\beta} - L) * D + (\eta u * D + \varepsilon_2),$$

where D identifies limit contributors. Under the assumptions of the GS model, the expected value of S can be written as

$$E(S) = X\gamma + \eta(X\beta - L) * D + \eta E(u \,|\, u > L - X\beta) * D$$
$$+ \, E(\varepsilon_2 \,|\, u > L - X\beta) * D + E(\varepsilon_2 \,|\, -X\beta < u < L - X\beta) * (1 - D).$$

Using standard results, we can write

$$(21) \qquad E(u \,|\, u > L - X\beta) = \sigma_u \frac{\phi[(L - X\beta)/\sigma_u]}{1 - \Phi[(L - X\beta)/\sigma_u]} = \sigma_u \lambda_1,$$

$$(22) \qquad E(\varepsilon_2 \,|\, u > L - X\beta) = \rho\sigma_\varepsilon \frac{\phi[(L - X\beta)/\sigma_u]}{1 - \Phi[(L - X\beta)/\sigma_u]} = \rho\sigma_\varepsilon \lambda_2,$$

$$(23) \quad E(\varepsilon_2 \,|\, -X\beta < u < L - X\beta)$$

$$= \rho\sigma_\varepsilon \frac{\phi[(L - X\beta)/\sigma_u] - \phi(-X\beta/\sigma_u)}{\Phi(-X\beta/\sigma_u) - \Phi[(L - X\beta)/\sigma_u]} = \rho\sigma_\varepsilon \lambda_3.$$

Under the assumptions of the GS model, consistent estimates can be obtained by estimating

36. The multiplication of terms in X is also likely to make identification tenuous.

Table 1.18   **Values of η Estimated from Two-Step Procedure by Specification**

| | Variables | | | |
| | In IRA and Other | | | Standard |
Specification	Saving Equations	In η	Estimated η	Error
1	Income	Constant	−1.193	1.879
2	Income and NIFA	Constant	0.835	1.828
3	All Xs excluding NIFA	Constant	−1.668	1.762
4	All Xs including NIFA	Constant	0.103	1.712
5	Income	Income, no constant	−1.591[a]	
6	Income and NIFA	Income and NIFA, no constant	−0.413[a]	
7	All Xs excluding NIFA	All Xs excluding NIFA, no constant	−1.889[a]	
8	All Xs including NIFA	All Xs including NIFA, no constant	0.192[a]	
9	All Xs excluding NIFA	All Xs excluding NIFA, plus constant	−1.668[a]	
10	All Xs including NIFA	All Xs including NIFA, plus constant	0.103[a]	

[a]Evaluated at the mean of predicted η for limit contributors.

$$S = X\gamma + \eta(X\beta + \sigma_u\lambda_1 - L) * D + D * \rho\sigma_\varepsilon\lambda_2 + (1 - D) * \rho\sigma_\varepsilon\lambda_3$$

$$= X\gamma + \eta(X\beta + \sigma_u\lambda_1 - L) * D + \rho\sigma_\varepsilon[D * \lambda_2 + (1 - D) * \lambda_3],$$

where β and σ_u are estimated from the first-stage Tobit equation and γ, η, and $\rho\sigma_\varepsilon$ are estimated in the second stage.

We have estimated several specifications using this procedure, and the estimated values of η are reported in table 1.18. The equations use a variety of covariates X, ranging from income only to the full set of variables used by GS, and use several different specifications of η. There are two important features of these results. First, in the most inclusive specifications, η is small. The estimate is 0.10 in specification 4 and 0.192 in specification 8. Specification 8 is analogous to the GS specification. If only a constant is included in the set of explanatory variables η, the resulting estimate is $\eta = 0.103$. Second, the inclusion of 1983 non-IRA financial assets (NIFA) produces a large jump in the estimated value of η. This is a feature of both the two-stage procedure and the maximum likelihood procedure discussed next.

Why does the inclusion of the 1983 level of NIFA lead to such large changes in η? For illustration, we compare specifications 7 and 8. Non-IRA financial assets are included presumably to control for past saving behavior. In specification 8, aside from income, NIFA is the only statistically significant variable

Table 1.19   **Predicted Underlying Other Saving, Total Other Saving, and Actual Other Saving For Limit and Nonlimit Contributors, Based on Two-Step Estimates**

Contributor Type and Specification	Predicted Underlying Other Saving		Predicted Other Saving: $X\gamma$ Plus λ_2 and λ_3 and λ_1 (3)	Actual Other Saving (4)
	$X\gamma$ Only (1)	$X\gamma$ Plus λ_2 and λ_3 (2)		
Nonlimit				
Specification 7	−2,452	2,084	2,084	1,989
Specification 8	682	2,149	2,149	1,989
Limit				
Specification 7	759	10,782	2,455	3,089
Specification 8	−1,959	1,287	2,920	3,089

of the 11 variables in the non-IRA saving equation for IRA contributors. Its estimated coefficient is *negative*, −3.447 with a *t*-statistic of 9.429. Taken literally, this result says that the greater the level of non-IRA assets in 1983—controlling for age, income, and other variables—the *lower* the level of saving over the subsequent three years. Thus NIFA is clearly not serving as a control for past saving behavior. Instead, it seems apparent that the coefficient reflects enormous error in the measurement of 1983 NIFA. Recall that saving is inferred from 1983 and 1986 NIFA balances, using a variant of $S = \text{NIFA}_{1986} - \text{NIFA}_{1983}(1 + r)^3$. Thus any error in NIFA_{1983} will impart a negative bias to the coefficient on this variable, and in this case the measurement error is surely very large—large enough to more than offset the intended role of NIFA as a control for heterogeneity.

The effect of NIFA on η can be understood by considering the components of the specification that determines η. It is useful to recall that to a first order of approximation, η can be thought of as

$$\eta = [(\text{Actual other saving}) - (\text{Underlying other saving})]/(I^* - L),$$

where underlying other saving refers to other saving as a function of X before the IRA limit is reached. The important aspect of this formula is that, given actual other saving, if the prediction for underlying saving is arbitrarily low, η will be arbitrarily large to compensate for the low underlying saving. In particular, if predicted underlying saving for limit contributors is lower than the actual saving of limit contributors, the shortfall between underlying and actual saving can be bridged by a large value of η. We show that adding NIFA to the specification yields implausible estimates of underlying saving and corresponding large offsetting increases in η. Column (1) in table 1.19 shows the mean value of estimated $X\gamma$. Column (2) shows $X\gamma + \rho\sigma_e[D * \lambda_2 + (1 - D) * \lambda_3]$ and represents the predicted value of *underlying* saving for limit and nonlimit contributors. Column (3) shows predicted values of other saving, accounting for the upper slope component of other saving for limit contributors.

It is easy to see from this table why the effect of NIFA is so large. Without NIFA (specification 7) the systematic component of underlying saving $(X\gamma)$ for nonlimit contributors is predicted to be $-2,452$ and for limit contributors 759. When NIFA is added the predicted underlying saving for limit contributors is *reduced* from 759 to $-1,959$ and for nonlimit contributors is *increased* from $-2,452$ to 682. Including the λ_2 and λ_3 terms, without NIFA, predicted underlying saving for limit contributors is substantially higher than for nonlimit contributors (10,782 vs. 2,084). But when NIFA is added, predicted underlying saving of limit contributors is *reduced* from 10,782 to 1,287 and underlying saving for nonlimit contributors is increased somewhat from 2,084 to 2,149. With reference to figure 1.8, the underlying saving function for limit contributors is lowered. In particular, predicted underlying saving is now lower for limit than for nonlimit contributors, which is inconsistent with the prevailing heterogeneity concern, that is, that contributors want to save more in all forms than noncontributors and that limit contributors want to save more than contributors. This means that η, the slope of the portion above the kink point, must be increased to compensate for the low predicted value of underlying saving for limit contributors. Indeed, the difference is made up by the larger η. The average predicted value of total other saving for limit contributors is close to the actual average—2,920 versus 3,089. Taken literally, specification 7 says that limit contributors save more in non-IRA financial assets than nonlimit contributors, as might be expected. But specification 8, with NIFA included, says just the reverse, that limit contributors have a lower propensity than nonlimit contributors to save in other forms.

This feature of the specification is created by the large negative coefficient on NIFA, which seems clearly to reflect error in measurement and not, as intended, a control for saving propensity. Thus the error in measurement of this variable imparts substantial bias to the results. We show below that this feature of the specification applies equally to the joint maximum likelihood estimation.

Joint Maximum Likelihood Estimation

If the GS model specification is a correct representation of the data, then both the two-step procedure and joint maximum likelihood estimation provide consistent estimates of the model parameters.[37] This, of course, is not true if the specification does not capture the empirical regularities in the data. As with the two-step procedure, we begin by using only one X variable—income—and then expand the specification to include the full set of variables used by GS.

---

37. In appendix A of their paper, GS describe the components of the likelihood function used in their analysis. The third component for limit contributors is incorrect. The numerator of the first term should include $\hat{S}_1 - L$, but the L is not included. We assume that this is only a typographical error in the paper and that the likelihood function is in fact programmed correctly.

Table 1.20   **Joint Maximum Likelihood Estimates of η By Specification**

	Variables			
Specification	In IRA and Other Saving Equations	In η	Estimated η	Standard Error
A	Income	Constant	−0.790	0.180
B	Income and NIFA	Constant	4.644	0.887
C	All Xs excluding NIFA	Constant	−1.468	1.115
D	All Xs including NIFA	Constant	4.355	0.904
E	**All Xs excluding NIFA**	**All Xs, no constant**	**−0.209**[a]	
F	**All Xs including NIFA**	**All Xs, no constant**	**1.170**[a]	
G	All Xs excluding NIFA	All Xs, plus constant	−0.006[a]	
H	All Xs including NIFA	All Xs, plus constant	1.254[a]	
I	All Xs excluding NIFA	All Xs, no constant	−0.222[a]	
J	All Xs including NIFA	All Xs, no constant	1.116[a]	

Note: β is fixed at single-equation Tobit estimates, except in specifications I and J.
[a]Evaluated at the mean of the X values for limit contributors.

To emphasize the key features of the model, in most specifications, we fix the β parameters at those obtained in a single-equation Tobit estimate of the IRA equation.[38] The results are presented in table 1.20.

As with the two-step estimates, the results change dramatically when NIFA is included among the X variables. No matter what the model specification, the estimated η jumps wildly when NIFA is added. For example, when NIFA is added to the specification including all X variables but with η estimated as a constant, the estimated value of η jumps from −1.468 to 4.355 (specification D vs. C).

Although we were unable to match the GS sample precisely, specification J is the same specification used by GS, and specification I is the GS specification excluding NIFA. Key parameters of these specifications along with the GS estimates are summarized in table 1.21, for four key variables: income, debt, nonliquid assets, and NIFA. (None of the estimated coefficients on the six other variables included in the GS analysis is statistically different from zero in any of these relationships.) The model J parameter estimates are very close to the estimates presented by GS, although our estimate of η differs somewhat from the value obtained by GS—1.116 versus 1.85 reported by GS. The difference arises for two reasons. First, our estimation sample differs from the GS sample (107 vs. 117 limit contributors). Second, η is parameterized without a constant, and estimated values are extremely sensitive to even small changes in the X values that may arise from slight differences in the sample. (This feature of the estimation procedure is documented below.) The critical features

38. This has very little effect on the results. In specifications I and J in table 1.20, β is estimated jointly with all other model parameters.

Table 1.21   Model I without NIFA, Model J with NIFA (GS Equivalent), and GS Estimates: **Selected Coefficients**

Variable	Noncontributor Other Saving Equation			Contributor Other Saving Equation			η Equation		
	Without NIFA	With NIFA	GS Estimate	Without NIFA	With NIFA	GS Estimate	Without NIFA	With NIFA	GS Estimate
Income	5.654	5.638	6.012	**−0.963**	**7.765**	7.784	**−0.322**	**−2.773**	−3.170
	(0.952)	(1.243)	(1.026)	(1.026)	(1.505)	(1.391)	(0.693)	(0.821)	(0.836)
Debt	1.175	1.187	1.056	1.412	1.154	1.151	−0.735	−0.486	−0.466
	(0.126)	(0.142)	(0.248)	(0.332)	(0.356)	(0.373)	(0.248)	(0.255)	(0.192)
Nonliquid assets	−3.874	−3.866	−3.998	0.419	−0.120	−0.599	1.094	0.802	0.471
	(0.330)	(0.357)	(0.492)	(0.712)	(1.375)	(0.577)	(0.885)	(0.869)	(0.541)
NIFA		−0.001	0.077		**−3.512**	−3.686		**0.782**	0.985
		(0.045)	(0.059)		(0.281)	(0.402)		(0.182)	(0.235)

Note: Numbers in parentheses are *t*-statistics.

of the maximum likelihood estimates are the same as those of the two-step procedure.

Estimates for the key variables in table 1.21 indicate that the influence of NIFA is enormous. In the contributor saving equation—the underlying level of saving for IRA contributors that have not reached the limit—NIFA has a large and negative coefficient (our estimate is -3.512 and the GS estimate is -3.686). This suggests that a one standard deviation increase in the 1983 NIFA level (about \$100,000) is associated with a *decrease* in saving of over \$35,000 in the 1983–86 period! Apparently the measurement error in 1983 NIFA, from which the dependent variable is constructed, swamps any role NIFA might play as a control for heterogeneity.

On the other hand, when NIFA is added to the η equation the estimated coefficient is large and positive, offsetting the large negative effect in the underlying saving equation. The size of the coefficient (0.782 in our model J and 0.985 in GS) is implausibly large, implying that a one standard deviation increase in the 1983 NIFA level (about \$100,000) will increase η by almost 10!

As above, we can understand better the effect of NIFA on η by considering predicted values of underlying saving with and without this variable in the specification. The appropriate predictions are shown in table 1.22. Without NIFA, predicted underlying saving of limit contributors is higher than that of nonlimit contributors (4,533 vs. 1,651). But when NIFA is added, the underlying saving of limit contributors is *lowered* from 4,533 to -760, leaving a large gap between underlying and actual other saving, which is 3,089. The underlying saving of nonlimit contributors is increased somewhat, from 1,651 to 1,713. Once again, to fit the actual saving data, the gap between underlying and actual saving of limit contributors is bridged by the large estimated value of η. In this case, predicted other saving of limit contributors is well above actual other saving—4,461 versus 3,089.[39] That is, when underlying saving is depressed, the slope η of S_L must be raised. With reference to figure 1.8: when S is reduced to S', S_L must be increased to S'_L. Or the measurement error in NIFA biases the underlying saving downward, and this is offset by an upward bias in η. Thus, at least in the presence of NIFA, no behavioral interpretation can be ascribed to the estimated value of η.

Although the addition of NIFA has an enormous effect on the other saving equation for contributors, the addition of this variable has virtually no effect on estimates in the other saving equation for families who do not contribute to an IRA, as shown in the first two columns of table 1.21.

In addition to the artificial increase in η caused by the introduction of NIFA, the GS parameterization of η—excluding a constant term—means that predicted changes in η with changes in X are likely to have little meaning. Without

---

39. GS do not report predicted other saving of limit and nonlimit contributors separately, but the predicted value for all contributors, which they do report, is far less than actual other saving of contributors (\$806 vs. \$2,184).

Table 1.22   **Predicted Underlying Other Saving, Total Other Saving, and Actual Other Saving for Limit and Nonlimit Contributors, Based on Maximum Likelihood Estimates**

Contributor Type and Specification	Predicted Underlying Other Saving		Predicted Other Saving: $X\gamma$ Plus λ_2 and λ_3 and λ_1 (3)	Actual Other Saving (4)
	$X\gamma$ Only (1)	$X\gamma$ Plus λ_2 and λ_3 (2)		
Nonlimit				
Specification I				
(excludes NIFA)	704	1,651	1,651	1,989
Specification J				
(includes NIFA)	1,082	1,713	1,713	1,989
Limit				
Specification I				
(excludes NIFA)	1,082	4,533	3,298	3,089
Specification J				
(includes NIFA)	−2,160	−760	4,461	3,089

a constant term in the specification, the expected value of η, given X, is not captured by $X\hat{\delta}$ unless the constant is in fact zero.[40] Predictions of η vary wildly in response to small changes in X variables. Indeed, by judicious selection of X values, a wide range of results can be obtained. GS have highlighted the estimated values of η based on selected X values. For example, GS show values for a "typical 35-year-old," defined by particular X values. The "typical 35-year-old" does not have an IRA in 1983 and does not have an employer-provided pension. Their "predicted" value of η is 0.68. But if, in addition to the X values GS use, the person is defined to have an IRA and a pension, the value of η is −1.565. Based on other X values, almost any η could have been emphasized. Table 1.23 makes the possibilities clear. For each specified change in an X variable the table gives the change in η implied by *the GS estimates*, reported in their table 5. For each of the continuous variables, the indicated change in the X variable is approximately one standard deviation. Thus the GS estimates themselves yield implausible responses to changes in household characteristics.

As indicated above, estimation results may vary enormously based on the sample used in estimation. Since the results depend critically on the small number of limit contributors—117 in the GS estimates—any selection that changes this number can change the results enormously, especially given the vast variation in assets and saving. The reported estimates are based on a sample deleting households with inferred 1983–86 saving less than or greater than

---

40. Specifications G and H in table 1.20 are estimated including a constant term in η, as well as the X variables. Although the constant in these specifications is not significantly different from zero, it is measured extremely imprecisely and identification is tenuous.

Table 1.23   **Change in η for Selected Changes in *X*, Based on GS Estimates**

Change	Variable	Change[a]	Change in η
1	Age	Increase by 12 years	0.331
2	Income (3 years)	Increase by $120,000	−3.170
3	Pension	No to yes	−1.376
4	Education	Increase by 3 years	0.666
5	Family size	Increase by 1.5 persons	1.424
6	1983 NIFA	Increase by $100,000	9.850
7	Debt	Increase by $40,000	−1.864
8	Nonliquid assets	Increase by $200,000	0.942
9	IRA in 1983	No to yes	−0.869

[a]For each of the continuous variables the indicated change in the *X* variable is approximately one standard deviation.

$100,000. Although they do not report the η values with samples based on different saving thresholds, GS do report their estimates of the proportion of an increase in IRA saving, resulting from an increase in the IRA limit, that would be net new saving. Here are their examples, which document how sensitive their results are to the choice of a saving threshold.

Sample Saving Deletions	Net Saving (%)
More or less than ±$75,000	−17.5
More or less than ±$100,000	2.1
More or less than ±$200,000	−382.2

Based on our estimates of the GS model (including NIFA), small differences in this critical sample selection criterion yield very different values of η. Estimates for selection thresholds ranging from ±$50,000 to ±$200,000 are shown in figure 1.9. Not only is the variation great, but most of the estimates are very small, even including NIFA.

1.7.5 Summary

In our judgment, a descriptive summary of the data used by GS suggests very strongly that the contributions of participants to the IRA program between 1983 and 1986 represented largely new saving. It is also clear from these data that the typical IRA contributor had not been saving close to the typical annual IRA contribution of $2,300 per year. Simple predictions of 1986 non-IRA financial assets based on the 1983 cross-sectional relationship between age, income, and non-IRA financial assets (and accounting for differences in rate of return) bolster the message of the raw data, suggesting that most IRA contributions must have represented new saving. These "reality checks" would seem to be inconsistent with the GS results.

But GS frame their conclusions in terms of the effect of an increase in the IRA limit, arguing that virtually none of the increase in IRA contributions

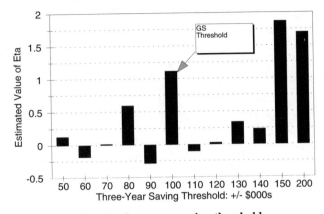

Fig. 1.9   Estimated η values by three-year saving threshold
Note: GS = Gale and Scholz (1994).

resulting from a limit increase would represent new saving. The summary data also suggest that this conclusion is inconsistent with the underlying data. A large fraction—60 to 85 percent—of annual IRA contributions are at a family or an individual IRA limit. Thus most of the increase in net saving that seems evident from the summary data must be attributed to persons who contributed at the limit. And it seems implausible to conclude that if the limit had been higher these people would not have increased their saving even more.

GS acclimatize the reader to their conclusion by highlighting the 1986 non-IRA financial assets of persons at a constructed IRA limit. GS must *infer* IRA contributions from 1983 and 1986 IRA balances, and from these inferred contributions, they infer limit status in the three consecutive years between 1983 and 1986. They classify 117 families in this group and conclude that about 22 percent of contributors are at this "constructed three-year limit." They point to the rather large non-IRA financial assets of this group, suggesting that because these families did have assets that could be transferred to an IRA, that is what they would do if the IRA limit were reached. Even with this unverified possibility in mind, the number GS highlight is misleading for several reasons: (1) While GS point to the assets of 22 percent of participants at a constructed limit, the proportion of contributions at either an individual or a family annual limit is three or four times this large. It is the assets of this much larger group that are relevant. (2) GS further exaggerate relevant non-IRA financial assets by including the assets of all families over age 25, including those over age 65, who are unlikely to contribute to an IRA. GS also use a very inclusive definition of financial assets, including assets that we believe are unlikely to be substituted for IRA assets. (3) Finally, GS emphasize 1986 asset levels. The 1986 data are relevant if one is drawing attention to what might be expected from a "future" increase in the IRA limit. But the 1986 number is at the same time misleading because there was a substantial increase in non-IRA financial assets of contributors during the 1983–86 period, during which IRA contributions were made. In considering the summary data, we emphasize 1983 assets, drawing attention to the fact that contributors had not been saving at the typical IRA annual contribution rate before the advent of the program. Indeed, the median level of the non-IRA financial assets of 1983 IRA contributors was only about 20 percent of the assets of inferred "three-year limit contributors" emphasized by GS. And the median 1983 non-IRA financial assets of the persons who contributed at an IRA limit during the 1983–86 period was probably less than 40 percent of the level emphasized by GS.

The formal GS results are not based on summary data, however, but rather on a complex estimation method. Having reproduced their estimation procedure and analyzed it closely, we conclude that the data provide little support for their conclusions. The value of η, the key substitution parameter reported by GS, is estimated with substantial bias because of measurement error in 1983 non-IRA financial assets. Furthermore, because the parameterization of η used by GS does not include a constant term, the reported variations in η by family attributes have no behavioral meaning whatsoever. These features of the GS estimation procedure, together with values of η that vary wildly with small changes in the sample used in estimation, mean that judicious choice of sample family attributes at which to evaluate η can produce virtually any result.

But can any specification of the GS model be given credence? In particular, can estimates that exclude NIFA and that estimate a constant η be viewed with confidence? We know that even in this case, the estimates vary widely depending on the sample selected for estimation. This is especially critical given that the key parameter η is essentially determined by limit contributors. Excluding NIFA, all specifications yield a negative value of η, which in many but not all instances is not significantly different from zero. We also find that although inclusion of NIFA changes the estimated value of η, it does not change the residual correlation between IRA and other non-IRA financial asset saving. When all X variables other than NIFA are used, the estimated correlation is essentially zero. And when NIFA is added the correlation remains essentially zero. Thus NIFA does not seem to serve its intended goal of providing further control for heterogeneity but does impart substantial bias. It seems evident that the results provide little support for a positive η, and thus little support for substitution of non-IRA financial asset saving for IRA saving. But the results obtained without NIFA may also be so fragile as to provide unreliable evidence of no effect.

1.8   Conclusions

Over the past several years we have undertaken a series of analyses of the effect of IRA and 401(k) contributions on net personal saving. We have summarized this research here, together with additional results. Saver heterogeneity is the key impediment to determining the saving effect of these plans, and in our studies we have used different methods to address this issue. We have organized the discussion according to the method used to correct for heterogeneity. We emphasize that no single method can provide sure control for all forms of heterogeneity. Taken together, however, we believe that the analyses address the key complications presented by heterogeneity. In our view, the weight of the evidence, based on the many nonparametric approaches discussed here, provides strong support for the view that contributions to both IRA and 401(k) plans represent largely new saving. Some of the evidence is directed to the IRA program, other evidence to the 401(k) plan, and some of the evidence to both plans jointly. We believe that the evidence is strong in all cases.

Several other investigators have used different methods to consider the effect of these retirement saving programs on personal saving and in some cases have reached very different conclusions from ours. Thus we have devoted particular effort to explaining why different approaches, sometimes based on the same data, have led to different conclusions. In some instances, we believe that the limitations of the methods used by others have undermined the reliability of the results. Particular attention is devoted to a paper by Gale and Scholz (1994) that is widely cited as demonstrating that IRAs have no saving effect. Based on our analysis of the data used by Gale and Scholz, including calculations based on a replication of their model, we find that their conclusions are at odds with the patterns of asset holding and saving in the raw data.

Appendix A
Cohort and Period Effects

Although the data make clear that the timing of housing market trends and trends in mortgage debt do not coincide, the apparent market, or "period," effects in the housing market complicate the estimation of precise housing data cohort effects. For example, the mortgage data by cohort between 1984 and 1987 show very small cohort effects. But if only the 1987 and 1991 data are considered, it would appear that there were substantial cohort effects. But it is likely that these within-cohort changes reflect period effects that can show up as cohort effects. This is illustrated in figure 1A.1, which shows mortgage debt for the C42 and C48 cohorts. Looking at the 1984 and 1987 data only, no cohort effect is apparent, as shown by the narrow line. But if the data are fitted by cohort, including the 1991 values, there appears to be a cohort effect. If a 1991 year effect were accounted for, the apparent cohort effect would essentially disappear. Suppose the increase in mortgage debt between 1987 and 1991 resulted from the Tax Reform Act of 1986. Then the data might be interpreted this way: The 1986 legislation induced an increase in the debt of the

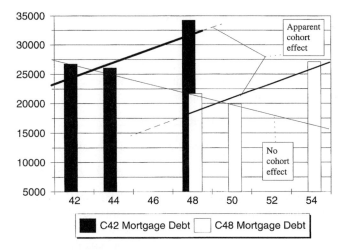

Fig. 1A.1   Period vs. cohort effect?

younger cohorts between ages 44 and 48. For the older cohort, the increase was induced between ages 50 and 54. This period effect raises the debt of the younger cohort at age 48 and the debt of the older cohort at age 54. This creates the illusion of a cohort effect, illustrated by the vertical distance between the two heavy lines. In this case, the apparent cohort effect is really a period effect and should be distinguished from a true cohort effect. But with so few observation per cohort, we have not tried to do that.[41]

Appendix B
Rate-of-Return Effects

The potential magnitude of the rate-of-return effect can be approximated as follows: Consider the predicted (by eq. [13]) assets of persons aged $a+3$ in 1983. The average asset level predicted by the 1983 cross-sectional regression could—if the appropriate data were known—be decomposed this way:

$$(B1) \qquad A_{a+3} = A_a(1 + r_-)^3 + S(A_a, Y; r_-).$$

---

41. As is well known, it is not possible to distinguish age effects from time effects within the same cohort. But if age effects are assumed not to depend on cohort—as is assumed when the effect of age is parameterized as in eq. (11) in n. 16—then, in principle, time effects can be estimated. In effect, shifts that correspond to changes between years are interpreted as year effects rather than within-cohort age effects. It is seems evident from the summary graphs that the data is somewhat more complicated than this, because the year effects seem in some cases to have a differential effect on young versus older cohorts.

Here A_a represents the assets that persons aged $a+3$ had three years earlier. The r_- pertains to the rate of return that applied during the three years preceding 1983. New saving, $S(A_a, Y; r_-)$, is some function of income over the three-year period. The r_- in this function recognizes that people might save less if r is higher, because the gain from existing assets is greater. Similarly, the assets of persons aged a could be decomposed as

(B2) $$A_a = A_{a-3}(1 + r_-)^3 + S(A_{a-3}, Y; r_-).$$

The difference between assets at $a+3$ and assets at a can then be described as

(B3) $$A_{a+3} - A_a = (A_a - A_{a-3})(1 + r_-)^3 + S(A_a, Y; r_-) - S(A_{a-3}, Y; r_-).$$

Accounting for the change in income between 1983 and 1986, the difference predicted by equation (14) could be decomposed this way. But the rate of return that determines the difference in assets with a three-year age difference in 1983 may be different from the rate that obtained in the next three years. To predict over the next three years, we would want to use the rate that applied during those years. In this case, we would have

(B4) $$A_{a+3} - A_a = (A_a - A_{a-3})(1 + r^+)^3 + S(A_a, Y; r^+) - S(A_{a-3}, Y; r^+),$$

where r^+ is the rate of return that applied between 1983 and 1986. The difference between the two predictions is

(B5) $$(A_a - A_{a-3})[(1 + r^+)^3 - (1 + r_-)^3] + [S(A_a, Y; r^+) - S(A_a, Y; r_-)]$$
$$- [S(A_{a-3}, Y; r^+) - S(A_{a-3}, Y; r_-)].$$

Assume that the last two terms approximately cancel. Then the difference is given by the first term. Consider, for example, the AAA bond rate in 1980–82 versus 1983–85. The average during the first period was 13.30, and during the second period 12.04. The second component of this term is thus negative. So correction for the rate of return would *reduce* the estimated increase. The return on other assets may give a different sign, but it seems evident that differences in the rate of return could not account for much of the difference between 1983 and 1986 non-IRA financial assets.

Appendix C

Table 1C.1   **Conditional Median Asset Balances by 401(k) Eligibility and Income**

Asset Category and Eligibility Status	Income						
	<10	10–20	20–30	30–40	40–50	50–75	>75
A. Results for 1991 (1991 dollars)							
Total financial assets							
Eligible	2,033	4,045*	5,499*	8,683*	14,470*	26,093*	51,080*
Not eligible	1,378	1,997	2,558	3,256	6,206	10,080	29,842
Non–IRA-401(k) assets							
Eligible	538	1,138	1,500	2,835*	4,724	8,699*	18,188*
Not eligible	663	1,063	1,411	2,052	4,250	5,437	17,000
401(k) assets							
Eligible	1,171	1,008	1,211	2,092	3,073*	4,833*	14,300*
Not eligible	0	0	0	0	0	0	0
IRA assets							
Eligible	0	0	0	0	0	1,437	6,029*
Not eligible	0	0	0	0	0	978	2,882
B. Results for 1987 (1987 dollars)							
Total financial assets							
Eligible	2,061	2,404	4,206*	9,062*	12,588*	24,384*	57,348*
Not eligible	1,581	1,902	2,624	4,605	6,726	14,108	30,971
Non–IRA-401(k) assets							
Eligible	591	1,029	1,711	3,398*	5,663*	10,776*	24,044*
Not eligible	799	1,004	1,554	2,904	4,246	8,462	20,383
401(k) assets							
Eligible	456	474	607	895	1,255*	1,755*	8,056*
Not eligible	0	0	0	0	0	0	0
IRA assets							
Eligible	0	0	0	0	0	3,564	9,064*
Not eligible	0	0	0	0	0	2,770	4,950
C. Results for 1984 (1984 dollars)							
Non–IRA-401(k) assets							
Eligible	561	1,042	1,988	3,861*	5,027	11,683*	28,824*
Not eligible	754	1,138	1,746	3,076	5,082	10,846	21,485
IRA assets							
Eligible	0	0	0	0	0	2,250	3,181
Not eligible	0	0	0	0	0	1,484	2,084

Source: Poterba, Venti, and Wise (1995).

*Difference between eligibles and noneligibles is statistically significant at the 95 percent confidence level.

Table 1C.2 Summary of Cohort Trends in Home Value, Home Mortgage, and Home Equity

								Cohort							
Age	C42	C44	C46	C48	C50	C52	C54	C56	C58	C60	C62	C64	C66	C68	C70
A. Mean Home Value Cohort Data															
42	73,740														
44	65,869	72,052													
46		65,675	70,479												
48	80,294	80,102	65,741	71,084											
50				66,224	71,091										
52			83,570		68,135	75,685									
54				81,275		68,374	73,289								
56							70,817	71,229							
58					80,829			70,456	68,968						
60						79,290			69,293	68,201					
62							78,785			70,564	70,842				
64								81,552			68,824	68,734			
66											80,365	69,097	65,632		
68									85,807			82,451	73,018	58,343	
70										79,437			79,269	70,354	62,770
72														84,061	64,279
74															
76															84,089
B. Mean Home Mortgage Cohort Data															
42	26,737														
44	26,066	24,380													
46		23,955	23,415												
48	34,244	31,920	21,311	21,648											
50				19,919	19,219										
52			29,717		18,139	16,901									

Age												
54	27,106											
56		23,021	16,267	14,462								
58			20,710	14,262	12,316							
60				17,234	12,482	11,855						
62					15,876	10,721	10,466					
64						15,022	9,822	8,857				
66							12,935	6,683	7,217			
68								9,550	5,823	6,572		
70									12,811	5,150	5,009	
72										13,505	5,150	3,683
74											10,189	5,044
76												5,766

C. Mean Home Equity Cohort Data

Age																		
42	47,003																	
44		39,802	47,672															
46			41,720	47,064														
48				46,050	44,430	49,436												
50					48,182	46,305	51,872											
52						53,853	49,996	58,784										
54							54,169	52,107	58,827									
56								57,808	56,554	58,914								
58									58,580	57,974	57,113							
60										61,551	58,572	57,735						
62											65,675	60,742	61,984					
64												70,784	62,141	61,516				
66													66,502	63,273	59,059			
68														70,815	67,867	53,334		
70															69,640	65,204		
72																65,764	59,087	
74																	73,873	59,235
76																		78,323

Note: All values are in 1991 dollars.

Table 1C.3   Conditional Median Asset Balances by 401(k) Eligibility and Income, 1984

Asset Category and Eligibility Status	Income Interval[a]						
	<10	10–20	20–30	30–40	40–50	50–75	75+
Non–IRA-401(k) financial assets							
Eligible	147	550	1,454	2,404	4,732	7,901	31,485
Not eligible	220	545	1,034	2,043	3,748	7,059	21,778
Difference	–73	6	420*	361*	985*	842*	9,708*
Net non–IRA-401(k) financial assets							
Eligible	–1,288	–651	302	716	2,815	6,241	22,068
Not eligible	–607	–348	130	775	2,080	5,208	17,802
Difference	–681	–304	172	–60	735*	1,034*	4,267*
Home equity							
Eligible	11,377	16,210	17,486	26,138	31,101	43,185	65,232
Not eligible	12,384	13,725	16,007	25,123	30,833	34,348	52,746
Difference	–1,007	2,486	1,478	1,014	268	8,837*	12,486*

Net non–IRA-401(k) financial assets less mortgage debt						
Eligible	−5,329	−4,328	−12,021	−16,737	−16,163	−15,560
Not eligible	−4,468	−4,386	−7,810	−14,317	−18,665	−10,264
Difference	−861	58	−4,212*	−2,420*	2,503*	−5,297*
Net non–IRA-401(k) financial assets plus home equity						
Eligible	16,616	21,371	28,136	38,799	53,060	104,748
Not eligible	14,398	18,632	28,461	36,327	44,462	83,338
Difference	2,218	2,739	−325	2,472	8,598*	21,410*
IRA						
Eligible	0	0	0	0	1,083	5,100
Not eligible	0	0	0	0	0	4,200
Difference	0	0	0	0	1,083	900

Note: Evaluated at the medians of age, marital status, and education.

[a]Income intervals are indexed to 1987 dollars.

*Difference between eligibles and noneligibles statistically significant at the 95 percent confidence level.

Table 1C.4 Conditional Median Asset Balances by 401(k) Eligibility and Income, 1991

Asset Category and Eligibility Status	Income Internal[a]						
	<10	10–20	20–30	30–40	40–50	50–75	75+
Total financial assets							
Eligible	2,323	2,473	5,443	10,263	19,628	37,166	70,954
Not eligible	563	1,030	1,630	3,863	5,523	15,109	42,953
Difference	1,760*	1,443*	3,813*	6,400*	14,105*	22,057*	28,002*
Net total financial assets							
Eligible	1,102	1,073	2,464	7,554	17,022	34,726	67,878
Not eligible	-483	-57	370	2,307	3,652	11,597	39,218
Difference	1,585	1,130*	2,094*	5,247*	13,370*	23,129*	28,660*
Non–IRA-401(k) financial assets							
Eligible	488	616	1,325	3,128	5,692	11,487	21,414
Not eligible	264	544	1,086	2,504	3,973	8,944	27,120
Difference	224	72	239*	624*	1,719*	2,543*	-5,709*
Net non–IRA-401(k) financial assets							
Eligible	-491	-262	-95	1,089	3,094	8,838	18,925
Not eligible	-327	-142	116	907	1,968	5,667	26,909
Difference	-164	-120	-211	182	1,126*	3,171*	-7,984*
Home equity							
Eligible	8,105	10,973	13,937	20,293	25,400	44,839	76,176
Not eligible	9,210	11,044	11,863	18,751	27,132	34,834	58,420
Difference	-1,105	-71	2,073*	1,541	-1,732	10,005*	17,756*

Net total financial assets plus housing equity							
Eligible	14,509	14,150	20,538	32,875	49,361	84,511	151,834
Not eligible	9,185	13,121	15,106	28,502	38,139	60,945	122,341
Difference	5,324	1,029	5,432*	4,373*	11,222*	23,566*	29,499*
Net non-IRA-401(k) financial assets less mortgage debt							
Eligible	-7,112	-7,534	-10,790	-23,701	-41,359	-39,584	-63,414
Not eligible	-5,800	-5,689	-7,795	-22,799	-29,345	-38,977	-16,320
Difference	-1,312	-1,845*	-2,995*	-902	-12,014*	-607	-47,094*
Net non-IRA-401(k) financial assets plus home equity							
Eligible	9,030	10,361	14,017	24,168	34,682	61,358	108,290
Not eligible	8,059	11,557	13,522	25,468	35,275	56,360	105,924
Difference	971	-1,196	495	-1,300	-593	4,998*	2,366
IRA							
Eligible	0	0	0	0	0	0	0
Not eligible	0	0	0	0	0	0	0
Difference	0	0	0	0	0	0	0
401(k)							
Eligible	405	431	1,164	2,072	4,053	6,942	15,832
Not eligible	0	0	0	0	0	0	0
Difference	405	431	1,164*	2,072*	4,053*	6,942*	15,832*

Note: Evaluated at the medians of age, marital status, and education.

[a] Income intervals are indexed to 1987 dollars.

*Difference between eligibles and noneligibles statistically significant at the 95 percent confidence level.

Table 1C.5   Mean Demographic Characteristics by Income Interval, Eligibility, and Year

Eligibility Status and Characteristic	Income Interval[a]							
	<10	10–20	20–30	30–40	40–50	50–75	75+	All
				1984				
401(k) Eligible								
Income	6,641	16,276	25,418	34,733	44,772	59,170	97,115	41,393
Age	40.8	41.5	41.5	40.9	40.5	43.0	46.2	41.8
Education	12.9	12.1	13.0	13.5	14.1	14.4	15.2	13.6
Married	0.28	0.42	0.64	0.75	0.86	0.93	0.98	0.76
Number	31	140	243	306	212	262	96	1,290
401(k) Not eligible								
Income	6,562	15,163	25,009	34,528	44,539	58,600	96,893	29,276
Age	40.8	40.0	39.4	41.3	41.9	43.2	45.4	40.8
Education	11.9	12.0	12.6	12.9	13.4	14.1	14.8	12.7
Married	0.23	0.45	0.66	0.84	0.88	0.90	0.91	0.65
Number	712	1,820	1,875	1,388	798	645	188	7,426
				1991				
401(k) Eligible								
Income	7,415	15,594	24,876	34,573	44,695	59,565	91,499	38,895
Age	41.0	40.2	40.0	41.4	41.9	43.0	43.6	41.4
Education	12.5	12.2	13.2	13.7	14.2	14.7	15.6	13.7
Married	0.21	0.37	0.55	0.75	0.82	0.90	0.93	0.69
Number	84	543	807	784	564	633	266	3,681
401(k) Not eligible								
Income	6,631	14,949	24,525	34,521	44,623	59,506	92,111	26,533
Age	40.0	40.2	40.4	40.6	41.3	43.3	45.3	40.7
Education	11.6	12.3	13.1	13.5	14.1	14.8	15.3	12.9
Married	0.28	0.41	0.63	0.78	0.84	0.90	0.89	0.58
Number	853	1,928	1,487	880	507	404	171	6,230

[a]The income intervals are indexed to 1987 dollars.

References

Attanasio, Orazio, and Thomas De Leire. 1994. IRAs and household saving revisited: Some new evidence. NBER Working Paper no. 4900. Cambridge, Mass.: National Bureau of Economic Research, October.

Bernheim, B. Douglas. 1994. Comments on: Do saving incentives work? *Brookings Papers on Economic Activity* 1:152–66.

Bickel, Peter J., Eugene A. Hammel, and J. William O'Connell. 1975. Sex bias in graduate admissions: Data from Berkeley. *Science* 87:398–404.

Burman, Leonard, Joseph Cordes, and Larry Ozanne. 1990. IRAs and national savings. *National Tax Journal* 43:259–83.

Engelhardt, Gary V. 1996a. House prices and homeowner saving behavior. *Regional Science and Urban Economics* 26:313–36.

———. 1996b. Tax subsidies and household saving: Evidence from Canada. *Quarterly Journal of Economics* 61:1237–68.

Engen, Eric M., and William G. Gale. 1995. Debt, taxes and the effects of 401(k) plans on household wealth accumulation. Washington, D.C.: Brookings Institution. Unpublished.

Engen, Eric, William G. Gale, and John Karl Scholz. 1994. Do saving incentives work? *Brookings Papers on Economic Activity* 1:85–151.

Feenberg, Daniel, and Jonathan Skinner. 1989. Sources of IRA saving. In *Tax policy and the economy*, vol. 3, ed. L. Summers, 25–46. Cambridge, Mass.: MIT Press.

Gale, William G. 1995. The effects of pensions on wealth: A re-evaluation of theory and evidence. Washington, D.C.: Brookings Institution. Mimeograph.

Gale, William G., and John Karl Scholz. 1994. IRAs and household saving. *American Economic Review* 84:1233–60.

Hoynes, Hilary, and Daniel McFadden. 1994. The impact of demographics on housing and non-housing wealth in the United States. NBER Working Paper no. 4666. Cambridge, Mass.: National Bureau of Economic Research, March.

Hubbard, R. Glenn. 1984. Do IRAs and Keoghs increase saving? *National Tax Journal* 37:43–54.

Hubbard, R. Glenn, and Jonathan S. Skinner. 1995. The effectiveness of saving incentives: A review of the evidence. Hanover, N.H.: Dartmouth College. Mimeograph.

Joines, Douglas H., and James G. Manegold. 1995. IRAs and saving: Evidence from a panel of taxpayers. Los Angeles: University of Southern California. Mimeograph.

Kotlikoff, Laurence J., and David A. Wise. 1985. Labor compensation and the structure of private pension plans: Evidence for contractual versus spot labor markets. In *Pensions, labor, and individual choice*, ed. D. Wise. Chicago: University of Chicago Press.

———. 1988. Pension backloading, wage taxes, and work disincentives. In *Tax policy and the economy*, vol. 2, ed. L. Summers. Cambridge, Mass.: MIT Press.

———. 1989. Employee retirement and a firm's pension plan. In *The economics of aging*, ed. D. Wise. Chicago: University of Chicago Press.

Papke, Leslie E. 1995. Does 401(k) introduction affect defined benefit plans? *Proceedings of the National Tax Association–Tax Institute of America*, 173–77. Columbus, Ohio: NTA-TIA.

Papke, Leslie E., Mitchell Petersen, and James M. Poterba. 1996. Did 401(k) plans replace other employer provided pensions? In *Advances in the economics of aging*, ed. D. Wise. Chicago: University of Chicago Press.

Poterba, James M., Steven F. Venti, and David A. Wise. 1994a. 401(k) Plans and tax-deferred saving. In *Studies in the economics of aging*, ed. D. Wise. Chicago: University of Chicago Press.

————. 1994b. Targeted retirement saving and the net worth of elderly Americans. *American Economic Review* 84:180–85.

————. 1995. Do 401(k) contributions crowd out other personal saving? *Journal of Public Economics* 58:1–32.

Shefrin, Hersh M., and Richard H. Thaler. 1988. The behavioral life-cycle hypothesis. *Economic Inquiry* 26:609–43.

Skinner, Jonathan. 1994. Housing and saving in the United States. In *Housing markets in the United States and Japan,* ed. Y. Noguchi and J. Poterba. Chicago: University of Chicago Press.

————. 1996. Is housing wealth a sideshow? In *Advances in the economics of aging,* ed. D. Wise, 241–68. Chicago: University of Chicago Press.

Skinner, Jonathan, and Daniel Feenberg. 1990. The impact of the 1986 Tax Reform Act on personal saving. In *Do taxes matter? The economic impact of the Tax Reform Act of 1986,* ed. J. Slemrod. Cambridge, Mass.: MIT Press.

Thaler, Richard H. 1990. Saving, fungibility, and mental accounts. *Journal of Economic Perspectives* 4:193–205.

Thaler, Richard H., and H. M. Shefrin. 1981. An economic theory of self-control. *Journal of Political Economy* 89:392–406.

Venti, Steven F., and David A. Wise. 1986. Tax-deferred accounts, constrained choice, and estimation of individual saving. *Review of Economic Studies* 53:579–601.

————. 1987. IRAs and saving. In *The effects of taxation on capital accumulation,* ed. M. Feldstein. Chicago: University of Chicago Press.

————. 1990. Have IRAs increased U.S. saving? Evidence from consumer expenditure surveys. *Quarterly Journal of Economics* 55:661–98.

————. 1991. The saving effect of tax-deferred retirement accounts: Evidence from SIPP. In *National saving and economic performance,* ed. B. D. Bernheim and J. B. Shoven. Chicago: University of Chicago Press.

————. 1992. Government policy and personal retirement saving. In *Tax policy and the economy,* vol. 6, ed. J. Poterba. Cambridge, Mass.: MIT Press.

————. 1995a. Individual response to a retirement saving program: Results from U.S. panel data. *Ricerche Economiche* 49:235–54.

————. 1995b. RRSPs and saving in Canada. Mimeograph.

————. 1997. The wealth of cohorts: Retirement saving and the changing assets of older Americans. In *Public policy toward pensions,* ed. S. Schieber and J. Shoven. Cambridge, Mass.: MIT Press.

Wise, David A. 1987. Individual retirement accounts and saving. In *Taxes and capital formation,* ed. M. Feldstein. Chicago: University of Chicago Press.

Comment   David Laibson

What does behavioral economics have to say about the savings incentives debate? That is the question that David Wise assigned me when he asked me to

David Laibson is assistant professor of economics at Harvard University and a faculty research fellow of the National Bureau of Economic Research.

This work has been supported financially by the National Science Foundation (SBR-95-10985) and the MacArthur Foundation. The author is grateful to Yu-Chin Chen and Xiaomeng Tong for excellent research assistance, and to Richard Zeckhauser for thoughtful and copious comments.

be the official discussant of his survey paper coauthored with Jim Poterba and Steven Venti.[1] I imagine that behavioral economics still does not have a lot of name recognition, so it may be helpful to start by defining my terms. In practice, behavioral economists tend to emphasize experimental evidence,[2] validation of modeling assumptions, synergies between psychology and economics, and skepticism regarding strong rationality assumptions. Why might this perspective be helpful?

First, let me address the economists who believe that the IRA-401(k) debate is unresolved (i.e., economists who believe that it is not yet empirically clear to what extent IRAs and 401(k)s increase aggregate savings). Where would these economists direct future research? More tests with heroic identification assumptions? Efforts to gather new data (e.g., data on pension offsets)? Truly random eligibility experiments? Such proposals have merit, but I propose another alternative: test the theoretical microfoundations of the purported efficacy of IRAs and 401(k)s. First, those microfoundations must be identified. But the microfoundations will not be found in mainstream economic models, as Engen, Gale, and Scholz (1994) have argued in theory and shown with simulations. These simulations imply that during the first decades after an IRA or 401(k) is introduced, most of the investment in the asset will reflect asset shifting. Even after 30 years, the IRA or 401(k) generates no new net capital accumulation. By contrast, psychological models suggest a host of reasons why IRAs and 401(k)s—particularly 401(k)s—can work to quickly generate higher levels of net savings. Identifying these psychological factors—for example, commitment and social modeling—and directly testing their impact may help to move the IRA-401(k) debate forward.

Other economists believe that Poterba, Venti, and Wise have already won the IRA-401(k) debate. These economists should still be interested in the behavioral perspective for three practical reasons suggested by Bernheim (1996). First, understanding why IRAs and 401(k)s work is necessary for welfare analysis. For example, mainstream models do not measure the possible welfare gains that would arise if a defined contribution plan helped a consumer overcome a self-control problem. Second, knowing why IRAs and 401(k)s work is necessary for policy analysis. Proposals to improve or expand these instruments can be analyzed ex ante only if we have theories about which features of these instruments drive their effectiveness. For instance, are the savings effects driven by marginal interest effects on rates or self-control effects arising from

1. Engen, Gale, and Scholz (1996a, 1996b) have already written critiques of the Poterba, Venti, and Wise manuscript. Bernheim (1996) and Hubbard and Skinner (1996) have also published surveys that evaluate the Poterba, Venti, and Wise research program. My comments build on the insights of Thaler (1994) and Bernheim (1996), who also relate the behavioral economics research program to the savings incentives debate.

2. However, behavioral economists do not view experimental evidence as a substitute for field data. Behavioral economists value both kinds of evidence and recognize that high-quality field data always trump laboratory evidence.

penalties and commitment? Third, understanding why IRAs and 401(k)s work may generate general insights about consumer behavior that will be applicable in domains far removed from the savings incentives literature. For example, evidence on self-control problems in the savings domain may have implications for self-regulation in other areas, such as teenage promiscuity, procrastination in the workplace, and drug addiction, and may suggest successful public or private interventions to combat these problems.[3]

Finally, a third group of economists believe that Engen, Gale, and Scholz are basically right. These economists need not read on, as standard economic theory is consistent with the Engen, Gale, and Scholz results. However, the behavioral perspective may be compatible with their findings. As I will point out below, behavioral models sometimes predict that 401(k)s and IRAs are not efficacious. Perhaps the most widely discussed example is target behavior. If savers have a target level of retirement savings, they will respond to higher after-tax interest rates by saving less. Such target behavior has been formally documented in the daily actions of cabdrivers deciding when to end their workdays. On days when the shadow wage is high, cabdrivers work shorter hours (Camerer et al. 1997). In the analysis that follows I discuss behavioral arguments that both support and oppose the claim that IRAs and 401(k)s raise net national savings.

I now turn to the general set of insights that behavioral economics brings to the IRA-401(k) discussion. The body of these comments discusses four categories of behavioral phenomena: bounded rationality, self-control problems and dynamic inconsistency, peer group sensitivities, and overoptimistic beliefs. Three caveats apply to this classification. First, in identifying these categories, I have looked for psychological primitives—foundational theories of cognition and motivation. Important behavioral phenomena like mental accounts will be discussed in relation to their associated primitives—in this case bounded rationality and self-control problems. Second, I imagine that some of the primitives may be interpreted as derivative of others. For example, anomalously high sensitivities to peer group behavior may result from bounded rationality: "It's hard to calculate the optimal policy, but it's easy to mimic my neighbor." Third, my list of primitives is undoubtedly incomplete. The psychology literature is vast, and it would be foolhardy to believe that behavioral economists have already identified all of the relevant phenomena in that enormous parallel literature. This observation should reinforce the obvious conclusion that the behavioral research program is just getting started.

The first section discusses the four behavioral phenomena identified above. The second analyzes empirical strategies motivated by this behavioral theory. The third section concludes.

---

3. See O'Donoghue and Rabin (1997a, 1997b) for a discussion of procrastination and incentives.

Four Behavioral Phenomena

Bounded Rationality

A number of commentators (e.g., Zeckhauser 1986; Thaler 1994; Bernheim 1994, 1995) have noted that classical arguments for rationality fall short when applied to the life cycle savings problem. Retirement savers do not get a second chance to correct or learn from their mistakes. There is little recourse for the 75-year-old who finds herself short of assets. Moreover, we should expect such mistakes to be made often since the lifetime accumulation problem is extraordinarily complex.[4] Expert advice only further complicates the picture. The advice offered by professional financial planners bears little resemblance to the prescriptions of economic theory (Bernheim 1994). Expert advice is usually organized around simple rules of thumb—for example, save 15 percent of your income each year. But simple rules of thumb do not come close to approximating the accumulation dynamics predicted by current optimization theory. Finally, suboptimal retirement savings does not drive the consumer out of the market. How can an arbitrageur exploit someone else's mistaken decision to underaccumulate for retirement?

These arguments, and many others like them in the articles cited above, suggest that lifetime consumption behavior may be poorly approximated by the predictions of the rational actor model. But it is not at all clear what alternative to adopt. There are no well-studied and generally applicable psychological replacements for the rational choice model.[5] Although behavioral economics cannot offer a general replacement for the rational choice model, there are two widely held behavioral principles that are useful for thinking about choices in a boundedly rational world: simplification and salience. I will discuss each of these areas in turn.

Consumers simplify their decision problems by adopting rules of thumb and heuristics (e.g., never go into debt). One particularly important heuristic is to

4. Assuming only three state variables, Hubbard, Skinner, and Zeldes (1995) were compelled to use the Cornell supercomputer to compute optimal lifetime consumption rules.

5. Reinforcement models, in which decision makers repeat actions that have had relatively high payoffs in the past, have only just begun to be studied empirically by economists (e.g., Roth and Erev 1995; Erev and Roth 1997) and extended to incorporate limited forward-looking properties (Camerer and Ho 1996). Moreover, most of this work analyzes subject choices in repeated games, where subjects receive payoffs at the end of every round. Even if we had confidence in such models in the repeated game setting, the reinforcement model would be difficult to apply to the savings context since it is not at all clear why savings is rewarding in the short run. How can reinforcement models explain savings activity that generates payoffs that are not realized for several decades? Other leading psychological models of choice, like Herrnstein's "melioration and matching" paradigm suffer from similar critiques about the timing of rewards (see Rachlin and Laibson, 1997, for a survey). Melioration predicts that decision makers always choose the activity with the highest instantaneous felicity, ignoring future consequences. Such radically myopic psychological models seem to be inherently ill equipped for application to savings behavior. Such models could explain savings activity if the primary return to saving were the intrinsic rewards of the process, but that seems unlikely.

partition the decision problem into simpler subproblems, just as economists work with partial equilibrium analysis despite spillovers beyond the arena studied. Such partitioning generates separate "mental accounts" for day-to-day consumption needs and retirement accumulation (Thaler and Shefrin 1981; Thaler 1985) and associated anomalous wealth nonfungibilities (Thaler 1990). For example, consumers may feel that it is appropriate to consume a wage windfall (e.g., overtime pay), but inappropriate to increase consumption at all in response to an equally large capital gain windfall in their retirement account.

The second behavioral principal is information salience. Salient information and rewards disproportionately influence behavior (e.g., see the surveys by McArthur 1981; Taylor and Fiske 1978). Current rewards are more salient than future rewards. When one spends $15 on a CD it is hard to imagine the retirement consumption sacrifice that this current splurge necessitates. This creates a bias for current consumption over retirement savings.

Instruments like 401(k)s and IRAs engage these two behavioral principles. For example, a retirement account should be viewed as a mental account that has been coded as off-limits to current consumption. Thaler (1994) points out that investments in these accounts may raise long-term accumulation levels, even if the original investment was generated by asset shifting. These long-run effects arise because the asset is moved from an account with a high marginal propensity for consumption (MPC)—say a demand deposit—to a retirement account with a low MPC. More generally, providing retirement accounts like 401(k)s and IRAs creates new "basins of attraction" for savings that would otherwise eventually be consumed. Hence, mental accounting arguments suggest that 401(k)s and IRAs raise accumulation levels. Similarly, salience effects generally strengthen the case for 401(k)s and IRAs. These savings instruments directly (through their existence) and indirectly (through the associated activities of firms and coworkers) focus attention on retirement needs.

Other decision-making heuristics, however, imply that special savings instruments will lower savings. For example, target saving—as discussed above—implies that higher returns would lower current contributions. Likewise, a fixed savings rule—save 15 percent of my gross income every year—implies that 401(k)s and IRAs lower net national savings, due to the tax break associated with these instruments.

Simplification and salience effects coexist in the behavioral mechanisms discussed by Ross and Nisbett (1991). These leading social psychologists emphasize that behavior is powerfully influenced by subtle situational factors that they call "channel factors." The success of behavioral interventions "depends not just on persuading people to hold particular beliefs, or even to develop particular intentions, but also on facilitating a specific, well-defined path or channel for action" (Ross and Nisbett 1991, 47). The channel factors that prove most effective drastically simplify the action space available to the decision maker. This simplification occurs on two fronts. An effective channel factor first narrows and simplifies the choice set and second strongly discourages the option of postponing the decision. Hence, the channel factor makes the action salient.

Ross and Nisbett cite numerous examples of effective channel factors, including the techniques used during the 1940s U.S. war bond campaigns. As Cartwright (1949) reports, these campaigns proved most successful when they identified a clear action (buy an extra $100 bond) and a specific time at which to implement that action (buy it when the solicitor at your workplace asks you to sign up). As Cartwright notes, "The essential function of solicitation lay in the fact that it required the person to make a decision" (1949, 266). The Home Shopping Network also seems to have adopted these lessons. Consider the flashing phone number that accompanies an announcement that a discount will expire in x minutes. Or consider a TV charity telethon that solicits an immediate phone call to lift the fund-raising drive over some "critical" threshold: "Once you take that initial step by making the phone call, they take care of everything. In other words, they create a behavioral channel that very reliably transforms a long-standing but vague intention, or even a momentary whim, into a completed donation" (Ross and Nisbett 1991, 48).[6]

Channel factors lower the action hurdle for cognitively overloaded decision makers. If decision makers were sufficiently cognitively sophisticated, channel factors such as arbitrary deadlines, or a narrowing of the choice set, would not work. By contrast, boundedly rational decision makers would be expected to respond to the simpler and immediate choices associated with channel factors.

For my purposes, the most important attribute of channel factors is their close correspondence to 401(k)s, and to a lesser degree IRAs. A 401(k) simplifies the choice set by (1) identifying a narrow range of contribution rates (zero to 15 percent of income), (2) identifying a specific salient contribution level (e.g., the highest contribution rate at which the firm will match the employee), and (3) identifying a narrow set of investment options (e.g., five mutual funds). In addition, 401(k)s provide a sign-up deadline, discouraging the option of postponing action. The salary reduction forms are distributed to employees in early December and are due back to the fringe benefits office by the end of the month. In this way 401(k)s transform a vague intention to save into a series of concrete events (automatic withdrawals). Analogous arguments can be made for IRAs. This analysis emphasizes that IRAs and 401(k)s increase accumulation by facilitating and focusing attention on the retirement accumulation decision.

Self-Control and Dynamically Inconsistent Preferences

There is a substantial gap between actors' long-term intentions and their short-term actions. When two rewards are both due far away in time, decision makers will generally choose the larger later reward over the smaller earlier

---

6. For another interesting example of a channel factor at work see Leventhal, Singer, and Jones (1965).

reward (e.g., the $100 restaurant meal in 150 weeks is preferred to the $90 meal in 145 weeks). But, when both rewards are brought forward in time, preference tilts toward the earlier reward (the $90 meal in one week is preferred to the $100 meal in six weeks). Experiments of this form have been done with a wide range of real rewards, including money, durable goods, fruit juice, sweets, video rentals, relief from noxious noise, and access to video games.[7] Such reversals should be well understood by academics, whose long-term intentions, "revising that paper over the summer," often conflict with their actual choices, "I had too many interruptions and didn't end up finding time for it until January." Invariably, our long-term intentions to delay gratification are at least partially defeated by our day-to-day temptations to seize immediate payoffs.

This gap between intentions and actions also arises in the life cycle savings domain. Three types of evidence highlight this gap. First, popular and professional financial advice emphasizes the need to commit oneself to a savings plan. For example, "Use whatever means possible to remove a set amount of money from your bank account each month before you have a chance to spend it" (Rankin 1993). Or "If you wait until the end of the month to put your money into investments, you'll probably encounter months in which there's nothing left over. To keep this from happening, pay yourself first by having money set aside from each paycheck into a savings account or 401(k) plan" (American Express 1996). Financial planners routinely advise their clients to cut up credit cards, to put credit cards in a safe deposit box, to use excess withholding as a forced savings device,[8] and to use Christmas clubs, vacation clubs, and other low-interest, low-liquidity goal clubs to regulate savings flows. American consumers deposited their holiday savings in roughly 10 million Christmas club accounts in 1995 (Simmons Market Research Bureau 1996). Such commitment devices are only appealing because consumers recognize their self-control problems.

Self-reports about preferred consumption paths provide a second type of evidence for the gap between intentions and actions. Consumers generally report a preference for flat or rising real consumption paths, even when the real interest rate is zero (Barsky et al. 1997; see Loewenstein and Sicherman, 1991, for related evidence). But consumers actually implement downward-sloping consumption paths when they are not effectively liquidity constrained (Gourinchas and Parker 1996). Moreover, the typical baby boomer household is saving at one-third the rate required to finance a standard of living during retirement comparable to the standard of living that the household enjoys today (Bernheim 1995).[9] Hence, U.S. consumers report a preference for rising consump-

---

7. See Solnick et al. (1980), Navarick (1982), Millar and Navarick (1984), King and Logue (1987), Kirby and Herrnstein (1995), Kirby and Marakovic (1995, 1996), Kirby (1997), and Read et al. (1996). See Ainslie (1992) for a partial review of this literature.

8. For interesting evidence on the relatively widespread use of intentional overwithholding, see Shapiro and Slemrod (1995).

9. Bernheim points out that this calculation assumes a best-case scenario. He assumes that all savings is available for retirement and that mortality rates, tax rates, social security benefits, Medicare benefits, and health care costs do not change during the next 50 years.

tion profiles—holding the net present value constant—but actually implement profiles that are downward sloping.

Finally, comparison of target and actual savings rates provides a third type of evidence for the gap between intentions and actions. Baby boomers report a median target savings rate of 15 percent and a median actual savings rate of 5 percent (Bernheim 1995). Baby boomers apparently understand that they save less than they should.

Numerous authors have used multiple-self frameworks to formally model the gap between intentions and actions (e.g., Thaler and Shefrin 1981; Schelling 1984; Hoch and Loewenstein 1991; Akerlof 1991; Ainslie 1992; Laibson 1996, 1997; O'Donoghue and Rabin 1997a, 1997b). These models highlight the contest between the short-run desire for instantaneous gratification and the long-run desire to be patient. IRAs and 401(k)s provide a set of commitment technologies that enable and encourage the present self to lock in choices that ensure that one's long-term, patient interests are heeded in the future. For example, 401(k)s compel consumers to set up an automatic deposit system; changes to the preset deposit levels are sometimes difficult or impossible to make on short notice. Assets in IRAs and 401(k)s are partially protected from splurges since preretirement withdrawals from these accounts generally face a 10 percent penalty. Finally, for limit contributors, withdrawals cannot be redeposited, implying that the consumer is penalized by both the 10 percent penalty and the loss of future tax deferrals.

Laibson (1996) shows that an appropriate combination of penalties and tax deferrals will implement the first-best consumption path for a multiple-self consumer with a "hyperbolic" discount function—a discount function characterized by short-term impatience and long-term patience. This work also demonstrates that currently enacted penalty and subsidy magnitudes are approximately optimal with respect to the calibrated model. Moreover, if consumers have hyperbolic preferences, the welfare gains associated with 401(k) availability are quite large—approximately equal to one year of output. However, this theoretical work needs to be generalized to more realistic economic environments that allow for uncertainty and assume the availability of other preexisting commitment devices, like defined benefit pensions.

What do these self-control models predict when 401(k)s are introduced into an economy in which self-control mechanisms already exist? Might consumers simply shift their assets or their marginal savings from preexisting self-control assets—for example, an illiquid asset like home equity or a defined benefit pension plan—to the new 401(k)? Perhaps mental accounts provide enough implicit self-control to make 401(k)s redundant. A 401(k) might not provide any additional commitment if a sufficient array of commitment technologies are already available in its absence. In such cases, 401(k) availability might lower savings, since the 401(k) would simply have an income effect without any corresponding marginal impact on the capacity for commitment.

However, 401(k)s probably provide better commitment opportunities than other widely discussed commitment mechanisms. Consider home equity;

401(k)s are often harder to borrow against and better diversified than home equity, making 401(k)s a more desirable retirement savings instrument for an actor with a self-control problem. Moreover, 401(k)s may also be more effective than mental accounts; 401(k)s create external penalties that are far more forceful than the psychic costs that regulate mental accounting rules. Mark Twain tried to use mental accounts to limit himself to one cigar per day: "I was getting cigars *made* for me—on a yet larger pattern. . . . Within the month my cigar had grown to such proportions that I could have used it as a crutch" (Twain [1899] 1906, 10).[10] W. C. Fields (n.d.) also had trouble effectively implementing mental accounting rules. Fields viewed alcohol as nothing more than a snakebite remedy, "which I always keep handy." He only permitted himself a drink "after first being bitten by a snake . . . which I also keep handy." Mental accounts may be far too labile to provide meaningful self-discipline. Other commitment mechanisms, like defined benefit pension plans, and other illiquid assets should be evaluated as possible substitutes for 401(k)s. The 401(k) will increase net savings to the extent that 401(k)s provide new, more effective, and more valued commitment technologies relative to these preexisting retirement instruments.

Finally, it is useful to revisit the discussion of channel factors in light of the self-control issues raised in this subsection. I have already noted that 401(k)s and IRAs reduce the complexity of the accumulation decision. In addition, 401(k)s and IRAs should be interpreted as channel factors that help would-be savers overcome self-control problems, especially procrastination.

Like the war bond solicitation techniques analyzed by Cartwright (quoted above), 401(k)s and IRAs impose decision-making deadlines. For procrastinators who would rather postpone any difficult or unpleasant task until tomorrow, such deadlines may make an important difference in their outcomes. Ross and Nisbett conclude that the most effective interventions are "channel factors that facilitate the link between positive intentions and constructive actions" (1991, 227). Whether the behavioral hurdle is problem complexity or a self-control problem like procrastination, 401(k)s and IRAs serve as canonical channel factors that make it easier to do the right thing.

Peer-Group Sensitivities

"When trying to get people to change familiar ways of doing things, social pressures and constraints exerted by the informal peer group represent the most . . . powerful inducing force than can be exploited to achieve success" (Ross and Nisbett 1991, 9). Myriad studies have shown that social modeling can have a disproportionate impact on outcomes. For example, Borgida and Nisbett (1977) gave undergraduates mean course evaluations based on ratings of students who had already taken the courses. This information did not influence

---

10. The Twain quote and the Fields quote that follows were brought to my attention by Ainslie (1992).

subsequent course choices. By contrast, brief face-to-face comments about the courses had a substantial impact. Rushton and Campbell (1977) showed that requests for blood donation pledges that were successful 25 percent of the time in the absence of any social model produced a positive response 67 percent of the time when an unknown confederate made a pledge just before the subject was asked. In addition, none of the subjects in the no-model condition showed up to give blood, while half of the subjects who agreed to give blood in the model condition ultimately did.[11] "The lesson is among social psychology's most important ones. When we want people to translate their positive intentions into equally positive actions, and when exhortations and reasoned appeals seem to be of limited effectiveness, a little social demonstration can be invaluable" (Ross and Nisbett 1991, 222–23).[12]

Social demonstration effects interact with 401(k)s in two ways. First, 401(k)s increase social learning. Contrast a firm in which all workers invest on their own to one in which all workers invest in the same 401(k) plan. In the 401(k) firm, the workers face similar narrow choice sets, making it easier to learn from each others' experiences. Hence, the 401(k) effectively coordinates all of the employees' investment decisions and enhances learning externalities. Moreover, in the 401(k) firm, dialogue about the investment decision is more likely to be formally and informally encouraged at the workplace, thereby facilitating social learning and increasing the salience of savings choices and the attention devoted to such decisions.

Second, 401(k)s increase social competition in the savings domain. Frank (1985) summarizes a wide range of evidence that actors care about their relative social ranking. Such competition is more likely in domains where choices are easily compared, like consumption. In a firm with a 401(k), workers can also compare their retirement savings with those of other workers. The workers share a common savings benchmark—the contribution rate—and a workplace norm that is likely to encourage discussion about savings choices. Such communications augment interworker competition in the savings domain, generating a predicted increase in accumulation rates. However, this increase is mitigated by the fact that the competition is likely to be focused exclusively on the 401(k) accumulation choice, generating an incentive for asset shifting out of other less public savings categories.

Overoptimism

When subjects evaluate their past performance, future prospects, and attributes, they consistently exhibit self-enhancing beliefs. Although there exists substantial controversy over the source of this bias—the biased beliefs may be

---

11. Rushton and Campbell's results need to be replicated with a larger sample. They report results for 35 subjects, but only 8 of these subjects were in the no-model condition.

12. Other dramatic social demonstration effects have been documented by Sherif (1937), Asch (1951, 1952, 1955, 1956), Lewin (1952), Rohrer et al. (1954), Jacobs and Campbell (1961), Bryan and Test (1967), and Aronson and O'Leary (1983).

"motivated," like wishful thinking, or they may be unmotivated cognitive errors—the bias itself is well documented. Only depressed subjects appear to have correctly calibrated beliefs (Taylor and Brown 1988).

In one commonly used test of self-enhancing beliefs, researchers ask subjects to rate themselves relative to a comparison group. For example, Svenson (1981) asks subjects to evaluate their skill and safety as drivers in comparison to the other subjects in the study; 49 percent of the subjects reported that they were above the 70th percentile in skill and 68 percent of the subjects reported that they were above the 70th percentile in safety. Weinstein (1980) asks subjects to evaluate whether they were more or less likely than their peers to experience a set of positive and negative life events (e.g., starting salary > $15,000 or not finding a job for six months). The beliefs reflected a self-enhancing bias for 88 percent of the life events. Studies like these have been replicated dozens of times.[13]

A small set of papers have evaluated these biases in settings where real rewards were at stake. For example, Ito (1990) analyzes the forecasts made by foreign exchange experts employed by Japanese firms. Forecasters whose firms benefit from depreciations tend to forecast a weaker yen than forecasters whose firms benefit from an appreciation. Kidd and Morgan (1969) and Kidd (1970) report the forecasts made by plant engineers regarding completion times for plant repairs. Actual completion times usually fell outside of the 99 percent confidence intervals estimated by the engineers. This bias persisted during the study period, despite repeated educational initiatives and the establishment of incentives for accurate reporting. Lovallo and Camerer (1996) conduct a laboratory experiment in which subjects decide whether to enter a market in which they compete based on their answers to trivia questions. The subjects repeatedly exhibit overentry, generating negative average payoffs across entrants.

Such biases seem to influence the retirement accumulation decision as well. Bernheim (1995) reports that the typical baby boomer expects his or her standard of living in retirement to be about the same as it is today. But Bernheim's calculations suggest that this subjective belief is unwarranted. As discussed above, the typical baby boomer household is saving at one-third the rate required to finance a standard of living during retirement comparable to the one enjoyed today.

If consumers are overoptimistic, 401(k)s will raise their retirement accumulation levels. Consider a consumer who overoptimistically forecasts too few negative wealth shocks (e.g., car or home repairs, medical and dental bills). In the absence of a 401(k), the overoptimistic consumer will forecast a level of

---

13. The literature on self-enhancing beliefs is quite large. Some of the more prominent experimental papers include those of Marks (1951), Irwin (1953), Fischhoff and Beyth (1975), Langer (1975), Miller (1976), Snyder, Stephan, and Rosenfield (1976), Stephan, Rosenfield, and Stephan (1976), Larwood and Whittaker (1977), Sicoly and Ross (1977), Riess et al. (1981), Zakay (1983), Alicke (1985), Brown (1986), Campbell (1986), and Perloff and Fetzer (1986). For helpful reviews, see Zuckerman (1979) and Taylor and Brown (1988).

savings that she will not be likely to attain. Such consumers may end up generating negligible accumulations. However, in the presence of a 401(k), such consumers will "lock in" a high savings rate at the beginning of each year. When the inevitable negative income shocks occur, the consumer will be more likely to cut consumption rather than savings. Such effects will be weakened to the extent that the consumer can either dissave from non-401(k) forms of financial wealth or readily reduce her 401(k) contribution rate.

Field Data Tests: A Few Suggestions

The behavioral perspective on 401(k)s suggests numerous empirical strategies. Some of these have already been explored. For example, Bayer, Bernheim, and Scholz (1996) find that participation in and contributions to voluntary savings plans are significantly higher when employers offer retirement seminars. Of course, perfectly rational (and fully informed) consumers would not be affected by such initiatives. Bayer et al. also find that *written* materials, such as newsletters and summary plan descriptions have no effects on savings, providing support for social psychology theories that emphasize the central role of social demonstration and group participation. Bernheim and Garrett (1996) find complementary evidence that financial education at the workplace increases household retirement accumulation levels.

Other sources of variation should be used to test behavioral hypotheses. For example, many of the commitment properties of 401(k) plans, discussed above, vary across plans. Some plans enable participants to quickly and frequently fine-tune their contribution levels, while other plans make such changes difficult or effectively impossible to implement. Borrowing rules also differ across plans, with variation arising in the consumption categories for which borrowing is allowed (e.g., tuition, medical expenses, home purchase, cars, vacations), as well as the simplicity or speed of the borrowing procedure.[14] As one pension consultant describes it, in certain cases "all employees do is punch a couple of numbers into the phone and a check magically appears" (quoted in Schultz 1995). Behavioral theories predict that plans with weaker commitment properties will tend to engender less long-run wealth accumulation. However, there may be a trade-off here. Extremely low levels of flexibility may discourage contributions in the first place.

Default features of 401(k) plans provide another useful source of variation. Many plans at large firms now make plan participation the default assignment. Moreover, within this set of firms, the default contribution levels vary substan-

---

14. BancOne recently developed a program to give 401(k) participants credit cards with which they could borrow against their 401(k) accumulations. Such a simple borrowing procedure would dramatically undermine the commitment properties of this instrument. Perhaps this is why the proposal was opposed by U.S. Representative Charles Schumer, who introduced a bill to restrict such cards, foreshadowing BancOne's decision to cancel the program ("BankOne drops Credit Card" 1996).

tially. Differences in the default assignment should be used to test the behavioral hypotheses that boundedly rational consumers tend to take the path of least resistance, or that consumers fear the consequences of changes, or weigh heavily the regret of errors of commission versus those of omission. Samuelson and Zeckhauser (1988) call such propensities status quo bias.

Social demonstration effects may also vary in measurable ways across firms. Some types of workers have relatively few opportunities for interemployee communication—for example, mail and package delivery workers and interstate truck drivers—while other workers have substantial opportunities for interaction. In addition, some firms organize savings discussion groups among their employees. Finally, some firms may actually encourage cross-worker savings comparisons by publicizing the distribution of their employees' contribution rates. An inexpensive experiment could be run along these lines, by actually asking a treatment group of firms to publicize this information at the workplace.

There may also be important sources of systemic variation in the tax-deferred instruments under study. For example, the Canadian retirement savings system adopted a new set of rules in 1992: workers who did not make the maximum allowable contribution in a given year could now carry forward the difference, enabling them to contribute more than the maximum in subsequent years.[15] Standard economic theory suggests that this policy change should increase steady state contribution levels (since the choice set has been expanded), while behavioral theories, which emphasize self-control problems and procrastination, would predict a deterioration in asset accumulation.

Beyond institutional and environmental variation, it may also be productive to exploit variation in household demographics. Households whose heads have relatively low levels of education will be more sensitive to many of the behavioral effects described above. Social demonstration and learning effects will be strongest for households who do not have extensive financial knowledge and preexisting active investment strategies. Likewise households with limited budgeting experience and lots of "unpredictable" expenses—for example, young households with children or new home owners—may be most susceptible to the overoptimism biases discussed above and hence will be most likely to increase their accumulation rate as a result of 401(k) availability.

The behavioral approach also suggests that empiricists focus more attention on little-studied psychological variables like the gap between savings intentions and savings outcomes (Bernheim 1995). Is this gap smaller for 401(k) eligible savers? Is this gap smaller for employees who receive free financial advice at the workplace? Standard economic theories cannot explain the existence of this gap, let alone its likely variation with environmental variables. By contrast, behavioral theories are based on the existence of such gaps and have much to say about the mechanisms that open and close them.

---

15. I am indebted to Gary Engelhardt for pointing out this set of issues to me.

This short list of empirical examples is guided by the unifying principle that it may be possible to specifically test the behavioral microfoundations of IRA and 401(k) efficacy. Such tests will be useful in determining whether—and, if the answer is affirmative, why—these instruments work.

Conclusion

Most of the behavioral analysis that I have reviewed implies that tax-deferred retirement instruments will raise net national savings. However, I want to conclude with four notes of caution. First, as I have repeatedly emphasized, behavioral arguments sometimes work against IRA and 401(k) efficacy (e.g., target saving).

Second, almost all of the behavioral effects reviewed above will be at least partially offset by asset shifting. For example, even if 401(k)s provide an excellent commitment device for actors with poor self-control, 401(k)s will only raise accumulation if this commitment device is not a close substitute for pre-existing commitment devices like home equity or mental accounts. Likewise, even if 401(k)s generate social demonstration or competition effects, which elevate contribution rates, this may simply draw away accumulation from other less public savings categories.

Third, many of the strongest behavioral arguments in support of tax-deferred investment vehicles apply only to 401(k)s. For example, IRAs generate less commitment, since they are rarely funded with a preannounced automatic deposit scheme. IRAs function less well as a channel factor, since they are not associated with workplace solicitation. IRAs generate fewer peer group effects, since they are less likely to be discussed with coworkers. Finally, IRAs benefit less from overoptimism effects than do 401(k)s, since 401(k) allocations are preannounced before the resolution of uncertainty.

Behavioral economics emphasizes learning, which leads to a fourth note of caution. In a simple laboratory experiment, subjects are usually given a chance to participate in mock trials of a game before any rewards are actually at stake or any data is recorded. Once the game is played "for real," the experimenters almost always repeat the game for several rounds—usually at least 10. In most games, the play at round 1 looks very little like the play 10 rounds later. It takes subjects a long time to learn how to play, despite the extraordinary simplicity of almost all laboratory experiments.

By comparison, the 401(k) experiment is effectively little more than 10 years old. Moreover, most of the empirical data that Poterba, Venti, and Wise have analyzed to date is from the first half of this experiment, when relatively sophisticated investors presumably represented a large share of the participant pool. Note that these sophisticated investors would be the least likely to exhibit many of the behavioral effects outlined in this essay. Hence, the Poterba-Venti-Wise results may be biased *against* finding 401(k) efficacy. On the other hand, whatever behavioral effects have arisen may weaken over time, as investors eventually learn how to shift assets optimally, or learn how to subvert the commitment properties of 401(k)s. Will savers eventually grow quite comfortable borrowing against their 401(k)s, just as they have grown more comfortable taking out home equity credit lines? Further complicating the picture, the 401(k) experiment has coincided with over a decade of abnormally high equity returns; 401(k) popularity could depend on a booming stock market. It is probably necessary to conclude that the existing empirical analysis of 401(k) effectiveness may tell us little about steady state responses to this new asset category.

Nevertheless, the prospects for 401(k)s and similar tax-deferred retirement instruments seem bright. Social psychology research has identified a core set of features of successful behavioral interventions. The 401(k) seems to have been designed by someone who intuitively or formally understood those lessons.

References

Ainslie, George. 1992. *Picoeconomics: The strategic interaction of successive motivational states within the person.* Cambridge: Cambridge University Press.

Akerlof, George. 1991. Procrastination and obedience. *American Economic Review Papers and Proceedings* 81:1–19.

Alicke, Mark D. 1985. Global self-evaluation as determined by the desirability and controllability of trait adjectives. *Journal of Personality and Social Psychology* 49:1621–30.

American Express. 1996. A commonsense guide to personal money management.

Aronson, Elliot, and Michael O'Leary. 1983. The relative effectiveness of models and prompts on energy conservation: A field experiment in a shower room. *Journal of Environmental Systems* 12:219–24.

Asch, S. E. 1951. Effects of group pressures upon the modification and distortion of judgment. In *Groups, leadership, and men,* ed. H. Guetzkow. Pittsburgh: Carnegie Press.

———. 1952. *Social psychology.* New York: Prentice-Hall.

———. 1955. Opinions and social pressure. *Scientific American,* November, pp. 31–35.

———. 1956. Studies of independence and conformity: A minority of one against a unanimous majority. *Psychological Monographs* 70 (9, Whole no. 416).

Banc One drops credit card tied to 401(k). 1996. *New York Times,* 26 December.

Barsky, Robert B., F. Thomas Juster, Miles S. Kimball, and Matthew D. Shapiro. 1997. Preference parameters and behavioral heterogeneity: An experimental approach in the Health and Retirement Study. *Quarterly Journal of Economics* 112:537–80.

Bayer, Patrick J., B. Douglas Bernheim, and John Karl Scholz. 1996. The effects of financial education in the workplace: Evidence from a survey of employers. NBER Working Paper no. 5655. Cambridge, Mass.: National Bureau of Economic Research, July.

Bernheim, B. Douglas. 1995a. Do households appreciate their financial vulnerabilities? An analysis of actions, perceptions, and public policy. In *Tax policy for economic growth in the 1990s,* 1–30. Washington, D.C.: American Council for Capital Formation.

———. 1994b. Personal saving, information, and economic literacy: New directions for public policy. In *Tax policy for economic growth in the 1990s,* 53–78. Washington, D.C.: American Council for Capital Formation.

———. 1996. Rethinking saving incentives. Stanford Economics Working Paper no. 96–009. Stanford, Calif.: Stanford University.

Bernheim, B. Douglas, and Daniel M. Garrett. 1996. The determinants and consequences of financial education in the workplace: Evidence from a survey of households. NBER Working Paper no. 5667. Cambridge, Mass.: National Bureau of Economic Research, July.

Borgida, Eugene, and Richard E. Nisbett. 1977. The differential impact of abstract vs. concrete information on decisions. *Journal of Applied Social Psychology* 7:258–71.

Brown, Jonathan D. 1986. Evaluation of self and others: Self-enhancement biases in social judgments. *Social Cognition* 4:353–76.

Bryan, J. H., and M. A. Test. 1967. Models and helping: Naturalistic studies in aiding behavior. *Journal of Personality and Social Psychology* 6:400–407.

Camerer, Colin, Linda Babcock, George Loewenstein, and Richard Thaler. 1997. Labor supply of New York City cabdrivers: One day at a time. *Quarterly Journal of Economics* 112:407–42.

Camerer, Colin, and Teck-Hua Ho. 1996. Experience-weighted attraction learning in games: A unifying approach. Pasadena: California Institute of Technology. Working paper.

Campbell, Jennifer D. 1986. Similarity and uniqueness: The effects of attribute type, relevance, and individual differences in self-esteem and depression. *Journal of Personality and Social Psychology* 50:281–94.

Cartwright, Dorwin. 1949. Some principles of mass persuasion: Selected findings of research on the sale of United States War Bonds. *Human Relations* 2:253–67.

Engen, Eric M., William G. Gale, and John Karl Scholz. 1994. Do saving incentives work? *Brookings Papers on Economic Activity* 1:85–180.

———. 1996a. The effects of tax-based saving incentives on saving and wealth. NBER Working Paper no. 5759. Cambridge, Mass.: National Bureau of Economic Research.

———. 1996b. The illusory effects of saving incentives on saving. *Economic Perspectives* 10:113–38.

Erev, Ido, and Alvin E. Roth. 1997. Modeling how people play games: Reinforcement learning in experimental games with unique, mixed strategy equilibria. Pittsburgh, Pa.: University of Pittsburgh. Working paper.

Fields, W. C. n.d. *The temperance lecture.* Proscenium Records.

Fischhoff, Baruch, and Ruth Beyth. 1975. "I knew it would happen": Remembered probability of once-future things. *Organizational Behavior and Human Performance* 13:1–16.

Frank, Robert H. 1985. *Choosing the right pond.* New York: Oxford University Press.

Gourinchas, Pierre-Olivier, and Jonathan A. Parker. 1996. Consumption over the life-cycle. Cambridge: Massachusetts Institute of Technology. Mimeograph.

Herrnstein, Richard J. 1997. *The matching law: Papers in psychology and economics.* Cambridge, Mass.: Harvard University Press.

Hoch, Stephen J., and George Loewenstein. 1991. Time-inconsistent preferences and consumer self-control. *Journal of Consumer Research* 17:429–507.

Hubbard, R. Glenn, and Jonathan S. Skinner. 1996. Assessing the effectiveness of saving incentives. *Economic Perspectives* 10:73–90.

Hubbard, Glenn, Jon Skinner, and Stephen Zeldes. 1995. Precautionary saving and social insurance. *Journal of Political Economy* 103:360–99.

Irwin, Francis W. 1953. State expectations as functions of probability and desirability of outcomes. *Journal of Personality* 21:329–35.

Ito, Takatoshi. 1990. Foreign exchange rate expectations: Micro survey data. *American Economic Review* 80:434–49.

Jacobs, R. C., and D. T. Campbell. 1961. The perpetuation of an arbitrary tradition through several generations of a laboratory microculture. *Journal of Abnormal and Social Psychology* 62:649–58.

Kidd, John B. 1970. The utilization of subjective probabilities in production planning. *Acta Psychologia* 34:338–47.

Kidd, John B., and J. R. Morgan. 1969. A predictive information system for management. *Operational Research Quarterly* 20:149–70.

King, G. R., and A. W. Logue. 1987. Choice in a self-control paradigm with human subjects: Effects of changeover delay duration. *Learning and Motivation* 18:421–38.

Kirby, Kris N. 1997. Bidding on the future: Evidence against normative discounting of delayed rewards. *Journal of Experimental Psychology* 126:54–70.

Kirby, Kris N., and R. J. Herrnstein. 1995. Preference reversals due to myopic discounting of delayed reward. *Psychological Science* 6:83–89.

Kirby, Kris N., and Nino N. Marakovic. 1995. Modeling myopic decisions: Evidence for hyperbolic delay-discounting within subjects and amounts. *Organizational Behavior and Human Decision Processes* 64:22–30.

———. 1996. Delay-discounting probabilistic rewards: Rates decrease as amounts increase. *Psychonomic Bulletin & Review* 3:100–104.

Laibson, David I. 1996. Hyperbolic discount functions, undersaving, and savings policy. NBER Working Paper no. 5635. Cambridge, Mass.: National Bureau of Economic Research.

———. 1997. Golden eggs and hyperbolic discounting. *Quarterly Journal of Economics* 112:443–77.

Langer, Ellen J. 1975. The illusion of control. *Journal of Personality and Social Psychology* 32:311–28.

Larwood, Laurie, and William Whittaker. 1977. Managerial myopia: Self-serving biases in organizational planning. *Journal of Applied Psychology* 62:194–98.

Leventhal, Howard, Robert Singer, and Susan Jones. 1965. Effects of fear and specificity of recommendation upon attitudes and behavior. *Journal of Personality and Social Psychology* 2:20–29.

Lewin, Kurt. 1952. Group decision and social change. In *Readings in social psychology,* ed. G. E. Swanson, T. M. Newcomb, and E. L. Hartley, 459–73. New York: Holt.

Loewenstein, George, and Nachum Sicherman. 1991. Do workers prefer increasing wage profiles? *Journal of Labor Economics* 9:67–84.

Lovallo, Dan, and Colin Camerer. 1996. Overconfidence and excess entry: An experimental approach. California Institute of Technology Working Paper no. 975. Pasadena: California Institute of Technology.

Marks, Rose W. 1951. The effect of probability, desirability, and "privilege" on the stated expectations of children. *Journal of Personality* 19:332–51.

McArthur, Leslie Zebrowitz. 1981. What grabs you? The role of attention in impression formation and causal attribution. In *Social cognition: The Ontario symposium,* vol. 1, ed. E. T. Higgins, C. P. Herman, and M. P. Zanna, 201–46. Hillsdale, N.J.: Erlbaum.

Millar, A., and D. J. Navarick. 1984. Self-control and choice in humans: Effects of video game playing as a positive reinforcer. *Learning and Motivation* 15:203–18.

Miller, Dale T. 1976. Ego involvement and attributions for success and failure. *Journal of Personality and Social Psychology* 51:1208–17.

Navarick, D. J. 1982. Negative reinforcement and choice in humans. *Learning and Motivation* 13:361–77.

O'Donoghue, Ted, and Matthew Rabin. 1997a. Doing it now or later. Evanston, Ill.: Northwestern University. Working paper.

————. 1997b. Incentives for procrastinators. Evanston, Ill.: Northwestern University. Working paper.

Perloff, Linda S., and Barbara K. Fetzer. 1986. Self-other judgments and perceived vulnerability to victimization. *Journal of Personality and Social Psychology* 50: 502–10.

Poterba, James M., Steven F. Venti, and David A. Wise. 1996. How retirement saving programs increase saving. *Economic Perspectives* 10:91–112.

Rachlin, Howard, and David I. Laibson, eds. 1997. *The matching law: Papers in psychology and economics by Richard J. Herrnstein.* New York: Russell Sage Foundation; Cambridge, Mass.: Harvard University Press.

Rankin, Deborah M. 1993. How to get ready for retirement: Save, save, save. *New York Times,* 13 March, p. 33.

Read, Daniel, George Loewenstein, Shobana Kalyanaraman, and Adrian Bivolaru. 1996. Mixing virtue and vice: The combined effects of hyperbolic discounting and diversification. Pittsburgh, Pa.: Carnegie-Mellon University. Working paper.

Riess, Marc, Paul Rosenfeld, Valerie Melburg, and James T. Tedeschi. 1981. Self-serving attributions: Biased private perceptions and distorted public descriptions. *Journal of Personality and Social Psychology* 41:224–31.

Rohrer, J. H., S. H. Baron, E. L. Hoffman, and D. V. Swinder. 1954. The stability of autokinetic judgment. *Journal of Abnormal and Social Psychology* 49:595–97.

Ross, Lee, and Richard E. Nisbett. 1991. *The person and the situation: Perspectives of social psychology.* New York: McGraw-Hill.

Roth, Alvin E., and Ido Erev. 1995. Learning in extensive-form games: Experimental data and simple dynamic models in the intermediate term. *Games and Economic Behavior* 8:164–212.

Rushton, J. Phillipe, and Anne C. Campbell. 1977. Modeling, vicarious reinforcement and extroversion on blood donating in adults: Immediate and long-term effects. *European Journal of Social Psychology* 7:297–306.

Samuelson, William, and Richard J. Zeckhauser. 1988. Status quo bias in decision making. *Journal of Risk and Uncertainty* 1:7–59.

Schelling, Thomas C. 1984. The intimate contest for self-command. *Choice and consequence: Perspective of an errant economist,* 57–82. Cambridge, Mass.: Harvard University Press.

Schultz, Ellen E. 1995. More workers are cracking their nest eggs. *Wall Street Journal,* 17 August.

Shapiro, Matthew D., and Joel Slemrod. 1995. Consumer response to the timing of income: Evidence from a change in tax withholding. *American Economic Review* 85:186–200.

Sherif, M. 1937. An experimental approach to the study of attitudes. *Sociometry* 1: 90–98.

Sicoly, Fiore, and Michael Ross. 1977. Facilitation of ego-biased attributions by means of self-serving observer feedback. *Journal of Personality and Social Psychology* 35:734–41.

Simmons Market Research Bureau, Inc. 1996. The 1996 study of media and markets. New York: Simmons Market Research Bureau, Inc.

Snyder, Melvin L., Walter G. Stephan, and David Rosenfield. 1976. Egotism in males and females. *Journal of Personality and Social Psychology* 33:435–41.

Solnick, J., C. Kannenberg, D. Eckerman, and M. Waller. 1980. An experimental analysis of impulsivity and impulse control in humans. *Learning and Motivation* 2:61–77.

Stephan, Walter G., Davis Rosenfield, and Cookie Stephan. 1976. Egotism and attribution. *Journal of Personality and Social Psychology* 34:1161–67.

Svenson, Ola. 1981. Are we all less risky and more skillful than our fellow drivers? *Acta Psychologia* 47:143–48.

Taylor, Shelley E., and Jonathan D. Brown. 1988. Illusion and well-being: A social psychological perspective on mental health. *Psychological Bulletin* 103:193–210.

Taylor, Shelley E., and Susan T. Fiske. 1978. Salience, attention, and attribution: Top of the head phenomena." In *Advances in experimental social psychology,* vol. 11, ed. L. Berkowitz, 249–88. New York: Academic Press.

Thaler, Richard H. 1985. Mental accounting and consumer choice. *Marketing Science* 4:199–214.

———. 1990. Saving, fungibility, and mental accounts. *Journal of Economic Perspectives* 4:193–205.

———. 1994. Psychology and savings policies. *American Economic Review* 84:186–92.

Thaler, Richard H., and H. M. Shefrin. 1981. An economic theory of self-control. *Journal of Political Economy* 89:392–406.

Twain, Mark. (1899) 1906. Following the equator. In *The complete works of Mark Twain,* vol. 13, 9–10. New York: Harper.

Weinstein, Neil D. 1980. Unrealistic optimism about future life events. *Journal of Personality and Social Psychology* 39:806–20.

Winston, G. C. 1980. Addiction and backsliding: A theory of compulsive consumption. *Journal of Economic and Behavior Organization* 1:295–324.

Zakay, Dan. 1983. The relationship between probability assessor and the outcomes of an event as a determiner of subjective probability. *Acta Psychologia* 53:271–80.

Zeckhauser, Richard J. 1986. Comments: Behavioral versus rational economics: What you see is what you conquer. *Journal of Business* 59:435–49.

Zuckerman, Miron. 1979. Attribution of success and failure revised, or: The motivational bias is alive and well in attribution theory. *Journal of Personality* 47:245–87.

2   Implications of Rising Personal Retirement Saving

James M. Poterba, Steven F. Venti, and David A. Wise

The individual retirement account (IRA) and 401(k) programs were introduced in 1982 to encourage personal saving for retirement.[1] Contributions to IRAs grew rapidly until 1986, when $38 billion was contributed to these accounts. The Tax Reform Act of 1986 curtailed this program, and by 1990 contributions had fallen to only $10 billion. They were only $8 billion in 1994. On the other hand, the 401(k) program has grown unimpeded since 1982. Now contributions to the 401(k) plan alone are greater than contributions to traditional employer-provided defined benefit and defined contribution plans combined. In 1993, 401(k) plan contributions exceeded $69 billion. Approximately 45 to 50 percent of employees were eligible for 401(k) plans in that year, and over 70 percent of those who were eligible to contribute did in fact make contributions.

The increase in personal retirement saving can have important implications for the accumulation of retirement saving for future generations of retirees. Now a large fraction of families approach retirement with virtually no personal financial asset saving. The median of personal financial assets of Health and Retirement Survey (HRS) families—whose heads were aged 51–61 in 1992—was approximately $7,000. This includes all financial assets held outside IRAs, 401(k)s, and related retirement saving accounts. Perhaps half of all families rely almost exclusively on social security benefits for support in retirement.

James M. Poterba is professor of economics at the Massachusetts Institute of Technology and director of the Public Economics Research Program at the National Bureau of Economic Research. Steven F. Venti is professor of economics at Dartmouth College and a research associate of the National Bureau of Economic Research. David A. Wise is the John F. Stambaugh Professor of Political Economy at the John F. Kennedy School of Government, Harvard University, and the director for Health and Retirement Programs at the National Bureau of Economic Research.

The authors acknowledge the support of the National Institute on Aging, the National Science Foundation, and the National Bureau of Economic Research.

1. The IRA program was in fact first introduced for persons without employer-provided pensions in 1974 and was expanded to include all employees in 1981 legislation. The 401(k) program was introduced in 1978 but was not used until IRS clarifying regulations were adopted in 1981.

The spread of 401(k) plans in particular could change this picture substantially. In this paper we simulate the 401(k) assets of future generations of retirees and compare these assets with the social security and other assets of the households who are approaching retirement now.

2.1 Overview of Method

Our goal is to project 401(k) assets of households who will retire 35 or 40 years from now. We direct attention in particular to the cohort that was age 33 in 1993, and will be age 65 in 2025. We compare the projected 401(k) assets of this cohort to the assets of the HRS respondents. We first trace backward to obtain approximate lifetime earnings histories of the HRS respondents. Lifetime earnings are grouped into 10 deciles, assuming that over their careers household earnings were in the same decile. Contributions to 401(k) plans are projected for each lifetime earnings decile. Thus we are able to ask what level of 401(k) assets such families would have accumulated, in 1992 dollars, had they had the same earnings histories as the HRS respondents but different amounts of contributions to 401(k) plans. We base the projections on the past growth in 401(k) participation rates and on the fraction of earnings contributed to the plans. The growth in participation since their inception, however, has been enormous, and simple projections—based on recent increases in participation—are not very meaningful. Therefore, we make what we believe to be plausible inferences about future participation. We actually make three projections. The first projection is for the cohort that was age 25 in 1993. The second is for a younger cohort with higher assumed participation rates. For comparison, the third projection is under the assumption of universal adoption of 401(k) plans.

In section 2.2 we document the growth of 401(k) plans and consider evidence on the amount of contributions as a percentage of earnings. We then describe the foundation for our projections and the method that is used. Finally, we discuss the projections and compare the results with the assets of the current HRS respondents.

2.2 The 401(k) Data and Estimation

2.2.1 The Growth of 401(k) Plans

We first document the growth in 401(k) contributions since the program's inception in 1982. Evidence on employee contributions and employer matching rates is presented in section 2.3. There are two principal data sources for 401(k) eligibility and participation rates. The first is the Survey of Income and Program Participation (SIPP). From the six panels of this survey data can be obtained for 1984, 1987, 1991, and 1993. The second is the Employee Benefits Supplement to the Current Population Survey (CPS). Data for this survey are available for 1988 and 1993. The participation rates assumed in the simulation analysis rely most heavily on the CPS data, but in discussing the growth in participation we first present data based on the SIPP.

The unit of observation in both the SIPP and the CPS is an individual. We have grouped the individual responses to form families. Unmarried persons are treated as single-person families and spouses are matched to recreate two-person family units. A family is eligible for (or participates in) a 401(k) plan if at least one member of the family is eligible (or participates) in a plan. Since 401(k)s are employer-sponsored saving programs, we restrict the sample to families with at least one member employed. Further discussion of these surveys and the sample definitions are contained in appendix A.

The first panel of table 2.1 shows eligibility rates, participation given eligi-

Table 2.1   **SIPP: Eligibility, Participation Given Eligibility, and Participation Rates by Age and Year**

	Year			
Age	1984	1987	1991	1993
	Eligibility			
25–29	0.089	0.142	0.228	0.406
30–34	0.130	0.169	0.307	0.434
35–39	0.132	0.202	0.354	0.444
40–44	0.151	0.225	0.379	0.461
45–49	0.146	0.203	0.344	0.441
50–54	0.129	0.219	0.359	0.423
55–59	0.152	0.186	0.305	0.377
60–64	0.091	0.151	0.233	0.297
All	0.126	0.185	0.317	0.423
	Participation Given Eligibility			
25–29	0.476	0.498	0.690	0.556
30–34	0.498	0.540	0.729	0.630
35–39	0.469	0.583	0.695	0.630
40–44	0.607	0.673	0.671	0.645
45–49	0.632	0.689	0.683	0.693
50–54	0.674	0.634	0.735	0.684
55–59	0.721	0.716	0.692	0.671
60–64	0.627	0.715	0.746	0.649
All	0.570	0.613	0.700	0.638
	Participation			
25–29	0.04	0.071	0.157	0.226
30–34	0.064	0.091	0.224	0.274
35–39	0.062	0.117	0.246	0.280
40–44	0.092	0.151	0.255	0.297
45–49	0.092	0.140	0.235	0.305
50–54	0.087	0.139	0.264	0.290
55–59	0.110	0.133	0.211	0.253
60–64	0.057	0.108	0.174	0.193
All	0.072	0.113	0.222	0.270

Source: Based on the Survey of Income and Program Participation.

bility, and participation rates by age interval for four years, based on the SIPP data. In 1984, according to these data, 12.6 percent of employees were eligible to contribute to a 401(k) plan; they worked for employers who offered a 401(k) plan. By 1993, over 42 percent were eligible. Eligibility rates are greatest for households with heads aged 40–44; rates are somewhat lower for younger as well as older households. The rates of participation given eligibility increased from 57 percent in 1984 to 70 percent in 1991, as shown in the middle panel of table 2.1. But, according to these data, the conditional participation rate declined to 64 percent in 1993. (The CPS data, discussed below, show a substantial increase in conditional participation, from 62 percent in 1988 to 72 percent in 1993, and we are inclined to doubt the apparent decline based on the SIPP data.) In 1984 and 1987 there was a noticeable increase in conditional participation rates with age, until age 55 or so. By 1991 and 1993, however, the correspondence between age and conditional participation was not very pronounced. Finally, unconditional participation rates, shown in the last panel of table 2.1, increased from about 7 percent in 1984 to 27 percent in 1993.

Eligibility and participation rates are shown by income decile in table 2.2. Earnings deciles are calculated separately for each year, and thus the data are comparable from one year to another. Although eligibility is only moderately related to age, there is a consistent increase in eligibility with earnings decile. For example, in 1993, about 17 percent of households in the lowest decile and almost 60 percent of those in the highest decile were eligible. Conditional participation given eligibility also increases with earnings, although the relationship is not as pronounced as for eligibility. For example, in 1993, 44 percent of household in the lowest decile who were eligible also contributed; in the top decile 77 percent contributed. Combining eligibility and participation given eligibility yields a substantial relationship between participation and earnings, as shown in the last panel of table 2.2.

Eligibility and participation are shown by both earnings decile and age interval in appendix table 2B.1 for 1993. These data show little interaction between eligibility and participation rates by earnings decile and age. Thus the simpler tables for age and earnings separately provide a good summary of the more detailed data.

Table 2.3 shows eligibility and participation rates by age interval based on the CPS data. These data show eligibility rates somewhat larger than the SIPP numbers. According to the CPS data, eligibility increased from 40 percent in 1988 to 50 percent in 1993. These data also show a substantial increase in participation given eligibility, from 62 percent in 1988 to 71 percent in 1993. Furthermore, the increase is apparent for all age groups. A comparable increase in conditional participation rates is shown in table 2.4 by earnings decile. These data show an increase in all but the lowest earnings decile. This is an important result, which suggests an increase in individual retirement saving propensity. It is consistent with the recent findings of Bernheim and Garrett (1996), Bayer, Bernheim, and Scholz (1996), and Clark and Schieber (1996),

Table 2.2   **SIPP: Eligibility, Participation Given Eligibility, and Participation Rates by Earnings Decile and Year**

Earnings Decile	Year			
	1984	1987	1991	1993
Eligibility				
1st (lowest)	0.035	0.046	0.071	0.166
2d	0.052	0.065	0.152	0.231
3d	0.070	0.108	0.208	0.298
4th	0.082	0.124	0.240	0.37
5th	0.114	0.154	0.305	0.41
6th	0.134	0.179	0.366	0.468
7th	0.143	0.228	0.408	0.525
8th	0.166	0.276	0.444	0.557
9th	0.213	0.322	0.474	0.602
10th (highest)	0.23	0.322	0.481	0.589
All	0.126	0.185	0.317	0.423
Participation Given Eligibility				
1st (lowest)	0.448	0.524	0.650	0.437
2d	0.616	0.517	0.651	0.483
3d	0.429	0.551	0.629	0.520
4th	0.514	0.561	0.649	0.515
5th	0.463	0.525	0.595	0.570
6th	0.515	0.618	0.671	0.614
7th	0.493	0.592	0.721	0.651
8th	0.584	0.615	0.705	0.68
9th	0.64	0.619	0.749	0.751
10th (highest)	0.692	0.728	0.798	0.777
All	0.570	0.613	0.700	0.638
Participation				
1st (lowest)	0.02	0.024	0.046	0.072
2d	0.032	0.034	0.099	0.111
3d	0.030	0.060	0.131	0.155
4th	0.042	0.069	0.156	0.191
5th	0.053	0.081	0.181	0.231
6th	0.069	0.111	0.246	0.288
7th	0.070	0.135	0.294	0.34
8th	0.097	0.170	0.313	0.38
9th	0.136	0.199	0.355	0.45
10th (highest)	0.162	0.234	0.384	0.46
All	0.072	0.113	0.222	0.27

Source: Based on the Survey of Income and Program Participation.

who conclude that employer education programs increase saving. It would of course also be consistent with a more general increase in saving propensity over time, although we know of no evidence of such a trend independent from personal retirement saving.

Like the SIPP data, the CPS data show a substantial increase in eligibility

Table 2.3   **CPS: Eligibility, Participation Given Eligibility, and Participation Rates by Age and Year**

	Year	
Age	1988	1993
Eligibility		
25–29	0.344	0.461
30–34	0.410	0.515
35–39	0.459	0.521
40–44	0.424	0.546
45–49	0.423	0.531
50–54	0.433	0.487
55–59	0.393	0.450
60–64	0.318	0.413
All	0.404	0.501
Participation Given Eligibility		
25–29	0.551	0.588
30–34	0.580	0.673
35–39	0.596	0.700
40–44	0.612	0.740
45–49	0.723	0.744
50–54	0.702	0.771
55–59	0.683	0.799
60–64	0.705	0.763
All	0.624	0.708
Participation		
25–29	0.170	0.241
30–34	0.215	0.318
35–39	0.252	0.344
40–44	0.243	0.373
45–49	0.294	0.375
50–54	0.280	0.350
55–59	0.250	0.336
60–64	0.206	0.286
All	0.232	0.328

Source: Based on the Employee Benefits Supplement to the Current Population Survey.

with earnings, and a noticeable increase in conditional participation with earnings. Thus unconditional participation also increases with earnings decile. Appendix table 2B.2 presents eligibility and participation rates by earnings and age interval jointly for 1993. This table is comparable to the presentation in appendix table 2B.1 based on SIPP data. As with the SIPP data, there appears to be no substantial interaction between age and eligibility or participation rates by earnings decile. Thus the simple text tables provide a reasonable summary of the relationship between age and earnings on the one hand and eligibility and participation rates on the other.

For convenience, the SIPP and CPS eligibility and participation rates for 1993 are compared in table 2.5. Both eligibility and conditional participation

Table 2.4   **CPS: Eligibility, Participation Given Eligibility, and Participation Rates by Earnings Decile and Year**

	Year	
Earnings Decile	1988	1993
Eligibility		
1st (lowest)	0.148	0.169
2d	0.227	0.249
3d	0.305	0.363
4th	0.378	0.477
5th	0.386	0.495
6th	0.435	0.529
7th	0.469	0.628
8th	0.527	0.665
9th	0.557	0.712
10th (highest)	0.600	0.715
All	0.404	0.501
Participation Given Eligibility		
1st (lowest)	0.425	0.357
2d	0.477	0.498
3d	0.540	0.592
4th	0.520	0.625
5th	0.600	0.629
6th	0.593	0.686
7th	0.647	0.757
8th	0.665	0.776
9th	0.673	0.808
10th (highest)	0.773	0.837
All	0.624	0.708
Participation		
1st (lowest)	0.055	0.052
2d	0.097	0.109
3d	0.146	0.186
4th	0.177	0.272
5th	0.208	0.290
6th	0.243	0.335
7th	0.281	0.446
8th	0.330	0.484
9th	0.358	0.548
10th (highest)	0.437	0.580
All	0.232	0.328

Source: Based on the Employee Benefits Supplement to the Current Population Survey.

rates reported in the CPS are somewhat larger than those reported in the SIPP. The SIPP overall average is 27 percent, and the CPS average is 33 percent. Differences in the wording and ordering of the eligibility and participation questions in the two surveys may account for differences in the results. The survey differences are discussed further in appendix A.

We will compare our simulation results with the assets of the 1992 HRS

Table 2.5   **SIPP and CPS Compared: Eligibility, Participation Given Eligibility, and Participation Rates by Age and by Earnings Decile, 1993**

Age or Earnings Decile	Eligibility		Participation Given Eligibility		Participation	
	SIPP	CPS	SIPP	CPS	SIPP	CPS
Age						
25–29	0.406	0.461	0.556	0.588	0.226	0.24
30–34	0.434	0.515	0.630	0.673	0.274	0.32
35–39	0.444	0.521	0.630	0.700	0.280	0.34
40–44	0.461	0.546	0.645	0.740	0.297	0.37
45–49	0.441	0.531	0.693	0.744	0.305	0.38
50–54	0.423	0.487	0.684	0.771	0.290	0.350
55–59	0.377	0.450	0.671	0.799	0.253	0.336
60–64	0.30	0.41	0.65	0.76	0.19	0.29
All	0.423	0.501	0.638	0.708	0.270	0.33
Earnings decile						
1st (lowest)	0.17	0.169	0.437	0.357	0.07	0.05
2d	0.23	0.25	0.483	0.498	0.111	0.109
3d	0.298	0.36	0.52	0.59	0.16	0.19
4th	0.37	0.477	0.515	0.625	0.191	0.272
5th	0.41	0.50	0.570	0.629	0.231	0.290
6th	0.468	0.53	0.61	0.69	0.29	0.34
7th	0.525	0.628	0.651	0.757	0.342	0.45
8th	0.557	0.665	0.683	0.776	0.381	0.484
9th	0.602	0.712	0.751	0.808	0.452	0.548
10th (highest)	0.589	0.715	0.777	0.837	0.458	0.580
All	0.423	0.501	0.638	0.708	0.270	0.33

Sources: Based on the Survey of Income and Program Participation and the Employee Benefits Supplement to the Current Population Survey.

respondents. The HRS also obtained data on 401(k) participation, but not eligibility, and on 401(k) balances. Because of the way the relevant questions are asked, however, the data on participation may be the least reliable of the three data sources. This issue is discussed further in appendix A. Nonetheless, for the age groups covered by the HRS, the participation rates calculated from the HRS 1992 responses are close to those reported for 1993 in the SIPP, as shown in table 2.6. The HRS rates are also not very different on average from the CPS responses. For households with heads aged 51–61 in 1992, the HRS overall participation rate is 26 percent, which is the same as the SIPP rate for 1993. The CPS participation rate for 1993 is 33 percent.

2.2.2 Contribution and Matching Rates

Participating employees make tax-deductible contributions to 401(k) accounts. Many employers also make matching contributions. The only survey that provides both employee contribution rates and employer matching rates is

Table 2.6   **SIPP and CPS Compared with HRS: Eligibility, Participation Given Eligibility, and Participation Rates by Age and by Earnings Decile, 1993 for SIPP and CPS and 1992 for HRS**

Age or Earnings Decile	Eligibility[a]		Participation Given Eligibility[a]		Participation		
	SIPP	CPS	SIPP	CPS	SIPP	CPS	HRS
Age							
51–55	0.43	0.466	0.67	0.771	0.29	0.334	0.292
56–61	0.35	0.45	0.67	0.776	0.236	0.32	0.22
All	0.391	0.456	0.669	0.77	0.261	0.33	0.26
Earnings decile							
1st (lowest)	0.14	0.115	0.42	0.559	0.06	0.057	0.027
2d	0.20	0.204	0.494	0.655	0.101	0.119	0.093
3d	0.282	0.297	0.611	0.679	0.173	0.175	0.152
4th	0.364	0.416	0.596	0.659	0.217	0.251	0.219
5th	0.388	0.425	0.553	0.712	0.215	0.297	0.228
6th	0.424	0.535	0.635	0.771	0.269	0.368	0.292
7th	0.488	0.609	0.662	0.837	0.323	0.470	0.33
8th	0.488	0.636	0.741	0.812	0.362	0.492	0.37
9th	0.576	0.684	0.791	0.808	0.46	0.531	0.44
10th (highest)	0.561	0.657	0.797	0.862	0.45	0.554	0.45
All	0.391	0.456	0.669	0.773	0.261	0.329	0.26

Sources: Based on the Survey of Income and Program Participation, the Employee Benefits Supplement to the Current Population Survey, and the Health and Retirement Survey.
[a]HRS does not obtain data on eligibility.

the 1993 CPS. Because of nonresponses, however, several assumptions must be made to infer employer matching rates for all employees. Basically, we use the available responses for a given age to impute missing match rates for that age. Further details on these imputations are contained in appendix A.

Employee contribution and employer matching rates are reported in table 2.7. These are earnings-weighted *family* rates, averaged over rates for both members of a two-person family, for example. Based on these estimates, the average family contribution rate of plan participants is 6 percent of family earnings. The average contribution rate of an individual employee is 7.1 percent. The rate increases only mildly with age and shows little relationship to earnings decile. The employer matching rate is 2.7 percent overall and bears little relationship to either age or earnings decile. Based on individuals (rather than families), the employer matching rate is 3.1 percent overall and 4.6 percent among employees that match. Thus the average total family contribution—counting both employee and employer contributions—is 8.7 percent.

Combining the total contribution rates with employee earnings, we obtain dollar contributions, which are reported in table 2.8. Overall, the average combined contribution of plan participants and their employers is $4,467. The aver-

Table 2.7   **Employee Contribution Rates and Employer Matching Rates by Age and by Earnings Decile, 1993**

Age or Earnings Decile	Employee Contribution	Employer Matching Rate	Total Contribution Rate
Age			
25–29	0.056	0.029	0.086
30–34	0.056	0.028	0.084
35–39	0.054	0.025	0.080
40–44	0.059	0.024	0.083
45–49	0.063	0.027	0.090
50–54	0.064	0.025	0.089
55–59	0.069	0.030	0.099
60–64	0.074	0.031	0.106
All	0.060	0.027	0.087
Earnings decile			
1st (lowest)	0.064	0.031	0.095
2d	0.062	0.029	0.092
3d	0.058	0.031	0.089
4th	0.061	0.029	0.090
5th	0.063	0.025	0.088
6th	0.061	0.026	0.087
7th	0.057	0.025	0.082
8th	0.061	0.026	0.087
9th	0.057	0.024	0.080
10th (highest)	0.062	0.030	0.092
All	0.060	0.027	0.087

Source: Based on the Employee Benefits Supplement to the Current Population Survey.

age ranges from $3,040 for the youngest age group to $5,508 for the 55–59 age group. The variation by earnings decile is much greater, as similar contribution rates would imply: the average for the lowest earnings decile is $591 and for the highest decile is $9,399.

Employee contribution and employer matching rates by both earnings decile and age are shown in appendix table 2B.3. Employee and employer dollar contributions are shown in appendix table 2B.4 by both earnings decile and age.

2.2.3   Estimation

The Approach

To understand the assumptions we make to simulate 401(k) assets of future retirees, it is useful to consider a cohort representation of the data. Figure 2.1 shows 401(k) eligibility rates for six cohorts based on SIPP data for 1984, 1987, 1991, and 1993. The cohorts are defined by their ages in 1984, so C27, for example, means the cohort aged 27 in 1984. (In fact, for the purposes of this figure, each cohort is a group of families with heads born in a five-year

Table 2.8   **Employee and Employer Contribution Amounts by Age and by Earnings Decile, 1993**

Age or Earnings Decile	Employee Contribution	Employer Contribution	Total Contribution
Age			
25–29	2,048	992	3,040
30–34	2,468	1,165	3,633
35–39	2,832	1,534	4,366
40–44	3,455	1,444	4,899
45–49	3,700	1,606	5,306
50–54	3,410	1,339	4,749
55–59	3,837	1,670	5,508
60–64	3,451	1,477	4,928
All	3,075	1,392	4,467
Earnings decile			
1st (lowest)	404	186	591
2d	805	363	1,167
3d	1,122	589	1,711
4th	1,522	732	2,254
5th	1,911	731	2,642
6th	2,162	898	3,060
7th	2,394	1,059	3,453
8th	3,113	1,322	4,434
9th	3,612	1,483	5,095
10th (highest)	6,258	3,141	9,399
All	3,075	1,392	4,467

Source: Based on the Employee Benefits Supplement to the Current Population Survey.

interval. So the C27 cohort includes families aged 25–29 in 1984, e.g.) The C27 cohort is identified by the square symbols. The eligibility rate of this cohort was less than 10 percent in 1984, when the cohort was 27 years old (on average), but had risen to almost 45 percent by 1993, when the cohort was 35 years old. A similar increase in eligibility is evident for each of the other six cohorts—C32, C37, C42, C47, C52, and C57. It is also clear that there is a very large "cohort effect": at any age each successively younger cohort has a higher contribution rate than the cohort five years older. This difference is approximately 20 percentage points. For example, 44 percent of the C27 cohort was eligible when this cohort was 35 years old. But the rate was only about 20 percent for the C32 cohort that was age 35 five years earlier. The cross-sectional relationship between age and eligibility can also be identified in the figure; cross-sectional relationships in 1984 and 1993 are shown by the solid lines.

Suppose that we wanted to predict the future 401(k) eligibility of the youngest—C27—cohort. One might be tempted simply to extrapolate the cohort trend to future ages. But it is clear that this could quickly lead to eligibility

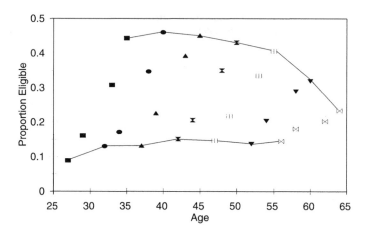

Fig. 2.1   401(k) Eligibility by cohort, 1984, 1987, 1991, and 1993

rates of over 100 percent. On the other hand, it is equally clear that when the C27 cohort reaches age 40 its eligibility rate will be greater than that of the C32 cohort at age 40.

At this point it is useful to revisit the problem of trying to distinguish age, cohort, and year effects. Suppose

$$A = \text{age},$$

$$C = \text{cohort} = \text{age in } 1984,$$

$$T = \text{year} = \text{calendar year} - 1984.$$

Then $A = C + T$. In a simple regression, if we relate eligibility to age, cohort, and year, as for example $E = aA + cC + tT$, it is not possible to isolate all three effects. In particular, it is not possible to identify age, cohort, and year effects for each age, cohort, and year. If one of the variables—say age—is parameterized, however, it is in principle possible to identify both cohort and time effects.

We parameterize the relationship between age and eligibility, but we do not try to identify separate cohort and year effects. Instead, we assume that the apparent cohort effects in the figure are time—or year—effects and simply represent the spread of 401(k)s with time. With reference to figure 2.1, this means that we estimate eligibility by allowing the cross-sectional relationship to shift upward over time. In fact, even if both cohort and year effects are estimated, the cohort effects are often not statistically different from zero, and most of the explanatory power comes from the year effects. We give more details of the specification below.

Now return to the problem of predicting future eligibility of the C27 cohort in the figure. (When we come to actual simulations, we will in fact work with the C25 and the C15 cohorts.) If 401(k) plans continue to spread, then the 1993

Table 2.9   **Aggregate 401(k) Participants and Contributions, 1988**

	From Form 5500		From CPS		
Year	Participants (millions)	Contributions (billion $)	Eligibility Rate	Participation Given Eligibility	Participation Rate
1988	15.203	39.412	0.380	0.630	0.229
1989	17.337	46.081	–	–	–
1990	19.548	48.998	–	–	–
1991	19.126	51.533	–	–	–
1992	22.404	64.345	–	–	–
1993	23.138	69.322	0.486	0.713	0.332
Percentage change 1988–93	52.20	75.90	28	13	45

Sources: U.S. Department of Labor (1997) and the Employee Benefits Supplement to the Current Population Survey.

relationship between eligibility and age will clearly understate future eligibility of the C27 cohort as it ages. In part this is simply because the program will undoubtedly continue to expand. But, in addition, the 1993 relationship is determined in part by how the past spread occurred. If, for example, the diffusion of plans has been disproportionately in small firms, with younger workers, the cross-sectional relationship would tend to look as it does in the figure. In the 1993 cross section there is a noticeable reduction in eligibility with age. This is much less apparent in the 1984 cross section. Thus we can only use formal estimates as a guide to future patterns. Our approach is to assume that 20 years from now, when members of the C27 cohort will be age 55, their eligibility rate will be x percent higher than the eligibility rate of the cohort that was age 55 in 1993.

To guess at a reasonable value for x, it helps to consider the recent aggregate increase in participants and contributions, as well as the recent increase in eligibility and participation rates, discussed above. These data for 1988–93 are shown in table 2.9. The data on aggregate participants and contributions come from so-called Form 5500 reports.[2] According to these data, the number of participants increased over 50 percent over the five-year period between 1988 and 1993. Employment grew by 4 percent over this period. The CPS data show a 45 percent increase in the participation rate, which together with the 4 percent employment increase is rather consistent with a 52 percent increase in the number of participants. Aggregate contributions increased by over 76 percent, much more than the 52 percent increase in participation. Aggregate earnings

2. The Form 5500 reports tabulate contributions to private sector 401(k) plans. They do not include contributions to related 457 (public sector) or 403(b) (nonprofit) plans, nor do they include contributions to 401(k) plans by public sector employees.

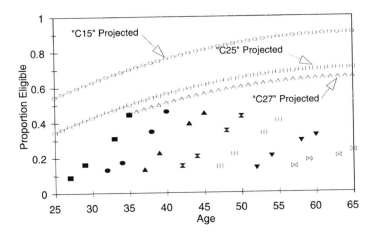

Fig. 2.2   401(k) Eligibility by cohort with illustrative projections

increased about 25 percent over this period, which—together with a 52 percent increase in participation—would imply an increase in aggregate contributions of 77 percent, if the average fraction of earnings contributed did not change. Taken at face value, this comparison suggests that the fraction of earnings contributed may have increased by as much as 1 percent. For the illustration at hand, the most relevant number is the 28 percent increase in the eligibility rate over this recent five-year period.

If the C27 cohort when it is age 55, 20 years from now, will contribute 50 percent more than 55-year-olds contributed in 1993, then the projected C27 eligibility rates would look something like those shown in figure 2.2. For convenience, we make actual projections for the C25 cohort, which is just two years younger than the C27 cohort. In principle, we might suppose that projections for this younger cohort would be somewhat higher than those for the C27 cohort, as depicted in figure 2.2—showing C25 rates .05 higher than the C27 rates. In fact, we make projections for this cohort assuming that when its members are age 55—22 years in the future—they will contribute 50 percent more than 55-year-olds contributed in 1993. We also want to make a reasonable assessment of eligibility rates for younger generations. Suppose that over the subsequent 10 years, the eligibility rate were to increase 20 percentage points (above the C25 rate) but the age pattern remain as shown for the C25 projection. That would yield an eligibility pattern represented by "C15 projected" in figure 2.2. The 20-point increase for cohorts 10 years apart is rather modest compared to the approximate 20-point increase for cohorts 5 years apart in figure 2.1. For future reference, we summarize in table 2.10 the age-year profiles of the cohorts mentioned above.

To check the implications of our cohort eligibility rates—together with contribution rates—against actual 401(k) balances, we will use the cohort data to

Table 2.10   **Age-Year Profiles for C27, C25, and C15 Cohorts**

Cohort	Age in 1984	Age in 1993[a]	Year Will Be 55	Year Will Be 65
C27	27	35	2013	2023
C25	25	33	2015	2025
C15	15	23	2025	2035

[a]Age at the time of the 1993 survey, which is approximated eight years older than age at the time of the 1984 survey.

obtain simulated balances for the HRS respondents. These simulated balances can then be compared to the actual balances of the respondents. The basic method we use, which is described below, is different from the approach used to project for future cohorts, as described above. In this case, the method relies directly on the cohort data as shown in figure 2.1. Thus the method can also be explained with reference to figure 2.1. The HRS respondents were age 51–61 in 1992—or 43–53 in 1984, which is the first year of the SIPP data. Thus their past eligibility rates should be reflected approximately in the C42 and C52 cohort rates shown in figure 2.1. To simulate the HRS respondent balances, we essentially predict their eligibility (and participation) from the past eligibility and participation rates for cohorts in this age range. For example, a person in the HRS sample who was age 60 at the time of the survey (in 1992) is a member of the C52 cohort. The experience of that cohort is used to predict HRS balances for people in that cohort.

In principle, we could go through a similar process for participation given eligibility, and for participation. In practice, we work with the participation rate from the beginning and pass over the decomposition into eligibility and participation given eligibility. We must assume contribution rates of participants, expressed as a fraction of earnings. To make projections like those described above, we use CPS, rather than SIPP, data as a base. Thus it is useful to see the CPS data organized by cohort. Eligibility, participation given eligibility, and participation rates based on these data are shown in figures 2.3, 2.4, and 2.5, respectively.

Fitting Cross-Sectional Age Profiles

As described in the previous section, we do not make projections by direct extrapolation of an estimated model. Rather, the data are used as a base that can be combined with eligibility and participation assumptions to produce future projections. Perhaps the most important reason for fitting the cross-sectional profiles is to estimate the relationship between earnings decile and eligibility and participation. We use a specification of the form

$$Y_{it} = \beta_{1t}A + \beta_{2t}A^2 + \sum_{i=1}^{10} \gamma_{it}D_{it} + \varepsilon_{it},$$

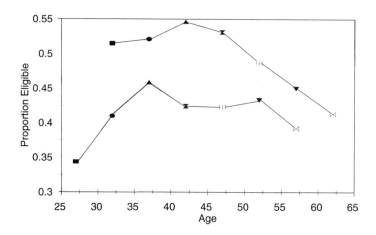

Fig. 2.3   401(k) Eligibility by cohort, 1988 and 1993

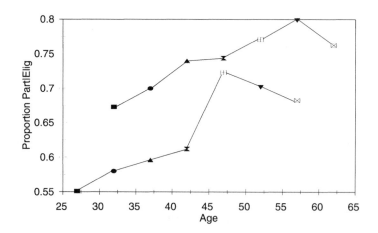

Fig. 2.4   401(k) Participation given eligibility by cohort, 1988 and 1993

where D is an indicator variable indicating earnings decile and A is age. The most important estimates are the γ_{it}, which indicate the effect of earnings decile on Y. We have estimated a probit specification of this form for eligibility, participation given eligibility, and participation. The estimates are reported in appendix table 2B.5.

The estimates, like the tabular data above, show large increases in eligibility, participation given eligibility, and participation with earnings decile. The estimates also suggest that the difference by earnings decile, in eligibility and participation rates, increased between 1988 and 1993. The implied age profiles for the 1st, 4th, 7th, and 10th earnings deciles in 1993 are shown in figures 2.6, 2.7, and 2.8A for eligibility, participation given eligibility, and participation, respectively.

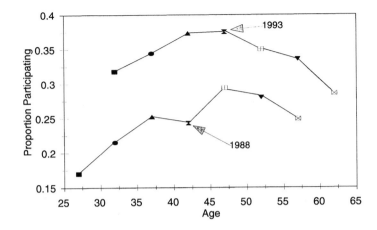

Fig. 2.5   401(k) Participation by cohort, 1988 and 1993

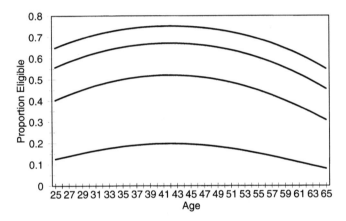

Fig. 2.6   Eligibility fitted 1993 profiles for 1st, 4th, 7th, and 10th income deciles
Note: Lowest curve corresponds to 1st decile, highest curve to 10th decile.

Participation Projections

For the projections in this paper, we assume no change in participation rates given eligibility, and therefore the participation and eligibility rate percentage increases are the same. Thus we discuss projections for participation only. Following the approach outlined above, to project future participation rates for the C25 cohort, we assume that when this cohort is 55 years old (in 2015) it will have participation rates 50 percent higher than the participation rate of the cohort that was age 55 in 1993. We further assume that the participation rate at age 65 will be 5 percent higher than this, that is, 55 percent higher than the participation rate of the cohort that was age 55 in 1993. Figure 2.8*B* is the same as figure 2.8*A* but includes these projections. The projections exhibit a widening difference between the participation rates of high- and low-income

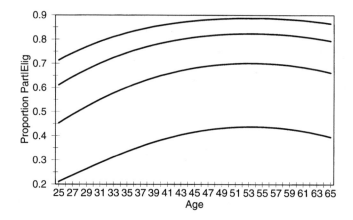

Fig. 2.7   Participation given eligibility fitted 1993 profiles for 1st, 4th, 7th, and 10th income deciles

Note: Lowest curve corresponds to 1st decile, highest curve to 10th decile.

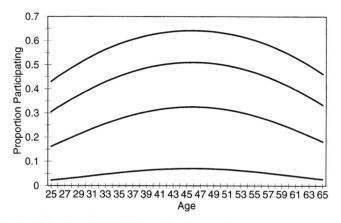

Fig. 2.8*A*   Participation fitted 1993 profiles for 1st, 4th, 7th, and 10th income deciles

Note: Lowest curve corresponds to 1st decile, highest curve to 10th decile

families as they age. We believe such spreading is plausible, but the extent of this dispersion is likely to be one of the most uncertain of the projection features.

We also make projections for the C15 cohort, whose members were 15 years old in 1984. Even looking ahead just 10 years further, however, makes plausible assumptions about future 401(k) participation even more problematic. Thus we think of these projections as representing what the 401(k) accumulation would be if participation were substantially higher than the C25 projections but considerably short of universal coverage. They cannot be taken to be what we believe will happen. These projections are based on the assumption

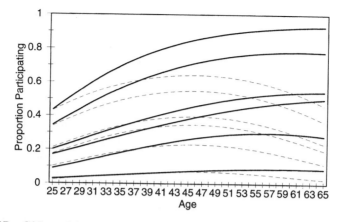

Fig. 2.8B   C25 participation projections for 1st, 3d, 5th, 6th, 8th, and 10th income deciles

Note: Lowest curve corresponds to 1st decile, highest curve to 10th decile. Dashed lines are participation fitted 1993 profiles for 1st, 3d, 5th, 6th, 8th, and 10th income deciles (cf. fig. 2.8A).

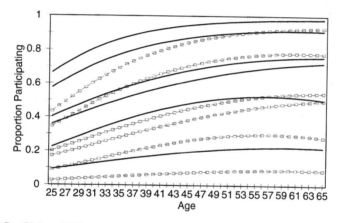

Fig. 2.8C   C15 vs. C25 participation projections for 1st, 3d, 5th, 6th, 8th, and 10th income deciles

Note: Lowest curve corresponds to 1st decile, highest curve to 10th decile. Dashed, boxed lines are C25 participation projections for 1st, 3d, 5th, 6th, 8th, and 10th income deciles (as in fig. 2.8B).

that participation rates for the median wage earner are 20 percentage points greater than the C25 rates. Rates for the highest and lowest decile increase somewhat less than this.[3] Figure 2.8C shows the C15 projections in compari-

---

3. The actual procedure was to add a constant term to the probit equation used to describe the C25 projections that would increase the C25 projections for the 5th and 6th income deciles by 20 percentage points. The same constant term was added to the probit equations for each of the other deciles. The highest deciles do not increase by 20 points because of the upper limit of 100 percent. The lower deciles are increased less than 20 points—because of the properties of the probit functional form—but, relative to the C25 projections, much more than the higher deciles.

son to those for the C25 cohort. Finally, we make projections assuming universal 401(k) participation.

2.3   Projected 401(k) Balances and Comparison with HRS Sample

2.3.1   Wealth of the HRS Respondents

To judge the relative importance of potential 401(k) contributions, we compare projected 401(k) assets of future generations with the current (1992) assets of the HRS sample. The 1992 assets of the HRS respondents when they were age 51–61 are shown in table 2.11, by earnings decile. As is typically true for wealth data, there is a very large difference between mean and median assets, especially for financial assets. For example, the mean of all personal retirement assets is $30,465 and the mean of 401(k) assets is $10,808. The medians are $3,200 and zero, respectively—fewer than half of HRS respondents have 401(k) accounts. The 401(k) projections discussed below are based on averages—for example, estimates of average contribution rates—and thus can only be compared to the HRS means. We do not capture the substantial differences that are likely between mean and median values within earnings deciles. The principle comparison we make is with social security wealth, however, and the means and medians of social security assets do not differ greatly. Social security wealth is evaluated by estimating the accrued wealth at age 65, were the person to work until that age.[4] These accrued levels are converted to 1992 dollars using the Social Security Administration's intermediate forecast of the average annual interest rate provided by the Board of Trustees of the OASDI Trust Fund. For comparability, the projected 401(k) balances discussed below also assume that a person works until age 65. The actual HRS 401(k) balances reported in table 2.11, however, are 1992 balances when the respondents were age 51–61. Personal retirement balances could easily double by the time the respondents attain age 65.

2.3.2   Estimation of Earnings Histories

We need earnings histories to project 401(k) assets of future cohorts of families—like those in the HRS sample, but who have different 401(k) participation rates. We have divided the HRS sample into earnings deciles according to their 1992 earnings. In principle, the social security earnings histories of the HRS respondents can be used to determine average earnings by age within each decile. As discussed by Venti and Wise (1996), however, there is one important limitation to this method: historical earnings are reported only up to the social security earnings limit. Actual earnings in the top two or three deciles may be substantially higher than social security reported earnings.

---

4. A family's social security wealth is the simple sum of the mortality-weighted present value of each member's benefit stream. We do not consider here the present value for a single family member including survivor benefits.

Table 2.11   Mean and Median 1992 Assets of HRS Respondents by Earnings Decile and Category

				Asset Category				
Earnings Decile	Total Wealth	Total Wealth Excluding Social Security	Total Retirement Excluding Social Security	Employer Pension Assets	Total Personal Retirement	Nonretirement Financial	401(k) Assets	Social Security Wealth
				Means				
1st	270,238	208,721	48,841	39,162	9,679	44,964	620	61,517
2d	228,538	154,438	51,117	40,002	11,114	27,692	1,025	74,100
3d	251,170	167,115	44,251	34,394	9,857	27,194	2,648	84,055
4th	269,872	176,423	47,335	36,749	10,586	29,904	2,192	93,449
5th	301,348	199,755	73,276	52,522	20,754	36,609	4,049	101,593
6th	378,252	270,121	97,228	75,745	21,483	45,592	6,366	108,131
7th	415,763	301,077	125,606	94,361	31,245	46,029	11,322	114,686
8th	479,383	354,268	145,595	105,368	40,228	61,423	13,514	125,115
9th	590,440	458,410	177,464	133,091	44,373	84,192	19,767	132,030
10th	1,007,740	864,328	328,495	219,055	109,441	148,277	48,709	143,412
All	415,833	312,441	112,677	82,212	30,465	54,724	10,808	103,392

(*continued*)

Table 2.11 (continued)

Earnings Decile	Total Wealth	Total Wealth Excluding Social Security	Total Retirement Excluding Social Security	Employer Pension Assets	Total Personal Retirement	Nonretirement Financial	401(k) Assets	Social Security Wealth
				Asset Category				
				Medians				
1st	128,615	69,674	0	0	0	5,000	0	55,114
2d	128,744	56,959	2,086	0	0	4,020	0	69,208
3d	169,828	90,500	7,782	0	0	5,000	0	81,383
4th	185,142	95,090	18,000	6,000	0	6,500	0	92,699
5th	247,204	148,500	36,934	10,847	3,200	10,400	0	103,783
6th	285,606	178,685	57,438	32,641	6,000	12,000	0	111,740
7th	341,419	215,422	73,270	42,671	10,000	15,100	0	117,699
8th	380,870	236,560	97,655	51,053	12,000	23,000	0	126,130
9th	471,370	331,019	107,000	61,011	21,900	30,000	0	130,993
10th	749,567	613,061	261,503	17,625	53,000	72,000	0	136,390
All	284,229	175,000	44,010	15,913	3,200	13,000	0	106,808

Note: Social security wealth is calculated for each respondent assuming the respondent works through normal retirement. The calculation reported above is based solely on each respondent's expected benefits. No account is made of spouse survivor benefits. Sample includes families with head aged 51–61, at least one member employed, and having matched social security records.

Because of this limitation of the social security data, we make calculations based on the annual March CPSs, which report earnings well above the social security maximum.[5] This is the procedure we use: (1) We identify earnings deciles, as described above, using the 1992 earnings of each HRS family. (2) Using the annual March CPSs we calculate earnings deciles by age for the years 1964–91. Using published data on median earnings prior to 1964, we extrapolate this series back to 1956. Thus we obtain CPS earnings histories by decile for the years 1956–91. (3) We assign each HRS household to a CPS decile according to the household's 1992 earnings decile. The CPS earnings histories begin at age 25, and a given household is assumed to have been in the same decile since age 25. As described in the next two subsections, we use these earnings profiles, together with projected 401(k) participation and contributions rates and rate-of-return assumptions, to calculate accumulated 401(k) assets through age 65.

2.3.3   HRS 401(k) Assets and Cohort Data

Before projecting the 401(k) accumulation of future cohorts, we first determine the extent to which the current 401(k) balances of HRS respondents appear to be consistent with the SIPP cohort data on participation, together with the CPS data on contributions. While the extent of this correspondence is not necessarily an indicator of the confidence that should be attached to our projections, we are inclined to give more credence to the projections if the cohort data that serve as a basis for our projection assumptions are roughly consistent with the HRS balances with which they can be compared.

When the 401(k) program began in 1982, members of the 1992 HRS sample were 41–51 years old. Suppose that in 1982 these families began to participate in 401(k) plans at rates estimated from the SIPP and to contribute at rates estimated from the CPS. We ask how close simulated balances based on these assumptions are to the actual 1992 balances of the HRS respondents. We first use the SIPP data to estimate participation profiles by age for each of two cohorts from whose members the HRS respondents were drawn: the cohorts whose members were age 51–55 and 56–60 in 1992—at the time of the HRS. The SIPP estimates allow us to predict the probability of participation for each HRS family beginning in 1982, when 401(k)s were first available and when the two HRS cohorts were age 41–45 and 46–50, respectively.

To estimate contributions, we use family earnings histories, derived as described above. Within each earnings decile, beginning in 1982, we randomly assign families to participation status, based on SIPP estimates of participation by age and earnings decile for each of the two cohorts.[6] Based on our estimates

5. The ratio of the CPS maximum to the social security maximum has ranged from a low of just under 2 in 1981 to a high of over 20 in 1964. In 1991 the CPS reported earnings up to a maximum of $200,000; the social security maximum was $53,400 in that year.

6. As a means of estimation, we actually construct a "synthetic HRS" sample of persons aged 41–51 in each of the 10 earnings deciles in 1982. This sample is "aged" through 1992, assigning

from the CPS data, we assume a contribution rate of 8 percent. This is somewhat less that the average rate of 8.7 percent—including both employee and employer matching contributions—estimated for 1993 from the CPS data. There is some evidence that earlier contribution rates were lower than this, as explained in appendix A. In the projections for future cohorts discussed below, we assume a contribution rate of 9 percent.

We calculate accumulated 401(k) balances for three different rates of return: the observed return on corporate bonds in each year, the return on large company stocks in each year, and the return assuming the contributor invests half in bonds and half in stocks. The observed rates of return are compiled from Ibbotson Associates (1997). Some families invest 401(k) assets in money market funds and may obtain returns lower than any of these.

Simulated 401(k) balances through 1992 are shown in table 2.12, by earnings decile, along with the actual reported 401(k) balances of the HRS respondents. On average, the simulated values do not differ greatly from the observed balances reported in the HRS. Using the bond rate of return seems to give the closest match. Even the simulated balances by earnings decile are typically not far from the HRS reported balances. This exercise must necessarily be tentative. By assuming a different contribution rate, for example, we would realize a different correspondence between simulated and reported values. As a basis for judgments about the future, the results help to give some credence to short-run projections, but future behavior could be very different from reasonable expectations based on historical trends. For example, contribution rates could be substantially different from 1993 rates.

2.3.4 401(k) Assets of Future Generations

Taking the lifetime earnings described above to be the actual past earnings of the HRS families, we estimate what they would have accumulated in a 401(k) had they had the participation rates that we project for the C25 and the C15 cohorts, and had there been universal 401(k) coverage. (The members of the C25 cohort were age 33 in 1993, and the members of the C15 cohort were age 23 in 1993.) As above, we suppose that once contributions begin they continue until retirement, at age 65. Within an earnings decile, we probabilistically assign persons to a beginning participation age, as discussed in the previous subsection. So, for example, say the projected participation rate at age 25 is 35 percent. We randomly assign a fraction .35 to begin at that age. If the projected rate at age 26 is 35.5 percent, we randomly assign .005 to start contributing at

---

families to participate and contribute to a 401(k) at rates determined by the estimates from the SIPP and the CPS. The estimated age-participation profiles are used to determine which sample members contribute in 1982 and in subsequent years. Once a family contributes, we assume the family continues to contribute in subsequent years. Thus, if the estimated participation rate for a particular age and earnings decile is 10 percent in 1982, we randomly assign 10 percent of the families to begin contributing in 1982. If the probability is 11 percent in 1983, then another 1 percent are randomly chosen to begin contributing in that year.

Table 2.12   **Mean Simulated and Reported HRS 401(k) Balances**

Earnings Decile	HRS Observed	Simulated		
		Bonds	50/50	S&P 500
All Families				
1st	620	248	266	284
2d	1,025	869	931	993
3d	2,648	2,104	2,262	2,418
4th	2,192	3,475	3,740	4,002
5th	4,049	4,992	5,376	5,753
6th	6,366	7,855	8,466	9,067
7th	11,322	11,232	12,113	12,980
8th	13,514	16,291	17,581	18,851
9th	19,767	23,542	25,425	27,280
10th	48,709	34,555	37,275	39,955
All	10,808	10,516	11,344	12,158
Contributor Families				
1st	21,693	2,923	3,135	3,343
2d	9,893	7,775	8,337	8,888
3d	14,116	13,062	14,044	15,010
4th	11,747	18,057	19,436	20,793
5th	15,387	23,307	25,098	26,861
6th	37,219	29,694	32,001	34,273
7th	33,735	37,103	40,012	42,876
8th	39,505	46,126	49,778	53,375
9th	49,877	59,354	64,101	68,777
10th	95,199	85,493	92,224	98,853
All	42,271	42,310	45,638	48,915

age 26, and so forth. And, once a family starts to contribute, we assume participation will continue in subsequent years. Some will never be assigned to participation status.

We assume a family contribution rate (including employee plus employer contributions) of 9 percent, based on CPS rates for 1993 discussed above. Our intention is that the C25 projection in particular be a conservative estimate of what actual participation is likely to be. The C15 projection may also be conservative, but that is harder to judge.

For each of the projections, we assume three different rates of return: the average rate of return on corporate bonds since 1926 (6 percent), the average rate of return on the Standard and Poor's (S&P) 500 over the same period (12.7 percent), and the rate of return assuming that a person is invested half in bonds and half in the S&P 500.

The results for these three projections are reported in table 2.13. As indicated above, our estimates of historical participation and contribution rates,

Table 2.13   Projected Mean 401(k) Assets by Cohort, Rate of Return, and Earnings Decile, Plus 1992 HRS 401(k) and Age 65 Social Security Wealth

Earnings Decile	401(k)	Social Security Wealth	Cohort 25			Cohort 15			Universal Coverage		
			Bond	50/50	S&P 500	Bond	50/50	S&P 500	Bond	50/50	S&P 500
1st	620	61,517	950	1,798	3,628	2,395	4,651	9,628	14,805	30,771	68,016
2d	1,025	74,100	5,360	10,023	20,001	11,080	21,365	44,037	39,404	80,923	177,665
3d	2,648	84,055	11,937	22,237	44,419	20,901	40,267	83,286	57,762	117,340	255,793
4th	2,192	93,449	21,651	40,307	80,848	34,393	66,423	138,213	74,497	149,579	323,179
5th	4,049	101,593	28,544	52,493	104,283	44,721	85,280	175,645	91,051	180,471	385,935
6th	6,366	108,131	38,669	71,104	141,321	57,726	109,535	224,829	107,786	211,260	447,924
7th	11,322	114,686	59,815	110,672	221,511	80,512	153,324	316,185	125,877	244,385	513,988
8th	13,514	125,115	77,702	143,218	286,004	99,724	188,596	386,876	148,264	284,878	594,106
9th	19,767	132,030	102,627	187,939	373,204	127,541	239,432	488,196	179,757	341,624	705,768
10th	48,709	143,412	153,852	276,406	540,450	188,657	346,466	693,668	255,144	473,216	957,672
All	10,808	103,392	50,111	91,620	181,567	66,765	125,534	256,056	109,435	211,445	443,005

Note: Social security wealth balances are calculated for each respondent assuming the respondent works through normal retirement. The HRS 401(k) assets are at the time of the survey in 1992. Both are reported in 1992 dollars. The calculation reported above is based solely on each respondent's expected benefits. No account is made of spouse survivor benefits. The sample includes families with head aged 51–61, at least one member employed, and having matched social security records. Projections use 1926–96 average rates of return on bonds and the S&P 500.

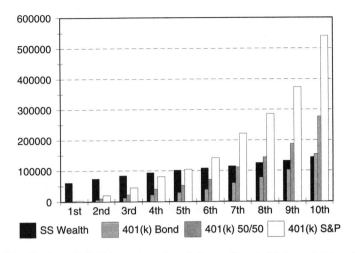

Fig. 2.9A   Projected 401(k) assets and social security wealth by cohort and earnings decile: C25 projections

and thus our projections, are based on means. The comparable HRS 401(k) and social security assets, shown in the first two columns of the table, are also means. The 401(k) assets, however, are accumulated tax free; taxes would be paid when funds are withdrawn. No tax will be paid on most social security benefits.

The C25 projections yield 401(k) assets at retirement ranging from $50,111 to $181,567, depending on the rate of return. These levels are very large relative to average social security wealth of $103,392 and are much larger than the HRS respondent mean 401(k) balance of $10,808 in 1992, when the respondents were age 51–61. Under the C15 assumptions, the means range from $66,765 to $256,056. Universal coverage would yield mean 401(k) balances at age 65 ranging from $109,439 to $443,005, depending on the rate of return.

For each projection, however, the ratio of projected 401(k) to social security wealth varies a great deal depending on lifetime earnings. Perhaps the easiest way to see this is by looking at figures 2.9A through 2.9C, which show projected 401(k) assets and social security wealth by earnings decile for each of the projections. Because the C25 projections assume continued very low participation rates in the lowest income deciles, the 1st and 2d deciles accumulate very little in 401(k) assets, no matter what the rate of return. Beginning with the 3d decile, however, 401(k) assets at retirement would likely be substantial relative to social security wealth, and for families with incomes above the median 401(k) balances would be likely to exceed social security wealth. (The increase in social security wealth with earnings is very small once earnings exceed the 4th earnings decile. Thus it is not surprising that saving based on a

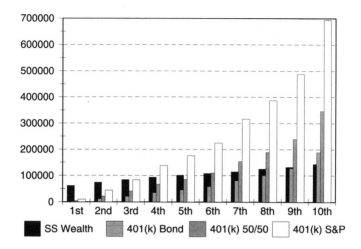

Fig. 2.9B   Projected 401(k) assets and social security wealth by cohort and earnings decile: C15 projections

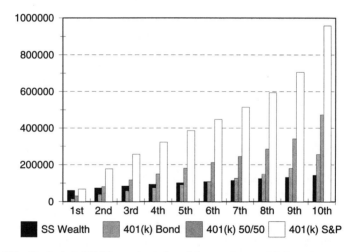

Fig. 2.9C   Projected 401(k) assets and social security wealth by cohort and earnings decile: Universal projections

percentage of income would exceed social security wealth at higher income levels.)

The C15 projections imply substantially large 401(k) assets, relative to social security wealth, for the lower earnings deciles. Under these projections, even the families in the 2d decile could accumulate 401(k) assets that could be an important fraction of social security wealth. Universal coverage could yield 401(k) assets that would exceed social security wealth in every lifetime earnings decile. And 401(k) assets would almost surely represent an important share of social security wealth even in the lowest decile.

As emphasized above, however, the projected differences in participation rates by earnings decile could well be far from realized experience, even if the average participation rates are realistic. Our sense is that the current C25 projections underestimate future 401(k) participation by low-income households. There seems to be no way to convincingly narrow this uncertainty. Of course, simulating results under alternative assumptions could provide further information about the implications of different rates of participation dispersion by earnings decile.

2.3.5 Risk

A concern about individual retirement saving is the risk associated with fluctuations in the rate of return. Of course there are important risks associated with conventional employer-provided pension plans and government programs such as social security as well, but they may be more difficult to evaluate. We can, however, provide an empirical measure of the rate-of-return risk associated with private saving accounts. To do this, we have calculated the asset accumulation that would been realized under the C25 assumptions, but based on the range of actual returns from 1926 to 1996. We calculate the asset accumulation that would have resulted over each 40-year career: the first beginning in 1926 and the last beginning in 1956. We do this for each of the investment options used above: bonds, the S&P 500, and half and half. This is very similar to the procedure followed by MaCurdy and Shoven (1992) to explore the returns on stock versus bond investments through TIAA-CREF.

The results are shown in figure 2.10. The median accumulation from stock investment is almost four times as large as the median return from bond investment. Yet the relative range of accumulations is much greater for bonds than for stocks. The largest bond accumulations are about four times as large as the smallest. The largest stock accumulations are about twice as large as the smallest accumulations. Put another way, a bond investor counting on the median could end up with half that much or twice that much. On the other hand, a stock investor counting on the median could end up with one-third less or one-third more than the median. Indeed, of the 31 possible 40-year careers since 1926, the *lowest* stock accumulation is about the same as the *highest* bond accumulation!

Whether this suggests high or low risk is a matter of opinion. It does not seem large relative to job change or job loss risk associated with defined benefit pension plans, for example. Job change could easily lead to benefits less than half of benefits that would result from a lifetime career in the same firm. Samwick and Skinner (1995) conclude that defined contribution plans are less risky than defined benefit plans because they depend on average earnings over the entire career rather than over the last few years of employment.

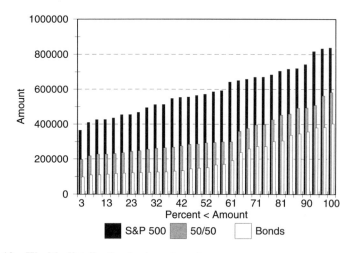

Fig. 2.10   Wealth distribution by investment

Persons who started work in 1956 are now receiving social security benefits that are much higher than they would have received under 1956 social security provisions. In many countries, it is likely that future social security benefits will be much less than those provided under current legislation. Perhaps the issue is not that some forms of preparation for retirement are risky while others are not, but rather how future retirees might best gain maximum returns on average while protecting themselves against very bad outcomes.

2.4   Conclusions

We have projected the accumulation of 401(k) assets at retirement for the cohort that was 25 years old in 1984 and the cohort that was 15 years old in 1984. The C25 projections are based on what we hope are plausible assumptions about future 401(k) participation rates. Indeed, our intention is that these projections be conservative and thus likely to underestimate realized contributions. The C15 projections are further from historical rates but we hope are also based on plausible assumptions about potential future participation. We are, however, more uncertain about the correspondence between projected rates and actual realized contributions for the C15 cohort; actual participation could easily exceed or fall short of these projections. For comparison, we have also made projections assuming universal 401(k) coverage.

In each case, the accumulation of 401(k) assets is large compared to current wealth at retirement. Because a large fraction of current retirees depend almost entirely on social security benefits for support in retirement, we have compared future 401(k) assets to social security wealth. Our C25 projections suggest that when this cohort reaches retirement age—they will be 65 years old in 2025— their average 401(k) assets are likely to exceed their average social security assets. But the projections also suggest that relative to social security wealth, 401(k) assets will vary a great deal with lifetime earnings. While this is surely true, we are quite uncertain about the exact magnitude of the variation by earnings decile. The projections suggest that the lowest earnings decile may have very little in 401(k) assets. But for families with lifetime earnings above the lowest two or three deciles, 401(k) assets are likely to be a substantial fraction of social security wealth. For families with lifetime earnings above the median, 401(k) assets could exceed social security wealth, and this would almost surely be true for families in the top four earnings deciles.

Universal 401(k) participation would likely yield 401(k) assets at retirement greater than social security wealth for all but the lowest lifetime earnings decile, and possibly for the lowest decile as well. The intermediate C15 projections yield 401(k) accumulations that could represent a substantial fraction of social security wealth for lifetime earnings histories as low as the 2d decile. Thus we believe that 401(k) assets will almost surely be an important component of the retirement wealth of future generations of retirees and could be the dominant component for a large fraction of them.

Appendix A
Data

The three principal data sources used in the analysis are the Survey of Income and Program Participation (SIPP), the Current Population Survey (CPS), and the Employee Benefits Supplement to the CPS. The unit of observation in each of these surveys is the person. For the present analysis we have grouped the individual data to obtain data for family units, by matching married partners in the sample. A family is included in the sample if it meets the following criteria:

- Head aged 25–65
- At least one family member employed
- Earnings available for both family members

A family participates (or is eligible) if at least one member participates (or is eligible). Based on the CPS data, the 401(k) contribution and the employer matching contribution are both calculated at the person level and then aggregated to obtain family amounts. Details on each of the samples are presented below.

CPS

We use the May 1988 and April 1993 surveys. Several missing data issues had to be addressed.

1. *Rates of 401(k) participation and eligibility.* These data come from two questions asked of currently employed workers. Respondents are first asked if they participate. If they answer "no" or "don't know" (DK) they are then asked if their employer offered a 401(k) plan. Of the respondents who said they did not participate in a 401(k), 11.5 percent did not know if their employer offered such a plan. We have chosen to treat these DK responses as missing data for the eligibility calculations only. One consequence is that the sample used in "participant" calculations will exceed the sample used for "eligible" calculations. Also, since information on eligibility is only missing for nonparticipants (all participants are eligible), it is likely that the conditional participation rate is biased upward.

2. *The percentage of gross pay contributed to a 401(k):* In both years slightly over 25 percent of the 401(k) participants failed to answer this question. To impute these missing amounts we calculated a table of percentage of gross pay contributed by five-year age intervals from the nonmissing observations. This table was used to impute the missing observations.

3. *The employer match percentage (1993 only):* Respondents were asked, "If you were to contribute $100 to this plan, how much would your employer contribute?" About 65 percent of the sample provided a dollar amount; another 17 percent indicated that their employer matched but could not provide an amount. The remaining 17 percent of the sample failed to answer the question. To impute dollar amounts for all participants we tabulated dollar amounts by five-year age intervals for the 65 percent of the sample providing a complete answer. If a respondent indicated that his or her employer matched but could not provide an amount, we imputed an amount using the mean by age interval from the distribution of matching amounts greater than zero. If a respondent failed to answer the question we imputed the amount from the distribution of matches including zero match rates.

SIPP

We used data from the 1984, 1985, 1986, 1990, 1991, and 1992 panels of the SIPP. Since the SIPP panels are overlapping we are sometimes able to obtain data for a single time period from more than one panel. The panels that were used, the survey wave within each panel, and the interview months corresponding to each panel are shown in table 2A.1. There are approximately 28 months separating the 1984 and 1987 interviews. In the cohort analyses we treat this interval as a two-year period. The 1984–91 interval is assumed to span six years. The 1984–93 interval is assumed to span eight years.

SIPP versus CPS

The SIPP responses imply eligibility and participation rates somewhat below those found in the CPS (see table 2.5 in the text). The difference may be due in part to the more inclusive wording of the 401(k) questions in the CPS. The SIPP asks:

Table 2A.1   **SIPP Panels**

Panel	Wave	Interview Months
1984	4	September–December 1984
1985	7	January–April 1987
1986	4	January–April 1987
1990	4	February–May 1991
1991	7	February–May 1993
1992	4	February–May 1993

Does your employer offer a 401(k) or thrift plan? Such a plan allows employees to defer part of their salary and not have to pay taxes on the deferred salary until they retire or withdraw the money.

If the respondent answers "yes," then the following question is asked:

Do you participate in this plan?

As noted above, the CPS reverses the order and inquires about participation first (1993 version):

Some retirement plans allow workers to make tax-deferred contributions to the plan. For example, you might choose to have your employer put part of your salary into a retirement savings account and then you don't pay earnings taxes on this money until you take it out or retire. These plans are called by different names, including 401(k) plans, pre-tax plans, salary reduction plans, and 403(b) plans. Do you participate in a plan like this?

If the respondent answers "no" or "don't know," then:

Does your employer *offer* you a plan like this? [emphasis in original]

HRS

The HRS does not inquire about eligibility for a 401(k) plan. It does ask about participation. All employed persons are asked if they are "included in any such pension, retirement, or tax-deferred plan with [their] employer." If yes, they are asked to distinguish between defined benefit ("benefits are usually based on a formula involving age, years of service, and salary") and defined contribution ("money is accumulated in an account for you") type plans. If they indicate coverage by a defined contribution plan, they are prompted to distinguish between 401(k) and non-401(k) plans. For a number of reasons some respondents were able to indicate coverage by a defined contribution plan but could not distinguish between a 401(k) and a traditional defined contribution plan. We treat these respondents as not participating in a 401(k) plan. The principal categories of defined contribution plan types are "thrift or savings," "401(k), 403(b), or SRA," "profit sharing or ESOP," and "other." It is perhaps unclear to the respondent whether the "thrift or savings" category includes 401(k)-type plans. We have included them as 401(k) plans.

Appendix B

Table 2B.1   SIPP: Eligibility, Participation Given Eligibility, and Participation Rates by Earnings Decile and Age in 1993

					Age				
Earnings Decile	25–29	30–34	35–39	40–44	45–49	50–54	55–59	60–64	All
				Eligibility					
1st (lowest)	0.245	0.171	0.156	0.154	0.179	0.130	0.119	0.115	0.166
2d	0.250	0.262	0.234	0.252	0.205	0.208	0.209	0.131	0.231
3d	0.275	0.293	0.304	0.339	0.336	0.317	0.255	0.192	0.298
4th	0.374	0.330	0.376	0.430	0.404	0.391	0.367	0.204	0.370
5th	0.329	0.403	0.463	0.454	0.432	0.417	0.361	0.277	0.405
6th	0.416	0.445	0.499	0.516	0.524	0.471	0.444	0.363	0.468
7th	0.436	0.568	0.515	0.590	0.595	0.524	0.481	0.398	0.525
8th	0.506	0.583	0.623	0.610	0.555	0.572	0.472	0.369	0.557
9th	0.548	0.644	0.613	0.659	0.623	0.625	0.533	0.439	0.602
10th (highest)	0.610	0.616	0.628	0.587	0.543	0.583	0.538	0.497	0.589
All	0.406	0.434	0.444	0.461	0.441	0.423	0.377	0.297	0.423

Participation Given Eligibility

	1	2	3	4	5	6	7	8	9
1st (lowest)	0.353	0.534	0.404	0.533	0.393	0.432	0.554	0.235	0.437
2d	0.417	0.527	0.526	0.507	0.428	0.476	0.463	0.440	0.483
3d	0.409	0.510	0.490	0.483	0.611	0.566	0.207	0.487	0.520
4th	0.540	0.414	0.481	0.510	0.554	0.577	0.603	0.563	0.515
5th	0.535	0.519	0.556	0.620	0.675	0.629	0.506	0.354	0.570
6th	0.500	0.574	0.623	0.636	0.689	0.632	0.659	0.649	0.614
7th	0.557	0.642	0.623	0.681	0.693	0.717	0.635	0.708	0.651
8th	0.567	0.691	0.676	0.670	0.756	0.764	0.708	0.711	0.683
9th	0.662	0.747	0.756	0.726	0.809	0.795	0.802	0.822	0.751
10th (highest)	0.677	0.782	0.779	0.795	0.856	0.803	0.793	0.820	0.777
All	0.556	0.630	0.630	0.645	0.693	0.684	0.671	0.649	0.638

Participation

	1	2	3	4	5	6	7	8	9
1st (lowest)	0.086	0.091	0.063	0.082	0.070	0.056	0.066	0.027	0.072
2d	0.104	0.138	0.123	0.128	0.088	0.099	0.097	0.057	0.111
3d	0.113	0.150	0.149	0.164	0.205	0.179	0.183	0.094	0.155
4th	0.202	0.137	0.181	0.219	0.224	0.226	0.221	0.115	0.191
5th	0.176	0.209	0.257	0.281	0.291	0.262	0.183	0.098	0.231
6th	0.208	0.256	0.311	0.328	0.361	0.298	0.293	0.236	0.288
7th	0.243	0.365	0.321	0.402	0.412	0.376	0.306	0.282	0.342
8th	0.287	0.403	0.421	0.408	0.420	0.437	0.334	0.263	0.381
9th	0.363	0.481	0.464	0.478	0.504	0.497	0.427	0.360	0.452
10th (highest)	0.413	0.482	0.489	0.466	0.465	0.468	0.426	0.408	0.458
All	0.226	0.274	0.280	0.297	0.305	0.290	0.253	0.193	0.270

Source: Based on the Survey of Income and Program Participation.

Table 2B.2 CPS: Eligibility, Participation Given Eligibility, and Participation Rates by Earnings Decile and Age in 1993

Earnings Decile	25–29	30–34	35–39	40–44	45–49	50–54	55–59	60–64	All
				Eligibility					
1st (lowest)	0.20	0.196	0.123	0.216	0.209	0.115	0.097	0.138	0.169
2d	0.24	0.214	0.304	0.254	0.303	0.181	0.257	0.181	0.25
3d	0.234	0.442	0.355	0.461	0.421	0.339	0.344	0.220	0.363
4th	0.445	0.502	0.488	0.552	0.519	0.484	0.380	0.259	0.477
5th	0.417	0.481	0.566	0.559	0.529	0.501	0.389	0.409	0.495
6th	0.479	0.480	0.592	0.522	0.593	0.623	0.432	0.474	0.529
7th	0.622	0.669	0.613	0.662	0.629	0.581	0.618	0.553	0.628
8th	0.591	0.634	0.657	0.768	0.683	0.727	0.614	0.606	0.665
9th	0.649	0.759	0.770	0.718	0.691	0.670	0.753	0.614	0.712
10th (highest)	0.686	0.738	0.744	0.745	0.734	0.682	0.617	0.70	0.72
All	0.46	0.515	0.521	0.546	0.531	0.487	0.450	0.41	0.50
				Participation Given Eligibility					
1st (lowest)	0.22	0.320	0.399	0.412	0.248	0.394	0.703	0.641	0.357
2d	0.21	0.439	0.418	0.659	0.548	0.712	0.777	0.363	0.498
3d	0.376	0.528	0.581	0.532	0.762	0.733	0.672	0.788	0.592
4th	0.487	0.505	0.659	0.654	0.713	0.726	0.671	0.740	0.625
5th	0.554	0.578	0.639	0.590	0.691	0.659	0.735	0.766	0.629
6th	0.592	0.677	0.650	0.684	0.743	0.698	0.794	0.806	0.686
7th	0.597	0.737	0.786	0.804	0.779	0.849	0.845	0.755	0.757
8th	0.677	0.742	0.792	0.821	0.781	0.787	0.835	0.814	0.776
9th	0.677	0.805	0.818	0.866	0.846	0.887	0.80	0.78	0.808
10th (highest)	0.779	0.828	0.759	0.925	0.865	0.847	0.928	0.83	0.837
All	0.588	0.673	0.700	0.740	0.744	0.771	0.799	0.76	0.71

	Participation								
1st (lowest)	0.03	0.052	0.044	0.078	0.051	0.041	0.061	0.076	0.052
2d	0.039	0.083	0.120	0.156	0.136	0.119	0.170	0.061	0.109
3d	0.074	0.200	0.184	0.205	0.288	0.204	0.205	0.159	0.186
4th	0.188	0.228	0.292	0.323	0.370	0.326	0.231	0.180	0.272
5th	0.211	0.240	0.355	0.305	0.358	0.312	0.295	0.245	0.290
6th	0.247	0.306	0.366	0.342	0.417	0.382	0.312	0.354	0.335
7th	0.362	0.474	0.433	0.480	0.480	0.475	0.466	0.378	0.446
8th	0.369	0.431	0.503	0.603	0.496	0.538	0.516	0.422	0.484
9th	0.412	0.600	0.598	0.580	0.556	0.581	0.568	0.443	0.548
10th (highest)	0.504	0.594	0.546	0.668	0.628	0.548	0.564	0.569	0.58
All	0.241	0.318	0.344	0.373	0.375	0.350	0.336	0.286	0.33

Source: Based on the Employee Benefits Supplement to the Current Population Survey.

Table 2B.3 **Employee Contribution and Employer Matching Rates by Earnings Decile and Age in 1993**

					Age				
Earnings Decile	25–29	30–34	35–39	40–44	45–49	50–54	55–59	60–64	All
				Employee Contribution Rate					
1st (lowest)	0.065	0.057	0.043	0.075	0.072	0.061	0.067	0.075	0.064
2d	0.064	0.086	0.054	0.052	0.063	0.060	0.056	0.106	0.062
3d	0.060	0.054	0.055	0.051	0.064	0.062	0.062	0.070	0.058
4th	0.049	0.060	0.051	0.069	0.059	0.072	0.061	0.071	0.061
5th	0.061	0.058	0.059	0.056	0.070	0.070	0.076	0.063	0.063
6th	0.061	0.056	0.056	0.055	0.059	0.065	0.085	0.074	0.061
7th	0.049	0.053	0.051	0.054	0.053	0.066	0.076	0.075	0.057
8th	0.056	0.056	0.054	0.061	0.066	0.066	0.059	0.090	0.061
9th	0.054	0.048	0.054	0.057	0.064	0.055	0.074	0.066	0.057
10th (highest)	0.059	0.058	0.056	0.062	0.067	0.062	0.068	0.073	0.062
All	0.056	0.056	0.054	0.059	0.063	0.064	0.069	0.074	0.060
				Employer Matching Rate					
1st (lowest)	0.054	0.028	0.018	0.029	0.035	0.025	0.021	0.046	0.031
2d	0.120	0.037	0.021	0.023	0.025	0.024	0.022	0.005	0.029
3d	0.032	0.031	0.023	0.026	0.033	0.031	0.044	0.041	0.031
4th	0.026	0.032	0.028	0.025	0.030	0.039	0.027	0.026	0.029
5th	0.029	0.033	0.023	0.019	0.019	0.028	0.028	0.021	0.025
6th	0.032	0.030	0.022	0.020	0.019	0.024	0.041	0.029	0.026
7th	0.026	0.029	0.025	0.022	0.023	0.021	0.028	0.034	0.025
8th	0.031	0.029	0.024	0.022	0.027	0.028	0.021	0.033	0.026
9th	0.024	0.024	0.020	0.026	0.027	0.015	0.034	0.020	0.024
10th (highest)	0.026	0.022	0.037	0.030	0.033	0.027	0.030	0.044	0.030
All	0.029	0.028	0.025	0.024	0.027	0.025	0.030	0.031	0.027

				Total Contribution Rate					
1st (lowest)	0.120	0.085	0.061	0.104	0.107	0.086	0.089	0.120	0.095
2d	0.184	0.124	0.075	0.075	0.088	0.083	0.078	0.111	0.092
3d	0.092	0.086	0.079	0.077	0.098	0.093	0.106	0.111	0.089
4th	0.075	0.092	0.079	0.095	0.089	0.111	0.088	0.097	0.090
5th	0.091	0.092	0.082	0.075	0.090	0.097	0.104	0.084	0.088
6th	0.093	0.086	0.078	0.075	0.078	0.089	0.126	0.104	0.087
7th	0.075	0.082	0.076	0.076	0.076	0.087	0.104	0.108	0.082
8th	0.087	0.085	0.078	0.082	0.093	0.094	0.080	0.123	0.087
9th	0.078	0.072	0.074	0.082	0.090	0.070	0.108	0.086	0.080
10th (highest)	0.085	0.080	0.093	0.093	0.100	0.089	0.099	0.117	0.092
All	0.086	0.084	0.080	0.083	0.090	0.089	0.099	0.106	0.087

Source: Based on the Employee Benefits Supplement to the Current Population Survey.

Table 2B.4   Employee and Employer Contribution Amounts by Earnings Decile and Age in 1993

Earnings Decile	25–29	30–34	35–39	40–44	45–49	50–54	55–59	60–64	All
Employee Contribution									
1st (lowest)	233	286	258	538	673	315	511	338	404
2d	532	886	722	847	946	781	711	784	805
3d	738	879	1,122	1,124	1,436	1,226	1,248	872	1,122
4th	835	1,277	1,327	1,925	1,730	1,916	1,537	1,272	1,522
5th	1,307	1,551	1,847	1,897	2,525	2,243	2,296	1,515	1,911
6th	1,584	1,765	2,030	2,187	2,491	2,569	3,088	2,079	2,162
7th	1,398	1,965	2,248	2,538	2,705	3,126	3,338	2,774	2,394
8th	1,990	2,516	2,786	3,396	4,008	3,759	3,088	3,939	3,113
9th	2,446	2,632	3,400	3,936	4,822	3,803	5,123	4,132	3,612
10th (highest)	3,708	4,915	5,872	7,430	7,842	6,760	8,091	7,012	6,258
All	2,048	2,468	2,832	3,455	3,700	3,410	3,837	3,451	3,075
Employer Contribution									
1st (lowest)	188	87	116	246	343	132	163	205	186
2d	955	404	288	364	365	324	287	36	363
3d	388	506	470	565	749	631	815	541	589
4th	426	688	718	706	868	1,025	659	513	732
5th	603	884	728	663	684	872	855	491	731
6th	836	939	812	776	795	964	1,584	822	898
7th	760	1,071	1,101	1,056	1,149	1,009	1,218	1,255	1,059
8th	1,101	1,284	1,249	1,226	1,680	1,575	1,084	1,421	1,322
9th	1,065	1,308	1,270	1,777	2,001	1,029	2,380	1,192	1,483
10th (highest)	1,643	1,879	4,567	3,311	3,867	3,043	3,660	3,759	3,141
All	992	1,165	1,534	1,444	1,606	1,339	1,670	1,477	1,392

	Total Contribution								
1st (lowest)	421	373	373	784	1,016	447	674	543	591
2d	1,487	1,290	1,010	1,210	1,311	1,104	998	820	1,167
3d	1,127	1,385	1,593	1,690	2,185	1,858	2,063	1,413	1,711
4th	1,261	1,965	2,046	2,631	2,598	2,940	2,195	1,785	2,254
5th	1,909	2,435	2,575	2,560	3,209	3,115	3,151	2,006	2,642
6th	2,420	2,704	2,842	2,964	3,286	3,533	4,672	2,900	3,060
7th	2,158	3,036	3,350	3,594	3,855	4,135	4,556	4,029	3,453
8th	3,090	3,800	4,034	4,622	5,688	5,334	4,173	5,360	4,434
9th	3,511	3,940	4,670	5,713	6,823	4,833	7,503	5,325	5,095
10th (highest)	5,351	6,794	10,439	10,741	11,709	9,803	11,751	10,771	9,399
All	3,040	3,633	4,366	4,899	5,306	4,749	5,508	4,928	4,467

Source: Based on the Employee Benefit Supplement to the Current Population Survey.

Table 2B.5   **Parameter Estimates for Eligibility, Participation Given Eligibility, and Participation**

Variable or Earnings Decile	Eligibility Estimate	Eligibility T-Statistic	Participation Given Eligibility Estimate	Participation Given Eligibility T-Statistic	Participation Estimate	Participation T-Statistic
Age 1988	0.09	8.84	0.05	3.09	0.10	9.06
Age 1993	0.087	9.43	0.086	6.05	0.113	12.08
Age squared 1988	−0.103	8.81	−0.043	2.22	−0.104	8.35
Age squared 1993	−0.104	9.70	−0.080	4.84	−0.124	−11.41
1988 Deciles						
1st	−2.839	−13.44	−1.498	−4.20	−3.713	−16.21
2d	−2.539	−12.11	−1.377	−3.92	−3.412	−15.08
3d	−2.301	−11.01	−1.219	−3.51	−3.165	−14.10
4th	−2.103	−10.06	−1.274	−3.68	−3.038	−13.56
5th	−2.079	−9.97	−1.075	−3.10	−2.917	−13.07
6th	−1.953	−9.37	−1.100	−3.18	−2.803	−12.57
7th	−1.871	−8.95	−0.962	−2.78	−2.696	−12.06
8th	−1.721	−8.26	−0.899	−2.61	−2.547	−11.44
9th	−1.645	−7.90	−0.887	−2.58	−2.471	−11.11
10th	−1.535	−7.37	−0.552	−1.61	−2.257	−10.17
1993 Deciles						
1st	−2.678	−13.704	−2.444	−8.04	−4.071	−20.092
2d	−2.400	−12.328	−2.095	−6.98	−3.683	−18.382
3d	−2.065	−10.671	−1.853	−6.22	−3.335	−16.820
4th	−1.777	−9.162	−1.759	−5.94	−3.050	−15.418
5th	−1.730	−8.949	−1.746	−5.91	−2.992	−15.162
6th	−1.645	−8.505	−1.592	−5.40	−2.862	−14.522
7th	−1.387	−7.187	−1.359	−4.65	−2.571	−13.088
8th	−1.291	−6.675	−1.323	−4.50	−2.478	−12.608
9th	−1.149	−5.957	−1.188	−4.07	−2.309	−11.776
10th	−1.148	−5.935	−1.076	−3.67	−2.235	−11.373

References

Bayer, Patrick, B. Douglas Bernheim, and John Karl Scholz. 1996. The effects of financial education in the workplace: Evidence from a survey of employers. NBER Working Paper no. 5655. Cambridge, Mass.: National Bureau of Economic Research, July.

Bernheim, B. Douglas, and Daniel M. Garrett. 1996. The determinants and consequences of financial education in the workplace: Evidence from a survey of households. NBER Working Paper no. 5667. Cambridge, Mass.: National Bureau of Economic Research, July.

Clark, Robert L., and Sylvester J. Schieber. 1996. Factors affecting participation rates and contribution levels in 401(k) plans. Paper presented at the spring symposium of the Pension Research Council, Wharton School, University of Pennsylvania, Philadelphia.

Ibbotson Associates. 1997. *Stocks, bonds, bills and inflation: 1997 Yearbook.* Chicago: Ibbotson Associates.

MaCurdy, Thomas E., and John B. Shoven. 1992. Stocks, bonds, and pension wealth. In *Topics in the economics of aging,* ed. David A. Wise. Chicago: University of Chicago Press.

Samwick, Andrew A., and Jonathan Skinner. 1995. How will defined contribution pension plans affect retirement income? Hanover, N.H.: Dartmouth College. Mimeograph.

U.S. Department of Labor. Pension and Welfare Benefits Administration. 1997. *Private pension plan bulletin: Abstract of 1993 Form 5500 annual reports,* no. 6. Washington, D.C.: U.S. Department of Labor, Winter.

Venti, Steven F., and David A. Wise. 1996. Lifetime earnings, saving choices, and wealth at retirement. Paper presented at symposium to honor F. Thomas Juster, Ann Arbor, Mich., December.

Comment   Sylvester J. Schieber

In their paper, Poterba, Venti, and Wise use a disparate set of data and methods to estimate the implications of the growth in 401(k) savings for the retirement security of various cohorts of current workers. The paper is so packed with information that it is difficult at times to keep track of everything that is happening at specific points in the story and how each particular piece of information fits into the whole.

The authors begin by developing an analysis of the growing prevalence of participation in 401(k) plans from 1984 through 1993. They develop the story line in pieces, first looking at growth in coverage, then growth in participation rates given coverage, and finally participation rates across the whole workforce. They then proceed to apply measured contribution rates to estimate contributions. Finally, they accumulate contributions under a set of investment scenarios to project the potential accumulation of 401(k) retirement savings for workers currently at or near the beginning of their careers.

While the authors present their coverage and participation data in a series of numerical tables, looking at it graphically gives a better visual perspective on what has been occurring in the world they are attempting to describe. Figures 2C.1*A*, 2C.1*B*, and 2C.1*C* are simply plots of the data points from the top, middle, and bottom panels, respectively, of the authors' table 2.1.

The authors note the clear pattern of coverage growth shown in figure 2C.1*A*. The picture makes it clear that the growth was consistent both across time and across age groups. The authors also note the growth in participation given coverage during the early years, and the confusing story in the 1993 Survey of Income and Program Participation (SIPP) data, contradicted by the Current Population Survey (CPS) data analyzed separately. The graphic story in figure 2C.1*B* shows that the early growth in participation given coverage occurred at lower age levels, with little variation over the whole period in

Sylvester J. Schieber is vice president of research and information for Watson Wyatt Worldwide.

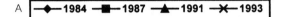

Portion of workforce eligible to participate in a plan

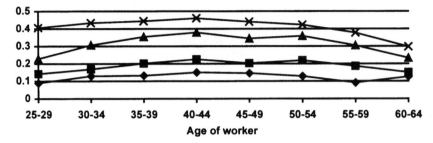

B **Portion of covered workforce participating in a 401(k) plan**

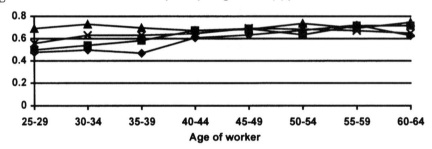

C **Portion of total workforce participating in a 401(k) plan**

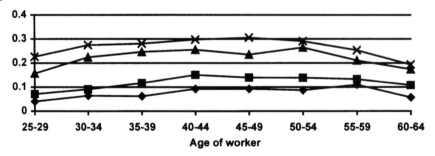

Fig. 2C.1 401(k) Coverage and participation by age and year
Source: Survey of Income and Program Participation as reported in table 2.1.
Note: (*A*) Percentage of workers covered by 401(k) plans. (*B*) Percentage of covered workers participating in a 401(k) plan. (*C*) Percentage of all workers participating in 401(k) plans.

participation rates of those over age 40 once they were offered the opportunity to participate in a plan. The combination of the evolving pictures shown in figures 2C.1*A* and 2C.1*B* make it quite clear that the growth in overall participation rates during the period shown in figure 2C.1*C* was more largely driven by the increases in coverage than the increases in participation once coverage was offered. This is an important point to keep in mind for later.

In table 2.2 of the paper and the discussion around it, the authors go through the same regimen as in table 2.1, except that they look at coverage and participation by earnings decile. Plotting those data results in a moving picture that is essentially the same as that shown in the age-based figures, so it is not repeated here. The one piece that the earnings perspective adds is that participation given coverage reported in the 1993 SIPP was substantially below that reported in the 1991 survey for the bottom 40 percent of the wage distribution, was somewhat less than but not as much so for the next 30 percent, and was equivalent for the top 30 percent.

After the discussion of the growing levels of participation in 401(k) plans, the authors turn to a discussion of estimation techniques that serve as the basis for the assumptions used in projecting future levels of benefits that might be provided by the system. They begin by looking at future potential increases in coverage under 401(k) plans. Here they are troubled by the profiles that are reflected in their figure 2.1 because older workers do not seem to have made the same kind of coverage gains as younger ones, and because workers in later years have much lower coverage rates than their younger counterparts. The authors hypothesize that the 1993 profile might look the way it does because "the diffusion of plans has been disproportionately in small firms, with younger workers." This hypothesis has major implications for the results found in the paper, given subsequent assumptions about pension coverage growth used to project the potential effect of 401(k) plans on future retirement income.

An alternative explanation for the 1993 profile of 401(k) coverage reported in figure 2.1 might be that the early initiation of 401(k) plans took place in firms that provided relatively generous retirement benefits in general. Those firms and their generous retirement plans encouraged the early retirement of workers in their mid- to late 50s during the late 1980s and early 1990s. As workers in their late 50s and early 60s with these generous retirement packages retired, they left behind a smaller number of similarly aged counterparts working for less generous firms, many of which had not yet sponsored a 401(k) plan. In essence, it is likely that the retirement of those with early 401(k) coverage drove down the coverage rate among the age group in question because those continuing to work had never had coverage. If this same phenomenon continues into the future, and I suspect that those with significant retirement savings in the future (i.e., mainly those covered by retirement plans) will continue to retire earlier than those without such savings (i.e., mainly those not covered by such plans), then the authors' hypothesis that the 1993 profile will not represent the future profile is simply wrong.

In their projections, the authors "assume" that each succeeding cohort of workers will have higher coverage rates at any attained age than earlier cohorts had achieved by that age. For example, they assume that workers aged 25 in 1993 will have higher coverage rates when they are age 55 than the 55-year-old cohort had in 1993. They assume that participation rates given eligibility are constant over time and thus that overall participation rate increases are driven by increased coverage. Following these general conditions, they assume that when the cohort of workers aged 25 in 1993 reaches age 55 it will have a participation rate that is 50 percent higher than that of the 55-year-old cohort in 1993 and that this cohort's participation rate will continue to grow until its members reach age 65.

The implicit assumption here is that we will continue to realize significant increases in 401(k) coverage rates. According to CPS tabulations in the paper, the coverage rate of 55-year-olds in 1993 was approximately 45 percent. To get the kind of growth that the authors are assuming, the coverage rate for 25-year-olds in 1993 would have to grow at a rate of 1.4 percent per year for 30 years. I have reservations about this growth assumption and its implications for personal retirement saving for two reasons.

First, the growth in 401(k) plans during the 1980s partly reflected the shift from defined benefit to defined contribution plans. In some cases there was a direct substitution of one type of plan for another. In many, the shift was a more subtle curtailment of a defined benefit plan as the 401(k) was offered. In 1993, 61 percent of the active participants in 401(k) plans worked for an employer that sponsored another retirement plan; 82 percent of them were in 401(k) plans with more than 1,000 active participants, while fewer than 3 percent were in plans with less than 100 active participants (U.S. Department of Labor 1997, 50). The explicit and implicit shifting from defined benefit to defined contribution plans has been mostly a large-employer phenomenon. At some juncture, both types of shifting will decline because of the saturation of 401(k) plans in large firms. To the extent that it has gone on thus far, it has not necessarily resulted in an increase in retirement saving but more likely a change in the way we are doing it.

Second, I believe that continued expansions in 401(k) coverage that represent new retirement savings are likely to be harder and harder to achieve in the future. Between 1984 and 1993, the number of 401(k) plans in operation grew from 17,303 to 154,527. Over the same period, the number of active participants in these plans grew from 7.5 million to 23.1 million (U.S. Department of Labor 1997, 95). The result was a steady decline in the number of active participants per plan over the period (shown in fig. 2C.2), indicating that the new plans added each year were smaller and smaller. Of the increase in the number of 401(k) plans offered during 1993, 86 percent of them were the sole plan being offered by the sponsor, and of these, 88 percent had fewer than 100 active participants (U.S. Department of Labor 1996, 47; 1997, 49). The recent growth in 401(k) plans has largely been a small-employer phenomenon, and it generally represents new coverage. The big ones have largely been harvested

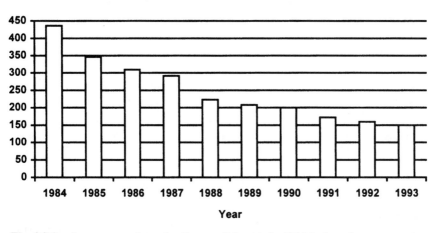

Active participants per plan

Fig. 2C.2   Average number of active participants in 401(k) plans for selected years
Source: U.S. Department of Labor (1997, 95).

already, and it will be increasingly difficult to get smaller employers to offer plans in the future at rates that will continue to drive up coverage rates significantly. The rate of growth of the number of active participants in 401(k) plans slowed from 19.2 percent per year from 1984 to 1988 to 7.5 percent per year from 1989 to 1993. It is likely that the rate of growth of coverage will continue to decline.

Beyond the underlying assumptions about future coverage and participation rates, there are other assumptions that have a significant bearing on the final projections in the paper that are worthy of comment. In simulating asset accumulations, the assumption is that once a household begins to contribute to a 401(k) plan it will continue to contribute until retirement age. This may not be a serious problem in projecting mean accumulations for cohorts of workers, but it does fail to take into account the considerable variation in participation that must occur among lower wage workers from year to year or the leakage in retirement savings that occurs as workers terminate employment early in their careers and take cash distributions that are used for preretirement consumption. This could be particularly important for variations in accumulations across the income spectrum.

The accumulation projections are developed using three alternative portfolios. In some recent work that I have done with a colleague we explored the variation in 401(k) asset allocations at three different wage levels by workers in their 20s, 30s, 40s, 50s, and 60s. The results are shown in table 2C.1. While this is a cross-sectional distribution of investment patterns, there is no reason to believe that it is not reflective of the investment patterns of workers across their life cycles to the extent that they spend their lives in a particular segment

Table 2C.1   **401(k) Asset Allocation by Age and Wage Level of Plan Participants (percentage of assets invested in equities)**

	Age of Participant				
Annual Wage	20s	30s	40s	50s	60s
Less than $15,000	68.1	65.1	57.8	49.0	35.6
$35,000–$45,000	72.1	66.2	61.4	56.0	46.0
$60,000–$75,000	84.0	76.1	69.9	65.6	56.2

Source: Gordon P. Goodfellow and Sylvester J. Schieber, "Social Security Reform: Implications of Financial Market Risk for Individual Accounts and the Distribution of Benefits," paper presented at the 1997 Pension Research Council Symposium, Wharton School, University of Pennsylvania, 12 May 1997.

of the wage spectrum. The more conservative investment style of lower wage workers, especially if it persists over the whole life cycle, suggests that they will tend to end up with asset accumulations toward the pure bond investing end of the projections while their higher wage counterparts will end up further along the spectrum toward the mixed or pure stock portfolios.

Another issue that the projections fail to account for is net rates of return that take into consideration the costs of investing. Access Research, Inc., estimates that current asset levels in 401(k) plans in mid-1997 stand at approximately $865 billion and that the annual administrative fees for both record keeping and asset management for the year will be $6.7 billion, or 77 basis points (Wuelfing 1997). While these fees are not borne by the participants in all cases, in many cases they are. My impression is that the trend is toward having the participants bear these costs.

Having been fairly critical of various aspects of this work, I want to close by saying that the goal being pursued here is a worthy one. The voluntary defined contribution system is relatively new, and it is impossible to judge its potential contribution to retirement security of today's workers by looking at current retirees or workers close to retirement. This effort is to be applauded in having begun to project the implications of the 401(k) system for workers who will be exposed to a full lifetime of the opportunity that it provides.

References

U.S. Department of Labor. Pension and Welfare Benefits Administration. 1996. *Private pension plan Bulletin: Abstract of 1993 Form 5500 annual reports,* no. 5. Washington, D.C.: U.S. Department of Labor, winter.

———. 1997. *Private pension plan bulletin: Abstract of 1993 Form 5500 annual reports,* no. 6. Washington, D.C.: U.S. Department of Labor, winter.

Wuelfing, Robert G. (CEO, Access Research, Inc.). 1997. Speech given at the national conference of the Society of Professional Administrators and Recordkeepers, Washington, D.C., 23 June.

3   The Taxation of Pensions: A Shelter Can Become a Trap

John B. Shoven and David A. Wise

3.1   Introduction and Motivation

The recent legislation that raised the minimum wage was accompanied by the Small Business Job Protection Act of 1996, which, among other things, temporarily (for years 1997–99) suspends the 15 percent excise tax on "excess distributions" from qualified pension plans. Surely few people know about the excise tax in the first place, let alone its suspension. In fact, while people are keenly aware that pensions allow them to save before-tax dollars and compound their investment returns without current taxation, it is our impression that very few people know how pension assets are taxed on withdrawal or on the death of the owner of the pension. In this paper we present a comprehensive examination of the taxation of pensions, with particular emphasis on large pension accumulations. The analysis answers a number of questions: (1) How do the excess distribution excise tax and its companion excess accumulation excise tax work? How do these taxes interact with the personal income tax systems and the estate tax? (2) Should only high-income individuals be concerned about these taxes or might they be imposed on people with relatively modest incomes? (3) Are pension plans still attractive saving vehicles once these excise taxes are applicable? For example, should someone whose base pension plan is likely to trigger either the excess distribution tax or the excess accumu-

John B. Shoven is the Charles R. Schwab Professor of Economics and dean of the School of Humanities and Sciences, Stanford University, and a research associate of the National Bureau of Economic Research. David A. Wise is the John F. Stambaugh Professor of Political Economy at the John F. Kennedy School of Government, Harvard University, and the director for Health and Retirement Programs at the National Bureau of Economic Research.

The authors are grateful to Henry Aaron, Joel Dickson, John Freidenrich, Steven Lockwood, Tom MaCurdy, Jim Poterba, and Seth Weingram for helpful comments and discussions. Jon Rork provided superb research assistance. The authors acknowledge the support of Charles Schwab and BZW Barclays Global Investors (Shoven), the National Institute on Aging and the Hoover Institution (Wise), and the National Bureau of Economic Research.

Table 3.1   **Average and Marginal Tax Rates Faced on a $1.9 Million Estate (in 1996 dollars)**

Date of Death	Average Combined Estate and Excise Tax Rate (%)	Marginal Combined Estate and Excise Tax Rate on Supplemental Plan (%)	Marginal Combined Estate, Excise, and Income Tax Rate on Supplemental Plan (%)
1982	4.17	0	39.23
1984	28.31	43	69.75
1988	22.62	43	69.75
1996	29.16	53.25	85.40

lation tax participate in a supplemental 401(k) plan? (4) Are pensions equally advantageous for stock investments and bond investments? If not, which assets should be held inside a pension plan and which should be held outside the plan? (5) Does it always make sense to delay distributions from pension plans as long as possible, thereby maximizing the tax deferral advantage that they offer? (6) How are pension accumulations treated when they are part of an estate? We focus on these microeconomic issues without discussing the social desirability of current tax policy. However, we should acknowledge at the outset that we see little economic merit in a penalty excise tax applying to people who save "too much" through the pension system. Most observers of the U.S. economy agree that the country's saving rate is too low. Since we know that savers only capture a fraction of the social return on their investments, it is unclear why the biggest savers in the economy should be penalized.

The Small Business Job Protection Act of 1996 is just the latest in a series of bills over the past 15 years that has changed the way pensions are taxed. To illustrate how radically the rules have changed, consider four different individuals with exactly the same wealth (and composition of wealth) at the time of their deaths, each of whom died at age 70. The four cases differ only in the date of death. The estates, all valued at $1.9 million in 1996 dollars, were composed of $600,000 in nonpension assets including a house, $1.2 million in a defined contribution pension plan, and $100,000 in a supplemental plan such as an individual retirement account (IRA) or a Keogh plan. Table 3.1 shows the tax rates faced by estates processed in 1982, 1984, 1988, and 1996. The estates of these individuals faced radically different tax laws. We cannot present all of the details in this introduction, but one important difference is that before 1983 pension accumulations were completely exempt from the estate tax. In addition, beneficiaries could take advantage of 10-year forward averaging on their income tax if the inherited pension plan funds were withdrawn in a lump sum. The result is that in 1982 the heir was able to consume more than 60 percent of the value of the inherited supplemental pension plan; the combined tax rate was less than 40 percent.

In contrast, consider the inheritance of the beneficiary in 1996. Because the estate tax exclusion of pensions assets was limited to $100,000 as of 1983 and eliminated in 1985, and because the excess accumulation tax became effective in 1987 (and 10-year averaging was replaced with 5-year averaging), the 1996 heir can spend less than 15 percent of the value of the inherited supplemental plan. This case is far from extreme. We will describe cases in which the total marginal tax rate on assets in qualified pension plans passing through an estate ranges from 92 to 96.5 percent. The highest such rate we have seen exceeds 99 percent. The numbers in table 3.1 immediately suggest at least two things. First, any pension saving strategy adopted more than a few years ago needs to be reviewed, given how drastically the rules have changed. And second, large pension accumulations are taxed very heavily when they pass through estates. So heavily, in fact, that withdrawing pension assets before death, if at all possible, needs to be considered.

The next section of the paper outlines the various tax systems that affect pensions, including the excess distribution tax, the federal and state income tax systems, and the estate tax system. Most important, it describes how these tax systems interact to determine the effective combined marginal tax rates. Section 3.3 explores the combinations of pension plan generosity, career length, investment returns, and income levels that can lead to pension accumulations subject to the excess distribution tax or excess accumulation tax. It becomes clear that people with relatively modest incomes (e.g., $30,000 to $40,000 at age 50) can face these taxes if they have long careers and relatively generous contribution rates. These taxes are certainly not limited to the "rich." In fact, due to the power of compound interest rates, the group that is the most likely to face the penalty taxes are long-term, lifetime savers.

In section 3.4 we present analysis of the relative attractiveness of saving through the pension system versus conventional saving in a taxable account. We consider whether the pension laws continue to encourage saving once the excess distribution and excess accumulation taxes are taken into account. We also evaluate lifetime supplemental participation and one-time extra contributions. Bond and stock investments are considered separately. In addition, we examine the outcomes of saving with and without pensions in terms of both retirement resources and net assets left to beneficiaries.

In section 3.5 we consider the choices available to someone who has already accumulated more than enough to trigger the penalty excise taxes. The question is whether a person in such a situation should take distributions sufficiently large to require the payment of the excess distribution tax or should leave the money in the pension and risk the excess accumulation tax. We demonstrate that the taxation of large pension accumulations is much more burdensome when they pass through an estate—so much so, that it is almost always better to incur the excess distribution tax and avoid the excess accumulation levy.

In section 3.6 we examine the efficient allocation of assets between pension accounts and taxable accounts. This is important because the returns on assets held outside a pension plan are taxed very differently. However, all asset returns are taxed identically inside a pension account. We show that extremely large efficiency gains are possible simply by locating different assets optimally. Our conclusions are summarized in section 3.7.

3.2   The Tax Systems and How They Interact for Pensions

Pensions are almost universally thought to be attractive tax shelters. Indeed, since the 1986 tax reform, pensions along with owner-occupied housing and municipal bonds are sometimes thought to be the only significant tax shelters remaining. As emphasized above, however, large pension withdrawals or large pension accumulations at death are hardly sheltered from taxes—in fact the tax rates they face are among the highest in our society. To understand the taxation of large pension distributions and accumulations, one needs to have a basic knowledge of the various tax systems operating in the United States. This section presents some essential facts about the major tax systems that impinge on pension assets: the excess distribution tax and the excess accumulation tax, the federal and state income tax systems, and estate taxes. We discuss how they can interact to generate total marginal rates over 95 percent.

3.2.1   The Excess Distribution and the Excess Accumulation Taxes

The excess distribution and the excess accumulation taxes were enacted as part of the Tax Reform Act of 1986 (TRA86). Their purpose was to penalize people who use the favorable tax treatment of pensions to accumulate wealth beyond what is reasonably required for a comfortable retirement. Effectively, beginning in 1987, any withdrawals from qualified pension plans exceeding $150,000 per year face a 15 percent additional income tax. The $150,000 figure was left unchanged between 1987 and 1995 but was raised to $155,000 for 1996 and now is effectively indexed for inflation. It will be increased from time to time in minimum increments of $5,000 to reflect inflation. The 15 percent surtax is not deductible against either federal or state income taxes, so it simply adds 15 points to a household's marginal income tax rate on pension withdrawals. It is often referred to as the "success tax" since it can be triggered by particularly successful investment returns or by career earnings success.

A companion 15 percent excess accumulation tax was also part of TRA86. It applies to the estates of people who die with pension accumulations deemed excessive. Excessive accumulation is defined as assets that exceed the value of a single life annuity paying out $155,000 per year,[1] for someone with the life expectancy of a person the same age as the deceased. Assets in qualified plans over this amount face the extra 15 percent tax. The government gives guidelines regarding the permissible rate of interest to use in determining the value

---

1. This number will be adjusted for inflation in the future in exactly the same manner as the withdrawal number for the excess distribution tax.

Table 3.2   **Federal Marginal Income Tax Rates for 1996**

Marginal Tax Rate (%)	Range of Taxable Income ($)	
	Single	Married
15	0–24,000	0–40,100
28	24,000–58,150	40,100–96,900
31	58,150–121,300	96,900–147,700
36	121,300–263,750	147,700–263,750
39.6	263,750+	263,750+

of a single life annuity and also provides a table of life expectancies. The borderline between "allowable" and "excessive" accumulations depends on age. Using the currently allowed life expectancy tables and the permissible 8.2 percent interest rate gives the following limits: $1,243,612 at age 65, $1,165,166 at age 70, $955,358 at age 75, and $794,158 at age 80. The excess accumulation tax can be deferred if assets are transferred to a surviving spouse, so it only affects single people, widows and widowers, and married individuals who name a nonspouse as a beneficiary.

3.2.2   The Federal Income Tax

A potential advantage of pension saving relative to conventional saving is that the marginal income tax rate in retirement may be lower than the rate when contributions are made. However, this advantage almost certainly does not apply to someone facing the excess distribution tax. Since the excess distribution tax only applies if the individual is withdrawing more than $155,000 of taxable funds from qualified pension plans and since such a person would also almost always face income taxes on 85 percent of social security income, the person would be in one of the top two federal income tax brackets.

The 1996 federal income tax brackets are shown in table 3.2. The actual marginal tax rates can be higher than shown, however, especially for high-income households. The $2,550 per person personal exemptions are phased out between adjusted gross incomes (AGIs) of $117,950 and $240,450 for singles and between $176,950 and $299,450 for married couples filing jointly. In these income ranges, the effective marginal rate is increased by approximately 0.72 percent for each personal exemption, meaning that a family of four in the published 36 percent rate category actually would face a 38.88 percent marginal tax rate. Further, when AGI exceeds $117,950 ($58,975 for singles), there is a partial phaseout of itemized deductions. The total of itemized deductions is reduced by 3 percent of the amount by which the taxpayer's AGI exceeds $117,950, with the limit of the reduction being 80 percent of itemized deductions. Since the vast majority of taxpayers with incomes above $117,950 are itemizers (property taxes and state and local income taxes alone make this advantageous), this partial phaseout of itemized deductions raises the effective marginal tax rates. The phaseout of itemized deductions alone raises the 36 percent bracket to 37.08 percent and the 39.6 percent bracket to approximately 41 percent. In conjunction with the phaseout of personal exemptions, the 36 percent bracket can effectively involve a 40 percent marginal tax rate for a family of four. The final factor raising effective marginal tax rates is the 2.9 percent Medicare tax that applies to labor income. This tax is shared 50–50 between employer and employee, with a self-employed person paying the full 2.9 percent. A high-income individual can face a marginal federal tax rate on self-employment income of nearly 44 percent (taking only the treatment of itemized deductions and the Medicare tax into account), even though 39.6 percent is listed as the highest tax bracket. As recently as 1992 the top effective marginal tax rate was 31 percent. It is clear that the 1993 Deficit Reduction Act, which introduced the 36 and 39.6 percent brackets and the phaseout of personal exemptions and itemized deductions, significantly raised the marginal tax rates on high-income taxpayers.

One aspect of the income tax law that does not apply to pension assets but that does affect investments outside the pension system is the treatment of capital appreciation. Increases in the value of assets are not taxed until the gains are realized. Realized gains resulting from the sale of assets are taxed at ordinary income tax rates (although realized gains can be offset with realized losses on the sale of other assets in the same year) with one important exception: the maximum rate applying to capital gains is 28 percent. Finally, the cost basis for inherited assets is reset to the value of the assets at the time of their transfer, implying that the appreciation of these assets completely escapes income taxation.

3.2.3   State Income Taxes

It is hard to generalize about state income taxes. Forty-three of the 50 states impose state income taxes of varying design and with marginal rates as high as 12 percent. State income taxes are deductible from federal income taxes. In the examples in this paper, we often use the 1996 California top marginal income tax rate of 9.3 percent (it had been 11 percent before 1996), which applies to taxable income over $31,700 for singles and $63,400 for married couples filing a joint return. For a Californian facing the 39.6 percent federal rate, the total federal and state marginal tax rate is 46.41 percent, taking into account the partial phaseout of itemized deductions. If this individual withdrew more than $155,000 from qualified pension plans, and thus faced the 15 percent excess distribution tax, then the total marginal tax rate on withdrawals above the $155,000 would be 61.41 percent. These 46.41 and 61.41 percent marginal rates appear in a number of our later examples.

3.2.4   Federal and State Estate Taxes

The federal schedule of estate taxes is shown in table 3.3. This schedule actually applies to cumulative lifetime taxable gifts as well as to assets trans-

Table 3.3   **Federal Marginal Estate Tax Rates for 1996**

Marginal Tax Rate (%)	Fair Market Value of Estate at Time of Transfer ($)
37	600,000–750,000
39	750,000–1,000,000
41	1,000,000–1,250,000
43	1,250,000–1,500,000
45	1,500,000–2,000,000
49	2,000,000–2,500,000
53	2,500,000–3,000,000
55	3,000,000–10,000,000
60	10,000,000–21,040,000
55	21,040,000+

ferred at death. The table reflects both the unified credit that basically exempts lifetime transfers of $600,000 or less and the phaseout of the graduated rates and unified credit that occurs between taxable transfers of $10 million and $21 million. This phaseout of the benefit of the graduated rates is what causes the effective marginal rate to be 60 percent in this range. Because of this phaseout, both the *average* and the marginal tax rates are 55 percent for estates above $21.04 million. One extremely important feature of the federal estate tax is that there is an unlimited marital deduction, which basically means that the tax does not apply to transfers between spouses.

The federal estate tax allows a limited credit for state estate and inheritance taxes. The amount of the allowed credit depends on the size of the estate. For instance, for estates valued between $2,040,000 and $2,540,000 the allowable credit for state death taxes is $106,800 plus 8 percent of the amount by which the estate exceeds $2,040,000. This means that a state could levy estate taxes of this amount without increasing the total taxation of the estate. Many states design their death duties with this in mind and charge precisely the amount that the federal government will credit against the federal tax. Such state estate taxes are referred to as "soak up" taxes. The "soak up" refers to the allowed credits (and not the wealth of the estate!). Some states (New York, e.g.) have estate taxes that exceed the amount that can be credited against the federal estate tax. We do not consider such cases in this paper, but it should be clear that this would simply make the high marginal tax rates we compute even higher.

The estate tax treatment of pension accumulations changed dramatically with the passage of the Tax Equity and Fiscal Responsibility Act of 1982. Before this aspect of the 1982 law became effective in 1983, benefits payable to a beneficiary from qualified accounts (both defined benefit and defined contribution plans, IRAs, Keoghs, etc.) were completely excluded from the taxable estate. The 1982 act limited the exclusion of pension assets from taxable estates to $100,000. Even that limited exclusion was repealed with the Deficit

Reduction Act of 1984. The effect of the 1982 and 1984 law changes is that pension wealth, which was completely sheltered from the estate tax for people who died before 1983, was completely taxable for deaths occurring after 1984.

3.2.5   The Interaction of the Taxes on Pensions

We have already discussed the taxation of distributions from qualified retirement plans in retirement. All distributions are subject to full ordinary income taxation at both federal and state levels. Distributions over $155,000 are subject to the additive 15 percent excess distribution tax. Since the excess distribution tax is not deductible with respect to federal and state income taxes, it is equivalent to an additional state income tax (which would be deductible from the federal income tax) of approximately 25 percent. The combined excess distribution tax and federal income tax rates go up to about 56 percent, and the total marginal rate (including state-level taxation) can be roughly 61.5 percent.

The taxation at death is more complicated. First, the excess accumulation tax is calculated on the amount by which total wealth in qualified plans exceeds the value of a single life annuity as previously described. Federal and state estate taxes are then computed, deducting the amount of the excess accumulation tax from the taxable estate. If the estate exceeds $3 million, for instance, and is therefore in the 55 percent federal estate tax category and state estate taxes do not exceed the amount creditable against the federal tax, then the combined marginal rate of an estate facing the 15 percent excess accumulation tax is 61.75 percent (note that $.15 + (.85)(.55) = .6175$).

This is not the end of the story, however. Keep in mind that personal income taxes have never been paid on the qualified assets being transferred through the estate. The beneficiary is still liable for these taxes, and much of the 61.75 percent estate and excess accumulation tax is not deductible in calculating the amounts. The excess accumulation tax is not deductible from either the state or the federal income tax. Generally, only the state portion of the estate tax is deductible in determining state income taxes. For example, a Californian who was the beneficiary of a qualified plan that was part of a $3 million estate and who faced a state income tax rate of 9.3 percent would have to pay state income taxes on 91.84 percent of the value of the inherited qualified plans, even though these plans may have already triggered estate and excess accumulation taxes amounting to 61.75 percent of the value of the plans. This adds another 8.54 percent to the 61.75 percent, bringing the total tax bill to 70.29 percent. But there is more. We still have to calculate the federal income tax on the inherited money. Only the federal portion of the estate tax and the state income tax are deductible for federal income tax purposes; this means that the beneficiary will have to pay federal income tax on 52.87 percent of the value of the inherited qualified plans even though previous taxes amounting to 70.29 percent of the value of the qualified plans have already been paid. An effective federal marginal tax rate of 41 percent on this 52.87 percent requires us to add another 21.67 percentage points to our calculation, bringing the total marginal tax triggered by each incremental dollar in qualified plans to 91.97 percent. This is not even an extreme case. The tax rate would be several points higher if the estate were in the 60 percent estate tax bracket; the rate would also be higher in New York or any other state that has an estate tax exceeding the amount the federal government will allow as a credit against the federal obligation. The most extreme case we have examined involves a total marginal tax rate of 99.73 percent. This case involves a resident of New York with excess accumulations in qualified plans, a total estate between $10 and $21 million, and heirs in the top income tax bracket.

3.3   How Rich or Successful Do You Have to Be in Order to Face the "Success" Tax?

Are the extraordinarily high marginal tax rates that can result from "excessively large" pensions only a problem for the extremely rich or for those with unusually good fortune in terms of financial returns? The answer is no. These tax rates are not limited to those with very high incomes or with large windfall gains. Rather they are imposed on people who save systematically through pensions over long periods of their work lives. Even savers of modest income may find that they are penalized for their thrift.

The wealth that accrues in a defined contribution pension plan is easy to compute. There are two key determinants—the contributions that are made at each age and the rate of return earned on those contributions. If we let $C(t)$ be the contributions at age t and r be the real rate of return earned on those contributions, then accumulated wealth at age A, $W(A)$, is simply given by

(1) $$W(A) = \sum_{t=a}^{A} C(t)(1 + r)^{A-t},$$

where a is the age at which contributions commence. If contributions are a fixed fraction f of labor income and if real labor income grows at rate g per year, then

(2) $$C(t) = f Y(a)(1 + g)^{t-a} \quad \text{for all } t \geq a,$$

and therefore

(3) $$W(A) = f Y(a) \sum_{t=a}^{A} (1 + g)^{t-a}(1 + r)^{A-t}.$$

The continuous compounding version of equation (3) is simply

(4) $$W(A) = f Y(a) \int_{a}^{A} e^{g(t-a)} e^{r(A-t)} \, dt = f Y(a) e^{rA-ga} \left[\frac{e^{(g-r)A} - e^{(g-r)a}}{g - r} \right].$$

With these simple compound interest equations, we can determine what combinations of initial income, contribution rate, rate of salary increase, real

Table 3.4   **Examples of Pension Plans**

Variable	Example 1	Example 2	Example 3
Age of initial contribution a	25	40	25
Initial salary $Y(a)$	$50,000	$100,000	$25,000
Salary increases g	.02	.02	.02
Salary at age 50 $Y(50)$	$82,030	$121,899	$41,015
Contribution rate f	.10	.15	.10
Asset allocation	S&P 500[a]	S&P 500[a]	Growth stocks[a]
Rate of return r	.08	.08	.10

[a]The assumed rates of return are conservative relative to actual realized rates of return between 1926 and 1995. Ibbotson Associates (1996) reports that the arithmetic average of real returns on the S&P 500 was 9.2 percent, while the geometric mean was 7.2 percent. The arithmetic mean is appropriate for estimating the expected or average future outcome, whereas the geometric mean of the distribution gives the median future outcome. For small company stocks, the arithmetic mean of real returns was 14.1 percent, whereas the geometric mean was 9.1 percent.

Table 3.5   **Pension Accumulations for Examples 1, 2, and 3**

Accumulation	Example 1	Example 2	Example 3
Wealth at 50 $W(50)$	$476,911	$272,066	$320,149
Wealth at 55 $W(55)$	$751,673	$513,289	$542,086
Wealth at 60 $W(60)$	$1,160,690	$879,542	$902,275
Wealth at 65 $W(65)$	$1,767,524	$1,424,334	$1,485,406
Wealth at 70 $W(70)$	$2,665,623	$2,224,813	$2,427,904

rate of return, and career length can generate sufficient pension accumulations to require the payment of the excess distribution or excess accumulation tax. Table 3.4 summarizes three examples that will be discussed. The wealth accumulations in these pension plans at various ages, $W(A)$, are shown in table 3.5. The numbers in the table are generated using the discrete annual compounding of equation (3).

Consider first example 1, someone who is starting a job at age 25, having just completed an MBA. The initial salary is $50,000. The basic employer-provided pension plan is a defined contribution plan involving a contribution of 10 percent of salary (perhaps funded partly by the employer and partly by the employee). The employee expects to continue to work with this employer, or for an employer with an equivalent plan, for his or her entire career. Future salary increases are expected to be 2 percent above inflation, implying that the salary will reach $82,030 by age 50 in real dollars. The employee is allowed to choose how to allocate the investments, and this person chooses to invest in the Standard and Poor's (S&P) 500. We have assumed an 8 percent real rate of return for the S&P 500, which is well below its 1926–95 average of 9.2 percent.

While the hypothetical person in example 1 enjoys a relatively high income, most people would not classify this individual as rich. Nonetheless, by age 70

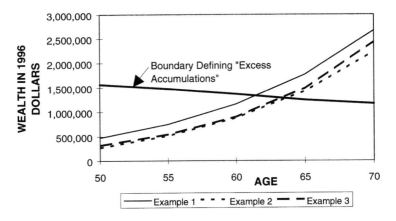

Fig. 3.1   Pension accumulations in examples 1, 2, and 3

this person would accumulate pension wealth in excess of $2.6 million and would almost certainly face the excess distribution or excess accumulation tax. If he or she should die at age 70 with this accumulation, the marginal rate faced by the estate and heirs would exceed 90 percent.

Example 1 is a person who began pension saving at the relatively young age of 25. Example 2 is an individual who does not begin saving until age 40 but then has a relatively generous plan (with 15 percent contributions) and a high salary ($100,000). This person also invests in the S&P 500 and accumulates more than $2.2 million in pension wealth by age 70.

Example 3 is a person who earns much less, earning $41,000 at age 50. This person contributes 10 percent of income to a pension plan and places the money in growth stocks that earn 10 percent over inflation. This is well below the 14.1 percent average real return earned on small company stocks over the 1926–95 period. This person would also accumulate almost $2.5 million in the pension plan by age 70. If the person in example 3 had earned an 8 percent rate of return (as assumed in examples 1 and 2), the accumulation at age 70 would have been $1.33 million, still enough to trigger the success tax.

The wealth accumulations of examples 1, 2, and 3, together with the amount above which accumulations are considered to be excessive, are shown in figure 3.1. As can be seen, all three of these individuals have excessive assets before age 65 and have over $1 million in the excessive category by age 70.

Each of the above examples uses hypothetical returns and assumes only stock investments. We now turn to a fourth individual and consider the outcomes under three alternative asset allocations: all stocks (S&P 500), all bonds, and a 50–50 allocation between stocks and bonds. This person is a leading-edge baby boomer, who was born in 1946 and entered the workforce in 1971. We refer to this person as "the software engineer." His salary in 1971 was $15,000 (in nominal terms), and he has always contributed 10 percent of salary

Table 3.6   **Example 4 with Alternative Asset Allocations**

	Example 4A	Example 4B	Example 4C
Initial nominal salary in 1971 at 25	$15,000	$15,000	$15,000
Salary in 1996 at 50	$102,579	$102,579	$102,579
Future real raises	1%	1%	1%
Contribution rate	10%	10%	10%
Asset allocation	100% S&P 500	100% Corporate bonds	50–50
Rates of return	Actual 1971–95, 8% thereafter	Actual 1971–95, 4% thereafter	Actual 1971–95, 8% stocks and 4% bonds thereafter
Wealth at 50 $W(50)$	$675,672	$440,045	$557,858
Wealth at 55 $W(55)$	$1,054,698	$592,586	$823,642
Wealth at 60 $W(60)$	$1,614,769	$781,095	$1,197,932
Wealth at 65 $W(65)$	$2,441,017	$1,013,510	$1,727,244
Wealth at 70 $W(70)$	$3,658,535	$1,299,503	$2,479,019

to his pension plan. His real salary grew at 2.5 percent per year between 1971 and 1995. In 1996 our software engineer is age 50 and has a salary of $102,579. His pay is projected to grow in real terms at 1 percent per year thereafter. The rates of return earned between 1971 and 1995 (ages 25–49) are the actual returns earned by the S&P 500 and by a diversified portfolio of high-grade long-term corporate bonds. The returns are taken from Ibbotson Associates (1996). The assumed real returns from age 50 onward are 8 percent for the stock portfolio and 4 percent for the bonds. Thus, in these examples, at least half of the returns are, not hypothetical, but actual returns realized in the market since 1971. Table 3.6 shows the specifics of examples 4A, 4B, and 4C, including the wealth accumulation at various ages.

The same wealth accumulation information is plotted in figure 3.2. There it is clear that our software engineer can face the success tax with any of the three asset allocations. With 100 percent stocks, the assets are too large at roughly age 58, with a 50–50 allocation at age 61, and the all-bond investor qualifies as an excess accumulator at age 68. There is nothing extreme about any of these examples. All pertain to diversified portfolios (not, e.g., to a single stock that appreciated 1,000-fold). All of the salaries are well under the $150,000 that can be used to compute pension benefits in employer-provided defined contribution pension plans. None of the examples assume a supplemental plan (e.g., 401(k) plan) in addition to the basic pension plan, and reasonable contribution rates are assumed in each case.

Equation (3) clarifies that the wealth accumulated at any particular age depends on five variables (salary levels, contribution rates, starting age, rate of salary growth, and rate of return on investments). The examples have shown that sufficient wealth can be accumulated to trigger the excess accumulation tax without extreme parameter values. Figures 3.3 and 3.4 further clarify the

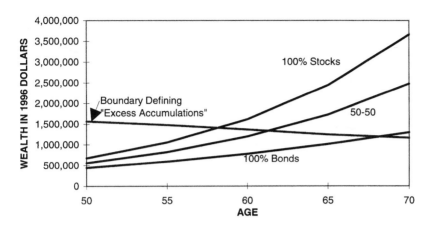

Fig. 3.2   Software engineer's pension accumulations (example 4)

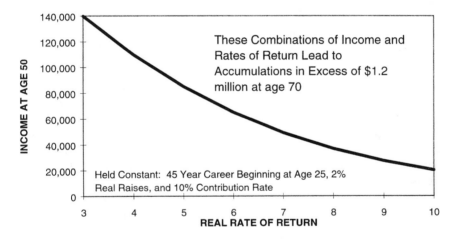

Fig. 3.3   Rates of return and income levels generating "excess accumulations"

range of parameter values that can lead to the imposition of the 15 percent tax.

Any combination of parameters above the curves in figures 3.3 and 3.4 leads to the accumulation of more than $1.2 million at age 70, which is roughly the dividing line between allowable and excess accumulations. It is not difficult or unusual to face these situations. Figure 3.3 pertains to a person who begins work at age 25, experiences annual salary increases of 2 percent above inflation, contributes 10 percent to a pension plan, and works until age 70. The figure shows the combinations of income at age 50 and realized rates of return that would yield excessive accumulations at age 70 under these assumptions. For instance, a person who earns $85,000 at age 50 and who realizes a 5 percent real rate of return on pension investments would accumulate $1.2 million

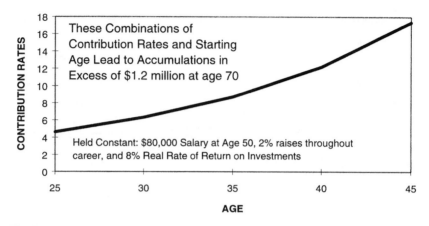

Fig. 3.4   Ages at which contributions commence and contribution rates generating "excess accumulations"

by age 70 and would face the excess accumulation tax. Any salary trajectory that is higher or rate of return that is better will land this person in excess accumulation territory.

Figure 3.4 pertains to a person who earns $80,000 at age 50, experiences 2 percent real salary increases throughout his or her career, and realizes an 8 percent return on pension investments. Under these assumptions, the figure shows the combinations of contribution rates and ages at which contributions begin that lead to excess accumulations. For example, under these assumptions a person who begins contributing 8.7 percent of salary to a pension plan at age 35 will attain the excess accumulation boundary by age 70. On the other hand, someone with these circumstances who waits until age 40 to begin pension saving would have to contribute about 12 percent to reach the excess accumulation range by age 70. Any combination of contribution rate and age of contribution commencement lying above the curve in figure 3.4 will lead to asset accumulations facing the success tax.

The rates of return assumed in this section have all been real rates (above inflation). The $1.2 million boundary between excessive and allowable accumulations is in 1996 dollars. Implicitly, our calculations recognize that the amounts that trigger the success tax are indexed for inflation. Nonetheless, we find that the success tax is not only a problem for those with extremely high incomes. It is a consideration for large numbers of lifetime savers, even those with incomes near the median of the society. The real income profile of example 3, for instance, is roughly at the 70th percentile of earnings, meaning that about 30 percent of all American workers earn more. Even our higher income examples, which are certainly in the top 5 percent of U.S. workers, are relevant to millions of individuals. We are presently doing research to further clarify how many people need to pay attention to the considerations of this paper. Even at this stage, however, we know that it is a large number of people who account for a very large fraction of the total personal saving in the United States.

3.4   When Are Pensions a Tax Shelter? When a Tax Trap?

Whether it pays to save through a pension plan depends on the retirement consumption that could be supported through wealth accumulated in this way compared to the retirement consumption that would be provided by "conventional" saving—outside a pension plan. Of course, people presumably realize that they face some mortality risk and may also care how their heirs would fare under the two saving alternatives. In this section we consider the relative performance of pensions and conventional saving in providing retirement resources and in transferring wealth to heirs. We consider separately cases in which bonds and stocks are purchased. We also examine both systematic lifetime saving and one-time supplemental saving. The potential impact of the excess distribution tax and the excess accumulation tax on the relative advantage of pension saving is examined.

3.4.1   Lifetime Saving: Investment in Bonds

The formulas that describe asset accumulation through pension and conventional saving for retirement are straightforward. To be precise about the basic calculations and variants of them, we set out the formulas here. First, some notation:

a	Age at which retirement saving starts
A	Retirement age
$C(t)$	Pension contributions at age t
$W_P(A)$	Wealth accumulation using pensions at retirement age A
$S(t)$	Saving outside of pensions, set to equal the after-tax cost of $C(t)$ so that the same consumption pattern can be enjoyed while working
$W_S(A)$	Wealth accumulation using nonpension saving at retirement age A
B_P	After-tax benefit stream enjoyed in retirement from pension saving
B_S	After-tax benefit stream enjoyed in retirement from nonpension saving
f	Fraction of wages contributed to pensions
$Y(t)$	Labor income at age t
g	Nominal rate of wage growth
r	Nominal rate of return on investments
L	Length of benefit payouts in retirement (could be life expectancy)
T_Y	Combined state and federal marginal tax rate on labor income
T_R	Combined state and federal marginal tax rate on pension payouts
T_I	Combined state and federal marginal tax rate on dividends or interest
T_C	Combined state and federal marginal tax rate on realized capital gains

Using this notation we consider first the net-of-tax retirement income stream, B_p, that can be supported through pretax contributions $C(t)$ under a pension plan. The equations are easier to manipulate if we use the continuous time formulation and therefore continuous compounding. The pension contribution as a function of time is given by

(5)
$$C(t) = fY(t) = fY(a)e^{g(t-a)},$$

where we assume that labor income grows at rate g. The accumulated pension wealth at retirement age A is then

(6)
$$W_p(A) = \int_a^A C(t)e^{r(A-t)}\, dt.$$

Assuming a constant nominal payment over L years, the (fair) after-tax annuity payment that this wealth could finance is given by

(7)
$$B_p = (1 - T_R)\frac{r}{1 - e^{-rL}} W_p(A)$$

$$= (1 - T_R)\frac{r}{1 - e^{-rL}} fY(a)e^{rA-ga}\int_a^A e^{(g-r)t}\, dt,$$

where the $r/(1 - e^{-rL})$ term is the annuity payment that \$1 of wealth can support for L years. The alternative strategy is to save for retirement outside the pension system. In this case the saving has to be done with after-tax dollars. Leaving consumption unchanged, the amount of saving that can be done as a function of time is therefore

(8)
$$S(t) = (1 - T_Y)fY(a)e^{g(t-a)}.$$

The wealth accumulated by retirement in this case is given by

(9)
$$W_S(A) = \int_a^A S(t)e^{r(1-T_I)(A-t)}\, dt.$$

The annuity payment that this wealth can finance is

(10)
$$B_S = \frac{r(1 - T_I)}{1 - e^{-r(1-T_I)L}} W_S(A)$$

$$= \frac{r(1 - T_I)}{1 - e^{-r(1-T_I)L}} (1 - T_Y)fY(a)e^{r(1-T_I)A-ga}\int_a^A e^{(g-r(1-T_I))t}\, dt.$$

The advantage of pension plan saving versus conventional saving for retirement is given by the ratio of B_p to B_S. Although there are many parameters in equations (7) and (10), the formulas are easily evaluated for any particular set of values. Table 3.7 presents several different parameter combinations that describe the circumstances of different savers. Note that f and $Y(a)$ are not included in the parameters describing each case. They appear in both equations (7) and (10) in such a way as to drop out of the expression for B_p/B_S. Note also

Table 3.7   **Advantage of Using Pensions for Retirement Saving: Eight Cases with Bond Investments**

Parameter	Case 1	Case 2	Case 3	Case 4	Case 5	Case 6	Case 7	Case 8
a	30	30	30	30	30	40	40	40
A	70	70	70	70	70	70	70	70
r	.08	.08	.08	.08	.08	.08	.08	.08
g	.06	.06	.06	.06	.06	.06	.06	.06
L	15	15	15	15	1	15	1	15
T_Y	.4641	.4641	.4641	.383	.383	.383	.383	.4641
T_R	.4641	.4641	.6141	.586	.586	.586	.586	.6141
T_I	.4641	.28	.28	.28	.28	.28	.28	.28
B_P/B_S	2.680	1.847	1.330	1.240	1.090	1.096	0.963	1.176

that equations (7) through (10) apply a single tax rate to particular kinds of income, rather than the progressive rates in the tax code. Thus the equations and the results in table 3.7—as well as those in table 3.8 below—are best interpreted as relevant for a particular marginal calculation. Rather than indicating whether a person should have a pension at all, the results are better interpreted as indicating whether additional lifetime saving should be done through a pension plan (such as a supplemental 401(k) plan) or whether supplemental saving should be done outside of the pension system. Or the calculations can be interpreted as indicating whether to contribute an additional amount to a pension plan (say increase the contribution rate from 10 to 11 percent) or to save the marginal 1 percent outside the pension system.

Under case 1 there is a tremendous advantage to saving even incremental amounts through a tax-sheltered pension plan. It is probably such an example that most financial advisers have in mind when they recommend participating in qualified pension plans to the maximum extent possible. Case 1 is a person who is participating in a defined contribution pension plan (or possibly a supplemental 401(k) plan) between ages 30 and 70 and who is investing the contributions in corporate bonds that yield an 8 percent return. This person receives a 6 percent nominal wage increase each year. The analysis in this section is in nominal terms because it is nominal income that is taxed. After retirement, an equal nominal amount of money is withdrawn each year between ages 70 and 85. This person faces a combined federal and state income tax rate of 46.41 percent, before and after retirement, on both labor income and interest income. Under these assumptions, the 2.680 number at the bottom of the case 1 column indicates that the person who saves in pension plans will be able to spend 168 percent more from retirement savings than the person who accumulated taxable bonds outside the pension system. This is an enormous advantage to pension saving, particularly when the consumption that was forgone to save while working is the same under both saving modes.

This case, however, is not very realistic, particularly for high-income individuals with high marginal tax rates. For this group, taxable corporate bonds are a poor investment outside a pension plan. Instead, they could invest in tax-free municipal bonds with an implicit tax rate of approximately 28 percent (which is the approximate difference between the rate of return on corporate vs. municipal bonds). Under case 2 the tax rate on bond investments outside the pension is lowered to 28 percent, reflecting the fact that municipal bonds dominate corporate bonds for high-tax-rate investors. Now, the net advantage of pension saving is reduced to 85 percent, still very large. But what if this person will face the excess distribution tax on retirement benefits? In this case, the marginal tax rate on money withdrawn from pension accumulations can be 61.41 percent. This is case 3, under which the advantage of pension corporate bond saving is only 33 percent over municipal bond saving.[2]

The first three cases are for very high income individuals who are in top tax brackets both while working and in retirement. However, the previous section of the paper showed that one need not have an income nearly so high to face the excess distribution tax on marginal pension contributions. Cases 4 through 7 are for someone in the 31 percent federal marginal tax bracket during his or her work career and in the 36 percent federal marginal tax bracket in retirement. In these cases the individual faces the 15 percent success tax and a 9.3 percent state income tax. The advantage of saving with pensions is reduced relative to cases 1, 2, and 3 because cases 4 through 7 face higher basic tax rates in retirement than while working. Case 4 shows someone who spends incremental retirement accumulation over 15 years. This person gains 24 percent from using pensions for retirement saving. Case 5 shows that if he or she took the money out in the first year of retirement, the advantage of using pensions would fall to only 9 percent. Case 6 returns to withdrawing the money over 15 years, but the extra contributions do not begin until age 40. In this case, the benefit of using pensions is 9.6 percent. Case 7 shows that even a long-term bond accumulator can be worse off for having used the pension system. This individual takes the money out in the first year of retirement and actually has 3.7 percent less to spend than if he or she had been accumulating municipal bonds yielding 5.76 percent.

The last case in table 3.7 is a very high income individual (like those in cases 1, 2, and 3), who starts saving at age 40 and faces the excess distribution

---

2. Mankiw and Poterba (1996) report an implicit tax rate for municipal bonds well below the 28 percent figure here. They compare the yields on 20-year Treasury bonds with the yield on high-quality municipals of the same maturity. The implicit tax rate in 1987–94 averaged 17.21 percent. The interest on Treasury bonds is not subject to taxation at the state level, however, and therefore they are not an ideal instrument to hold in pension accounts. The Mankiw-Poterba evidence, however, might indicate that the correct implicit tax rate to apply for municipal bonds vs. corporate bonds is about 20 percent. A 20 percent implicit tax rate on municipals, rather than the 28 percent that we assumed, would make using pensions for retirement saving less attractive. E.g., the B_p/B_s figures for cases 2, 3, and 4 would have been 1.559, 1.123, and 1.046, respectively.

tax. In fact, cases 3 and 8 are identical except that the person in case 3 saves for 40 years whereas the person in case 8 saves for 30 years. The net advantage of using the pension system to buy corporate bonds versus accumulating municipal bonds amounts to 17.6 percent.

The general message of table 3.7 is that once the option of investing in municipal bonds is recognized and also once the fact that extra pension saving is likely to face the excess distribution tax is taken into account, the advantage of using pensions for retirement saving is much more modest than the 168 percent of case 1. In fact, the advantage may be positive or negative, but it is unlikely to exceed the 33 percent of case 3. Most of these cases assume that the individuals receive pension benefits until age 85. We have so far not examined what happens to these accounts if the individual dies before they are depleted below the amount that would trigger the excess accumulation tax. We examine that case a little later.

3.4.2   Lifetime Saving: Investment in Stocks

We now turn to accumulating incremental wealth with stocks. The pension accumulation formulas (5) through (7) are unchanged because all money taken from pension accumulations is taxed the same regardless of how it was generated. However, outside savers face different tax rates depending on how investment returns are paid (e.g., dividends, capital gains, municipal bond interest). Equations (8) through (10) assumed that all of the return on the bond investments took the form of interest payments. With stock investments, we need to treat accrued capital gains, realized capital gains, and dividends separately.

Consider a stock portfolio or mutual fund portfolio whose total return r is divided into three components

$$(11) \qquad\qquad r = r_d + r_c + r_a,$$

where r_d is the dividend yield, r_c represents the rate of realized capital gains, and r_a represents accrued or deferred capital gains. Dividends are taxable as ordinary income, realized capital gains are taxed at preferential rates (with a maximum rate of 28 percent), and the taxes on accrued gains can be deferred and possibly escaped (such gains are never taxed if the asset passes through an estate). If we let

$$(12) \qquad\qquad R = r_d(1 - T_I) + r_c(1 - T_C) + r_a$$

be the after-tax rate at which equities compound, then equation (9) can be modified to

$$(13) \qquad\qquad W_S(A) = \int_a^A S(t)e^{R(A-t)}\, dt$$

and equation (10) can be modified to

(14)
$$B_S = \frac{(1 - T_K)RW_S(A)}{1 - e^{-RL}},$$

where T_K is the effective capital gains tax rate payable as the money is spent in retirement. That is, T_K is given by

(15)
$$T_K = \frac{T_C(W_S(A) - C_S(A))}{W_S(A)},$$

where $C_S(A)$ is the cost basis of the stock portfolio when the saver is age A. If we let $\hat{R}$ be the currently taxable part of the portfolio's return, that is,

(16)
$$\hat{R} = r_d(1 - T_I) + r_c(1 - T_C),$$

then at the time of retirement the cost basis of the portfolio would be

(17)
$$C_S(A) = \int_a^A S(t)e^{\hat{R}(A-t)}\, dt.$$

With these equations we can look once again at the ratio of B_P to B_S. Several cases are described in table 3.8.

Once again, the first case shows a very big advantage to saving for retirement, or incremental saving for retirement, through a pension plan. Case 1 is a person saving for retirement between ages 30 and 70, investing in a stock portfolio with an annual dividend yield of 2 percent, and realizing capital gains of 2 percent per year. The remaining 7 percent of the return takes the form of unrealized or accrued capital gains. Again, the retirement accumulation is spent over the 15 years between ages 70 and 85. This individual has very high income while working and in retirement and always faces top tax rates. Case 1 does not take into account the excess distribution tax, however. It shows that the net advantage of saving with pensions is 101.2 percent.

This large benefit to pensions is eroded considerably if the success tax is applicable, as in case 2 where the advantage of pensions is reduced to 44.9 percent. Examining cases 2, 3, and 4 reveals the advantage of investing in stock portfolios that minimize taxable distributions when equities are held outside of a pension. The only difference between the three cases is the composition of returns between dividends, realized capital gains, and unrealized capital gains. The portfolio held in case 3 is more tax efficient than that held in case 2, and hence the advantage of using pensions is much smaller, 18.5 percent instead of 44.9 percent. The portfolio in case 4 generates only unrealized capital gains, and it actually provides more retirement income if assets are accumulated outside the pension system. The reason is that the rate of compounding is identical inside and outside a pension in this case, but the total tax burden is less for outside saving. Cases 5, 6, and 7 again reveal the advantage of tax-efficient stock portfolios, although this time for a lower income saver (someone in the 31 percent federal marginal tax bracket before retirement and in the 36 percent bracket after retirement). Pensions are less advantageous for someone

Table 3.8 Advantage of Using Pensions for Retirement Saving: Nine Cases with Stock Investments

Parameter	Case 1	Case 2	Case 3	Case 4	Case 5	Case 6	Case 7	Case 8	Case 9
a	30	30	30	30	30	30	30	30	40
A	70	70	70	70	70	70	70	70	70
r	.11	.11	.11	.11	.11	.11	.11	.11	.11
r_d	.02	.02	.01	0	.02	.01	0	.02	.01
r_c	.02	.02	.01	0	.02	.01	0	.02	.01
r_a	.07	.07	.09	.11	.07	.09	.11	.07	.09
g	.06	.06	.06	.06	.06	.06	.06	.06	.06
L	15	15	15	15	15	15	15	15	1
T_Y	.4641	.4641	.4641	.4641	.383	.383	.383	.383	.383
T_R	.4641	.6141	.6141	.6141	.586	.586	.586	.586	.586
T_I	.4641	.4641	.4641	.4641	.383	.383	.383	.383	.383
T_C	.28	.28	.28	.28	.28	.28	.28	.14	.28
B_P/B_S	2.012	1.449	1.185	0.956	1.287	1.078	0.891	1.042	0.958

with this pattern of tax rates. The case 7 person ends up with 11 percent less if he or she acquires stocks inside a pension rather than simply buying stocks or equity mutual funds outside the pension system. Case 8 is the same as case 5, except that the maximum capital gains tax rate has been lowered to 14 percent before the retirement saving is withdrawn. This significantly reduces the advantage of saving within a pension, since only assets held outside a pension can take advantage of the lower capital gains tax rate. This example is a reminder that all of these calculations are vulnerable to changes in the basic tax structure. Pension saving, which is taxed only upon distribution is particularly vulnerable to future changes in the tax rules. Case 9 is the same as case 6, with two exceptions: first, saving is not begun until age 40, and second, the money is withdrawn in 1 year instead of 15. This person still saves for retirement for 30 years. The final column of the table indicates that this person would be approximately 4 percent worse off with pension rather than conventional saving.

The lesson of tables 3.7 and 3.8 is that the advantage of systematically contributing more to a pension plan over an entire career depends crucially on the investment chosen, the length of the career, and the precise tax rate that will be applied when benefits are withdrawn. If the 15 percent tax on excess distributions is triggered, then the net advantage of pensions is greatly reduced and may be negative.

3.4.3 One-Time Contribution, One-Time Withdrawal: Investment in Bonds

We now turn to a somewhat different margin and a simpler set of cases. Instead of considering a slightly higher contribution rate over the entire career, consider someone who is debating whether to make a one-time supplementary pension contribution. The opportunity to make this contribution may come from temporarily taking a second job or from self-employment. For simplicity, we assume that the saver will withdraw the proceeds from the contribution at a known age. If the potential contribution would be made at age a_1 and withdrawn at age a_2, which is more than 59 ½, then each dollar contributed would permit retirement consumption of

$$(18) \qquad (1 - T_R)e^{r(a_2-a_1)}.$$

If the investment is a bond and if the person in question faces a combined federal and state marginal income tax rate in excess of 28 percent, then the reasonable alternative for an outside investor is municipal bonds yielding approximately $.72r$. In this case, each before-tax dollar would permit retirement consumption of

$$(19) \qquad (1 - T_Y)e^{.72r(a_2-a_1)}.$$

Clearly, one difference between expressions (18) and (19) is that (18) depends on the future income tax rate while retired, whereas (19) depends on the current income tax rate on labor income. If $T_R \leq T_Y$, then clearly expression (18) exceeds expression (19) and using the pension vehicle is advantageous, more so for longer periods of time $(a_2 - a_1)$ between contribution and distribution. However, if $T_R \geq T_Y$ either because tax rates are increased or because of the excess distribution tax, then by equating expressions (18) and (19) we can solve for the break-even period of time $a_2 - a_1$.

$$(20) \qquad a_2 - a_1 = \frac{1}{.28r} \ln\left(\frac{1 - T_Y}{1 - T_R}\right).$$

For reasonable parameters for a high-income person facing the success tax (i.e., $T_Y = .4641$, $T_R = .6141$, and $r = .08$), the break-even holding period is 14.7 years. For periods greater than that, using the pension system will provide more retirement consumption.[3] After 25 years, for instance, the pension system will produce 26 percent more money than municipal bonds held outside the pension system, even accounting for the excess distribution tax. The advantage of using municipal bonds rather than taxable corporate bonds outside of a pension is shown by this result: the break-even period of time is only 8.85 years if both the inside and the outside investments are made in corporate bonds.

3.4.4   One-Time Contribution, One-Time Withdrawal: Investment in Stocks

For stocks, we once again must use the R and $\hat{R}$ previously defined. Equation (19) must be replaced with

$$(21) \qquad (1 - T_K)(1 - T_Y)e^{R(a_2-a_1)},$$

where

$$(22) \qquad T_K = T_C \frac{e^{R(a_2-a_1)} - e^{\hat{R}(a_2-a_1)}}{e^{R(a_2-a_1)}}.$$

Table 3.9 evaluates the break-even holding period, $a_2 - a_1$, as a function of the tax and return parameters. A comparison of equations (18) and (21) shows that using pensions for this saving dominates conventional saving if $T_R \leq T_Y$, so we do not report such cases. The interesting circumstances occur when the excess distribution tax is part of T_R. Once again, we are reminded that even though all investments are treated the same in a qualified pension account, they are taxed quite differently if they are held outside. Case 1 shows a stock or stock mutual fund with a total nominal return of 11 percent, split between a 2 percent dividend yield, a 2 percent return of realized capital gains, and a 7

---

3. If the implicit tax rate on municipal bonds is 20 percent instead of 28 percent, the break-even period would be 20.5 years instead of 14.7 years.

Table 3.9   **Break-Even Holding Period for Using Pensions for Investments in Stocks**

Parameter	Case 1	Case 2	Case 3	Case 4	Case 5	Case 6
r	.11	.11	.11	.11	.11	.11
r_d	.02	.01	0	.02	.01	.01
r_c	.02	.01	0	.02	.01	.01
r_a	.07	.09	.11	.07	.09	.09
T_R	.6141	.6141	.6141	.586	.586	.586
T_Y	.4641	.4641	.4641	.383	.383	.383
T_C	.28	.28	.28	.28	.28	.14
Break-even period (years)	11	14	Never	15	20	48

percent return of unrealized capital gains. With the tax parameters shown, including a 28 percent tax rate on realized capital gains and a 15 percent excess distribution tax, the break-even holding period is 11 years. Case 3 shows just how sensitive this result is to the payout characteristics of the stock portfolio. With the same tax rates, it never makes sense to hold a stock portfolio that yields only unrealized capital gains inside a pension plan. The reason is that the tax deferral feature of the pension plan is completely redundant and the total taxes are actually slightly less if the asset is not put in a pension. In terms of the notation that we have developed, notice that for case 3, $R = r$ and at $T_Y = .4641$, $T_C = .28$, and $T_R = .6141$, $(1 - T_C)(1 - T_Y) > (1 - T_R)$. Cases 4 and 5 pertain to someone with somewhat more modest income levels. Once again, we see that the pension system is less attractive for this person than for the richer persons in cases 1 and 2, with the break-even periods being considerably longer. Case 6 is the same as case 5, except that the capital gains rate has been reduced, making pensions far less attractive, with the break-even period being an extraordinarily long 48 years.

3.4.5 Pension Accumulations that Pass through an Estate

We now turn to the situation in which the supplemental saver dies before spending the money. Take the example of someone who saves some money at age a_1 over and above base pension plan contributions and is considering whether to use a supplemental pension vehicle such as a 401(k) account. Assume that the person anticipates facing either the excess distribution tax when withdrawals are made or realizes that the estate would face the excess accumulation tax if he or she dies before spending the money. The person cares about his or her beneficiaries in the event that death occurs before the money is spent. Since it is quite simple to transfer wealth including qualified accounts to one's spouse without tax, we consider a single person or someone who will ultimately be the surviving spouse.

In order to calculate what the heirs would inherit in the two cases (pension saving vs. outside saving) we need to introduce yet more notation. The following definitions are useful:

T_X Tax rate on excess distributions and excess accumulations
T_E Marginal estate tax rate
T_E^f Federal marginal estate tax rate
T_E^s State marginal estate tax rate
T_Y^f Federal marginal income tax rate of beneficiary
T_Y^s State marginal income tax rate of beneficiary
$H_p(t)$ Net-of-tax amount received by the beneficiary from pension saving that took place t years before death
$H_S(t)$ Net-of-tax amount received by the beneficiary from conventional saving that took place t years before death

Consider someone contemplating an extra \$1 contribution to a 401(k) plan at age a_1. If that person dies at age a_2, the extra money that the beneficiary can spend because of this saving is given by

$$(23) \quad e^{r(a_2-a_1)}[(1 - T_X)(1 - T_E) - \Pi_S - (1 - (1 - T_X)T_E^r)(1 - \Pi_S)T_Y^f],$$

where Π_S is the state income tax owed and is given by

$$(24) \qquad\qquad \Pi_S = (1 - (1 - T_X)T_E^s)T_Y^s.$$

Note that the excess distribution tax is not deductible against state and federal income taxes and that only some of the regular estate taxes are deductible. Only the state portion of the estate tax is deductible from the base of the state income tax, and only the federal portion is deductible against the base of the federal income tax. If the extra saving had not been invested in the 401(k) but an equivalent before-tax amount had been used to purchase municipal bonds, then the beneficiary would have netted

$$(25) \qquad\qquad e^{.72r(a_2 - a_1)}(1 - T_Y)(1 - T_E),$$

where T_Y is still the combined federal and state marginal income tax rate of the saver and we are assuming that municipal bonds have an implicit tax rate of 28 percent. On the other hand, had the money been used to purchase a stock portfolio held outside of the pension system, the beneficiary would have received (after all taxes)

$$(26) \qquad\qquad e^{R(a_2-a_1)}(1 - T_Y)(1 - T_E),$$

where

$$R = r_d(1 - T_Y) + r_c(1 - T_C) + r_a.$$

Equations (23), (25), and (26) illustrate that the advantage of using pensions is that, in general, the money compounds at a faster rate. However, the complicated string of taxes that are applied to pension accumulations passing through

Table 3.10   **Supplemental Saving with Bonds: Three Cases Where the Money Passes through an Estate**

Parameter	Case 1	Case 2	Case 3
Total estate (million $)	3.1	1.6	10.1
r	.08	.08	.08
T_x	.15	.15	.15
T_E	.55	.45	.60
T_E^s	.096	.072	.16
T_E^f	.454	.378	.440
T_Y^s	.093	.093	.093
T_Y^f	.41	.37	.41
T_Y	.4641	.429	.4641
Total tax rate on incremental			
401(k) dollar (%)	91.97	83.86	96.41
$H_p(30)/H_s(30)$	.653	1.005	.329
Break-even period (years)	49	30	80

an estate may more than offset this advantage. Tables 3.10 and 3.11 show the net advantage to the beneficiary of using pensions for bonds and stocks, respectively.

Case 1 of table 3.10 shows someone who has a total estate of $3.1 million, with sufficient accumulations in qualified plans to face the excess accumulation tax, and whose beneficiary is in top federal and state income tax brackets. If the money were saved in 8 percent bonds and held for 30 years before the saver died, then the beneficiary would net only 65.3 percent as much as if the original saver had invested in 5.76 percent municipal bonds. So, in this case, the use of a 401(k) plan would significantly reduce the net inheritance. The total tax rate faced by the money in the incremental 401(k) account is 92 percent. The break-even period for the two strategies (401(k) vs. municipal bonds) is 49 years. Case 2 is someone whose estate consists primarily of an "overstuffed" set of qualified plans but who is not as wealthy as the person in case 1. The heir is also in a lower federal income tax bracket. In this case the total tax rate faced by the incremental pension accumulation is 84 percent. The beneficiary only gains from the pension saving strategy over the municipal bond strategy if the holding period is 30 years or longer. The individual depicted in case 3 is much wealthier and faces the federally imposed estate tax rate of 60 percent. Some states (such as New York) impose state death duties that exceed the amount that can be credited against the federal estate tax and hence impose higher tax rates than in case 3. Even so, the combined effective tax rate on the case 3 incremental 401(k) account is 96.41 percent. The beneficiary gets only 3.5 percent of the accumulation, with the government taking 96.5 percent. This person was going to face high estate taxes and income taxes with any strategy, but the pension saving choice provides the beneficiary with less than one-third as much as the municipal bond strategy, even after 30 years.

Table 3.11   **Supplemental Saving with Stocks: Six Cases Where the Money Passes through an Estate**

Parameter	Case 1	Case 2	Case 3	Case 4	Case 5	Case 6
Total estate (million $)	3.1	3.1	1.6	1.6	10.1	10.1
r	.11	.11	.11	.11	.11	.11
r_d	.02	0	.02	0	.02	0
r_c	.02	0	.02	0	.02	0
r_a	.07	.11	.07	.11	.07	.11
T_X	.15	.15	.15	.15	.15	.15
T_E	.55	.55	.45	.45	.60	.60
T_E^s	.096	.096	.072	.072	.16	.16
T_E^f	.454	.454	.378	.378	.44	.44
T_Y^s	.093	.093	.093	.093	.093	.093
T_Y^f	.41	.41	.37	.37	.41	.41
T_C	.28	.28	.28	.28	.28	.28
Total tax rate on incremental 401(k) dollar ($)	91.97	91.97	83.86	83.86	96.41	96.41
$H_p(30)/H_s(30)$	.522	.334	.803	.513	.262	.168
Break-even period (years)	74	Never	45	Never	120	Never

Turning now to the cases involving stock investments shown in table 3.11, one can see that using pensions for supplemental saving is never a good choice for beneficiaries, at least not for the cases shown involving the excess accumulation tax being added to the estate tax. The first two cases refer to the same individual as in case 1 of table 3.10. The only difference between case 1 and case 2 of table 3.11 is that case 2 involves a stock portfolio generating only unrealized capital gains, whereas case 1 has some current dividends and realized capital gains. In case 1, with a 30-year holding period, the heir ends up with almost twice as much money if pensions are avoided, and in case 2, three times as much.

Cases 3 through 6 show other possible circumstances. Case 6 is the most extreme, with the beneficiary receiving only one-sixth as much money via the supplemental pension accumulation as he or she would have if the stock portfolio had been kept outside the pension system.

One feature of cases 2, 4, and 6 that may not be obvious is that the ratio $H_p(t)/H_s(t)$ is independent of t. In cases where the investment itself offers complete tax deferral, the advantage or disadvantage of using pensions for saving (at least in terms of how much money your heirs will receive) is independent of how many years before death the saving takes place. This implies, for instance, that if a 70-year-old with the wealth and tax circumstances of case 2 makes an extra contribution to a pension plan and then dies, the heir would receive only one-third as much as if the money had been kept out of the pension system. This same one-third figure applies after 30 years or 50 years if the investment is in land or growth stocks whose return comes completely in the

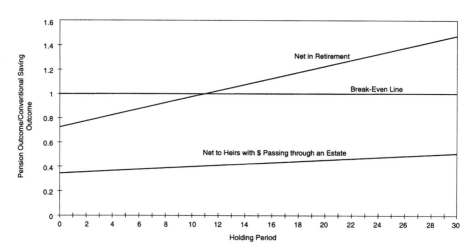

Fig. 3.5   Pensions vs. conventional saving: net proceeds in retirement and to heirs

Note: Assumptions: 15 percent excess distribution tax and excess accumulation tax, 55 percent estate tax, 41 percent federal income tax, 9.3 percent state income tax, 28 percent capital gains tax, 11 percent nominal return on stocks, including 2 percent dividends and 2 percent realized capital gains.

form of unrealized capital gains. For case 6, pension saving results in a net inheritance of one-sixth as much as conventional saving.

The lesson from the analysis of this section of the paper is that once one faces the excess distribution tax or excess accumulation tax, the gain from pensions in providing for retirement is modest at best and the loss in terms of the amount that one's beneficiaries will receive can be very significant. This is graphically illustrated in figures 3.5 and 3.6. Note that figure 3.5 pertains to someone with the same wealth and tax parameters as case 1 in both tables 3.9 and 3.11. That is, this is someone facing the success tax and high income and estate tax rates. The action being considered is a supplemental investment in a conventional stock mutual fund with an 11 percent nominal return composed of 2 percent dividends, 2 percent realized capital gains, and 7 percent unrealized capital gains. For holding periods up to 11 years, pension saving provides less retirement income than conventional saving; for longer holding periods pension saving provides more. For all holding periods, the inheritance of heirs is less with pension than with conventional saving. Even with holding periods of greater than 11 years, the gain in retirement income is less than the loss in the inheritance of the heirs.

The contrast between figure 3.5 and figure 3.6 illustrates the importance of the tax efficiency of stock portfolios held outside of pension accounts. The only difference is that the investment vehicle is now an asset that generates only unrealized capital gains. Now, for all periods of 30 years or less, conven-

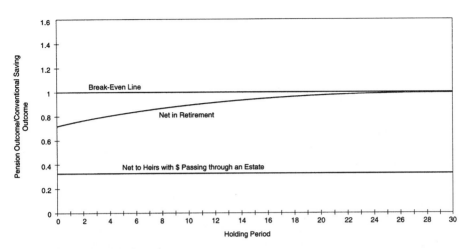

Fig. 3.6   Pensions vs. conventional saving: net proceeds in retirement and to heirs with non-dividend-paying growth stocks

Note: Assumptions: 15 percent excess distribution tax and excess accumulation tax, 55 percent estate tax, 41 percent federal income tax, 9.3 percent state income tax, 28 percent capital gains tax, 11 percent nominal rate of return on stocks, all in the form of unrealized capital gains.

tional (supplemental) saving dominates pension saving; if the money is withdrawn in retirement, there is more net money to spend if conventional saving is chosen, although the outcome is very nearly the same for periods of 20 years or more. If the individual dies before spending the money, the heirs receive three times as much if conventional saving is used than if a supplemental qualified pension plan is used. The reason that the outcome ratio shown in figure 3.6 is flat for the case when the money passes through an estate is that the compounding effect is the same whether or not the money is put in a pension (even conventional saving has complete tax deferral), so the ratio of outcomes is completely determined by the alternative tax burdens.

Figure 3.6 makes clear that it would not make economic sense for someone facing the success tax to make supplementary contributions to pension plans and invest the money in non-dividend-paying growth stocks. Better outcomes can be achieved with conventional saving. In this sense, the pension system does not offer this person any extra incentive to save. While figure 3.5 is not as unambiguous, it still indicates that it makes no sense to use pension saving for that particular type of stock portfolio, for holding periods of less than 11 years, and probably not for much longer periods if the saver cares about what heirs will receive in the event that he or she dies before depleting this account. Our conclusion is that once a person is on a trajectory that will trigger the success tax, there is little or no economic incentive to save additional money in pension plans.

3.5   The Incentives to Take Distributions

The previous section demonstrated that the tax system, particularly the excess distribution tax and the excess accumulation tax, effectively removes the incentive to save supplemental amounts via the pension system for people who already anticipate pension accumulations that will be deemed excessive. In this section we consider a separate question: should someone who has already accumulated more than enough to trigger the success tax accelerate distributions, perhaps incurring the excess distribution tax, or should he or she leave the money in the pension system as long as possible and defer the payment of taxes?

We consider first a person who retires at age 65 and who has pension assets exceeding $2 million. The software engineer in example 4A (table 3.6) would have been in such a position by age 65. Should such a person begin withdrawals immediately and reduce the funds subject to the excess distribution tax (and potentially the excess accumulation tax) or should this person maximize the deferral advantage of pensions by waiting until age 70½ to begin withdrawals and then distribute only the minimum amounts required by the IRS? In analyzing this question we follow the method of analysis of Lockwood (1993).

Consider two alternative strategies for someone with large pension accumulations at age 65: strategy 1, withdraw $155,000 per year between ages 65 and 69, and strategy 2, roll over $155,000 per year between ages 65 and 69 from existing defined contribution pension plans into a new, separate IRA. We assume that the individual has a combined marginal state and federal income tax rate of 46.41 percent. We also assume that the minimum distributions from the IRA beginning at age 70½ under strategy 2 face the excess distribution tax and hence a combined marginal tax rate of 61.41 percent. The IRA is invested in corporate bonds earning an 8 percent nominal return. In order to keep track of which strategy is the more advantageous, we assume that the after-tax distributions of strategy 1 are invested in a municipal bond fund earning 5.76 percent. The results are shown in table 3.12.

The after-tax accumulation in the municipal bond fund reaches $466,004 with the final distribution from the primary pension plan at age 69. If these funds were left untouched and continued to earn 5.76 percent, they would total $1,350,507 by age 88. Contrast that with the outcome under strategy 2. By age 70½, the separate IRA would have grown to $982,069, and minimum distributions would have to commence. We have used an 18-year-term-certain payout in calculating the minimum distributions, following the example in Lockwood (1993). The 18 years is the joint life expectancy of the owner of the IRA and his or her spouse. The initial distribution at age 70 is $51,687. The minimum payouts continue to grow each year until the IRA is exhausted with the final payout of $206,538 at age 88. The net after-tax proceeds of these distributions are again invested in a municipal bond fund paying 5.76 percent. After the final distribution is added to the fund, the balance stands at $1,262,351. The

Table 3.12   **Early Distribution vs. Maximum Deferral**

| | Strategy 1: Early Distribution | | | Strategy 2: Maximum Deferral | |
Age	Taxable Distribution	After-Tax Accumulation	IRA Account	Minimum Distribution	After-Tax Accumulation
65	155,000	83,065	155,000		
66	155,000	170,914	322,400		
67	155,000	263,823	503,192		
68	155,000	362,083	698,447		
69	155,000	466,004	909,323		
70		492,846	982,069	51,687	19,946
71		521,234	1,004,812	55,823	42,637
72		551,257	1,024,909	60,289	68,358
73		583,009	1,041,789	65,112	97,423
74		616,590	1,054,811	70,321	130,171
75		652,106	1,063,249	75,975	166,988
76		689,667	1,066,257	82,020	208,258
77		729,392	1,062,975	88,581	254,437
78		771,405	1,052,345	95,668	306,011
79		815,838	1,033,211	103,322	363,509
80		862,830	1,004,281	111,587	427,509
81		912,529	964,109	120,514	498,640
82		965,091	911,082	130,155	577,588
83		1,020,680	843,401	140,567	665,102
84		1,079,471	759,061	151,813	761,996
85		1,141,649	655,828	163,957	869,158
86		1,207,408	531,221	177,073	987,554
87		1,276,955	382,480	191,240	1,118,237
88		1,350,507	206,538	206,538	1,262,351

difference between the fund balances of strategy 1 and strategy 2 at age 88 is $88,156, which represents the net advantage of the early withdrawal choice. So the message from table 3.12 is that the early withdrawal strategy (where the five $155,000 distributions avoid the excess distribution tax) is more advantageous than the strategy of postponing distributions to the maximum extent possible in order to take advantage of the deferral feature of pensions. This conclusion depends on the age of the pension owner and on the rates of return that can be earned both inside and outside the pension plan. However, it clearly indicates that withdrawing money before age 70½ can be advantageous for someone facing the success tax. It would be worthwhile for any such person to do a calculation like the one illustrated in table 3.12.

So far, we have seen that the early withdrawal choice is in the interest of this particular couple should the surviving spouse live to age 88. It is even more advantageous if the widow or widower should die before that age. For instance, at age 75 strategy 1 has a municipal bond fund worth $652,106 whereas strategy 2 has an IRA with a balance of $1,063,249 and a municipal bond fund of $166,988. If the owner and spouse died at this age, the net inherited funds for the beneficiaries would be significantly greater with strategy 1. Depending on the precise size of the total estate, the tax rate of the beneficiaries, and their state of residence, the difference could easily exceed $100,000. We conclude, then, that people over age 59½ who have very large pension accumulations face strong incentives to withdraw the money early. If, in contrast to these examples, they do not reinvest the money outside the pension, this incentive for early distributions may translate to an incentive to consume rather than save.

The example of table 3.12 does not take into account the recently legislated three-year (1997–99) moratorium on the excess distribution tax mentioned in section 3.1. In this period, distributions can be taken in any amount from qualified plans without triggering the excess distribution tax. This obviously significantly enhances the advantage of taking large distributions during this time window. In fact, the optimal policy for the person in the above example would be to distribute more than $155,000 per year during 1997–99 so as to minimize or eliminate the possibility that the pension funds will face either the excess distribution tax or the excess accumulation tax. The legislation did not suspend the excess accumulation tax applying to large pension accumulations passing through estates. This magnifies the incentive to get funds out of the pension.

We now turn to a different case, someone who is considerably older and who still has pension assets that the government classifies as excessively large. Consider, for example, a single person who has $2 million in pension assets at age 75, roughly $1.05 million beyond the amount that would trigger the excess accumulation tax. If this person dies without withdrawing the $1.05 million, the heirs may receive a net benefit of $84,300 from its existence. Even this is not the extreme case, as earlier in the paper we have shown cases where this money would face tax rates of over 96 percent rather than the 91.97 percent rate assumed here. However, if the money were withdrawn (and the individual died before spending any of it) the beneficiaries would receive at least $182,300 even if all of the money withdrawn faced the excess distribution tax. If the $1.05 million were withdrawn during the 1997–99 window, the heirs would receive more than $310,000 after all taxes due to the moratorium on the excess distribution tax. In either case (with or without the moratorium), the tax system is not neutral with respect to the distribution decision: in fact, it favors taking distributions in retirement and strongly penalizes those dying with large pension assets.

We conclude from the two examples just discussed that pension tax law is not only antisaving with respect to additional contributions for people with substantial pension assets, it also is antisaving in that it gives such people a strong incentive to withdraw their funds in retirement (even if such withdrawals trigger the excess distribution tax) rather than leave them in the pension plan and let them pass through an estate. Thus the consistent saver has an incentive to withdraw funds from the saving pool even in the absence of any need or desire to use the proceeds for consumption. The combination of the taxes triggered by withdrawals (even excess distributions) with the estate tax later applying to the unspent money held outside the pension system is considerably less than the taxes faced by excessively large pension accumulations passing through an estate.

Throughout the paper, we have been calculating the outcomes for nonspouse beneficiaries as if they withdrew the inherited accumulations immediately. In some circumstances the plan can be set up so that the heirs are permitted to take distributions from the inherited plans over their own life expectancies,[4] thus extending the tax deferral nature of the account. The excess accumulation tax and the estate taxes cannot be deferred, but the income taxes of the heirs would not be payable immediately, but rather payable as the distributions are taken from the account. The government requires that the beneficiary begin distributions immediately, but in some cases they can be extended over the entire life expectancies of the heirs. If this option is available, it may be very advantageous. Of course, if the heirs are to use the inherited IRA over their own lifetimes, then they must find a source for the estate tax and excess accumulation tax other than the pension money itself. These options involve detailed financial planning and depend on specific circumstances that we cannot describe exhaustively in this paper.

3.6   Asset Allocation: Which Assets Should Be Held inside a Pension Plan?

In this section we deal with a related question concerning the often ignored issue of asset allocation. The previous sections have indicated that lifetime savers are likely to face either the excess distribution or the excess accumulation tax and therefore may want to hold some investments outside of the pension system. Now we address the issue of which assets should be held where. Where should one hold corporate bonds or growth stocks? Does it make a difference? The tax system operates in such a way that it can make a big difference.

The intuition regarding this kind of asset allocation goes as follows. Recall that the tax treatment of pensions is completely independent of the type of assets in the account. Before-tax money can be saved, but all withdrawals are taxed as ordinary income. While it is true that there is the success tax to worry about, even that and the estate tax do not differentiate between the type of income that was generated inside the account (capital gains, interest, dividends, rents, etc.). The reason that it makes a difference which assets are held inside the pension account and which are held outside is not that they are taxed differently inside of a pension account but that different types of income are

---

4. If the owner of an IRA had begun distributions before his or her death, a nonspouse beneficiary (or a spouse who elects not to roll over the account into his or her own name) inheriting the IRA must take distributions at least as rapidly as under the method being used at the owner's death. However, if the owner had not begun distributions, and if the plan is explicitly set up to allow it, the beneficiary may be able to take distributions extended over his or her lifetime.

taxed very differently when the assets are held outside, in taxable accounts. For instance, municipal bonds can be free of state and federal income taxation but carry an implicit tax (or lower interest yield) of about 28 percent. Realized capital gains are taxed more lightly than ordinary income; currently, the maximum rate on realized capital gains is 28 percent, and there have been many proposals to lower this rate further. Accrued capital gains (perhaps resulting from retained earnings) are tax deferred (i.e., they face no taxes until the gain is realized). Further, the cost basis of appreciated assets held outside of pensions is reset when they pass through an estate, so these capital gains can completely escape taxation. This resetting of the basis occurs, whether or not the estate is large enough to pay estate taxes.

The basic answer to the question of how to allocate one's assets between those held inside a pension and those held outside is to hold inside those assets that would be taxed most harshly on the outside. For instance, if you want to hold a total portfolio consisting of zero- or low-dividend growth stocks, high-dividend utility stocks, and long-term corporate bonds, it makes sense to place all of the corporate bonds and utility stocks inside the plan before any of the relatively lightly taxed growth stocks are placed inside. Further, the outside taxation of the growth stock portfolio depends on how one manages the realization of capital gains. This does not say that it is irrational to have all stocks or even all growth stocks both inside the pension and outside. What it does say is *if* you are going to have some highly taxed assets such as corporate bonds or utility stocks, *then* they first belong inside the qualified plan. They are the assets that gain the most from the tax deferral feature of the plan. Growth stocks, to the extent that they yield unrealized capital gains, already have that feature.

A person who is making investments both in a currently taxable environment and through pension accumulations may not only want to allocate the assets of a given portfolio in terms of where they are held but may also find it profitable to change the composition of the portfolio itself. For instance, someone who wants the risk-return trade-off of large-capitalization stocks (such as offered by the S&P 500) may be able to achieve that position or something very close to it with a portfolio consisting of high-grade corporate bonds and low-dividend small-capitalization growth stocks. By appropriately positioning the bonds and growth stocks (bonds first in the pension fund and growth stocks first outside of the pension fund) the net-of-tax return can be enhanced relative to holding the S&P 500 in both environments.

There is a second asset allocation effect that generally reinforces the one just discussed. The second consideration involves risk allocation. Because of the excess distribution tax and the excess accumulation tax, the marginal tax rates faced by assets in pensions are more progressive than those faced by outside investments. This extra progressivity differentially reduces the expected return on riskier assets relative to safer ones. The success tax discour-

Table 3.13   **Comparing "Balanced Portfolios" inside the Pension Plan and outside of It with a Tax-Efficient Asset Allocation**

	Inefficient Saving	Efficient Saving
Pension account	50% Growth stocks 50% Corporate bonds	100% Corporate bonds
Nonpension saving	50% Growth stocks 50% Municipal bonds	100% Growth stocks
Retirement advantage without excess distribution tax		2.6%
Retirement advantage with excess distribution tax		12.7%
Beneficiary's advantage without excess accumulation tax		15.2%
Beneficiary's advantage with excess accumulation tax		25.5%

Note: Assumptions: Corporate bonds yield 8 percent, municipal bonds yield 5.76 percent, stocks earn 13 percent, with 1 percent dividend yield and 1 percent realized capital gains. Individual has a combined federal and state marginal income tax rate of 46.41 percent and saves between ages 25 and 70. Saving is proportional to labor income, which grows at 6 percent per year.

ages one from taking risks that might lead to "success," at least within the pension environment. The optimal response is to hold riskier assets outside of the pension system and safer ones within it.

One question regarding these asset allocation effects is whether they involve minor adjustments in returns or whether they amount to important considerations. The best way to answer that is to consider some examples. The issue is interesting only if someone is saving sizable amounts both inside the pension system and outside of it. Consider someone who contributes an amount to a pension fund equal to the amount saved outside of the fund, and assume this is done for the entire career. He or she might, for instance, save 5 percent of income in pensions and 5 percent conventionally. This person chooses to invest half of the total money in bonds and half in common stocks. Two strategies are depicted in table 3.13. The first, labeled "inefficient saving," involves devoting half of the saving to growth stocks and bonds, both inside the pension system and outside of it. The second strategy, which involves the same total asset allocation and therefore the same total risk, allocates all of the pension saving to bonds and all of the nonpension saving to growth stocks. This second strategy is more tax efficient because all of the relatively lightly taxed stocks are kept in the taxable environment whereas all of the more heavily taxed bonds are placed in the tax-deferred accounts. The advantage is not as great as might be expected because of the existence of municipal bonds, which, by assumption, involve an implicit tax rate of only 28 percent. Nonetheless, there is a noticeable net advantage to the more efficient asset allocation strategy, and this ad-

Table 3.14   **Efficiently Allocating Two Equity Mutual Funds between Pension Accounts and Nonpension Savings Accounts**

	Inefficient Saving	Efficient Saving
Pension account	50% Growth stock fund	100% Equity income fund
	50% Equity income fund	
Nonpension saving	50% Growth stock fund	100% Growth stock fund
	50% Equity income fund	
Retirement advantage without excess distribution tax		9.0%
Retirement advantage with excess distribution tax		15.7%
Beneficiary's advantage without excess accumulation tax		16.9%
Beneficiary's advantage with excess accumulation tax		23.8%

vantage can be obtained with little or no change in risk exposure. If, in retirement, the money is withdrawn and does not trigger the excess distribution tax, the withdrawals would be 2.6 percent higher with the efficient strategy. If the 15 percent excess distribution tax applies to these withdrawals, then the efficient saver ends up with almost 13 percent more net retirement income.

If the saving is not withdrawn in retirement but instead becomes part of an estate, the advantage to the beneficiaries of efficiently allocating assets is even greater. In this case, the advantage grows to 15.2 or 25.5 percent depending on whether the excess accumulation tax is involved or not. The reason that efficient asset allocation is even more advantageous in this case is that the unrealized capital gains on assets held outside of pension plans completely escape taxation when the assets pass through an estate. Thought of as pure efficiency gains, the numbers in table 3.13 are impressively large. Remember these are gains with little or no cost. A person might, for instance, receive 13 percent more from retirement saving simply because he or she had allocated assets in an efficient manner.

Table 3.14 illustrates that this is not just a stocks-versus-bonds phenomenon. In fact, what table 3.14 shows is another lifetime saver who saves an equal amount in pension accumulations and in a taxable environment. This person wants to invest in a balanced portfolio of equities consisting half of growth stocks and half of income-oriented stocks such as utilities. A growth stock mutual fund is once again modeled as having a nominal return of 13 percent, including a 1 percent dividend yield and 1 percent realized capital gains. This fund would have to be tax conscious in order to hold the realized capital gains to this level. The second fund is an equity income fund with a nominal yield of 11 percent, including a 6 percent dividend rate and 1 percent realized capital gains. The stocks in such a fund might include utilities and preferred issues.

The naive or inefficient policy for this saver would be to have the same 50–50 allocation between these two types of funds both inside the pension and in the outside taxable environment. The much more efficient strategy is to place the fund generating the most currently taxable income inside the pension and place the fund generating the most unrealized capital gains in the taxable environment. Table 3.14 indicates that the gain to placing these investments efficiently is even greater than in the stocks-versus-bonds case just discussed.

The reason that the gain is in general larger in this case is that the effect of taxes on the return of the equity income fund is more than the 2.24 percent difference between the yield on taxable and municipal bonds. This means that there is a larger advantage to efficiently locating the income mutual fund than there is to efficiently locating bonds in the previous example. The 9 to 16 percent improvement in retirement income reflected in table 3.14 strikes us as an extremely large potential payoff for such a simple adjustment in asset allocation.

3.7   Conclusions and Final Remarks

Pensions are thought to be one of the few remaining tax shelters providing attractive incentives for people to save for retirement. The excess distribution tax and the excess accumulation tax were included in the Tax Reform Act of 1986 to prevent people from taking advantage of the favorable tax treatment of pensions to amass wealth beyond what is thought to be reasonably necessary for a comfortable retirement. The wisdom of this policy is open to question. People who increase saving because of the tax shelter opportunity offered by pension plans, or for other reasons like the payroll deduction feature of many pension plans, do not reduce the resources available to the rest of the population. In fact, individual savers reap only a portion of the social return of the incremental capital. If the extra pension saving results in extra capital for the economy, then this extra capital pays corporation income taxes and the pension saver ultimately pays personal income taxes, which improves the overall budget picture for everyone in the economy. The social return to the capital significantly exceeds the private return received by the pension saver.

For the most part, we have refrained from evaluating current tax policy toward pensions from a social perspective and have simply analyzed how the tax system operates and how an individual might optimally respond. This analysis has led to several striking results:

- The tax rates faced by pensions deemed "too large" can be extraordinarily high. The marginal rate on distributions over $155,000 can be roughly 61.5 percent. The effective marginal tax rate faced by large pension accumulations passing through an estate can dwarf this rate, however, reaching 92 to 96.5 percent.

- These high tax rates, which include the excess distribution and excess accumulation taxes, can be faced by savers who do not have extraordinarily high incomes. The success tax is not limited to the rich, but rather primarily affects lifetime savers. For example, someone who works between ages 25 and 70, makes $40,000 at age 50, and contributes 10 percent to a pension plan invested in the S&P 500 will likely be penalized by the success tax for overusing the pension provisions.

- The advantage of pensions relative to conventional saving is greatly reduced and in many cases eliminated once accumulations exceed the amounts that will trigger the success tax. Even in cases where additional pension saving still provides more resources in retirement than conventional saving, when the plan owner dies, the heirs get less than they would have if the saving had been done outside of a pension plan.

- The advantage of pension saving is reduced by the availability of tax-advantaged investments outside of pension plans. Examples are tax-free municipal bonds and tax-efficient low-dividend stock portfolios.

- Not only is there little, if any, incentive to continue to save via pensions once the excess distribution and excess accumulation taxes become applicable, there is a strong incentive to withdraw money while living rather than risk the nearly confiscatory tax rates faced by pension assets transferred through estates. This means that there is an incentive to consume more in retirement than would otherwise be the case.

- Individuals can realize significant efficiency gains by allocating their investments appropriately between pension accounts and outside holdings. Simply locating assets in their most advantageous environment could improve the net proceeds of saving by almost 25 percent.

These findings are sufficiently important to warrant more consideration of the tax treatment of large pension accumulations on several fronts. First, we are currently engaged in further research to clarify the number of future elderly households who need to be concerned about the excess distribution and excess accumulation taxes. We know that it is a distinct minority of the population, but we are also quite sure that it is a large number of households who account for a significant portion of total personal saving. Second, further attention needs to be given to the transfer of pensions through estates. The estate taxation of pensions changed dramatically in the 1982–86 period with almost no study or evaluation. Now that it is recognized that pensions are the primary vehicle for personal saving in the economy, a careful reconsideration of the legislation of the early and mid-1980s is called for. As this paper has demonstrated, once the excess distribution and excess accumulation taxes are understood, these taxes are likely to become quite effective at discouraging pension saving and hence they will reduce economic welfare in an economy that surely has lower than optimal saving now.

References

Ibbotson Associates. 1996. *Stocks, bonds, bills, and inflation: 1996 Yearbook.* Chicago: Ibbotson Associates.
Lockwood, Steven G. 1993. Tax planning opportunities for large qualified plan and IRA balances. *ERISA and Benefits Law Journal* 2:201–9.
Mankiw, N. Gregory, and James M. Poterba. 1996. Stock market yields and the pricing of municipal bonds. NBER Working Paper no. 5607. Cambridge, Mass.: National Bureau of Economic Research, June.

Comment   Alan J. Auerbach

This paper is a good illustration of the miracle of compound interest. An upper-middle-income person who saves consistently throughout his or her life in a pension plan will quite possibly be subject to very heavy taxes on withdrawal of funds in retirement or when passing assets through an estate. It will be useful to break my comments down into two areas, regarding methodology and assumptions.

Methodology

The paper's basic approach is to consider, for different portfolios, the tax implications of a variety of marginal decisions: saving for retirement in a pension plan versus outside a pension plan, saving to leave a bequest in a pension plan versus outside, withdrawing funds from a pension plan as soon as possible rather than letting them accumulate, and so forth. To illustrate the effects of these choices, the authors examine the outcomes for people in different situations with respect to age, income level, and pension plan generosity. They find that, in many cases, the individual will be subject to an excise tax on excess accumulations (if he or she dies) or excess distributions (if he or she uses the funds during retirement) and that, facing excise tax, the individual may wish not to save in a sheltered form or may wish to withdraw funds from a sheltered form as soon as it is possible to do so without additional penalty.

The basic algebra seems correct to me, although I think the intuition for some of the results could stand further development. For example, pensions look so much worse for funds passing through an estate than for those used in retirement (cf. figures 3.5 and 3.6) because of the additional benefit of the step-up in basis at death that accrues only to assets held outside pension funds.

How much do these comparisons tell us about behavioral distortions? Not as much as they might appear to do. We are learning about marginal tax rates in certain situations, not how likely these situations are to occur or, of equal

Alan J. Auerbach is the Robert D. Burch Professor of Economics and Law at the University of California, Berkeley, and a research associate of the National Bureau of Economic Research.

importance, how difficult it would be to avoid them. That is, how likely is it that these outcomes will occur, for an empirically reasonable pattern of wage growth and pension accumulation? How much less must one contribute to pension accounts to avoid the penalty thresholds? How much do we need to give our children annually to avoid estate tax? And so forth.

Ideally, we would like this analysis to be placed in a model of life cycle saving that takes account of the probabilities of reaching each state being considered here and the further avoidance activity that can increase the probability of more favorable (from a tax perspective) states. This is not an easy task, and the paper's calculations provide valuable information simply by illustrating the *possibility* of very high marginal tax rates facing the decisions being studied. Ultimately, though, the seriousness of these potential distortions depends critically on what motivates saving—for example, on the extent to which estates represent the byproduct of precautionary saving as opposed to planned bequests to heirs.

Assumptions

Now let us consider the paper's underlying assumptions. I have already mentioned the need to consider the likelihood that pension accumulations will actually follow the paths for which examples are presented. It is a likely conjecture that, in the past, very few individuals accumulated enough pension assets to be very concerned about encountering the Shoven-Wise penalties. But the private pension system is evolving, and the paper's projections may be reasonable for some group of individuals. But then we must ask whether we believe that current estate tax and excise tax rules will not change.

Presumably, virtually no one now would be subject to excise tax. Similarly, at present, only a couple of percent of estates are subject to tax. This is not surprising, with the $600,000 exemption, which effectively becomes $1.2 million for a married couple. With real growth, even the indexed excise tax threshold will not be enough, and the nominal estate tax threshold looms as even more significant. But it seems implausible that these penalties will remain as they are if they catch an ever increasing share of the population over time. The issue, then, is how one should define "current policy." Current policy may, implicitly, be one that adjusts these thresholds to keep a certain share of the population subject to them, in the way that social security benefits and income tax brackets were "indexed" before being indexed explicitly by law. While the current excise tax moratorium may have more to do with the shifting of revenue into the "budget window," it does suggest legislative flexibility. The same is illustrated for the estate tax by currently pending legislation that would raise the exemption level over time.

Is this just a question of semantics? No, because what is ultimately relevant for current saving is what people believe will happen. I do not think very many people need to worry about these tax rates. Of course, such insouciance may be rational in part *because* Shoven and Wise have written this paper.

II Health: Spending Patterns and Implications and Effect on Work

4 The Medical Costs of the Young and Old: A Forty-Year Perspective

David M. Cutler and Ellen Meara

It is widely known that medical costs have increased over time. In the United States, as in most of the developed world, medical spending growth has exceeded income growth by several percentage points per year for three decades or longer (Levit et al. 1994). In country after country, the cost of medical care has become a major public sector issue.

But much less is known about what medical spending is buying us. Is medical spending valuable or wasteful? Should we want to limit total spending or increase it? The answer to this question is by no means clear. On the one hand is voluminous evidence that medical spending conveys great value. Randomized clinical trials, for example, routinely document the benefits of new pharmaceuticals and medical devices. And we would venture to guess that most people would prefer today's medical system to the medical system of 30 years ago, even given the much higher cost of medical care today. This suggests that people are on net better off with the additional medical care spending than they would be without it.

On the other hand is a great sense that medical care often brings little in the way of health benefit. Nearly one-third of Medicare spending occurs in the last six months of life (Lubitz and Riley 1993), which has been interpreted as evidence that a lot of medical care is wasted on those who will not in any case survive.[1] Other studies, such as the RAND Health Insurance Experiment (Newhouse et al. 1992), show that putting people in less generous insurance

David M. Cutler is professor of economics at Harvard University and a research associate of the National Bureau of Economic Research. Ellen Meara is a doctoral candidate in economics at Harvard University.

This paper was prepared for the National Bureau of Economic Research Conference on Aging, April 1997. We are grateful to the National Institute on Aging for research support.

1. Of course, since people who are sick are more likely to die than people who are healthy, medical care spending will naturally be skewed to those near death. Still, the magnitude of the skewness is large.

policies reduces their spending on medical services but does not affect their health. And direct estimates of the value of medical care typically find that, at the margin, a substantial amount of medical care has little or no health benefit (Chassin et al. 1987; Greenspan et al. 1988; Winslow et al. 1988a, 1988b; Kahn et al. 1990; Newhouse et al. 1992; Cutler 1995; Staiger and Gaumer 1994; McClellan and Newhouse 1995).[2]

Our goal is to understand why medical care has become so expensive over time and what has been its value to society. We focus particularly on medical spending by age. Many of the concerns about the medical care system are associated with changes in the age distribution of medical resources and an increase in the share of resources going to the elderly (Lubitz et al. 1995). And the most pressing cost problem in the medical care economy is the pending insolvency of trust funds to provide medical care for the elderly. Further, growth in spending by age is important in forecasting medical costs as society ages (Lubitz et al. 1995). If patterns of medical spending by age are changing over time, projections of spending based solely on the number of people of different ages will be inaccurate.

Our analysis is based on periodic surveys of national health expenditures conducted in 1953, 1963, 1970, 1977, and 1987. The surveys have large numbers of people (from 8,000 to 40,000 people per survey) and aggregate all of acute care spending.

Our analysis of age-based spending documents two conclusions. First, there has been a dramatic change in the distribution of medical spending over time. While spending on medical care has increased for all people, it has increased disproportionately for the very young (those under 1 year old) and the old (those 65 years old or older). Over the 24-year period from 1963 through 1987, per person spending on infants increased by 9.8 percent per year, and per person spending on the elderly increased by 8.0 percent per year, compared to a rise of only 4.7 percent per year for the "middle-aged" (1–64 years old). The share of medical care spending for infants and the elderly doubled from 17 to 36 percent.

We further show that essentially all of the disproportionate growth of spending for the very young and the old is accounted for by high-cost users within those groups. For infants, 89 percent of the excess spending increase over the middle-aged is accounted for by the top 10 percent of the spending distribution. For the elderly, the equivalent share is 66 percent. Thus, in understanding the concentration of medical spending by age, we need to understand the concentration of spending among high-cost users.

In section 4.3, we consider who are the high-cost users of medical care. We show that a substantial amount of high-cost medical use is associated with the

---

2. Cutler and Staiger (1996) review the evidence on the marginal and average value of medical spending.

increasing technological capability of medicine. Among infants, high-cost users are premature babies with substantial respiratory or other acute conditions. For the elderly, high-cost users are generally patients with severe cardiovascular problems or cancer. For both infants and the elderly, the capacity to devote many more resources to the most pressing cases has increased over time.

In section 4.4, we look at how health outcomes for premature infants and the sick elderly have changed over time. We find substantial health improvements in most of the categories of high-cost medical care. Infant mortality among very low birth weight infants has fallen substantially at exactly the time when the cost of these infants has risen most rapidly. And mortality improvements among the elderly have been especially prominent in cardiovascular care, where spending increases have been dramatic. Our analysis is not causal; we do not have any direct link between the technologies we discuss in section 4.3 and the outcomes we analyze in section 4.4. But our results suggest such a link is plausible.

We begin in the next section with some basic facts about the distribution of medical spending over time. In section 4.2, we look at the age distribution of medical care utilization. Section 4.3 focuses in more detail on high-cost users of medical care. Section 4.4 looks at trends in medical outcomes over time. Section 4.5 concludes.

4.1 The Basics of Medical Spending

Much of our knowledge about individual spending on medical services is based on periodic surveys of national medical expenditures that have been conducted over time. In the post–World War II period, there have been seven such surveys: the 1953 and 1958 National Surveys of Family Medical Costs and Voluntary Health Insurance in the United States; the 1963 and 1970 Surveys of Health Services Utilization and Expenditures; the 1977 and 1980 National Medical Care Utilization and Expenditure Surveys; and the 1987 National Medical Expenditure Survey (NMES). Beginning with the 1963 survey, all of the surveys are available in machine-readable form; for data from the 1950s, we are forced to use published tabulations from the survey authors (Anderson, Collette, and Feldman 1963; Anderson and Feldman 1956). In the absence of microdata, we omit consideration of the 1958 survey. We also omit the 1980 survey because we are interested in long-term trends, so differences between 1977 and 1980 data are less important for this analysis. We would clearly like to have more recent data for our analysis; while there is a more recent survey being conducted (the 1996 NMES), these data are not yet available.

The surveys all gather information on the range of acute care medical expenditures in a one-year period. Several features of the data are important to note. Newborn hospital admissions for delivery are counted as part the mother's admission unless the newborn is discharged on a later date than the mother, in

Table 4.1   **Characteristics of Medical Spending**

Year	Number of Observations	Average Spending[a]	Average Spending Change (%)	Share of Spending by Percentile (%)		
				Below 50th	50th–90th	90th+
1953	8,846	278	–	–	–	<43[b]
1963	7,803	385	3.3	5	36	59
		(17)				
1970	11,619	668	7.9	4	30	66
		(43)	(0.7)			
1977	38,815	874	3.8	3	27	70
		(16)	(0.9)			
1987	34,456	1,521	5.5	3	25	72
		(40)	(0.4)			

Note: Numbers in parentheses are standard errors.

[a]Average spending is in real (1987) dollars adjusted using the GDP deflator.

[b]According to Anderson and Feldman (1956), the top 11 percent of the health spending distribution consumed 43 percent of all health care dollars in 1953. Without microdata it is impossible to know exactly what share of medical spending the top 10 percent consumed.

which case the newborn is recorded as having a separate admission.[3] In all cases, the institutionalized population is not included in the survey, and any information on long-term care is excluded. With the exception of the 1987 NMES long-term care supplement, the surveys give no information about nursing home spending, including spending on nursing homes for those now living in the community.

Table 4.1 shows summary statistics about the data. The sample sizes are large: 8,846 in 1953, 7,803 in 1963, 11,619 in 1970, 38,815 in 1977, and 34,456 in 1987. Table 4.1 also shows basic statistics about medical care spending. In real (1987 dollar) terms, medical spending rose from $278 per person in 1953 to $1,521 per person in 1987. Growth was 3.3 percent per year in the 1953–63 period. Growth was most rapid in the 1963–70 period (7.9 percent per year), when Medicare and Medicaid were created and insurance coverage for the privately insured population expanded as well. In the next seven years, growth slowed to 3.8 percent per year. In the 1980s, spending growth increased again, to 5.5 percent per year. The average change over the entire period is 5.0 percent per year.

The remaining columns of table 4.1 document another frequently noted fact about medical spending (Berk and Monheit 1992): medical spending has become more concentrated among high-cost users over time. In 1953, the top 10 percent of the spending distribution accounted for less than 43 percent of total spending; by 1987, that share was 72 percent. Most of the increase occurred in

3. In the 1987 data, attempts were made to assign costs separately to newborns and mothers in all cases, but there are cost variables that assign the newborn's costs to the mother for normal deliveries where the newborn's stay does not exceed that of the mother.

the 1950s and 1960s; since 1970, the distribution of overall medical spending has been relatively stable.

4.2 Medical Spending by Age

While the aggregate facts about medical spending are well known, much less is known about the distribution of medical spending by age or disease. Ideally, we would construct a set of "national disease accounts"—accounts that measure spending on particular diseases over time.[4] But the surveys do not include detailed diagnosis codes for spending prior to 1977. Instead, we consider first medical spending by age.

We denote spending for age group a at time t by $C_t(a)$. We divide the population into 11 age groups: under 1, 1–4, 5–14, 15–24, 25–34, 35–44, 45–54, 55–64, 65–74, 75–84, and 85+.[5] Table 4A.1 in the appendix shows average spending for survey years between 1963 and 1987, as well as average annual growth rates within age groups. To examine differential spending by age over time, we define relative age-specific spending as

$$(1) \qquad C_t^r(a) = \frac{C_t(a)}{C_t(35\text{--}44)}.$$

Figure 4.1A shows relative medical spending by age for each of the five surveys. The data show a clear pattern: relative to spending on 35–44-year-olds, spending for the very young (those less than age 1) and the old (those above age 65) has increased dramatically over time. The trend for infants is startling. In 1953, per capita spending on those under age 5 was less than half of per capita spending on middle-aged adults. In 1963, this figure was 53 percent, and in 1970, 64 percent. By 1977, per capita spending on infants was 97 percent of spending on middle-aged adults. After 1977, spending on infants soared. By 1987, the average infant used 2.3 times the medical services that middle-aged adults did. Figure 4.1B shows relative spending plus or minus one standard error for 1963 and 1987. Given that there are relatively few infants in each survey year (200 to 500), it is not surprising that relative spending for infants is measured imprecisely. Still, the dollar amounts are staggering; real average spending for high-cost infants above the 90th percentile tripled in the 1977–87 period, from $6,690 to $21,505.

Figure 4.2 shows the implied growth rates of spending. If we define the "middle-aged" as those aged 1–64, spending on the middle-aged rose 4.7 percentage points per year between 1963 and 1987, while spending on infants rose by 9.8 percentage points per year.

---

4. The current national health accounts tabulate spending by payer and sector of medical care provision (hospitals, physicians, etc.). For a set of disease accounts for 1995, see Triplett (1997).

5. The 1953 data are only available for more aggregated age groups: 0–5, 6–17, 18–24, 25–34, 35–54, 55–64, and 65+.

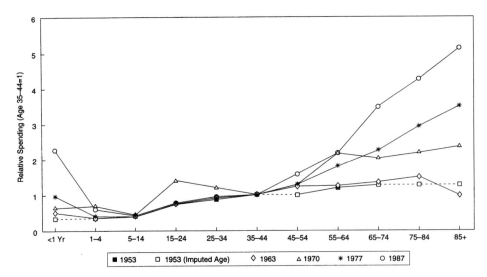

Fig. 4.1A   Age distribution of medical spending, 1953–87

Note: The 1953 age groups are 0–5, 6–17, 18–24, 25–34, 35–54, 55–64, and 65+. Relative spending for 5–24-year-olds was constructed assuming a uniform age distribution. Dashed lines for 1953 connect all age groups that were combined when calculating relative spending.

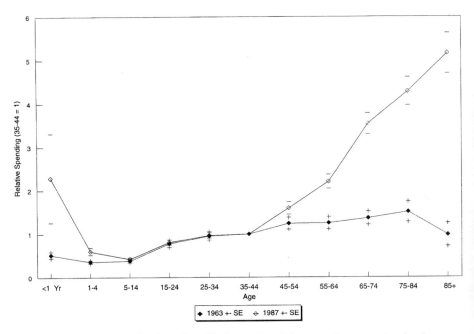

Fig. 4.1B   Age distribution of medical spending (plus or minus one standard error), 1963 and 1987

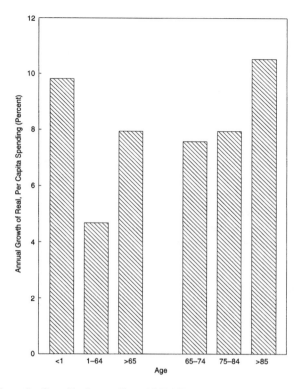

Fig. 4.2   Growth of medical spending, 1963–87

The change in relative spending for the elderly is equally dramatic but less concentrated in time. In 1953 and 1963, spending on the elderly was less than 30 percent higher than spending on the middle-aged. In addition, among the elderly population, spending declined at increasingly older ages during our sample period. Where the 75–84-year-olds used $689 per person in 1963, those aged 85 or over used only $447 per person. Over time, spending for the elderly has increased, particularly among the oldest old. By 1970, average spending on the elderly was twice the amount for 35–44-year-olds, by 1977 it was 2.6 times, and by 1987 it was 4 times. Further, within the elderly population, spending on the population aged 85 and over increased even more dramatically than spending among the younger old. In 1963 per capita spending on those aged 85 or over equaled average spending on 35–44-year-olds. By 1987, spending for the average person over age 85 was 5.2 times average spending for 35–44-year-olds. As figure 4.2 shows, the growth of per person spending on the elderly averaged 8.0 percent annually between 1963 and 1987, including a rate of over 10 percent annually for the oldest old.

Recall that spending on the elderly excludes long-term care services, which have also increased over time; total medical spending has thus become even more skewed than these data suggest.[6]

Figure 4.1A also shows a temporary increase in spending on 15–24-year-olds in 1970 that is eliminated by 1977. In the 1970 sample, two young men aged 19 and 20 have unusually high charges, which causes average spending for this group to be skewed.

The disproportionate growth of medical care spending for the elderly and the very young is substantively quite large. In 1963, spending on infants and the elderly accounted for 17 percent of total spending (1.6 percent for infants and 15.1 percent for the elderly). By 1987, spending on these two groups accounted for 36 percent of total spending (2.7 percent for infants and 33.2 percent for the elderly). We are not the first to document such a trend. Anderson et al. (1963) document a similar trend over the 1953–58 period. In the 1953 and 1958 surveys, spending grew most rapidly for those under age 6 and those over age 65. Although the authors are unsure about the causes of this rapid growth, they note that insurance enrollment grew more rapidly for the aged than for others over this period. The trend of rapid spending growth for the young and the old has continued throughout our sample.

As an alternative metric, figure 4.3 shows a simulation of medical spending if growth for the elderly and infants had matched growth for the middle-aged. The upper line graphs actual per capita medical spending. The lower line graphs spending under the alternative scenario. By 1987, the disproportionate growth of spending for infants and the elderly accounted for over $300 in spending per person, or over one-quarter of the total increase in medical spending since 1953.

Why has spending for infants and the elderly increased so rapidly? Has the increase been concentrated among high-cost users or has it been spread more uniformly through the distribution? The views about wasteful spending suggest that disproportionate spending growth ought to be concentrated among the very high cost users in these groups.

We address this question by considering aspects of the distribution of spending broader than just the mean. Suppose we consider percentile q of the distribution of spending within each age group. That is, $C_t^q(a)$ is spending at the qth percentile of age group a at time t. We can define relative spending at the qth percentile of the distribution as

$$(2) \qquad C_t^{r,q}(a) = \frac{C_t^q(a)}{C_t^q(35-44)}.$$

Figure 4.4 shows relative spending at the 50th and 90th percentiles of the spending distribution. For infants, neither the 50th nor the 90th percentile of

---

6. Real spending on nursing homes has increased from $3.9 billion in 1960 to $41.9 billion in 1985. Since 90 percent of nursing home residents are 65 years old or older, this implies that spending has become even more skewed toward the elderly.

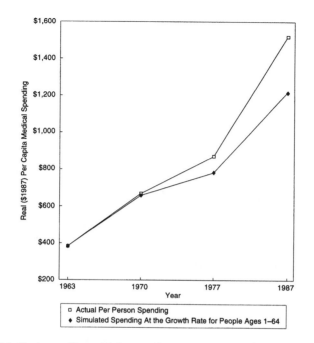

Fig. 4.3   Medical spending with less rapid cost growth for infants and elderly

spending increases much relative to middle-aged adults. Even in 1987, the 90th percentile of spending for infants is only just above spending for 35–44-year-olds, while the mean was over two times higher. The implication is that essentially all of the growth in spending occurs among the very high cost users—those above the 90th percentile. For the elderly, spending for the median person increases substantially less than spending for the mean person, and spending at the 90th percentile increases by only the amount of the mean. Thus, for the elderly as well there appears to be an increasing concentration of the distribution among high-cost users.

We can be more precise about how much spending at different points in the distribution contributes to overall growth in spending. To do this, we first divide the sample into three age groups: under 1, or infants; 1–64, or "middle-aged"; and 65 and older, or elderly. We then define "excess spending growth" as the increase in per capita spending resulting from more rapid growth of spending for infants (or the elderly) than for the middle-aged population. In other words, we ask the question, What would spending on infants (or the elderly) be in 1987 if it grew at the same rate as spending on the middle-aged over the 1963–87 period? The difference between actual spending on infants (or the elderly) in 1987 and this hypothetical spending at middle-aged growth rates is total excess spending growth for an age group. Using infants as an example:

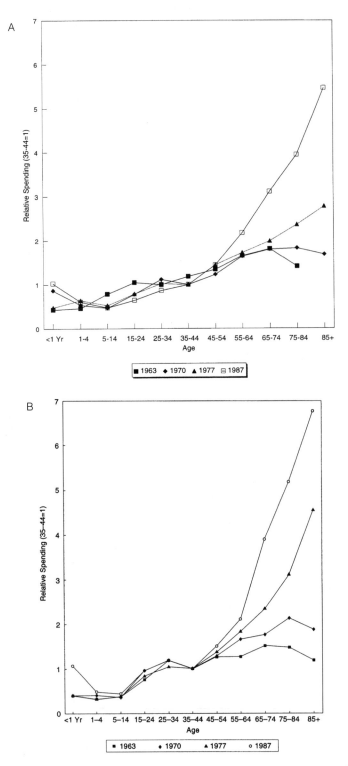

Fig. 4.4 Age distribution of medical spending at 50th percentile (*A*) and 90th percentile (*B*), 1963–87

(3)   Excess spending (<1) = $\text{Spend}_{1987}(<1)$

$$- \text{Spend}_{1963}(<1)\left(\frac{\text{Spend}_{1987}(1-64)}{\text{Spend}_{1963}(1-64)}\right),$$

where $\text{Spend}_t(a)$ is average spending in age group a in year t. We then divide each age group into four subgroups: those in the bottom 50 percent of the spending distribution, those in the 50th to 75th percentiles of the spending distribution, those in the 75th to 90th percentiles of the distribution, and those above the 90th percentile. For each age group, we calculate what share of excess spending is attributable to different parts of the spending distribution.

Consider spending on the bottom 50 percent of the distribution. For infants, this is

(4) $$\text{Spend}_t^{0-50}(<1) = \frac{1}{N_t(<1)} \int_{q=0}^{50} C_t^q(<1),$$

where we have divided total spending in the bottom half of the distribution by the total number of infants $N_t(<1)$ so that this amount is the contribution of this set of infants to average spending. If spending for the bottom 50 percent of the distribution had increased at the same rate as spending for the bottom 50 percent of the middle-aged population, in 1987 this group would have spent

(5)   Hypothetical $\text{Spend}_{1987}^{0-50}(<1)$ = $\text{Spend}_{1963}^{0-50}(<1)\left(\frac{\text{Spend}_{1987}^{0-50}(1-64)}{\text{Spend}_{1963}^{0-50}(1-64)}\right).$

We subtract this figure from $\text{Spend}_{1987}^{0-50}$ and divide the result by total excess spending growth for infants to determine what share of excess spending growth for infants is attributable to infants in the bottom half of the distribution.

Figure 4.5A shows the contribution to excess spending growth for infants and the elderly made by faster growth in different parts of the distribution. In both cases, the excess growth in medical care spending is particularly concentrated among high-cost users. For infants, 89 percent of the excess spending growth is a result of excess spending increases in the top 10 percent of the population.[7] For the elderly, 66 percent of excess spending growth results from higher cost growth in the top 10 percent of the distribution.

The highly concentrated spending growth at the top of the distribution for infants and the elderly reflects concentrated spending growth on the very ill in all age groups. Figure 4.5B shows the annual percentage change in spending from 1963 to 1987 for different age groups and at different points in the spending distribution within each age group. In all age groups, spending growth rises with percentile in the spending distribution. For those aged 1–64, spending

---

7. Indeed, 60 percent of spending growth is attributable to above average growth in the top 2 percent of the distribution. Because the number of infants is so small, however, the uncertainty about this estimate is high.

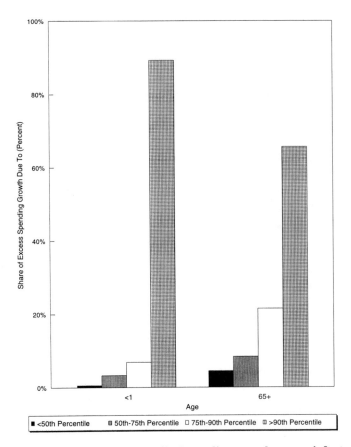

Fig. 4.5A   Accounting for excess medical spending growth among infants and elderly

grew at an average rate of 4.7 percent per year, yet even at the 95th percentile, spending is growing more slowly, at 4.6 percent per year. This implies that as for infants and the elderly, spending growth for the middle-aged is highly concentrated at the top of the distribution. However, spending growth is much slower for the middle-aged than for infants and the elderly, even above the 90th percentile of spending.

An alternative way to examine whether our trends reflect rapid spending growth for the ill of all ages is to choose a constant dollar amount and compare spending growth for all those who spend more than this amount. This allows us to look only at the most severely ill respondents in all age groups. Because the 1–64-year-old population is a healthier group than infants and the elderly, even those in the 95th percentile of the distribution are likely to be relatively healthy and therefore spend little. We want to examine the tendency for spending on the very ill at all ages to grow much more rapidly than per capita spend-

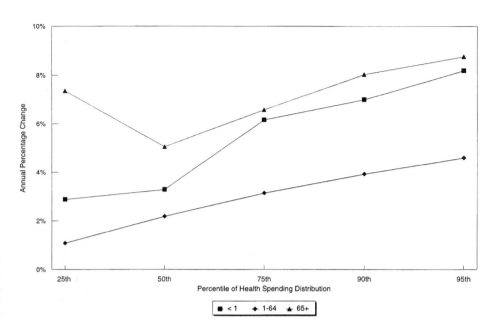

Fig. 4.5*B*   Annual percentage change in spending by age group and percentile of spending, 1963–87

ing in an age group. We looked at spending growth for those with real spending over $2,000. Measured in 1987 dollars, this is well above 90th percentile spending for all three groups in 1963 but below 90th percentile spending for all groups in 1987. Average spending for all infants spending over $2,000 grew 7.8 percent annually between 1963 and 1987. The figure was 4.9 percent for the elderly and 2.4 percent for those aged 1–64. The differences in growth rates among the very ill of different ages show that, although the trend of highly concentrated spending growth at the top of the spending distribution may occur within all age groups, it is most striking for infants and the elderly.

It is thus clear that in understanding why medical care has become so concentrated by age, we need to understand why it has become so much more concentrated among high-cost users within any age. We turn to this next.

4.3   Who Are the High-Cost Users?

Understanding why high-cost users spend more than they used to is hampered by data problems. Only the 1977 and 1987 surveys contain detailed information about diagnoses. Thus, we cannot look at the distribution of high-cost users over more than a 10-year period. Still, there was a substantial increase in concentration among high-cost users between 1977 and 1987, and we proceed with this analysis.

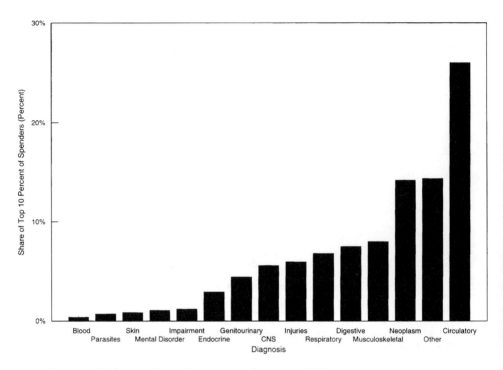

Fig. 4.6   High-cost elderly by primary diagnosis, 1987

4.3.1   High-Cost Elderly

We begin with an analysis of the high-cost elderly. We divide acute care spending and spending on prescription medicines for the elderly into 14 groups and one category for other diagnoses based on the chapters of the *International Classification of Diseases,* 9th rev., as adapted for use in the Health Interview Survey (National Center for Health Statistics 1979). The categories include parasites and infections, neoplasms, endocrine, blood, mental disorders, central nervous system (CNS), circulatory system, respiratory system, digestive system, genitourinary system, skin, musculoskeletal system, injuries and poisoning, impairments, and other. Because the surveys use impairment codes and often do not code congenital anomalies, we omit the congenital anomaly category and use the NMES category for impairments. Because we are focusing on those over age 65, conditions relating to pregnancy and the perinatal period are omitted. For each person, we sum all costs associated with each diagnosis group. We then assign each person a "primary diagnosis," or the diagnosis group that accounts for the largest amount of spending. In most cases (particularly for high-cost users), this is a fairly clear delineation.

Figure 4.6 shows the distribution of primary diagnoses for the top 10 percent of elderly spenders in 1987. The most common diagnosis in this group is cir-

Table 4.2   **Growth Rate of Costs for Primary Diagnosis of Circulatory Disorders or Neoplasms**

Percentile	Average Spending[a]		Annual Growth Rate of Real Average Spending (%)
	1977	1987	
	Circulatory Disorders		
All	2,001	8,634	14.6
	(259)	(721)	(1.4)
Below 50th	126	706	17.2
	(3)	(49)	(0.7)
50th–75th	449	5,171	24.4
	(11)	(155)	(0.4)
75th–90th	2,443	15,203	18.3
	(103)	(493)	(0.5)
Above 90th	14,546	46,593	11.6
	(2,045)	(3,579)	(1.6)
	Neoplasms		
All	5,552	8,590	4.4
	(611)	(946)	(1.6)
Below 50th	492	788	4.7
	(56)	(54)	(1.3)
50th–75th	4,232	5,610	2.8
	(401)	(298)	(1.1)
75th–90th	10.689	15,657	3.8
	(438)	(595)	(0.6)
Above 90th	25,079	43,886	5.6
	(2,281)	(4,272)	(1.3)

Note: Numbers in parentheses are standard errors.
[a]Spending is in real (1987) dollars adjusted using the GDP deflator.

culatory system disorders, accounting for 26.1 percent of the top spenders. Next in importance is other, then neoplasms (which includes benign and cancerous growths), with 14.4 and 14.2 percent, respectively. The other diagnoses generally have 5 to 10 percent of the top spenders.

The primary diagnoses of top spenders did not change substantially over the 1977–87 period. In 1977, the most common diagnosis was also circulatory system disorders (25.7 percent of high cost users), followed by other (11.4 percent) and neoplasms (11.3 percent). We suspect, however, that if we were able to look at spending in the 1950s or 1960s, we would observe more change in primary diagnoses.

We examined growth in spending on circulatory disorders and cancers to see how it contributed to overall spending growth. We wanted to know whether costs grew more rapidly for these conditions than for overall spending. In addition, we examined whether cost growth differed at different points in the spending distributions for these conditions. The top panel of table 4.2 shows growth in spending for individuals with a primary diagnosis of circulatory system disorder.[8] Costs for the average patient with this primary diagnosis grew 14.6 percent per year. This rapid growth occurred throughout the distribution of spending on circulatory disorders, with growth in spending ranging from 11.6 to 24.4 percent at different parts of the distribution. The bottom panel of table 4.2 shows a similar trend for patients with a primary diagnosis of neoplasm. Overall spending for patients with this primary diagnosis grew at an average annual rate of 4.4 percent. Growth was highest among the top 10 percent of spenders with a primary diagnosis of neoplasm, where real growth averaged 5.6 percent per year.

Since circulatory disorders were by far the most common primary diagnosis among the high-cost elderly, we examined them more closely by dividing circulatory disorder diagnoses into 16 detailed groups using the Clinical Classifications for Health Policy Research (CCHPR). We were forced to collapse categories relating to ischemic heart disease into a single category and categories relating to cerebrovascular disease into a single category because coding procedures used for the NMES did not distinguish between these groups. Table 4.3 shows the individual CCHPR categories included under ischemic heart disease and cerebrovascular disease. Figure 4.7 shows the distribution of detailed diagnoses for the high-cost elderly with a primary diagnosis of circulatory disorder. Within this group, half had a diagnosis of ischemic heart disease in connection with their most expensive medical event. Cerebrovascular disease was diagnosed for 8.4 percent of the high-cost elderly during their most expensive medical event. In 1987, the average cost for an expensive medical event relating to ischemic heart disease was $18,548 among the high-cost elderly. Cerebrovascular conditions were slightly less costly, averaging $16,566 for expensive medical events among the high-cost elderly.

To gain a clearer picture of why these diseases are so costly, we looked at procedure codes in 1987. Unfortunately, most expensive medical events have no procedure codes. For the 30 percent of expensive events with procedure codes, the most common procedures are unspecified "other operations on vessels" occurring during 39.9 percent of these expensive medical events. "Other operations on heart and pericardium" and "operations on vessels of heart" are also common, occurring during 20.7 percent and 19.8 percent of coded expensive medical events, respectively. These procedure categories are broad, but they include bypass surgery, peripheral bypass surgery, and other operations performed to treat ischemic heart disease. Not surprisingly, the procedures that make circulatory disorders expensive are operations to treat circulatory diseases, particularly ischemic heart disease and other vascular diseases.

Using high-technology care to treat even common diagnoses contributes to

---

8. The trends shown in table 4.2 do not change when one looks at all respondents with a circulatory disorder instead of limiting the sample to those with a primary diagnosis of circulatory disorder.

Table 4.3   **Individual Diagnoses Included in Ischemic Heart and Cerebrovascular Diseases**

Diagnosis Group[a]	CCHPR Recode[b]	Examples
Ischemic heart disease	Acute myocardial infarction (heart attack)	
	Coronary atherosclerosis (hardening of arteries)	Postmyocardial infarction syndrome Intermediate coronary syndrome Old myocardial infarction Angina pectoris Other specified forms of chronic ischemic heart disease
	Other and ill-defined heart disease	Aneurysm of heart Myocardial degeneration Cardiovascular disease, unspecified Cardiomegaly Rupture of chordae tendinae Rupture of papillary muscle Acquired cardiac septal defect
Cerebrovascular disease	Acute cerebrovascular disease	Subarachnoid hemorrhage Intracerebral hemorrhage Other and unspecified intracranial hemorrhage
	Occlusion or stenosis of precerebral arteries	
	Other and ill-defined cerebrovascular disease	Cerebral atherosclerosis Other generalized ischemic cerebrovascular disease Hypertensive encephalopathy Cerebral aneurysm, nonruptured Cerebral arteritis Moyamoya disease Nonpyogenic thrombosis of intracranial venous sinus Transient global amnesia
	Transient cerebral ischemia Late effects of cerebrovascular disease	

[a]Used in the 1987 National Medical Expenditure Survey.
[b]Based on Clinical Classifications for Health Policy Research (CCHPR) recodes from the Agency for Health Care Policy and Research.

the growth in relative spending for the elderly. For example, during the period 1984–91, the share of Medicare patients with acute myocardial infarctions receiving catheterization, angioplasty, bypass surgery, or some combination of these, grew from 11 percent to 41 percent (Cutler et al. 1996). The proliferation of technology to treat cardiovascular disease probably drives much of the spending growth for the high-cost elderly with circulatory disorders.

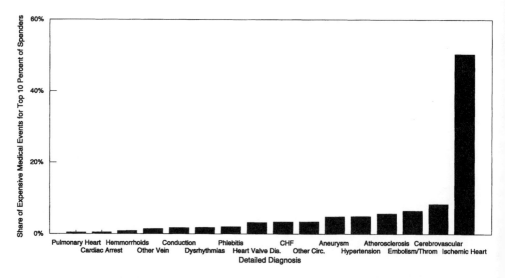

Fig. 4.7   Detailed diagnoses for high-cost elderly with primary diagnosis of circulatory disorder, 1987

4.3.2   High-Cost Infants

Understanding the reasons for increased spending among high-cost infants is more difficult than it is for the high-cost elderly. Generally, the surveys omit diagnosis codes for infants, and procedure codes are rarely used. This makes it impossible for us to use the "primary diagnosis" approach to understand high-cost users. Nor does the survey contain information such as birth weight of the infant or subsequent infant death.

However, the survey does provide some clues about what makes high-cost infants different from other infants. Sixty percent of high-cost infants experienced their most expensive medical event at the time of birth. It is much rarer for postbirth medical problems to lead to high spending. Two-thirds of high-cost infants did not undergo any surgery during their most expensive medical event.

Perhaps most striking is how long high-cost infants were in the hospital. The average length of stay for high-cost infants during their most expensive medical event was 23 nights in 1987. That was a dramatic increase over 1977, when high-cost infants stayed in the hospital only 13 nights during their most expensive stay.

Indeed, figure 4.8 shows the distribution of lengths of stay for all infants at the time of birth. Although the share of births requiring one-night or zero-night stays increased in 1987 compared with 1977, the upper tail of the distribution also increased in 1987 compared to 1977. For example, only 1 percent of births in 1977 were in the hospital over 30 days, compared to 6 percent in 1987.

The reason for a long stay at birth is generally complications related to pre-

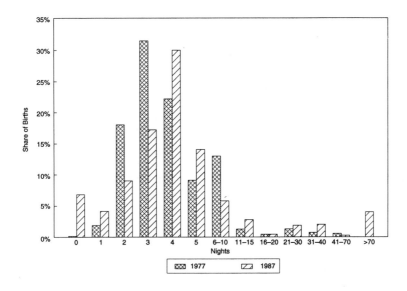

Fig. 4.8   Length of stay at time of birth, 1977–87

mature delivery. Infants born very prematurely tend to have respiratory or other developmental problems that either result in immediate death or require long hospital stays. Over time, as the technology available to treat these infants has improved, more of them may be surviving premature birth but requiring longer hospital stays.

This is consistent with the sketchy evidence that is available on the diagnosis of high-cost infants. Fifty-seven percent of high-cost episodes had a diagnosis code. Of these events, 24 percent had a condition code indicating that the baby was born prematurely—between 1,000 and 2,400 grams at birth. Among babies who were not high cost, less than 1 percent have a diagnosis code indicating that they were born prematurely.

The most common conditions among high-cost infants were disorders involving the respiratory system. Thirty-five percent of the high-cost sample had a respiratory condition in connection with their most expensive medical event. These ranged from postbirth respiratory disease to congenital respiratory anomalies and a variety of lower respiratory diseases. Respiratory conditions (pneumonia excepted) are a frequent complication of premature birth.

The evidence seems consistent with a story of increasing costs related to low birth weight. As technology to treat premature babies has improved, the costs of low-birth-weight children—and thus the overall costs of infants—have increased.

Historical trends in the proliferation of neonatal care support this contention. In particular, the increasing cost of infants after the mid-1970s is consistent with the major technological innovation of this period—the diffusion of neo-natal intensive care units (NICUs). NICUs are intensive care facilities specially designed for complications arising shortly after birth, such as respiratory failure or incomplete physical development. In 1976, the first year that the American Hospital Association kept data on this technology, 8 percent of hospitals had an NICU, and there were 5,630 NICU beds in total. By 1990, 19 percent of hospitals had an NICU, and the number of NICU beds had nearly doubled.[9] Among the largest hospitals (those with 400 or more beds), two-thirds had an NICU in 1990.

Although we cannot be certain with our data, we suspect that the diffusion of NICUs and their associated technologies explains much of the cost explosion for infants. Medical technology is buying us, in the crudest sense, care for infants who previously died at birth.

4.4   The Value of Medical Spending

Understanding the sources of cost growth is only one concern; determining the value of this spending is a second. In this section, we look at crude measures of outcomes to see whether there is some contemporaneous relation between spending increases and health. We do not interpret these data as causal. Instead, we are interested in examining whether the basic facts about health outcomes are consistent with the cost trends. If increased spending on cardiovascular disease and neoplasms in the elderly is not associated with better outcomes for patients with these diseases in the aggregate, it will be hard to argue that medical spending is buying much in the way of improved health. In future work, we intend to examine the causality issue in more detail.

4.4.1   The Health of the Elderly

Given that over 40 percent of the high-cost elderly have primary diagnoses relating to circulatory disorders or malignant neoplasms, one can look to mortality rates for these diseases for evidence on how outcomes for patients with these diseases have changed over time.

Figure 4.9 shows death rates for four groups of diagnoses: diseases of the heart, cerebrovascular disease, malignant neoplasms, and all other diagnoses. Over the three decades between 1960 and 1990, death rates for heart disease and cerebrovascular disease have plummeted. In 1960, the age-adjusted death rate due to heart disease was 287 per 100,000. This figure fell by nearly half, to 152 per 100,000, by 1990. Similarly, deaths due to cerebrovascular disease fell by 60 percent, from 80 per 100,000 in 1960 to 28 per 100,000 in 1990. This is certainly consistent with improved, but high-cost, medical care.

---

9. In both of these years, the number of NICUs is slightly understated because hospitals that had neonatal intensive care services as part of their medical/surgical ICU were not counted. The understatement is not likely to be large, however.

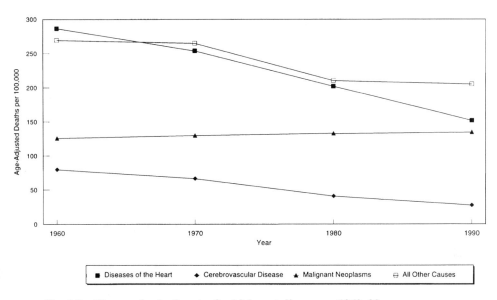

Fig. 4.9   Changes in death rates for high-cost diagnoses, 1960–90
Source: National Center for Health Statistics, *Trends in the Health of Older Americans: United States, 1994* (Hyattsville, Md., 1994).

In contrast to the improvements in outcomes for major circulatory diseases, deaths attributable to malignant neoplasms followed a slow but steady rising trend during this period, with deaths per 100,000 rising from 125 to 135. While mortality due to neoplasm has declined for younger ages, mortality rates have increased for those over age 50 (Cohen and Van Nostrand 1995). Similar trends in cancer mortality have been documented in Canada (Berkel 1995). Clearly, we have made little progress in preventing death from cancer over this period.

Of course, the technologies that have increased costs may not have been the ones that extended life. The source of reduced mortality for cardiovascular disease is the subject of great debate. The general consensus in the literature (Hunink et al. 1997) is that high-tech medicine has been less important in improved health than have been lifestyle modifications and pharmaceuticals that provide better primary prevention (reduced incidence of disease at all) and secondary prevention (reduced incidence of disease reoccurrence). But the contributions of these different factors are likely to change over time, and there has been much less analysis of the reasons for improved health over the past decade than in previous periods.

4.4.2   The Health of Infants

The most readily available measure of health outcomes for infants is infant mortality; we consider what has happened to mortality in the first year of life as spending has increased. Rather than look at overall infant mortality, how-

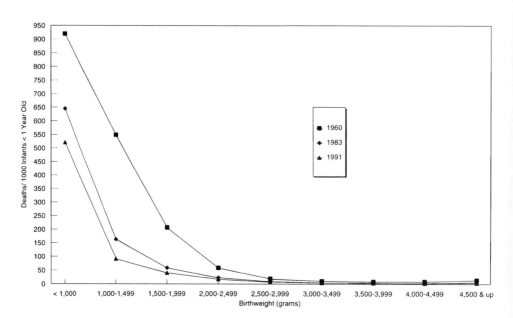

Fig. 4.10   Infant mortality by birth weight, 1960–91
Sources: National Center for Health Statistics, "A Study of Infant Mortality from Linked Records by Birth Weight, Period of Gestation and Other Variables: United States, 1960 Live Birth Cohort" (Rockville, Md., 1972); National Center for Health Statistics, *Health: United States 1995* (Hyattsville, Md., 1972).

ever, we examine infant mortality by birth weight. There are two reasons for this. First, to the extent that technological changes are concentrated among premature infants, mortality reductions should be concentrated in this group as well. In addition, exogenous changes in birth weights for infants will naturally affect infant mortality, and we want to purge these from our estimates.

Figure 4.10 shows infant mortality rates (deaths per 1,000 live births) in the years 1960, 1983, and 1991. Over the period 1960–91, dramatic gains were made in mortality outcomes for low-birth-weight babies, particularly those under 2,000 grams. Among babies born between 1,500 and 1,999 grams, deaths per 1,000 dropped 75 percent, from 207 to 40. Among the 1,000–1,499 gram babies, deaths per 1,000 dropped by 80 percent, from 549 to 91, over these three decades. Among those born under 1,000 grams, deaths per 1,000 fell by half, from 919 to 521.

In Figure 4.11 we show the annual percentage decline in infant mortality by birth weight from 1960 to 1983 and from 1983 to 1991. The most prominent feature in this graph is the way the decline in infant deaths occurs most rapidly in the low-birth-weight ranges, particularly in the 1,000–1,999 gram range. This is especially pronounced for the 1983–91 period. From 1960 to 1983, infant mortality reductions were greater among lighter infants but not by a large amount. The decline was about 5.5 percent per year for the lighter infants

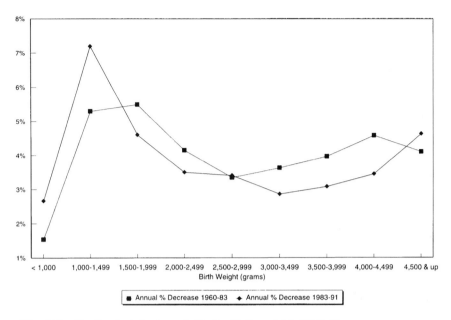

Fig. 4.11 Decline in infant mortality by birth weight, 1960–91
Sources: National Center for Health Statistics, "A Study of Infant Mortality from Linked Records by Birth Weight, Period of Gestation and Other Variables: United States, 1960 Live Birth Cohort" (Rockville, Md., 1972); National Center for Health Statistics, *Health: United States 1995* (Hyattsville, Md., 1972).

and perhaps 4 percent per year for the normal-birth-weight infants. After 1983, however, infant mortality reductions were particularly concentrated among the lightest infants. Mortality for infants born between 1,000 and 1,499 grams, for example, declined by 7 percent per year, compared to 3 percent per year for normal-birth-weight infants.

The increasing emphasis on mortality reductions for the lightest infants over the 1980s is consistent with the diffusion of medical care designed for very low birth weight infants. Recall that the costs of very expensive infant care increased most rapidly from the late 1970s to the late 1980s and that NICUs expanded most rapidly in this period. Thus, the evidence is certainly consistent with a fair return to medical spending.

The one exception to this story is the very lightest group—those born under 1,000 grams. For these infants, reductions in mortality have been low in all periods. We suspect that one reason we do not observe such rapid improvements in infant mortality for babies born under 1,000 grams is the way live births were counted. Although nothing changed in the official definition of live births over the 1960–91 period, it is plausible that very premature infants who died minutes after birth were not counted as live births when there was no technology available to treat them. Now that technology offers more possibilities for saving very low birth weight babies, these babies are more likely to be counted as live births so that the number of live births has increased in low-birth-weight ranges.[10]

Some evidence for this is provided by the increasing number of very low birth weight live births over time. The ratio of births below 1,000 grams to births between 1,000 and 1,499 grams has been increasing over time, even as the ratio of births between 1,000 and 1,499 grams and 1,500 and 1,999 grams has been relatively constant.

One drawback of using infant mortality to measure gains in infant health is that it provides no evidence about long-term outcomes for low-birth-weight babies. There is considerable evidence that low-birth-weight babies who survive the neonatal period are much more likely than heavier infants to have problems that continue throughout childhood and later in life (Institute of Medicine 1985; Saigal et al. 1996). The evidence presented here does not capture this component, which should be included in any evaluation of the costs and benefits of increased medical spending on infants.

4.5   Conclusions

Although growth and concentration in health care spending have been well documented, until now we have known little about the nature of this growth and the high-cost spenders that drive it. Our analysis shows a striking trend in the growth of health care spending. Not only is spending at a point in time highly concentrated at the top of the spending distribution, but growth in health care spending is highly concentrated as well. We find that growth is most rapid among the young, those less than 1 year old, and the old, those 65 years old or older. Within these rapid growth groups, increased spending is largely driven by those at the top of the spending distribution. We find that 89 percent of excess spending growth for infants originates from tremendous growth in health care spending for the top 10 percent of the spending distribution of infants. For the elderly, 66 percent of excess spending growth originates from high-cost users. Among the young, this spending often is associated with birth, and a connection with premature birth seems likely. Among the old, circulatory disorders and neoplasms are the most common primary, or high-cost, diagnoses.

In our initial attempts to see whether gains in health outcomes are consistent with increased spending, we find that high spending growth on a particular population or condition is accompanied by gains in health outcomes for these conditions over time. While overall infant mortality has plummeted since 1960, the reductions are largest among low-birth-weight babies. In our analysis of diseases driving high-cost elderly spending, we find that deaths due to circula-

---

10. Across types of medical care, diagnosis of a disease is strongly associated with ability to treat the disease. See Cutler and Richardson (1997).

tory disorders have decreased dramatically over time, even during periods when mortality due to other causes is relatively constant. The trend in mortality for malignant neoplasms is an exception to the broad finding that where spending is most concentrated gains in health outcomes are great. Future research should try to determine whether the correlation between high spending and health gains is causal. Regardless of whether this relationship is causal, our findings suggest that one can understand more about the growth in health care spending by learning more about technologies aimed at helping very ill infants and elderly.

Our results also have implications for forecasting medical spending growth over time. Common forecasts of medical spending do not account for changes in relative spending by age over time. Our results suggest that this understates the future growth of costs, since the fastest growing age group, the population aged 85 and over, is also the group whose costs are growing most rapidly.

Finally, determining what caused the shift in resources toward infants and the elderly is important. Clearly, the advent of Medicare and Medicaid and the increased generosity of private health insurance coverage have played a role in raising the share of medical spending on infants and the elderly. However, little is known about the mechanism that transforms increased insurance coverage into technological improvements, and ultimately gains in health. Answering these questions should be part of any agenda to contribute to debates on medical spending.

Appendix

Table 4A.1   Average Spending by Age Group 1963–87

Age Group	1953[a]	1963	1970	1977	1987	Average Annual Percentage Change 1953–87	Average Annual Percentage Change 1963–1987
Under 1	119.32	236.12 (28.06)	353.45 (56.37)	789.71 (273.84)	2,502.64 (1,117.01)	9.0	9.8 (1.9)
1–4	119.32	163.53 (11.41)	391.09 (137.23)	333.80 (20.63)	654.75 (82.33)	5.0	5.8 (0.5)
5–14	157.68	175.17 (11.94)	246.91 (21.93)	322.56 (17.67)	465.51 (27.80)	3.2	4.1 (0.3)
15–24	257.40	353.48 (28.77)	791.35 (218.94)	588.03 (19.25)	880.55 (49.74)	3.6	3.8 (0.4)
25–34	298.31	434.84 (28.87)	672.93 (51.63)	773.44 (30.21)	1,057.75 (45.22)	3.7	3.7 (0.3)
35–44	340.92	456.33 (35.56)	553.70 (48.46)	810.53 (37.84)	1,095.19 (51.33)	3.4	3.6 (0.4)
45–54	340.92	566.35 (44.70)	728.57 (62.80)	1,043.4 (46.44)	1,742.03 (135.66)	4.8	4.7 (0.5)
55–64	409.11	570.96 (56.29)	1,207.54 (209.88)	1,476.35 (86.06)	2,410.35 (137.86)	5.2	6.0 (0.4)
65–74	434.68	622.08 (49.62)	1,124.76 (82.19)	1,835.15 (96.26)	3,874.34 (191.32)	6.4	7.6 (0.4)
75–84	434.68	688.66 (92.64)	1,217.90 (147.28)	2,400.05 (207.79)	4,694.39 (280.08)	7.0	8.0 (0.6)
85+	434.68	447.46 (117.04)	1,310.52 (508.05)	2,845.54 (357.94)	5,650.04 (433.79)	7.5	10.6 (1.1)

Notes: Average spending is in real (1987) dollars using the GDP deflator. Numbers in parentheses are standard errors.

[a]The 1953 age groups are 0–5, 6–17, 18–24, 25–34, 35–54, 55–64, and 65+. Average spending for 5–24-year-olds was constructed assuming a uniform age distribution.

References

Anderson, Odin W., Patricia Colette, and Jacob Feldman. 1963. *Changes in family medical care expenditures and voluntary health insurance: A five-year resurvey.* Cambridge, Mass.: Harvard University Press.

Anderson, Odin W., and Jacob Feldman. 1956. *Family medical costs and voluntary health insurance: A nationwide survey.* New York: Blackstone Division.

Berk, M. L., and A. C. Monheit. 1992. The concentration of health expenditures: An update. *Health Affairs* 11 (4): 145–49.

Berkel, H. J. 1995. Progress against cancer . . . ? *Journal of the Louisiana Medical Society* 147 (10): 449–57.

Center for Health Administration Studies and National Opinion Research Center. 1965 and 1972. *Survey of Health Services Utilization and Expenditures* 1963 & 1970 data tapes. Chicago: National Opinion Research Center.

Chassin, Mark, et al. 1987. Does inappropriate use explain geographic variations in the use of health care services? *Journal of the American Medical Association* 258: 2533–37.

Cohen, R. A., and J. F. Van Nostrand. 1995. Trends in the health of older Americans: United States, 1994. *Vital and Health Statistics,* vol. 3, no. 30. Rockville, Md.: National Center for Health Statistics.

Cutler, David M. 1995. The incidence of adverse medical outcomes under prospective payment. *Econometrica* 63:29–50.

Cutler, David M., Mark McClellan, Joseph P. Newhouse, and Dahlia Remler. 1996. Are medical prices declining? NBER Working Paper no. 5750. Cambridge, Mass.: National Bureau of Economic Research.

Cutler, David M., and Elizabeth Richardson. 1997. Measuring the health of the United States population. Cambridge, Mass.: Harvard University, June. Mimeograph.

Cutler, David M., and Douglas Staiger. 1996. Measuring the benefits of medical progress. Cambridge, Mass.: Harvard University. Mimeograph.

Greenspan, Allan M., et al. 1988. Incidence of unwarranted implantation of permanent cardiac pacemakers in a large medical population. *New England Journal of Medicine* 318:158–63.

Hunink, Maria G. M., et al. 1997. The recent decline in mortality from coronary heart disease, 1980–1990: The effect of secular trends in risk factors and treatment. *Journal of the American Medical Association* 227 (7): 535–42.

Institute of Medicine. Committee to Study the Prevention of Low Birthweight. 1985. *Preventing low birthweight.* Washington, D.C.: National Academy Press.

Kahn, Katherine L., et al. 1990. Comparing outcomes of care before and after implementation of the DRG-based Prospective Payment System. *Journal of the American Medical Association* 264:1984–88.

Levit, Katharine R., et al. 1994. National health spending trends, 1960–1993. *Health Affairs* 13 (5): 14–31.

Lubitz, James D., and Gerald F. Riley. 1993. Trends in Medicare payments in the last year of life. *New England Journal of Medicine* 328:1092–96.

Lubitz, James D., et al. 1995. Longevity and Medicare expenditures. *New England Journal of Medicine* 332:999–1003.

McClellan, Mark, and Joseph P. Newhouse. 1995. The marginal benefits of medical technology. Cambridge, Mass.: Harvard University. Mimeograph.

National Center for Health Statistics. 1979. *Medical coding manual: National Health Interview Survey.* Hyattsville, Md.: U.S. Department of Health and Human Services, Public Health Service.

———. 1979 and 1989. *National Medical Expenditure Survey 1977 & 1987 public use tapes.* Hyattsville, Md.: U.S. Department of Health and Human Services, Public Health Service.

Newhouse, Joseph P. 1993. *Free for all? Lessons from the RAND Health Insurance Experiment.* Cambridge, Mass.: Harvard University Press.

Newhouse, Joseph P., et al. 1992. Medical care costs: How much welfare loss? *Journal of Economic Perspectives* 6 (3): 3–21.

Saigal, Saroj, et al. 1996. Self-perceived health status and health-related quality of life of extremely low-birth-weight infants at adolescence. *Journal of the American Medical Association* 276 (6): 453–59.

Staiger, Douglas, and Gary Gaumer. 1994. Prospective payment and hospital mortality. Cambridge, Mass.: Harvard University. Mimeograph.

Triplett, Jack E. 1997. What's different about health? Human repair and car repair in national accounts. Washington, D.C.: U.S. Bureau of the Census, Bureau of Economic Analysis. Mimeograph.

Winslow, Constance M., et al. 1988a. The appropriateness of carotid endarterectomy. *New England Journal of Medicine* 318:721–27.

———. 1988b. The appropriateness of performing coronary artery bypass surgery. *Journal of the American Medical Association* 260:505–10.

Comment   David Meltzer

This paper examines the distribution of medical care costs among and within age groups over a 40-year period in order to try to better understand why medical care has become so expensive over time and what its value to society has been. It comes to three basic conclusions:

1. Costs have increased disproportionately for the young and the very old.

2. Most of these costs are associated with "technically" intensive aspects of medicine—the care of premature babies and adults with cardiovascular disease or cancer.

3. With respect to the value of these treatments, there is some evidence that mortality has decreased in the areas where expenditures have increased.

The first part of the paper makes two basic points. The first is that costs have increased disproportionately for the very young and old compared to the "middle-aged" (ages 1–64!). The second is that essentially all of the disproportionate growth in spending on the very young and old is accounted for by high-cost users in those groups.

These are important facts and may suggest where we will need to look if we are to control health care costs. Nevertheless, it seems possible that the two points may really be condensed into just one: that health care expenditures in all age groups have risen because of a few high-cost users. The growth in costs among the middle-aged may be relatively smaller because there may be pro-

David Meltzer is assistant professor in the Section of General Internal Medicine, Department of Economics, and Harris Graduate School of Public Policy at the University of Chicago and a research associate of the National Bureau of Economic Research.

portionately fewer very sick people in the middle-aged group—yet just as much rapid growth in costs among those who are very sick. It is hard to distinguish these two possibilities from the paper because all the results are normalized relative to that middle group.

This suggests that it would be useful to break down spending at each point in time by age group and percentile within each age group then trace the growth in these amounts over time. This procedure would describe, for example, the annual percentage growth in expenditures for the 90th percentile of middle-aged individuals—a rate that is hidden by the normalization in the current calculations. These numbers could be reported either in per capita terms or as total spending for the age group. If reported as changes in total spending, the changes could then be decomposed into changes in the numbers of people in the age group and changes in per capita expenditures conditional on age and percentile in the spending distribution within that age group.

I suspect that this would show that the sickest middle-aged people have also had extremely fast growth in costs. Such a finding could help provide some further insight into why spending among middle-aged people has grown less quickly than spending among the very young and old. One possibility is that we have increased our aggressiveness in treating the very young and old. However, it is equally plausible that, if a smaller percentage of middle-aged people tend to be sick than of the very young or the elderly, a given percentile among the middle-aged will be healthier than the same percentile among the other age groups. The middle-aged group would thus be less likely to have rapid growth in costs if most cost growth is among the very sick. Examination of the growth of expenditures among the highest percentiles across these age groups might help distinguish these hypotheses.

This also suggests that it may be useful to analyze cost growth across the life cycle over time by examining the percentage of costs due to people with costs above some level in real terms (e.g., $1,000 in 1994 dollars). Another approach would be to look at growth in the costs of treating specific conditions arising at different ages—for example, heart attacks at ages 40, 50, 60, 70, and so on. The comparison would then change from an age-normalized one to an objective one not affected by the relative health of others of the same age.

With appropriate longitudinal data, one could then begin to trace out lifetime costs. This could be particularly useful in instances where changes in expenditures lead to changes in survival that, in turn, induce future expenditures. Some of the work I have done on future costs in medical cost-effectiveness analysis suggests that these costs may be nontrivial (Meltzer 1997). Future costs such as these might imply that the costs associated with an intervention performed in a particular age group could appear in other age groups. This could provide some insight into why costs have increased so greatly among the very sick by separating changes in survival from technical change, changes in prices, and other causes of increased health care costs.

The second part of the paper examines particular diagnoses for these high-cost users: heart disease and cancer for the old and premature birth for the young. There are no surprises here; these diagnoses are well recognized to be the most common causes of serious illness in these age groups. Of course, it is worth remembering that these conditions may be to some extent acute manifestations of chronic conditions. For example, heart disease may result from diabetes, or premature birth may result from maternal substance abuse. This fact is important because it is a reminder that the most effective and efficient way to decrease the costs of caring for the extremely ill may, in some cases, be prevention.

The third part of paper shows that mortality has tended to decrease in those areas where costs have increased. The authors are careful not to say that this relationship is causal, but the motivation is clearly to suggest that medical expenditures in these areas may be of value. I suspect that this is correct but agree with the authors that other interpretations are possible. Expenditures may have increased because mortality has decreased. For example, imagine that we observe decreased cardiovascular mortality at the same time that costs increase. It could be that high spending to save patients from heart attacks leads to decreased mortality. On the other hand, it could also be that the accidental discovery of an inexpensive intervention that saves lives (e.g., administration of an aspirin in the emergency room to a patient with chest pain) also leads to prolongation of life and years of interventions with questionable value at the margin (e.g., cardiac catheterizations and treatment for congestive heart failure). To take another example, cancer can sometimes cause elevations in the amount of calcium in the blood (hypercalcemia) and can sometimes present itself first with the symptoms of hypercalcemia. Hypercalcemia can be fatal in the absence of good treatments, but effective and fairly inexpensive treatments are now available. The consequence, however, could be that people with cancer survive long enough to receive chemotherapy and incur the high costs associated with it. Even if chemotherapy had no effect on survival, we could observe that chemotherapy expenditures increase at the same time that cancer mortality decreases, but there would be no causal connection between the two, and most of the expenditures would be wasted.

Still, it seems likely that health care expenditures on the seriously ill have often had substantial payoffs. The vast body of literature from randomized clinical trials suggests that there is value in a wide range of medical interventions. The question is ultimately not whether medical interventions have had any value in improving health, but the magnitude of their contributions compared to other causes of improving health, such as expenditures on public health and increases in income and education. With respect to tuberculosis, there is evidence that the largest decreases in the burden of disease resulted from improvements in nutrition and public health that occurred before the development of effective treatments (McKeown 1988). With respect to cardiovascular mortality, older work suggested that treatment might not have been as important as prevention in reducing mortality, but some of the newest work suggests that more recent trends have been more heavily influenced by high-tech interventions. For example, a recent study suggests that more than three-fourths of the increase in survival after heart attacks in Minneapolis in the 1980s was due to acute interventions (McGovern et al. 1996). Of course, this is survival after a heart attack, and prevention may have a much bigger overall effect on cardiovascular mortality than does treatment. With cancer death rates not declining for the most part, it is hard to argue that huge strides have been made in that area (Bailar 1997). Certainly, it is possible that we would have done better with an emphasis on prevention and screening rather than an emphasis on acute treatment.

As a brief aside about the relatively slow decline in death rates for very low birth weight babies, it is worth noting that, while this could reflect changes in definitions of live versus still births, as suggested by the authors, it could also reflect the fact that existing technology is often simply not able help these infants.

I would like to make two last points about the implications of this research. First, the fact that health care costs are highly concentrated among high-cost users and are remaining so over time suggests that cost containment will have to come by controlling costs among this group. To the extent that this is accomplished through changes in the financing and organization of health care as opposed to cost-reducing medical technologies, it is likely to be difficult without managed care or prospective payment for inpatient care because most deductibles in traditional insurance are too small to be relevant for these sorts of large expenditures. One possible exception is medical savings accounts with very high deductibles. These arrangements might be effective, but there are still many questions concerning their intertemporal aspects as well as their effects on adverse selection. This may be somewhat less true to the extent that decreases in outpatient coverage can decrease inpatient utilization as suggested by the RAND Health Insurance Experiment (Manning et al. 1987). However, the RAND experiment lasted only a relatively short time, and it is quite possible that policies that try to lower expenditures by limiting outpatient expenditures would backfire by increasing preventable illness and hospitalization over the long run.

The second point is that patterns and trends in health care expenditures over the past 40 years may or may not be a good guide to the future. The increasingly popular view of health care as part of wellness—ranging from prevention to sports medicine—could cause much more growth in costs to occur among the well than among the severely ill. That seems unlikely, however.

References

Bailar, John. 1997. Cancer undefeated. *New England Journal of Medicine* 336 (22): 1569–74.

Manning, Willard, Joseph Newhouse, Naihua Duan, et al. 1987. Health insurance and the demand for medical care: Evidence from a randomized experiment. *American Economic Review* 77:251–77.

McGovern, P. G., et al. 1996. Recent trends in acute coronary heart disease—mortality, morbidity, medical care, and risk factors. *New England Journal of Medicine* 334 (14): 884–90.

McKeown, Thomas. 1988. *The origins of human disease.* Cambridge: Blackwell.

Meltzer, David. 1997. Accounting for future costs in medical cost-effectiveness analysis. *Journal of Health Economics* 16 (1): 33–64.

5 Diagnosis and Medicare Expenditures at the End of Life

Alan M. Garber, Thomas MaCurdy, and Mark McClellan

5.1 Introduction

Expenditures for health care at the end of life (EOL) have been the object of considerable policy interest. To many observers, aggressive health care administered shortly before death is wasteful, at least in retrospect, and there is no doubt that elderly Americans use health care heavily before they die. In 1990, the 6.6 percent of Medicare recipients who died accounted for 22 percent of program expenditures (Lubitz and Riley 1993). Some question the benefits of such care, especially because severe morbidity and disability may compromise any years of life potentially gained from such treatments in the very old (Verbrugge 1984). The increasing use at advanced ages of costly and aggressive health interventions, whose impact on both the quality and length of life is often unknown, exacerbates these concerns. For example, the use of radical prostatectomy for invasive prostate cancer increased threefold between 1983 and 1989 (Lu-Yao and Greenberg 1994), and the rate at which both new and old major operations are performed in the elderly increased dramatically from 1972 to 1981 (Valvona and Sloan 1985) and 1984 to 1991 (McClellan and Skinner 1994). These phenomena have helped to stimulate a growing literature on the significance and policy implications of EOL health care utilization and expenditures (Bayer et al. 1983; Lubitz and Prihoda 1984; Scitovsky 1984,

Alan M. Garber is a Health Services Research and Development Senior Research Associate of the Department of Veterans Affairs, associate professor of medicine, economics, and health research and policy at Stanford University, and a research associate and director for the Health Care Program at the National Bureau of Economic Research. Thomas MaCurdy is professor of economics at Stanford University and a research associate of the National Bureau of Economic Research. Mark McClellan is professor of economics and medicine at Stanford University and a faculty research fellow of the National Bureau of Economic Research.

This research was supported in part by grants AG07651, AG11706, and AG05842 from the National Institute on Aging, by grant 96170 from the Commonwealth Fund, and by grant 26749 from the Robert Wood Johnson Foundation.

1988, 1994; Lubitz and Riley 1993; Schneiderman and Jecker 1993; Emanuel and Emanuel 1994). Because nearly all the elderly are insured by Medicare, federal funds pay for most EOL medical costs.

Despite the provocative findings of this literature, the policy significance of EOL care is uncertain. Although they consume a large share of health dollars, patients nearing death are not the main source of large Medicare payments. Most high-cost elderly patients are survivors, not decedents. In 1990, for example, the 8 percent of Medicare enrollees with over $10,000 in Medicare costs accounted for 65 percent of all Medicare expenditures. Even if every enrollee who died that year generated more than $10,000 in payments, they could have been responsible for at most one-third of this total (Helbing 1993). In addition, some studies suggest that the elderly who are most likely to die are not responsible for the greatest expenditures; for the very old, for example, the ratio of spending for decedents to that for survivors narrows, and more of the excess costs are for nursing home care, which presumably is an unavoidable expense (Scitovsky 1988).

An even more important limitation of an exclusive focus on EOL expenditures is its implicitly retrospective nature. If health care providers knew ex ante which patients would die despite their interventions, expenditures on dying patients could potentially be reduced. Yet often it is impossible, even with detailed clinical records, to predict *individual* patient mortality with sufficient specificity to influence medical decision making. Even after days of detailed intensive care unit (ICU) measurements, systems such as APACHE can reliably predict death in only a small minority of ICU patients (Atkinson et al. 1994), and such systems have not been shown to lead to more cost-effective decisions than expert physicians would otherwise make. Furthermore, specific policies designed to reduce EOL expenditures, such as advance directives and "do not resuscitate" orders, seem to have had only a modest impact on overall expenditures. As a result, some analysts have recently argued that attempts to limit EOL expenditures through both of these methods are unlikely to reduce health expenditures substantially (Emanuel and Emanuel 1994). Simpler rationing rules, such as age-based rationing of costly operations or ICU admissions, are even less likely to lead to selective reductions in "futile" care, since there are no simple characteristics such as age or disease that clearly predict whether interventions are likely to be worthwhile.

Moreover, such rationing rules would have large effects on expenditures only if implemented at ages when life expectancy remains substantial, such as below age 70 (Garber and Fuchs 1992). Finally, some of the expenditures at the end of life are for treatments designed to provide comfort rather than to prevent death. Refinements in methods to predict death and avoid inappropriately aggressive care would not reduce these expenditures.

Although there is growing disenchantment with policies designed to identify and avert "futile care" at the *individual* patient level, the consequences of population-level policies merit further exploration. Little is known about the impact on the cost and outcomes of elderly populations with major illnesses of policies that would lead to a generally more parsimonious approach to health care delivery. Would efforts designed to limit major operations, aggressive diagnostic approaches, or care delivered in ICUs lead to an increase in mortality rates, health complications, and other adverse outcomes in the populations with major illness? Would substantial cost savings result from associated reductions in technology use? Further analysis of alternative patterns of care for severe illness might also reveal why policies designed to reduce EOL expenditures have had such disappointing results. Perhaps decedents consume substantial care because it is not clear until very late in the course of their illnesses that they will die. Even if they are known to suffer from illnesses that are nearly always fatal, it may be neither feasible nor desirable to reduce expenditures for their health care. For example, advance directives may not save money because they induce the substitution of one set of services (such as nursing home or hospice care) for another (hospital care), because high-intensity care at the end of life does not prolong life for long enough to generate large increases in expenditures, or because intensive spending is already concentrated on treatments that have a significant chance of improving outcomes.

As a first step toward addressing these questions, we sought to explore the basic characteristics of Medicare recipients during the time approaching their deaths. The magnitude of health expenditures for Medicare enrollees with major illnesses and uncertainty about their impact on costs and outcomes underscores the need for basic information about the prevalence, causes, and concomitants of the conditions that commonly lead to death among the U.S. elderly. What characteristics of patients are associated with high-cost care and high probability of death? Can these characteristics be used to identify individuals and populations with major illnesses prospectively, to guide policies on the use of intensive treatments? What is the distribution of costs and survival across high-risk illnesses, and across individuals with a given illness, and how are they correlated? In this study, we report the results of analyses of expenditures patterns for Medicare decedents, investigating in particular the diseases and demographic characteristics of decedents and the associated Medicare expenditures.

5.2   Analytic Data Files

Our analysis builds from linked Medicare Part A (hospital) and Part B (physician and other services) claims files. These files include information regarding all covered services (inpatient, hospital outpatient, ambulatory and physician care, durable medical equipment, home care, hospice care, and skilled nursing and rehabilitation care), key discharge information (discharge destination and condition), and demographic information (including residence information at the zip code level). Demographic information is updated annually.

Failure to meet deductible or out-of-pocket limits for the year will rarely lead to omission of significant utilization data in the major illness population that we study. EOL Medicare expenditures and disease incidence figures are calculated from patients in the Medicare 5 percent beneficiary sample (obtained from the Health Care Financing Administration [HCFA]) who died between 1986 and 1990 and who also received inpatient treatment for cancer, cardiovascular, cerebrovascular, "fatal," or "frailty" disorders during the last year of their lives. The specific diagnostic groupings are based on an aggregation scheme developed by McClellan to map primary diagnosis codes into one of 155 disease groupings. In this approach, a "cancer patient" is someone who, at any point during the last year of life, was admitted to a hospital with a primary diagnosis of oropharyngeal, upper gastrointestinal, colorectal, intraabdominal, upper respiratory tract, lung, thoracic, bone/connective tissue, skin, breast, genital, prostate, central nervous system, or other primary solid cancers; secondary solid cancer/metastasis; leukemia/lymphoma; or malignancies of the bladders, kidneys, or urinary tract. Similarly, anyone with a primary diagnosis of acute myocardial infarction, old myocardial infarction, ischemic heart disease, cardiac valve disorders, cardiac conduction defects, cardiac arrhythmia, ventricular arrhythmia, supraventric/unspecified arrythmia, atrial fibrillation, or heart failure is a "cardiovascular patient." "Cerebrovascular patients" are those with a primary diagnosis of hemorrhagic stroke, occlusive stroke, transient cerebral ischemia, or chronic cerebrovascular deficits. "Fatal" disorders are colorectal cancer, lung cancer, breast cancer, prostate cancer, acute myocardial infarction, ischemic heart disease, ventricular arrhythmia, heart failure, occlusive stroke, chronic obstructive pulmonary disease (which includes chronic bronchitis, emphysema, and some forms of asthma), and hip fracture. Finally, the "frailty" conditions we consider are septicemia, endocrine/metabolic disorders (except diabetes), pneumonia, pyelonephritis, cystitis/lower urinary tract infections, and failure to thrive/malnutrition. (For each of tables 5.11 through 5.13, below, the percentage in the upper left-hand corner indicates the percentage of those who died who fall into these diagnosis groupings.)

We merge the Part A (MEDPAR), Part B (BMAD), and outpatient (OUTPAT) files to calculate total Medicare reimbursements for each patient during the indicated periods. For Part A and outpatient claims, we use the HCFA reported reimbursement amounts. For a Part B claim, reimbursed amounts are calculated as 0.8 times allowed charges. All claims are deflated to 1990 dollars by the CPI. We sum these three components to calculate total reimbursements for each person during the period. The "Percentage of Total Medicare Expenditures" sums total reimbursements for the group and expresses this sum as a fraction of total reimbursements for all patients in the HCFA 5 percent sample from 1986–90. Thus the cost figures reported are based on reimbursements and do not include the patient's out-of-pocket expenditures for noncovered services, copayments, or deductibles.

To calculate disease incidence among the group in any time period, we count by disease type all primary diagnoses of beneficiaries in the specified sub-sample during that time period, rank the diseases, and report the 14 most prevalent as percentages. In other words, the 28.1 percent number reported in table 5.12 for heart failure during the last year of life for cardiovascular patients means: of all the hospital admissions for cardiovascular patients during the last year of life, 28.1 percent of the admissions had a primary diagnosis of heart failure.

Sample selection is based on gender and age during the year that the patient dies. As a means of summarizing the presentation efficiently, we allocate age at death into three categories: 65–74, 75–84, and 85–99. It bears repeating that there are a few sample restrictions that we place on every analysis we do. To be in *any* of our tables, patients must be between the ages of 65 and 99. We also exclude all prior or current HMO members.

5.3   Results

Table 5.1 shows basic characteristics of Medicare beneficiaries who die. Approximately 15 percent of all Medicare beneficiaries will die in a five-year period. As the age and sex distribution of decedents shows, women tend to be

Table 5.1   **Characteristics of Medicare Beneficiaries Who Die, 1986–90**

Characteristic	Percentage
Age and Sex Distribution (% Male/% Female)	
65–69	7.9/5.4
70–74	9.7/7.1
75–79	10.4/9.11
80–84	9.0/10.3
80–84	9.0/10.3
85–89	6.2/10.1
90–100	4.2/10.6
Racial Distribution (%)	
White	89.0
Black	8.2
Asian	1.1
Percentage of Beneficiaries Who Die Each Year	
1986	4.59
1987	4.58
1988	4.67
1989	4.61
1990	4.54
1986–90	15

somewhat older when they die than men, and deaths are distributed fairly evenly over the five-year age intervals. Approximately 90 percent of all decedents are white, the rest being predominantly black. A high percentage—roughly 5 percent—of all Medicare beneficiaries die each year, greatly exceeding the annual mortality rates for other segments of the population.

Table 5.2, which reports overall Medicare expenditures before death, shows that the vast majority of Medicare recipients have claims in the year before they die. Only about 4 percent do not have claims. The mean expenditures in the last year of life over the 1986–90 period total about $13,000, more than half of which occurred in the last three months of life. The 50th percentile, however, is only about $8,000 in the last year of life, reflecting the influence of the upper tail of the distribution of expenditures, which can reach very large amounts. Reimbursements of $8,000 can easily be incurred in a single hospitalization.

Panel B of table 5.2 shows the percentage of deaths associated with several of the most common diagnoses. These are expressed in three ways. The column labeled "first" gives the percentage of times the given diagnosis was listed as the primary diagnosis during the first hospital admission of the year of death. "Last" refers to the same figure, except for the final admission during the year, rather than the first. To the extent that patients have a single hospital admission during the last year of life, these figures should be similar. The columns labeled "all year" and "all period" refer to the percentage of times the given diagnosis was the principal diagnosis during any admission during the corresponding time period.

For most diagnoses, it does not matter which of these definitions of prevalence is used. Among the exceptions to this general observation are conditions that cause death in elderly women who are already chronically ill with one or more other diseases. For example, in the last year of life, the prevalence of pneumonia as a diagnosis rises from 5.61 percent as initial diagnosis to 7.07 percent if the final diagnosis is the basis for the prevalence estimate. Similarly, the percentage of deaths attributable to septicemia nearly doubles if the final admission is the basis for the diagnosis. Some other diagnoses, such as hip fracture, are more common as first than as last diagnoses. The shifts in rankings reflect the characteristics of these disorders. Septicemia, which refers to disseminated bloodstream infection, ordinarily causes death in the setting of one or more other chronic diseases and would more often be the final blow that fells a severely ill man or woman than a deadly disease occurring in isolation. Pneumonia is another condition that frequently causes death when associated with multiple other chronic diseases or a general state of debilitation. This is particularly true of aspiration pneumonia, which is caused by inability to swallow and cough appropriately. It is often the final cause of death in individuals suffering from stroke, Alzheimer's disease, prolonged mechanical ventilation, and numerous other conditions that depress neurological or respiratory function. Pneumonia, septicemia, and related conditions can indeed cause death,

Table 5.2   Medicare Expenditures and Diagnoses for the Elderly during Periods before Death, 1986–90

	A. Expenditures before Death		
	Last Year of Life	Last Six Months	Last Three Months
Fraction without expenditures (%)	3.68	4.70	6.19
Expenditures within group (1990 $)			
10th Percentile	350.03	147.06	56.34
25th Percentile	3,161.21	1,570.99	617.50
50th Percentile	8,386.09	6,103.53	4,724.39
75th Percentile	17,418.53	13,358.85	10,244.88
90th Percentile	29,744.18	23,109.15	18,146.77
Mean	12,833.99	9,857.08	7,709.81
Percentage of total Medicare expenditures due to category	24	18	14

(*continued*)

Table 5.2 (continued)

B. Percentages of Deaths Associated with Most Prevalent Diagnoses[a]

Primary Diagnosis	Last Year of Life			Last Six Months			Last Three Months		
	First	All Year	Last	First	All Period	Last	First	All Period	Last
Heart failure	6.57	6.66	6.62	6.38	6.33	6.23	6.01	6.02	6.38
Pneumonia	5.61	6.18	7.07	5.65	6.11	6.73	5.72	6.02	6.38
Acute myocardial infarction	4.48	4.56	4.91	4.56	4.60	4.79	4.52	4.57	4.70
Occlusive stroke	4.46	4.36	4.52	4.25	4.20	4.30	4.00	3.99	4.06
Secondary solid cancer/ metastasis	2.85	3.28	3.91	3.21	3.44	3.78	3.32	3.43	3.57
Metabolic disorders	2.39	2.80	3.10	2.45	2.75	2.93	2.50	2.64	2.72
Lung cancer	2.31	2.13	2.23	2.14	2.06	2.14	1.96	1.96	2.03
Ischemic heart disease	2.19	1.90	1.43	1.80	1.60	1.30	1.47	1.35	1.18
Hip fracture	2.12	1.86	1.62	1.83	1.62	1.43	1.57	1.42	1.27
Septicemia	1.28	1.78	2.48	1.45	1.86	2.39	1.62	1.93	2.30
Acute respiratory failure	1.36	1.71	2.27	1.49	1.80	2.22	1.62	1.86	2.16
Cystitis/lower urinary tract infection	1.43	1.57	1.57	1.40	1.44	1.42	1.30	1.30	1.27
Intestinal diseases	1.52	1.55	1.55	1.45	1.46	1.44	1.37	1.36	1.33
Colorectal cancers	1.43	1.22	1.12	1.17	1.07	1.01	0.99	0.95	0.93

[a]"First" ("last") refers to the primary diagnosis associated with the first (last) hospital admission reported in the specified period, and "all year" (or "all period") refers to the average number of times the diagnosis is reported as the primary diagnosis for all hospital visits during period.

yet prevention or successful treatment of these conditions, because they so frequently occur as complications of other severe illnesses, might not prolong survival substantially.

No single condition stands out as a dominant cause of death among Medicare recipients. Only two diagnostic categories account for more than 6 percent of the deaths in any of the time periods, and the single most common diagnosis for any of the time periods before death is pneumonia, which only reaches a prevalence of 7.07 percent as the last listed diagnosis in the last year of life. Congestive heart failure, the most prevalent diagnosis in the last year of life under most definitions, is a disorder of highly variable severity. Under some circumstances, it can be rapidly fatal, but more often, it is a chronic disease with a moderately high mortality rate. It often occurs in association with acute myocardial infarction, or with a diagnosis of coronary artery disease. But its frequency as a cause of death may reflect the high prevalence of the disorder rather than a very high mortality rate.

Tables 5.3 through 5.10 present similar figures for the following groups: all women, all men, women in three different age groups, and men in three different age groups. These tables demonstrate that women have causes of death that are broadly similar to those of men, with an upward shift in the age distribution. Of course, there are obvious exceptions, such as some of the cancers. There are also distinct age trends in the prevalence of differing causes of death.

As tables 5.3 (women) and 5.4 (men) demonstrate, overall Medicare expenditures in the periods before death are similar for men and women. About half of the expenditures are for Part A, and median expenditures in the last year of life are somewhat higher than $8,000 for both men and women. Similarly, mean expenditures are between $12,000 and $13,000. The two genders display similar trends of increasing use of resources as death approaches, as can be seen in the shorter intervals before death represented as one moves to the right on each of these tables. The prevalences of specific causes of death are also similar. However, men are much more likely to die of lung cancer, reflecting the greater prevalence of this disease in current cohorts of the elderly, while hip fracture is much more common among women.

Some of the differences in the prevalences of disorders may also reflect differences in the distribution of age at death. Because women survive longer than men, disorders that are common in far advanced age, such as hip fracture, are more likely to be a cause of death in women. Some hints of this phenomenon can be seen in the results stratified by age, which appear in tables 5.5 through 5.10. Tables 5.5, 5.6, and 5.7 give EOL expenditures and diagnoses for women in the 65–74, 75–84, and 85–99 age ranges, respectively. Tables 5.8, 5.9, and 5.10 give results for men in the same age categories. A comparison of the tables for women shows that median Medicare expenditures in the last year of life, and in the shorter intervals before death, decline substantially with advancing age, from about $11,000 for ages 65–74 to less than $6,000 for ages

Table 5.3   **End-of-Life Medicare Expenditures and Diagnoses for All Women Aged 65–99, 1986–90**

A. Expenditures before Death

	Last Year of Life	Last Six Months	Last Three Months	Last One Month
Fraction without expenditures (%)	2.5	3.3	4.1	9.0
Expenditures within group (1990 $)				
10th Percentile	401.11	175.85	97.09	13.61
25th Percentile	3,185.39	1,666.49	810.72	139.65
50th Percentile	8,022.81	5,947.50	4,814.41	3,328.49
75th Percentile	16,445.12	12,784.59	10,141.22	6,480.02
90th Percentile	28,087.96	22,034.09	17,799.71	12,644.80
Mean	12,241.14	9,498.38	7,689.52	5,247.92
Percentage of total Medicare expenditures due to category	12.0	9.3	7.5	5.1
Percentage hospitalized	77.8	72.7	67.6	59.0

B. Percentages of Deaths Associated with Most Prevalent Diagnoses[a]

Primary Diagnosis	All Year	All Period	All Period	All Period
Heart failure	8.8	9.1	9.1	9.1
Pneumonia	7.1	7.7	8.1	8.7
Acute myocardial infarction	5.4	6.2	6.6	7.4
Occlusive stroke	6.1	6.5	6.6	6.8
Secondary solid cancer/metastasis	4.0	4.8	5.2	5.2
Metabolic disorders	3.9	4.1	4.2	4.2
Lung cancer	1.8	1.9	1.9	1.9
Ischemic heart disease	2.4	2.0	1.8	1.6
Hip fracture	3.3	2.9	2.6	2.3
Septicemia	2.4	2.8	3.2	3.7
Acute respiratory failure	2.0	2.4	2.7	3.1
Cystitis/lower urinary tract infection	2.4	2.4	2.3	2.1
Intestinal diseases	2.4	2.4	2.4	2.4
Colorectal cancers	1.7	1.5	1.4	1.3

[a]See table 5.2 note.

Table 5.4 **End-of-Life Medicare Expenditures and Diagnoses for All Men Aged 65–99, 1986–90**

A. Expenditures before Death				
	Last Year of Life	Last Six Months	Last Three Months	Last One Month
Fraction without expenditures (%)	5.5	6.7	7.9	13.0
Expenditures within group (1990 $)				
10th Percentile	226.34	94.73	43.44	0
25th Percentile	2,927.27	1,434.64	757.66	157.21
50th Percentile	8,334.66	6,164.09	4,944.61	3,395.49
75th Percentile	17,659.02	13,740.51	10,872.33	6,892.18
90th Percentile	30,183.92	23,775.41	19,187.10	13,666.71
Mean	12,888.78	10,064.74	8,168.33	5,618.38
Percentage of total Medicare expenditures due to category	11.4	8.9	7.2	5.0
Percentage hospitalized	76.6	71.9	67.1	59.2

B. Percentages of Deaths Associated with Most Prevalent Diagnoses[a]				
Primary Diagnosis	All Year	All Period	All Period	All Period
Heart failure	8.1	8.4	8.3	8.2
Pneumonia	8.5	9.3	9.8	10.6
Acute myocardial infarction	5.9	6.5	6.9	7.6
Occlusive stroke	4.9	5.0	5.1	5.2
Secondary solid cancer/metastasis	3.8	4.7	5.0	5.0
Metabolic disorders	3.0	3.4	3.6	3.6
Lung cancer	3.6	3.9	4.0	4.1
Ischemic heart disease	2.9	2.5	2.2	2.0
Hip fracture	1.6	1.5	1.5	1.4
Septicemia	1.9	2.3	2.5	2.9
Acute respiratory failure	2.1	2.5	2.8	3.2
Cystitis/lower urinary tract infection	1.6	1.5	1.5	1.4
Intestinal diseases	1.6	1.6	1.6	1.6
Colorectal cancers	1.6	1.4	1.4	1.3

[a]See table 5.2 note.

Table 5.5 **End-of-Life Medicare Expenditures and Diagnoses for Women Aged 65–74, 1986–90**

A. Expenditures before Death

	Last Year of Life	Last Six Months	Last Three Months	Last One Month
Fraction without expenditures (%)	4.7	5.5	6.3	10.8
Expenditures within group (1990 $)				
10th Percentile	431.77	183.23	92.47	0
25th Percentile	4,504.67	3,178.22	1,821.63	324.16
50th Percentile	11,453.55	8,431.85	6,305.00	4,124.64
75th Percentile	22,387.00	17,226.08	13,378.95	8,171.44
90th Percentile	36,636.28	28,422.45	22,905.77	16,128.67
Mean	16,354.99	12,654.92	10,141.49	6,855.78
Percentage of total Medicare expenditures due to category	3.8	2.9	2.4	1.6
Percentage hospitalized	81.1	77.1	72.5	64.2

B. Percentages of Deaths Associated with Most Prevalent Diagnoses[a]

Primary Diagnosis	All Year	All Period	All Period	All Period
Heart failure	6.8	6.9	6.9	6.6
Pneumonia	4.5	4.8	5.1	5.4
Acute myocardial infarction	5.7	6.4	6.9	7.7
Occlusive stroke	4.0	4.1	4.2	4.5
Secondary solid cancer/metastasis	7.6	8.9	9.4	9.4
Metabolic disorders	3.2	3.6	3.7	3.9
Lung cancer	3.7	3.9	3.9	3.9
Ischemic heart disease	3.0	2.6	2.4	2.3
Hip fracture	1.0	0.8	0.8	0.7
Septicemia	1.8	2.1	2.4	2.8
Acute respiratory failure	2.8	3.3	3.6	4.1
Cystitis/lower urinary tract infection	1.1	1.1	1.1	1.0
Intestinal diseases	1.9	2.0	2.0	2.0
Colorectal cancers	1.9	1.5	1.4	1.3

[a]See table 5.2 note.

Table 5.6   **End-of-Life Medicare Expenditures and Diagnoses for Women Aged 75–84, 1986–90**

A. Expenditures before Death				
	Last Year of Life	Last Six Months	Last Three Months	Last One Month
Fraction without expenditures (%)	1.8	2.6	3.3	8.1
Expenditures within group (1990 $)				
10th Percentile	615.44	262.96	137.26	18.47
25th Percentile	3,970.87	2,690.80	1,442.65	223.77
50th Percentile	9,134.01	6,666.91	5,333.75	3,689.92
75th Percentile	17,626.68	13,729.12	10,928.20	6,905.76
90th Percentile	29,344.14	23,065.35	18,599.56	13,262.79
Mean	13,175.82	10,201.44	8,260.60	5,610.56
Percentage of total Medicare expenditures due to category	4.8	3.7	3.0	2.0
Percentage hospitalized	81.2	76.2	71.2	62.3

B. Percentages of Deaths Associated with Most Prevalent Diagnoses[a]				
Primary Diagnosis	All Year	All Period	All Period	All Period
Heart failure	8.7	9.0	9.1	9.0
Pneumonia	6.3	6.8	7.3	7.8
Acute myocardial infarction	6.2	7.1	7.6	8.5
Occlusive stroke	6.2	6.6	6.7	7.0
Secondary solid cancer/metastasis	4.0	4.9	5.2	5.1
Metabolic disorders	3.6	3.8	3.8	3.8
Lung cancer	1.8	1.9	2.0	2.0
Ischemic heart disease	2.6	2.2	2.0	1.7
Hip fracture	2.7	2.4	2.2	2.0
Septicemia	2.2	2.6	3.0	3.5
Acute respiratory failure	2.1	2.5	2.8	3.3
Cystitis/lower urinary tract infection	2.2	2.2	2.2	2.0
Intestinal diseases	2.4	2.4	2.4	2.4
Colorectal cancers	1.9	1.7	2.0	1.6

[a]See table 5.2 note.

Table 5.7 **End-of-Life Medicare Expenditures and Diagnoses for Women Aged 85–99, 1986–90**

	A. Expenditures before Death			
	Last Year of Life	Last Six Months	Last Three Months	Last One Month
Fraction without expenditures (%)	1.8	2.6	3.4	8.7
Expenditures within group (1990 $)				
10th Percentile	307.03	140.25	79.62	13.32
25th Percentile	1,798.76	667.94	390.78	80.00
50th Percentile	5,857.67	4,463.64	3,715.98	2,334.00
75th Percentile	12,172.60	9,582.33	7,709.30	5,284.47
90th Percentile	20,463.42	16,330.76	13,574.97	9,933.94
Mean	8,874.33	6,928.36	5,669.62	3,934.56
Percentage of total Medicare expenditures due to category	3.4	2.7	2.2	1.5
Percentage hospitalized	72.5	66.7	61.3	52.8

	B. Percentages of Deaths Associated with Most Prevalent Diagnoses[a]			
Primary Diagnosis	All Year	All Period	All Period	All Period
Heart failure	10.1	10.6	10.8	11.0
Pneumonia	9.7	10.6	11.1	12.0
Acute myocardial infarction	4.4	5.1	5.5	6.1
Occlusive stroke	7.3	8.0	8.2	8.4
Secondary solid cancer/metastasis	1.5	1.9	2.1	2.1
Metabolic disorders	4.7	4.9	5.0	4.9
Lung cancer	0.4	0.5	0.5	0.4
Ischemic heart disease	1.7	1.3	1.1	1.0
Hip fracture	5.5	4.7	4.4	3.8
Septicemia	3.0	3.5	3.9	4.6
Acute respiratory failure	1.4	1.7	1.9	2.3
Cystitis/lower urinary tract infection	3.5	3.5	3.4	3.1
Intestinal diseases	2.8	2.7	2.6	2.6
Colorectal cancers	1.4	1.3	1.2	1.1

[a]See table 5.2 note.

Table 5.8   End-of-Life Medicare Expenditures and Diagnoses for Men Aged 65–74, 1986–90

A. Expenditures before Death

	Last Year of Life	Last Six Months	Last Three Months	Last One Month
Fraction without expenditures (%)	9.5	11.1	12.5	17.9
Expenditures within group (1990 $)				
10th Percentile	25.44	0	0	0
25th Percentile	1,609.77	756.13	474.95	105.76
50th Percentile	8,707.63	6,389.96	4,975.84	3,224.83
75th Percentile	19,775.05	15,418.45	12,042.93	7,319.49
90th Percentile	34,208.76	26,970.12	21,359.53	15,016.63
Mean	14,035.75	10,951.27	8,797.96	6,000.79
Percentage of total Medicare expenditures due to category	4.6	3.6	2.9	2.0
Percentage hospitalized	72.4	68.1	63.7	56.5

B. Percentages of Deaths Associated with Most Prevalent Diagnoses[a]

Primary Diagnosis	All Year	All Period	All Period	All Period
Heart failure	7.3	7.4	7.4	7.3
Pneumonia	5.9	6.4	6.8	7.3
Acute myocardial infarction	6.4	7.0	7.4	8.1
Occlusive stroke	4.1	4.1	4.2	4.3
Secondary solid cancer/metastasis	5.5	6.6	7.1	7.3
Metabolic disorders	2.4	2.8	3.0	3.2
Lung cancer	5.6	6.0	6.0	6.3
Ischemic heart disease	3.7	3.2	2.9	2.6
Hip fracture	0.6	0.5	0.5	0.5
Septicemia	1.5	1.8	2.1	2.4
Acute respiratory failure	2.4	2.8	3.1	3.6
Cystitis/lower urinary tract infection	0.8	0.8	0.8	0.7
Intestinal diseases	1.4	1.4	1.5	1.5
Colorectal cancers	1.6	1.4	1.4	1.3

[a]See table 5.2 note.

Table 5.9 **End-of-Life Medicare Expenditures and Diagnoses for Men Aged 75–84, 1986–90**

A. Expenditures before Death

	Last Year of Life	Last Six Months	Last Three Months	Last One Month
Fraction without expenditures (%)	3.4	4.4	5.4	10.4
Expenditures within group (1990 $)				
10th Percentile	455.60	201.80	102.81	0
25th Percentile	3,701.15	2,432.73	1,186.08	245.34
50th Percentile	9,090.48	6,667.19	5,298.82	3,665.82
75th Percentile	18,091.57	14,026.89	11,213.21	7,156.25
90th Percentile	30,197.42	23,889.06	19,361.26	13,925.42
Mean	13,370.19	10,419.25	8,495.22	5,853.86
Percentage of total Medicare expenditures due to category	4.8	3.8	3.1	2.1
Percentage hospitalized	79.8	75.0	70.1	61.9

B. Percentages of Deaths Associated with Most Prevalent Diagnoses[a]

Primary Diagnosis	All Year	All Period	All Period	All Period
Heart failure	8.3	8.6	8.5	8.4
Pneumonia	8.6	9.4	9.9	10.7
Acute myocardial infarction	6.1	6.8	7.2	8.0
Occlusive stroke	5.1	5.3	5.4	5.5
Secondary solid cancer/metastasis	3.6	4.4	4.6	4.5
Metabolic disorders	2.9	3.3	3.4	3.4
Lung cancer	3.3	3.6	3.7	3.7
Ischemic heart disease	2.8	2.4	2.2	2.0
Hip fracture	1.5	1.4	1.4	1.3
Septicemia	1.8	2.2	2.5	2.9
Acute respiratory failure	2.2	2.7	3.0	3.4
Cystitis/lower urinary tract infection	1.6	1.5	1.5	1.3
Intestinal diseases	1.7	1.6	1.6	1.6
Colorectal cancers	1.7	1.5	1.4	1.4

[a]See table 5.2 note.

Table 5.10   **End-of-Life Medicare Expenditures and Diagnoses for Men Aged 85–99, 1986–90**

A. Expenditures before Death

	Last Year of Life	Last Six Months	Last Three Months	Last One Month
Fraction without expenditures (%)	2.9	3.9	4.8	9.8
Expenditures within group (1990 $)				
10th Percentile	351.14	155.77	84.68	7.57
25th Percentile	2,908.81	1,447.23	719.24	125.18
50th Percentile	6,816.93	5,219.88	4,346.01	3,100.67
75th Percentile	13,637.80	10,715.21	8,695.29	5,938.30
90th Percentile	22,748.42	18,461.93	15,359.66	11,019.81
Mean	10,061.70	7,912.15	6,500.39	4,536.90
Percentage of total Medicare expenditures due to category	2.0	1.5	1.3	0.9
Percentage hospitalized	77.7	72.3	67.3	58.9

B. Percentages of Deaths Associated with Most Prevalent Diagnoses[a]

Primary Diagnosis	All Year	All Period	All Period	All Period
Heart failure	8.9	9.4	9.5	9.5
Pneumonia	12.4	13.8	14.5	15.6
Acute myocardial infarction	4.6	5.1	5.4	6.0
Occlusive stroke	5.7	6.0	6.1	6.2
Secondary solid cancer/metastasis	1.8	2.3	2.3	2.3
Metabolic disorders	4.3	4.6	4.7	4.7
Lung cancer	1.1	1.2	1.2	1.2
Ischemic heart disease	1.8	1.5	1.3	1.1
Hip fracture	3.5	3.4	3.2	2.9
Septicemia	2.6	3.1	3.4	3.7
Acute respiratory failure	1.3	1.7	1.9	2.4
Cystitis/lower urinary tract infection	2.7	2.7	2.5	2.4
Intestinal diseases	1.8	1.7	1.7	1.7
Colorectal cancers	1.4	1.3	1.3	1.3

[a]See table 5.2 note.

85–99. Mean expenditures also drop, from $16,000 to $9,000. Similar declines with age are seen using different time periods—the last six months, the last three months, and the last one month—instead of the last year of life.

The diagnoses associated with death also show a distinct age trend. Heart failure becomes an increasingly common cause of death as age advances, and the same is true of pneumonia and occlusive stroke. Secondary solid cancer/ metastasis and lung cancer become less common with advancing age as causes of death, as does acute respiratory failure.

Mean Medicare expenditures in the last year of life do not decline as much for men as for women, and median expenditures in the last year of life decline from about $9,000 in men aged 65–74 to $7,000 in men aged 85–99, a less dramatic decline than for women. A higher fraction of men aged 65–74 than women of the same ages die without having Medicare reimbursements in the last year of life, possibly reflecting the influence of sudden and unexpected deaths that are more likely at the earlier ages than at far advanced ages. The prevalence of congestive heart failure as a cause of death does not rise as rapidly for men as for women, but pneumonia and septicemia do become considerably more common at the most far advanced ages, while lung cancer and other cancers decline in prevalence as causes of death at the far advanced ages. The most dramatic age-related increase in prevalence is for hip fracture, rising from 0.6 percent in the last year of life for men aged 65–74 to 3.5 percent for men aged 85–99.

These figures provide few surprises about the causes of death, but they demonstrate that the most common causes of death are the most prevalent chronic diseases among the elderly, rather than diseases that have intrinsically very high mortality rates. Furthermore, it appears likely that some of the causes that are acute, such as pneumonia and septicemia, cannot always be anticipated, and at the time of onset of these conditions, dramatic reductions in expenditures may not be possible, because the time until death is fairly short.

Further evidence about EOL expenditures for individuals with specific diseases appears in tables 5.11 through 5.13. Table 5.11 presents findings similar to those of the previous tables, except that only men and women with a principal diagnosis of a common cancer during the last year of life are included. The fraction of decedents who did not have Medicare expenditures in the last year of life appears in the first row, which shows that it is a rare phenomenon. However, more than 5 percent have no expenditures in the last month, perhaps because many were not hospitalized and received little medical care during the terminal phases of their illnesses. Mean expenditures in the last year of life for cancer decedents approach $20,000, a fairly high number, but expenses tend to be lower in the last month of life than for many other conditions.

Panel B of table 5.11 shows the prevalence of different diagnoses listed during hospital admissions of enrollees with cancer during the last year of their lives. Not surprisingly, most of the diagnoses are of cancers. But other common conditions also appear in the list of leading diagnoses, such as pneumonia and

Table 5.11 **Medicare Expenditures and Diagnoses for Patients Admitted with Cancer in Last Year of Life, 1986–90**

A. Expenditures before Death

17.1% of Deaths	Last Year of Life	Last Six Months	Last Three Months	Last One Month
Fraction without expenditures (%)	0.1	0.4	0.9	5.1
Expenditures within group (1990 $)				
10th Percentile	5,732.81	3,914.83	2,059.53	71.33
25th Percentile	9,799.36	6,753.64	4,776.79	2,095.94
50th Percentile	16,086.52	12,037.71	8,874.29	4,865.29
75th Percentile	24,920.66	19,082.74	14,711.08	8,961.63
90th Percentile	36,127.09	28,012.59	21,943.31	19,291.27
Mean	19,349.31	14,635.81	11,138.30	6,767.55
Percentage of total Medicare expenditures due to category	6.2	4.7	3.6	2.2

B. Percentages of Deaths Associated with Most Prevalent Diagnoses[a]

Primary Diagnosis	All Year	All Period	All Period	All Period
Secondary solid cancer/ metastasis	15.9	18.2	20.2	21.9
Lung cancer	9.8	10.6	11.6	13.1
Cancer therapy	8.6	6.8	4.4	2.0
Colorectal cancers	5.0	4.9	5.0	5.5
Leukemia/ lymphoma	4.6	5.1	5.7	6.7
Intra-abdominal cancers	3.8	4.3	4.8	5.5
Pneumonia	3.3	3.5	3.7	4.0
Metabolic disorders	3.2	3.7	4.0	4.1
Prostate cancer	2.6	2.2	2.1	2.1
Upper gastrointestinal cancers	2.4	2.6	2.8	3.0
Heart failure	1.9	1.8	1.8	1.6
Genital cancers	1.8	1.7	1.7	1.8
Bladder cancer	1.8	1.5	1.3	1.1
Intestinal diseases	1.7	1.7	1.6	1.4

Note: "Cancer" includes admissions with the following principal diagnoses: oropharyngeal cancer, upper gastrointestinal cancer, colorectal cancer, intra-abdominal cancer, upper respiratory tract cancer, lung cancer, other respiratory tract cancer, thoracic cancer, bone/connective tissue cancer, skin cancer, breast cancer, genital cancer, prostate cancer, central nervous system cancer, bladder cancer, kidney cancer, urinary tract cancer, leukemia/lymphoma, and secondary solid cancer/metastasis.

[a]See table 5.2 note.

metabolic disorders, which can be complications of cancer, and heart failure, which is less frequently a complication. Because heart failure is so common at advanced ages, it may have been an unrelated coexisting disorder in many of the Medicare recipients who had cancer. Thus just under 60 percent of the diagnoses in the last year of life were of a common form of cancer. The remaining 40 percent were a combination of complications, coexisting conditions that may have been unrelated, and less common cancers.

Table 5.12 reports analogous findings for decedents with cardiovascular diseases. These diseases as a group were somewhat less expensive than the cancers. The diagnoses listed as most prevalent are primarily subsets of cardiovascular diseases. However, other common acute and chronic conditions (e.g., pneumonia, metabolic disorders, chronic obstructive pulmonary disease, intestinal diseases, cystitis, and septicemia) listed as leading diagnoses during the last year of life are not cardiovascular diseases and may only be related insofar as the cardiovascular diseases can be debilitating. For example, a patient who suffers a stroke—which is a form of cardiovascular disease—may develop a partial paralysis, which can subsequently lead to skin breakdown, wound infection, and septicemia. Thus a cardiovascular disorder can lead to debilitation, which in turn predisposes the patient to an "unrelated" infectious condition.

Septicemia is one of the chronic disorders that we refer to as "frailty diseases" (see table 5.13). This is a loosely grouped set of diagnoses that can be considered markers for debility or, in the case of malnutrition and failure to thrive, debilitating conditions in their own right. Most often the elderly Medicare enrollees who are admitted to hospitals with one of these diagnoses have multiple chronic health problems. All of these patients have at least one hospital admission during the last year of life, and mean Medicare expenditures for their care is similar to the mean for cancers and cardiovascular diseases. Pneumonia is the most prevalent diagnosis in this group, presumably because it is one of the most common of the frailty diseases and because it often coexists with other frailty diseases.

All of the preceding tables describe characteristics of decedents. Table 5.14 presents information about the importance of decedents within the population of high-cost Medicare enrollees. Several categories of high-cost users are listed in the column headings—those who have the highest 2 percent of expenditures in a given year, the top decile, and the top two deciles over varying periods. Note that about 20 percent of all beneficiaries in a five-year period will be in the top decile during one year. Note also that a relatively high fraction of the high-cost users die during the relevant time period, and that those who are most consistently high-cost users (top 2 percent during a year, top decile in any year, top two deciles in any two years) have mortality rates approaching one-third, but that all of the high-cost users have high mortality rates. Mean expenditures are highest for those in the top 2 percent, at more than $33,000 per year, but the top decile has mean expenditures of more than $17,000. This figure is similar to the mean expenditures for the decedents, even though most

Table 5.12   **Medicare Expenditures and Diagnoses for Patients Admitted with Cardiovascular Diseases in Last Year of Life, 1986–90**

A. Expenditures before Death

22.1% of Deaths	Last Year of Life	Last Six Months	Last Three Months	Last One Month
Fraction without expenditures (%)	0.1	0.3	0.7	2.7
Expenditures within group (1990 $)				
10th Percentile	4,254.72	3,199.37	2,195.08	206.57
25th Percentile	6,624.80	5,037.50	4,175.30	2,913.64
50th Percentile	12,361.06	9,056.24	6,987.58	4,847.17
75th Percentile	22,403.30	16,830.47	12,980.01	8,178.35
90th Percentile	36,519.65	28,488.52	22,781.68	15,574.22
Mean	17,458.70	13,397.50	10,733.55	7,427.60
Percentage of total Medicare expenditures due to category	7.2	5.5	4.4	3.1

B. Percentages of Deaths Associated with Most Prevalent Diagnoses[a]

Primary Diagnosis	All Year	All Period	All Period	All Period
Heart failure	28.1	28.5	28.4	27.4
Acute myocardial infarction	12.9	15.1	17.7	22.3
Ischemic heart disease	8.6	7.9	7.3	6.6
Pneumonia	4.0	4.1	4.1	4.2
Occlusive stroke	2.5	2.5	2.5	2.7
Atrial fibrillation	2.3	2.2	2.0	1.7
Metabolic disorders	2.2	2.2	2.2	1.9
Cardiac conduction defects	2.1	2.0	1.8	1.7
Acute respiratory failure	1.6	1.7	1.8	1.9
Chronic obstructive pulmonary disease	1.1	1.0	0.9	0.7
Intestinal diseases	1.0	0.9	0.8	0.7
Cystitis/lower urinary tract infection	1.0	0.9	0.9	0.7
Acute upper respiratory disease	1.0	0.8	0.7	0.4
Septicemia	0.9	1.0	1.1	1.3

Note: "Cardiovascular diseases" includes admissions with the following principal diagnoses: acute myocardial infarction, old myocardial infarction, ischemic heart disease, cardiac valve disorders, cardiac conduction defects, supraventric/unspecified arrhythmia, atrial fibrillation, cardiac arrhythmia, ventricular arrhythmia, and heart failure.

[a]See table 5.2 note.

Table 5.13　　　**Medicare Expenditures and Diagnoses for Patients Admitted with "Frailty" Diseases in Last Year of Life, 1986–90**

A. Expenditures before Death

21.7% of Deaths	Last Year of Life	Last Six Months	Last Three Months	Last One Month
Fraction without expenditures (%)	0	0.2	0.6	2.8
Expenditures within group (1990 $)				
10th Percentile	4,549.24	3,261.04	2,057.93	122.30
25th Percentile	7,692.76	5,465.55	4,256.39	2,627.57
50th Percentile	13,825.57	10,229.51	7,692.10	4,761.35
75th Percentile	23,459.67	17,639.38	13,450.94	8,225.17
90th Percentile	36,502.35	27,604.00	21,229.83	13,851.48
Mean	18,263.36	13,714.02	10,596.77	6,693.77
Percentage of total Medicare expenditures due to category	7.4	5.6	4.3	2.7

B. Percentages of Deaths Associated with Most Prevalent Diagnoses[a]

Primary Diagnosis	All Year	All Period	All Period	All Period
Pneumonia	21.0	23.0	25.7	30.3
Metabolic disorders	10.5	11.6	12.4	12.9
Septicemia	6.3	7.3	8.5	10.6
Cystitis/lower urinary tract infection	6.1	6.1	6.1	5.7
Heart failure	5.7	5.4	5.0	4.5
Occlusive stroke	2.6	2.4	2.3	2.1
Cancer therapy	2.6	2.0	1.2	0.4
Metastatic cancers	2.2	2.4	2.4	2.1
Lung cancer	1.6	1.7	1.7	1.6
Ischemic heart disease	1.4	1.1	0.8	0.6
Acute upper respiratory disease	1.4	1.2	1.0	0.7
Chronic obstructive pulmonary disease	1.4	1.2	1.1	1.0
Acute respiratory failure	1.4	1.6	1.8	2.1
Intestinal diseases	1.4	1.3	1.2	1.0

Note: "Frailty" includes admissions with the following principal diagnoses: septicemia, endocrine/metabolic disorders, pneumonia, pyelonephritis, cystitis/lower urinary tract infections, and failure to thrive/malnutrition.

[a]See table 5.2 note.

Table 5.14   High-Cost Users of Medicare and Their Share of Reimbursements

		Intensity and Duration of Utilization				
	Top 2% in Any Year	Top Decile in Any Year	Top Decile in Only One Year	Top 2 Deciles in Any Two Years[a]	Top 2 Deciles in Any Three Years[a]	Top 2 Deciles in Any Four Years[a]
Percentage of all beneficiaries	7.3	30.01	20.97	16.51	7.13	2.47
Percentage who die at end of period	29.8	27.8	25.03	33.2	31.6	28.59
Age and Sex Distribution (% Male/% Female)						
65–69	4.7/3.6	6.1/6.0	6.9/6.6	4.4/4.7	3.2/3.8	2.3/3.3
70–74	11.4/9.2	11.2/11.3	11.1/11.1	10.9/11.6	10.7/12.2	10.5/13.7
75–79	10.9/9.6	10.9/12.2	10.6/11.9	11.4/12.9	11.7/14.0	11.7/15.3
80–84	7.1/7.8	8.1/11.1	7.9/10.8	8.6/12.1	8.8/12.9	8.5/13.3
85–89	3.7/5.2	4.8/8.4	4.8/8.4	5.0/9.0	5.0/9.3	4.7/9.2
90–100	12.6/14.2	2.8/6.9	2.8/7.18	2.7/6.6	2.5/6.1	2.2/5.3
Racial Distribution (%)						
White	87.1	88.3	88.9	88.9	88.3	88.3
Black	9.1	7.8	7.3	7.8	8.1	8.8
Other	1.6	1.5	1.4	1.3	1.2	1.2
Expenditures before Death						
Expenditures within group (1990 $)						
10th Percentile	21,989.94	7,604.16	7,338.59	6,403.11	6,070.53	4,844.91
25th Percentile	24,152.80	9,369.49	8,661.23	7,872.77	7,528.66	6,097.30
50th Percentile	28,804.05	13,204.98	11,682.84	10,972.00	10,407.46	8,334.82
75th Percentile	36,924.66	20,398.70	17,472.55	16,389.00	15,118.08	11,920.88
90th Percentile	49,040.28	31,018.88	26,947.36	23,797.24	21,521.56	16,890.92
Mean	33,340.62	17,080.72	15,046.58	13,613.08	12,580.79	12,429.15

(continued)

Table 5.14   (continued)

		Intensity and Duration of Utilization				
	Top 2% in Any Year	Top Decile in Any Year	Top Decile in Only One Year	Top 2 Deciles in Any Two Years[a]	Top 2 Deciles in Any Three Years[a]	Top 2 Deciles in Any Four Years[a]
Percentage of total Medicare expenditures due to category	25	52.79	32.42	46.19	27.63	15.78
		Percentage of Deaths Associated with Most Prevalent Diagnoses				
Heart failure	4.94	4.41	4.05	5.39	6.00	6.38
Ischemic heart disease	13.63	6.19	6.00	5.72	6.00	6.57
Pneumonia	3.56	4.21	4.12	4.67	4.84	4.88
Occlusive strike	3.09	4.08	4.40	3.87	3.38	2.76
Chronic obstructive pulmonary disease	1.62	1.58	1.33	2.02	2.53	3.30
Acute myocardial infarction	4.48	3.88	4.26	3.01	2.42	1.96
Intestinal diseases	2.36	2.37	2.23	2.32	2.40	2.47
Hip fracture	1.99	4.81	5.31	3.08	2.20	1.58
Endocrine/metabolic disorders	1.66	1.78	1.68	2.05	2.14	2.09
Acute pulmonary	2.49	2.04	1.89	1.75	1.70	1.69
Cystitis/lower urinary tract infection	1.06	1.12	1.05	1.46	1.64	1.66
Acute upper respiratory disease	0.74	0.86	0.70	1.22	1.61	2.09
Colorectal cancers	2.17	2.77	2.93	1.69	1.18	0.82
Secondary solid cancer/metastasis	2.08	1.78	1.75	1.56	1.13	0.80

[a]10th Decile ≥ 1 year.

of the high-cost users did not die. The distribution of prevalent diagnoses is broadly similar to the distribution for decedents, except that ischemic heart disease is responsible for a disproportionate share of expenditures among the top 2 percent.

5.4 Conclusions

The results reported here are among the preliminary findings from a study of Medicare expenditures for the care of the severely ill elderly. The limitations of Medicare claims files, which constitute the primary data source for this research effort, are well known: the reliability of some of the diagnostic coding is uncertain, there is little clinical detail, there is no information about noncovered services (such as outpatient pharmacy use and many forms of long-term care), and detailed socioeconomic characteristics (such as income, occupational or educational history, and living arrangements) are not recorded. But the claims files have many advantages for descriptive analyses of health expenditures and other phenomena at the end of life. They include a representative sample of all elderly Americans, the diagnostic codes are likely to be reasonably accurate guides to the overall prevalence of various health conditions at death, and they include information about virtually all hospitalizations and office visits among Medicare recipients.

Because the data analyzed here are from the late 1980s, few Medicare patients were enrolled in HMOs or covered by capitated contracts. Thus our analysis does not address current concerns that incentives to limit costs and utilization under managed care might lead to undertreatment of Medicare recipients. Our planned analyses of more Medicare data from the 1990s will investigate these issues, which are of particular concern for the most vulnerable Medicare recipients—those with chronic or severe illnesses. Under Medicare's traditional fee-for-service reimbursement arrangements, such patients generated a high level of utilization, which often meant substantial revenues for physicians and possibly for hospitals (Medicare's Prospective Payment System, which reimburses hospitals a fixed amount per admission, makes hospital incentives ambiguous). Under capitation, such patients are undesirable. Because the altered incentives may have their most prominent manifestations in care administered near the end of life, comparisons of care for decedents between managed care and fee-for-service based on recent data may be illuminating.

Like previous investigators, we found that Medicare expenditures for decedents decline with advancing age. Health expenditures not covered by Medicare, such as nursing home expenses, tend to rise with age for both decedents and "survivors." Scitovsky, who examined nursing home as well as typical Medicare-covered services, reported that the decline with age in decedent expenses for Medicare was largely offset by increases in expenses for noncovered services (Scitovsky 1988). Recent changes in Medicare reimbursement policy appear to have increased substantially the expenditures for home health, hospice, and other nonhospital services; these may alter the pattern of expenditures for decedents in ways that were not apparent during the late 1980s. Such expenses may vary by diagnosis, a possibility that we will be able to explore with more recent claims files.

Overall, our results confirm that decedents have disproportionately high Medicare expenses. But a comparison with high-cost users suggests that many of the characteristics of decedents are similar to those of high-cost Medicare enrollees who do not die during a given period. This suggests that, at least based on the information available in Medicare claims files, it will be difficult to formulate policies to limit expenditures for individuals in the last year of life without simultaneously limiting health care delivered to sick Medicare recipients who have the potential to survive. A detailed study of sophisticated mortality prediction models in the severely ill elderly (SUPPORT; Murphy and Cluff 1990) implies that more comprehensive clinical information is unlikely to change this conclusion.

References

Atkinson, S., D. Bihari, et al. 1994. Identification of futility in intensive care. *Lancet* 344:1203–6.

Bayer, R., D. Callahan, et al. 1983. The care of the terminally ill: Mortality and economics. *New England Journal of Medicine* 309:1490–94.

Emanuel, E., and L. Emanuel. 1994. The economics of dying: The illusion of cost savings at the end of life. *New England Journal of Medicine* 330 (8): 540–44.

Garber, A., and V. Fuchs. 1992. Health expenditures for older Americans: 1990–2040. Stanford, Calif.: Stanford University. Working paper.

Helbing, C. 1993. Medicare program expenditures. *Health Care Financing Review,* 1992 (Suppl.): 23–54.

Lubitz, J., and R. Prihoda. 1984. The use and costs of Medicare services in the last two years of life. *Health Care Financing Review* 5:117–31.

Lubitz, J., and G. Riley. 1993. Trends in Medicare payments in the last year of life. *New England Journal of Medicine* 328 (15): 1092–96.

Lu-Yao, G., and E. Greenberg. 1994. Changes in prostate cancer incidence and treatment in USA. *Lancet* 343:251–54.

McClellan, M., and J. Skinner. 1994. The lifetime distribution of Medicare benefits. Cambridge, Mass.: Harvard University. Working paper.

Murphy, D., and L. Cluff. 1990. SUPPORT: Study to understand prognoses and preferences for outcomes and risks of treatment. *Journal of Clinical Epidemiology,* 1990 (Suppl.): 43–63.

Schneiderman, L., and N. Jecker. 1993. Futility in practice. *Archives of Internal Medicine* 153:437–41.

Scitovsky, A. 1984. "The high cost of dying": What do the data show? *Milbank Memorial Fund Quarterly* 62:591–608.

———. 1988. Medical care in the last twelve months of life: The relation between age, functional status, and medical care expenditures. *Milbank Quarterly* 66 (4): 640–60.

———. 1994. "The high cost of dying" revisited. *Milbank Quarterly* 72 (4): 561–91.

Valvona, J., and F. Sloan. 1985. DataWatch: Rising rates of surgery among the elderly. *Health Affairs* 4 (3): 108–19.

Verbrugge, L. 1984. Longer life but worsening health? Trends in health and mortality of middle-aged and older persons. *Milbank Memorial Fund Quarterly* 62:475–519.

Comment   David M. Cutler

Garber, MaCurdy, and McClellan have written an interesting paper on medical care expenditures at the end of life. It is well known that a lot of medical care resources (up to one-third of Medicare dollars) are spent in the last year of life. It has also long been suspected that not all of this care is truly necessary. Thus, it seems natural to search for cost savings by eliminating unnecessary medical expenditures at the end of life.

Garber et al. cast doubt on the possibility of large savings in end-of-life care. They note that the diagnoses associated with large end-of-life care expenditures are similar to the diagnoses associated with high spending in general. For example, much care at the end of life is provided to patients with pneumonia; but pneumonia is not a particularly good indicator that a patient is about to die. Thus, it would make little sense to ration care to patients with pneumonia as a way of limiting unnecessary end-of-life medical expenses.

Garber et al. point out valuable facts about end-of-life expenditures. The ease of deciding to save money through reduced end-of-life care is surely overstated. But the paper is too quick to dismiss potential end-of-life care savings. I say this for two reasons.

The first reason is statistical. While Garber et al. look at medical spending by diagnosis, they do not relate medical spending to the underlying disease of the patient. Consider a simple observation: a person with severe heart failure is more likely to catch pneumonia than a person with a well-functioning heart. Garber et al. note that most pneumonia diagnoses are not for people with very severe heart failure; therefore, it makes little sense to ration care to patients with pneumonia as a way of saving money for those with severe heart failure. But suppose we instead associate the spending on pneumonia for the patient with severe heart failure with heart failure itself, rather than with pneumonia. Then we might be able to ration care to patients with severe heart failure and save money.

The key issue is whether we want to group spending by immediate diagnosis or underlying medical condition. Garber et al. group spending by immediate diagnosis. It seems more fruitful, and technically possible, to group spending by the underlying condition of the patient. Such a grouping could change views about end-of-life care dramatically.

David M. Cutler is professor of economics at Harvard University and a faculty research fellow of the National Bureau of Economic Research.

The second issue concerns the information that is available to care providers versus researchers. Garber et al. find little difference in observable characteristics between those who are about to die and those farther away from death. My impression from talking with physicians is that with more information one can do a better job of forecasting death. This is probably not true for all patients: for a vast majority of patients, ultimate survival is not known with any certainty. But for some patients, physicians are reasonably sure that the patient will die.

Many of these patients, however, wind up spending a lot of money: they are in an ICU for many months, they get intensive surgeries, and they receive many diagnostic tests. Often, this care is provided because there is no coordination mechanism for dealing with the patient. The patient is not alerted to nonhospital alternatives, or physicians who know the wishes of the patient are not present when these decisions are made. Thus, among physicians I have spoken to there is a strong sense that substantial resources could be saved for a small number of patients who are near death but still receiving intensive treatments. This does not mean that we can save a lot of money for the average patient; Garber et al. show that this is not the case. But for many patients, medical care is overprovided and society could spend much less without a great deal of loss. Eliminating this care could save substantial resources.

6   The Impact of Intrafamily Correlations on the Viability of Catastrophic Insurance

Matthew J. Eichner

This paper explores the relationship between health care expenditures of spouses. If expenditures are due largely to random shocks, the household's medical expenditures are smoothed when two or more family members each draw from the distribution. On the other hand, if shocks are positively correlated, the potential exists for negative wealth shocks that are greater than those that would be predicted based on studies of the persistence of individual medical expenditures over time. Under traditional systems of insurance, with relatively low coinsurance levels, the consequences of any putative positive correlation across family members in expenditures are relatively mild. But under the sort of high-deductible insurance that is currently attracting interest from the policy community, wealth and utility effects may be appreciable. And under systems that include both high-deductible insurance and medical savings accounts, intrafamily correlations might dramatically change the accumulation of wealth in such accounts over a working lifetime.

Intrafamily correlations might exist for medical, economic, or behavioral reasons. Certain conditions, such as those related to contagious diseases or automobile accidents, might affect multiple members of a family. In addition, and as described in Eichner (1997), spending by one family member under most traditional employer-provided insurance plans lowers the price of care faced by other family members and may thereby induce additional expenditure. Finally, there may be fundamental differences in behaviors across families. Some individuals may make choices about their lives that lead, in the short

Matthew J. Eichner is assistant professor of finance and economics at Columbia University Graduate School of Business and a faculty research fellow of the National Bureau of Economic Research.

The author thanks Jeffrey Brown, Jeffrey Kling, James Poterba, and David Wise for helpful comments, and the National Institute on Aging, the Sloan Foundation, and the National Bureau of Economic Research for financial support.

run or the long run, to lower health care expenditures. And such individuals may seek out, as partners, individuals with similar values. In extreme cases, behaviors exhibited by one family member may directly affect expenditures by a spouse. The recently documented consequences of secondhand smoke provide such an example. Equally important, individuals may display different levels of inclination to initiate contact with the health care system. And again, there is every reason to suppose that individuals with particular levels of "taste for medical care" will choose similar individuals as partners.

The empirical strategy used in this paper will seek to differentiate between these various explanations for intrafamily correlations. To do this, I will look at individuals covered under different sorts of insurance plans and their expenditures for different sorts of care. By comparing the correlation between spousal expenditures in plans with coinsurance to the correlation between spousal expenditures in plans without coinsurance, I can measure the extent of the price effect. And by comparing the correlation between spouses for different sorts of expenditures, I can at least begin to sort out how much of the observed correlation in expenditures is due to factors other than taste. For example, the correlation in total medical expenditures between spouses may well be driven by correlation in expenditures for routine care. But if I restrict attention to expenditures related to surgical interventions, the effects of contagious disease and certain taste parameters are likely eliminated.

I also seek to determine where in the distribution of expenditures the correlations appear to be strongest. For example, there may be large correlations at lower expenditure levels produced by taste parameters, price effects, or contagious diseases. But the correlation could diminish higher in the distribution. In other words, there may be a great deal of information about whether a husband spends nothing or $300 on medical care in whether his wife spends nothing or $300. But there is likely less information concerning the husband's spending patterns in whether the wife spends $300 or $30,000.

The remainder of this paper is divided into six sections. Section 6.1 uses a simple framework to demonstrate the effect of intrafamily correlations on the standard microeconomic insurance problem. The analysis suggests that substantial intrafamily correlations can dramatically alter the value to individuals of insurance against the risk of medical expenditures. Section 6.2 introduces the data consisting of claims records of employees of two Fortune 500 firms and their spouses. The critical distinction between these two firms is that the first provides medical coverage with standard coinsurance provisions consisting of copayments and deductibles, while the other provides first-dollar coverage of almost all expenditures. In order to measure correlations for specific sorts of expenditures, it is necessary to adopt a strategy for aggregating claims that are likely due to the same medical condition. Section 6.3 describes the strategy I adopt in this paper and provides some descriptive evidence that it accomplishes the stated goal. Section 6.4 introduces the basic econometric framework utilized in this work. Rather than trying to faithfully capture the extremely long right tail of the expenditure distribution, I seek to estimate the probability that an individual's expenditure falls above a particular threshold. And most important, I will explore whether the fact that an individual's expenditures exceed a threshold provides information about the spending of his or her partner. In section 6.5, I consider the possibility that correlations may change over a working lifetime as a function of the aging process. Finally, section 6.6 presents some illustrative utility calculations and discusses the implication of the estimation results for systems of medical savings accounts and catastrophic insurance.

6.1   Risk, Insurance, and Intrafamily Correlation

This section presents the traditional microeconomic insurance problem, but modified to allow for the possibility of losses that are correlated among family members covered under a single insurance policy. I will show that positive correlation in losses within families unambiguously increases the value to families of purchasing insurance. This is reflected in their willingness to pay larger spread, or risk premium, over the expected loss.

Consider first a single risk-averse individual with a concave utility function $U(\cdot)$ such that $U'(\cdot) > 0$ and $U''(\cdot) < 0$. The standard insurance problem considers the expected utility of this individual integrated over all possible losses, which are assumed to follow some density $f_L(l)$:

$$E \; U(M - L) = \int_L U(M - l)f_L(l) \, dl,$$

where M is income. Willingness to pay for insurance coverage is usually expressed in terms of a certainty equivalent, the amount an individual would pay with probability one to avoid drawing some realization l from the density $f_L(l)$. This certainty equivalent c is found by solving

$$U(M - c) = \int_L U(M - l)f_L(l) \, dl.$$

If the certainty equivalent c equals the expected value of the loss, then the individual is unwilling to pay for insurance. But if $U(\cdot)$ is concave as assumed above, c will always exceed the expected loss. As developed in Arrow (1971), the individual is then willing to pay a risk premium to avoid the uncertainty in drawing from the density $f_L(l)$.

Now I consider the same problem, but modified to consider, not an individual facing a loss with density function $f_L(l)$, but a married couple facing a realization of two losses l_1 and l_2 with the joint density function $f_{L_1,L_2}(l_1, l_2)$. The critical issue, of course, is how the joint density function affects the certainty equivalent and hence the risk premium that the family is willing to pay to avoid the uncertainty of drawing l_1 and l_2 from $f_{L_1,L_2}(l_1, l_2)$. In particular, the issue will be the correlation coefficient between l_1 and l_2 implied by the joint density function.

Suppose a second joint density $g_{L_1,L_2}(l_1, l_2)$ differs from $f_{L_1,L_2}(l_1, l_2)$ only in that the correlation between l_1 and l_2 is higher, so $\rho_g > \rho_f$. The expected loss L is the same under either of the functions, since $E(L) = E(l_1) + E(l_2)$ does not depend on the correlation between the two individual losses. But the variance of the family loss L, $V(L) = V(l_1) + V(l_2) + 2\rho\sigma_{l_1}\sigma_{l_2}$, is an increasing function of the intrafamily correlation ρ.

If both density functions $g_{L_1,L_2}(l_1, l_2)$ and $f_{L_1,L_2}(l_1, l_2)$ yield the same expected loss but the loss under $g_{L_1,L_2}(l_1, l_2)$ has higher variance than the loss under $f_{L_1,L_2}(l_1, l_2)$, a risk-averse family will always prefer to face density function $f_{L_1,L_2}(l_1, l_2)$ rather than $g_{L_1,L_2}(l_1, l_2)$. Both imply the same expected loss, but the variance under $g_{L_1,L_2}(l_1, l_2)$ is greater. This intuitive idea can be formalized using the idea of second-order stochastic dominance. The density $f_{L_1,L_2}(l_1, l_2)$ is said to second-order stochastically dominate $g_{L_1,L_2}(l_1, l_2)$ if both have the same expected value and

$$\int_0^{l_1} \int_0^{l_2} G_{L_1,L_2}(l_1, l_2)\, dl_2\, dl_1 \geq \int_0^{l_1} \int_0^{l_2} F_{L_1,L_2}(l_1, l_2)\, dl_2\, dl_1$$

for any l_1 and l_2, where G and F are the distribution functions corresponding to density functions g and f, respectively. This condition will always be satisfied if the variance of the total loss, the sum of l_1 and l_2, described by the density $g_{L_1,L_2}(l_1, l_2)$ exceeds the variance of the total loss described by $f_{L_1,L_2}(l_1, l_2)$. As shown in Rothschild and Stiglitz (1970), second-order stochastic dominance is sufficient to establish

$$\int_{L_1,L_2} f_{L_1,L_2}(l_1, l_2) U(Y - l_1 - l_2)\, dl_1\, dl_2$$

$$> \int_{L_1,L_2} g_{L_1,L_2}(l_1, l_2) U(Y - l_1 - l_2)\, dl_1\, dl_2$$

or, equivalently, that the expected utility is higher if the loss follows $f_{L_1,L_2}(l_1, l_2)$ rather than $g_{L_1,L_2}(l_1, l_2)$.

This result suggests that the utility consequences of insurance schemes, and particularly those that involve relatively high potential out-of-pocket payments, may look quite different when evaluated on a family rather than on an individual basis. In particular, schemes that may have acceptable consequences for the utility of a single individual under all states of nature might have the potential to impose ruinous losses on families if substantial intrafamily correlations in medical expenditures exist. The empirical analysis described in this paper is an effort to measure the extent of these potentially important intrafamily (and particularly spousal) correlations in medical expenditures.

6.2   Firm Claims Data

The empirical analysis described in this paper uses claims data from two Fortune 500 firms. The firms differ along several dimensions. Most important for this analysis, firm 1 offers its employees a plan that requires them to bear none of the cost of their medical care, while firm 2 offers its employees a

Table 6.1   **Summary Data Description**

	Firm 1	Firm 2
Mean employee spending in 1992 ($)	1,355	1,832
Standard deviation of employee spending in 1992 ($)	5,177	7,968
Mean spousal spending in 1992 ($)	1,176	2,084
Standard deviation of spousal spending in 1992 ($)	4,253	8,872
Mean employee age	43.7	41.0
Mean spouse age	41.2	40.1
Mean difference in ages (employee age minus spouse age)	2.58	0.94
Percentage of male employees	95.04	74.69
Number of married couples	13,273	6,313

choice of plans all of which incorporate more traditional coinsurance provisions. In addition, firm 1 employees are located at a single site, while firm 2 employees are spread over six locations. All of the insurance plans at both firms incorporate limited case management for certain high-cost medical conditions and concurrent reviews of hospital stays. None cover pharmacy charges, mental health treatment, substance abuse treatment, or dental care, which are all covered separately under "carve-out" arrangements.

Married couples were formed from all individuals filing claims between 1990 and 1993 who could be unambiguously matched with a spouse. The analysis was then restricted to those married couples formed by employees between ages 25 and 55 whose spouses were aged 20 to 60. In firm 1, 13,273 such couples were identified, while the corresponding number from firm 2 was 6,313. Table 6.1 shows some basic descriptive information about the data. Thus, on average, the employee at firm 2 is younger, is more likely to be female, and spends more in 1992.

Claims data provide excellent information on the timing and nature of contacts with the health care system, as well as who in the family received treatment. Claims data are less useful in determining who was covered by the insurance plan during a particular period. Only by observing an individual filing a claim do I know that an individual is present. And when an individual does not file a claim during a particular period, it is presently impossible to discern whether the individual has received no treatment or has separated from the firm. I hope that the impact of this issue is minimized by studying firms that have stable workforces and individuals who have not yet reached ages at which retirement is likely. To address this issue more directly, additional enrollment data is required that will become available in the near future.

6.3   Classification of Claims

Most contacts with the health care system generate multiple claims. For example, the individual who visits the doctor complaining of stomach pains might receive an examination, blood tests, and an X-ray. Each of these may generate separate and, in some cases, multiple claims. Each claim may carry a diagnosis code, a procedure code, both, or neither. Continuing with the above example, the examination may be coded for a digestive disorder (diagnosis) and a medical procedure (examination), while the blood test may be coded as a laboratory procedure without a diagnosis. The empirical work described in this paper seeks to demonstrate that, for certain types of care, intrafamily correlations are greater than for other types of care. To do this requires grouping claims together by procedure and diagnosis in a sensible way, so that all claims stemming from the stomach pain scenario sketched above can be classified as a single treatment episode.

The idea of grouping claims to form treatment episodes dates to the RAND experiment in the 1970s. As described in Newhouse (1993), clinicians participating in the study made notes that explicitly indicated which claims were related. This information, along with the chronological spacing of treatments, allowed all charges to be grouped that "reflect[ed] decisions about the same medical problem." These episodes were then assigned to one of four categories: hospital, physician and supplies, dental, and pharmacy.

Because claims data lack the explicit links relied upon by the RAND investigators, I have taken a different approach. Furthermore, since the claims data explicitly exclude pharmacy and dental charges, their classification of episodes into one of four categories does not lend itself to my purpose. Instead, I have adopted an algorithm using exclusively chronological criteria to group episodes. The algorithm is fairly simple, yet as I will argue, it produces episodes that are internally consistent, as well as consistent with reasonable priors about health care delivery.

Under this typology, an outpatient episode begins on the date an outpatient treatment is received, and a window of 14 days is opened. Any further claims during that period are grouped with the initial treatment. When each additional treatment is received, the window is extended for an additional two weeks from the date of service. When two weeks pass during which no additional claims are filed, the outpatient episode is deemed complete. The procedure with respect to inpatient episodes is similar, although the window is 28 rather than 14 days in length. If an episode begins with an outpatient claim, a subsequent inpatient claim for treatment lengthens the window measured from all further claims in the episode from 14 to 28 days.

Once episodes are defined, I then group them using a hierarchy of the ICD-9 and CPT codings, which designate particular diagnoses and procedures, respectively. At the top of the hierarchy are episodes related to injuries and poisonings, as reflected by the presence in the grouping of at least one claim with an ICD-9 code corresponding to such a diagnosis. The next level consists of those episodes containing at least one claim referencing an inpatient or outpatient surgical procedure. Lower still are episodes with an inpatient or outpatient medical procedure, again as indicated by the presence of an appropriately coded claim. Another level consists of episodes that consist of at least one claim indicative of a diagnostic test. And, finally, there is the residual.

Table 6.2   **Treatment Episodes by Type**

	Firm 1			Firm 2		
Episode Type	Percentage of Episodes	Percentage of Cost	Mean Cost ($)	Percentage of Episodes	Percentage of Cost	Mean Cost ($)
Injury/poisoning	12.47	21.46	1,526	10.93	24.81	1,863
Surgical	18.78	43.40	2,068	18.15	48.46	2,191
Medical	35.41	26.46	669	49.35	19.56	325
Diagnostic	18.62	4.54	218	8.80	2.95	276
Residual	14.71	4.34	264	12.77	4.22	271

Table 6.3   **Treatment Episodes by Length**

	Firm 1			Firm 2		
Episode Length	Percentage of Episodes	Percentage of Cost	Mean Cost ($)	Percentage of Episodes	Percentage of Cost	Mean Cost ($)
1 Day	66.21	14.20	192	61.69	11.96	159
< 1 Week	10.79	14.93	1,238	10.79	11.21	852
< 2 Weeks	10.28	14.54	1,266	11.40	11.23	807
< 3 Weeks	5.17	9.34	1,619	6.25	8.70	1,141
< 4 Weeks	2.19	7.20	2,943	2.97	6.80	1,878
< 6 Weeks	2.39	10.53	3,937	2.97	9.31	2,575
< 8 Weeks	1.01	5.63	4,988	1.34	6.24	3,835
< 3 Months	1.09	8.93	7,348	1.45	10.67	6,049
> 3 Months	0.88	14.70	15,027	1.15	23.89	17,109

Note that in this typology each level subsumes the levels below. An individual receiving only a cardiogram would produce an episode coded as a diagnostic procedure. If he or she had a cardiogram and also a medical examination, the episode would be categorized as medical. A cardiogram and medical examination followed by open heart surgery would be classified as a surgical episode.

Table 6.2 shows the breakdown of episodes constructed from claims filed by employees and spouses at the two firms during the 1990–92 period. In both firms, injury/poisoning and surgical episodes account for a disproportionate share of expenditures. For example, only 18 percent of the episodes of treatment for firm 2 employees are classified as surgical, but these account for almost one-half of expenditures. On the other hand, the more numerous medical episodes account for less of the total cost. Again referring to firm 2, the 49 percent of episodes classified as medical account for only 20 percent of expenditures. In both firms, the importance of the so-called residual episodes, those that cannot be classified elsewhere in the hierarchy, is relatively small as the cost share of these episodes is below 5 percent.

Table 6.3 describes the treatment episodes, defined using the algorithm and classifications outlined above, in terms of their length, that is, the number of days from the treatment that initiates the episode to the final treatment included in the grouping. The distribution of episode lengths is quite similar across the two firms. And, as in table 6.2, the category that contains most of the episodes accounts for a relatively small percentage of the cost.

6.4   Estimation of Intrafamily Correlations

A primary goal of this work is to assess empirically the magnitude of intrafamily correlations in medical expenditures. In this section, I outline three possible approaches to this analysis and describe the bivariate probit model that I choose to apply. I then show how the results of the bivariate probit analysis can be easily interpreted using the concept of conditional probability.

One option in measuring the correlation is to estimate a system of two regressions, one for the employee and one for the spouse, and to allow some covariance structure between the equations. This sort of estimation is generally referred to as seemingly unrelated least squares (SUR). The problem is fundamentally complicated by the fact that both equations, employee expenditures and spousal expenditures, are censored, with a substantial proportion of individuals spending nothing. Estimation of an SUR system with censored dependent variables requires restrictive assumptions concerning the distribution of both expenditures and the disturbance terms and would still prove computationally intractable because construction of the likelihood function would require evaluating "hybrid" density and distribution functions for the assumed bivariate distribution.

Another approach estimates the joint distribution function at particular points. For example, controlling for demographic factors, I might estimate the probability that the spouse spends more than $1,000 while the employee spends more than zero. This is done using the bivariate probit specification. The assumption of joint normality is relatively harmless since I do not need to claim that I accurately capture the shape of the probability mass between any two points of support. The probability in which I am interested is the only parameter of the relevant Bernoulli distribution. In other words, I care only about whether expenditures are above or below some threshold. The exact nature of the distribution above and below this threshold is unimportant; only how much of the density is above and below the threshold is critical.

A third possibility involves a bivariate ordered probit model. Instead of estimating the joint probability that the spouse's expenditures exceed some level and the employee's expenditures exceed some level, I would estimate the joint probability that the spouse's expenditures fall in a particular range and that the employee's expenditures fall in a particular range. Here the assumption of joint normality is more restrictive, since the outcome of interest is not simply whether a realization falls above or below some threshold.

Another troublesome implication of the bivariate ordered probit is that the correlation is constrained to be equal across the entire expenditure distribution.

One might imagine that positive expenditures by a spouse are correlated with positive expenditures by an employee. But it is unlikely that the correlation persists higher in the distribution and that expenditures above $1,000 by a spouse are as correlated with expenditures above $1,000 by an employee. The results are therefore very sensitive to the choice of expenditure ranges. I will opt to avoid this issue by using the simple bivariate probit framework to estimate the probabilities of exceeding certain points in the joint distribution.

A simple probit model of expenditures is written

$$P(Y > y) = P(Z\beta + \varepsilon > 0),$$

where y is a particular threshold of interest (often zero) and Z is a vector of independent variables including a constant. Making the distributional assumption that ε follows a normal distribution, the relation can be rewritten

$$P(Y > y) = \Phi(Z\beta),$$

where Φ is the distribution function that gives the probability in the lower tail of the normal distribution.

This framework is easily modified to deal with a system of two equations. Suppose

$$P(Y_1 > y_1 \text{ and } Y_2 > y_2) = P(\beta_1 Z_1 + \varepsilon_1 > 0 \text{ and } \beta_2 Z_2 + \varepsilon_2 > 0),$$

where the subscripts 1 and 2 refer to the equations. The distributional assumption is then

$$\begin{pmatrix} \varepsilon_1 \\ \varepsilon_2 \end{pmatrix} \sim N\left(\begin{pmatrix} 0 \\ 0 \end{pmatrix}, \begin{pmatrix} 1 & \rho \\ \rho & 1 \end{pmatrix} \right),$$

and the relevant probability can be written

$$P(Y_1 > y_1 \text{ and } Y_2 > y_2) = \Phi_2(\beta_1 Z_1, \beta_2 Z_2, \rho),$$

where Φ_2 is the distribution function for the bivariate normal distribution written above.

The parameters β_1, β_2, and ρ can be estimated using standard maximum likelihood methods. The exact specifications for firm 1 are

$$Z_i \beta_i = \alpha_i + \beta_{i1} \text{Age}_i + \beta_{i2} \text{Male}_i + \beta_{i3} \text{Age}_i * \text{Male}_i.$$

For firm 2, five location and two plan indicators are added for each member of the couple:

$$Z_i \beta_i = \alpha_i + \beta_{i1} \text{Age}_i + \beta_{i2} \text{Male}_i + \beta_{i3} \text{Age}_i * \text{Male}_i$$

$$+ \beta_{i4} 1(\text{Plan} = 1) + \beta_{i5} 1(\text{Plan} = 3) + \sum_{k=1}^{5} \beta_{i(k+5)} 1(\text{Loc} = k).$$

Table 6.4   **Bivariate Probit Estimates**

Variable	Firm 1		Firm 2	
	$P(Y_i > 0)$	$P(Y_i > 500)$	$P(Y_i > 0)$	$P(Y_i > 500)$
Employee				
Age	0.0044	0.0087	0.0198**	0.0213**
	(0.0070)	(0.0068)	(0.0040)	(0.0039)
Male	−0.8722**	−0.7100*	−0.3841*	−0.6720**
	(0.3035)	(0.2998)	(0.1815)	(0.1845)
Age*Male	0.0113	0.0063	0.0043	0.0062
	(0.0072)	(0.0071)	(0.0045)	(0.0045)
Constant	0.3362	−0.5680	−0.3036	−0.8075
Spouse				
Age	0.0227**	0.0167**	0.0211**	0.0153**
	(0.0015)	(0.0016)	(0.0022)	(0.0022)
Male	−0.2051	−0.5640	−0.5999**	−0.8340**
	(0.2780)	(0.3325)	(0.1697)	(0.1877)
Age*Male	−0.0058	0.0056	−0.0017	−0.0056
	(0.0062)	(0.0073)	(0.0040)	(0.0044)
Constant	−0.7805	−1.3413	0.6905	−0.7984
Rho	0.4097**	0.2183**	0.6905**	0.3995**
	(0.0122)	(0.0151)	(0.0133)	(0.0189)
Other covariates	None	None	Five location and two plan indicators	Five location and two plan indicators

Note: Numbers in parentheses are standard errors.
*Statistically distinct from zero ($p < 0.05$).
**Statistically distinct from zero ($p < 0.01$).

The aim is to ensure that ρ, the parameter of interest, does not capture correlation related to both employee and spouse living in the same location, receiving care under the same plan, or being roughly the same age.

I begin by considering whether the sum of expenditures for all treatment episodes exceeds zero. I then continue by increasing the threshold from zero to $500 and then to $1,000. Results from this estimation are shown in table 6.4. The correlations between employees and spouses are large and quite precisely measured. In addition, the correlation decreases at higher levels of expenditure. For firm 1 couples, the correlation drops from 0.41 to 0.22 when the threshold is raised from zero to $500. A similar pattern is evident for firm 2 couples. This can be explained by the decreasing importance of taste parameters higher in the distribution. Whether a spouse chooses to visit the doctor with a common cold is likely correlated with whether an employee would make a similar choice. But whether a spouse would spend larger sums is likely less a function of the taste parameters that account for at least some of measured intrafamily correlations.

Finally, the estimated correlations for firm 1 are appreciably smaller than for firm 2. An obvious explanation for this regularity involves price effects that are present in firm 2 but not in firm 1. Recall that firm 2, unlike firm 1, requires coinsurance payments for standard medical care. These coinsurance payments take the form of a deductible that must be satisfied before insurance payments begin as well a copayment that continues from the point at which the deductible is met to some stop loss limit. As a result of the deductible and copayment requirements, each family faces a nonlinear price schedule for medical care, with the price falling once the deductible is satisfied and again once the stop loss limit is reached. Since the coinsurance provisions apply to the family as a whole, spending by one spouse can reduce, under plans like those in firm 2, the price of care faced by the other spouse.

Table 6.5 shows the correlation coefficients from additional estimation of joint probability distributions. Specifications are similar to those in table 6.4, but with additional expenditure thresholds and varying subsets of claims. As in table 6.4, the correlations are uniformly higher for couples covered by firm 2, suggesting the existence of substantial price effects. Furthermore, the correlations are largest when all episodes are included in the estimation. As episodes are restricted to those of the medical type, the correlations fall. Correlations between employee and spousal spending for surgical episodes, which are closer to the top of the hierarchy introduced in section 6.3, fall further. This suggests that moving up the hierarchy reduces the influence of taste parameters relative to external factors such as health shocks and provider decisions. Estimation results related to injury/poisoning episodes are an exception to this pattern, largely because a substantial fraction of injury/poisonings affect multiple family members.[1]

Increasing the threshold for each type of episode decreases the estimated correlation. Again, this is related to the relative importance of taste parameters as determinants of spending for different levels of expenditure. Both spouses may well opt to have the dermatologist remove benign growths within the same time frame. Expenditures for surgical removal of malignant tumors are much less likely to be correlated. Thus the correlation of 0.1628 for spending on surgical episodes above zero falls to essentially zero for spending on surgical episodes above $4,000.

To facilitate interpretation of these estimated correlations, it is useful to express them as conditional probabilities. This is done using the basic definition of conditional probability:

---

1. These results may seem to contradict the arguments presented in Eichner (1997) concerning the exogeneity of injuries and poisonings to family members. But those results were predicated on excluding all injury and poisoning claims that affected multiple family members. In addition, much of the exogenous variation was produced by injuries and poisonings to children, who are not included in the present analysis.

Table 6.5   **Estimated Correlations**

Spending	Firm 1	Firm 2
All Episodes		
Above zero	0.4097	0.6905
	(0.0121)	(0.0133)
Above $500	0.2183	0.3995
	(0.0151)	(0.0189)
Above $1,000	0.2036	0.3150
	(0.0173)	(0.0215)
Above $2,000	0.1434	0.2200
	(0.0214)	(0.0261)
Above $4,000	0.1273	0.1396
	(0.0272)	(0.0351)
Medical Episodes		
Above zero	0.2724	0.5730
	(0.0145)	(0.0159)
Above $500	0.1997	0.3022
	(0.0231)	(0.0256)
Above $1,000	0.1705	0.2635
	(0.0318)	(0.0333)
Above $2,000	0.1180	0.2221
	(0.0462)	(0.0523)
Above $4,000	0.1578	0.1111
	(0.0583)	(0.1168)
Surgical Episodes		
Above zero	0.1628	0.3182
	(0.0177)	(0.0216)
Above $500	0.1283	0.2328
	(0.0241)	(0.0274)
Above $1,000	0.0914	0.1400
	(0.0278)	(0.0333)
Above $2,000	0.0688	0.0873
	(0.0336)	(0.0415)
Above $4,000	−0.0082	0.0447
	(0.0482)	(0.0552)
Injury/Poisoning Episodes		
Above zero	0.2515	0.2732
	(0.0188)	(0.0271)
Above $500	0.2349	0.2312
	(0.0333)	(0.0373)
Above $1,000	0.1974	0.2039
	(0.0445)	(0.0455)
Above $2,000	0.0992	0.2747
	(0.0644)	(0.0540)
Above $4,000	0.1085	0.2399
	(0.0801)	(0.0727)

Note: Numbers in parentheses are standard errors.

$$P(Y_e > y \mid Y_s > y) = \frac{P(Y_e > y \text{ and } Y_s > y)}{P(Y_s > y)} = \frac{\Phi_2(Z_e\beta_e, Z_s\beta_s, \rho)}{\Phi(Z_s\beta_s)},$$

where the subscript e refers to the employee and the subscript s to the spouse. The conditional probability is evaluated for a couple with particular demographic characteristics. Here I will consider a 45-year-old male employee married to a woman of the same age. Table 6.6 shows the conditional probabilities for different thresholds and subsets of episodes and again makes clear that the correlations are strongest in the lower portions of the distributions. For example, a spouse with positive expenditures increases the probability of the employee's incurring positive expenditures by 0.2689. But a spouse with expenditures exceeding $2,000 only increases the probability of the employee's exceeding that level by 0.06.

6.5   Age-Dependent Correlations

In evaluating the effects of medical savings accounts in combination with catastrophic health insurance, a critical issue involves accumulation of balances in the accounts over a working lifetime. Intrafamily correlations, which potentially depend on the age of the couple, could have major effects on accumulation, particularly if the correlation increases with age so that the relation is strongest during the years in which the largest medical expenditures are likely to occur. This might occur if the effect of certain behavior decisions made over a lifetime produce increasingly important health consequences as a couple ages. For example, smoking (either first- or secondhand) is surely such a behavioral factor, and the deleterious consequences of smoking become manifest, not when individuals are in their 20s and 30s, but when they have reached more advanced stages of life.

I can easily reparametrize the bivariate probit model to allow for the dependence of the correlation coefficient on the age of the employee:

$$P(Y_e > y \text{ and } Y_s > y) = \Phi_2(\beta_e Z_e, \beta_s Z_s, \rho(\text{Age})),$$

where $\rho(\text{Age})$ is a simple linear function:

$$\rho(\text{Age}) = \gamma_0 + \gamma_{\text{Age}}.$$

Estimates of β_e, β_s, and γ are obtained as before using maximum likelihood.

The results of this estimation, presented in table 6.7, show that correlation decreases with employee age, although in most cases the coefficient on age is not statistically distinct from zero. For example, each additional year is predicted to decrease the correlation in the bivariate normal distribution for positive expenditures in firm 1 by -0.0016. As shown in table 6.8, the implied correlations for couples with employees of ages 30, 40, and 50 are 0.4334, 0.4174, and 0.4014, respectively.

Table 6.6 **Conditional Probabilities**

	Firm 1	Firm 2
All Episodes		
$P(Y_e > 0 \mid Y_s > 0)$	0.6768	0.8118
$P(Y_e > 0 \mid Y_s < 0)$	0.4079	0.3303
$P(Y_e > 500 \mid Y_s > 500)$	0.3646	0.5441
$P(Y_e > 500 \mid Y_s < 500)$	0.2380	0.2885
$P(Y_e > 1,000 \mid Y_s > 1,000)$	0.2745	0.4077
$P(Y_e > 1,000 \mid Y_s < 1,000)$	0.1699	0.2241
$P(Y_e > 2,000 \mid Y_s > 2,000)$	0.1761	0.2596
$P(Y_e > 2,000 \mid Y_s < 2,000)$	0.1161	0.1534
$P(Y_e > 4,000 \mid Y_s > 4,000)$	0.1193	0.1349
$P(Y_e > 4,000 \mid Y_s < 4,000)$	0.0765	0.0867
Medical Episodes		
$P(Y_e > 0 \mid Y_s > 0)$	0.4357	0.6938
$P(Y_e > 0 \mid Y_s < 0)$	0.2667	0.3044
$P(Y_e > 500 \mid Y_s > 500)$	0.1924	0.2955
$P(Y_e > 500 \mid Y_s < 500)$	0.1051	0.7045
$P(Y_e > 1,000 \mid Y_s > 1,000)$	0.1198	0.2060
$P(Y_e > 1,000 \mid Y_s < 1,000)$	0.0629	0.0949
$P(Y_e > 2,000 \mid Y_s > 2,000)$	0.0684	0.1122
$P(Y_e > 2,000 \mid Y_s < 2,000)$	0.0394	0.0463
$P(Y_e > 4,000 \mid Y_s > 4,000)$	0.0610	0.0339
$P(Y_e > 4,000 \mid Y_s < 4,000)$	0.0269	0.0179
Surgical Episodes		
$P(Y_e > 0 \mid Y_s > 0)$	0.2354	0.4376
$P(Y_e > 0 \mid Y_s < 0)$	0.1584	0.2457
$P(Y_e > 500 \mid Y_s > 500)$	0.1323	0.2516
$P(Y_e > 500 \mid Y_s < 500)$	0.0875	0.1420
$P(Y_e > 1,000 \mid Y_s > 1,000)$	0.0967	0.1562
$P(Y_e > 1,000 \mid Y_s < 1,000)$	0.0697	0.1035
$P(Y_e > 2,000 \mid Y_s > 2,000)$	0.0649	0.0909
$P(Y_e > 2,000 \mid Y_s < 2,000)$	0.0490	0.0665
$P(Y_e > 4,000 \mid Y_s > 4,000)$	0.0287	0.0488
$P(Y_e > 4,000 \mid Y_s < 4,000)$	0.0299	0.0402
Injury/Poisoning Episodes		
$P(Y_e > 0 \mid Y_s > 0)$	0.2811	0.2886
$P(Y_e > 0 \mid Y_s < 0)$	0.1480	0.1459
$P(Y_e > 500 \mid Y_s > 500)$	0.1226	0.1684
$P(Y_e > 500 \mid Y_s < 500)$	0.0485	0.0803
$P(Y_e > 1,000 \mid Y_s > 1,000)$	0.0806	0.1169
$P(Y_e > 1,000 \mid Y_s < 1,000)$	0.0324	0.0551
$P(Y_e > 2,000 \mid Y_s > 2,000)$	0.0375	0.1093
$P(Y_e > 2,000 \mid Y_s < 2,000)$	0.0216	0.0362
$P(Y_e > 4,000 \mid Y_s > 4,000)$	0.0304	0.0748
$P(Y_e > 4,000 \mid Y_s < 4,000)$	0.0159	0.0242

Table 6.7	Bivariate Probit Estimates: Correlation Parametrized as a Function of Employee Age			
	Firm 1		Firm 2	
Variable	$P(Y_i > 0)$	$P(Y_i > 500)$	$P(Y_i > 0)$	$P(Y_i > 500)$
Employee				
Age	0.0053	0.0087	0.0196**	0.0211**
	(0.0070)	(0.0069)	(0.0040)	(0.0039)
Male	−0.8365**	−0.7134*	−0.3896*	−0.6748**
	(0.3045)	(0.3008)	(0.1816)	(0.1844)
Age*Male	0.0105	0.0063	0.0045	0.0063
	(0.0072)	(0.0071)	(0.0045)	(0.0045)
Constant	0.2992	−0.5653	−0.2966	−0.7988
Spouse				
Age	0.0227**	0.0166**	0.0211**	0.0152**
	(0.0015)	(0.0016)	(0.0022)	(0.0022)
Male	−0.2051	−0.5505	−0.5960**	−0.8299**
	(0.2781)	(0.3322)	(0.1698)	(0.1874)
Age*Male	−0.0059	0.0053	−0.0017	−0.0056
	(0.0062)	(0.0073)	(0.0040)	(0.0044)
Constant	−0.7814	−1.3381	0.5027	−0.7975
Rho				
Age	−0.0016	−0.0050*	−0.0007	−0.0037
	(0.0018)	(0.0023)	(0.0018)	(0.0022)
Constant	0.4814**	0.4393**	0.7177**	0.5547**
	(0.0814)	(0.1015)	(0.0814)	(0.0950)
Other covariates	None	None	Five location and two plain indicators	Five location and two plain indicators

Note: Numbers in parentheses are standard errors.
*Statistically distinct from zero ($p < 0.05$).
**Statistically distinct from zero ($p < 0.01$).

Thus correlations appear likely to be lower in the later years of life when big expenditures typically occur. Such a pattern is at least partially explained by the fact that when individuals are relatively young and healthy the taste parameters that are presumably at least partially jointly determined between partners are relatively more important than in later life, when health shocks and provider decisions play a larger role in determining health outlays. And, based on this empirical estimation, the cumulative effect of behavior over the life cycle appears to be swamped by the random shocks in the later stages of life.

Table 6.8   **Estimated Correlations Parametrized as a Function of Age:
All Expenditures**

Spending	Age	Constant	$\rho(30)$	$\rho(40)$	$\rho(50)$
		Firm 1			
Above zero	−0.0016	0.4814**	0.4334	0.4174	0.4014
	(0.0018)	(0.0814)			
Above $500	−0.0050	0.4393**	0.2893	0.2393	0.1893
	(0.0023)	(0.1015)			
Above $1,000	−0.0006	0.2308*	0.2128	0.2068	0.2008
	(0.0026)	(0.1175)			
Above $2,000	−0.0010	0.1896	0.1596	0.1496	0.1396
	(0.0032)	(0.1444)			
Above $4,000	0.0046	−0.0798	0.0582	0.1042	0.1502
	(0.0041)	(0.1882)			
		Firm 2			
Above zero	−0.0007	0.7177**	0.6967	0.6897	0.6827
	(0.0017)	(0.0687)			
Above $500	−0.0037	0.5547**	0.4437	0.4067	0.3697
	(0.0022)	(0.0950)			
Above $1,000	−0.0074**	0.6274**	0.4054	0.3314	0.2574
	(0.0025)	(0.1080)			
Above $2,000	−0.0078*	0.5492**	0.3142	0.2372	0.1592
	(0.0031)	(0.1328)			
Above $4,000	−0.0076	0.4665**	0.2385	0.1625	0.0865
	(0.0042)	(0.1826)			

Note: Numbers in parentheses are standard errors.
*Statistically distinct from zero ($p < 0.05$).
**Statistically distinct from zero ($p < 0.01$).

6.6   Utility Consequences of Intrafamily Correlation

In this section, I will provide some illustrative calculations detailing the cost of correlation between partners under a prototypical catastrophic insurance plan. The key provision of the plan I consider is a $2,000 annual individual deductible so that a married couple can, at most, suffer a $4,000 out-of-pocket loss. And once again, I will focus on the case of a 45-year-old male employee and his wife of the same age. My empirical approach has thus far abstracted from the continuous nature of the expenditure distribution, and I will continue to do so in this context by assigning individuals to be either at or below the $2,000 individual annual deductible.

I will first consider the joint distribution defined by the following four probabilities: $P(Y_e \geq \$2,000$ and $Y_s \geq \$2,000)$, $P(Y_e \geq \$2,000$ and $Y_s < \$2,000)$, $P(Y_e < \$2,000$ and $Y_s < \$2,000)$, and $P(Y_e < \$2,000$ and $Y_s \geq \$2,000)$. This distribution is obtained from the previously estimated probit specification. For firm 1, this distribution can be written

	$Y_e < \$2,000$	$Y_e \geq \$2,000$
$Y_s < \$2,000$	0.7671	0.1008
	(0.0698)	(0.0151)
$Y_s \geq \$2,000$	0.1089	0.0233
	(0.0670)	(0.0193)

The standard errors appearing in parentheses below each estimated probability are obtained from the bivariate probit estimation results using the Taylor series approximation referred to as the delta method.

The analogous bivariate distribution for firm 2 is

	$Y_e < \$2,000$	$Y_e \geq \$2,000$
$Y_s < \$2,000$	0.6568	0.1191
	(0.0564)	(0.0189)
$Y_s \geq \$2,000$	0.1660	0.0582
	(0.0527)	(0.0174)

For each firm, I also construct a second bivariate distribution that has the same expected value but correlation equal to zero. This is done by applying a basic definition of independence and taking the product of the appropriate marginal distributions obtained by summing over the joint distributions shown above. For firm 1, this distribution is

	$Y_e < \$2,000$	$Y_e \geq \$2,000$
$Y_s < \$2,000$	0.7602	0.1077
	(0.0712)	(0.0110)
$Y_s \geq \$2,000$	0.1157	0.0164
	(0.0712)	(0.0159)

while for firm 2 the tabular representation is

	$Y_e < \$2,000$	$Y_e \geq \$2,000$
$Y_s < \$2,000$	0.6383	0.1375
	(0.0577)	(0.0148)
$Y_s \geq \$2,000$	0.1844	0.0397
	(0.0573)	(0.0151)

For each firm, I also calculate the mean expenditure for the appropriate ages and genders conditional on expenditures below $2,000. For firm 1, this conditional expectation is $340 for the employee and $374 for the spouse. The corresponding numbers for firm 2 are $234 and $240. I will take these figures to represent the loss when expenditures do not exceed $2,000 per person. Using these figures, the expected out-of-pocket loss for a firm 1 couple is $926, while the figure for firm 2 is $1,375. Note that these expected losses are identical under both the actual ($\rho > 0$) and constructed ($\rho = 0$) distributions.

My approach will compare the amount individuals are willing to pay to avoid facing the actual distribution with the amount they will pay to eliminate the uncertainty embodied in the constructed distribution. The difference I will interpret as some measure in dollars of the utility cost of intrafamily corre-

Table 6.9   **Estimated Cost of Correlations**

Income		Risk Premium ($)	Risk Premium if ρ Equals Zero ($)	Percentage Change
		Firm 1		
$30,000	$U(M) = \ln M$	13.12	12.32	6.10
	$U(M) = M^{0.25}$	9.80	9.20	6.12
	$U(M) = M^{0.5}$	6.50	6.11	6.00
	$U(M) = M^{0.75}$	3.24	3.04	6.17
$50,000	$U(M) = \ln M$	7.66	7.20	6.00
	$U(M) = M^{0.25}$	5.73	5.39	5.93
	$U(M) = M^{0.5}$	3.81	3.58	6.04
	$U(M) = M^{0.75}$	1.90	1.79	5.79
$70,000	$U(M) = \ln M$	5.41	5.09	5.91
	$U(M) = M^{0.25}$	4.05	3.81	5.93
	$U(M) = M^{0.5}$	2.70	2.54	5.93
	$U(M) = M^{0.75}$	1.35	1.27	5.93
		Firm 2		
$30,000	$U(M) = \ln M$	17.33	15.47	10.73
	$U(M) = M^{0.25}$	12.95	11.57	10.66
	$U(M) = M^{0.5}$	8.60	7.69	10.58
	$U(M) = M^{0.75}$	4.28	3.83	10.51
$50,000	$U(M) = \ln M$	10.08	9.01	10.62
	$U(M) = M^{0.25}$	7.54	6.75	10.48
	$U(M) = M^{0.5}$	5.02	4.49	10.56
	$U(M) = M^{0.75}$	2.50	2.24	10.40
$70,000	$U(M) = \ln M$	7.11	6.36	10.56
	$U(M) = M^{0.25}$	5.32	4.76	10.53
	$U(M) = M^{0.5}$	3.54	3.17	10.45
	$U(M) = M^{0.75}$	1.77	1.58	10.73

lation. The first step is to calculate the certainty equivalent, the amount the couple would be willing to pay to avoid facing the distribution. This is done by solving for c_a and c_c so as to equate utility with and without uncertainty:

$$U(M - c_a) = \sum_1^4 U(M - l_e - l_s) f_{L_e, L_s}(l_e, l_s, \rho),$$

$$U(M - c_c) = \sum_1^4 U(M - l_e - l_s) f_{L_e, L_s}(l_e, l_s, 0).$$

Here M is again income, L_e the loss incurred by the employee, L_s the loss incurred by the spouse, $f_{L_e, L_s}(l_e, l_s, \rho)$ denotes the actual distribution, and $f_{L_e, L_s}(l_e, l_s, 0)$ denotes the constructed distribution. Risk premiums can then be calculated assuming $f_{L_e, L_s}(l_e, l_s, \rho)$ and $f_{L_e, L_s}(l_e, l_s, 0)$ by subtracting the certainty equivalent under each distribution from the expected loss.

Table 6.9 shows these risk premiums for a variety of income levels under several different utility functions. These are surprisingly small. Under log utility and income of $30,000, for example, the risk premium for the actual firm 1 distribution is $13.12 while the risk premium for the constructed distribution is $12.32. The difference of $0.80 represents the cost of correlation under this set of assumptions. In this case, the cost of correlation represents 6.1 percent of the risk premium under the actual ($\rho > 0$) distribution. While the risk premium decreases with increasing income as expected, the fraction related to intrafamily correlation remains steady at about 6 percent for firm 1. A similar pattern is evident for firm 2, although the higher correlations due to price effects boost the cost of intrafamily correlation to about 10.5 percent of the risk premium.

I can also use the technique described above to investigate the counterfactual that the level of intrafamily correlation around the threshold of zero persists into the higher ranges of the distribution. I do this by looking at the probabilities that expenditures exceed zero and assuming that these instead reflect, as above, the probabilities that expenditures exceed $2,000. Obviously, the risk premiums will be larger. But my primary interest is, not the risk premiums themselves, but how much of the risk premium can be attributed to intrafamily correlation of expenditures.

The actual distribution relevant for these calculations and firm 1 is

	$Y_e < \$0$	$Y_e \geq \$0$
$Y_s < \$0$	0.2194	0.1008
	(0.0287)	(0.0151)
$Y_s \geq \$0$	0.1264	0.5461
	(0.0309)	(0.0367)

The distribution constructed from the marginal distribution is

	$Y_e < \$0$	$Y_e \geq \$0$
$Y_s < \$0$	0.1132	0.2143
	(0.0225)	(0.0420)
$Y_s \geq \$0$	0.2325	0.4400
	(0.0234)	(0.0425)

The corresponding distributions for firm 2 are

	$Y_e < \$0$	$Y_e \geq \$0$
$Y_s < \$0$	0.2394	0.1650
	(0.0502)	(0.0568)
$Y_s \geq \$0$	0.1927	0.4030
	(0.0516)	(0.0583)

and

	$Y_e < \$0$	$Y_e \geq \$0$
$Y_s < \$0$	0.1747	0.2297
	(0.0469)	(0.0615)
$Y_s \geq \$0$	0.2573	0.3383
	(0.0470)	(0.0616)

Table 6.10   **Estimated Cost of Correlations: Counterfactual Distribution**

Income		Risk Premium ($)	Risk Premium if ρ Equals Zero ($)	Percentage Change
		Firm 1		
$30,000	$U(M) = \ln M$	34.52	27.35	20.78
	$U(M) = M^{0.25}$	25.92	20.53	20.81
	$U(M) = M^{0.5}$	17.30	13.69	20.84
	$U(M) = M^{0.75}$	8.66	6.85	20.87
$50,000	$U(M) = \ln M$	20.04	15.86	20.90
	$U(M) = M^{0.25}$	15.04	11.90	20.90
	$U(M) = M^{0.5}$	10.04	7.94	20.92
	$U(M) = M^{0.75}$	5.02	3.97	20.93
$70,000	$U(M) = \ln M$	14.12	11.17	20.92
	$U(M) = M^{0.25}$	10.60	8.38	20.93
	$U(M) = M^{0.5}$	7.07	5.59	20.95
	$U(M) = M^{0.75}$	3.54	2.79	20.96
		Firm 2		
$30,000	$U(M) = \ln M$	32.13	21.96	31.64
	$U(M) = M^{0.25}$	24.16	16.49	31.72
	$U(M) = M^{0.5}$	16.15	11.01	31.79
	$U(M) = M^{0.75}$	8.09	5.51	31.87
$50,000	$U(M) = \ln M$	18.64	12.70	31.89
	$U(M) = M^{0.25}$	14.00	5.93	31.93
	$U(M) = M^{0.5}$	9.35	6.36	31.97
	$U(M) = M^{0.75}$	4.68	3.18	32.06
$70,000	$U(M) = \ln M$	13.13	8.93	31.99
	$U(M) = M^{0.25}$	9.86	6.70	32.02
	$U(M) = M^{0.5}$	6.58	4.47	32.05
	$U(M) = M^{0.75}$	3.29	2.24	32.08

With these distributions in hand, I can repeat the calculation of risk premiums, which is shown in table 6.10. Moving to a counterfactually more correlated distribution increases the fraction of the risk premium attributable to intrafamily correlation. For firm 1, the fraction rises to 21 percent, while for firm 2, with the presence of price effects, the fraction reaches 32 percent. Note, however, that the magnitudes of the risk premiums remain, as before, very small.

6.7 Summary and Conclusion

The empirical work in this paper suggests that, while correlation of expenditures among married partners is large at the low end of the expenditure distribution, the relation diminishes appreciably in the upper ranges. For example, I estimate correlations for positive expenditures of 0.41 for firm 1 and 0.69 for firm 2. But the correlations in expenditures above $4,000 are only 0.13 and

0.14, respectively. Thus, while these correlations may be important in the lower ranges of the expenditure distribution, they decrease appreciably in the ranges relevant for a discussion of catastrophic health insurance schemes. Furthermore, the utility cost of this correlation is quite small as a percentage of the risk premium required to induce an individual to face the uncertainty in a prototypical major risk policy. For the firm 1 plan, which like a prototypical catastrophic plan is structured so that spending by one family member does not reduce the price for care paid by other family members, only about 6 percent of the risk premium is due to intrafamily correlation. Thus the existence of intrafamily correlation is unlikely to appreciably complicate the analysis or implementation of catastrophic insurance coverage.

More generally, the calculations in this paper reveal that the entire risk premium, and not just the portion related to intrafamily correlation, is quite small under a set of standard assumptions about the form of the utility function. The risk premiums for the prototypical catastrophic plan, even abstracting from any behavior response to the greater cost sharing, are no more than $20 in the most extreme case. Such small numbers, of course, raise more general questions about why individuals are consistently observed paying a great deal in premiums to avoid relatively small amounts of additional risk. Additional insight into this behavior will be a major goal of future work involving the broader issue of plan choice.

References

Arrow, Kenneth A. 1971. *Essays in the theory of risk bearing*. Chicago: Markham.
Eichner, Matthew J. 1997. Incentives, price expectations, and medical expenditures: An analysis of claims under employer-provided health insurance. New York: Columbia University, Graduate School of Business. Mimeograph.
Newhouse, Joseph P. 1993. *Free for all: Lessons from the RAND Health Insurance Experiment*. Cambridge, Mass.: Harvard University Press.
Rothschild, M., and J. Stiglitz. 1970. Increasing risk I: A definition. *Journal of Economic Theory* 2:225–43.

Comment   Thomas J. Kane

Pooling risk within groups, such as firms or families, yields greater opportunity for utility gains when those risks are not positively correlated. In this chapter,

Thomas J. Kane is associate professor of public policy at the John F. Kennedy School of Government, Harvard University, and a faculty research fellow of the National Bureau of Economic Research.

Matt Eichner constructs a unique data set on family medical expenditures to study the implications of such correlation. He asks four questions: First, how correlated are medical expenditures within couples? Second, is that correlation different for large and small expenditures? Third, how is the degree of correlation related to deductibles and coinsurance? Fourth, what are the utility consequences of such correlation for the value of medical insurance?

The Data

The author has assembled an impressive set of claims data for two Fortune 500 firms, matching spouses' expenditures and aggregating the claims data by health episodes. As the author's recent work demonstrates, such data can prove extremely useful for studying a range of questions related to families' claims behavior and insurance purchasing behavior.

An interesting component of the data, which the author exploits in this paper as well as in other work, is the difference between the two firms' insurance plans. One firm requires various types of coinsurance (copayments, deductibles); the other does not. As long as the incentive structure is the only difference between the two firms that would be relevant for the intrafamily correlation in insurance behavior (one firm is not a major manufacturer of "bungee" jumping equipment, for instance), such variation can shed light on how couples behave when price incentives differ.

The Structure of the Problem

Insurance companies are worried not about the total variance in health expenditures but primarily about the variance that is not related to easily observable characteristics. If everyone in the sample had the same expected health expenditures, Eichner's problem would be the fairly straightforward exercise of describing the joint distribution of actual expenditures by couples. However, his work is complicated by the fact that easily observed demographic characteristics, such as age and gender, are clearly related to expenditures. Therefore, we are less interested in the distribution of total expenditures by each person (y_i and y_j) than in the distributions of the orthogonal components of health expenditures (e_i and e_j) below:

$$y_i = X_i\beta + e_i,$$

$$y_j = X_j\beta + e_j.$$

Faced with the task of having to estimate β in order to study e_i and e_j, Eichner chooses not to use a highly restrictive parametric form, such as the joint normal distribution with a single correlation parameter ρ, to describe the data. Rather, he specifies a series of thresholds ($500, $1,000, $2,000, and $4,000) and uses a bivariate probit estimator to model the likelihood that the expenditures of either member of the couple are above or below each threshold. Since joint normality of e_i and e_j would imply the same β and ρ regardless of the threshold used, Eichner's framework allows him to study correlation at various points in the joint distribution of expenditures, while providing a natural test for joint normality.

These results of the first part of the paper are summarized below:

1. For each type of expenditure, the estimated correlations were lower at higher expenditure thresholds, although the estimated correlations generally remained positive.

2. The intracouple correlations in expenditures were generally lower for surgical episodes than for other types of medical episodes.

3. The intracouple correlations at levels of expenditure below $4,000 tended to be greater in firm 2, which had fewer coinsurance features.

4. There was little evidence to suggest that intracouple correlations varied with the couple's age.

The author draws the plausible conclusion that shared tastes for medical care are more likely to produce covariance in small expenditures than in larger expenditures such as major surgeries. This conclusion is bolstered by the finding that the magnitude of intracouple correlation was higher at the firm with less coinsurance, primarily at lower spending thresholds.

Although the results are both plausible and interesting, I have two concerns with the first section of the paper. First, I could imagine that different forms of measurement error in health care expenditures would affect different parts of the joint distribution differently. For example, suppose that a couple's expenditures were truncated—such as when the employee left the firm, died, or started using his or her spouse's insurance. Any error that resulted in the simultaneous loss of both spouses' expenditure data would lead to greater correlation in expenditure at lower levels. Moreover, any errors in the assignment of claims to different types of episodes—surgical, medical, or injury/poisoning—could produce more "random" variation in various parts of the joint distribution, depending on the nature of the error.

Whether such errors in categorization are important would depend on the question being asked. For instance, an insurance company setting annual deductibles would not necessarily care about the impact of using an arbitrary accounting unit such as a year, which would produce both left- and right-censored expenditure episodes. For setting annual deductibles, it is the distribution of truncated or uncompleted spells that matters. However, for drawing conclusions about the influence of "tastes" on joint expenditures, sorting out the implications of various types of measurement error could be important.

Second, finding different correlation coefficients at different cut points may be a cause for concern—not just for the assumption that the distribution is joint normal throughout the range of expenditures, but even for whether the bivariate probit is the right specification. For instance, such findings may suggest that the joint distribution of e_i and e_j is also nonsymmetric. In future work, the author might experiment with other specifications of the distribution of e_i and e_j.

Utility Implications of Intracouple Correlation

In section 6.6 of the paper, the author explores the implications of intra-couple correlation for the value of an insurance policy with a $2,000 per person deductible. He calculates the certainty equivalent "cost" of that correlation in the following way. First, he uses his estimates to calculate the probability that a couple with a given set of characteristics would find themselves in each of four quadrants, with the employee spending above or below $2,000 and the spouse spending above or below $2,000. (Call these probabilities P^{00}, P^{01}, P^{10}, and P^{11}.) He then calculates the mean expenditures in each of the four quadrants. (Call these e^{00}, e^{01}, e^{10}, and e^{11}.) Using a log utility function with income M, the author calculates the risk premium under correlated expenditures by solving for c_a:

$$U(M - c_a) = P^{00}U(M - e^{00}) + P^{01}U(M - e^{01}) + P^{10}U(M - e^{10})$$
$$+ P^{11}U(M - e^{11}).$$

Having correlated medical expenditures means that the likelihood of falling into each of the quadrants is not equal to the product of the individual likeli-hoods that the employee or his spouse has expenditures above or below the relevant threshold. For example, the likelihood of both persons spending above $2,000 ($P^{11}$) is greater than the product of the probability that each individually has expenditures above $2,000. Such correlation can be costly for a couple, and Eichner seeks to estimate this cost. To do so, he then calculates a second certainty equivalent, c_c, to approximate the certainty equivalent with indepen-dent expenditures by solving the following equation:

$$U(M - c_c) = (P^{00} + P^{01}) * (P^{00} + P^{10})U(M - e^{00}) +$$
$$(P^{00} + P^{01}) * (P^{01} + P^{11})U(M - e^{01}) +$$
$$(P^{00} + P^{10}) * (P^{10} + P^{11})U(M - e^{10}) +$$
$$(P^{01} + P^{11}) * (P^{10} + P^{11})U(M - e^{11}).$$

The difference in risk premiums, $c_c - c_a$, provides an estimate of the "cost" to families of having correlated health expenditures. At a family income of $30,000, Eichner estimates that intrafamily correlation raises the risk premium by roughly 10 percent over what two individuals with uncorrelated expendi-tures would have been willing to pay.

However, the above calculation probably misstates the cost of intracouple correlation for at least two reasons: First, the method calculates only the utility cost of movements of probability mass *between* the four quadrants; it does not take into account the utility cost of movements of probability mass *within* each of the four quadrants. Particularly because expenditures are correlated below $2,000, much of the cost of the correlation presumably results from the in-

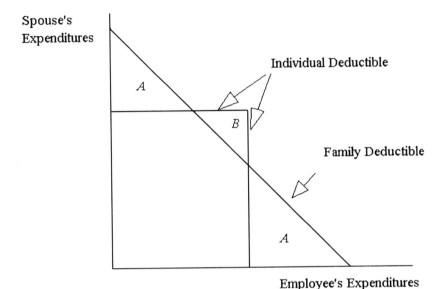

Fig. 6C.1   Families can trade individual risk (A) for less combined risk (B)

creased likelihood that the couple will face payments of $1,999 for each. Although Eichner's choice of the bivariate probit allows him to ignore the shape of the density surface within each of the quadrants, it also means that he is forced to focus only on between-quadrant shifts in density rather than the within-quadrant shifts.

Second, because the bonds of matrimony allow couples to enforce cost-sharing agreements better than two strangers with less correlated expenditures could do, they can avoid some of the costs of having correlated expenditures by purchasing a policy with a joint deductible. As illustrated in figure 6C.1, by buying a policy with a family deductible rather than an individual deductible, a family can trade off less insurance against individual risk (A) by buying more insurance against pooled risk (B). Here, the couple's deductible would be less than two times the individual deductible. Yet the insurance company's expected cost would be unchanged as long as the expected cost in the area B is just equal to the expected cost in the areas labeled A. Even though any two strangers on the street might also be able to benefit from pooling their resources and sharing the cost of health care, they lack the means that a family would have for enforcing it.

Conclusion

This paper is an early contribution to what promises to be an important line of research on families' claims behavior and insurance purchasing decisions. Expenditures among couples and for a given person over time are likely to be correlated. As Eichner points out, this may well have strong welfare implications for different types of insurance. Moreover, sorting out the source of the correlation is crucial. To the extent that expenditures are correlated *because* of price effects—for instance, having used up my family's deductible, I lower the cost for my wife's next procedure—rather than taste effects, such variation may also be a valuable source of exogeneity for studying the price elasticity of demand for medical care.

7   Health Events, Health Insurance, and Labor Supply: Evidence from the Health and Retirement Survey

Mark McClellan

7.1 Introduction

The economic consequences of health problems are reported to be enormous. For example, many investigators have concluded that the cost to society of common health problems such as heart disease, diabetes, and cancer is many billions of dollars per year in terms of lost work productivity, intensive medical treatments, and additional supportive care. However, these estimates have several important limitations. Few data sets have incorporated detailed information on health problems and economic circumstances such as retirement, medical and personal care expenditures, income, and wealth. Consequently, most existing studies have had to combine data from different sources, possibly missing important correlations between variables such as insurance availability and the occurrence of health problems. Many of these studies have been based on cross-sectional, descriptive comparisons of individuals with and without health problems. As a result, it is difficult to account for other differences besides health problems that might also have affected these outcomes. For example, individuals with health problems may have had chronically worse health status, or have lower-income backgrounds, or have other differences in preferences that might have led to differences in economic outcomes anyway.

Addressing these limitations of prior data for studying health and economic behavior was a major motivation for the new Health and Retirement Survey (HRS), which completed its third wave of longitudinal interviews in 1996 (Juster and Suzman 1995). Early analyses of the relatively detailed information on both health and economic outcomes collected in the HRS has already provided

Mark McClellan is professor of economics and medicine at Stanford University and a faculty research fellow of the National Bureau of Economic Research.

The author thanks Loren Mell for outstanding research assistance and the National Institute on Aging and the Olin Foundation for financial support. All errors are his own.

many new insights into the relationship between health status and economic outcomes (see, e.g., Bound, Schoenbaum, and Waidmann 1995). As more waves of the survey become available, the HRS promises to become an even richer foundation for understanding the interaction between health and economic outcomes.

This study uses the first two waves of the HRS to provide insights into how changes in health status affect two issues of considerable policy interest: health insurance coverage and labor supply for middle-aged Americans. These topics are linked for many reasons. The principal source of health insurance coverage for HRS respondents is private insurance, and the vast majority of private insurance coverage is obtained through employment (Employee Benefit Research Institute 1995). Indeed, the availability of health insurance coverage for middle-aged Americans with health problems, and the related problems of "job lock" or "retirement lock," has been the subject of considerable recent economic research (Gruber and Madrian 1995, 1996; Blau and Gilleskie 1997). Second, health insurance availability and the labor supply of household members in the event of health impairments are key determinants of households' capacity to smooth consumption of all other goods and services (Deaton 1992; Morduch 1995).

In addition, the methods that might be used to study both questions are similar and illustrate some of the opportunities and problems that arise in the analysis of complex questions with relatively rich data sets such as the HRS. Health problems are not "treatments" or policies that can be varied for individuals, so it may be difficult to develop methods that isolate the "effect" of health. This study uses difference-in-differences methods to examine the effects of changes in health on insurance coverage and labor supply. The amount of detail about respondents' health and economic characteristics may make it easier to identify such effects convincingly. These details also present new challenges in modeling the effects of multidimensional factors such as health status on complex decisions such as labor supply and insurance coverage.

7.2   Health Capital in Theory and Practice

Most economic studies of the consequences of health begin with a model of an individual's health capital. In Grossman's classic formulation (Grossman 1972), an individual chooses his or her investment in behaviors that influence health based on the investment's impact on discounted expected utility. Adverse health events are depreciations or negative investments in health, and they are not fully predictable. When a health change occurs, it may affect utility through many mechanisms: through its impact on individual productivity, through its impact on the utility received from consumption of various goods and services, and through its impact on the time available to enjoy these goods and services. For example, an adverse health event may either reduce or increase labor supply. If the event reduces an individual's marginal utility of income—for instance, if the individual is no longer able to enjoy relatively expensive consumption activities such trips abroad or dinners out, or if the event reduces expected survival time—then it will tend to reduce labor supply. On the other hand, if the event increases an individual's marginal utility of income—for instance, because of increased demand for medications or supportive care—then it will tend to increase labor supply. The direct effects of adverse health events on an individual's productivity may cause labor supply changes in either direction, depending on the relative magnitudes of the substitution and income effects of the resulting wage change.

This discussion suggests that different kinds of changes in health may have substantially different consequences for economic behavior. Many prior studies have been unable to distinguish these different kinds of effects because the measures of health status and changes in health status available have been limited (for a review of this earlier work, see Sammartino 1987). For example, some studies of retirement have examined the impact of a single overall measure of health status—"good" versus "bad" health—and have found that bad health is a strong predictor of retirement. Yet, depending on the underlying health problems involved, an individual's overall assessment of bad health today may not be a very good guide to the consequences of the adverse health state for an individual's consumption demands, work productivity, or expected survival time.

More recent studies have examined the impact of impairments in an individual's functional capabilities on labor supply (Stern 1989; Gertler and Gruber 1997). Yet such disability-based studies do not easily capture the behavioral consequences of health events through their impact on preferences and on expectations about future health. The development of diabetes, for example, may have no consequences at all for functional status today and possibly for a number of years to come, but it may have substantial implications for an individual's demand for many types of goods and services as well as survival time.

The behavioral consequences of health events also depend on government policies and past individual actions that provide various kinds of insurance against the consequences of adverse health events for consumption. For example, an extensive literature has examined the consequences of disability insurance and the eligibility for government-provided health insurance that may accompany it for both employee reports of health status and employee responses to the development of health problems (Bound 1989, 1991; Parsons 1980, 1991; Gruber 1996). Fewer studies have examined the actual consequences of health events for health insurance coverage: When adverse health events do occur, are individuals able to retain insurance coverage, and if so how? Does the availability of insurance differ across different kinds of health problems?

For these reasons, I focus on health problems per se, rather than disability or a single summary measure of an individual's current health state. Health problems are extremely diverse. Osteoarthritis of the knees, compressed intervertebral discs in the back, and coronary heart disease all have potentially different implications for an individual's demand for particular medical services and other services now and in the future, as well as potentially different implications for current and future functional capabilities. Moreover, each of these problems may vary greatly in severity, both from the standpoint of functional implications and from the standpoint of effects on demand. Additionally, different types of health problems may have different implications for the availability of insurance coverage. Unfortunately, no available data set has information on both health and economic variables and is large enough to permit detailed analysis of particular health problems. Consequently, feasible analysis of health changes requires aggregation across particular kinds of health problems.

This analysis aggregates health problems in two major dimensions. The first dimension is the extent to which the health event may lead to significant functional impairments *now*. For example, previous studies found small labor supply effects of new health conditions, particularly chronic health problems, in contrast to strong effects of functional status impairments (see, e.g., Gertler and Gruber 1997). Because of the possible consumption and life expectancy effects, as well as possible insurance eligibility effects, new health problems that do not result in functional impairments may either increase or decrease labor supply. These countervailing effects may explain why net effects on labor supply appear to be small. To address this concern, the second dimension considers the chronicity of the health problem, that is, the extent to which it is likely to remain present if not progress. As described in more detail below, this framework results in three broad classes of health problems: major health events, which frequently have major acute and long-term functional implications; new chronic illnesses, which are less likely to affect functional status dramatically today but which may have substantial long-term implications; and accidents, which may result in temporary or even permanent acute functional impairments but otherwise would be expected to have little long-term impact on preferences or future health expectations. Finally, to distinguish the effects of new health problems on expectations about consumption demands from their effects on work productivity, I consider the differential effects of new health problems that are and are not associated with current functional impairments.

This analysis presents preliminary results on the effects of new health events. It considers the economic factors that are associated with the development of new health problems, mainly to illustrate the baseline differences between individuals who do and do not experience health events. The analysis then considers the consequences of these health events for insurance coverage and labor supply for three different types of individuals: males in couples, females in couples, and single females. These three groups make up the bulk of the HRS-age population in the United States, and their different household resources and economic circumstances suggest that their responses to new health problems may differ substantially, depending on the nature of the problem and the extent of functional impairment involved.

7.3   Data and Preliminary Comparisons by Health Status Changes

Of the original sample of 12,756 individuals in wave 1 of the HRS, 229 individuals died before wave 2 and 1,160 individuals did not participate in the wave 2 survey. An additional 794 respondents were dropped for the following reasons: deaths (229 wave 1 respondents), nonintact households between the two waves, households with two members of the same sex, households with missing family status variables, and households with capital income over $1 million.

Measures of baseline respondent characteristics, health, functional status, health insurance, pension eligibility, labor supply, income, wealth, and changes in most of these variables between the first and second survey waves (approximately two years apart) were derived from the HRS wave 1 beta and wave 2 alpha survey releases. These variables are described in more detail elsewhere (see, e.g., Smith 1995; Wallace and Herzog 1995; and related papers). Tables 7.1 through 7.3 summarize these measures for three different groups: males in couples (tables 7.1A, 7.2A, and 7.3A, including 4,244 paired couples and 138 males whose spouses did not participate), females in couples (tables 7.1B, 7.2B, and 7.3B, including 4,244 paired couples and 214 females whose spouses did not participate), and single females (tables 7.1C, 7.2C, and 7.3C; 1,293 respondents).[1] The small sample size for single males (594 individuals) precludes any detailed analysis of health events for that group.

The tables report averages for each household group, both overall and by the occurrence of each type of health event. Three broad categories of health events were constructed. *Major health events* are serious diseases that often have substantial immediate and long-term effects on health status. These major events include heart attacks, which may be fatal or lead to subsequent heart failure; strokes, which may result in substantial neurologic impairments; and new diagnoses of cancer. While cancer itself involves chronic progression, cancer treatments—including surgery but especially systemic treatments such as chemotherapy and radiation therapy—commonly have a substantial impact on well-being in the months after diagnosis. Individuals who experience these major events are also at elevated risk of further health complications from these conditions in the future. *Chronic illnesses* are diseases that typically result in progressive loss of function of an organ system, and that may place the individual at increased risk for a range of major health events as well. They include diabetes, lung diseases (e.g., chronic obstructive pulmonary disease or asthma), arthritis, back pain, or heart failure. Typically, these illnesses result

---

1. Results for the three types of households are presented in all tables in this paper except table 7.4: males in couples (A tables), females in couples (B tables), and single females (C tables).

in only limited functional impairments initially, but they may result in more substantial impairments over time. *Accidents* are defined in the HRS wave 2 survey as occurrences of "accident or injury" since wave 1.[2] While accidents may result in substantial temporary functional impairments and possibly long-term impairments as well, in general they do not result in progressive deterioration over time, and they have only limited direct implications for an individual's future health prognosis.

A fourth type of health problem sometimes considered in studies of older populations is *frailty,* health impairments not associated with specific diseases of any organ system but rather with the result of gradual degeneration of the functional capacity of multiple systems. While frailty is a major concern in studies of the older elderly, it is likely to be rare among HRS respondents during the period of study.[3] Thus, no measures of frailty are constructed for the analyses presented here. Finally, *mental illnesses* are also important sources of functional impairments and potentially of adverse economic consequences, but they present special issues in characterizing new diagnoses and associated functional impairments and are not considered here because of space limitations. Though information on mental illnesses in the HRS is limited, similar methods could in principle be applied to study them.

Following many previous studies of the consequences of impairments in functional status (see, e.g., Smith and Kington 1997), I summarize the many dimensions of physical functioning in a unidimensional index. The index is obtained by constructing a raw functional status score based on one point for a minor impairment and two points for a major impairment in each of the following 11 dimensions of activities of daily living: walking across the room; walking several blocks; climbing one flight of stairs without resting; climbing several flights of stairs without resting; lifting or carrying a weight of over 10 pounds; pushing or pulling large objects (such as a living room chair); picking up a dime from a table; stooping, kneeling, or crouching; getting in and out of bed without help; bathing or showering without help; and eating without help. After the initial scores were constructed for respondents in each wave, they were converted to an index with a 0–100 scale using the formula[4]

$$100 \times (\text{respondent's score})/(\text{highest score} - \text{lowest score}).$$

Table 7.1 shows that the rates of new health events differ across the population groups. For males in couple households, approximately 28 percent of respondents had at least one health event during the two-year period between

---

2. A separate question asked about head injuries leading to unconsciousness in particular; it was not included in this definition. A total of 72 respondents in the entire survey said "no" to the injury question and "yes" to the head injury question.

3. E.g., well under 1 percent of HRS respondents had been admitted to a nursing home for a prolonged period, and even fewer reported such chronic degenerative diseases as dementia.

4. In both waves, the lowest raw functional status score was zero and the highest was 22 (the highest possible score).

Table 7.1A   **Respondent Characteristics for Couple Males**

Characteristic	All Respondents	Male Health Event Occurrence					
		None	All Types	Major Event	Chronic Illness	Accident	Death
Sample size	4,364	3,134	1,230	276	837	233	93
(%)	(100%)	(71.8%)	(28.2%)	(6.3%)	(19.2%)	(5.3%)	
Age[a]	57.1	56.9	57.6	59.1	57.4	56.4	60.1
	(4.7)	(4.6)	(4.8)	(4.9)	(4.7)	(4.5)	(6.2)
White	84.5	85.1	83.0	85.2	82.0	83.3	83.1
Black	8.0	7.9	8.1	8.0	8.0	6.8	13.2
Latino	5.5	5.1	6.5	5.1	7.2	7.7	3.4
Education in years[a]	12.5	12.6	12.1	11.9	11.9	12.3	11.3
	(2.9)	(2.8)	(3.0)	(2.8)	(3.1)	(2.9)	(2.9)
	Male Health and Functional Status						
History of major health event	13.7	11.2	20.0	39.1	20.3	11.5	52.6
History of chronic illness	58.0	56.8	61.0	74.8	56.4	70.1	75.9
Wave 1 functional status index[a]	6.5	5.5	9.1	14.9	9.4	7.6	24.4
	(10.8)	(9.6)	(12.9)	(15.9)	(13.2)	(12.5)	(18.6)
Change in functional status index[a]	−0.55	−1.3	1.3	3.4	1.4	1.8	
	(8.4)	(7.0)	(10.9)	(14.5)	(10.6)	(12.5)	
	Male Social Security and Pension Eligibility						
Participation in social security	93.4	93.3	93.7	93.3	92.8	95.4	94.7
Participation in private pension	57.6	57.1	59.0	53.1	58.5	65.3	44.9

[a]Numbers in parentheses are standard deviations.

Table 7.1B   **Respondents Characteristic for Couple Females**

Characteristic	All Respondents	None	All Types	Major Event	Chronic Illness	Accident	Death
					Female Health Event Occurrence		
Sample size	4,370	3,237	1,133	153	808	245	37
(%)	(100%)	(74.1%)	(25.9%)	(3.5%)	(18.5%)	(5.6%)	
Age[a]	53.2	53.0	53.7	54.9	53.7	52.9	54.3
	(5.0)	(5.1)	(4.9)	(4.7)	(4.9)	(4.8)	(4.8)
White	84.5	85.1	82.8	84.6	81.8	83.4	72.2
Black	7.9	7.6	8.7	5.9	9.4	9.4	18.6
Latino	5.6	5.3	6.6	7.4	7.0	4.9	7.2
Education in years[a]	12.4	12.5	12.1	11.6	11.9	12.5	10.6
	(2.4)	(2.3)	(2.5)	(2.3)	(2.6)	(2.1)	(2.4)
			Female Health and Functional Status				
History of major health event	9.9	9.0	12.7	29.5	11.1	13.5	56.7
History of chronic illness	57.1	57.1	57.3	70.0	53.9	63.3	72.2
Wave 1 functional status index[a]	9.2	8.5	11.4	16.4	11.5	11.1	30.7
	(10.9)	(10.2)	(12.6)	(14.5)	(12.5)	(13.6)	(16.0)
Change in functional status index[a]	−1.5	−2.2	0.75	4.0	0.84	0.39	
	(8.7)	(7.6)	(11.1)	(13.5)	(10.4)	(13.7)	
			Female Social Security and Pension Eligibility				
Participation in social security	89.2	89.5	88.1	87.3	87.5	88.8	91.8
Participation in private pension	51.9	51.8	52.0	48.6	51.9	52.4	46.2

[a]Numbers in parentheses are standard deviations.

Table 7.1C   **Respondent Characteristics for Single Females**

	All Respondents	None	All Types	Major Event	Chronic Illness	Accident	Death
					Health Event Occurrence		
Sample size	1,293	882	411	63	288	112	27
(%)	(100%)	(68.2%)	(31.8%)	(4.8%)	(22.3%)	(8.7%)	
Age[a]	55.8	55.8	55.8	56.5	56.2	54.9	56.1
	(2.8)	(2.9)	(2.7)	(2.8)	(2.6)	(2.8)	(2.6)
White	68.6	70.7	63.7	67.3	61.7	64.1	59.7
Black	21.9	20.5	25.1	24.6	25.8	24.9	34.3
Latino	6.7	5.9	8.6	7.0	8.9	9.4	3.0
Education in years[a]	12.1	12.2	11.6	11.3	11.5	11.6	11.5
	(2.7)	(2.6)	(2.7)	(2.7)	(2.8)	(2.4)	(1.7)
Health and Functional Status							
History of major health event	14.0	13.1	16.1	32.7	18.0	15.5	49.3
History of chronic illness	67.5	65.6	72.0	91.8	67.1	76.7	79.1
Wave 1 functional status index[a]	13.3	12.0	16.5	27.3	16.1	18.4	28.8
	(13.8)	(13.3)	(14.4)	(17.6)	(14.0)	(16.1)	(16.6)
Change in functional status index[a]	−0.81	−1.9	1.6	5.7	1.4	1.3	
	(9.8)	(8.4)	(12.0)	(14.8)	(12.2)	(10.9)	
Social Security and Pension Eligibility							
Participation in social security	92.6	92.4	93.0	96.5	94.0	90.3	88.1
Participation in private pension	55.8	54.7	58.6	71.3	53.3	60.2	59.3

[a]Numbers in parentheses are standard deviations.

waves 1 and 2. These events consisted of major acute events in 6.3 percent, new chronic illnesses in 19.2 percent, and accidents in 5.3 percent. Approximately 26 percent of couple females had health events, including major acute events in 3.5 percent, new chronic illnesses in 18.5 percent, and accidents in 5.6 percent. Health event rates were higher among single females. Almost 32 percent of single females had events, consisting of major acute events in 4.8 percent, new chronic illnesses in 22 percent, and accidents in 8.7 percent. Around 2 percent of both males and females in couples had health events in more than one category, and around 4 percent of single females had health events in more than one category.

7.3.1 Respondent Demographic Characteristics, Health Characteristics, and Pension Eligibility

In all three groups, individuals who have major acute events are somewhat older than average, and individuals who have accidents tend to be younger. Education levels were lower for virtually all health event groups. Most respondents also had a history of health problems at the beginning of the survey. For example, 58 percent of males reported at least one chronic health problem in wave 1, and 14 percent had experienced previous major health events. Among females in couples, 57 percent had chronic health problems in the baseline interview, and 10 percent had experienced major health events. The baseline health status of single females was worse: 68 percent had chronic health problems, and 14 percent had prior major health events.

Table 7.1 shows that the occurrence of different types of health events is at least weakly correlated with most of these individual characteristics. For all three groups, individuals who experienced major health events were slightly older (over one year older on average for couples, and 0.8 years older on average for single females), less educated, and significantly more likely to have had health problems and worse functional status at baseline. Individuals in couples who developed new chronic illnesses were also slightly older and less educated—though differences in these respects were more modest than for major health events—and had slightly worse baseline functional status. In contrast, single females with new chronic illnesses were slightly younger than average, perhaps because the baseline prevalence of chronic problems in this group was significantly higher to begin with. For all groups, individuals experiencing accidents were somewhat younger than those who did not have accidents but also had worse baseline health status compared to those who remained healthy between the two survey waves.

Table 7.1 begins to illustrate the consequences of health events by presenting average changes in functional status. For respondents with no new health events, functional status improved slightly on average (-1.3 points for couple males, -2.2 points for couple females, and -1.9 points for single females), so that average reported functional status for the whole sample actually improved slightly between waves 1 and 2. Health events were associated with significantly different trends in functional status. Individuals experiencing major health events reported declines in function on average. For females, the difference in trends compared to those without health events was around $+6$ to $+7$ points; for males, the difference in trends was around $+5$ points. The tables also confirm that the development of chronic illness is less likely to be associated with substantial decrements in function between the survey waves: while the trends are worse compared to those without health events, the difference in trends is only around $+2$ to $+3$ points. Similarly, accidents are also associated with small increases in functional impairment on average.

Finally, table 7.1 reports some general summary information on pension eligibility for each of the health status groups. Approximately 93 percent of couple males and single females are eligible for or expect to receive social security benefits, and a slightly lower percentage of couple females report current or future social security eligibility. These fractions do not differ much across the health event groups. Current or future private pension eligibility differs somewhat more across the health groups. For example, among couple males, approximately 53 percent of respondents with major health events and 65 percent of respondents with accidents report that they expect pension benefits at some time in the future. Somewhat fewer women report private pension eligibility, with similar correlations across the health event groups.

7.3.2   Health Insurance

Table 7.2 reports information on health insurance coverage and changes in health insurance coverage for the different health status groups. Baseline rates of insurance coverage were lower for both single and couple females than for males. They were slightly lower for males with health events compared to those without health events. Reflecting baseline health status, however, the sources of baseline health insurance coverage differed substantially between the groups. Males with health events were significantly less likely to be covered by private insurance (especially private insurance with retirement benefits) and were much more likely to be covered by Medicare (25 percent of those who experienced major events and 13 percent of those with new chronic illnesses, compared to 9 percent of those without health events). Couple females who had health events were much less likely to be covered by Medicare or Medicaid at baseline, and their coverage rates with private insurance were only slightly lower than those for couple females without health events. On the other hand, single females with health events had considerably lower private insurance coverage rates at baseline, and significantly higher rates of Medicare and especially Medicaid coverage.[5] These tabulations suggest that a relatively large portion of major health events for couple males and for single females involve government health insurance programs, while private insurance cover-

---

5. Some of the Medicare coverage, particularly for males, is the result of age eligibility for Medicare. For example, approximately 6 percent of male respondents in wave 1 and 9 percent of respondents in wave 2 were age 65 or older, and approximately 12 percent with major health events in wave 1 and 16 percent with major health events in wave 2 were age 65 or older. Elderly individuals are omitted from the regressions in tables 7.5 through 7.8 below.

Table 7.2A   Health Insurance Coverage Rates for Couples by Male Health Event Status

			Male Health Event Occurrence			
Coverage	All Respondents	None	All Types	Major Event	Chronic Illness	Accident
Male Health Insurance						
Uninsured at wave 1	8.4	8.2	9.0	9.5	9.1	10.9
Private with retirement health insurace at wave 1	51.6	52.8	48.5	40.8	48.7	49.6
Private, no retirement health insurance at wave 1	27.3	27.9	26.0	19.7	26.1	27.2
Medicare insurance at wave 1	10.4	9.2	13.3	24.7	13.5	7.7
Medicaid insurance at wave 1	0.51	0.38	0.83	1.5	0.88	0.27
Change in uninsured	−1.7	−1.5	−2.4	−6.3	−2.0	−1.8
Change in private with retirement health insurance	−0.81	−0.67	−1.2	−0.95	−0.39	−1.1
Change in private, no retirement health insurance	−3.5	−3.2	−4.3	−5.9	−4.3	−2.4
Change in Medicare insurance	5.4	4.8	6.9	10.3	6.2	4.2
Change in Medicaid insurance	0.47	0.31	0.88	1.3	0.73	0.55
Female Health Insurance						
Uninsured at wave 1	10.7	10.1	12.3	16.0	11.8	15.5
Private with retirement health insurance at wave 1	53.9	54.7	51.8	50.6	52.1	49.9
Private, no retirement health insurance at wave 1	30.6	31.0	29.7	26.3	29.9	28.8
Medicare insurance at wave 1	2.3	2.0	3.0	2.6	3.1	2.2
Medicaid insurance at wave 1	1.1	0.89	1.6	2.8	1.6	1.9
Change in uninsured	−1.5	−1.3	−2.0	−3.9	−1.7	−3.5
Change in private with retirement health insurance	1.6	1.7	1.4	1.5	0.48	2.7
Change in private, no retirement health insurance	−1.9	−2.0	−1.4	−2.7	−0.88	−0.71
Change in Medicare insurance	1.8	1.9	1.4	1.6	1.7	0.70
Change in Medicaid insurance	0.14	0.08	0.29	0.96	0.04	0.00

Table 7.2B   Health Insurance Coverage Rates for Couples by Female Health Event Status

Coverage	All Respondents	None	Female Health Event Occurrence			
			All Types	Major Event	Chronic Illness	Accident
Female Health Insurance						
Uninsured at wave 1	10.9	10.8	11.1	13.3	12.0	10.5
Private with retirement health insurance at wave 1	53.6	54.1	52.3	49.1	52.1	54.8
Private, no retirement health insurance at wave 1	30.9	31.2	30.0	28.8	28.9	29.0
Medicare insurance at wave 1	2.2	1.7	3.7	5.7	4.0	3.3
Medicaid insurance at wave 1	1.1	0.93	1.6	1.5	1.6	1.8
Change in uninsured	-1.5	-1.4	-2.0	-4.9	-1.6	-2.7
Change in private with retirement health insurance	1.5	1.3	2.0	0.65	1.4	2.1
Change in private, no retirement health insurance	-1.8	-1.4	-3.0	-5.4	-2.4	-4.0
Change in Medicare insurance	1.8	1.5	2.8	5.9	2.2	2.8
Change in Medicaid insurance	0.18	0.15	0.28	4.0	0.40	0.26
Male Health Insurance						
Uninsured at wave 1	8.4	8.3	8.8	8.7	9.7	8.9
Private with retirement health insurance at wave 1	50.9	50.9	51.1	50.0	50.1	54.0
Private, no retirement health insurance at wave 1	27.8	28.2	26.5	23.9	25.5	25.6
Medicare insurance at wave 1	10.5	10.4	10.7	14.8	10.9	8.7
Medicaid insurance at wave 1	0.51	0.51	0.51	0.42	0.49	0.51
Change in uninsured	-1.7	-1.5	-2.2	-1.8	-2.5	-2.9
Change in private with retirement health insurance	-0.87	-0.45	-2.1	-3.6	-1.6	-4.8
Change in private, no retirement health insurance	-3.6	-3.7	-3.3	-3.4	-3.3	-1.5
Change in Medicare insurance	5.5	5.1	6.7	5.5	6.2	8.5
Change in Medicaid insurance	0.47	0.27	1.1	2.7	1.3	0.26

Table 7.2C   Health Insurance Coverage Rates for Single Females

Coverage	All Respondents	None	Health Event Occurrence			
			All Types	Major Event	Chronic Illness	Accident
Uninsured at wave 1	16.4	16.7	15.7	12.1	15.9	19.8
Private with retirement health insurance at wave 1	39.2	39.8	37.6	38.6	35.3	39.8
Private, no retirement health insurance at wave 1	28.5	29.9	25.2	18.1	26.9	18.8
Medicare insurance at wave 1	5.9	4.9	8.0	7.3	8.1	9.8
Medicaid insurance at wave 1	8.0	6.2	11.9	20.6	12.5	10.2
Chane in uninsured	−0.69	−0.55	−1.0	−2.4	−0.53	−1.3
Change in private with retirement health insurance	−0.60	−0.39	−1.1	−4.7	−2.6	−3.2
Change in private, no retirement health insurance	−1.3	−1.5	−0.63	−5.9	−0.66	−1.3
Change in Medicare insurance	3.0	2.4	4.2	15.8	6.0	2.7
Change in Medicaid insurance	−0.41	−0.32	−2.1	−3.6	−2.4	−1.0

age (in many cases involving a spouse's employer) is more important for couple females who experience health events.

Differences in changes in insurance coverage between wave 1 and wave 2 provide further insights into the availability of insurance coverage for different types of new health events. For males experiencing health events, uninsurance rates declined slightly, so that 7 percent of males with and without health events reported no insurance coverage in wave 2 despite the slightly higher baseline uninsurance rate for the group with health events. The decline was substantial for males with major health events: the insurance rate increased by 6 percent, so that 4 percent were uninsured at wave 2. This increase in insurance coverage occurred despite a substantial decline in coverage by private insurance without retirement benefits (a reduction of 6 percent, compared to a reduction of only 3 percent for couple males with no health events). The reduced private insurance coverage was entirely offset by increases in Medicare and, to a lesser extent, primary Medicaid coverage. For couple males with chronic illnesses and accidents, coverage trends did not differ much from those for males with no health events.

The magnitude of differences in insurance coverage changes for females experiencing health events was somewhat smaller across the groups, compared to males. Couple females with health events had a decline in uninsurance rates slightly greater than that reported for females without events, and as with males the decline was particularly large for females with major health events. Also as with males, the decline occurred despite some reduction in coverage through private insurance that did not provide retirement benefits, because of increased coverage by Medicare and Medicaid. Medicare and Medicaid were also relatively important sources of increased insurance coverage among couple females with new chronic illnesses or accidents. For single females, increased Medicare coverage was particularly important in maintaining high insurance rates, especially for those with major health events. Finally, table 7.2A also shows that insurance coverage for female spouses of males with health events improved slightly over time, again because of relative increases in Medicare and Medicaid coverage.

7.3.3   Respondent Labor Supply, Income, and Wealth

Table 7.3 summarizes baseline labor supply, income, and wealth, as well as average changes in these economic variables, for the same groups presented in tables 7.1 and 7.2. The baseline differences across the groups in wave 1 are largely as expected from the demographic and health differences reported in table 7.1. Individuals who experienced health events were significantly less likely to be working in wave 1, and they were more likely to report being retired.[6] In part as a result of the lower work hours, their labor earnings

---

6. Note that a substantial number of individuals who report zero hours also report that they are not retired.

Table 7.3A Labor Supply, Income, and Wealth for Couples by Male Health Event Status

	All Respondents	Male Health Event Occurrence				
		None	All Types	Major Event	Chronic Illness	Accident
Male Labor Supply (%)						
Working >1,200 hours/year at wave 1	68.5	70.9	62.4	45.7	61.3	74.7
Working ≤1,200 hours/year at wave 1	5.3	5.3	5.2	4.4	5.2	4.4
Working zero hours at wave 1	26.2	23.8	32.4	49.9	33.4	20.9
Self-reported retirement at wave 1	20.6	19.2	24.2	36.2	23.7	14.5
Change in working >1,200 hours/year	−7.4	−6.3	−10.2	−17.3	−7.8	−9.3
Change in working >1,200 hours/year	0.9	1.0	0.8	−0.9	0.8	1.1
Change in working ≤1,200 hours/year	6.5	5.3	9.4	18.3	7.0	8.2
Change in working zero hours	11.0	10.7	11.7	14.6	9.7	9.6
Change to self-reported retirement						
Female Labor Supply (%)						
Working zero hours at wave 1	38.7	38.2	39.8	43.2	38.8	41.2
Change to working zero hours	3.7	3.2	4.9	6.1	3.7	3.6
Household Income[a]						
Male labor income at wave 1	33,059	34,307	29,844	23,621	28,170	33,984
	(42,174)	(42,186)	(42,027)	(45,952)	(38,878)	(37,794)
Female labor income at wave 1	12,803	13,048	12,170	11,434	12,426	11,470
	(14,765)	(15,144)	(13,740)	(12,450)	(13,929)	(13,507)

Nonlabor income at wave 1	18,718	18,610	18,995	20,330	19,134	15,967
	(33,508)	(35,651)	(27,309)	(24,257)	(28,962)	(22,073)
Total household income at wave 1	64,579	65,966	61,009	55,384	59,729	61,421
	(56,902)	(58,337)	(52,963)	(52,524)	(52,160)	(45,354)
Change in male labor income	−5,047	−4,505	−6,444	−6,899	−4,876	−8,165
	(44,076)	(42,816)	(47,128)	(35,448)	(49,806)	(37,865)
Change in female labor income	−200	−529	647	−414	1,203	767
	(15,313)	(13,259)	(19,583)	(11,575)	(22,654)	(10,193)
Change in nonlabor income	10,214	10,083	10,550	8,179	9,224	12,380
	(50,632)	(50,568)	(50,813)	(46,020)	(48,780)	(52,915)
Change in total household income	4,966	5,049	4,754	867	5,551	4,982
	(66,172)	(66,463)	(65,451)	(57,096)	(70,142)	(41,710)
Household Wealth[a]						
Housing assets at wave 1	109,511	112,154	102,704	84,333	98,057	107,311
	(97,207)	(96,776)	(98,081)	(70,914)	(95,242)	(105,232)
Nonhousing assets at wave 1	214,478	228,810	177,569	132,840	181,432	145,815
	(479,985)	(510,181)	(390,985)	(340,039)	(411,761)	(249,796)
Household net worth at wave 1	302,188	320,657	254,628	197,280	254,262	227,555
	(529,828)	(564,794)	(425,336)	(375,456)	(441,206)	(299,595)

Note: Numbers in parentheses are standard deviations.

[a]In current dollars.

Table 7.3B Labor Supply, Income, and Wealth for Couples by Female Health Event Status

	All Respondents	Female Health Event Occurrence				
		None	All Types	Major Event	Chronic Illness	Accident
Female Labor Supply (%)						
Working >1,200 hours/year at wave 1	50.1	51.0	47.2	40.9	44.6	53.9
Working ≤1,200 hours/year at wave 1	11.3	11.6	10.7	11.2	11.1	9.5
Working zero hours at wave 1	38.6	37.4	42.1	47.9	44.3	36.7
Self-reported retirement at wave 1	6.3	6.2	6.8	4.2	7.1	5.1
Change in working >1,200 hours/year	−3.2	−2.6	−5.1	−8.4	−4.8	−4.6
Change in working ≤1,200 hours/year	−0.7	−0.3	−1.8	−5.3	−1.9	−0.8
Change in working zero hours	3.9	2.9	6.9	13.7	6.7	5.4
Change to self-reported retirement	6.9	6.3	8.7	13.5	9.1	5.6
Male Labor Supply (%)						
Working zero hours at wave 1	26.3	25.3	29.1	35.0	29.7	26.0
Change to working zero hours	6.5	6.5	6.4	5.3	5.4	9.9
Household Income[a]						
Male labor income at wave 1	31,861	33,286	27,717	20,999	28,054	26,590
	(36,173)	(38,782)	(27,068)	(19,414)	(28,612)	(21,671)
Female labor income at wave 1	12,813	13,084	12,023	9,429	11,385	13,323
	(14,864)	(15,187)	(13,882)	(10,688)	(13,261)	(15,316)

Nonlabor income at wave 1	18,688	18,628	18,865	15,451	18,184	18,661
	(33,484)	(34,928)	(28,979)	(17,131)	(25,101)	(22,102)
Total household income at wave 1	63,362	64,999	58,604	45,879	57,623	58,574
	(52,242)	(54,832)	(43,764)	(27,092)	(42,360)	(34,509)
Change in male labor income	−4,384	−4,520	−3,987	−3,587	−4,047	−3,127
	(38,641)	(42,657)	(23,683)	(13,510)	(25,246)	(20,264)
Change in female labor income	−195	−15	−718	−909	−824	243
	(15,372)	(16,424)	(11,857)	(10,370)	(12,384)	(10,938)
Change in nonlabor income	9,910	10,097	9,367	10,242	8,296	15,634
	(50,321)	(50,256)	(50,524)	(39,796)	(42,007)	(67,929)
Change in total household income	5,332	5,563	4,662	5,746	3,425	12,660
	(63,678)	(65,788)	(57,246)	(39,873)	(50,904)	(71,306)
Household Wealth[a]						
Housing assets at wave 1	108,238	110,497	101,670	86,804	94,858	112,335
	(96,014)	(99,133)	(86,264)	(64,427)	(73,799)	(100,414)
Nonhousing assets at wave 1	209,989	214,590	196,611	150,481	198,972	189,777
	(463,453)	(472,008)	(438,077)	(282,031)	(468,437)	(384,503)
Household net worth at wave 1	296,777	304,269	275,000	217,936	271,539	274,967
	(511,868)	(522,968)	(478,441)	(327,118)	(500,916)	(440,412)

Note: Numbers in parentheses are standard deviations.

[a]In current dollars.

Table 7.3C   Labor Supply, Income, and Wealth for Single Females

		Health Event Occurrence				
	All Respondents	None	All Types	Major Event	Chronic Illness	Accident
Labor Supply (%)						
Working >1,200 hours/year at wave 1	61.3	64.0	55.1	46.2	54.0	50.8
Working ≤1,200 hours/year at wave 1	6.5	6.8	5.9	3.5	5.7	7.1
Working zero hours at wave 1	32.2	29.2	39.0	50.3	40.2	42.1
Self-reported retirement at wave 1	6.6	7.5	4.7	5.8	3.7	8.4
Change in working >1,200 hours/year	-7.0	-6.2	-8.7	-10.5	-9.5	-3.9
Change in working ≤1,200 hours/year	0.7	1.4	-1.0	-3.5	-1.2	-1.9
Change in working zero hours	6.3	4.9	9.7	14.0	10.7	5.8
Change to self-reported retirement	6.8	6.8	6.8	4.7	7.1	5.2
Household Income[a]						
Labor income at wave 1	16,066	16,770	14,453	10,819	13,205	15,376
	(13,803)	(14,423)	(12,281)	(10,768)	(11,764)	(12,738)
Nonlabor income at wave 1	12,646	12,443	13,110	12,690	14,236	11,484
	(19,185)	(17,995)	(21,537)	(22,710)	(22,992)	(14,461)

Total household income at wave 1	28,712	29,213	27,563	23,509	27,441	26,860
	(22,835)	(22,173)	(24,196)	(24,177)	(25,524)	(18,258)
Change in labor income	−1,362	−1,302	−1,498	−572	−1,731	−1,923
	(11,329)	(12,124)	(9,411)	(7,746)	(7,344)	(12,947)
Change in nonlabor income	596	1,262	−930	−1,454	−1,757	768
	(23,861)	(25,026)	(21,122)	(23,983)	(21,479)	(18,293)
Change in total household income	−766	−41	−2,428	−2,025	−3,488	−1,155
	(25,135)	(26,451)	(22,018)	(24,639)	(21,309)	(21,416)
Household Wealth[a]						
Housing assets at wave 1	56,966	61,203	47,255	39,372	43,208	49,389
	(68,208)	(73,845)	(53,394)	(47,758)	(47,428)	(57,372)
Nonhousing assets at wave 1	58,818	60,155	55,753	32,233	66,920	27,507
	(135,361)	(129,900)	(146,531)	(74,211)	(169,217)	(50,612)
Household net worth at wave 1	102,666	110,542	84,617	58,625	92,521	57,627
	(167,608)	(166,400)	(169,438)	(101,758)	(191,571)	(81,002)

Note: Numbers in parentheses are standard deviations.

[a] In current dollars.

in wave 1 were lower as well. The differences were particularly striking for those who experienced major health events but were also notable for those with chronic illnesses. In contrast, baseline labor supply for those who experienced accidents was very similar to that for individuals without health problems.

Total household income was also lower for individuals with health events, despite some offset in some groups through greater nonlabor income. Again, differences were particularly striking for those with major health events: for couple males, total income was around $10,000 lower; for couple females, it was around $20,000 lower; and for single females, whose baseline income is less than half of that of couples, it was almost $6,000 lower. While baseline income differences are less pronounced for individuals with chronic diseases or accidents, the patterns are similar. Corresponding differences exist in baseline household assets, and especially in net worth. For example, the baseline household net worth for couple males with major health events was around $197,000 and for those with accidents was around $228,000, compared to $320,000 for those without any health events. Differences in income and wealth are more modest between females with health events and those without. Indeed, the income differences for the male spouses of couple females are larger than the differences for the females themselves. In general, a much larger share of females reported working zero hours but not being "retired," presumably reflecting their lower lifetime labor force participation rates. As with males, however, the proportion of individuals working zero hours but not reporting retirement is relatively larger for those experiencing health events.

The table also provides some preliminary insights into the association between the occurrence of health events and changes in labor supply and income. In particular, changes to zero hours and from not reporting retirement to reporting it are much higher for individuals with major health events. Moreover, there is a substantial difference in trends for actual work hours and in reported retirement for this group. For example, for couple males, 18 percent of those with major health events moved from positive to zero hours, but only 15 percent reported becoming "retired." In contrast, among those with no health events, 5 percent moved from positive to zero hours, but 11 percent reported becoming "retired." Generally, major health events had a much more pronounced effect on actual work hours than they did on reported retirement status. Indeed, for single females, a smaller share with major health events reported "retiring" than among those without health events (5 percent vs. 7 percent), but a much larger share moved to zero hours (14 percent vs. 5 percent). Individuals who experienced accidents and new chronic illnesses were somewhat more likely to switch to zero hours than those who did not, but their self-reported "retirement" decisions did not differ much (and for these groups as well, single females with health events were less likely to report retirement). If the individuals' self-reports about retirement status reflect their beliefs, they seem to indicate that actual labor supply is much more responsive to changes in health status than are individuals' own perceptions about retirement following the occurrence of a major health event.

Health events were also associated with differences in spouse labor supply changes. In particular, the spouses of males with health events were more likely to change to zero hours of work than were spouses of males without health events (e.g., 5 percent vs. 3 percent overall, and 6 percent for spouses of men with major health events). No general patterns were evident for spouses of females with health events: men whose spouses experienced major events or new chronic illnesses were slightly less likely to retire (5 percent vs. 7 percent), and men whose spouses experienced accidents were somewhat more likely to retire (10 percent vs. 5 percent).

In association with the reduction in hours worked, labor income for individuals with health events declined more substantially between wave 1 and wave 2 compared to trends for individuals without health events. On average, these reductions in labor income were not offset by any increases in nonlabor income, except for couples with accidents.

These descriptive statistics highlight a number of important differences in trends in insurance coverage, labor supply, and income for individuals with different health experiences. The results suggest that health events may have important consequences for a range of economic outcomes. But the results also highlight considerable baseline differences among the groups with different health experiences, and significant differences across the different types of health problems. To develop a more complete understanding of the consequences of health events for trends in labor supply and insurance coverage, the remainder of the paper evaluates whether these differences in trends are robust to methods that try to compare individuals with and without health events in a more sophisticated way. These methods also permit a more sophisticated treatment of the functional consequences that may occur in association with health events.

7.3.4 Deaths

Table 7.1 also reports the number and characteristics of wave 1 survey respondents in each of the three groups that died between wave 1 and wave 2. Death rates were higher for older respondents and blacks, and those who died tended to have much lower education levels. These individuals were also in much worse health in wave 1: most had experienced major health events or chronic illnesses or both, and they had substantially worse functional status at baseline as well. Though death is obviously an important health event, households experiencing deaths are not included in the analysis that follows. The consequences of death for a household are different from the consequences of nonfatal health problems in a household member and are beyond the scope of this paper.

7.3.5   Health Events and Functional Status Changes

Table 7.4 summarizes the association between health events and functional status changes, for both males and females.[7] Table 7.4 shows that around 13 percent of all males reported an improvement in health status between waves 1 and 2, where improvement is defined as an improvement in functional status index of over 5 points. Only 9 percent of respondents had notable declines in functional status of 5 points or more: 5 percent had declines of 5 to 14 points, and 4 percent had declines of 15 points or more. The occurrence of health events was substantially correlated with these changes. Individuals with major health events were actually significantly more likely to have improvements in functional status: 17 percent of those with major health events reported improvements compared to 12 percent of those with no health events. This difference reflects the higher baseline prevalence of functional impairments in the major event group. A much larger share of the major event group (27 percent vs. 6 percent) experienced declines in function as well. Individuals with chronic illnesses and accidents had somewhat higher rates of functional decline, compared to those without events, but did not experience as severe impairments as did those with major events. Results for females were qualitatively similar, but health events of all types were somewhat more likely to lead to functional declines compared to males, and rates of improvement in functional status did not differ much among the groups.

Although table 7.4 suggests that the occurrence of health events and functional status changes are correlated, it is worth emphasizing that health events may have diverse consequences for functional status changes. Most individuals who report health events do not report decrements in function. Even among those who experienced major medical events, 73 percent of males and 65 percent of females reported no change or improvement in functional status between waves 1 and 2. Conversely, 6 percent of males and 8 percent of females who reported no new health events at all experienced functional declines. Because the share of respondents who report no health events is relatively large, a large share of respondents who report functional declines are in this category despite the low progression rate. For example, for males, approximately half of respondents reporting moderate or severe declines and approximately 45 percent of those reporting severe declines had no reported health events. This finding may result partly from measurement error and from the infeasibility of accurate survey questions about all possible health events. But it also probably results from the progression of old health problems: virtually all individuals that reported any functional decline had at least one previous chronic condition. Such long-term implications of health events imply that behavior today may be influenced by changes in expectations about future functional declines as well as changes currently associated with the health problem.

---

7. Results did not differ substantially between single and couple females.

Table 7.4A   Health Events and Functional Status Changes for Males

				Health Event Occurrence		
Functional Status (FS) Change	All Males	None	All Types	Major Event	Chronic Illness	Accident
Improvement (ΔFS index < -5)	12.5	12.2	13.5	16.8	13.6	12.3
No significant change	78.6	81.7	70.4	56.4	70.0	72.1
Minor impairment ($5 \leq \Delta$FS index < 15)	5.0	4.1	7.5	11.8	8.3	4.9
Major impairment (ΔFS index ≥ 15)	3.8	2.0	8.6	15.0	8.1	10.7

Note: Columns sum to 100 percent.

Table 7.4B   Health Events and Functional Status Changes for Females

				Health Event Occurrence		
Functional Status (FS) Change	All Females	None	All Types	Major Event	Chronic Illness	Accident
Improvement (Δ FS index < -5)	20.2	20.6	19.0	20.0	18.8	19.5
No significant change	68.2	71.2	59.8	44.7	60.1	59.6
Minor impairment ($5 \leq \Delta$FS index < 15)	7.1	5.3	12.2	19.1	12.2	10.8
Major impairment (ΔFS index ≥ 15)	4.5	2.9	9.0	16.3	8.9	10.1

Note: Columns sum to 100 percent.

7.4   Effects of Health Events: Difference-in-Differences Models

Tables 7.5 and 7.6 present estimates from difference-in-differences models of the effects of health events on insurance coverage and labor supply. In addition to individual fixed effects, the models include a number of controls for possible sources of differential trends besides the health and functional status effects of interest. The controls include age (age -45 and its square), education and its square, race (black or Latino), and private pension eligibility (eligibility for private pension benefits within one year of the wave 1 interview and eligibility for more benefits at some time in the future if work continues). Individuals aged 65 or over at the time of their wave 2 interviews were excluded. These specifications and other specifications with more complex treatment of age effects (e.g., age 62 effects for early social security eligibility) did not substantially affect the results presented here.

7.4.1   Health Insurance Coverage

Table 7.5 describes insurance coverage effects; for ease of interpretation, linear probability model results for effects on health insurance transitions are reported, with Huber-White heteroscedasticity-consistent standard errors. (Logit models gave virtually identical effect estimates.) Results are largely consistent with those reported in table 7.2 and extend them. Columns (1) and (2) describe net changes in insurance coverage for each health event group. In the model for couple males with effects for each type of health event only, individuals with new major events are slightly less likely to become uninsured (coefficient estimate of -1.5 percentage points with a t-statistic significant at the 10 percent level), while the estimates for the effects of chronic illnesses and accidents are smaller than 1 percentage point and insignificantly different from zero. With interactions for functional status declines included, no effects are statistically significant, though having major events and having substantial functional status declines are associated with insignificant reductions in the likelihood of losing insurance coverage. Uninsured males with major health events are significantly more likely (point estimate of 3 percentage points) to acquire health insurance coverage. In the interaction model, the occurrence of a major event regardless of functional status change remains associated with greater likelihood of obtaining health insurance (point estimate of 2.5 percentage points, t-statistic of 1.7), and accidents, major functional status deterioration, and interactions of functional status deteriorations with chronic illnesses and accidents are insignificantly associated with a greater likelihood of obtaining health insurance.

Columns (3) through (6) in the table consider the sources of these net changes in health insurance coverage. Those with all types of health events are insignificantly more likely to change to private insurance, and all effects are small in magnitude. The model with functional status interactions included shows that the interaction effects are concentrated in individuals with chronic illnesses and accidents (again, the results approach but do not reach statistical significance). Respondents with major events are slightly more likely to acquire private insurance. They are much less likely to continue private insurance policies, especially if major health events occur: with no functional status decline, they are 16 percentage points more likely to leave private insurance plans. In models with separate effects for the different types of private insurance policies (not shown), the transition rates are significantly greater for private insurance plans without retirement benefits. Individuals with major events are also more likely to continue in government insurance programs. Transitions to government insurance are substantial for males with major events: with no functional status decline, the coefficient estimate is 5.5 percentage points (*t*-statistic of 2.9).

In contrast, individuals with chronic illnesses and accidents without functional impairments are not much more likely to acquire government insurance. When separate effects for functional status changes are included, the overall average effect for major events regardless of functional status change largely persists. However, the effect is particularly large for those with substantial functional status declines in the absence of new health events (a total effect on likelihood of government coverage of 5.5 + 13.0 = 18.5 percentage points). In contrast, accidents are not more likely to result in new government insurance coverage by the time of the wave 2 interview.

Table 7.5B shows that the results for females in couples are qualitatively similar to those for males, though with less dramatic insurance coverage responses. Women with major events and accidents are insignificantly less likely to lose health insurance coverage, with the largest effects for women with major events who experience significant functional status declines. Women with major events and accidents are also insignificantly more likely to acquire health insurance coverage. The model with functional status interactions shows that these changes are concentrated primarily in women with significant functional status declines and no new health problems, with accidents, and (to a lesser extent) with new major events. In contrast to males, couple females with functional status declines and no new health events, and with major declines due to accidents, are slightly more likely to change to private insurance. In contrast, couple females with new major events and new accidents are significantly more likely to obtain government insurance coverage or to continue it. The model with functional status interactions shows that new government-provided insurance is particularly important for women with new major events leading to functional status declines.

Table 7.5C presents analogous results for single females. As with couple females, those with new major events are slightly less likely to lose insurance coverage, though results generally do not reach statistical significance. There are also no significant differences on average among groups with health events in changes from uninsured to insured status. In contrast to males, single females with significant functional status declines and new major events are sig-

Table 7.5A Health Events and Health Insurance Changes for Couple Males

Health Changes	Change to Uninsured (1)	Change to Insured (2)	Change to Private Insurance (3)	Continue Private Insurance (4)	Change to Government Insurance (5)	Continue Government Insurance (6)
New major health event	-1.5 (-1.5)	3.3 (2.6)	1.9 (1.6)	-14.7 (-6.0)	5.7 (3.5)	10.2 (6.0)
New chronic illness	0.19 (0.30)	-0.00 (-0.01)	0.60 (0.82)	-1.9 (-1.3)	0.44 (0.44)	0.87 (0.85)
Accident	0.73 (0.68)	0.92 (0.68)	0.92 (0.72)	-5.4 (-2.1)	0.16 (0.09)	1.9 (0.89)
Minor functional status impairment	0.46 (0.34)	-2.2 (-1.2)	-1.3 (-0.82)	-0.86 (-0.25)	-0.38 (-0.17)	5.4 (2.3)
Major functional status impairment	-1.4 (-0.75)	1.7 (0.73)	-4.5 (-2.1)	-13.7 (-3.1)	13.0 (4.4)	7.4 (2.4)
Major event* Minor FS impairment	-1.9 (-0.56)	6.1 (1.5)	0.80 (0.20)	11.1 (1.4)	0.73 (0.13)	-13.3 (-2.4)
Major event* Major FS impairment	2.2 (0.70)	-1.2 (-0.31)	1.0 (0.27)	9.0 (1.2)	-8.2 (-1.6)	-4.5 (-0.86)
Chronic*Minor FS impairment	0.14 (0.06)	2.4 (0.78)	5.0 (1.7)	-5.3 (-0.88)	0.69 (0.02)	-0.23 (-0.06)
Chronic*Major FS impairment	-1.7 (-0.66)	4.1 (1.3)	4.3 (1.4)	4.4 (0.70)	1.9 (0.44)	-5.8 (-1.4)
Accident*Minor FS impairment	-5.0 (-1.0)	4.1 (0.66)	-0.82 (-0.14)	22.5 (1.9)	-1.9 (-0.24)	-6.7 (-0.81)
Accident*Major FS impairment	0.88 (0.24)	-5.7 (-1.2)	6.4 (1.5)	10.2 (1.1)	-14.2 (-2.4)	-3.6 (-0.59)

Note: Sample consists of all nonelderly couple males. Coefficients are reported in percentage points, with *t*-statistics in parentheses. Regressions also include controls for age, education, race, and private pension eligibility.

Table 7.5B Health Events and Health Insurance Changes for Couple Females

Health Changes	Change to Uninsured (1)	Change to Insured (2)	Change to Private Insurance (3)	Continue Private Insurance (4)	Change to Government Insurance (5)	Continue Government Insurance (6)
New major health event	-1.2 (-0.84)	1.9 (1.1)	-0.59 (-0.35)	-8.1 (-2.6)	7.8 (5.6)	3.1 (2.1)
New chronic illness	0.05 (0.21)	-0.38 (-0.46)	-0.54 (-0.54)	-2.0 (-1.3)	0.06 (0.09)	2.3 (3.3)
Accident	-1.2 (-1.0)	0.89 (0.65)	0.37 (0.28)	-2.7 (-1.1)	2.1 (1.9)	1.7 (1.5)
Minor functional status impairment	0.29 (0.23)	2.6 (1.6)	2.9 (1.9)	-8.1 (-2.9)	0.47 (0.37)	1.3 (0.97)
Major functional status impairment	0.85 (0.47)	4.0 (1.9)	1.8 (0.88)	-16.0 (-4.1)	3.7 (2.1)	7.4 (4.0)
Major event* Minor FS impairment	-0.23 (-0.06)	-1.2 (-0.26)	-1.0 (-0.23)	-0.79 (-0.10)	0.58 (0.16)	1.9 (0.48)
Major event* Major FS impairment	-4.2 (-0.95)	-1.4 (-0.27)	-7.6 (-1.5)	7.3 (0.76)	10.1 (2.3)	-9.5 (-2.1)
Chronic*Minor FS impairment	-1.3 (-0.58)	-4.4 (-1.6)	-5.3 (-2.0)	10.9 (2.2)	1.8 (0.81)	-4.2 (-1.8)
Chronic*Major FS impairment	0.08 (0.03)	-4.5 (-1.3)	-0.45 (-0.14)	-5.3 (-0.88)	2.5 (0.90)	-0.26 (-0.09)
Accident* Minor FS impairment	3.4 (0.90)	-7.2 (-1.6)	-6.3 (-1.4)	4.7 (0.57)	-6.6 (-1.8)	4.2 (1.1)
Accident* Major FS impairment	3.4 (0.87)	8.0 (1.7)	5.1 (1.1)	-5.7 (-0.67)	-1.4 (-0.36)	-6.4 (-1.6)

Note: Sample consists of all nonelderly couple females. Coefficients are reported in percentage points, with t-statistics in parentheses. Regressions also include controls for age, education, race, and private pension eligibility.

Table 7.5C Health Events and Health Insurance Changes for Single Females

Health Changes	Change to Uninsured (1)	Change to Insured (2)	Change to Private Insurance (3)	Continue Private Insurance (4)	Change to Government Insurance (5)	Continue Government Insurance (6)
New major health event	-1.7 (-0.54)	0.10 (0.03)	-2.9 (-1.1)	-13.7 (-2.4)	8.7 (2.9)	13.4 (3.1)
New chronic illness	-1.1 (-0.69)	-1.7 (-0.98)	-0.69 (-0.49)	0.23 (0.08)	1.2 (0.78)	0.57 (0.26)
Accident	-0.04 (-0.02)	-0.36 (-0.15)	-0.85 (-0.42)	-4.8 (-1.1)	0.59 (0.26)	1.5 (0.46)
Minor functional status impairment	2.2 (0.69)	-0.30 (-0.09)	-3.9 (-1.4)	-3.4 (-0.59)	1.8 (0.59)	6.5 (1.5)
Major functional status impairment	2.8 (0.78)	5.3 (1.4)	-2.2 (-0.70)	-29.8 (-4.6)	20.7 (6.1)	4.5 (0.93)
Major event*Minor FS impairment	-3.3 (-0.36)	-7.2 (-0.75)	-4.0 (-0.53)	-25.4 (-1.6)	5.8 (0.66)	29.9 (2.4)
Major event*Major FS impairment	5.8 (0.73)	-17.3 (-2.1)	-3.9 (-0.55)	14.3 (0.98)	-21.8 (-2.9)	-0.02 (-0.00)
Chronic*Minor FS impairment	0.48 (0.09)	7.4 (1.3)	10.0 (2.2)	2.2 (0.22)	1.6 (0.30)	-8.8 (-1.2)
Chronic*Major FS impairment	-0.48 (-0.08)	4.7 (0.78)	5.9 (1.1)	22.1 (2.1)	-15.3 (-2.7)	-6.8 (-0.85)
Accident* Minor FS impairment	-2.1 (-0.27)	5.7 (0.71)	-4.7 (-0.70)	-6.6 (-0.47)	16.0 (2.2)	-17.0 (-1.6)
Accident* Major FS impairment	-10.3 (-1.3)	-0.59 (-0.07)	0.35 (0.05)	18.2 (1.3)	-8.9 (-1.2)	-10.9 (-1.0)

Note: Sample consists of all nonelderly single females. Coefficients are reported in percentage points, with t-statistics in parentheses. Regressions also include controls for age, education, race, and private pension eligibility.

nificantly less likely to acquire health insurance coverage. Instead, they are (insignificantly) more likely to continue private insurance coverage. Women with new chronic illnesses and functional status declines are also more likely to change to or continue private insurance coverage.

Taken together, the results on insurance coverage trends suggest that individuals with functional declines and new health events are less likely to continue private insurance plans than are those without new events or functional declines associated with existing illnesses. Rather, increased uptake of government-provided insurance is the primary source of an increase in insurance coverage rates following the occurrence of these health events. However, coverage changes differ significantly across health problems.

7.4.2 Labor Supply

Table 7.6 summarizes the effects of health events on changes in labor supply, using three different measures of labor supply: trends in whether the respondent provides any hours of work, trends in annual hours of work, and changes in self-reported "retirement" status. Only individuals who were working greater than zero hours in wave 1 are included in the analysis. As in table 7.5 for insurance coverage, the results show that different types of health events have different implications for labor supply.

For couple males, major health events have large impacts on labor supply: compared to changes in labor supply for individuals without events, rates of changing to zero hours are 26.3 percentage points higher, and hours worked decline by more than 600. These effects are concentrated in individuals with functional status impairments, particularly if those impairments occur in the setting of a new major health event. Males who experience new major events associated with substantial functional declines are more than 75 percentage points more likely to go to zero hours, and these individuals have average declines in work hours more than 1,700 hours greater than males with no health events. Reductions to zero work hours are also somewhat more common for males with chronic illnesses, provided that they are associated with minor or major functional impairments. Individuals with new chronic illnesses associated with minor reductions in function are 13.9 percentage points more likely to go from positive to zero hours, and those with major reductions are 35.3 percentage points more likely to go to zero hours. Accidents do not lead to significantly greater declines in actual labor supply overall, and even those associated with substantial functional declines are associated with only a 21 percentage point greater probability of moving to zero work hours.

In contrast to these substantial effects on actual labor supply, effects of health events on self-reported retirement status are modest. Those with major health events are only slightly (and insignificantly) more likely to report being retired, and even those with major events and substantial functional declines are only 7.1 percentage points more likely to report being retired. Those with new chronic illnesses and substantial functional declines are actually less

Table 7.6A Health Events and Labor Supply Changes for Couple Males

Health Changes	Full or Part Time to Zero Hours		Change in Work Hours per Year		Change to Self-Reported Retirement	
New major health event	26.3	17.4	-629	-412	2.27	3.6
	(8.7)	(5.0)	(-5.8)	(-3.3)	(1.0)	(1.1)
New chronic illness	1.8	-0.98	-1	61	-1.3	-0.55
	(1.1)	(-0.58)	(-0.02)	(1.0)	(-0.88)	(-0.36)
Accident	2.1	0.61	-173	-127	-2.0	-2.0
	(0.80)	(0.22)	(-1.9)	(-1.3)	(-0.87)	(-0.79)
Minor functional status impairment		0.10		-200		-3.6
		(0.03)		(-1.4)		(-1.0)
Major functional status impairment		32.1		-660		11.1
		(5.8)		(-3.3)		(2.2)
Major event*Minor FS impairment		10.2		-157		1.2
		(1.0)		(-0.44)		(0.13)
Major event*Major FS impairment		25.8		-719		-7.6
		(2.7)		(-2.1)		(-0.89)
Chronic*Minor FS impairment		13.8		-209		2.8
		(2.1)		(-0.87)		(0.47)
Chronic*Major FS impairment		3.2		-56		-17.3
		(0.43)		(-0.21)		(-2.6)
Accident*Minor FS impairment		0.24		2.25		-0.31
		(0.02)		(0.04)		(-0.02)
Accident*Major FS impairment		-10.8		-3		-4.0
		(-1.2)		(-0.01)		(-0.49)

Note: Sample consists of all nonelderly couple males working part time or full time in wave 1. Numbers in parentheses are *t*-statistics. Regressions also include controls for age, education, race, and private pension eligibility.

Table 7.6B Health Events and Labor Supply Changes for Couple Females

Health Changes	Full or Part Time to Zero Hours			Change in Work Hours per Year			Change to Self-Reported Retirement	
New major health event	17.5 (4.4)	4.7 (0.98)	3.3 (0.70)	−236 (−2.2)	45 (0.36)	72 (0.57)	6.8 (2.5)	3.0 (0.88)
New chronic illness	5.1 (2.8)	3.2 (1.6)	3.9 (2.0)	−68 (−1.4)	−28 (−0.53)	−39 (−0.74)	2.8 (2.2)	1.3 (0.90)
Accident	−1.2 (−0.42)	−3.3 (−1.1)	−4.2 (−1.3)	−77 (−1.0)	−28 (−0.33)	−16 (−0.19)	−2.4 (−1.2)	−3.1 (−1.4)
Minor functional status impairment		6.8 (1.8)	7.2 (2.0)		−231 (−2.4)	−238 (−2.4)		−4.0 (−1.5)
Major functional status impairment		17.8 (3.1)	16.9 (3.0)		−374 (−2.5)	−372 (−2.5)		−2.4 (−0.61)
Major event*Minor FS impairment		27.4 (2.7)	28.6 (2.6)		−666 (−2.5)	−701 (−2.4)		25.9 (3.4)
Major Event*Major FS impairment		44.4 (3.3)	45.3 (3.5)		−782 (−2.2)	−818 (−2.3)		−5.2 (−0.56)
Chronic*Minor FS impairment		2.0 (0.32)	2.5 (0.40)		−27 (−0.17)	−55 (−0.33)		10.9 (2.5)
Chronic*Major FS impairment		6.1 (0.69)	7.3 (0.84)		−49 (−0.21)	−34 (−0.15)		12.5 (2.0)
Accident*Minor FS impairment		16.1 (1.8)	18.0 (2.0)		−314 (−1.3)	−302 (−1.3)		8.1 (1.3)
Accident*Major FS impairment		−21.7 (−1.7)	−19.3 (−1.5)		366 (1.1)	350 (1.0)		−0.77 (−0.09)
Male retirement			11.1 (4.7)			−89 (−1.4)		9.4 (5.6)
Male Major health event			−1.9 (−0.59)			217 (2.5)		−1.1 (−0.59)
Male retirement*Major health event			−1.7 (−0.24)			−556 (−2.0)		−2.2 (−0.43)

Note: Sample consists of all nonelderly couple females working part time or full time in wave 1. Numbers in parentheses are *t*-statistics. Regressions also include controls for age, education, race, and private pension eligibility.

Table 7.6C   Health Events and Labor Supply Changes for Single Females

Health Changes	Full or Part Time to Zero Hours	Change in Work Hours per Year	Change to Self-Reported Retirement
New major health event	12.3 (1.8) −4.0 (−0.49)	141 (0.51) −241 (−1.1)	−8.1 (−1.5) −3.5 (−0.79)
New chronic illness	9.4 (3.0) 8.5 (2.5)	−204 (−1.8) −256 (−2.4)	−0.16 (−0.07) −0.92 (−0.44)
Accident	9.8 (2.1) 9.2 (1.8)	−182 (−1.1) −160 (−1.0)	1.1 (0.32) 1.4 (0.45)
Minor functional status impairment	13.4 (2.0)	−219 (−0.93)	−0.57 (−0.12)
Major functional status impairment	29.5 (3.4)	−325 (−1.1)	5.2 (0.90)
Major event*Minor FS impairment	56.2 (2.3)	−336 (−0.40)	20.7 (1.2)
Major event*Major FS impairment	21.8 (1.3)	−984 (−1.7)	11.9 (1.1)
Chronic*Minor FS impairment	−21.8 (−1.8)	229 (0.55)	−4.6 (−0.55)
Chronic*Major FS impairment	2.7 (0.21)	−472 (−1.1)	−11.9 (−1.4)
Accident*Minor FS impairment	−10.0 (−0.56)	139 (0.23)	7.1 (0.60)
Accident*Major FS impairment	−2.5 (−0.13)	308 (0.46)	−11.3 (−0.86)

Note: Sample consists of all nonelderly single females working part time or full time in wave 1. Numbers in parentheses are *t*-statistics. Regressions also include controls for age, education, race, and private pension eligibility.

likely than individuals without health problems to change to reporting that they are retired. The source of this discrepancy with only two waves of survey data is unclear: perhaps these individuals intend to return to work, or perhaps the question is misinterpreted. Future evidence on their behavior should help resolve this question, but it suggests that health events may result in substantial dissonance between individuals' perceptions of retirement status and actual work behavior.

Table 7.6B shows that the three types of health events also have substantially different implications for the labor supply of women. For women in couples, overall effects of major health events on movements to zero hours are more modest compared to males, but major health events associated with functional declines have comparably large effects. For example, women with new major health events and major impairments are 65 percentage points more likely to go to zero hours than are women with no health events or changes in impairments, and their average reduction in hours worked is over 1,100 hours greater. Also like males, major functional declines have less effect on labor supply changes associated with accidents, and functional declines in the absence of any new health events have an impact on labor supply similar to that of new chronic illnesses. In contrast to males, effects on self-reported retirement status generally do not differ substantially from effects on actual labor supply.

The last three rows of table 7.6B consider an alternative specification that includes the effect of a spouse's health event on the labor supply of females in couples. Table 7.6A showed that major health events in males have a substantial effect on male labor supply; to the extent that these effects may reduce household income, female labor supply may respond. Table 7.6B shows little net impact on the rate of movement to zero hours once controls for male retirement are included. These specifications suggest a strong joint retirement effect, but little differential effect of spouse health events on decisions to move to zero work hours. Despite this small effect on total retirement, there is a notable effect on average work hours associated with major illness in a spouse. In particular, women whose spouses have new major health events but do not retire tend to work more hours (coefficient estimate of 217 with a t-statistic of 2.5), while those whose spouses have new major events and do retire tend to work significantly fewer hours (coefficient estimate of -428 with a t-statistic of 2.6). These results suggest the presence of offsetting hours effects for the spouses of men with major health events, and more detailed regressions of effects on changes in work hours short of retirement confirm this effect.[8] In particular, spouses of men with health events who retire, but who do not retire themselves, are somewhat more likely to move from full- to part-time work, and spouses of men with health events who do not retire are somewhat less likely to move to part-time work.

---

8. The results are also somewhat stronger and more precisely estimated in the propensity model of table 7.8B.

Table 7.6C reports analogous estimates for the effects of health events on labor supply changes for single females who were working in wave 1. For single females, all three types of health events as well as decrements in functional status unrelated to new health events have notable and significant effects on movement to zero work hours. As for males, interactions between major events and functional status changes are important and have complex effects. Single women with major events associated with minor decrements in function are 65 percentage points more likely to retire, and those with major events associated with large decrements in function are 47 percentage points more likely to retire. For chronic illnesses and accidents, the effects on movement to zero hours are largely independent of the changes in function associated with the event. As with males, effects on self-reported retirement status are generally much more modest and insignificant than effects on actual hours of work. In addition, effects on changes in average hours of work are somewhat different, suggesting effects on part-time work similar to those described for couple females. As with couple females, major functional status declines associated with major events have the largest effects on average hours worked.

Together, these results show that the effects of health events on labor supply depend on both the type of change in health status as well as its consequences for physical function. While accidents have only limited independent effects, major events have dramatic effects on labor supply that extend well beyond their consequences for current functional status. The effects of chronic diseases tend to be intermediate. They are less often associated with substantial short-term functional declines, but in those cases they too can have substantial effects on labor supply. Major health events in spouses may also have important consequences for the hours worked of women in couples.

7.4.3   Propensity Score Models

Tables 7.7 and 7.8 present results analogous to those in tables 7.5 and 7.6 for models based on propensity score methods. These methods use an alternative approach to account for individual differences that might lead to differences in trends for reasons other than the occurrence of health events. Individuals were classified into five propensity groups on the basis of the propensity models for the occurrence of health events. The results of these classification models are summarized in appendix table 7A.1. Despite the different modeling framework, the results are virtually identical to those presented in tables 7.5 and 7.6.

7.5   Conclusion

This analysis of new health events in middle-aged Americans in the Health and Retirement Survey suggests several conclusions about the effects of health problems. First, new health events of all types are more prevalent in individuals with lower education, incomes, and wealth and are more prevalent in indi-

Table 7.7A   Propensity Score Model of Health Events and Health Insurance Changes for Couple Males

Health Changes	Change to Uninsured (1)	Change to Insured (2)	Change to Private Insurance (3)	Continue Private Insurance (4)	Change to Government Insurance (5)	Continue Government Insurance (6)
New major health event	−1.5 (−1.5)	2.5 (1.9)	2.1 (1.7)	−14.6 (−5.2)	5.8 (3.4)	10.2 (5.3)
New chronic illness	0.42 (0.68)	0.06 (0.08)	0.57 (0.77)	−0.93 (−0.55)	−0.19 (−0.19)	−0.38 (−0.33)
Accident	0.76 (0.72)	0.82 (0.60)	1.2 (0.97)	−2.1 (−0.73)	−0.55 (−0.31)	−1.5 (−0.76)
Minor functional status impairment	0.63 (0.46)	−2.5 (−1.4)	−1.2 (−0.71)	−4.7 (−1.2)	0.29 (0.12)	8.1 (3.1)
Major functional status impairment	−0.68 (−0.38)	2.3 (0.98)	−3.8 (−1.7)	−11.4 (−2.3)	11.7 (3.8)	2.6 (0.76)
Major event*Minor FS impairment	−1.9 (−0.58)	6.5 (1.5)	0.85 (0.21)	15.4 (1.7)	−0.31 (−0.06)	−16.2 (−2.6)
Major event*Major FS impairment	1.8 (0.58)	−2.0 (−0.51)	0.76 (0.20)	15.4 (1.8)	−8.9 (−1.7)	−7.0 (−1.2)
Chronic*Minor FS impairment	0.34 (0.14)	3.2 (1.0)	5.2 (1.8)	−2.2 (−0.32)	−0.97 (−0.24)	−4.4 (−0.95)
Chronic*Major FS impairment	1.5 (0.58)	4.9 (1.5)	4.2 (1.4)	−2.9 (−0.41)	3.3 (0.77)	−1.5 (−0.30)
Accident*Minor FS impairment	−4.3 (−0.87)	7.0 (1.1)	−0.16 (−0.03)	15.1 (1.1)	−1.8 (−0.22)	−4.0 (−0.43)
Accident*Major FS impairment	0.17 (0.05)	−7.0 (−1.5)	4.9 (1.1)	13.1 (1.3)	−13.5 (−2.2)	−2.0 (−0.30)

Note: Sample consists of all nonelderly couple males. Coefficients are reported in percentage points, with *t*-statistics in parentheses. Models include propensity score group effects.

Table 7.7B   Propensity Score Model of Health Events and Health Insurance Changes for Couple Females

Health Changes	Change to Uninsured (1)	Change to Insured (2)	Change to Private Insurance (3)	Continue Private Insurance (4)	Change to Government Insurance (5)	Continue Government Insurance (6)
New major health event	−1.6	1.9	−0.44	−5.3	7.1	1.8
	(−1.1)	(1.1)	(−0.26)	(−1.6)	(5.0)	(1.2)
New chronic illness	0.10	−0.11	−0.45	−2.4	0.04	2.0
	(0.14)	(−0.12)	(−0.56)	(−1.5)	(0.06)	(2.9)
Accident	−0.72	−0.67	0.26	−1.4	1.7	0.95
	(−0.64)	(−0.49)	(0.19)	(−0.53)	(1.5)	(0.82)
Minor functional status impairment	0.33	2.9	3.0	−9.9	0.89	1.4
	(0.25)	(1.9)	(2.0)	(−3.4)	(0.70)	(1.0)
Major functional status impairment	1.0	4.8	2.2	−19.2	4.1	7.3
	(0.56)	(2.2)	(1.1)	(−4.7)	(2.3)	(4.0)
Major event*Minor FS impairment	−0.18	−0.52	−0.43	0.05	0.26	1.2
	(−0.05)	(−0.11)	(−0.10)	(0.01)	(0.07)	(0.30)
Major event*Major FS impairment	−3.7	−0.62	−7.2	3.7	10.4	−8.9
	(−0.84)	(−0.12)	(−1.4)	(0.37)	(2.4)	(−2.0)
Chronic*Minor FS impairment	−0.95	−4.4	−5.2	10.2	1.5	−4.1
	(−0.42)	(−1.6)	(−1.9)	(2.0)	(0.67)	(−1.7)
Chronic*Major FS impairment	0.50	−4.3	−0.18	−8.4	2.7	1.0
	(0.18)	(−1.3)	(−0.06)	(−1.3)	(1.0)	(0.36)
Accident*Minor FS impairment	3.1	−6.5	−5.9	1.1	−6.1	5.0
	(0.82)	(−1.4)	(−1.3)	(0.13)	(−1.7)	(1.3)
Accident*Major FS impairment	2.9	7.5	4.9	−3.7	−1.9	−6.5
	(0.72)	(1.6)	(1.1)	(−0.41)	(−0.50)	(−1.6)

Note: Sample consists of all nonelderly single females. Coefficients are reported in percentage points, with *t*-statistics in parentheses. Models include propensity score group effects.

Table 7.7C Propensity Score Model of Health Events and Health Insurance Changes for Single Females

Health Changes	Change to Uninsured (1)	Change to Insured (2)	Change to Private Insurance (3)	Continue Private Insurance (4)	Change to Government Insurance (5)	Continue Government Insurance (6)
New major health event	-2.0 (-0.63)	2.6 (0.61)	-3.6 (-1.3)	-6.7 (-1.1)	8.0 (2.6)	8.3 (1.9)
New chronic illness	-1.0 (-0.74)	-3.3 (-1.7)	-0.78 (-0.55)	-0.73 (-0.23)	1.2 (0.75)	0.57 (0.25)
Accident	0.21 (0.09)	-0.27 (-0.10)	-1.6 (0.80)	-4.1 (-0.89)	0.20 (0.09)	-2.0 (-0.59)
Minor functional status impairment	2.4 (0.78)	0.06 (0.02)	-4.3 (-1.6)	-10.8 (-1.8)	2.1 (0.72)	11.0 (2.5)
Major functional status impairment	3.0 (0.84)	6.3 (1.7)	-2.2 (-0.69)	-34.0 (-4.8)	29.0 (6.2)	5.0 (1.0)
Major event*Minor FS impairment	-4.8 (-0.52)	-8.9 (-0.92)	-4.7 (-0.44)	-14.5 (-0.86)	4.9 (0.56)	21.8 (1.7)
Major event*Major FS impairment	6.0 (0.76)	-16.9 (-2.0)	-3.1 (-0.44)	14.7 (0.93)	-21.6 (-2.8)	-0.27 (-0.03)
Chronic*Minor FS impairment	0.93 (0.17)	9.2 (1.6)	11.2 (2.4)	-6.5 (-0.63)	3.5 (0.67)	-3.2 (-0.43)
Chronic*Major FS impairment	-0.10 (-0.02)	4.2 (0.69)	5.9 (1.2)	22.8 (2.0)	-15.1 (-2.7)	-6.4 (-0.79)
Accident*Minor FS impairment	-1.7 (-0.22)	5.0 (0.62)	-4.7 (-0.69)	-5.0 (-0.33)	16.0 (2.2)	-15.9 (-1.5)
Accident*Major FS impairment	-10.7 (-1.4)	-0.60 (-0.07)	1.1 (0.16)	16.3 (1.0)	-9.0 (-1.2)	-10.1 (-0.92)

Note: Sample consists of all nonelderly single females. Coefficients are reported in percentage points, with *t*-statistics in parentheses. Models include propensity score group effects.

Table 7.8A Propensity Score Model of Health Events and Labor Supply Changes for Couple Males

Health Changes	Full or Part Time to Zero Hours		Change in Work Hours per Year		Change to Self-Reported Retirement	
New major health event	25.5	16.9	−609	−396	2.7	4.0
	(8.2)	(4.8)	(−5.6)	(−3.2)	(0.95)	(1.2)
New chronic illness	1.0	−1.5	25	80	−1.9	−0.99
	(0.63)	(−0.84)	(0.43)	(1.3)	(−1.3)	(−0.62)
Accident	2.3	0.91	−167	−119	−2.2	−2.2
	(0.85)	(0.33)	(−1.8)	(−1.2)	(−0.91)	(−0.84)
Minor functional status impairment		0.47		−195		−2.6
		(0.12)		(−1.4)		(−0.72)
Major functional status impairment		29.6		−600		7.8
		(5.2)		(−3.0)		(1.5)
Major event*Minor FS impairment		12.6		−243		2.1
		(1.2)		(−0.68)		(0.23)
Major event*Major FS impairment		25.6		−723		−9.0
		(2.6)		(−2.1)		(−1.0)
Chronic*Minor FS impairment		11.5		−162		0.13
		(1.7)		(−0.67)		(0.02)
Chronic*Major FS impairment		3.4		−57		−16.5
		(0.46)		(−0.21)		(−2.4)
Accident*Minor FS impairment		−6.8		357		−9.2
		(−0.43)		(0.63)		(−0.63)
Accident*Major FS impairment		−7.7		−105		−0.83
		(−0.82)		(−0.32)		(−0.10)

Note: Sample consists of all nonelderly couple males working part time or full time in wave 1. Numbers in parentheses are *t*-statistics. Models include propensity score group effects.

Table 7.8B   Propensity Score Model of Health Events and Labor Supply Changes for Couple Females

Health Changes	Full or Part Time to Zero Hours			Change in Work Hours per Year			Change to Self-Reported Retirement	
New major health event	18.4 (4.6)	5.8 (1.2)	4.5 (0.93)	−255 (−2.4)	25 (0.20)	54 (0.42)	7.4 (2.6)	4.3 (1.2)
New chronic illness	4.8 (2.6)	2.7 (1.4)	3.5 (1.8)	−63 (−1.3)	−18 (−0.35)	−30 (−0.57)	2.5 (1.9)	1.0 (0.71)
Accident	−2.5 (−0.88)	−4.6 (−1.4)	−5.4 (−1.7)	−47 (−0.62)	0 (0.00)	13 (0.15)	−3.5 (−1.7)	−4.4 (−1.9)
Minor functional status impairment	6.7 (1.8)	7.1 (1.9)		−227 (−2.3)	−235 (−2.4)		−3.8 (−1.4)	
Major functional status impairment	18.6 (3.3)	17.6 (3.1)		−387 (−2.6)	−382 (−2.6)		−1.9 (−0.47)	
Major event*Minor FS impairment	27.6 (2.7)	29.1 (2.7)		−679 (−2.5)	−715 (−2.5)		26.6 (3.4)	
Major event*Major FS impairment	41.2 (3.1)	42.4 (3.2)		−712 (−2.0)	−751 (−2.2)		−10.0 (−1.0)	
Chronic*Minor FS impairment	2.5 (0.40)	3.0 (0.48)		−38 (−0.23)	−65 (−0.39)		10.6 (2.3)	
Chronic*Major FS impairment	6.3 (0.71)	7.7 (0.89)		−73 (−0.31)	−62 (−0.27)		12.8 (2.0)	
Accident*Minor FS impairment	16.0 (1.8)	18.9 (2.1)		−314 (−1.4)	−329 (−1.4)		10.7 (1.6)	
Accident*Major FS impairment	−22.4 (−1.7)	−19.9 (−1.6)		400 (1.2)	376 (1.1)		−2.8 (−0.31)	
Male retirement			12.3 (5.2)			−115 (−1.8)		11.4 (6.6)
Male major health event			−0.84 (−0.26)			196 (2.3)		−0.21 (−0.09)
Male retirement*Major health event			−5.1 (−0.72)			−485 (−2.6)		−6.3 (−1.2)

Note: Sample consists of all nonelderly couple females working part time or full time in wave 1. Numbers in parentheses are *t*-statistics. Models include propensity score group effects.

Table 7.8C   **Propensity Score Model of Health Events and Labor Supply Changes for Single Females**

Health Changes	Full or Part time to Zero Hours	Change in Work Hours per Year	Change to Self-Reported Retirement
New major health event	15.4	-316	-1.1
	(2.1)	(-1.4)	(-0.24)
New chronic illness	9.6	-233	-0.97
	(2.9)	(-2.2)	(-0.45)
Accident	8.9	-147	-0.36
	(1.8)	(-0.92)	(-0.11)
Minor functional status impairment	13.4	-261	-0.44
	(1.9)	(-1.1)	(-0.09)
Major functional status impairment	33.1	-444	6.4
	(3.7)	(-1.5)	(1.1)
Major event*Minor FS impairment	64.8	-463	29.9
	(2.5)	(-0.54)	(1.7)
Major event*Major FS impairment	18.2	-891	9.2
	(1.1)	(-1.6)	(0.81)
Chronic*Minor FS impairment	-21.6	179	-5.8
	(-1.7)	(0.42)	(-0.68)
Chronic*Major FS impairment	-2.9	-317	-13.9
	(-0.22)	(-0.71)	(-1.5)
Accident*Minor FS impairment	-10.5	225	7.7
	(-0.58)	(0.37)	(0.63)
Accident*Major FS impairment	-5.3	468	-12.4
	(-0.27)	(0.70)	(-0.91)

Note: Sample consists of all nonelderly single females working part time or full time in wave 1. Numbers in parentheses are *t*-statistics. Models include propensity score group effects.

viduals with other prior health conditions as well. These relationships persist after adjusting for age. Second, health events may be quite heterogeneous in nature, and thus in their consequences for functional status and expectations about future functional status, consumption, and survival. Only a minority of new health events lead to substantial short-term functional impairments, even for major events such as heart attacks and strokes. Old health problems (and possibly health problems for which information was not obtained in the HRS) are also important in explaining functional declines.

Third, different types of health events have quite different consequences for health insurance coverage and labor supply. Major health events have particularly large effects on retirement decisions, and these effects go well beyond the consequences of the events for functional status. For example, males with major events associated with major functional status declines leave the labor force at rates over 40 percentage points higher than males with major functional status declines in the absence of new health events. New chronic illnesses have milder, though significant, effects on increasing rates of labor force exit beyond their association with functional declines alone. In contrast, health problems that are unlikely to have long-term consequences for health (accidents) are not associated with additional labor force departures. Though these health events have enormous significance for labor force departure rates, they have only modest impact on individuals' self-reported retirement status, especially for males in couples and single females. Examining the subsequent labor supply of individuals with these events is thus a question of considerable importance for understanding the long-term impact of health events.

In conjunction with their effects on labor supply, health events also have substantial effects on health insurance coverage, especially for males. Health events are associated with small increases in the probability of having health insurance, despite the fact that they tend to lead to reductions in private insurance coverage, particularly for males and for individuals without retiree insurance coverage. These reductions in private insurance coverage are offset by increased coverage through government insurance programs, primarily Medicare, as a result of qualification through the disability insurance system. These insurance changes are more related to the actual occurrence of disability than the labor supply changes, though major health events do lead to more switches to government insurance regardless of functional status change.

These substantial effects of health events on labor supply and health insurance coverage raise further questions. What are the consequences for household expenditures on medical care and other types of consumption? Do the events substantially alter wealth accumulation? What are the long-term implications of these events for households, including the spouses of individuals with health events? Further analysis of the HRS should provide additional insights into these and other questions about the economic consequences of health events.

Appendix

Table 7A.1   **Propensity for Health Events**

Independent Variable	Couple Males		Couple Females		Single Females	
	Any	Major	Any	Major	Any	Major
Intercept	−1.06	−7.44	−2.38	−8.02	−14.0	−22.8
	(1.24)	(3.46)	(0.88)	(3.42)	(9.37)	(54.2)
Age at wave 1	−0.00	0.08	0.03	0.11	0.28	0.25
	(0.02)	(0.07)	(0.02)	(0.07)	(0.19)	(0.51)
Age squared	0.00	−0.00	0.00	−0.00	−0.00	−0.01
	(0.01)	(0.00)	(0.00)	(0.00)	(0.01)	(0.02)
Black	0.23	2.90	1.85	−28.7	5.19	7.77
	(1.64)	(3.23)	(1.40)	(280)	(3.31)	(48.5)
Latino	1.95	0.03	−0.43	−52.1	−0.74	−0.81
	(1.88)	(4.56)	(1.71)	(23.8)	(5.77)	(397)
Graduated high school	−0.01	0.01	−0.32	−0.37	−0.08	0.18
	(0.12)	(0.24)	(0.13)	(0.31)	(0.23)	(0.62)
Some college	−0.16	0.29	−0.44	−0.29	0.29	1.25
	(0.15)	(0.29)	(0.16)	(0.39)	(0.29)	(0.69)
Bachelor's degree only	−0.15	−0.49	−0.38	−0.35	0.07	0.73
	(0.17)	(0.43)	(0.21)	(0.56)	(0.36)	(0.97)
Post-baccalaureate degree	−0.15	0.26	−0.35	−0.43	−0.42	−0.41
	(0.17)	(0.39)	(0.24)	(0.69)	(0.39)	(1.35)
Black*Age	−0.00	0.04	−0.02	0.32	−0.11	0.03
	(0.03)	(0.05)	(0.03)	(0.15)	(0.06)	(0.16)
Latino*Age	−0.03	−0.01	0.01	0.89	−0.00	0.01
	(0.03)	(0.08)	(0.03)	(0.40)	(0.10)	(7.25)
Black*Postsecondary education	0.16	0.35	−0.20	−11.2	−0.25	−0.73
	(0.30)	(0.56)	(0.31)	(134)	(0.40)	(1.10)
Latino*Postsecondary education	0.18	0.53	0.86	−10.6	−1.52	−0.22
	(0.37)	(0.90)	(0.42)	(248)	(0.89)	(62.2)
U.S. born	−0.06	0.55	0.35	−0.13	−0.86	6.55
	(0.21)	(0.60)	(0.24)	(0.55)	(0.51)	(47.7)
Black*U.S. born	0.23	0.02	−0.57	10.7	0.79	−9.18
	(0.51)	(1.24)	(0.54)	(280)	(0.76)	(47.7)
Latino*U.S. born	−0.16	−0.15	0.17	0.59	1.65	−6.93
	(0.36)	(0.99)	(0.43)	(1.49)	(0.83)	(74.3)
Mother had postsecondary education	0.24	−2.06	−0.21	0.15	0.49	0.62
	(0.16)	(0.74)	(0.18)	(0.45)	(0.33)	(0.84)
Mother's education missing	−0.02	−0.03	−0.25	−1.60	0.58	0.93
	(0.20)	(0.37)	(0.29)	(0.74)	(0.48)	(0.85)
Black*Mother had post-secondary education	0.24	−11.86	0.87	−10.8	0.61	−5.28
	(0.16)	(1150)	(0.54)	(291)	(0.82)	(55.3)
Black*Mother's education missing	0.74	0.65	0.28	−10.7	−0.97	−9.39
	(0.48)	(1.00)	(0.54)	(170)	(0.70)	(32.0)
Father had postsecondary education	0.31	0.87	0.18	−0.61	−0.48	−0.72
	(0.15)	(0.31)	(0.16)	(0.52)	(0.35)	(1.22)
Father's education missing	0.22	0.66	−0.28	0.83	−0.52	1.28
	(0.18)	(0.34)	(0.25)	(0.47)	(0.39)	(0.68)

Table 7A.1   (continued)

Independent Variable	Couple Males		Couple Females		Single Females	
	Any	Major	Any	Major	Any	Major
Black*Father had post-	−1.56	−14.5	−0.06	−9.32	0.15	−5.78
secondary education	(1.11)	(1251)	(0.77)	(465)	(0.94)	(53.8)
Black*Father's	−1.10	−2.83	0.12	0.55	1.02	−1.12
education missing	(0.46)	(1.26)	(0.46)	(1.10)	(0.55)	(1.40)
Mother lived to age 70	−0.10	−0.23	−0.07	−0.20	−0.05	−0.55
	(0.09)	(0.20)	(0.10)	(0.27)	(0.19)	(0.47)
Mother's longevity missing	−0.32	0.48	−0.25	−12.1	−15.0	0.26
	(0.69)	(1.20)	(1.25)	(791)	(1628)	(164)
Father lived to age 70	−0.03	0.00	−0.01	−0.11	0.21	−0.07
	(0.09)	(0.18)	(0.28)	(0.25)	(0.17)	(0.45)
Father's longevity missing	0.59	−0.27	0.67	1.06	0.77	−7.52
	(0.37)	(0.82)	(0.42)	(0.74)	(0.60)	(49.1)
Household net worth	−0.03	−0.43	−0.01	−0.49	−0.56	−1.96
0–200,000	(0.26)	(0.44)	(0.28)	(0.64)	(0.29)	(0.57)
Household net worth	−0.06	−0.73	−0.11	−0.28	−0.34	−1.85
200,000–1,000,000	(0.27)	(0.48)	(0.29)	(0.67)	(0.37)	(0.84)
Household net worth	−0.27	−1.63	−0.15	0.09	−0.53	−8.43
>1,000,000	(0.33)	(0.78)	(0.36)	(0.88)	(0.89)	(72.9)
Household income	−0.16	−0.27	−0.26	−0.21	0.22	−0.02
15,000−75,000	(0.20)	(0.39)	(0.23)	(0.51)	(0.22)	(0.58)
Household income	−0.26	−0.56	−0.18	−0.66	0.06	0.14
75,000–200,000	(0.22)	(0.45)	(0.24)	(0.59)	(0.46)	(1.30)
Household income	−0.08	0.40	−0.60	−11.9	1.93	3.83
>200,000	(0.35)	(0.71)	(0.45)	(265)	(1.29)	(1.63)
History of major	0.40	0.92	0.19	1.03	−0.13	0.79
health event	(0.13)	(0.22)	(0.16)	(0.31)	(0.26)	(0.53)
History of chronic illness	−0.00	0.25	−0.12	−0.00	−0.15	1.27
	(0.09)	(0.20)	(0.10)	(0.27)	(0.18)	(0.62)
Wave 1 functional status	0.06	0.06	0.03	0.07	0.05	−0.00
index	(0.01)	(0.02)	(0.01)	(0.03)	(0.02)	(0.05)
Functional status index	−0.00	−0.00	−0.00	−0.00	−0.00	0.00
squared	(0.00)	(0.00)	(0.00)	(0.00)	(0.00)	(0.00)
Eligible to receive	0.28	−0.02	0.07	0.15	−0.24	0.87
pension benefits	(0.10)	(0.23)	(0.15)	(0.35)	(0.25)	(0.59)
Pension eligibility missing	0.07	0.08	0.05	−0.33	−0.05	0.35
	(0.16)	(0.34)	(0.15)	(0.49)	(0.24)	(0.68)

Note: Table presents results for logistic models with dependent variables at the column head. Numbers in parentheses are standard errors.

References

Blau, David, and Donna Gilleskie. 1997. Retiree health insurance and the labor force behavior of older men in the 1990s. NBER Working Paper no. 5948. Cambridge, Mass.: National Bureau of Economic Research.

Bound, John. 1989. The health and earnings of rejected disability applicants. *American Economic Review* 79:482–503.

———. 1991. The health and earnings of rejected disability applicants: Reply. *American Economic Review* 81:1427–34.

Bound, John, Michael Schoenbaum, and Timothy Waidmann. 1995. Race and education differences in disability status and labor force attachment in the Health and Retirement Survey. *Journal of Human Resources* 30 (Suppl.): S227–S267.

Deaton, Angus. 1992. *Understanding consumption.* Oxford: Clarendon.

Employee Benefit Research Institute. 1995. EBRI databook on employee benefits. Washington, D.C.: Employee Benefit Research Institute.

Gertler, Paul, and Jonathan Gruber. 1997. Insuring consumption against illness. NBER Working Paper. Cambridge, Mass.: National Bureau of Economic Research.

Grossman, Michael. 1972. *The demand for health: A theoretical and empirical investigation.* New York: National Bureau of Economic Research.

Gruber, Jonathan. 1996. Disability insurance benefits and the labor supply of older persons. NBER Working Paper. Cambridge, Mass.: National Bureau of Economic Research.

Gruber, Jonathan, and Brigitte Madrian. 1995. Health insurance availability and the retirement decision. *American Economic Review* 85:938–48.

———. 1996. Health insurance and early retirement: Evidence from the availability of continuation of coverage. In *Advances in the economics of aging,* ed. David Wise. Chicago: University of Chicago Press.

Juster, F. Thomas, and Richard Suzman. 1995. An overview of the Health and Retirement Survey. *Journal of Human Resources* 30 (Suppl.): S7–S56.

Morduch, Jonathan. 1995. Income smoothing and consumption smoothing. *Journal of Economic Perspectives* 9 (summer): 103–14.

Parsons, Donald. 1980. The decline of male labor force participation. *Journal of Political Economy* 88:117–34.

———. 1991. The health and earnings of rejected disability insurance applicants: Comment. *American Economic Review* 81:1419–26.

Sammartino, Frank. 1987. The effect of health on retirement. *Social Security Bulletin* 50 (2): 31–47.

Smith, James. 1995. Racial and ethnic differences in wealth in the Health and Retirement Survey. *Journal of Human Resources* 30 (Suppl.): S158–S183.

Smith, James, and Raynard Kington. 1997. Demographic and economic correlates of health in old age. *Demography* 34:159–70.

Stern, Steven. Measuring the effect of disability on labor force participation. *Journal of Human Resources* 24:361–95.

Wallace, Robert B., and A. Regula Herzog. 1995. Overview of the health measures in the Health and Retirement Study. *Journal of Human Resources* 30 (Suppl.): S84–S107.

Comment   Michael D. Hurd

Although there is a long history of using measures of health in behavioral estimation, most often the measure is self-assessed health, and its use has been criticized because it is said to be "endogenous." For example, models of retirement may use health status as an explanatory variable, but perhaps those who

Michael D. Hurd is professor of economics at the State University of New York, Stony Brook, a researcher at RAND, and a research associate of the National Bureau of Economic Research.

retire report poor health simply to have a socially acceptable reason for retiring. That is, the decision to retire causes the report of poor health, not the reverse. While I find this rather implausible because self-rated health predicts retirement many years later, this paper addresses this issue by using some of the wide range of data from the Health and Retirement Survey (HRS) that are plausibly more objective. An important aspect is whether results based on these more objective measures are similar to results based on more subjective measures. The paper also augments traditional analyses of the effects of health by studying the effects of changes in health as well as cross-sectional variation in health across individuals. This is likely to be important particularly for labor force participation because workers can adapt to long-term health problems either by job sorting or by accommodation on the job. Thus, the cross-sectional variation in participation as health varies may not be large. In contrast a change in health status may lead to large effects on retirement as the costs of finding a new job or making accommodation may be rather large in comparison to the value of a few extra years of work.

The main health measures used in this paper are health events, particularly major health events, and functional limitations. In principle, these are mainly objective. However, the frequency of health events is likely to be related to socioeconomic status because the form of the questions in the HRS is "In the last two years has a doctor told you that you have had a . . ." Thus, the detection and reporting are likely to be related to intensity of the use of health care services and economic status. A number of the functional limitations, such as limitations on activities of daily living, are quite subjective: the form of the questions is "Do you have any difficulty . . ." Nonetheless, these measures are likely to be more objective than self-assessed health status, although that does not especially mean they will be better predictors of behavior.

I consider the main results to be in tables 7.3 and 7.5. Here we see that among married men who had no health event between waves 1 and 2 labor force participation fell by 5.3 percent whereas among men who had a major health event participation fell by 18.3 percent. This decline comes on top of a much lower baseline participation rate (76.2 percent vs. 50.1 percent), so that following the major event the participation rates are very different. The results for women, both married and single are qualitatively similar. When the major health event is interacted with the change in functional impairment, as in table 7.6, the effects are very large, basically predicting that anyone with major functional impairment and a major health event will no longer be in the labor force. The conclusion is that health, as measured more objectively, has a substantial effect on labor force participation, which complements earlier results about retirement based on self-assessed health. These results show that health effects are not simply ex post rationalizations for retirement.

An interesting finding that shows the potential for this line of work is the effect of health events of the husband on the labor force participation of the wife. In table 7.3A when there was a major health event wives reduced their participation by 6.1 percent compared with a reduction of 3.2 percent when there was not a major health event. Although qualitatively consistent with the wife's leaving the labor force to care for her husband, the effect is not especially large in that there were only 276 cases out of 4,364. However as shown in table 7.6B the change in participation of wives is associated with the retirement of husbands, not with health events themselves: when husbands retired, participation by wives declined by 11.1 percent relative to wives whose husbands did not retire; yet the changes associated with the health events themselves are basically zero. This finding can be explained in two, not necessarily contradictory, ways: (1) It supports prior research that indicated a complementarity in the leisure of husbands and wives, leading to coordination of their retirement dates. (2) Even in the class of major health events there are gradations, and the most serious may lead to retirement by the husband and retirement by the wife to care for the husband. Of course both of these explanations could be relevant, although health events are unlikely to be as important quantitatively as the other determinants of retirement, such as social security and pensions.

The importance of socioeconomic status as measured by either income or wealth shows in the tables: for example, household wealth among all couples was $302,200; among couples where the husband had a major health event it was $197,300. This finding is consistent with the variation in wealth by self-assessed health.

I have some reservations about some of the results. The apparent improvement in functional status reported in table 7.1 could be due to sample selection between the waves, rather than to true average improvement in the population. The level of functional status in wave 1 was 6.5, which is about 1.4 points on average,[1] but with a standard deviation of 10.8. In that a point is assigned if a respondent has even some difficulty in performing tasks such as stooping, kneeling, or crouching, a substantial majority would have no points and be quite healthy. Thus, the index is low on average but is very highly skewed. The mean change in the index between the waves was 0.55, but with a standard deviation of 8.4. In this context the change is small: for example, it could be explained by mortality. Consider the contribution to the baseline index from the 93 husbands who died between the waves. They contributed 0.51 to the baseline level, which is about the amount of change between the waves. Furthermore, the response rate of HRS wave 2 was about 92 percent, and the nonrespondents had worse health than the average in wave 1. The highly skewed distribution at baseline and in the change, combined with differential sample retention, may well be the cause of the overall improvement. This view is reinforced by the fact that the overall patterns are the same over married men, married women, and single women.

I believe some of results are due to the special age range of the sample and

1. The index in table 7.1 is the score, which ranges from 0 to 22, multiplied by 100/22.

to a correlation between age and the probability of a health event. In particular, some of the HRS respondents were older than age 62 at baseline, and some reached age 62 between the waves. Their experience, especially with respect to labor force participation, is probably strongly influenced by their ages. For example, a health event may induce retirement or perhaps reinforce an already planned retirement that is financed by social security benefits. This option would not be available to the general population or even to the HRS respondents of younger ages. This scenario could be investigated through complete interactions with the age intervals less than 62 and 62–64. A health event inducing withdrawal from the labor force at age 62 is really about the effects of health on retirement, and the welfare effects are quite different from withdrawal from the labor force at younger ages.

A result that could benefit from additional explanation is the level and increase in Medicare coverage in table 7.2A. The sample is limited to those younger than 65, so the high level of Medicare eligibility (about 25 percent) among those who had a major event between the waves must be through the social security disability program, as it would also be for the additional 10 percent that became eligible for Medicare between the waves. This seems like a high rate of Medicare coverage. In the survey, Medicare coverage is determined from self-reports that may be subject to reporting error, but some verification could be made from data in other parts of the survey: section N has information about receipt of social security disability benefits, and section J has information about application and qualification for the social security disability program.

III   Methodological Innovations

Consumption and Savings Balances of the Elderly: Experimental Evidence on Survey Response Bias

Michael D. Hurd, Daniel McFadden, Harish Chand,
Li Gan, Angela Merrill, and Michael Roberts

> Collecting bracket responses without varying the anchors is criminally
> negligent.—Danny Kahneman, 1993

8.1 Psychometric Biases in Economic Survey Data

8.1.1 The Need for Accurate Data

A prerequisite for understanding the economic behavior of the elderly, and the impacts of public policy on their health and well-being, is accurate data on key economic variables such as income, consumption, and assets, as well as on expectations regarding future economic and demographic events such as major health costs, disabilities, and death. Standard practice is to elicit such information in economic surveys, relying on respondents' statements regarding the variables in question.

Economists are generally aware that stated responses are noisy. Item nonresponse is a common problem, and carefully done surveys are designed to minimize it. Well-designed analyses of economic survey data are careful about detecting implausible outliers, imputing missing values, and correcting for selection caused by dropping missing observations. Circumstances are recognized that tend to produce systematic biases in response, such as telescoping in recall of past events that arises from the psychophysical perception of time intervals, or overstatement of charitable contributions that arises from the incentive to project a positive self-image. Nevertheless, economic studies are

Michael D. Hurd is professor of economics at the State University of New York, Stony Brook, a researcher at RAND, and a research associate of the National Bureau of Economic Research. Daniel McFadden is professor of economics at the University of California, Berkeley, and a research associate of the National Bureau of Economic Research. Harish Chand is a graduate student at the University of California, Berkeley. Li Gan is a graduate student at the University of California, Berkeley. Angela Merrill is a graduate student at the University of California, Berkeley. Michael Roberts is a graduate student at the University of California, Berkeley.

This research was supported by a grant from the Institute on Aging of the National Institutes of Health to the National Bureau of Economic Research. The authors are indebted to Danny Kahneman, whose remarks on anchoring motivated this research.

often too sanguine about the reliability of subjects' statements regarding objective economic data.

8.1.2   Stated versus Revealed Economic Data

For many economic variables, it is possible in principle to obtain the accounting or administrative records necessary to verify stated responses. For example, subjects may be asked to consult or provide copies of utility bills, bank statements, or income tax records, or to give permission for linking to Medicare or social security records. In practice, this is rarely done because of the cost, the difficulty of obtaining compliance from the subjects, and privacy and disclosure issues surrounding government administrative records.

In cases where direct comparisons of stated and revealed economic data are available, the results are sobering. For example, Poterba and Summers (1986) find that misstatements regarding employment status lead to underestimates by a factor of two of the duration of unemployment. Cowing, Dubin, and McFadden (1982) found in an Energy Information Administration panel of houses that 5 percent of the basements reported in one wave of the survey disappeared in the next wave. There may be parallels between the "disappearing basement" problem and the "disappearing asset" problem following sales of homes in economic panels such as the Panel Study of Income Dynamics and the Health and Retirement Survey.

Other techniques for investigating the accuracy of economic survey responses are to compare survey aggregates with national administrative aggregates and to vary the survey by experimental design to obtain internal evidence on consistency of responses. An example of the first type is comparison of stated days of hospitalization with aggregate hospital statistics. This paper focuses on an example of the second type, in which the elicitation format for several economic questions in the survey of Asset and Health Dynamics among the Oldest Old (AHEAD) was varied by design.

8.1.3   Response Errors

There are at least five reasons that a subject may fail to give accurate information on an economic variable: question ambiguity, subject concerns about confidentiality of sensitive information, incentives for strategic misrepresentation, imperfect knowledge of the facts, and psychometric context effects. In addition, errors may be introduced in the coding of responses by interviewers and in processing the survey data.

Question Ambiguity

Questions about economic quantities may confuse subjects even if they are prepared to give accurate responses. Consider annual savings as an illustration. The question "How much did you save last year?" is not straightforward. Should accumulation of equity in durables such as real property be included? What about vehicles? Accumulated earnings and capital gains in asset accounts? Depreciation? Changes in checking account balances? Should changes in asset values be in nominal terms, or in inflation-corrected dollars? Is the year in question from the date of the interview, or the past calendar year? In the absence of detailed instructions, which would themselves be vulnerable to misunderstanding, even subjects with precise knowledge of their economic position may find such questions difficult to answer. The result may be nonresponse or a dispersion in responses resulting from different implicit assumptions about the definition of the economic variable. This paper will not address question ambiguity, but we note that it may be a significant source of error in economic surveys, and the elicitation and analysis methods used to moderate the impact of other sources of error do nothing to control these errors.

Confidentiality

Concerns of subjects about privacy and disclosure are likely to contribute to item nonresponse. In addition, survey organizations may be reluctant to ask sensitive questions because of the possibility of upsetting respondents and endangering the rest of the survey responses. However, the experience with AHEAD, the Longitudinal Study of Aging, and other contemporary panel studies is that subjects are remarkably willing to discuss areas that have traditionally been considered difficult areas for questioning, such as health events. While it is clearly essential to establish that the survey has a useful social purpose and that confidentiality will be maintained, it seems clear that establishing rapport between the interviewer and the subject and structuring the questionnaire so that sensitive questions are not surprising or boring will be sufficient to eliminate confidentiality concerns as a major source of error for most topics.

Strategic Misrepresentation

Economic theory suggests that when subjects anticipate a possible connection between their response and some economic outcome in which they have an interest, they may have strategic incentives to misrepresent information. To illustrate, subjects asked about their interest in nursing home insurance may overstate their willingness to pay (WTP) if they believe a large response will increase the probability they will have this service as an option without committing them to this cost. On the other hand, they may understate WTP if they believe that their actual cost will be tied to their response. In practice, most standard economic surveys have no linkage from response to subsequent economic events that would create incentives for misrepresentation. Further, there is at least fragmentary evidence that subjects are usually truthful when there are no positive incentives for misrepresentation, and even in some circumstances where there are such incentives (see Bohm 1972; Smith 1979). There are, however, some areas where there may be strong *nonpecuniary incentives* for misrepresentation. For example, subjects asked questions like "How often do you go to church?" or "How much did you contribute to charity last year?"

may give biased responses in order to project a more favorable image to the interviewer and to themselves. In contingent valuation surveys, this phenomenon is sometimes called the "warm glow" motivation for overstating WTP for public goods. There are some elementary precautions in economic survey design that decouple responses from economic consequences and eliminate obvious sources of *economic* incentives for misrepresentation. One way to control misrepresentation arising from nonpecuniary incentives is to present subjects with tasks that are "ethically neutral." For example, subjects may have no incentive to misrepresent trade-offs between different public goods, even when "warm glow" distorts their stated trade-off between public goods and personal private goods or money.

Imperfect Knowledge

Most economic surveys assume that subjects can readily and reliably recall household economic facts. This may be valid for regularly monitored quantities, such as checking account balances or monthly social security checks, and subjects may find that being truthful minimizes response effort. However, subjects are likely to be uncertain about quantities that are irregularly monitored or require them to process multiple numbers, such as net wealth or monthly consumption. In such circumstances, subjects may refuse to answer or may construct estimates. Svenson (1996) describes a decision process in which simple heuristics are used to produce a preliminary estimate, using *markers* and *editing* to simplify and group information (see Kahneman and Tversky 1979; Coupey 1994). Next, the decision maker engages in a process of differentiating the test estimate from alternatives through an internal dialogue in which ambiguities are resolved so that consistent aspects of the test estimate are emphasized, through sharpening of perceptions of the plausibility of the test estimate and implausibility of alternatives, and through restructuring of the task by adding or resurrecting alternatives. There may also be consolidation of perceptions following selection of a final estimate, to reduce dissonance and promote development of rules and principles for future decisions. It is a particular problem for analysis if constructed estimates are systematically biased.

Psychometric Bias

There is extensive evidence from psychological experiments that humans are vulnerable to systematic cognitive illusions when dealing with uncertainty (see Rabin 1998). Table 8.1 lists some of the cognitive errors that appear regularly in experimental settings and may be factors in economic survey responses. This paper will focus on biases induced by anchoring to prompts presented by questions on economic variables and will show that anchoring bias is a significant issue in consumption and savings variables of key interest for the study of the elderly.

Anchoring describes a family of effects observed in many psychological studies of beliefs about uncertain quantities, such as the length of the Amazon

Table 8.1	Cognitive Illusions
Effect	Description
Anchoring	Responses are influenced by cues contained in the question.
Availability	Responses rely too heavily on readily retrieved information, and too little on background information.
Context	Previous questions and interviewer interaction color perception.
Framing/reference point	Question format changes saliency of different aspects of the cognitive task.
Focal	Quantitative information is stored or reported categorically.
Primary/recency	Initial and recently experienced events are the most salient.
Projection	Responses are consonant with the self-image the subject wishes to project.
Prospect	The likelihoods of low-probability events are misjudged and treated either as too likely or as impossible.
Regression	Causality and permanence are attached to past fluctuations, and regression to the mean is underestimated.
Representativeness	High conditional probabilities induce overestimates of unconditional probabilities.
Rule-driven	Motivation and self-control induce strategic responses.
Saliency	The most salient aspects of the question are overemphasized.
Status quo	Current status and history are privileged.
Superstition	Elaborate causal structures are attached to coincidences.
Temporal	Time discounting is temporally inconsistent.

or the height of the tallest redwood (Tversky and Kahneman 1974). Subjects in these studies are asked to judge whether a particular value (the bid) is higher or lower than the uncertain quantity before stating their own estimates. A robust result is that subjects start from the bid and fail to adjust fully to their base beliefs, so that their estimates are pulled toward the bid. Open-ended responses that follow up a bid are pulled toward the bid, and in "yes/no" responses to the bid, minority responses are more prevalent than they would be if subjects were not influenced by the bid. Even an explicitly uninformative prompt, such as the output of a random device, can operate as an anchor. Large anchoring effects have been reported in diverse contexts and populations of respondents, including experts (e.g., see Northcraft and Neale 1987).

A psychological explanation for the phenomenon of anchoring is that a prompt creates in the subject's mind, at least temporarily, the possibility that the uncertain quantity could be either above or below the prompt. This could result from classical psychophysical discrimination errors or from a cognitive process in which the subject treats the question as a problem-solving task and seeks an appropriate framework for "constructing" a correct solution, utilizing the prompt as a cue. Both formal and informal education train individuals to use problem-solving protocols in which responses to questions are based not only on substantive knowledge but also on contextual cues as to what a correct response might be. Consequently, it should be no surprise if subjects apply these protocols in forming survey responses.

In psychological experiments, anchoring is found even when the bid amount is explicitly random, suggesting that there is more to anchoring than "rational" problem solving. This could happen because subjects are subrational, making cognitive errors and processing information inconsistently, or because they are "superrational," going beyond the substantive question to "model" the mind of the questioner and form superstitious beliefs about the behavior of nature.[1]

Several other effects in table 8.1 may be significant in economic survey responses and are topics for further research. *Focal* effects occur when the cognitive organization of quantitative information is categorical rather than extensive or when categorical approximations are used to minimize reporting effort. Open-ended responses on many economic variables exhibit the focal phenomenon, with responses piled up at rounded-off numbers. Travel times are usually reported in five-minute intervals, monthly income in multiples of $500, and so forth. One explanation of focal effects is that quantitative information is stored in a series of successively refined partitions, with increasing effort and uncertainty associated with retrieval from deeper levels. Survey responses may correspond to the finest partition the individual maintains or may correspond to a coarser level that can be accessed with less effort. We have found in AHEAD data that focal responses are more common among the cognitively impaired and that the probabilities of giving focal responses are correlated across questions. The focal response phenomenon can have significant effects on the analysis of economic data. Since focal responses concentrate at rounded-off dollar amounts, growth or inflation is captured mostly through switches between focal points, rather than marginal adjustments. Because focal responses are "sticky," questions stated in nominal dollars are likely to lead to an overestimate of money illusion. Similarly, "no change" may be a focal point in expectations questions. Focal effects interact with *framing* because changing the reporting periods or units change the focal points.

Several cognitive illusions are related to the effort required to retrieve various pieces of information; these might all be referred to as *availability* effects. Examples are *primacy/recency* effects, in which initial or most recent experiences are more readily recalled than those in between; *saliency* effects, in which the information that seems most important or relevant is emphasized to the exclusion of other information; and *status quo* effects, in which historical experience is more easily retrieved than hypothetical alternatives. Framing and anchoring phenomena may be related to availability as well, with the question itself providing immediately accessible information. The possible impacts on

---

1. It may seem a contradiction in terms to label superstition "superrational." However, systems of superstitious beliefs may well be consistent with a probability model for nature that contains elaborate patterns of causality and correlation too complex to effectively reject empirically. A complete Bayesian facing a complex world admits the possibility that apparently random events have a hidden structure of causation. There are powerful psychological forces, related to limited memory and recall and the cogency of coincidences, that reinforce complex, superstitious worldviews (see McFadden 1974).

economic survey responses are obvious: information on social security income is more accessible than asset income, so the former may provide an internal anchor for the latter; beliefs about mortality may be unduly influenced by the ages attained by relatives and friends, to the exclusion of baseline information from life tables; recent changes in health status may be weighed too heavily in predicting future health status, with insufficient allowance for regression to the mean.

Finally, several cognitive distortions related to motivation, self-control, and projection of self-image may affect the recall and filtering of information. Subjects may overestimate quantities associated with socially desirable behavior and positive self-image. For example, the elderly may overstate their ability to do the routine tasks asked for in IADL batteries and may underestimate their consumption of tobacco and alcohol. Individuals appear to establish rules that precommit themselves to strategically desirable behavior and then to shape perceptions so they are consonant with these rules.

8.2   Elicitation Protocols and the Unfolding Bracket Method

8.2.1   Elicitation Formats

The most direct way to ask about a quantitative economic variable is to request an open-ended quantitative response. A problem with this method is that it often results in relatively high item nonresponse, as well as implausible extreme responses. A popular alternative that is effective in reducing these problems is to use an *unfolding bracket* elicitation format, which converts the quantitative question into an unfolding series of "yes/no" questions. Subjects are presented with a series of gates, or bids, and at each bid are asked whether the quantity of interest is at least as large as the presented bid. The bids are determined sequentially; that is, a "yes" response is followed by a larger bid, a "no" response by a smaller bid. The sequence of bids and responses establishes a bracket for the quantity of interest.

There is considerable evidence that the unfolding bracket method is effective in reducing nonresponse rates. The method also avoids implausible extreme responses, although the confusion or inattention on the part of subjects that produces these problems in open-ended questions may also distort bracket responses. One reason that it works well may be that memory for quantitative data is organized in hierarchical categories, with recall at one level aiding (or anchoring) recall at the next. Then qualitative or range questions require relatively little effort, whereas increasing detail requires an increasingly complex web of interconnected facts and prompts.

A disadvantage of the unfolding bracket method is that the presentation of bids may influence beliefs or response protocols, so that the distribution of responses over brackets is sensitive to the unfolding design. For example, McFadden (1994) finds that unfolding bracket questions on WTP for natural resources contain anchoring distortions; Green et al. (1998) find similar results for both objective estimation and WTP tasks.[2]

8.2.2 A Model for Unfolding Bracket Responses

We shall be interested in an economic variable q, such as log monthly consumption or log savings balances, that can be related to a vector of covariates $\mathbf{x}$ via a linear model

$$(1) \qquad q = \mathbf{x}\beta - \upsilon,$$

where β is a vector of parameters and υ is a disturbance, independent of $\mathbf{x}$, that has mean zero and a cumulative distribution function $G(\upsilon)$.[3] Then $G(\mathbf{x}\beta - q)$ is the complementary cumulative distribution function (CCDF) of q, given $\mathbf{x}$, in the population.

In the case of an unfolding bracket response, an observation will be denoted

$$t, \ \mathbf{x}, \ (b_1, y_1), \ (b_2, y_2), \ldots, \ (b_K, y_K),$$

where t is a *treatment*, b_k is the kth bid, y_k is a response indicator for this bid (1 if "yes" and 0 if "no"), and K is the number of bid questions presented *and* answered. The treatment t determines the bids b_k, conditional on previous responses $y_1, \ldots, y_{k-1}$. Assume a "yes" response leads to a larger gate amount for the next question, and vice versa. Let q^{bot} and q^{top} denote bounds on beliefs, $-\infty \le q^{bot} \le q < q^{top} \le +\infty$, and augment the response pairs (b_k, y_k) with the pairs $(q^{bot}, 1)$ and $(q^{top}, 0)$. The notation $B = (b', b'')$ will be used for the interval determined by an unfolding bracket response; that is, $(b', 1)$ is the largest bid in an unfolding bracket sequence that elicits a "yes" response, and $(b'', 0)$ is the smallest bid that elicits a "no" response.

8.2.3 Outcomes When Responses Are Error-Free

If there are no response errors, then a subject asked an open-ended question will give the true value q, and a subject asked an unfolding bracket question will indicate correctly the bracket in which his latent q falls. The probability that q exceeds a bid b is

$$(2) \qquad P(y \mid \mathbf{x}) = G(\mathbf{x}\beta - b),$$

---

2. In a variety of tasks involving estimation of an unknown physical quantity, such as the height of the tallest redwood, the sample distribution of unprompted open-ended responses is presumably an unbiased estimator of the population distribution of beliefs about the quantity and the standard against which the accuracy of unfolding bracket responses should be judged. For economic questions such as WTP or asset balances, unprompted open-ended responses may themselves be biased for various reasons, and these tests should simply be interpreted as tests of whether open-ended and unfolding bracket questions yield the same distributions of responses.

3. For a variable such as savings balances that has a significant probability of being zero and is highly skewed, a bivariate selection model is a convenient setup. Assume $p = \mathbf{x}\alpha - \eta$, $S = 0$ if $p \le 0$, and $q \equiv \log S = \mathbf{x}\beta - \upsilon$ if $p > 0$, with (η, υ) having a bivariate distribution.

and the probability of observing a bracket $B = (b', b'')$ as a result of unfolding bracket responses under treatment t is

$$(3) \qquad P(B \mid \mathbf{x}, t) = G(\mathbf{x}\beta - b') - G(\mathbf{x}\beta - b'').$$

A completed sequence of gate responses will pick out a single final bracket; however, incomplete responses will span several final brackets.

When G can be placed in a parametric family, root N consistent asymptotically normal (RCAN) estimates of the parameter vector β and parameters of G can be obtained by maximum likelihood, subject to identification and regularity conditions. When G is normal, this reduces to least squares in the case of open-ended responses and ordered probit (with thresholds specified by the bracket boundaries) in the case of unfolding bracket responses; both β and the variance σ^2 of υ can be identified as long as there are at least three brackets or two treatments. Another case that permits parametric analysis occurs when there are no covariates; then $P(b', b'' \mid \mathbf{x})$ is a sum of multinomial probabilities, and one can estimate a *saturated* multinomial model.

Suppose G cannot be placed in a parametric family. Least squares remains a RCAN estimation method for β from open-ended data. Sample moments of q observations are RCAN estimates of the corresponding unconditional population moments. For a continuous function $r(q, \mathbf{x})$ for which the population conditional moment $\mathbf{E}_{q|x} r(q, \mathbf{x})$ exists, an estimator that is RCAN under mild regularity conditions is

$$(4) \qquad \hat{\mathbf{E}}_{q|x} r(q, \mathbf{x}) = \frac{1}{N} \sum_{i=1}^{N} r(q_i + (\mathbf{x} - \mathbf{x}_i)\beta, \mathbf{x}),$$

where $i = 1, \ldots, N$ indexes observations and $\hat{\beta}$ is the least squares estimator of β. Leading examples are $r(q, \mathbf{x}) = q^k$ and $r(q, \mathbf{x}) = e^{kq}$, the kth moments of q and e^q, respectively.

The case of unfolding bracket responses and nonparametric G presents a semiparametric estimation problem, with equation (3) specifying the probability of an observation, conditioned on $\mathbf{x}$. This falls within the general class of single-index models for which Horowitz and Neumann (1989), Ichimura (1993), Lee (1995), and others have provided RCAN estimators for β. When the distribution of bid levels specified by the experimental design has a positive density, as can be the case with a randomized design in which the bid levels are drawn from continuous distributions, Lewbel (1997) and Lewbel and McFadden (1997) give a simple weighted least squares estimator that is RCAN for β. However, this is not applicable to the AHEAD experiments, which followed a fixed design. An alternative when there are open-ended data available is to estimate β by least squares using this external data. This is the route we will follow in analyzing the AHEAD experiments. It should be noted that differences in question formatting and context between surveys could confound this analysis; we will introduce rescaling factors that will absorb some, although not necessarily all, of the effects of mismatches across surveys.

Given an external RCAN estimator $\hat{\beta}$ for β, it is possible to construct a simple RCAN estimator of the population moment $E_{q|x}r(q, x)$. For each subject in a sample $i = 1, \ldots, N$, define residuals $v'_i = x_i\hat{\beta} - b'_i$ and $v''_i = x_i\hat{\beta} - b''_i$, where b'_i is the highest bid at which the subject says "yes" and b''_i is the lowest bid at which the subject says "no." (By convention, we assume that q^{bot} would elicit a "yes" response and q^{top} would elicit a "no" response.) Consider the $2N$ pairs $(v'_i, 1)$ and $(v''_i, 0)$, sort them so the first arguments are in nondecreasing order, and let (v_m, y_m) denote the mth pair in this order, for $m = 1, \ldots, 2N$. Integration by parts gives

$$E_{q|x_0}r(q, x_0) = r(x_0\beta, x_0) + \int_{-\infty}^{+\infty} r'(x_0\beta - v, x_0) \cdot [G(v) - 1(v > 0)]\, dv$$

(5)
$$\approx r(x_0\beta, x_0) + \sum_{m=1}^{2N} r'(x_0\beta - v_m, x_0) \cdot [G(v_m) - 1(v_m > 0)]$$

$$\cdot \frac{v_{m+1} - v_{m-1}}{2} + O(N^{-2}),$$

with the last approximation obtained by application of the trapezoid rule for numerical integration, subject to some regularity conditions, including smoothness conditions on r, and tail conditions on G; tail values of v are defined by convention to take care of tail terms in the summation. Equation (5) suggests the estimator

(6) $$\hat{E}_{q|x_0}r(q, x_0) = r(x_0\hat{\beta}, x_0) + \sum_{m=1}^{2N} r'(x_0\beta - v_m, x_0) \cdot [y_m - 1(v_m > 0)]$$

$$\cdot \frac{v_{m+1} - v_{m-1}}{2},$$

where y_m is the average (in case of ties) of the ys corresponding to the value v_m. Lewbel and McFadden (1997) show that this estimator is RCAN under fairly mild regularity conditions. However, a critical requirement is that either the bids levels be drawn randomly from a positive density or the covariates have a continuous component with sufficient variation so that v_m has a positive density. This excludes the case of no covariates and fixed number of treatments without randomized bids. One cannot achieve a consistent estimator of the expectation of r for this case, but the estimator

(7) $$\hat{E}_{q|x_0}r(q) = r(0) + \sum_{m=1}^{2N} r'(b_m) \cdot [1(b_m < 0) - y_m] \cdot \frac{b_{m+1} - b_{m-1}}{2}$$

will have relatively satisfactory finite-sample properties because of the approximation properties of y_m and the trapezoid rule.

The models and estimators above developed for the case of no response error can be applied to data pooled across treatments under the null hypothesis of no treatment effects. Treatment effect parameters can then be used to test this hypothesis. Surveys in which the same bracket can be reached under alternative gating designs provide a simple but powerful nonparametric test of the hypothesis of no anchoring effects. McFadden (1994) uses this test to show that a two-gate protocol for eliciting WTP, also called a *double-referendum* elicitation, produces anchoring distortions. An empirical test for the hypothesis of no anchoring distortion in response can also be carried out by eliciting unprompted open-ended responses from one sample, using the empirical distribution of responses from this sample to estimate the bracket probabilities for a second sample where an unfolding bracket protocol is used, and calculating a goodness-of-fit test of the estimated probabilities to the second sample frequencies. An asymptotically efficient version of this test carries out maximum likelihood estimation of the probabilities of responses in each final bracket, separately for each sample and for the pooled samples, and calculates a likelihood ratio statistic.

8.2.4   Model for Anchoring to Unfolding Brackets

We develop a simple model for anchoring that combines features of a model proposed in Green et al. (1998) for anchoring to a starting point prompt and a model proposed by Hurd for unfolding brackets. The premise of this model is that beliefs are stationary: gate choices create a temporary *discrimination* problem, but past history has no effect on current discrimination tasks. When a subject with a belief q is presented with a sequence of gate amounts b_k, responses are based on a comparison of the latent q with $b_k + \eta_k$, where η_k is a *perception error.* We assume the errors η_k are distributed independently across successive gates and have CDFs $T_k(\cdot)$ that are symmetric about zero. Let $s_k = 2y_k - 1$ be a response indicator that is $+1$ for "yes" and -1 for "no." Then $s_k = 1$ if $b_k + \eta_k < \mathbf{x}\beta - \upsilon$, so that the probability of this event given υ is $T_k(s_k(\mathbf{x}\beta - b_k - \upsilon))$. We use the notation (b_k, y_k) and (b_k, s_k) interchangeably. The probability of an observation is then

$$P((b_1,s_1), (b_2 s_2),\ldots, (b_K, s_K) \mid \mathbf{x}, t)$$

(8)

$$= \int_{q^{bot}}^{q^{top}} \prod_{k=1}^{K} T_k(s_k(\mathbf{x}\beta - b_k - \upsilon)) \cdot G'(\upsilon)\, d\upsilon.$$

We will term this the *imperfect discrimination model of anchoring to unfolding brackets.* Imperfect discrimination is usually associated with physical stimuli, such as pitch or loudness of sounds or brightness of lights, and it is not obvious that it is relevant when the stimuli are precisely stated numbers. However, ambiguity about whether q and the gate amounts refer to precisely the same quantity, or whether there are differences in scope or scale, can induce perception errors. For example, in unfolding bracket questions about savings balances, the subject may be unsure whether balances in certificates of deposit or individual retirement accounts should be included.

This model is able to capture several of the stylized features of anchoring. First,

$$P((b_1,1) \mid \mathbf{x},t) = \int_{q^{\text{bot}}}^{q^{\text{top}}} T_1(\mathbf{x}\beta - b_1 - \upsilon) \cdot G'(\upsilon) \, d\upsilon \equiv R(\mathbf{x}\beta - b_1),$$

where R is the CDF of the random variable $\upsilon + \eta_1$. This is a mean-preserving spread of υ, so that the probability of minority responses to bids will be increased. Second, suppose two gate designs lead to the same bracket, for example, $((b', 1), (b'', -1))$ and $((b'', -1), (b', 1))$. The respective probabilities

$$P((b',1),(b'',-1) \mid \mathbf{x},t) = \int_{q^{\text{bot}}}^{q^{\text{top}}} T_1(\mathbf{x}\beta - b' - \upsilon) \cdot T_2(-\mathbf{x}\beta + b'' + \upsilon) \cdot G'(\upsilon) \, d\upsilon,$$

$$P((b'',-1),(b',1) \mid \mathbf{x},t) = \int_{q^{\text{bot}}}^{q^{\text{top}}} T_1(-\mathbf{x}\beta + b'' + \upsilon) \cdot T_2(\mathbf{x}\beta - b' - \upsilon) \cdot G'(\upsilon) \, d\upsilon,$$

can differ if $T_1 \neq T_2$. For example, if T_1 is more disperse than T_2 and $b' < \mathbf{x}\beta$, then

$$P((b',1),(b'',-1) \mid \mathbf{x},t) > P((b'',-1),(b',1) \mid \mathbf{x},t).$$

A parametric version of the model assumes that υ and the η_k are all normally distributed, with standard deviations σ and λ_k, respectively. Then discrimination follows a classical psychophysical model of Thurstone (1927). The probability of an observation in this *normal imperfect discrimination model* is then

(9) $P((b_1,s_1), (b_2,s_2),\ldots, (b_K,s_K) \mid \mathbf{x},t)$

$$= \int_{-\infty}^{+\infty} \prod_{k=1}^{K} \Phi\left(\frac{s_k(\mathbf{x}\beta - b_k - \upsilon)}{\lambda_k} \right) \cdot \phi\left(\frac{\upsilon}{\sigma} \right) \cdot \frac{d\upsilon}{\sigma},$$

The parameters of this model can be estimated by maximum likelihood, with numerical integration used to evaluate the integral. An overall assessment of the goodness of fit of the normal model can be performed by a likelihood ratio test against the saturated model. Rejection of the normal model could occur either because the discrimination process above is not adequate to describe anchoring behavior or because q is not normally distributed.

A relaxation of this parametric model retains the Thurstonian discrimination but takes G to be an empirical distribution obtained from external data. To assure that the model is well behaved numerically for small λs, these empirical distributions are interpolated. This can be interpreted probabilistically as sampling from piecewise uniform densities with breaks at the observations.

Consider an external open-ended sample of size J in which q is observed, along with covariates $\mathbf{x}$. Assume that least squares applied to the regression equation $q = \mathbf{x}\beta - \upsilon$ yields a RCAN estimate $\hat{\beta}$ of β, and define the least squares residuals $u_j = \mathbf{x}_j\hat{\beta} - q_j$. Assume these residuals are indexed so that

$u_1 \leq \ldots \leq u_J$. These residuals then define an empirical CDF G_J that can be used in the imperfect discrimination model. To avoid numerical analysis problems when discrimination is sharp, we use a linear spline smoothing of the empirical CDF, with $2J + 2$ knots placed at each u_j and at midpoints between the u_j, constrained so that the expectation of the smoothed distribution, conditioned on the interval formed by the knots bracketing u_j, equals u_j. For numerical integration, we choose evenly spaced points between successive knots. This construction preserves the mean-zero property of the residuals. Let (v_m, p_m) for $m = 1, \ldots, M$ denote the evaluation points and weights for the numerical integration. Add a parameter α to account for scaling differences between AHEAD and the external survey. Then the probability of an observation in the imperfect discrimination to unfolding brackets model is

(10)
$$P((b_1, s_1), (b_2, s_2), \ldots, (b_K, s_K) \mid \mathbf{x}, t)$$
$$= \sum_{m=1}^{M} p_m \prod_{k=1}^{K} T_k(s_k(\alpha + \mathbf{x}\hat{\beta} - b_k - v_m)).$$

In the case of normal discrimination, this becomes

(11)
$$P((b_1, s_1), (b_2, s_2), \ldots, (b_K, s_K) \mid \mathbf{x}, t)$$
$$= \sum_{m=1}^{M} p_m \prod_{k=1}^{K} \Phi\left(\frac{s_k(\alpha + \mathbf{x}\hat{\beta} - b_k - v_m)}{\lambda_k}\right).$$

The parameters of this model, α and the λ_j, can be estimated by maximum likelihood. We shall term expression (11) the *empirical prior normal discrimination model*.

8.3   An Experiment on Anchoring in the AHEAD Survey

8.3.1   The AHEAD Experiment

The AHEAD panel study, in progress to study the economic and health status of the elderly, provides the primary data for this paper.[4] Unfolding brackets are used as follow-up to nonresponse on a variety of economic questions regarding income and assets and have proved quite effective in reducing item nonresponse. To test for anchoring effects in these elicitations, an experimental module was introduced in the second wave of the panel, administered in fall 1995, that asked questions on savings account balances and on consumption, using seven alternative treatments, randomly assigned to each respondent. Each treatment specified a gating design for questions on savings balances

---

4. The survey is being conducted by the University of Michigan Survey Research Center on behalf of the Institute on Aging of the National Institutes of Health. The survey questionnaires and data are available at http://www.umich.edu//~hrswww/.

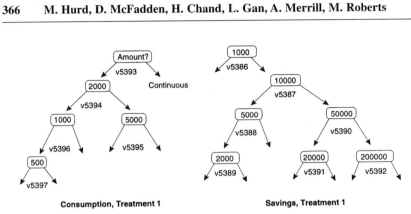

Consumption, Treatment 1   Savings, Treatment 1

Fig. 8.1   Treatment 1

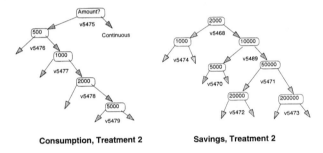

Consumption, Treatment 2   Savings, Treatment 2

Fig. 8.2   Treatment 2

and another design for monthly consumption. A total of 4,855 subjects were administered the experimental module. Figures 8.1 through 8.7 describe the unfolding bracket questions for each of the treatments; variable numbers (e.g., v5397) refer to the survey instrument. If there are no distortions in response due to the brackets, then the proportions of subjects appearing in the various brackets should be independent of treatment. Because of the random assignment of treatments, tests for anchoring can be carried out without considering covariates. However, when modeling the effects of anchoring, one will want to consider the effect of covariates that may affect the magnitude of anchoring effects.

8.3.2   Other Data

As external open-ended data supplements for the AHEAD questions on consumption and savings balances, we have analyzed consumption data from the fall 1994 Consumer Expenditure Survey (CES) and savings data from the 1989 Survey of Consumer Finances (SCF). We have selected measures from these surveys that closely match AHEAD variable definitions and have converted all dollar values to 1995 dollars using the CPI. For example, the mean age of

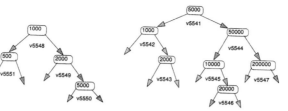

Consumption, Treatment 3

Savings, Treatment 3

Fig. 8.3 Treatment 3

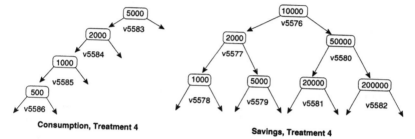

Consumption, Treatment 4

Savings, Treatment 4

Fig. 8.4 Treatment 4

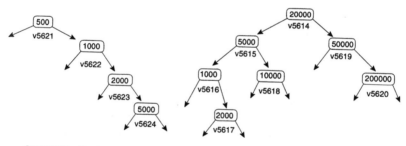

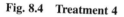
Consumption, Treatment 5

Savings, Treatment 5

Fig. 8.5 Treatment 5

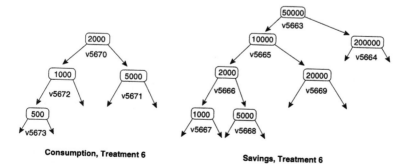

Consumption, Treatment 6

Savings, Treatment 6

Fig. 8.6 Treatment 6

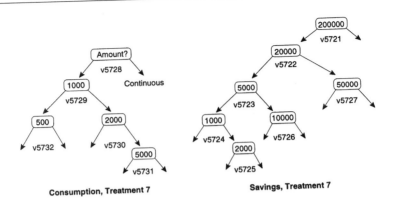

Fig. 8.7   Treatment 7

household heads in wave 1 of AHEAD was 76.2. In the subsamples of the CES and SCF with heads aged 70 or over, the mean ages of heads were 77.1 and 74.5, respectively. Marital status reveals some significant differences between the surveys: the proportions married among households with heads aged 70 or over are 0.561, 0.398, and 0.570 in AHEAD, the CES, and the SCF, respectively. Thus, CES includes a larger fraction of unattached individuals.

8.4   Consumption

8.4.1   Measuring Consumption

The level of consumption and its relation to the annuitized value of wealth are the key determinants of the economic well-being of the elderly, determining current and prospective poverty rates. Consumption data can be obtained from consumer expenditure surveys (which are typically panels with expenditure diaries), in household panels as the difference between stated income and the imputed savings required to account for stated changes in asset holdings, or by direct questions. Subjects are likely to monitor some consumption components, such as utilities, food expenditures, and major durable purchases, more closely than others, and inferring total consumption from the more reliably reported components is an alternative to asking directly for total consumption.

8.4.2   Data from the Consumer Expenditure Survey

A relatively reliable picture of the distribution of consumption can be obtained from the fall 1994 CES of the Bureau of Labor Statistics. This survey collects panel data on detailed expenditure categories, which then can be aggregated to total expenditure, and contains 772 households aged 70 or over.

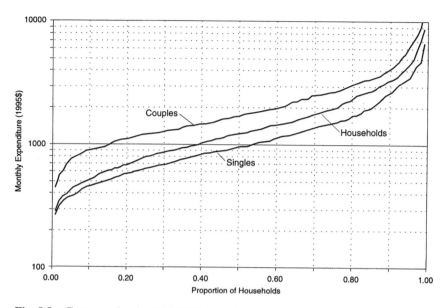

Fig. 8.8   Consumption in 1994 CES: households, singles, and couples aged 70 or over

We have constructed a total consumption measure from this survey that closely matches the definition of consumption used in the AHEAD survey. Figure 8.8 gives the empirical CDF of total consumption for these households, as well as separate CDFs for singles and couples. Figure 8.9 gives the Lorenz curve for household consumption. For all households aged 70 or over, the median monthly consumption level in 1995 dollars is $1,224, and the mean is $1,735, with a standard deviation of $1,801. The poverty level in 1995 was $768 per month for elderly couples and $609 for elderly singles. Then 5.2 percent of couples and 23.0 percent of singles were below the poverty level; in aggregate, 13.8 percent of households and unattached individuals over age 70 are below the poverty level. Note that the poverty comparisons are being made in terms of consumption rather than income. Some households who are below poverty levels of income can by decumulating assets have consumption levels above the poverty line. Then the 13.8 percent poverty rate defined in terms of consumption may be consistent with the official poverty rate of 16.3 percent among those aged 70 or over (see Hobbs 1996).

Subjects in wave 2 of the AHEAD panel who were given treatments 1, 2, and 7 were first asked an open-ended question about consumption, with an unfolding bracket follow-up to nonresponse. Figure 8.10 gives the distribution of open-ended responses, without correction for the selection effects of nonresponse. Consumption levels obtained from AHEAD are uniformly below those

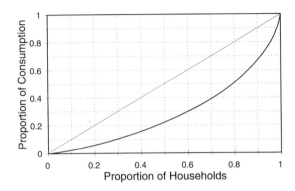

Fig. 8.9   **Lorenz curve for consumption in 1994 CES: households aged 70 or over**

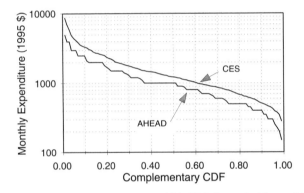

Fig. 8.10   **Consumption in AHEAD and 1994 CES: households aged 70 or over**

obtained from the CES, probably due to some combination of selection effects, differences in the definition of consumption between the CES and the understanding of AHEAD respondents, and response bias in the AHEAD data. Noteworthy is the frequency of focal responses in the AHEAD survey at $500, $1,000, $1,500, and $2,000, and the dispersion of responses in comparison to the CES. Table 8.2 provides some summary statistics on consumption, based on the CES survey. The CES data show substantially higher mean consumption than AHEAD, $1,738 versus $1,252, and somewhat lower dispersion, with a standard deviation of $1,833 versus $2,376. This pattern is repeated in the medians, $1,224 versus $1,000. An examination of the CES and AHEAD consumption distributions indicates that differences occur primarily in the tails. There is a significantly thicker lower tail in the AHEAD distribution, with the CES having 10.8 percent (S.E. = 1.1 percent) below $500 and AHEAD having 19.3 percent (S.E. = 1.1 percent) below this level. This suggests that very low income households have a strong tendency to underestimate consumption,

Table 8.2   **Consumption Summary Statistics**

Variable	Coding	Mean	Standard Deviation
log(Monthly expenditure)	1995$	7.160	0.730
Monthly expenditure	1995$	1,738	1,833
Head age	Years	77.058	5.987
Spouse age	Years	71.166	7.045
married	1 = Yes, 0 = No	0.398	0.490
Head some college	1 = Yes, 0 = No	0.272	0.330
Spouse some college	1 = Yes, 0 = No	0.331	0.471
Home owner	1 = Yes, 0 = No	0.769	0.412
Head sex	1 = Male, 0 = Female	0.462	0.499
Spouse sex	1 = Male, 0 = Female	0.097	0.296
Head minority	1 = Yes, 0 = No	0.105	0.307
Spouse minority	1 = Yes, 0 = No	0.086	0.281
Lives with kids	1 = Yes, 0 = No	0.023	0.151
Head high school graduate	1 = Yes, 0 = No	0.539	0.492
Spouse high school graduate	1 = Yes, 0 = No	0.721	0.449
No spouse	1 = Yes, 0 = No	0.624	0.485
Couples			
Monthly expenditure		2,429	2,444
Home owner		0.886	0.318
Lives with kids		0.062	0.242
No spouse			
Monthly expenditure		1,322	1,154
Home owner		0.699	0.459
Lives with kids[a]		0.000	0.000

Source: Fall 1994 Consumer Expenditure Survey.

[a]Unattached individuals living with kids are considered part of the kid's household.

perhaps because they fail to consider items such as consumption in kind that are included in the CES. However, the upper tail of the AHEAD open-ended responses is thinner than in the CES, with 23.2 percent (S.E. = 1.5 percent) of CES respondents above $2,000 and 18.4 percent (S.E. = 1.0 percent) of AHEAD respondents above this level. An economic explanation of this pattern would require that there be income expenditure components that are part of the CES definition of consumption but are not considered consumption by elderly households.

To determine the influence of demographics on consumption levels, we regressed log consumption on selected demographic variables, using the CES data. The results are given in table 8.3. There is an economically, but not statistically, significant decline in consumption with age, a combination of life cycle and cohort effects. Figure 8.11 shows this relationship. If the disturbances in the regression have median zero, then this can be interpreted as the relation of median consumption to age. We find significant positive effects of education, presumably tied to lifetime earnings and current income, and significant negative effects of living alone and of being a female head.

Table 8.3   Demographics and Consumption

Variable	Coefficient	Standard Error
Constant	7.8907	0.5256
Head age	−0.0103	0.0070
Pos(Head age − 80)[a]	−0.0176	0.0149
No spouse	−0.3334	0.0648
Head some college	0.3094	0.0587
Head high school graduate	0.1694	0.0540
Head male	0.2524	0.0621
Head minority	−0.0776	0.0743
R^2	0.2768	

Source: Fall 1994 Consumer Expenditure Survey.
Note: Ordinary least squares estimation; dependent variable is log(Monthly expenditure).
[a]Pos(x) = max(0,x).

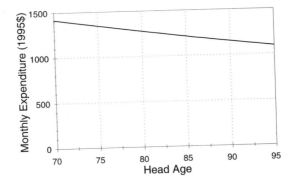

Fig. 8.11   Consumption vs. age in 1994 CES

8.4.3   The AHEAD Data

The consumption module asks for total monthly consumption expenditures. The experiment initially asks for an open-ended response under treatments 1, 2, and 7, with unfolding bracket follow-up for nonrespondents. We term the subjects who responded to these follow-up brackets the *residual bracket* respondents. The remaining treatments forced bracket responses. Gate starting values were $500, $1,000, $2,000, and $5,000. Figures 8.1 through 8.7 describe each consumption treatment and the gate designs. Subjects forced to give unfolding bracket responses (treatments 3 through 6) had a first gate response rate of 98.2 percent, and a complete bracket response rate of 93.5 percent. Of subjects asked the initial open-ended consumption question (treatments 1, 2, and 6), 64.2 percent gave a usable response. Nonrespondents were followed up with unfolding bracket questions, with a response rate on the first

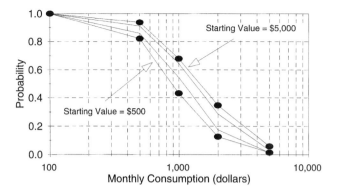

Fig. 8.12   Consumption CCDF by starting value: all bracket responses

gate question of 89.3 percent and a complete bracket response rate of 50.7 percent. The combined open-ended or first gate response rate was 96.2 percent, and the open-ended or complete bracket response rate was 84.0 percent. Un-folding brackets are therefore *very effective in reducing item nonresponse when used as a follow-up to an open-ended question.* However, subjects given an initial open-ended question have a higher rate of incomplete response than those facing only bracket questions, suggesting that once a subject admits to not knowing a quantity, there is more reluctance to give possibly speculative gate responses. The quality of bracket responses obtained from subjects who would be nonrespondents to an open-ended question remains an issue. Resid-ual bracket respondents complete the unfolding bracket sequence at a much lower rate than subjects in general, indicating that incomplete bracket response may in itself be a useful indicator of subject uncertainty.

Analysis is carried out in terms of log consumption and log bracket quanti-ties. Figure 8.12 gives the CCDF of consumption, for each starting value, for the subjects who give bracket responses, including incomplete responses. Higher starting values induce significantly higher responses. Table 8.4 gives sample sizes, medians, and means for the bracket responses for each treatment, as well as for the treatments grouped by starting value or by response for-mat (forced bracket vs. initial open ended). Means and medians are also given for the open-ended responses. *The location of the distribution of stated consumption rises sharply with starting value,* as can be seen by comparison of the treatments grouped by starting value in the second panel of the table: a starting value of $500 leads to median consumption of $886, while a starting value of $5,000 leads to median consumption of $1,455. A regression of the nonparametric mean of log consumption on the log starting value yields a coef-ficient of 0.235, with a standard error of 0.028, indicating that *a 100 percent increase in the starting value induces a 23.5 percent increase in stated con-sumption.*

Table 8.4   Consumption: Sample Sizes, Medians, and Means

Treatment	Starting Gate Amount	Sample Size	Number with Open-Ended Response	Percentage of Bracket Responses Completed	Medians Nonparametric[a]	S.E.[b]	Parametric[c]	S.E.[d]	Means Nonparametric[e]	S.E.[f]	Parametric[g]	S.E.[h]
1	2,000[i]	739	492	53.8	1,061	87	1,128	72	1,732	108	1,513	88
2	500[i]	689	422	51.3	861	53	864	53	1,261	87	1,139	63
3	1,000	627	0	92.8	1,146	39	1,104	37	1,508	49	1,365	40
4	5,000	782	0	94.0	1,455	56	1,486	52	2,161	65	1,979	62
5	500	707	0	92.9	895	31	934	31	1,311	45	1,180	35
6	2,000	594	0	94.1	1,415	53	1,392	51	1,946	61	1,764	57
7	1,000[i]	717	464	47.0	897	62	967	69	1,466	98	1,352	89
2 and 5	500	1,396	422	81.5	886	26	915	27	1,298	40	1,170	31
3 and 7	1,000	1,344	464	79.7	1,090	36	1,066	33	1,497	44	1,364	38
1 and 6	2,000	1,333	492	82.3	1,326	46	1,310	42	1,884	53	1,695	49
Open-ended first (1, 2, 7)		2,145	1,378	50.7	931	35	980	37	1,485	57	1,331	46
Forced (3, 5, 6)		1,928	0	93.3	1,129	25	1,167	25	1,572	30	1,523	29
Pooled (1, 2, 3, 5, 6, 7)		4,073	1,378	81.2	1,077	22	911	18	1,358	31	1,237	22
Open-ended responses			1,378		1,000	9			1,253	64		
Overall		4,855	1,378	84.0	1,163	21	1,170	19	1,696	26	1,534	22

Completed Log Likelihoods	Semiparametric	DF	Normal	DF
No anchoring	−4,522.4	4.0	−4,525.9	2
Saturated	−4,403.9	28.0	−4,426.6	14
Imperfect discrimination	−4,442.6	6.0	−4,442.6	4

[a] Exponential of linearly interpolated CCDF of log consumption, with the CCDF estimated using a "saturated" multinomial model for all respondents.

[b] Standard error is estimated by (median) × $(a − b)/(2 × (\text{prob. of bracket}) × (\text{root } N))$, where (b,a) is the log consumption bracket containing the estimator. This estimator assumes that log consumption is uniformly distributed within the bracket containing the median.

[c] Exponential of the mean of a log normal distribution fitted by maximum likelihood estimation to bracket frequencies of log consumption.

[d] Standard error is estimated by (median) × (SD) × root $(\pi/2 × N)$, where SD is the estimated standard error of log consumption.

[e] Sum of bracket midpoints times estimated bracket probabilities.

[f] Standard error is estimated by square root of (sum of squared bracket midpoints times bracket probabilities minus median squared)/N.

[g] Exponential of (mean) $+0.5 × (\text{sigma})^2$, where mean and sigma are estimates of the mean and standard deviation of log consumption.

[h] Standard error is estimated by (mean) × (SD) × root $(1 + 0.5 × (SD)^2)/\text{root } (N)$, where SD is the estimated standard error of log consumption.

[i] Subjects were first asked for an open-ended response, with unfolding brackets if there was no response to the open-ended question.

The median consumption among residual bracket responses ($931) is significantly lower than that for the forced bracket respondents ($1,129) facing the same starting values. In some combination, open-ended nonresponse may be associated with true lower consumption levels and with an effect in which an initial open-ended question acts to depress subsequent bracket responses. The mean open-ended response ($1,253) is significantly lower than the mean bracket response for the forced bracket respondents ($1,572), suggesting an overall tendency for bracket responses to be higher than open-ended responses. This finding is consistent with other studies of anchoring (Jacowitz and Kahneman 1995; Green et al. 1998), which find that for quantities with distributions skewed to the right, anchors in the middle or upper tail of the distribution tend on average to elevate bracket responses above open-ended responses. There is inconsistent evidence that anchors in the lower tail of the distribution have the reverse effect, lowering bracket response below open-ended response. In many, but not all, cases where the quantity has an objective value, open-ended responses appear to be located closer to the objective value than bracket responses. Comparing the CES data and the AHEAD open-ended responses with data from forced bracket responses in AHEAD, and taking the CES data to be closest to true consumption, we conclude that subjects' beliefs about consumption levels as reflected in the AHEAD open-ended responses are systematically biased downward, and the effect of forced brackets is to elevate responses compared with the open-ended distribution, reducing but not completely offsetting the initial bias in beliefs. The nonparametric and lognormal models without anchoring, or by treatment, give similar measures of location. Likelihood ratio tests reject the hypothesis of no anchoring at any conventional level of significance, while the hypothesis of lognormality, given the maintained hypothesis of no anchoring, is weakly rejected.[5]

Figure 8.13 compares the CCDF of the open-ended responses with the estimated CCDFs for pooled forced bracket responses and pooled residual bracket responses. The open-ended responses generally are more concentrated than the bracket responses, a pattern consistent with the implication of anchoring that minority responses are increased. There are significant focal points among open-ended responses, particularly at $400, $500, $1,200, $1,500, $2,000, and $2,500. The presence of significant focal points is itself an indication of response bias, as there are no factors operative in the economy that tend to cluster consumers at rounded-off consumption levels. An interesting psychometric

---

5. The completed log likelihood for the saturated model is $-4,403.90$. The completed log likelihood for the nonparametric model with no anchoring effects is $-4,522.39$. Then a likelihood ratio test statistic for the hypothesis of no anchoring effects is 236.98 with 24 degrees of freedom. This hypothesis is rejected at any conventional significance level. A normal parametric model with no anchoring effect has log likelihood $-4,525.92$. Then a likelihood ratio test statistic for the hypothesis that consumption is lognormal, given the maintained hypothesis of no anchoring, is 7.047 with 2 degrees of freedom. The hypothesis is rejected at the 5 percent level, but not at the 1 percent level.

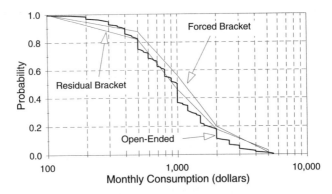

Fig. 8.13   Consumption CCDF for alternative elicitation formats: all responses

question still to be answered is whether individuals tend to do mental accounting on quantities in terms of focal categories, so the focal levels will also play a substantial role in bracket responses, or whether they represent a reporting shorthand for more continuous underlying beliefs. There is some psychological evidence for the former explanation, in which case the simple discrimination model for gate response requires elaboration.

The pattern in figure 8.13 in which both open-ended and selected bracket responses are lower than forced bracket responses suggests that both a *selection* effect, in which low-consumption individuals are more likely to be nonrespondents on the open-ended question, and a *psychometric* effect, in which responses to unfolding brackets are higher than to open-ended questions, may be operating. A test for the former effect, which may be confounded by the latter, can be carried out using a bivariate selection model. First, a binomial probit model for open-ended response is estimated as a function of subject characteristics, including sex, an indicator for whether the respondent handles the family finances, cognitive impairment, age, marital status, high school graduate, some college, and dummy variables for wealth quartile in the first wave of AHEAD. Then open-ended log consumption responses are regressed on these subject characteristics and on an inverse Mills ratio term constructed from the probit model. A test for endogenous selection effects can be carried out by testing whether the coefficient on the inverse Mills ratio variable is zero; this can be done using a conventional *T*-test. Table 8.5 gives the estimates of the two models. The probability that a respondent will answer an open-ended question is significantly higher if the respondent handles household finances, is not cognitively impaired, and is relatively young. Respondents with some college are more likely to respond, and respondents in the top wealth quartile are less likely to respond. Confidentiality may be a factor in the last effect, but the additional cognitive effort required to accumulate a larger number of ac-

Table 8.5   **Consumption: Selection in Open-Ended Responses**

Explanatory Variable	Probit Model (Dependent Variable: Whether Open-Ended Response)		Regression Model (Dependent Variable: Consumption)	
	Estimate	Standard Error	Estimate	Standard Error
Constant	0.084	0.258	−2,458.6	3,434.6
Sex	−0.067	0.039	27.5	145.7
Rfinance	0.165	0.047	−369.5	335.5
Cognition	−0.361	0.044	531.7	655.7
Age	−0.011	0.003	19.5	21.9
Married	0.045	0.046	304.8	120.4
High school graduate	0.075	0.045	−119.0	160.8
Some college	0.119	0.049	199.5	250.9
Wealth quartile 2	−0.038	0.048	141.7	102.5
Wealth quartile 3	−0.062	0.049	284.8	138.2
Wealth quartile 4	−0.156	0.056	825.5	319.0
Inverse Mills ratio			4696.8	4589.2
Log likelihood or R^2	−3,319.08		0.179	
No. of observations	6,722		1,368	

counts and activities may be more important. The level of consumption is significantly increased for respondents who are married, or whose wealth is in the upper two quartiles. The coefficient on the inverse Mills ratio is insignificant, indicating that there is no systematic bias in open-ended reported consumption explained by endogenous selection. However, the significant downward shift in consumption estimated from either open-ended or residual bracket responses indicates that there may be psychometric biases that tend to shrink open-ended responses and reduce "yea-saying" in residual bracket responses, relative to the case of forced brackets.

We have estimated the empirical prior normal imperfect discrimination model (11) for the AHEAD bracket respondents, using CES data to form the external prior G_m and using a five-point numerical integration procedure between the knots in the linear spline smoother of G_m. Table 8.6 gives the results for three alternative models. The first two models use the least squares parameters β estimated from the CES data to estimate $\mathbf{x}\beta$, so the only model parameters are the standard errors λ_k in the discrimination probabilities and the scaling factor α. In the first model, the restriction $\lambda_2 = \lambda_3 = \lambda_4 = \lambda_5$ is imposed; in the second model, this is relaxed to $\lambda_3 = \lambda_4 = \lambda_5$. The third model requires only $\lambda_4 = \lambda_5$ and estimates β directly from the AHEAD data. These models all indicate substantial discrimination errors, largest (e.g., λ smallest) for the initial bid and decreasing for each successive gate. Likelihood ratio tests show that model 2 is significantly better than model 1 and model 3 is significantly

Table 8.6   **Empirical Prior Imperfect Discrimination Model of Consumption: AHEAD Forced and Residual Bracket Responses**

	Model 1		Model 2		Model 3	
Parameter	Estimate	Standard Error	Estimate	Standard Error	Estimate	Standard Error
Lambda 1	0.687	0.042	0.685	0.042	0.487	0.042
Lambda 2	2.053[a]	0.127	1.505	0.147	1.040	0.091
Lambda 3	2.053[a]	0.127	2.610[b]	0.233	1.844	0.288
Lambda 4 and lambda 5	2.053[a]	0.127	2.610[b]	0.233	3.447	0.639
Alpha	0.268	0.025	0.257	0.025	−0.064	0.284
Married					0.353	0.048
Head some college					0.294	0.053
Spouse some college					0.394	0.052
Home owner					0.013	0.056
Head age					−0.012	0.004
Log likelihood	−4,180.243		−4,174.682		−3,991.677	

Note: The log likelihood with perfect discrimination (same as model 1 with lambdas constrained to be infinite) is −4,807.911

[a]Model 1 parameters constrained to be the same.

[b]Model 2 parameters constrained to be the same.

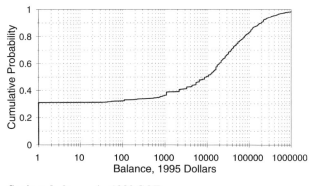

Fig. 8.14   Savings balances in 1989 SCF

better than model 2. Also, a likelihood ratio test shows that model 1 is much better than a model without anchoring errors, that is, with perfect discrimination.[6] *We conclude that there is a significant anchoring effect that is captured by the empirical prior imperfect discrimination model, with discrimination errors largest for the first bid and declining as the gate sequence continues.*

8.5   Savings

8.5.1   Savings Balances

The 1991 median net worth of households aged 70 or over, in 1995 prices, was $92,609, according to the U.S. Bureau of the Census (1994, table G). Savings balances, or interest-earning assets at financial institutions, represent an important component of the net worth of the elderly. The same source estimates that the distribution of net worth of households aged 65 or over is 41.5 percent home equity, 21.0 percent savings balances, 12.1 percent in other interest-earning assets such as checking accounts, U.S. savings bonds, IRA, or Keogh accounts, and 9.4 percent stocks and mutual funds. The 1989 SCF contains 625 households aged 70 or over. In this population, 31 percent had zero savings balances, and the distribution is highly skewed. Expressed in 1995 prices, the median savings balance is $9,130, the mean is $88,881, and the standard deviation is $299,920. Figure 8.14 shows the CDF for savings balances in the SCF, and figure 8.15 shows the Lorenz curve for this asset.

Table 8.7 provides some summary statistics on savings, based on the SCF. Table 8.8 gives a probit model for having positive savings, as a function of demographic variables, and a regression of log savings on demographic variables, for the subpopulation with positive savings, with an inverse Mills ratio

---

6. The log likelihood for the perfect discrimination model is −4,807.91, so that the likelihood ratio test statistic for model 1 against the perfect discrimination model is 1,255, with 2 degrees of freedom.

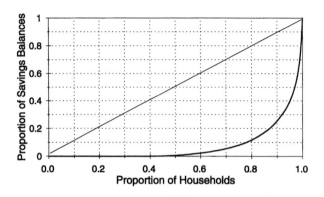

Fig. 8.15 Lorenz curve for savings in 1989 SCF

Table 8.7 **Savings Balances Summary Statistics**

Variable	Coding	Mean	Standard Deviation
Positive savings balance	1 = Yes, 0 = No	0.688	0.444
Savings balances	1995$	88,880	299,919
Head age	Years	74.522	5.784
Spouse age	Years	69.936	7.241
Married	1 = Yes, 0 = No	0.571	0.444
Head education	Years	11.840	3.819
Spouse education	Years	0.331	0.471
Home owner	1 = Yes, 0 = No	0.731	0.444
Head health			
Good	1 = Yes, 0 = No	0.376	0.485
Fair	1 = Yes, 0 = No	0.276	0.448
Poor	1 = Yes, 0 = No	0.122	0.327
Spouse health			
Good	1 = Yes, 0 = No	0.406	0.492
Fair	1 = Yes, 0 = No	0.235	0.424
Poor	1 = Yes, 0 = No	0.086	0.280
No spouse	1 = Yes, 0 = No	0.421	0.494
Couples			
Positive savings balance		0.754	0.431
Savings balances		133,539	384,681
Home owner		0.843	0.365
No Spouse			
Positive savings balance		0.597	0.491
Savings balances		27,411	61,569
Home owner		0.578	0.495

Source: 1989 Survey of Consumer Finances.

Table 8.8   **Demographics and Savings Balances**

Variable	Probit Model (Dependent Variable: Positive Savings Balance)		OLS on Positive Subsample (Dependent Variable: Log Savings Balances)	
	Coefficient	Standard Error	Coefficient	Standard Error
Constant	−1.246	1.069	7.611	1.947
Head age	0.007	0.001	−0.006	0.036
Pos(Head age − 80)[a]	−0.027	0.040	0.049	0.122
Married	0.266	0.119	0.081	1.075
Education	0.067	0.016	0.049	0.264
Home owner	0.205	0.128	−0.049	0.835
Head health				
Good	0.169	0.054	−0.881	2.044
Fair	0.252	0.062	−0.578	0.383
Poor	0.078	0.074	−0.801	0.579
Inverse Mills ratio			2.269	5.365
Log likelihood or R^2	−343.750		0.155	

Source: Fall 1994 Consumer Expenditure Survey.
[a]$Pos(x) = max(0,x)$.

term to control for selection. The probit model shows that being married, more educated, and in good health are all associated with higher savings balances. The omitted health category is excellent health, so that the coefficients suggest that those in the best and the worst health are most likely to have zero savings. Since net worth is positively correlated with health status, the results suggest that those reporting excellent health tend to keep their assets in less liquid forms than savings balances. The coefficient on poor health is explained by some combination of the positive correlation of health status and net worth and the drain on assets imposed by major health problems (see Smith 1995). The regression results indicate that savings balances for those with positive savings do not vary significantly with demographic variables. There is no evidence that selection is an issue. Figure 8.16 shows the profile of savings balances with age predicted by the regression model. The statistically insignificant upturn past age 80 is probably an artifact, although at advanced ages there may be conversion of assets, particularly housing equity, to more liquid form.

8.5.2   AHEAD Data

Recall that Figures 8.1 through 8.7 describe each of the savings gate designs. These designs forced a bracket response for subjects who indicated in a preliminary question that they had positive savings. The starting gate values were $1,000, $2,000, $5,000, $10,000, $20,000, $50,000, and $200,000. Table 8.9 gives the sample sizes for each treatment. A total of 4,855 subjects were admin-

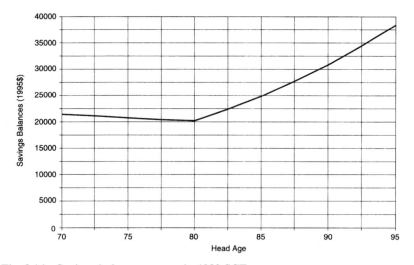

Fig. 8.16   Savings balances vs. age in 1989 SCF

istered the module containing the unfolding bracket treatments, with treatments assigned randomly. In the case of couples, both household members were given the questions, with treatments drawn independently for each.

In the sample, 69.6 percent of respondents indicated positive savings balances, and of these, 94.6 answered the first bracket question and 88.4 percent gave completed bracket responses; these response rates did not vary systematically with the first gate amount. Item response rates to open-ended questions on financial assets are typically in the 50–70 percent range, so that the unfolding bracket method is extremely effective in lowering nonresponse. Further, unfolding brackets reduce the problem of large reporting errors in open-ended responses. On the other hand, there is information loss from using bracket rather than continuous responses, and subject uncertainty that could produce large open-ended response errors could also contaminate bracket responses, and the presentation of gate cues may cause anchoring errors.

Parametric and nonparametric analyses of the savings data are carried out in terms of the log of savings balances and logs of gate amounts. The parametric analysis assumes that savings is lognormal, conditioned on treatment. The nonparametric analysis uses the saturated multinomial model. The CCDF of savings balances was estimated from the bracket frequencies in the sample, using the subsample of respondents that completed the sequence of unfolding bracket responses, and using all respondents, with final bracket probabilities obtained from the saturated model.

Figure 8.17 shows the CCDFs under the different treatments computed for all observations, including partial bracket response. There are economically significant anchoring effects, with the CCDFs from higher starting values showing substantially higher means and medians than those from lower start-

Table 8.9   Savings: Sample Sizes, Medians, and Means

Treatment	Starting Gate Amount	Sample Size	Number with Positive Savings[a]	Percentage of Bracket Responses Completed	Medians Non-parametric[b]	S.E.[c]	Parametric[d]	S.E.[e]	Means Non-parametric[f]	S.E.[g]	Parametric[h]	S.E.[i]
1	1,000	739	511	91.4	11,750	1,313	11,894	1,191	58,429	5,274	57,438	7,366
2	2,000	689	479	85.8	12,453	1,384	12,239	1,220	50,259	4,455	48,808	5,995
3	5,000	627	425	89.4	11,626	1,130	11,644	1,266	54,482	5,463	52,087	7,143
4	10,000	782	543	88.0	19,145	1,857	16,048	1,417	57,640	4,617	54,865	5,773
5	20,000	707	492	85.8	19,759	2,517	16,129	1,714	72,609	6,215	79,044	10,786
6	50,000	594	416	90.4	24,670	3,212	23,583	2,463	88,143	6,919	91,018	11,628
7	200,000	717	511	88.1	19,490	2,504	17,795	1,787	79,898	6,514	80,690	10,246
Overall		4,855	3,377	88.4	16,206	669	15,107	582	65,797	2,156	66,011	3,190

Completed Log Likelihoods	Semiparametric	DF	Normal	DF
No anchoring	-6,202.6	7	-6,216.8	2
Saturated	-6,123.0	49	-6,183.8	14
Imperfect discrimination	-6,188.1	9	-6,213.2	4

[a]Subjects were first asked whether they had positive savings, and affirmative respondents were then presented with unfolding bracket questions.

[b]Exponential of linearly interpolated CCDF of log saving, with the CCDF estimated using a "saturated" multinational model for all respondents.

[c]Standard error is estimated by (median) × (a − b)/(2 × (prob. of bracket) × (root N)), where (b,a) is the log savings bracket containing the estimator. This estimator assumes that log savings is uniformly distributed within the bracket containing the median.

[d]Exponential of the mean of a log normal distribution fitted by maximum likelihood estimation to bracket frequencies of log savings.

[e]Standard error is estimated by (median) × (SD) × root(2 × pi/N), where SD is the estimated standard error of log savings.

[f]Sum of bracket midpoints times estimated bracket probabilities.

[g]Standard error is estimated by square root of (sum of squared bracket midpoints times bracket probabilities minus median squared)/N.

[h]Exponential of (mean) + 0.5 × (sigma)², where mean and sigma are estimates of the mean and standard deviation of log savings.

[i]Standard error is estimated by (mean) × (SD) × root(1 + 0.5 × (SD)²/(root N), where SD is the estimated standard error of log savings.

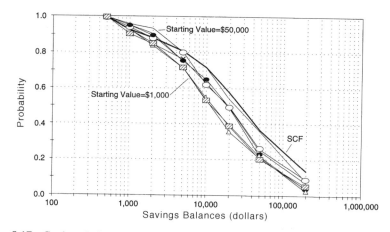

Fig. 8.17   Savings balance CCDF for AHEAD by starting value: all responses
Note: Starting values are $1,000 (*open inverted triangle*), $2,000 (*open triangle*), $5,000 (*open square*), $10,000 (*open circle*), $20,000 (*filled inverted triangle*), $50,000 (*filled triangle*), and $200,000 (*lined square*). Heavy line graphs SCF.

ing values.[7] However, the effects of anchoring are not uniform. The starting values of $1,000, $2,000, and $5,000 yield very similar CCDFs, and the starting value of $200,000 does not exert as much pull to the right as the starting value of $50,000. Table 8.9 gives the medians and means of these distributions; the pattern is consistent with that suggested by examining the CCDFs: the three lowest starting values lead to similar location measures, and the location measures then increase with starting value, except at the highest level. The distribution of savings is highly skewed, so that means are much larger than medians. The differences in location by starting value are strongly statistically significant; a likelihood ratio test rejects the hypothesis of no effect of gate design on response at any conventional level of significance.[8] A regression of the nonparametric mean of log savings on log starting value, weighted to reflect the different numbers of observations for each treatment, yields a coefficient of 0.1037, with a standard error of 0.0365. Thus, a 100 percent increase in starting value produces a statistically significant 10.4 percent increase in estimated mean savings. A lognormal savings model without anchoring produces mean and median estimates that are qualitatively similar to its nonparametric coun-

---

7. Nonparametric medians are estimated by log linear interpolation; this is equivalent to assuming that the density of log savings is uniform within each bracket. Nonparametric means are estimated assuming that savings is bounded between $1 and $800,000, and they are sensitive to the assumed upper bound. Standard errors on the nonparametric estimates of the mean are lower than their parametric counterparts. This is primarily due to the assumed upper bound on savings imposed on the nonparametric estimator, eliminating the upper tail that contributes significantly to the variance of the parametric estimates.

8. The completed log likelihood for the saturated model is −6,122.99, and the completed log likelihood for a multinomial model with no anchoring is −6,202.59. Then the likelihood ratio statistic is 159.19 with 42 degrees of freedom.

Table 8.10   **Empirical Prior Imperfect Discrimination Model of Savings Balances: AHEAD Forced Bracket Responses for Subjects with Positive Savings**

Parameter	Model 1		Model 2		Model 3	
	Estimate	Standard Error	Estimate	Standard Error	Estimate	Standard Error
Lambda 1	3.643	0.228	3.641	0.228	2.827	0.182
Lambda 2	10.273	1.820	10.280	1.823	8.499	1.129
Lambda 3	6.570[a]	0.918	6.611	1.030	6.113[b]	0.863
Lambda 4 and lambda 5	6.570[a]	0.918	6.481	1.499	6.113[b]	0.863
Alpha	−1.057	0.092	−1.058	0.092	−2.511	0.341
Married					0.893	0.161
Head education (years)					0.141	0.028
Spouse education (years)					0.143	0.027
Poor health					−1.979	0.245
Log likelihood	−6,293.610		−6,293.608		−6,177.115	

Note: The log likelihood with perfect discrimination (same as model 1 with lambdas constrained to be infinite) is −6,521.557.

[a]Model 1 coefficients constrained to be the same.

[b]Model 3 coefficients constrained to be the same.

terpart; however, the lognormal parametric specification is rejected using a likelihood ratio test.[9]

The empirical prior imperfect discrimination model was estimated for the AHEAD unfolding bracket data on savings, using the SCF empirical distribution of savings balances, and using five evaluation points between the knots in the linear spline smoothing of the empirical prior. The results are given in table 8.10. Discrimination errors are highest at the first gate (λ_1 lowest), with no significant variation in the λ_k for successive gates (model 2 vs. model 1). In general, the λs are larger for the savings data than for the consumption data, corresponding to fewer discrimination errors and less anchoring effects. A likelihood ratio test rejects the hypothesis of perfect discrimination. One caveat is that the discrimination functions and the parameter α are operating both to explain variations across treatments and to explain differences between measured savings balances in the SCF and beliefs about savings in AHEAD, and one cannot interpret the discrimination model parameters as arising solely from anchoring. Model 3 gives a significantly better fit than model 1, indicat-

9. The completed log likelihood for the lognormal model without anchoring is −6,216.79, and the likelihood ratio statistic for the lognormal vs. nonparametric models without anchoring is 28.24, with 5 degrees of freedom. When full interactions with treatments are allowed, so that log linear models estimated separately for each treatment are compared with the saturated model, a likelihood ratio test of the joint hypothesis that the lognormal specification is correct is rejected; the likelihood ratio statistic is 121.6 with 35 degrees of freedom.

ing that there are some significant differences in the β parameters between the SCF and AHEAD populations. Married couples and heads with more education have significantly higher savings balances, and poor health leads to significantly lower savings balances.

8.6 Conclusions

This study has used an experimental module in the AHEAD panel to establish that anchoring can cause significant biases in unfolding bracket questions on quantitative economic variables. In the case of savings, variation in starting values for unfolding brackets from $5,000 to $200,000 induces a 100 percent difference in estimated median savings. The anchoring is even stronger for consumption: increasing the starting value for unfolding brackets from $500 to $5,000 induces nearly a doubling of estimated median consumption.

A simple model in which each gate presented to the subject can induce discrimination errors is successful in explaining much of these anchoring effects. Thus, variation in unfolding bracket gates, in tandem with the discrimination model or an alternative model of anchoring, promises to be effective in identifying the effects of anchoring and undoing most of these effects. We recommend that survey researchers who wish to use unfolding bracket elicitations adopt experimental variations in their designs that permit identification and correction of anchoring biases and that they exercise caution in imputing economic variables based on stated brackets.

References

Bohm, P. 1972. Estimating willingness to pay: An experiment. *European Economic Review* 3:111–30.

Coupey, E. 1994. Restructuring: Constructive processing of information displays in consumer choice. *Journal of Consumer Research* 21:83–89.

Cowing, T., J. Dubin, and D. McFadden. 1982. The NIECS database and its use in residential energy demand modelling. MIT Energy Laboratory Discussion Paper no. MIT-EL-82-041 WP. Cambridge: Massachusetts Institute of Technology.

Green, D., K. Jacowitz, D. Kahneman, and D. McFadden. 1998. Referendum contingent valuation, anchoring, and willingness to pay for public goods. *Resource and Energy Economics,* forthcoming.

Hobbs, F. 1996. *65+ in the United States.* Current Population Report no. P23-190. Washington, D.C.: U.S. Department of Commerce, Bureau of the Census.

Horowitz, J., and G. Neumann. 1989. Computational and statistical efficiency of semiparametric GLS estimators. *Econometric Reviews* 8:223–35.

Ichimura, H. 1993. Semiparametric least squares (SLS) and weighted SLS estimation of single-index models. *Journal of Econometrics* 58:71–120.

Jacowitz, K., and D. Kahneman. 1995. Measures of anchoring in estimation tasks. *Personality and Social Psychology Bulletin* 21:1161–66.

Kahneman, D., and A. Tversky. 1979. Intuitive prediction: Biases and corrective procedures. *Studies in Management Science* 12:313–27.

Lee, L. 1995. Semiparametric maximum likelihood estimation of polychotomous and sequential choice models. *Journal of Econometrics* 65:381–428.

Lewbel, A. 1997. Semiparametric latent variable model estimation with endogenous or mismeasured regressors. Waltham, Mass.: Brandeis University. Working paper.

Lewbel, A., and D. McFadden. 1997. Estimating features of a conditional distribution from binomial data. Berkeley: University of California. Working paper.

Lowenstein, G. 1988. Frames of mind in intertemporal choice. *Management Science* 34:200–214.

McFadden, D. 1994. Contingent valuation and social choice. *American Journal of Agricultural Economics* 76:689–708.

Northcraft, G., and M. Neale. 1987. Experts, amateurs, and real estate: An anchoring-and-adjustment perspective on property pricing decisions. *Organizational Behavior and Human Decision Processes* 39:84–97.

Poterba, J., and L. Summers. 1986. Reporting errors and labor market dynamics. *Econometrica* 54:1319–38.

Rabin, M. 1998. Psychology and economics. *Journal of Economic Literature,* forthcoming.

Smith, J. 1995. Racial and ethnic differences in wealth in the Health and Retirement Survey. *Journal of Human Resources* 30 (Suppl.): S158–S183.

Smith, V. 1979. An experimental comparison of three public good decision mechanisms. *Scandinavian Journal of Economics* 81:198–215.

Svensson, O. 1996. On the modeling of human choices in descriptive behavioral decision theory. Working paper, Stockholm University.

Thurstone, L. 1927. A law of comparative judgment. *Psychological Review* 34:273–86.

Tversky, A., and D. Kahneman. 1974. Judgment under uncertainty: Heuristics and biases. *Science* 185:1124–31.

U.S. Bureau of the Census. 1994. *Household wealth and asset ownership.* Current Population Report no. P70-34. Washington, D.C.: U.S. Department of Commerce, Bureau of the Census.

Comment   James P. Smith

Let me go straight to the bottom line. This is a very good paper. It deals with an important problem, has the appropriate combination of technique and substance, is completely convincing in its main conclusion, and is constructive in offering remedies.

The paper argues (and I believe proves) that serious anchoring effects exists when household surveys use follow-up bracket questions after initial nonresponse to economic questions. Follow-up brackets are a sequence of "more than x or less than y" questions offered to respondents who initially refused or were unable to provide an exact value for, say, their assets or their income. Anchoring occurs when the content of the question itself conveys information about what the probable "correct" answer is. For example, if respondents were

James P. Smith is a senior economist at RAND.

This work was supported by grants 5P01-AG08291 and 1R01-AG12394 awarded by the National Institute on Aging.

asked about the size of their checking accounts, responses may be influenced by whether the first question was set at the $100 level, $1,000 level, or $10,000 level, even if the final set of categories offered will eventually be identical. Since respondents may assume that question designers know more than they do, the entry point may tell respondents something about what the "correct" answer is.

We know from recent research that unfolding brackets are an important survey research tool that can substantially reduce item nonresponse to economic questions. They also significantly improve estimates of missing values of respondent assets (see Juster and Smith 1997). For example, Juster-Smith report that item nonresponse for asset questions is reduced by almost 75 percent and estimates of mean nonhousing wealth increased by 18 percent by the use of brackets in the Health and Retirement Survey.

This paper takes this survey technology a step further by asking whether estimates of missing values are affected by the placement of the initial entry point in the bracket sequence. That is, even if the final set of bracket categories are the same, it may matter if we start respondents off at a very low entry number or a very high one. The reason the authors can test this question is that an experiment was performed in the survey of Asset and Health Dynamics among the Oldest Old (AHEAD) whereby respondents were randomly assigned different entry points to questions on monthly consumption and savings account balances. Although the entry points varied (randomly), all respondents eventually were presented the same set of final bracket categories for both questions. For the consumption measure, there were four different initial entry points: $500, $1,000, $2,000, and $5,000. After going through the full bracket sequence, all respondents will have been offered the option of placing their unknown consumption into the same five bracket categories: 0–$500, $501–$1,000, $1,001–$2,000, $2,001–$5,000, and more than $5,000. Similarly, there were seven initial entry points for savings accounts: 1, 2, 5, 10, 20, 50, 200 (all in thousands of dollars), but all respondents eventually were provided the same eight bracket categories in which their unknown values could be placed.

The evidence presented that entry points do in fact matter is overwhelming. Table 8C.1 summarizes this evidence by listing the authors' nonparametric estimates of how median values vary with initial entry point for the two measures. For example, their estimate of median household consumption is $895 when the initial entry point is $500 and $1,455 when the initial entry point was $5,000. This range represents a 62 percent difference, which is truly scary for those of us who fret about the quality of economic data. With tongue firmly in cheek, I cannot resist suggesting that a simple cure for high measured poverty is simply to use high entry points in bracket sequences on income. Similarly, the authors' estimate of median savings balances are $11,750 when the lowest entry point of $1,000 was used but rises to $19,590 for respondents who received the highest entry bid of $200,000 (a 66 percent range). The simplicity and beauty of their test is that, since respondents were selected randomly with

Table 8C.1   **Estimated Median Values by Initial Entry Point**

Consumption ($)		Savings ($)	
Entry Bracket	Median	Entry Bracket	Median
500	895	1,000	11,750
1,000	1,146	2,000	12,453
2,000	1,415	5,000	11,626
5,000	1,455	10,000	19,145
		20,000	19,759
		50,000	24,670
		200,000	19,490

respect to entry points, there should be no systematic differences across entry bids. That is obviously not the case.

In light of how persuasive their case is that entry point brackets matter, what are the remaining issues? There are two critical ones. First, how much can we and should we generalize from this evidence to other measures of economic well-being? Second, what can we do about the problem?

How far should we generalize to other measures of economic status? Maybe not too much, since these two items—consumption and savings accounts—probably represent worst-case scenarios. Total consumption and savings accounts are among the most difficult to measure economic constructs conceptually. This inherent difficulty in measurement is compounded by some quite imperfectly worded questions in surveys. For these reasons, consumption or savings accounts may exaggerate the extent of the problem.

For example, consumption is typically measured in economic surveys such as the Consumer Expenditure Survey (CES). These consumption surveys are lengthy, detailed, time consuming, and often involve the use of household diaries, and they appropriately worry about a host of thorny problems—the periodicity of measurement, how to treat consumer durables, and the jointness of many consumption items. By contrast, measurement of consumption in AHEAD relies on a single question. And consider the precise wording of the AHEAD consumption question.

> About how much did you and your household spend on everything in the past month? Please think about all bills, such as rent, mortgage loan payments, utility, and other bills as well as expenses such as food, clothing, transportation, entertainment, and other expenses you and your household may have.

Little wonder then that AHEAD respondents were more than a little unsure of what the interviewer wanted to know and what the answer would be even if they did know. Such vagueness and uncertainty makes respondents particularly sensitive to any clues (including entry bids) that they might obtain from the interviewer. One piece of evidence about the severity of this problem is that mean consumption in AHEAD is only 72 percent as high as that measured in the CES. AHEAD respondents apparently significantly understate total consumption. This understatement may also be partly a consequence of the limited set of items listed in the question after the phrase "such as food." For example, respondents' answers may have been different and larger if medical care was added to the list.

The conceptual and wording problems are just as severe with the savings account question. "Savings account" is an old-fashioned and perhaps outmoded term. Quite frankly, if I were the respondent, I would have no idea what the interviewer was asking. Savings accounts used to be interest-bearing accounts that were distinguished from checking accounts (on which one could write checks). But in today's world of interest-earning checking accounts, the distinction may have lost much of its original meaning. Similarly, the precise wording of the question on savings is of little help.

> I have a few more questions about how people are getting along financially these days. First, do you have any money in SAVINGS ACCOUNTS?

Alongside this question wording, there exists an instruction to interviewers to exclude checking accounts, money markets, mutual funds, and so forth. This may represent another situation in which most respondents are very unsure of exactly what question is being posed. Even if respondents knew what the question meant, they may not have much confidence that they actually know the correct (e.g., most accurate) answer. Once again, such vagueness maximizes the likelihood that respondents will be unusually sensitive to any clues or hints given by the interviewer to help answer the question. I believe that other constructs that economists care about—such as education, income, or even specific asset categories (stocks, house values)—would be less susceptible to the anchoring phenomenon. But to be fair, they are unlikely to be immune from it. Additional testing using the methodology spelled out in this paper should be a high priority for these other central economic constructs.

Finally, what can we do about the problem? Here the paper is quite unusual in not simply pointing out a serious survey methodological problem but also offering a constructive suggestion. The authors argue that the type of random variation in anchoring entry points used in the AHEAD experimental module should be a standard part of all surveys that rely on follow-up brackets. Experimental variation in entry gates allows researchers to statistically identify the biases caused by anchoring and to correct their parametric estimates for these biases.

I think their idea is excellent, but I would take it one step further. A respondent's answer or estimate of the unknown economic value (C^*) is a function of both his own prior beliefs (C_R^*) and any information advertently or inadvertently provided by interviews (C_I^*). In a simple linearized expression of this idea, we can write

$$C^* = a + bC_R^* + e(C_I^* - C_R^*) + f(C_I^* - C_R^*)^2.$$

In this formulation, if interviews (entry points) do not matter, then $e = f = 0$. Interviews will matter only if they provide departures from respondents' initial beliefs in some way, but big departures will probably get less weight ($f < 0$). The notion that large departures may get less weight receives some support from the savings column in table 8C.1. The big difference in median savings appears to depend only on whether the initial entry bid was higher or lower than $10,000, with little variation among bids below or above that threshold. Most people do not have accounts of $200,000, and they may not take seriously entry bids that start that high.

This formulation also suggests that the same set of variations in initial entry points may not be optimal for all respondents. If one could only use a single entry point, values close to the population median may minimize variances in estimation errors. But with modern survey methods, there is no reason not to center the variation in initial entry points around an individual respondent's expected value. To minimize mean square errors, this suggests that the set of random entry points chosen should vary across respondents. For example, the set of entry points chosen should be lower for respondents with asset values below the population median than for respondents with asset values above the median.

How can we know a priori which respondents might have low or high asset values? We must remember that these new economic wealth surveys are longitudinal in nature so that we have considerable information from prior waves about where individual respondents are likely to lie in the distribution. Variation across respondents in the set of entry points can be programmed into the computer-assisted telephone or personal interview technology.

Reference

Juster, F. Thomas, and James P. Smith. 1997. Improving the quality of economic data: Lessons form the HRS and AHEAD. *Journal of the American Statistical Association* 92(440):1268–78.

9 Stochastic Forecasts for Social Security

Ronald Lee and Shripad Tuljapurkar

Population aging is projected to have a major impact on the federal budget in the next century, in part through its effects on health costs through Medicare and Medicaid, and in part through its effect on the retirement system. Despite the inevitability of the aging of the baby boom, and its dramatic effect on the old age dependency ratio, a great deal of uncertainty remains about the extent of future population aging. On the one hand, we do not know how rapidly mortality will decline and how long people will be living, and on the other hand, we do not know what fertility will be, and therefore we do not know how large the labor force will be in the future. Immigration adds another layer of uncertainty, but we do not consider it in this paper. In addition to these demographic sources of uncertainty, there are economic variables with important effects on the future finances of the social security system, notably the rate of growth of productivity or real wages and the level of the real interest rate. Rational planning for the next century must somehow take into account not just our best guesses about the future but also our best assessments of the uncertainty surrounding these guesses.

Scenario-based forecasts are widely used to express the uncertainty of long-term forecasts. In these, the forecaster chooses, for each variable, a medium or best-guess trajectory, as well as high and low trajectories. Then one of these trajectories for each variable is grouped with others in a scenario, or collection

Ronald Lee is professor of demography and economics at the University of California, Berkeley. Shripad Tuljapurkar is president of Mountain View Research.

The authors are grateful to Bryan Lincoln, Timothy Miller, and Carl Boe for their research contributions to this project, and to Alan Auerbach and David Wise for helpful discussions at the planning stage. Participants in the Boulders NBER meeting also made helpful comments. Lee's research for this paper was funded by National Institute on Aging (NIA) grant AG11761. Tulja-purkar's research for this paper was funded by NICHD grant HD32124. The authors also acknowledge support by Berkeley's NIA-funded Center for the Economics and Demography of Aging.

of trajectories. These scenarios may, in turn, be described as "high," "medium," or "low," or by other terms such as "optimistic" and "pessimistic." A high scenario would typically be based on a high trajectory for fertility and net immigration and a low trajectory for mortality; this combination would yield high population growth. Alternatively, a "low cost" scenario for social security would bundle together high fertility and net immigration with high, rather than low, mortality; this scenario would generate the lowest old age dependency ratio. For the social security forecast, this low-cost demographic scenario would then be combined with high trajectories for productivity growth and (perhaps) for interest rates.

The scenario-based approach has several features worth noting. First, no probability is assigned to any of the trajectories or to the range that they cover, or to a scenario. Second, the trajectories are always high, or always low, or always middle; this means that fluctuations and structural shifts are assumed away. Third, the combinations of trajectories in scenarios are fixed to produce extreme outcomes. If there is some probability that fertility will follow the high trajectory, that must be higher than the probability that mortality will simultaneously follow its low trajectory; and that joint probability must be greater than the probability that productivity growth will simultaneously follow its high trajectory. Thus, even if we could attach some rough probability to the individual trajectories, we would have no clear way to attach probabilities to their combination. Fourth, any effort to attach probabilities to trajectories or to scenario outcomes would have to ignore many internal contradictions. For example, uncertainty about fertility is compounded by uncertainty about numbers of reproductive age women, but much of this uncertainty may cancel when it is transformed into uncertainty about numbers of annual births. Some uncertainty about annual births will cancel when it is summed into uncertainty about age group sizes or total population sizes. When demographic uncertainty is added to uncertainty from other sources, further cancellation should take place. Uncertainty is not additive in the way that it is assumed to be in scenario-based forecasts. These problems with the usual approach are very serious and have potentially serious consequences for planning and policy formation.

In this paper, we build on earlier work (Lee and Carter 1992; Lee 1993; Lee and Tuljapurkar 1994; Tuljapurkar and Lee, in press) to develop stochastic forecasts of the social security trust fund (assuming currently legislated changes in taxes and benefits), of summary actuarial balances, and of the "pay as you go" (PAYGO) payroll tax rate. These forecasts are based on stochastic models for fertility, mortality, productivity growth, and interest rates, which are fitted on historical data. For interest rates and productivity growth, the fitted models are constrained to conform in long-run expected value to the middle assumptions of the Social Security Administration (SSA; see Board of Trustees 1995). We have not attempted to build a simulation model for social security that is realistic in detail, which would be a major task. Instead we have sought to build a simple model that captures the core features of social security, and that can reproduce the social security forecasts when run with SSA specifications.

The Lee-Tuljapurkar (1994) stochastic population forecasts were used by the Congressional Budget Office (CBO) in its 1996 and 1997 reports to generate stochastic forecasts of the federal budget over the long term (CBO 1996). For an alternative approach to generating stochastic forecasts of social security finances, see Holmer (1995a, 1995b).

9.1   Forecasts of Fertility and Mortality

The evolution of the population depends on fertility, mortality, and net migration. In this analysis, we take fertility and mortality to be stochastic but have taken net migration to be fixed at the future levels assumed by the SSA. According to the sensitivity analysis done by the SSA (see Board of Trustees 1995, 32–42), in 2070 the effect on projected actuarial balance of the range of migration assumptions is only one-third as great as the effect of the fertility range, and only one-fifth as great as the range of the mortality assumptions.

Because our methods for forecasting fertility and mortality have been described in detail elsewhere (Lee and Carter 1992; Lee 1993), we only sketch them here. Both fertility and mortality are fitted by a model of the form

$$m_{x,t} = a_x + k_t b_x + \varepsilon_{x,t},$$

where $m_{x,t}$ is fertility of women aged x in year t, or the logarithm of the central death rate for age x in year t; a_x is an additive age-specific constant, reflecting the general shape of the age schedule; k_t is a period-specific index of the general level of fertility or mortality; b_x indicates the responsiveness of fertility or mortality at age x to variations in the general level; and $\varepsilon_{x,t}$ is the error in this approximation to the actual age schedule. There are some important issues in the estimation of this model, but they will not be discussed here. The key for forecasting is the period index, k. This is modeled as a stochastic time-series process, and the model is fitted to historical data. In the stochastic demographic forecasts, the stochastic model is used either to characterize the probability distributions for future fertility and mortality in analytic work or to generate sample paths for fertility and mortality through stochastic simulation. In either case, the coefficients a_x and b_x are then used to generate the age schedules for each t. In the case of fertility, it is necessary to constrain the model based on outside information; otherwise, the long-run behavior of the forecast is unsatisfactory, for reasons discussed later (see Lee 1993). The simplest and most satisfactory approach has been to constrain the long-term expected value of the fertility process to equal a specified level, such as 2.1 for the total fertility rate (TFR). Then the model conveys information about the variance and autocovariance of fertility around this long-term mean.

9.2   Forecasts of Productivity Growth and Interest Rates

The finances of the social security system depend not only on demographic variables but also on a whole range of economic and health variables: productivity growth rates, interest rates, inflation, disability uptake rates, and disability departure rates, to name only the ones for which the SSA performs a sensitivity analysis. From this list, we have chosen to focus on productivity growth rates and real interest rates. This choice is based partly on the sensitivity analysis reported in Board of Trustees (1995) and partly on the conceptual centrality of these variables for the retirement system.

Our analysis treats fertility, mortality, productivity growth, and the interest rate as stochastic. In addition to these four factors, the SSA performs sensitivity tests on assumptions about net migration, the rate of inflation, disability incidence, and disability termination. Analysis of the SSA projections and sensitivity tests (Board of Trustees 1995) indicates that the four variables we treat as stochastic account for 63, 70, and 76 percent of the width of the SSA low-cost–high-cost range in 2020, 2045, and 2070, respectively.[1]

In a pure PAYGO system, the interest rate would be irrelevant. However, the U.S. system has become partially funded, and interest on its growing reserve fund is an important inflow to the system. Also, in forecasts that imply negative reserve fund balances, it is appropriate to incorporate the cost of borrowing to cover the deficit.

Retirees receive benefits based on their earnings histories. When productivity growth is rapid, these histories are on average much lower than are the wages of the current workers. For this reason, rapid productivity growth reduces the tax rate necessary to fund the benefits of current retirees. The average age of receiving benefits is estimated to be 71 years old around 1990, whereas the level of benefits of a cohort is set by the level of the real wage when the cohort turns 60 years old. This 11-year age difference leverages the effects of changes in the rate of productivity growth.

Productivity growth and interest rates are economic variables that could be forecast in some highly structured way, based on the marginal products of labor and capital in an aggregate production function, with labor supply driven by the demographic forecasts, and with capital accumulation depending in part on savings behavior that might in turn be driven by our forecasts of demographic change, drawing on either life cycle saving theory or estimated age profiles of saving and dissaving. Such an approach could certainly be implemented. However, demographic change has shown limited power to explain saving rate variations in the past (see Aaron, Bosworth, and Burtless 1989); domestic saving does not explain all variations in capital accumulation, due in part to international capital flows, nor does the capital-labor ratio explain all

---

1. These are calculated from ranges in the sensitivity tests reported in Board of Trustees (1995, 132–42) and are for the summary actuarial balance. The total range when all vary is very close to the sum of the individual ranges when one varies and all others are held at their middle values.

variation in real interest rates; the capital-labor ratio is only one influence on labor productivity; technological progress is a great unknown; and on the whole, we have little confidence that such a structured approach would actually be very useful. Instead, we will simply model productivity growth and interest rates as single time series, without attempting to relate them to the economic structure believed to generate them. Provided that the trust fund does not become too large in absolute value relative to GNP, our no-feedback assumption may not be too bad. In principle we could model and forecast them as jointly evolving (e.g., VAR or cointegrated processes), but our empirical analysis turned up surprisingly little evidence that they were associated.

Productivity was measured as output per worker-hour, from the Bureau of Labor Statistics. This measure has a longer available time series than the alternatives, although there are sometimes fairly substantial differences between its rate of change and that of the social security covered wage series. In modeling productivity growth, we take into account the effect of changing age composition of the labor force on aggregate wages or productivity. The cross-sectional age profile of wages has a characteristic inverted U shape, peaking in the late 40s. This means that when there are disproportionately many young workers, for example, as in the 1970s and 1980s, there is downward pressure on aggregate wage levels or productivity per worker, arising purely from the compositional effect. We purged our productivity growth measure of age composition effects by dividing it by the summed age-by-age products of the average age profile of earnings times the year-specific proportional age-sex composition of the labor force.[2] Figure 9.1 shows the real productivity growth rate series from 1948 to 1994 *(line)* and the growth rate series with adjustment for demographic composition effects *(diamonds)*. Demographic adjustment typically alters the growth rate by less than $\pm.5$ percent. In addition, there may be a twist in the age distribution of earnings due to the well-known cohort size effect. However, we view this as a second-order effect and do not try to incorporate it.

Statistical time-series methods are not intended for long-term forecasts. Their purpose is instead to fit a highly simplified and parsimonious linear model with very short memory, which will mimic the behavior of the true generating process for a few steps into the future. Standard diagnostic and modeling procedures typically indicate that one should at least first-difference the time series before fitting it as an ARMA process. The first-differencing means that the original process is modeled as some sort of random walk, with a

---

2. The average wage profile by age and sex was calculated from the 1990 March Current Population Survey (CPS) supplement. The data on age-sex composition of the labor force are also taken from the CPS for 1948–94. If $N(i,j,t)$ is the number in the labor force for age category i, sex j, and year t, and the average wage from the 1990 CPS is $W(i,j)$, then the index $I(t)$ is

$$I(t) = \sum_i \sum_j W(i,j) N(i,j,t) / \sum_i \sum_j N(i,j,t).$$

The productivity series is then divided by $I(t)$ to remove the effects of changing age-sex composition of the labor force.

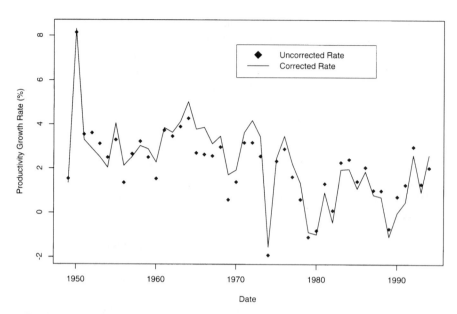

Fig. 9.1   Rate of productivity growth, with and without demographic adjustment, 1948–94

Note: Productivity is measured as output per worker-hour. Demographic adjustment removes the influence of the changing age-sex composition of the labor force, using the average age-sex earnings schedule over the period.

complicated innovation term and with drift. This often works well for short-run forecasts. For long-run forecasts, however, the drift (arising from any constant term in the differenced process) may lead to absurd levels at the same time that the random walk (or integrated) nature of the model leads to huge variances. For these reasons, long-term forecasts from these models can often be rejected as absurd. For example, in one of our fitted models, the forecast of the productivity growth rate for the year 2070 was 20 percent per year, plus or minus 60 percent.

The standard diagnostic and modeling procedures go quickly to first-differencing because it is simple, not because the data indicate that the process is truly a random walk. An alternative autoregressive model may fit just as well yet behave entirely differently in the long run, with no long-term trend and much smaller variance, relative to the integrated process. There is often too little information in the historical data to indicate which model is more correct. It may be necessary to turn to outside information, which is the route we take here.[3]

For some of our series, there is an additional problem: the consensus view

3. The level of productivity, of course, has a very strong trend and must be differenced (after taking the logarithm) to obtain the rate of productivity growth. The discussion in this section addresses the question of whether the rate of productivity growth should then be differenced once more, before modeling.

is that there have been structural changes in recent years such that the means of the fertility, productivity, and interest rate series will be different from the average of their past values. We initially attempted to deal with these purported structural changes formally, by fitting state space models with random trends (Harvey 1989). These efforts did not lead to plausible forecasts. After much experimentation, we found that apparently satisfactory models and forecasts were obtained by prespecifying the long-term means of the series, rather than estimating them from the data. In particular, we chose the long-term means of the real productivity growth and real interest rate series to equal the middle values assumed by the SSA: 1 percent per year and 2.3 percent, respectively. For better or for worse, this guarantees that the expected values of the forecasts will converge to the prespecified values, insuring consistency with the SSA middle scenarios. Since we wish to focus on the uncertainty rather than on the mean values, this feature is acceptable. Furthermore, with constrained means and an autoregressive (rather than differenced) specification, the probability bands for the forecasts of these rates appear very plausible, as we shall see below.

The trust fund for social security is held in special government securities, described as follows: "By law, the securities issued to Social Security for investment of the reserve fund bear an interest rate equal to the average yield, as of the last day of the prior month, on all outstanding Federal securities that are not due to mature for at least four years" (Foster 1994, 21). We constructed a historical interest rate series using the interest rate series for this special issue from 1961 to the present. Before 1961, social security interest rates were governed by different policies. Ideally, we would have constructed an equivalent measure for the period before 1961, since it would be most informative for forecasting purposes, whether or not it was actually the rate earned during the earlier period. In practice, having experimented with weighted averages of the three-month Treasury bill rate and the 10-year rate for best fit after 1961, we settled on using a within-sample regression fitted to predict the pre-1961 special issue rate from the simple three-month rate (bank discount basis). A Chow test accepted the null hypothesis that models fitted separately to the pre- and post-1961 data were the same. To convert these nominal interest rates into real rates, we used the Consumer Price Index for Urban Consumers (CPI-U).

As discussed earlier, we experimented with standard ARIMA models, random trend (structural time series) models, and ARMA constrained mean models (ARMA-CM), and chose the ARMA-CM models for the preferred estimates. To fit these models, one simply subtracts the constrained mean from the variable to be modeled and then fits an ARMA model in the usual way, but with no constant term.

The fitted model for productivity growth rate (PGR) is as follows:

$$PGR_t - .01 = .607(PGR_{t-1} - .01) + \varepsilon_t,$$

$$\sigma_\varepsilon = .021, \qquad R^2 = .50.$$

The fitted model for the real interest rate (I) is as follows:

$$I_t - .023 = .735(I_{t-1} - .023) + v_t,$$

$$\sigma_v = .018, \qquad R^2 = .17.$$

A standard ARIMA model leads to a long-term productivity growth rate forecast of .0210 for the raw series and .0225 for the series that was adjusted for age-sex structure, with 95 percent probability intervals $\pm.065$ and $\pm.072$, respectively. Our Kalman filter estimates of a random trend model yielded mean growth rates of about .016, with an interval of $\pm.16$. In both cases, the conventional mean forecast remains substantially higher than the social security mean forecast, and higher than many analysts would view as plausible. Additionally, the interval width for the Kalman filter estimate is greater than we find reasonable. The social security forecasts, as well as many analysts, assume that the productivity growth rate has undergone a structural decline to 1 percent per year. We therefore took this as the mean for our ARMA-CM models. These have mean productivity growth rates of .01, by assumption, with empirical interval ranges of .09 and .09, respectively.[4] Note that estimated errors are greater when there is no constant in the fitted model, leading to wider intervals than in the conventional models. Figure 9.2 shows the historical series of corrected growth rates together with the model forecast and 95 percent probability bands.

The SSA uses a productivity growth rate range of .005 to .015 per year, for an interval width of .01, only one-ninth as wide a range as in our preferred model, the ARMA-CM. But it is very important to realize that these intervals are not comparable. The SSA interval is intended to bracket some notion of the long-term tendency in the rate, while ours is intended to bracket year-to-year fluctuations. Over the time period 1948–94, the rate of real productivity growth had a high of more than 8 percent per year and a low of almost negative 2 percent, for a range of about 10 percent. This compares quite closely to the interval width of 9 percent estimated by the models[5] and obviously far exceeds the range assumed in the SSA forecast. For purposes of comparison, we also calculated the 95 percent probability interval for the average value of the productivity growth rate up to 2070. Instead of having a width of .09, it has a width of .0244, only about a quarter as great. It is narrower because a great deal of the year-to-year variation cancels out in the average. Note that the greater the positive autocorrelation, the less cancellation there will be, and the more similar will be the averaged and unaveraged brackets.

The SSA forecasts a real interest rate of .023, with a range of .015 to .030. Our ARIMA forecasts (actually a simple 1,0,0 model was chosen) have a long-

---

4. I.e., the difference between the upper and lower 95 percent bounds is .09.

5. We would expect to encounter a value at least as great as the 95 percent upper bound about once in a realization as long as 1948–94, and the same for the lower bound: each should be attained by about 2.5 percent, or one-fortieth, of the observations.

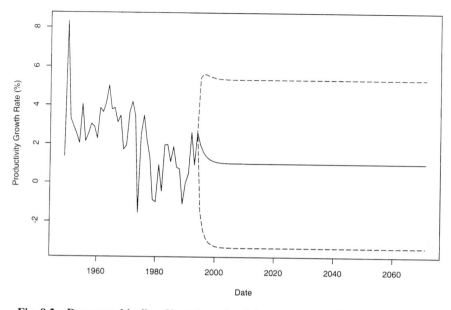

Fig. 9.2   Demographically adjusted productivity growth rates, actual and forecasted, with 95 percent probability interval, 1948–2070

Note: The long-term rate of productivity growth has been constrained to be 1 percent annually. See text for details.

run mean of .022, close to that of the SSA, with an interval width of about .12. The ARMA-CM estimates, with a constrained mean of .023 to match the SSA, also have an interval width of .12. These interval widths are very large, but the maximum-minimum range in the data series from 1948 to 1994 is even wider at 15 percent. As before, it is useful to calculate the interval width for the cumulative average values in 2070, and these are far narrower, at .045, or about a third the width. Figure 9.3 shows the historical series, the forecast, and the 95 percent probability interval for the special issue real interest rate.

The upshot, then, is that our preferred forecasts of productivity growth rates and interest rates have the same means as the SSA forecasts by assumption and are stochastic with 95 percent probability intervals for the cumulative averages that are about two and a half or three times as wide as the SSA scenario ranges. Like the SSA, we find forecasts of the real interest rate to be considerably more uncertain than those of the productivity growth rate.

9.3   The Tax and Benefit Schedules

The age schedules of payroll tax payments and receipt of benefits, when multiplied times the forecasted population age distribution and summed, determine the main flows into and out of the system. It is important to give careful consideration to the shapes and levels of these schedules.

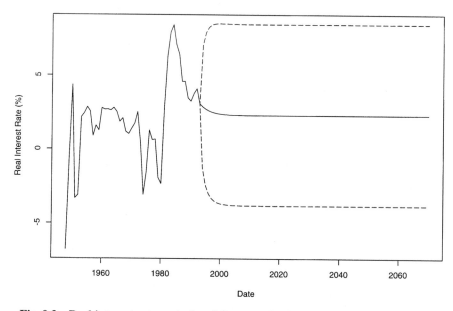

Fig. 9.3   Real interest rate, actual and forecasted, with 95 percent probability interval, 1948–2070

Note: Interest rate is for the special Treasury issue for social security from 1961 to 1994, with estimated values before 1961. It is deflated by CPI-U. The long-term real interest rate is constrained to be 2.3 percent. See text for details.

Our starting point will be the average age schedules of payroll taxes and benefits for 1994. For benefits, these are calculated from data in the *Annual Statistical Supplement* to the *Social Security Bulletin,* and for taxes, from the March CPS.[6] Figure 9.4 plots the age profiles of tax payments per capita for males and females. Figure 9.5 plots the corresponding data for receipt of benefits per capita. In figure 9.5, note the survivor's benefits received at ages under 20, and the survivor's and disability benefits received in growing amounts in the decades before the early retirement age of 62 is reached.

We will take into account the way in which productivity growth will affect the level and shape of the tax and benefit schedules. We will also take into

6. Data on the OASDI payments made by the SSA during 1994 are taken from the *Annual Statistical Supplement* to the *Social Security Bulletin* (SSA 1994). Estimates of OASI and DI payments by single year of age and by sex are generated from these data by assuming a constant per capita benefit level within the broad age categories provided in the published tables and allocating based on Census Bureau estimates of the 1994 U.S. resident population. These sex-age profiles of OASI and DI benefits are then adjusted by a constant factor so that the population-weighted sum equals the total benefit paid by OASI and DI as reported in the *Annual Statistical Supplement.* Data on the amount of OASDI taxes paid are derived from estimates of OASDI-taxable income taken from the March 1994 CPS. The sex-age profile of OASDI taxes paid is then adjusted by a constant factor so that the population-weighted sum equals the total taxes received by the OASI and DI trust funds as reported in the SSA's *Annual Statistical Supplement.*

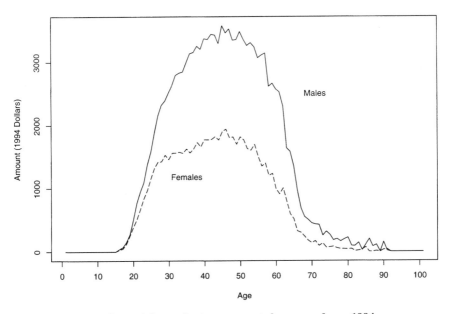

Fig. 9.4   Per capita social security tax payments by age and sex, 1994

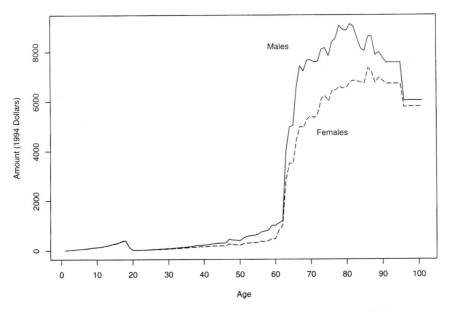

Fig. 9.5   Per capita social security benefits received by age and sex, 1994

account the effect of planned changes in the normal retirement age on these schedules. As mortality declines, there will be fewer survivors to claim benefits, and compositional effects of widowhood and selectivity (to be discussed later) will be reduced. We have not attempted to incorporate these effects of mortality decline. There will doubtless be other changes in the level and shape of these schedules that will occur over the next 75 years arising from changes in labor supply behavior due to causes other than the changes in social security regulations, and perhaps also arising from changes in the age structure of wages due to the changing age distribution of the labor force (young workers becoming less plentiful relative to older workers). There may also be further, currently unscheduled, changes in the social security regulations that will affect taxes and benefits. We have attempted neither to anticipate any of these changes nor to include measures of the uncertainty to which they give rise.

9.3.1   The Effect of Postponing the Normal Retirement Age

First consider the effects of the planned changes in the normal retirement age. The early age at retirement will remain at 62, but the age of retirement with full benefits will be raised gradually from age 65 to age 67. Since benefits will be reduced in an actuarially fair way for those retiring before age 67, benefits at age 62 will be lower than they are now, other things equal. In addition, it is planned to make actuarially fair adjustments to benefits for those who continue working past the normal retirement age, which should lead to some additional postponement of retirement.

A number of econometric studies attempt to assess the effects on retirement behavior of these planned changes (e.g., Lumsdaine and Wise 1994; and studies reviewed in Hurd 1990). Most analysts conclude that the effects of the planned changes will probably be relatively minor, but there is no consensus on details.

We have taken a mechanical approach to adjusting the age schedules. Our procedure is illustrated by the adjustment to benefits for the full two-year shift in the normal retirement age. We assume that at age 61, there will be no change at all in the tax or benefit schedules. At ages 70 and over, as discussed by the SSA, all beneficiaries will have started taking benefits. The levels of taxes and benefits that now obtain at ages 62–70 are assumed to shift in a smooth fashion, toward a profile in which the benefits at a given age before the shift are obtained two years later after the shift. At intermediate points, the amount of the age shift is interpolated proportionately.[7]

---

7. More generally, let the size of the shift in the normal retirement age be Y years (Y is 2 in the above example). Then the final benefit or tax schedule at age x will interpolate between its starting value at that age and its starting value at age $x + Y$, with an interpolation factor that depends on $(x - 62)/(70 - 62)$ for $62 \leq x \leq 70$. We assume that the new benefit profile phases out the old one evenly over the time period specified under law. The tax profile is adjusted in a similar way to incorporate additional wage-earning years before the new retirement age.

9.3.2   The Effect of Productivity Growth

We assume that the tax cutoff will be raised in proportion to the general level of wages, so we ignore it except to the extent that it is already reflected in the level and shape of the tax payment age profile. Thus we assume that the age schedule of taxes shifts upward proportionately at the same rate as productivity grows. These rising age schedules of payroll taxes are applied to projected population age distributions, thereby capturing the influence of the changing age distribution of the labor force on tax revenues in addition to the influence of productivity growth itself. The procedure restores the age composition effects that were initially purged from our measure of productivity.[8]

The effect of productivity growth on the benefit schedule is more complicated to model. The base-year age profile of benefits reflects many factors:

- Timing of retirement, and the way that the benefit level changes as a consequence

- Effect of widowhood and other factors on the proportion of beneficiaries that are single, since the per capita benefit is lower for married couples with only one primary beneficiary

- Effects of productivity change in the past, since more rapid productivity growth reduces the benefit level of older beneficiaries relative to younger ones

- Selectivity of mortality at higher ages, as those with lower lifetime incomes tend to have shorter lives and lower benefits

- Overgenerous adjustment for inflation led to rapidly rising benefits for some cohorts, and disappointment for the notch generations

We wish to retain the influences of all these factors except the last. In principle we should purge the profile of the effects of the notch generations, since these are relevant only for certain cohorts that will die out before many years have passed. In practice we have not yet attempted to do so.

Our approach is to modify the base-year benefit schedule in such a way that it is constantly updated to reflect the changing effects of past and future productivity change. For a person retiring at any age who turned 60 in year t, benefits depend on the average of his or her 35 highest annual earnings totals, with earnings before age 60 in year $t - s$ multiplied by the factor $w(t)/w(t - s)$, where $w(t)$ refers to economy-wide average wage levels. Because of the averaging and adjusting of wages, it happens that the primary benefit amount will depend almost entirely on the average wage level when the cohort

---

8. By first purging the measure of age effects, then modeling and forecasting it, and then reintroducing the effects of age composition change on tax revenues, we achieve two goals. First, we derive a measure of productivity growth that should be more amenable to time-series modeling, since once source of long swings has been removed. Second, we obtain a measure that can appropriately be multiplied times the tax age schedule, which would not otherwise be true.

turned age 60, and not on average wage levels in earlier years. To be more exact, for someone who retires at age 62, and whose highest earnings were in the last 35 of those years, the primary benefit will reflect the sum of (a) wages earned in the 33 years through age 59, each year's wages being inflated to the wage levels when the person is 60, and (b) the sum of wages at ages 61 and 62.

We have developed an algorithm to adjust the shape of the benefit schedule to reflect changes in the growth rate of productivity or wages while retaining the other important aspects of the shape of the benefit profile, as catalogued earlier. Let $B(x, t)$ be the benefit level for a person aged $x \geq 62$ in year $t \geq 1995$. We will define the benefit level for $B(x, t)$ recursively in terms of the benefit level at the same age in the previous year, $B(x, t - 1)$. These two benefit levels will differ because those aged x in t retired one year later than those aged x in $t - 1$, and therefore their benefits will be higher by a factor of $w(t - (x - 60))/w(t - 1 - (x - 60))$, or by the rate of productivity growth (or wage growth) in the year just before they turned age 60. Therefore

$$B(x,t + 1) = \{w(t - (x - 62) - 1)/w(t - 1 - (x - 62) - 1)\} \, B(x,t).$$

This simple equation ignores a term that depends on productivity change between ages 60 and 61, but this has very little effect on the results.

Note that when the rate of productivity growth continues at a constant rate that was also the rate of change in the past, then this algorithm simply raises the whole age profile by the same multiplicative factor each year. However, even if the projected future rate is constant, yet differs from the past constant rate, this procedure will change the shape of the benefit profile as time passes, as it should. Generally, more rapid productivity growth will tilt the age profile downward to the right, so that older people get relatively lower benefits than younger retirees. Because in fact productivity growth has recently been slower than in the more distant past, and because it is expected to be slower in the future as well, the age profile of benefits will be made to tilt upward to the right, so that older beneficiaries receive relatively higher benefits.

Figure 9.6 shows the projected age profile of taxes for the years 2005 and 2045, at which time the normal retirement age will have been raised by one full year and by two full years, respectively. It, and figure 9.7, are plotted on the assumption that productivity growth after 1994 is fixed deterministically at 1 percent per year. Figure 9.6 therefore reflects the effects of both productivity growth and the increase in the normal retirement age. Figure 9.7, which shows benefits received by age, is also affected by these factors. Because past productivity growth was generally more rapid than 1 percent, the assumed slowdown of productivity growth tilts the profiles upward toward the right. But the striking increase of benefits with age that is shown in figure 9.7 also reflects compositional change. The average real benefit received per surviving member of a retirement cohort actually rises with age and time following retirement, because survival is selective of those who had higher earnings while working,

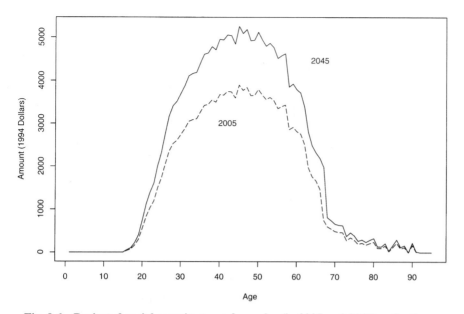

Fig. 9.6   **Projected social security taxes for males (in 2005 and 2045), reflecting 1 percent productivity growth rate and legislated increases in retirement age**

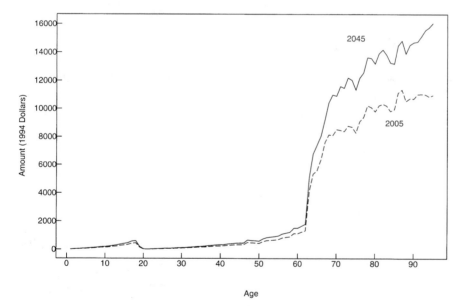

Fig. 9.7   **Projected social security benefits received for males (in 2005 and 2045), reflecting 1 percent productivity growth rate and legislated increases in retirement age**

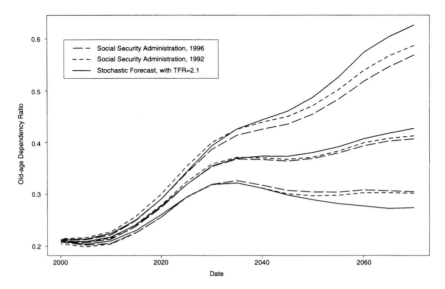

Fig. 9.8   Projected old age dependency ratios to 2070 with brackets
Note: SSA brackets are high- and low-cost variants. Stochastic forecast brackets are 95 percent probability intervals.

and because benefits are higher per capita for those living alone than for those living as married couples, so that increasing widowhood raises the average benefit.

9.4   Forecasts of the Reserve Fund under Legislated Schedule Changes

Having discussed the way in which fertility, mortality, productivity growth, and interest rates are modeled as stochastic processes, we are now ready to discuss the way these are used to generate forecasts of the social security reserve fund. We do this through stochastic simulation. Although it is conceivable that we could derive an analytic solution for the forecasts and their moments, as we have done elsewhere for the population forecasts (Lee and Tuljapurkar 1994), that would be extremely difficult. Stochastic simulation is a straightforward and convenient method for arriving at results for particular models.

The first step is to generate a large set of stochastic simulations of the population from the present to 2070, the end date of our forecasts. We have simulated 750 populations in this way. Our methods follow those in Lee and Tuljapurkar (1994), except that we have increased the migration levels to the intermediate levels in SSA forecasts (Board of Trustees 1996) and have used the SSA initial population for midyear 1994 as the starting population.

Figure 9.8 plots the 95 percent projection intervals for the old age dependency ratio, containing 95 percent of our simulated trajectories. Also plotted

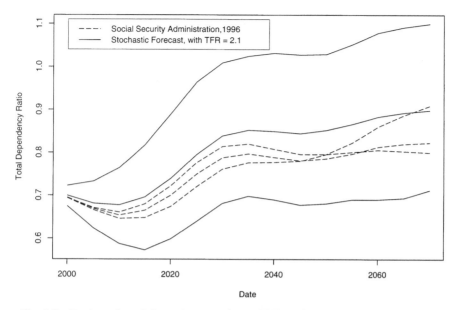

Fig. 9.9   Projected total dependency ratios to 2070 with brackets

Note: SSA brackets are high- and low-cost variants. Stochastic forecast brackets are 95 percent probability intervals.

are the SSA 1992 and SSA 1996 projections and intervals (Board of Trustees 1992, 1996). Their projections and ours are evidently quite similar, with our higher fertility assumption compensating for our lower mortality forecast. It is particularly interesting to note that the fixed scenarios used by the SSA generate a range of dependency ratios that is almost as wide as the 95 percent intervals in the stochastic projection.

Any comfort produced by the similarities in figure 9.8 is dispelled by figure 9.9, which displays the total dependency ratio. Whereas the stochastic projections again yield wide projection intervals in distant years, the SSA scenarios are very close to each other throughout the 75-year forecast period. This remarkable closeness results from intrinsic contradictions in the scenario-based approach. In order to indicate what is construed to be an appropriate amount of uncertainty in the old age dependency ratio, the variable of prime concern to the SSA, low fertility and low mortality are combined in the high-cost scenario, and high fertility and high mortality in the low-cost scenario. But low fertility means few children, while low mortality means many elderly, so that when they are combined in the total dependency ratio, they offset one another. For this reason, the SSA high and low total dependency ratios are very close to one another.

For each simulation, we also stochastically simulate a trajectory for real productivity growth and another for interest rates. The productivity growth rate

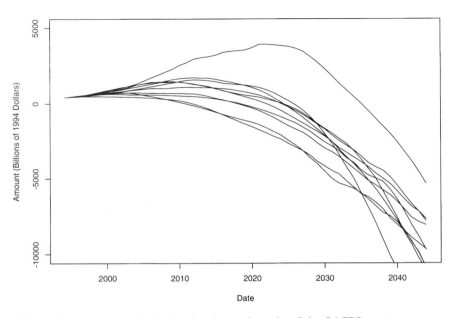

Fig. 9.10   Ten stochastically simulated sample paths of the OASDI trust fund balance

simulation is then used in the ways discussed to alter the tax and benefit profiles, which are next applied to the population age distribution simulation for that year. That generates gross flows of payroll taxes and benefit payments. Additional inflows to the reserve fund come from the simulated interest rate times the reserve fund at midyear, plus revenues from income taxes on benefits.[9] Additional outflows are for administrative costs of the system, and of the separate railroad fund. The difference between total inflows and total outflows, the net flow, is added to the value of the reserve fund. In this way, the state of the system is updated each year, and the level of the reserve fund is calculated for one particular simulated sample path. This process is repeated for each of the 750 stochastic simulations of population, interest rate, and productivity growth. Each simulation assumes that no policy action is taken to adjust tax or benefit rates in response to trends in the reserve fund.

Figure 9.10 plots 10 randomly chosen simulated sample paths out of the total of 750. These lines often cross one another, indicating that the same line is not always the best or always the worst, as would be the case under scenario-

9. This procedure slightly exaggerates the influence of interest rate movements on the finances of the system in the short run, because once bonds are purchased by the trust fund, the nominal interest rate is fixed for the life of the bond. Subsequent fluctuations in the nominal rate will not affect the money earned on that bond. However, most of the volatility in the real interest rate series that we use is due to variation in the rate of inflation. The rate of inflation affects the real rate of return on bonds no matter when they were purchased, consistent with the specification we use.

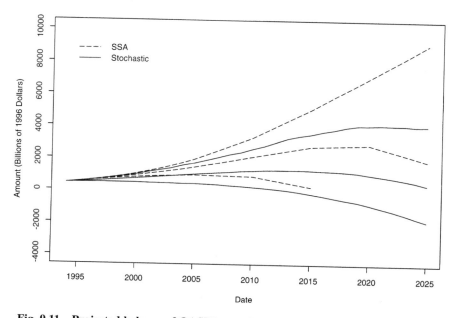

Fig. 9.11   Projected balance of OASDI trust fund (1995 to 2025) with brackets from SSA and stochastic forecasts
Note: SSA brackets are high- and low-cost variants. Stochastic forecast brackets are 95 percent probability intervals.

based forecasting. Based on the full set of 750 (or a larger set of simulations if we wished) we can calculate the mean of sample paths in each year, and we can also find for each year the level of the reserve fund that is greater than 97.5 percent of the paths and the level that is greater than only 2.5 percent of the paths. These two levels then define the 95 percent probability band for each year.

Figure 9.11 shows the forecast only for the first 30 years, up to 2025, for purposes of comparison to the SSA forecast. There are noticeable differences. Although we cannot see it, the simulated mean crosses the line of zero reserves in 2026, four years earlier than in SSA forecasts. The main message, however, is uncertainty about this crossing point: the 95 percent interval includes exhaustion in 2014, as well as exhaustion in 2037, beyond the range of this plot. The level of the reserve fund peaks at $1.3 trillion on average, but the upper bound peaks at $4.0 trillion, and the lower bound at only $0.57 trillion, not much more than it is now.

Figure 9.12 shows the mean and 95 percent probability band for the forecast of the reserve fund, now all the way out to 2070. Because we have not modeled any economic or policy feedbacks and the forecasted fund debt becomes enormous, these forecasts should not be taken at face value. The debt could not actually grow so large without serious consequences for the economy, which

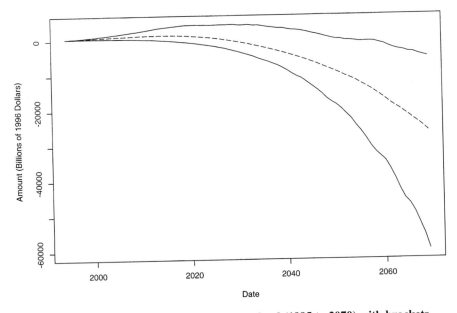

Fig. 9.12   Projected balance of OASDI trust fund (1995 to 2070) with brackets from stochastic forecast
Note: Stochastic forecast brackets (*solid lines*) are 95 percent probability intervals.

would in turn cause changes in interest rates and productivity growth, or lead to policy changes in taxes or benefits.

In figure 9.12, the mean fund balance dips to a debt of $26 trillion by 2070 (all dollars are expressed in 1996 U.S. dollars). The 95 percent range spans debts in 2070 of $6 to $60 trillion. The SSA only publishes fund projections for trajectories above zero, but their low-cost forecast for the fund in 2070 is a positive $9 trillion dollars—a more optimistic projection than ours, despite our assumed expected TFR of 2.1. The most important message from this plot is not the trend in the mean, which should not be far different from other forecasts of the same quantity. The important message is rather the great deal of uncertainty surrounding the mean forecast, and the explicit quantification of the probabilities.

We do not, in fact, mean to suggest that the trust fund will actually go to zero, let alone to debts of trillions of dollars. As the fund begins to fall toward zero, action will be taken to raise the tax schedule, reduce benefits, delay retirement, further tax benefits, invest the reserves in equities yielding higher returns than government bonds, privatize the system, or in some other way prevent the system from going into debt. These forecasts, conditional on the future tax and benefit rules conforming to current plans, are rather intended to shed light on the consequences of those plans. Section 9.5 takes up a different kind of calculation that we believe to be more interesting.

Table 9.1   **Summary Actuarial Balance According to SSA and the Current Model (percentage increase in payroll tax rate necessary to restore actuarial balance)**

	Summary Actuarial Balance, by Period		
Source of Projection	1995–2020	1995–2045	1995–2070
SSA 1996	.36	−1.39	−2.19
LT: SSA mortality and fertility, deterministic	.82	−1.28	−2.31
LT: SSA mortality, TFR = 2.1, deterministic	.82	−1.25	−2.14
LT: LC mortality, TFR = 2.1, stochastic	.50	−2.00	−3.33

Notes: In deterministic simulations, the discount rate is 2.3 percent; in the stochastic simulation, the discount rate for each sample path is the corresponding simulated rate. "SSA mortality" corresponds to life expectancy of 80.7 years in 2070; "LC mortality," for Lee and Carter (1992) mortality, corresponds to life expectancy of 86.1 years in 2070. "SSA fertility" corresponds to TFR = 1.9. In our simulations, SSA mortality is a mortality trajectory calculated using the Lee-Carter model, but with an imposed rate of decline resulting in the SSA life expectancy level in 2070. Details of the age pattern of decline and the timing of decline differ from SSA assumptions.

9.5   Long-Term Actuarial Balance and Tax Increases

The SSA employs a summarized measure of the long-term status of the trust funds, based on what are called summarized cost rates and summarized income rates. The basic measure, the long-term actuarial balance, is roughly speaking equal to the difference between the present value of the stream of tax revenues and benefit payments over the projection period, divided by the present value of the stream of total payroll. It can be interpreted as the amount by which the payroll tax rate would have to be raised, immediately and permanently, to equalize these two present values, taking into account the existing reserve fund at the start and the target reserve fund at the end. We will use the SSA calculations of actuarial balance as a kind of benchmark against which to test the long-term performance of our model. We will also use this measure as a convenient metric for representing the relative importance of different sources of uncertainty in our stochastic forecasts.

Table 9.1 reports on the calculated summary actuarial balance based on four different models and for each of the four shows the calculated balance over three different periods. The first row reports the balance according to the SSA (Board of Trustees 1996). This report concludes that the system would be in balance through 2070 if the payroll tax rate were immediately and permanently raised from 12.4 percent (for OASDI) to 14.59 percent (= 12.4 + 2.19). We attempt to replicate this result by running a deterministic simulation in which TFR is set at the SSA level of 1.9 children per woman and mortality is assumed to decline at a constant rate (distributed by age according to the Lee and Carter, 1992, model) such as to achieve the SSA projected life expectancy in 2070. Interest rates and productivity growth rates are assumed fixed at the SSA levels of 2.3 percent and 1 percent. The result is shown in the second row, resulting in a figure of −2.31 versus −2.19, which we view as excellent agreement, given our very different approach to projecting the tax and benefits schedules. Additional experiments, not reported here, show that deterministic sensitivity analyses using our model yield results very similar to those reported by SSA.

The third row of table 9.1 shows another deterministic simulation, which differs from the previous one only in that TFR is now set at 2.1, as in Lee and Tuljapurkar (1994). The agreement with SSA is very slightly worse in the medium term, but somewhat closer in the long term. Finally, the last row shows the mean result from the set of stochastic simulations, this time with TFR = 2.1 and mortality declining at the faster pace of Lee and Carter (1992), resulting in roughly twice the gain in life expectancy projected by the SSA. Because of this more rapid mortality decline, the actuarial balance for 1995–2070 is now −3.33, or about 1.2 percent worse than with the SSA mortality.

The SSA (Board of Trustees 1996, 23) gives a range for this summary actuarial balance from +.46 percent to −5.67 percent, with an interval width of 6.13 percent (= .46 + 5.67). The standard deviation of our stochastic summary actuarial balance is 1.58 percent, leading to a 95 percent probability interval ranging from −.17 percent to −6.49 percent, for an interval width of 6.3 percent, very similar to the SSA's. This indicates that the SSA's low-cost–high-cost range for 2070 has an approximate 95 percent probability coverage, assuming it is correctly centered. However, our interval is centered at −3.33, versus −2.19 for theirs, a fairly substantial difference. The difference arises from the more rapid mortality decline in the stochastic simulation.

9.6   Fund Exhaustion and Tax Increase

According to the SSA projections, a 2.19 percent increase in the OASDI tax rate should restore the system to long-term balance, under the intermediate set of assumptions. We can use our stochastic simulation (as reported in the last row of table 9.1) to assess the likelihood that exhaustion would occur in any case. Panel *A* of figure 9.13 shows the probability distribution of dates of exhaustion of the OASDI trust fund if taxes were immediately raised by 1 percent, to 13.4 percent. In this case, 93.4 percent of the sample paths reach fund exhaustion before the end of the period in 2070, and the median fund balance in 2070 is −$17 trillion (1996 dollars). Panel *B* shows the corresponding probability distribution assuming an immediate 2 percent increase in the tax rate, to 14.4 percent. In this case, three-quarters of the sample paths still end in exhaustion by 2070, and the median fund balance then is −$8 trillion.

We could search for the permanent tax increase necessary to achieve a 95 percent probability of nonexhaustion by 2070. However, the requirement that there be no subsequent tinkering with taxes and benefits to achieve balance in the future, as more is learned about actual demographic and economic developments, is unappealingly rigid. Instead we pursue a different approach, going to the opposite extreme of adjusting taxes on a year-by-year basis to meet costs.

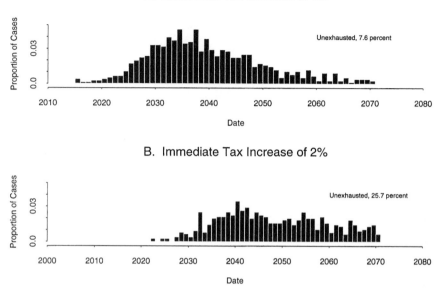

A. Immediate Tax Increase of 1%

B. Immediate Tax Increase of 2%

Fig. 9.13   Histograms of dates of exhaustion

9.7   Forecasts of the Payroll Tax Rate under Reserve Fund Constraints

Suppose that instead of fixing a tax rate to hold for the next 75 years, we set the tax rate each year to maintain the reserve fund at a level exactly sufficient to cover one year's benefit payments? We can do this calculation in two ways. One is to leave the currently legislated 12.4 percent tax rate in place until the reserve falls to 100 percent of anticipated year-ahead outflows and thereafter raise or lower the tax rate as necessary to leave the reserve at this level. We call this "eventual pay as you go." The other way is to let the reserve fund immediately fall to 100 percent of outflow (which takes only a couple of years of zero or very low taxes) and thereafter adjust it as necessary. This approach gives us the pure PAYGO rate.

We present results only for the first calculation, eventual PAYGO. We hold constant the 12.4 percent rate until the reserve fund drops to the target level. The results are shown in figure 9.14, which plots lines giving varying probability coverages. For example, in any year, 60 percent of the sample lines lie below the line labeled .6. The median line (not shown) would lie roughly halfway between the .4 and .6 lines. It would remain at 12.4 percent until 2022, rise rapidly as the baby boom retires, and then rise more slowly to 24 percent in 2070. The lines labeled .025 and .975 bound the region with 95 percent probability coverage. The lower .025 bound remains at 12.4 percent until 2043

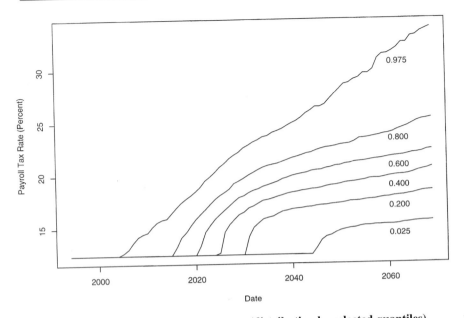

Fig. 9.14   Tax rate for year-ahead balance (distribution by selected quantiles)

and then rises modestly to 16 percent in 2070. The upper 97.5 percent bound rises roughly linearly after 2003, to 34 percent in 2070.

In sum, with the eventual PAYGO system with variable tax rates the median tax rate would double by 2070 and still be rising slowly at that point, reflecting continuing mortality decline. There is a 2.5 percent chance that the tax rate would have to rise to 34 percent of earnings by the end of the forecast in 2070. A 34 percent payroll tax rate, plus additional taxes for Medicare and Medicaid, plus other state, local, and federal taxes, would be a terribly heavy burden.

These results may be compared to annual cost estimates by the SSA (Board of Trustees 1996, 170–71) for 2070, which gives a high-medium-low range of 28.0, 18.8, and 13.1 percent, respectively. The range widths are again similar: 15 percent for SSA versus 18 percent for the stochastic simulation, indicating that the SSA probability coverage would be somewhat less than 95 percent if the range were correctly centered. However, the stochastic simulation gives a median tax in 2070 of 24 percent, versus 18.8 percent for the SSA. The increase from the initial tax of 12.4 percent is nearly twice as great in the stochastic simulation as in the SSA projection. This difference arises from the more rapid decline in mortality incorporated in the stochastic simulation.

9.8   How Much Uncertainty Does Each Component Contribute?

We have seen that there is a great deal of uncertainty about the long-term finances of the system. Where does this uncertainty originate? What would we

Table 9.2   **Sources of Uncertainty in Forecasts of Summary Actuarial Balance (standard errors when one variable at a time is stochastic)**

	Standard Error of Summary Actuarial Balance, by Period		
Stochastic Variable	1995–2020	1995–2045	1995–2070
Fertility	.02	.27	.86
Mortality	.19	.39	.54
Productivity growth rate	.90	.90	.80
Interest rate	.14	.50	.69
Fertility and mortality	.19	.48	1.02
All	.93	1.18	1.58

Note: The discount rate is 2.3 percent, except when the interest rate is stochastic, in which case the simulated trajectory of interest rates is used for each sample path.

need to know to reduce it? The Board of Trustees (1996) reports a sensitivity analysis for its forecasts, showing the effect on the long-run balance of the system when one factor varies across the specified high-low range, while holding all others at their mean values. The outcome, of course, depends on the sensitivity of the projection to each variable, but it also depends on the amount of change that is examined for each variable—the width of the range. We can avoid arbitrary assumptions about this range by using our stochastic simulation model. Holding all but one of the variables (fertility, mortality, interest rates, and productivity growth rates) fixed at their mean trajectories, we allow the fourth to vary stochastically in the usual way. The resulting widths of the probability bands can then be compared. Results of this exercise are reported in table 9.2, which gives the standard deviation of the summary actuarial balance in each case, for each of three time periods.

From the last column of the table, we see that fertility contributes the greatest uncertainty through 2070, followed by the productivity growth rate, the interest rate, and finally mortality. It is striking that whereas our model puts uncertainty about mortality *last* in importance, the SSA analysis (Board of Trustees 1996, 132–34) puts it *first*. And whereas we put fertility *first* in importance, the SSA puts it *last* (tied with the interest rate).

It is also interesting to note how the relative and absolute contributions to uncertainty change with the period over which actuarial balance is assessed. Fertility makes only a trivial contribution over the period 1995–2020 because there is a long lag between birth and labor force entry, while the productivity growth rate makes by far the strongest contribution over this period. Interest does not matter much because the trust fund is not very large, and mortality, which operates cumulatively on survival rates, has insufficient time to make much difference.

The fifth row of the table shows the standard deviation of the actuarial balance when both fertility and mortality are stochastic but the economic variables are fixed, and the last row gives the result when all four variables are stochastic. Comparing these, we see that over the 25-year horizon, demographic uncertainty generates a standard deviation only one-fifth as wide as the fully stochastic model. However, over a 75-year horizon, demographic uncertainty alone generates a standard deviation almost two-thirds as wide as the fully stochastic model. Evidently, demographic uncertainty becomes far more important over the long run than it is over the shorter run.

9.9   Conclusion

We are still developing the methods used for these stochastic simulations, and there will doubtless be future changes. Nonetheless, this macrosimulation model replicates quite closely the key SSA results, when run in deterministic mode using SSA assumptions. This confirms that the basic simulation model is mechanically sound. Most of the material we present is based on stochastic models of fertility, mortality, interest rates, and productivity growth rates, with expected values that conform closely to the SSA intermediate assumptions. The exception is mortality, for which we believe the SSA projected rate of decline is too slow. Our fitted stochastic mortality model foresees twice as great gains in life expectancy by the year 2070 as do the SSA projections.

We considered long-term stochastic projections of the trust fund balance, the summary actuarial balance, and the PAYGO tax rate. Because we do not incorporate economic or policy feedbacks in our model, outcomes in which large positive or negative trust fund balances occur are bound to be quite unrealistic. With that caveat, our 95 percent probability intervals for 2070 were as follows: for the trust fund, in 1996 dollars, $-\$6$ to $-\$60$ trillion; for the summary actuarial balance, $-.2$ to -6.5 percent of the present value of payroll; and for the PAYGO balanced budget tax rate in 2070, 16 to 34 percent of payroll.

Because of the more rapid expected rate of mortality decline used in our stochastic simulations, our financial projections are somewhat more pessimistic than those of the SSA. For example, our expected summary actuarial balance is -3.33 percent of the present value of payroll, versus -2.19 for the Board of Trustees (1996). However, the width of the SSA high-cost–low-cost ranges, to which no probability interpretation is attached, are surprisingly close to the width of our 95 percent probability intervals, when compared for horizons of 2020, 2045, and 2070. These widths are much greater than the differences in means between the stochastic simulation projections and the SSA projections, which is reassuring.

According to our simulations, if currently legislated tax and benefit rates are unchanged, there is a 95 percent chance of trust fund exhaustion between 2014 and 2037. There is only a 2.5 percent chance that the trust fund balance in 2070 will exceed $-\$6$ trillion (1996 dollars). If the tax rate were immediately and permanently raised by 1 percent, there would still be a 92 percent probability of trust fund exhaustion before 2070. If the tax were raised by 2 percent, close to the 2.19 percent that the SSA suggests would be needed to achieve long-term balance, we find that there would still be a 75 percent chance that the trust fund would be exhausted before 2070.

We have also computed the implicit rate of return that the generation born in 1980–84, and therefore just about to enter the labor force, will receive through OASDI. We project an expected real rate of return of 1.6 percent, with a 95 percent probability interval of .2 to 2.8 percent.

When we examined the relative contributions of our four stochastic factors to uncertainty in the projections, the results disagreed sharply with the SSA sensitivity analysis. For example, we found fertility to be by far the greatest source of uncertainty about the long-run finances of the system, while the SSA found it to be least important. We found mortality to be least important in the long run, while the SSA found it to be most important. Our results also showed clearly that demography matters most in the long run, where its tidal forces have a cumulative impact.

We are still at early stages of digesting our stochastic forecasts of the finances of the social security system and are still exploring new ways in which these forecasts and experiments might be useful and informative. One promising use, not yet implemented, will be to test the consequences of a range of strategies and policy options for dealing with uncertainty. Is it better to wait and see, adjusting policy continuously as we gain information? Or is it better to accumulate large reserves early on, to provide a buffer against unlikely but possible transitory insults to the system? Or should policy simply be set to deal reasonably with the mean trajectory, ignoring the uncertainty? How about keying the level of benefits to life expectancy at retirement, as in the Swedish system, or tying cohort benefit levels to cohort fertility, as has sometimes been suggested? Stochastic simulations could provide a useful laboratory for testing these alternative policies in relation to goals such as achieving intergenerational equity, avoiding rapid changes in taxes or benefits, and keeping the trust fund above zero.

References

Aaron, Henry, Barry Bosworth, and Gary Burtless. 1989. *Can America afford to grow old? Paying for social security.* Washington, D.C.: Brookings Institution.

Board of Trustees. Federal Old-Age and Survivors Insurance and Disability Insurance Trust Funds. 1992. *1992 Annual report of the Board of Trustees of the Federal Old-Age and Survivors Insurance and Disability Insurance Trust Funds.* Washington, D.C.: Government Printing Office.

———. 1995. *1995 Annual report of the Board of Trustees of the Federal Old-Age and Survivors Insurance and Disability Insurance Trust Funds.* Washington, D.C.: Government Printing Office.

————. 1996. *1996 Annual report of the Board of Trustees of the Federal Old-Age and Survivors Insurance and Disability Insurance Trust Funds.* Washington, D.C.: Government Printing Office.

Congressional Budget Office. 1996. *The economic and budget outlook: Fiscal years 1997–2006.* Washington, D.C.: Government Printing Office.

Foster, Richard S. 1994. A stochastic evaluation of the short-range economic assumptions in the 1994 OASDI trustees report. Actuarial Study no. 109 (SSA Publ. no. 11-11502). Washington, D.C.: U.S. Department of Health and Human Services, August.

Harvey, Andrew. 1989. *Forecasting, structural time series models and the Kalman filter.* Cambridge: Cambridge University Press.

Holmer, Martin. 1995a. Briefing on trust-fund asset-allocation policy: Stochastic simulation model. SSA Contract no. 95-22582.

————. 1995b. Overview of SSASIM: A long-run stochastic simulation model of social security. SSA contract no. 95-22582.

Hurd, Michael. 1990. Research on the elderly: Economic status, retirement, and consumption and saving. *Journal of Economic Literature* 28:565–637.

Lee, Ronald D. 1993. Modeling and forecasting the time series of U.S. fertility: Age patterns, range, and ultimate level. *International Journal of Forecasting* 9:187–202.

Lee, Ronald D., and Lawrence Carter. 1992. Modeling and forecasting the time series of U.S. mortality. *Journal of the American Statistical Association* 87:659–71.

Lee, Ronald D., and Shripad Tuljapurkar. 1994. Stochastic population forecasts for the U.S.: Beyond high, medium and low. *Journal of the American Statistical Association* 89:1175–89.

Lumsdaine, Robin L., and David A. Wise. 1994. Aging and labor force participation: A Review of trends and explanations. In *Aging in the United States and Japan,* ed. Yukio Noguchi and David Wise, 7–41. Chicago: University of Chicago Press.

Shripad, Tuljapurkar, and Ronald Lee. In press. Demographic uncertainty and the OASDI fund. In *Intergenerational economic relations and demographic change,* ed. Andrew Mason and Georges Tapinos. Oxford: Oxford University Press.

Social Security Administration (SSA). Office of Research and Statistics. 1994. *Social security bulletin annual statistical supplement.* Washington, D.C.: Government Printing Office.

Comment   Sylvester J. Schieber

The basic premise in Ronald Lee and Shripad Tuljapurkar's (hereafter L-T) paper is that the planning surrounding major government entitlement commitments in general, and social security in particular, must not only take into account our best estimates about the future costs and cost drivers of these programs but also must consider the uncertainty surrounding those estimates. On the basis of this premise, they develop a set of stochastic forecasts of the future operations of social security.

L-T's approach to forecasting social security operations in the paper has been supported by various groups in the past, including some in advisory roles to the Social Security Administration (SSA). For example, the Technical Panel

Sylvester J. Schieber is vice president of research and information for Watson Wyatt Worldwide.

on Assumptions and Methods that supported the 1994–96 Social Security Advisory Council recommended the "implementation of stochastic analysis procedures for presenting and evaluating the uncertainty in OASDI projections" (Technical Panel 1996, 137). Following on the recommendations of the Technical Panel, the Advisory Council itself recommended that such "modeling should be used as a tool for recognizing explicitly the uncertainty surrounding the . . . demographic and economic assumptions" used in valuing the program's operations (Advisory Council 1997, 22).

While the approach that L-T have recommended and the analysis that they have done may receive relatively widespread support among policy analysts in general, it is still a debated approach within social insurance policy analysis circles, and it is not a path that has been taken by the social security program's actuaries in developing official cost estimates. Robert J. Myers, former chief actuary of the SSA, believes that the deterministic scenario-based modeling that is currently used in projecting social security operations is adequate and that the high- and low-cost estimates give a reasonable range of costs that might be expected under the program.

Myers has laid out a rationale for continued use of the deterministic approach and makes three points to support it. First, he believes that "experienced judgment" is superior to "blind mathematical analysis of past experience" in developing these estimates. Second, he believes that the present practice of lumping together the low-cost (high-cost) assumptions to develop low-cost (high-cost) program projections produces a reasonable "range" of cost estimates in the aggregate. Third, he argues that "any large changes . . . should be phased in over a period of years, so that there is a reasonable certainty that they should be made in their entirety" (Technical Panel 1996, 267–68). In the last point, it is not clear whether Myers is arguing that changes in *assumptions* should be phased in slowly or whether changes in *program costs* should be recognized on a phased basis. To a certain extent, phasing in changes in assumptions over a period of annual valuations will result in the slow recognition of changing cost estimates. Regardless of his precise meaning on the third point, Myers's arguments for staying with the current valuation methodology offer a framework for reviewing the work reported in L-T's paper.

Accuracy of Prior Estimates

One way to judge the quality of the current approach to projecting social security costs or whether it might be desirable to move to a stochastic modeling approach is to review prior projections to see how they have comported with ultimate experience. In this regard, the results are mixed. Estimates of OASI program costs developed by the program's actuaries after the passage of the 1939 amendments to the Social Security Act projected the cost of OASI in 1970 at 6.33 percent of covered payroll based on "original assumptions" and at 8.54 percent of payroll based on "probable maximum cost assumptions." The respective projections for 1980 were 7.21 percent and 10.60 percent of covered payroll (Bronson 1939). The actual cost of OASI benefit payments in 1970 was 6.98 percent of covered payroll (Board of Trustees 1971), and in 1980 it was 9.39 percent (Board of Trustees 1981).

Based on this evidence, it seems the early estimates of long-term program costs were reasonable predictions of the ultimate tax burden to support it. While the SSA's actuaries likely never dreamed of the rapid expansion of benefits during the 1970s, their 1939 "maximum probable cost" estimate for 1980 still bounded the actual cost of the program. The early history of the program and its related cost projections, however, might not be instructive for the future that we now face. It seems there was a general sense among the early advocates of social security that the economy and the public would or could bear cost rates up to 12 percent of covered payroll. The managers of the program were fully cognizant that costs would rise over time as a growing share of the working population attained "insured" status under the program. Over the years, benefits were increased repeatedly but always within the constraints that estimated cost rates allowed. In this environment, the 1939 cost projection for 1970 became a self-fulfilling prophecy. It was accepted from the earliest days of the program as being a reasonable cost, and benefit levels were merely adjusted periodically to move toward it. The target cost rate could be achieved without being exceeded because the program was run on a nominal basis. If costs started to get out of hand, inflationary forces could bring them back into line with acceptable rates. This all changed with the 1972 amendments that automatically indexed benefits and resulted in the double indexing of initial benefit awards for new beneficiaries. These amendments made the program particularly susceptible to price inflation, especially to the extent that it significantly exceeded the rate of growth of wages.

Social Security has always been run largely on a pay-as-you-go basis. Under such a financing regime, revenues must roughly equal expenditures from year to year. In simple mathematical terms,

$$(1) \qquad t \cdot N_w \cdot W = N_b \cdot B,$$

where t is the payroll tax rate, N_w the number of workers who are covered by the system, W their average covered wages, N_b the number of beneficiaries, and B their average benefit levels. Stated in another way,

$$(2) \qquad t = (N_b/N_w) \cdot (B/W),$$

where the ratio of beneficiaries to workers can be thought of as the dependency ratio and the ratio of benefits to wages might be thought of as the benefits ratio or, in the parlance of retirement plans, the system's average wage replacement level.

Table 9C.1 compares the midrange economic assumptions used in developing the SSA's cost projections for the 1972 Board of Trustees report with actual experience for the five years from 1972 through 1976. As a result of the

Table 9C.1   **Comparison of Five-Year Economic Assumptions in the 1972 OASDI Trustees Report with Actual Experience**

| Year | CPI Increase (%) | | Real Wage Increase (%) | | Unemployment Rate (%) | |
	Assumed[a]	Actual	Assumed[a]	Actual	Assumed[a]	Actual
1972	2.75	3.3	2.25	4.0	4.2	5.6
1973	2.75	6.2	2.25	0.7	4.2	4.9
1974	2.75	11.0	2.25	−3.6	4.2	5.6
1975	2.75	9.1	2.25	−2.5	4.2	8.5
1976	2.75	5.8	2.25	2.5	4.2	7.7
Total	14.53	40.6	11.77	1.0	4.2[b]	6.5[b]

Sources: 1972 Annual Report of the Board of Trustees of the Federal Old-Age and Survivors Insurance and Disability Insurance Trust Funds (Washington, D.C.: Government Printing Office, 1972) and *Economic Report of the President* (Washington, D.C.: Government Printing Office, 1982).

[a]Midrange assumptions.

[b]Estimates for five-year unemployment totals and five-year averages.

1972 social security amendments and what was going on in the economy at the time, benefits absolutely exploded relative to wage levels, and the beneficiary-to-worker ratio was adversely affected by the higher than expected unemployment levels. There was a clear breakdown in the reliability of the cost estimation process at this point in social security's history. It is conceivable that stochastic modeling would have helped catch the problems introduced in the 1972 amendments before their passage, but it is also quite possible that it would not have.

The 1977 social security amendments were intended to bring benefits back into line with their more traditional levels and to stabilize the relationship between benefits and wages looking forward, subject to the variations noted by L-T in their analysis. The 1977 amendments proved to be insufficient to deal with the continuing adverse economic conditions of the late 1970s and early 1980s, and the program had to be rebalanced once again in the 1983 amendments. The actuaries' projections after the adoption of the 1983 changes predicted that the trust fund balances would accumulate to more than $20 trillion but would ultimately be depleted in 2063 (Ballantyne 1983). Subsequent projections in the annual Board of Trustees reports have consistently ratcheted down the trust fund accumulation, with the latest projection that it would only accumulate about $2.8 trillion at its peak and would be depleted by 2029 (Board of Trustees 1997). The 1997 intermediate projection actually turned out to be somewhat less optimistic than the pessimistic projection from 1983.

The point of this discussion is that since social security has matured and the benefit structure been indexed, the cost projections for the program have become somewhat more sensitive to economic and demographic variations than they had been in the past. Recent projections have suggested an unwarranted level of certainty about future costs that have often proved to be badly out of range, and "worst case" scenarios have proved to be optimistic. In short, the projection game has changed, and the old methods no longer seem adequate to the task of providing realistic cost estimates in some cases, or a sense of the vulnerability of those estimates to varying experience under the program.

Stochastic Projections versus Reliance on Experienced Judgment

In Myers's defense of the current SSA projection methods he argues that the "experienced judgment" behind current projections is better than "blind mathematical analysis" of the past. The implication is that stochastic modeling necessarily relies solely on mindless projection of past trends with the historical variation around those trends built into the projections that are being developed. The work by L-T shows that this does not have to be the case. For several of the important variables used in determining social security's long-term costs, L-T constrain their projections to mean distributions that are equivalent or close to the best-guess estimates used by the SSA actuaries in their long-term projections.

However, the results of the L-T stochastic simulations raise a question about the superiority of such projections over the current scenario-based deterministic projections that are formally used in monitoring and projecting social security operations. For example, the close correspondence between the L-T 95 percent probability intervals for the aged dependency ratios and those generated in the high- and low-cost projections developed by the SSA actuaries suggests a similar correspondence in long-term cost projections, given the importance of this dependency ratio in determining costs, as shown in equation (2) above. Indeed, L-T report that the range of their cost estimates from 95 percent probability levels corresponds closely to the range in the low- and high-cost estimates published by the Board of Trustees. L-T's costs are generally higher than those from the SSA largely because of the difference in their assumptions about continued improvements in life expectancy. Earlier work by Ronald Lee and Lawrence Carter (1994) supports the contention that the SSA is being overly optimistic in its assumptions about future life expectancy—that is, it is assuming slower increases in life expectancy than many demographers think is reasonable. The Technical Panel for the 1994–96 Advisory Council was very critical of the assumptions being used by the SSA in its projections (Technical Panel 1996, 251–62).

The criticism that current formal SSA projections are not based on proper assumptions does not necessarily mean that the actuaries' current cost projection methods are inferior to a stochastic approach. But this issue of appropriate assumptions cuts directly against the first of the points that Robert Myers makes in arguing for the current projection methodology over stochastic modeling of the future. If we are to rely on the "experienced judgment" of those doing projections, no matter what their method of projecting that judgment should not blindly ignore the past unless there is a powerful reason for doing

Percent of covered payroll

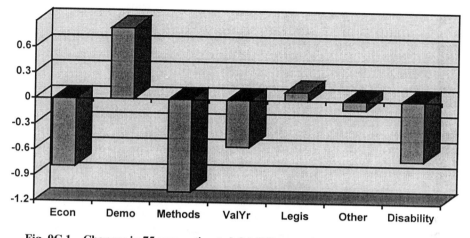

**Fig. 9C.1 Changes in 75-year estimated OASDI actuarial balance as a
percentage of covered payroll over projection years 1983–95**
Source: U.S. Department of the Treasury, Office of the Assistant Secretary for Economic Policy.

so. If the actuaries were using stochastic projection techniques, it is likely that
they would use more formal processes in projecting important variables such
as life expectancy than they seem to be using now. They would also have to
provide a much better rationale than they do now in relying on their "experienced judgment" when such judgment goes against historical trends.

Projecting a Reasonable Range of Outcomes

Robert Myers's second argument for the SSA's staying with its current
method of projecting future OASDI costs is that the scenarios project a reasonable range of cost estimates. As noted earlier, the L-T range of projections
starting from a base year of 1995 does correspond closely with those of the
SSA actuaries. While the range of the two sets of projections may be relatively
close, another way to consider the variance in the projections from the respective models is to look at how they might be used in choosing public policies
and whether the two approaches would lead to different potential conclusions.

The last time that we undertook a major review of SSA policies that led to
significant policy changes was in 1983. After the 1983 social security amendments were adopted, the program actuaries estimated that the program would
be in actuarial balance—that is, aggregate revenues plus assets would equal
aggregate expenditures—for the next 75 years. Over the years since then, the
annual projections of the system have consistently estimated larger and larger
actuarial deficits for the program. Figure 9C.1 summarizes, by reason of
change, the changes in projected actuarial balances under the formal projections over the period.

A natural question that arises from figure 9C.1 is whether the evolution of SSA projections between 1983 and 1995 would have been any different in a stochastic modeling world than under the deterministic process now used. While it is impossible to be certain, there is some likelihood that the actuaries would have used similar economic and demographic assumptions whether they were doing stochastic or deterministic projections. Beyond the economic and demographic assumptions (Econ and Demo), both models would likely have been plagued by similar experiences. The costs attributed to changing methods (Methods) relate to the discovery of calculation errors or different ways of looking at cost calculations. The change in costs attributed to differences in valuation year (Val Yr) are related to doing 75-year forecasts and the demographic structure of the population; namely, each year we give up one good year in the projection and add a bad one. The cost changes attributed to disability relate to growing incidence rates of such benefits, and it is not clear that explicit modeling of disability on a stochastic basis would have anticipated these increases any more quickly than the actuaries have. L-T are not explicitly stochastically modeling disability at this time, but given the sensitivity of cost estimates to these claims, it would seem like a valuable addition to make to the program.

Given the close correspondence between the L-T and SSA aged dependency ratios noted earlier, the significant divergence in total dependency ratios under the two projection methods is curious. It is easy to understand why L-T would get greater variance in total dependency than the SSA actuaries. The latter, in their low-cost estimates, pair high fertility rates with low improvements in life expectancy, and in their high-cost estimates, pair low fertility rates with high improvements in life expectancy. In some of L-T's simulations, high fertility rates get paired with high improvements in life expectancy resulting in high total dependency rates, a situation that never arises in the actuaries' deterministic projections. The larger variance in the total dependency ratio in the L-T stochastic projections results from the underlying variations in fertility rates in their alternative simulations. But conventional wisdom suggests that the high-fertility scenarios, which would initially drive up the total dependency ratio, should ultimately drive down the aged dependency ratio as the greater number of children being born under the scenario age and enter the workforce. The inconsistency in the results in these two dependency ratios either deserves more analysis or more explanation.

Clearly, stochastic projection models can produce ranges of estimates for programs like social security that are as much within the boundaries of reasonable expectations as the models that are currently being used. They have the possible added benefit that they give a new perspective on how variations in various demographic or economic variables can drive overall program costs. L-T raise this issue in their analysis of the comparative sensitivity of cost estimates to variations in fertility, mortality, productivity growth, and interest rates, although they do not fully explain why their stochastic results are so different from those generated by deterministic projections.

Modeling and Implementing Policy Changes

It is not clear what Robert Myers meant when he wrote in support of the current projection methodology used by the SSA that "large changes . . . should be phased in" gradually. Certainly it makes sense to implement significant policy changes on a phased basis in many cases. It makes no sense, however, to phase in our understanding of the financial obligations that our entitlement programs present and the uncertainties associated with those obligations for our citizens in the future. Policymakers and citizens alike should understand the implications of current policy as soon as policy analysts have relative confidence in their own understanding of these programs.

One of the problems in developing public policy estimates that are bounded by degrees of uncertainty is that policymakers do not like uncertainty. When a problem arises, they want to be able to solve it, or at least to adopt policy changes that they can describe to their constituents as solving it. When social security was in financial crisis in the early 1980s, the deterministic model allowed policymakers to claim that they had solved the problem by adopting the 1983 amendments because the actuaries' projections showed that they had. It is not clear how the same policies would have been greeted under the headline "Congress Adopts Changes That Have a 60 Percent Probability of Solving the Social Security Financing Problem." In retrospect, the public probably would have been better off if something like that had been the message, but putting probability distributions on policy prescriptions may further complicate the process of policy making itself.

We are now at a point in the evolution of our public entitlement programs that there is a fairly widespread consensus that they are seriously underfinanced. The sense of concern about these programs has reached the point that policy analysts are now making proposals to reform them in ways that heretofore were never seriously considered. Many of the proposals that are now being put on the table would likely have significant effects on the economy that go beyond the rebalancing of the entitlement programs themselves.

Possibly the greatest weakness of the deterministic model used to project social security's costs is its relative inability to consider feedback effects that relate to OASDI's overall effects on the economy. Currently, the L-T model suffers from the same problem. In their conclusion the authors note that one potential use of their stochastic model is testing policy options in the context of our ability to limit uncertainty under the programs and proposals to reform them. L-T are absolutely correct in their assessment of the potential usefulness of these kinds of models, but before their model can be used in this way, it must be able to consider feedback effects. They note in the presentation of their results that some of the scenarios they estimate with the current model are implausible because the trust fund deficits become so large that they would undoubtedly have implications for the larger economy. Many of the solutions for the current underfunding of social security anticipate significant increases in trust fund or savings levels that would also have significant macroeconomic effects. These must ultimately be considered in the testing of policy options.

Social security is not the only program around which the issues raised by L-T in this paper might be considered. Under the actuaries' midrange projections, social security benefit claims are expected to rise from around 4.5 percent of GDP today to about 6.5 percent of GDP by 2030. Comparable projections for Medicare would have its claims rising from around 2.5 percent of GDP today to 7.5 percent of GDP by 2030. In reviewing the assumptions used in making this projection, the Medicare actuaries are assuming that the excessive inflation that has plagued this program from its outset will somehow be ameliorated around 2010. Beyond that, they assume the rate of growth in costs beyond pure demographic effects will be at the rate of growth in the economy. In other words, Medicare's actuaries are assuming a significant reduction of inflation in this sector of the economy just as the baby boomers make their largest claims on Medicare and the health delivery system. The uncertainties and risks associated with Medicare far outweigh those in social security and are deserving of the kind of scrutiny that L-T are advocating in their paper.

This work by Ronald Lee and Shripad Tuljapurkar is a good beginning in helping us to understand some of the uncertainty surrounding social security cost projections. The authors should be encouraged to continue the development of their model and to apply it to other public programs.

References

Advisory Council on Social Security. 1997. *Report of the 1994–1996 Advisory Council on Social Security.* Washington, D.C.: Social Security Administration.

Ballantyne, Harry C. 1983. Long-range projections of social security trust fund operations in dollars. *Social Security Administration Actuarial Notes,* no. 117 (October): 2.

Board of Trustees. Federal Old-Age and Survivors Insurance and Disability Insurance Trust Funds. 1971. *1971 Annual report of the Board of Trustees of the Federal Old-Age and Survivors Insurance and Disability Insurance Trust Funds.* Washington, D.C.: Government Printing Office.

———. 1981. *1981 Annual report of the Board of Trustees of the Federal Old-Age and Survivors Insurance and Disability Insurance Trust Funds.* Washington, D.C.: Government Printing Office.

———. 1997. *1997 Annual report of the Board of Trustees of the Federal Old-Age and Survivors Insurance and Disability Insurance Trust Funds.* Washington, D.C.: Government Printing Office.

Bronson, Dorance C. 1939. Social Security Board internal memorandum, 31 August. Files of the Social Security Board. National Archives, Washington, D.C.

Lee, Ronald D., and Lawrence Carter. 1994. Modeling and forecasting the time series of U.S. mortality. *Journal of the American Statistical Association* 87:659–71.

Technical Panel on Assumptions and Methods. 1996. *Report of the Technical Panel on Assumptions and Methods.* Washington, D.C.: Social Security Administration.

IV   Views of Inequality

10   Health, Income, and Inequality over the Life Cycle

Angus Deaton and Christina Paxson

10.1   Introduction

In previous work, Deaton and Paxson (1994, 1997), we used data from the United States, Great Britain, Taiwan, and Thailand to document that inequality increases within cohorts with age, for consumption, income, and earnings. In this paper, we extend the analysis to two health-relevant measures, the body-mass index and self-reported health status. We use data on more than 500,000 adults in the United States to track birth cohorts over time and to document the evolution of the two measures with age, looking at both cohort means and within-cohort dispersion. We also consider the life cycle profile of dispersion in income and health jointly, presenting evidence separately for men and women, and for blacks and whites.

Our original work on consumption and income inequality was motivated by the prediction of the standard theory of autarkic intertemporal choice that within-cohort inequality in consumption and income (although not necessarily earnings) should increase with cohort age, at least up to the date of retirement. Although the theory has no immediate extension to processes other than income and consumption, there are a number of reasons to extend the analysis to health status.

First, we wish to investigate the generality of the proposition that dispersion

Angus Deaton is the William Church Osborn Professor of Public Affairs and professor of economics and international affairs at Princeton University and a research associate of the National Bureau of Economic Research. Christina Paxson is professor of economics and public affairs at Princeton University and a research associate of the National Bureau of Economic Research.

The authors are grateful to Sudhir Anand, David Meltzer, Amartya Sen, Burt Singer, and Jim Smith for helpful discussions during the preparation of this paper. Research assistance was ably provided by Shelley Clark. The authors gratefully acknowledge financial support from the National Institute on Aging and from the John D. and Catherine T. MacArthur Foundation. Errors, omissions, and incompleteness are the responsibility of Benjamin Paxson Gabinet, born 25 March 1997.

increases with age. For the four countries where we have looked, it is true of income, consumption, and earnings. We are curious as to whether the proposition is true for other state variables, such as weight, the body-mass index, self-reported health status, dexterity, intelligence, or ability to complete specified tasks.

Second, while health status is interesting as an example, it is also important in its own right. Inequalities in income and consumption are of concern because they are important components of welfare. But as we move from a narrow, economic measure of well-being toward broader definitions, health status has the most immediate claim on our attention. Nor is health status independent of economic status; indeed, there is a well-documented but poorly understood "gradient" linking socioeconomic status to a wide range of health outcomes (Adler et al. 1994), as well as changes in wealth and changes in health among the elderly (Smith 1995). Income or its correlates (smoking, obesity, social status, and various types of behaviors) may directly affect health, and where health care is expensive, the ability to pay may give access to superior health services. There are also mechanisms that operate in the opposite direction; health status affects the ability to work and, among the elderly, the timing of retirement. There is also a literature linking health status to relative deprivation, or to the income distribution: Wilkinson goes so far as to claim that "mortality rates in the developed world are no longer related to per capita economic growth, but are related instead to the scale of income inequality in each society" (1994, 61). Yet there has been no research of which we are aware that tracks these relationships over the life cycle, or that looks at the life cycle patterns for clues to directions of causality.

Third, it is plausible that the theoretical reasons that consumption, income, and earnings processes disperse also apply to health status. This requires a little explanation. In Deaton and Paxson (1994), we started from the implication of (some) theories of intertemporal choice that individual consumption should follow a martingale process; Hall (1978) showed that under appropriate assumptions, consumption is the cumulative sum of uncorrelated increments. The same will be true of earnings if employers pay workers their expected marginal product (see Farber and Gibbons 1996). It is also plausible that, at least in part, health status should be a cumulative process, determined by the "piling up of adverse life experiences" (Singer and Ryff 1997) offset by recuperative processes. Although some health shocks will have only temporary effects, others will leave a permanent residue, so that even if this residue is a small component of the original shock, the resulting health status will be nonstationary. Because most of the effects of most health shocks wear off over time, there is no reason to suppose that health status is a martingale; on the contrary, health status of individuals will generally revert to its individual trend after positive or negative shocks. But the trend will itself be stochastic since it is the cumulative sum of the permanent residues of a lifetime of shocks. If so, and provided the shocks to different individuals are not perfectly correlated, the health of members of a cohort will disperse over time, just as do their incomes, consumptions, and earnings.

We use data from the National Health Interview Survey (NHIS) for the 12 years 1983–94. This survey collects data on around 50,000 freshly drawn adults every year (as well as data on children), from which we use information on income, on a ordinal self-reported health status (SRHS) measure that ranges from 1 (excellent) to 5 (poor), on body-mass index (BMI), typically defined as weight in kilograms divided by the square of height in (square) meters, on race (black or white), and on sex. The arguments for using SRHS and BMI as measures of health status are discussed in the next section. Our procedure is the same as in Deaton and Paxson (1994, 1997); we create cohort data by following birth cohorts through the members of the cohorts that are randomly drawn into each year's surveys. For each year and for each cohort of men or women, black or white, we select income and health status information, from which we can create measures of central tendency, of dispersion, and of correlation for each cohort in each year. We present these data, typically as plots against age, with each cohort shown separately. We also decompose the plots into age and cohort effects, so as to isolate the trend effects that operate from one cohort to the next from age effects that are common to all cohorts as they age. A major focus is how these age patterns differ by race and by sex.

10.2   Self-Reported Health Status and the Body-Mass Index

It is difficult to define and measure a state variable that adequately captures health status during the life cycle. Much of the work on health status and income has focused on mortality, which is perhaps the only well-defined and straightforward measure, but which is useless for our purposes. Self-reported "days of illness" or "doctor visits" are themselves conditioned by socioeconomic status and often show perverse correlations with income, with better-off people apparently perceiving and treating their illnesses more seriously. Direct measures of function, activities of daily living (ADLs) and instrumental activities of daily living (IADLs), have been used to overcome these problems and provide a possible alternative to the measures used here. We start with a brief literature review that documents the links between the self-reported measures we use and other health outcomes. We conclude the section with a brief discussion of what is meant by inequality in health outcomes, and of the relevance of inequality measures derived from SRHS and BMI.

10.2.1   Self-Reported Health Status and Health Outcomes

There is a large literature that examines the relationship between SRHS and subsequent mortality. The earliest papers use data from Canada (Mossey and Shapiro 1982) and California (Kaplan and Camacho 1983). Subsequently, there have been similar studies for a variety of countries (work surveyed in Idler and Kasl 1995). Virtually all of these studies support the idea that reports of poor health are significantly related to higher risk of mortality. Furthermore, the risk of mortality is higher for a substantial period of time (i.e., six-year and even nine-year mortality). There has been some dispute over whether self-reported health is associated with mortality in elderly populations, with the majority of researchers finding a strong association.

The standard approach in the literature has been to start by establishing the positive correlation between SRHS and mortality. Researchers then examine whether this correlation disappears on the introduction of controls for other variables, such as socioeconomic status (often quite crudely defined), as well as "objective" measures of health status and life style factors. Appels et al. summarize as follows: "Most authors are mainly concerned with the possibility that the observed associations [between self-rated health and mortality] are spurious. Eaker, for example, suggests that the female participants in the Framingham study who perceived their health as poor may have based their evaluation on their knowledge of family history of disease. Others suggest that the rating of one's health as poor may reflect a still subclinical disease and/or an unhealthy life-style" (1996, 682). Appels et al. then go on to suggest an "alternative explanation," that people who think of themselves as healthy build up more positive self-images, which positively affect health. The fact that SRHS is still typically correlated with mortality even after controlling for other health and lifestyle factors is often taken as support for these more psychosociological explanations, although an obvious alternative reading is that the controls are not fully effective and that people have private information about their health. For our current purposes, it is the raw correlations between self-rated health and mortality (possibly age adjusted) that are of interest, since we are trying to identify a variable that can serve as a single summary measure of health status.

The methods and results of the various studies are generally consistent, although the estimates of the size of the "effect" of poor health on mortality vary across studies, which is hardly surprising given that the groups under study often have very different characteristics. For example, in a study of people aged 70 and older, the relative risk of dying within 36 months of the initial survey is 3.5 times greater for women who report themselves in poor health relative to those in excellent/good health, and 2.5 times greater for men (Grant, Piotrowski, and Chappell 1995). Adding controls for age, education, race, marital status, ADL difficulties, and other health measures reduces the increase in relative risk to 1.5 for women in poor health and eliminates the increase in relative risk for men in poor health. A study of Lithuanian and Dutch middle-aged men indicates that, controlling for age only, those that report their health status as poor have a 23 to 80 percent increase in the risk of mortality (over 10 years) relative to those who reported good health (Appels et al. 1996).

In addition to the work on SRHS and mortality, there is growing interest in the relationship between SRHS and other health measures. Idler and Kasl (1995) find that the elderly with poor SRHS are more likely to develop ADL difficulties. Marmot et al. (1995) use the British Whitehall II study to examine whether British civil servants who report poor health miss more work. They find that people with poor SRHS have significantly more and longer absences from work than those who report themselves in good health. Overall, the research literature supports the conclusion that SRHS is a useful health measure, in that it is correlated with and predicts health outcomes such as illness, disability, and death.

10.2.2   Body-Mass Index and Health Outcomes

The literature on BMI and health status focuses almost exclusively on the relationship with mortality. There is less consensus here than in the literature on self-reported health and mortality. Some work shows strong relationships between weight and mortality; other work shows none, or relationships only for certain groups (e.g., white women and black men, but not black women or white men; see Stevens et al. 1992a, 1992b). Many of the studies suffer from small sample sizes (which yield very few deaths) or from the use of nonrandom samples (e.g., members of a particular insurance plan or coronary heart disease study).

Our own reading of the literature is that the most convincing studies find significant effects on mortality of both very high and very low BMIs, especially for men, but that once the investigators eliminate subjects who died shortly after the survey started, or who were smokers at the time of the initial survey, the relationship between low body mass and subsequent mortality either disappears or is substantially weakened. This general result is supported by Troiano et al. (1996), which contains a literature review and "meta-analysis" of the relationship. Two specific studies that support this conclusion are Seidell et al. (1996) and Lee et al. (1993). The first studies a random sample of over 48,000 Dutch adults, aged 30–54 at the baseline, who were tracked for 12 years. (Note that because the sample is fairly young, there are still only 1,300 deaths.) The second uses a sample of over 19,000 (male) Harvard graduates for whom self-reported health information was collected between 1962 and 1966, and who were tracked until 1988. The second of these samples is obviously not representative of the overall population, but the study appears to be carefully done and uses a large sample.

The Dutch study indicates that very overweight men (defined as those with BMI greater than 30) have significantly higher rates of all-cause mortality, controlling for age. For example, those with a BMI in excess of 30 are 46 percent more likely to die than those with a BMI of between 18.5 and 25 (defined to be the baseline group). The raw data also indicate that very underweight men are more likely to die; the relative risk of mortality for those with a BMI of less than 18.5 is 2.6. However, among a sample of nonsmokers who did not die within five years of the initial period, the low-weight men do not have higher mortality. (Most of the mortality among smokers in the first five years of the survey is from lung cancer.) The Dutch results for women are not clear-cut. Overweight women have a significantly higher risk of mortality from coronary heart disease and cardiovascular disease but do not have a significantly higher risk of all-cause mortality. A potential problem here may be that relatively few—only 500—women died, so that nothing is estimated very precisely. The Harvard study finds that, using the full sample and controlling for age only, the underweight and the overweight are at significantly greater risk of mortality than other groups. For example, with the baseline defined to be thin men with BMIs of less than 22.5, the relative risk of mortality first falls as weight rises, to 0.92 for those with BMI between 23.5 and 24.5, and then rises to 1.12 for overweight men with BMIs in excess of 26.0. When the sample is limited to those who never smoked and who did not die in the first five years, the age-adjusted relative risk of mortality increases monotonically with age and is 67 percent higher for the group with the highest BMI relative to the group with the lowest.

10.2.3   Inequality in Health Outcomes

Although the literature provides a firm basis for the relevance of SRHS and BMI as indicators of health status, it is not sufficient by itself to justify their use in the investigation of inequalities in health status. Although we may be curious to know whether BMIs become more dispersed with age—or since height varies very little, whether weight becomes more dispersed with age—we are a good deal more interested in health outcomes, so that we need to know what dispersion in BMI tells us about dispersion in health. By this token, SRHS is of more direct interest than BMI, since it contains direct information about individual welfare. Even so, there are serious difficulties in interpreting the dispersion of both measures.

Consider first a seemingly technical difficulty. When we look to see whether distributions (of income or health) are dispersing over time, the ideal criterion is that of (second-order) stochastic dominance. If distribution F_1 stochastically dominates distribution F_2, then it will be measured as more equal by any inequality measure that satisfies the principle of transfers, effectively by any sensible inequality measure. But stochastic dominance is not preserved under monotone transformations, and our measure of SRHS is an ordinal one, so that unless we can somehow restrict allowable transforms of the 1–5 scale, we have no nonarbitrary basis for making statements about changes in inequality. The problem for BMI is less immediate but is just as serious. Because BMI is a cardinal measure, we can make well-defined statements about changes in its dispersion, or about changes in the dispersion of body weights. But since the relationship between BMI and health status is almost certainly nonlinear and possibly nonmonotonic, statements about changing dispersion in BMI have no obvious implications for changes in the dispersion of health status. One interpretation of the literature is that BMI is irrelevant for health status up to some cutoff, say 30, after which mortality risk increases monotonically with BMI. Given such a relationship, there is no reason to suppose that statements about changes in the dispersion of BMI, well defined though they are, will have any implications for changes in mortality risk.

More serious than the problems associated with our *specific* measures is the *general* problem of what we mean when we talk about inequality in health status, and what sort of indexes might adequately capture that meaning. The possibilities are addressed by Anand and Sen (1997), with generally pessimistic conclusions. The natural (money) cardinalizations of income and consumption that permit the development of index numbers of inequality are not applicable to other concepts, such as range of functional capabilities associated with health status. Some of the literature on health inequality has focused on inequality in life expectancy—see Wilkinson (1986) for British evidence—but life expectancy, important as it is, does not capture many aspects of health status, particularly quality of life.

If we were to accept the limited goal of looking at the mean and dispersion of life expectancy, then one avenue of progress is to subject our indicators to the transformation that best predicts life expectancy, thus translating our measures into that metric. But the empirical literature, impressive as it is, is hardly adequate to establish the appropriate functional form. Even the correlations are subject to some dispute, and we are still some way from definitive conclusions about functional form (see in particular the debate on whether BMI is or is not even monotonically related to mortality). However, if we can establish that, conditional on age, life expectancy is a concave and monotone increasing function of health status as measured, and if we are concerned with average life expectancy, or with the average of any concave function of life expectancy, then an increase in the dispersion of health status is a bad thing. This is the same argument for being concerned with the distribution of income because we weight increases in income more highly the poorer the recipient. Although the point is hardly established, our reading of the literature is consistent with the view that changes in SRHS along the five-point scale have larger implications for mortality when health status is poor than when it is good or excellent. If so, increasing the dispersion of SRHS as reported here will lower average life expectancy and lower any measure based on life expectancy that values increases in life expectancy more at lower starting points. A similar argument can be constructed for BMI, at least provided we dismiss the evidence that low BMI is associated with increased mortality. For example, if we were to construct a measure such as $z = \ln 50 - \ln$ BMI, life expectancy is a monotone increasing function of z and increases rapidly with increases in z at low levels—that is, among those with high BMI—becoming relatively flat thereafter. Once again, increased dispersion of z generates lower life expectancy or lower welfare if we care more about increases in life expectancy among those who have shorter life spans.

10.3   Empirical Results

10.3.1   Preliminaries

Most of our empirical results will be presented graphically, and most are straightforward transformations of the data from the 12 years of the NHIS. These surveys collect an enormous amount of information on health and on medical conditions, but very little on the economic status of individuals. In particular, there is a single family-income question, the answers to which are presented in bracketed form. The brackets are sufficiently detailed for our purposes but have the serious deficiencies that they are constant in nominal terms and that the top of the highest bracket is $50,000, again with no change for inflation over the period 1983–94. In order to use these data, we first allocate to each individual the family income of the household in which he or she resides, using the midpoint of the bracketed range, and then convert to logarithms. Our procedures for handling the top-coding and for measuring variances are described below.

We use individuals aged 20–70, inclusive. Cohorts are typically defined by the exact year of birth, although for some of the analysis that follows we define cohorts using (nonoverlapping) five-year birth intervals, and we identify cohorts by the midpoint of their ages in a specified year. When we use exact year of age, there are 62 cohorts and 612 cohort-year cells. Not all cohorts are observed in all years because their ages must be between 19 and 71. When we use five-year age bands, there are 11 cohorts and 120 cohort-year pairs. For each cohort, sex, and, for some of the analysis, race group in each of the 12 survey years, we assemble (individual) data on the logarithm of family income, SRHS, and the logarithm of BMI. (We actually define BMI in units of pounds per inches squared rather than kilograms per meters squared, so the log of the BMI differs from the conventional measure by a constant.) From these raw data we calculate the various quantiles in the usual way on a cell-by-cell basis. In some of what follows we examine the joint distributions of health and income. To obtain means and variances of the log of income, and the covariance between income and health, taking into account the top-coding of family income, we assume bivariate normality for the pairs (log income, log BMI) or (log income, SRHS). We then fit the distributions to the data for each cohort-year cell, taking account of the censoring of log income at the log of $50,000. This is conveniently done by fitting a Tobit model containing a constant and either SRHS or the logarithm of BMI on the right-hand side and computing moments and comoments using standard formulas for conditional normal distributions.

In some of the figures we show, not the raw data, but age effects. These are constructed by regressing the cohort-year means, variances (constructed as above), medians, or quantiles on a set of age, cohort, and year dummies. Since age is equal to the calendar year minus the year of birth, these effects must be

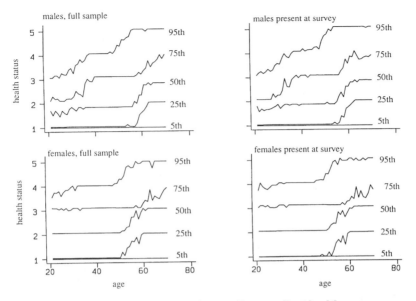

Fig. 10.1 **Percentiles of health status by age (1 = excellent health,
5 = poor health)**

restricted in some way. Most often this is done by omitting either year or cohort effects, and we shall explain in each case the procedures that were adopted and their influence on the results.

10.3.2 Univariate Analysis of Self-Reported Health Status, Body-Mass Index, and Income

Figures 10.1, 10.2, and 10.3 describe the univariate life cycle behavior of our three measures, separately for males and females, but pooled over all races. Figure 10.1 plots the profiles in the 5th, 25th, 50th, 75th, and 95th percentiles of SRHS, by males and by females, for all those covered in the sample and for only those present at the time of the survey. This last distinction is to allow for the possibility that reports made on behalf of others may be less reliable or systematically biased. In fact, the right- and left-hand sides of the figure are very similar, and we do not make further reference to this division of the sample. The age effects shown here were obtained by forming the percentiles for each cohort-year-sex cell and then regressing each on a set of age and year dummies; the plots show the coefficients on the age dummies. The year effects show little statistical significance, and the age effects are little affected if year dummies are replaced by cohort dummies; all of the systematic variance in these data are in the age effects, and there is little change over time at any given age.

Figure 10.1 shows that SRHS deteriorates with age—recall that 1 is "excellent" and 5 is "poor"—and that, as the initial hypothesis predicts, dispersion

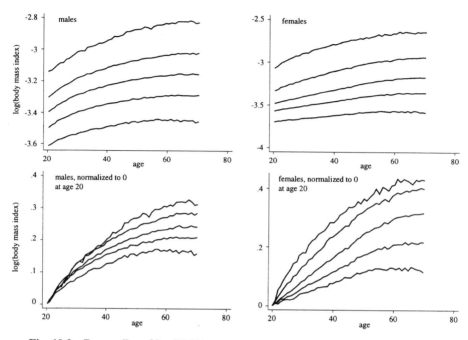

Fig. 10.2   Percentiles of log BMI by age

increases with age; see the difference between the 25th and 75th percentiles, or between the 5th and 95th percentiles. The age profiles for men and women are broadly similar, although SRHS is both worse and more variable among young women than among young men. We imagine that some of this difference is associated with pregnancy, which is not recorded in the surveys. That SRHS worsens with age is perhaps not surprising, but it implies that when people report their health status, they do not "norm" their answers with respect to the experience of those at the same age or at least they only do in part.

Figure 10.2 shows the corresponding age profiles of the same percentiles for the logarithm of BMI. The top panels—for males and females—are the coefficients of the age dummies in regressions on age and cohort dummies. There are strong cohort effects in BMI, with younger cohorts consistently heavier than their elders. Given that BMI is continuously measured, these graphs are much smoother than those for SRHS, and they also trend upward with age. At the median BMI, these graphs correspond to weight gains of about 0.3 lbs per year of age for men and 0.45 lbs per year of age for women. Women have lower BMIs than men but have greater dispersion—note the different scales on the right- and left-hand sides of the figure.

As does SRHS, BMI becomes more dispersed with age. This can be seen directly from a comparison of percentiles in the top half of the figure, but it is more clearly seen in the bottom two panels, which are constructed from the

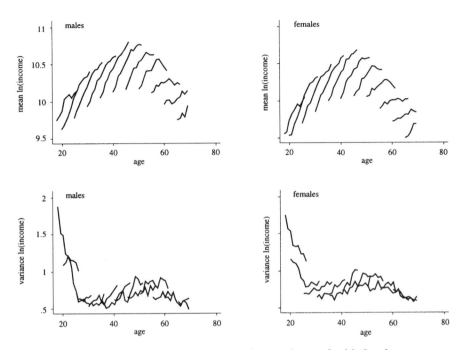

Fig. 10.3   Mean and variance of log family income by age for birth cohorts

top panels by shifting the age profiles vertically so that all are zero at age 20. The more rapid dispersion of BMI for women is then very clear in the bottom right-hand panel. But recall from section 10.2 that the links between BMI and mortality are likely much weaker for women than for men, so that their greater rate of weight dispersion may have only very limited consequences for the dispersion of health status.

Figure 10.3 plots the data on the means and variances of the logarithm of (nominal) family income, obtained from fitting the censored lognormal distributions. These figures show the raw data for each cohort, and the connected lines follow the experience of a single cohort observed year by year as it ages. The logarithm of income rises over time for each cohort and is higher for more recently born cohorts than for less recently born cohorts at the same age. The top panels also show the slower rate of growth of cohort family income in later years, a rate of growth that actually turns negative for the oldest cohorts. Note too that family incomes are lower for women than for men, a finding that does not come from distinguishing men's and women's incomes within each family—all members of a family are attributed the same family income—but rather reflects the fact that there are more women in families with lower incomes. Note finally that incomes have not been deflated for price inflation, so that the growth within and between cohorts is nominal, not necessarily real.

The bottom panels plot the estimated within-cohort variances of the loga-

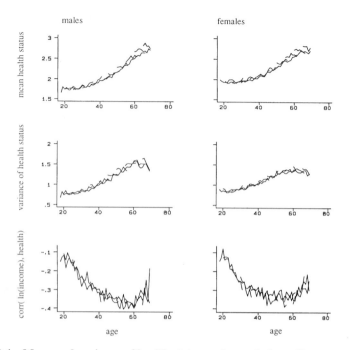

males   females

Fig. 10.4   Mean and variance of health status and correlation of income and health by age for birth cohorts

rithm of income, again on a cohort-by-cohort basis. (Unlike the levels, these variances are unaffected by inflation.) As in our previous work, which used a household rather than an individual basis, the variance of logarithms rises with age after age 25 or so until around the age of retirement, after which the variance ceases to rise or fall. The rapid falls in variance at very young ages reflect no more than the process of family formation. There are also distinct cohort effects reflecting the well-documented increases in income inequality among American families over this period.

We present this figure, less for its own interest—since it contains no information about health status—than to confirm that the income information in the NHIS, in spite of its (increasingly severe) top-coding problems and the marginality of income in the survey, can be used to reproduce the same patterns of cohort and age inequality that we obtain from higher quality income surveys, such as the Consumer Expenditure Survey and (especially) the Current Population Survey, as used in our previous work.

10.3.3   Bivariate Analysis of Health Measures and Income

Figure 10.4 shows cohort-level plots for the mean and variance of SRHS, and for its correlation coefficient with the logarithm of family income. The top two panels replicate in different form the age profiles in means and variances that we have seen in the percentile plots in figure 10.1. Most interesting here are the two bottom plots, which document the negative correlations between SRHS and income; people with higher incomes consistently report that they are in better health. Moreover, this correlation is different at different ages; it is quite weak among those in their early 20s but becomes steadily larger (in absolute value), reaching a peak value of around -0.4 between ages 50 and 60. There are only slight differences between men and women—the correlation goes on increasing for men until age 60, whereas for women there is a plateau from around age 45 to age 60—but in both cases the correlation weakens after age 60 as SRHS deteriorates in general. This is not simply a matter of all the elderly having poor health status. As the top panels show, health status deteriorates with age, but the middle panels show only a slight decrease in the variance after age 60. It is more that, after age 60, differences in SRHS are much less well predicted by income.

These patterns of correlations between health status and income at different ages hold some clues to possible causal mechanisms. That the negative correlation should have the same age profile as the level of income (or earnings) is what would be predicted if health shocks cause income changes through participation effects or ability to work. The same health shock will have a larger effect on earnings when earnings are high, which is in the middle period of the life cycle. Against this story is the similarity of the age profiles of health-income correlation between men and women, in spite of the lower level of labor force participation among the latter.

Figure 10.5 (for males) and figure 10.6 (for females) present the correlations between SRHS and income in a way that permits us to map variance and correlation simultaneously, as well as to track different cohorts as they age. The ellipses in these figures are computed from the variance covariance matrices of log income and SRHS as follows. For each cohort-year-sex cell, we estimate the variance covariance matrix V from fitting the censored bivariate logarithmic distribution to the individual data. If z is the vector $(y, x)'$, where y is log income and x SRHS, then the points on each ellipse satisfy

(1) $$z'V^{-1}z = 1.$$

The ellipse cuts the x-axis at (plus and minus) the standard deviation of SRHS and cuts the y-axis at (plus and minus) the standard deviation of the logarithm of income. The distance from the origin to the ellipse along a ray can be interpreted as the standard deviation of the corresponding linear combination of x and y. The ellipses are negatively sloped—as here—when health status and income are negatively correlated and would be positively sloped if the two were positively correlated. The ellipses can also be thought of as representing the direction and width of the joint scatter of x and y.

In both figures 10.5 and 10.6 the ellipses replicate the negative correlations in the bottom panel of figure 10.4. Each diagram shows two ellipses for the same birth cohort, one for 1983 and one for 1994, and there are diagrams for each of seven cohorts, with the youngest cohorts at the top left, and the oldest at the bottom. For the older cohorts, the ellipses are narrower and more elon-

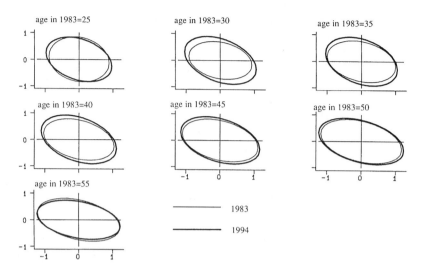

Fig. 10.5   Males, correlation of income and health by birth cohort for 1983 and 1994

Note: Log income is plotted on the *y*-axis, health status on the *x*-axis.

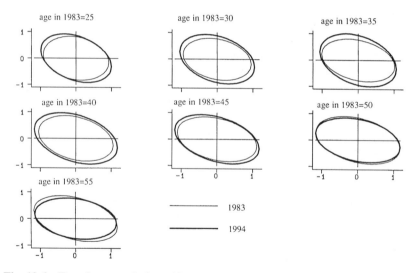

Fig. 10.6   Females, correlation of income and health by birth cohort for 1983 and 1994

Note: Log income is plotted on the *y*-axis, health status on the *x*-axis.

gated, which shows again that SRHS and income are more negatively correlated at higher ages. But within each cohort, the later (1994) ellipse—the heavier line—is typically outside the earlier (1983) ellipse as well as being more elongated. The joint distribution of income and health status becomes more negatively correlated and more (jointly) dispersed with age. This finding of

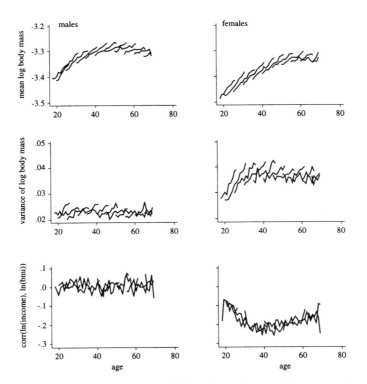

Fig. 10.7   Mean and variance of log BMI and correlation of income and body mass by age for birth cohorts

bivariate spreading generalizes and strengthens the earlier univariate findings in figures 10.1 and 10.2. Note finally that, as in these earlier findings, the rate of increase of joint dispersion diminishes with age so that, for the oldest cohorts, the earlier and later ellipses are essentially superimposed on one another.

Figures 10.7, 10.8, and 10.9 repeat the analysis with the logarithm of BMI replacing SRHS. The finding of increasing joint dispersion is replicated, but the age profiles and other patterns are otherwise quite different for the two measures. The top panels of figure 10.7 complement figure 10.2 by showing the raw cohort data for means and variance, and they repeat (with some variations) the patterns we have already seen. Weight increases with age, and there are pronounced cohort effects, with younger cohorts having higher BMIs. The age-cohort profiles of variances of the logarithm of BMI also display cohort effects; younger cohorts are not only heavier relative to height but also more variably heavy. These cohort effects obscure the positive age effects for both men and women in the middle panels, but note the generally positive slope of each cohort segment. As was the case for the interpercentile ranges in figure 10.2, the variances of logs show dispersion increasing with age, with much faster dispersion from a higher base among women.

The correlations between the logarithms of BMI and income are quite differ-

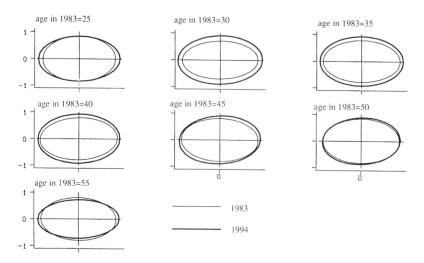

Fig. 10.8   Males, correlation of income and body mass by birth cohort for 1983 and 1994

Note: Log income is plotted on the *y*-axis, body mass on the *x*-axis.

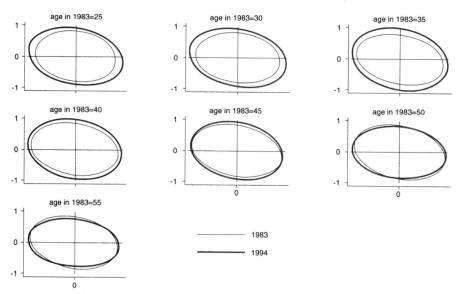

Fig. 10.9   Females, correlation of income and body mass by birth cohort for 1983 and 1994

Note: Log income is plotted on the *y*-axis, body mass on the *x*-axis.

ent from those between SRHS and log income. The bottom panels of figure 10.7 show that there is essentially no correlation between income and BMI for men at any age or for any cohort, while for women, the correlation is negative and becomes more so with age until around 40, at which age it reaches its largest (negative) value. We strongly suspect that these differences between men and women have little to do with different relationships between income and health status by sex but reflect rather the different social consequences of greater than normal weight for men and women.

In the absence of a correlation between BMI and income, the ellipses for men in figure 10.8 lie flat and, as before, move outward with age, at least among the middle-aged cohorts. Those for women in figure 10.9 are negatively inclined and show evidence of increasing joint dispersion with age among the young and middle-aged cohorts.

10.3.4   Race, Health Status, and Income

In this final subsection, we turn to differences in health status by race, and the role of income in accounting for these differences. Table 10.1 presents the raw data on SRHS by race, age, and sex. The table shows, for all years taken together, the fractions of people at each age in each of the five self-reported health categories; the numbers add to one across the rows for each sex and age. For both races, and both sexes, there is a gradual deterioration in SRHS with age. However, black males and black females are more concentrated on the right-hand side of the table than are white males and white females. At all ages, and for both sexes, there are higher fractions of whites in the "excellent" and "very good" columns, and higher fractions of blacks in the "good," "fair," and "poor" columns. That these differences are significant is confirmed by the very large χ^2 statistics in the final column.

The corresponding evidence for incomes is reported in table 10.2, although instead of showing fractions in each group by age, we show the fractions for five cohorts at two ages, 10 years apart, for each. The patterns are very much the same as for SRHS in table 10.1; blacks are consistently and significantly more heavily represented in the lower income groups.

The graphical analysis of these data begins in figure 10.10, which plots the age profiles of percentiles of the SRHS distribution for whites and blacks by sex. Within races, we see the same patterns as before, with (negative) levels and dispersions of health status increasing with age. But there are also differences by race, with the black distributions worse and more variable, even at early ages. Among whites aged 20–30, the median SRHS is "very good"; among the same age group of blacks, it is only "good." Increasing dispersion— or what is close to the same thing, increasing incidence of poor health—starts at much earlier ages for blacks than for whites. A quarter of white men report themselves in excellent health until their late 50s, and a quarter of white women until their early 50s. Among blacks, the same points are reached before age 40 among males, and in the 20s for females.

Table 10.1   Fractions of People with Various Self-Reported Health Measures by Age, Race, and Sex

| | Self-Reported Health | | | | | | | | | | |
| | Excellent | | Very Good | | Good | | Fair | | Poor | | |
Age	Whites	Blacks	Whites	Blacks	Whites	Blacks	Whites	Blacks	Whites	Blacks	$\chi^2(4)$
					Males						
20	0.522	0.424	0.293	0.245	0.158	0.272	0.023	0.053	0.005	0.007	124.9
25	0.514	0.441	0.304	0.260	0.152	0.245	0.025	0.049	0.006	0.004	86.0
30	0.491	0.398	0.305	0.281	0.160	0.248	0.036	0.059	0.007	0.014	85.8
35	0.481	0.359	0.300	0.259	0.172	0.253	0.037	0.099	0.010	0.030	173.0
40	0.427	0.321	0.306	0.276	0.198	0.287	0.052	0.076	0.016	0.040	106.7
45	0.408	0.266	0.300	0.252	0.198	0.299	0.070	0.139	0.024	0.045	132.6
50	0.367	0.199	0.282	0.229	0.235	0.341	0.077	0.146	0.039	0.085	122.6
55	0.307	0.222	0.276	0.218	0.265	0.282	0.096	0.188	0.056	0.091	80.0
60	0.263	0.156	0.250	0.182	0.281	0.288	0.116	0.229	0.090	0.146	79.3
65	0.219	0.115	0.231	0.184	0.306	0.276	0.161	0.240	0.083	0.186	73.7
70	0.192	0.105	0.225	0.172	0.318	0.266	0.179	0.301	0.085	0.157	56.5
					Females						
20	0.400	0.301	0.328	0.305	0.224	0.303	0.042	0.079	0.006	0.013	112.6
25	0.407	0.325	0.338	0.306	0.212	0.285	0.037	0.074	0.007	0.010	119.9
30	0.414	0.309	0.336	0.253	0.197	0.321	0.044	0.103	0.008	0.015	286.5
35	0.403	0.275	0.323	0.261	0.212	0.308	0.049	0.125	0.012	0.030	256.5
40	0.382	0.228	0.312	0.239	0.234	0.347	0.056	0.146	0.015	0.040	341.9
45	0.360	0.186	0.293	0.242	0.251	0.313	0.073	0.197	0.023	0.062	261.8
50	0.331	0.174	0.279	0.227	0.266	0.292	0.088	0.204	0.037	0.104	246.3
55	0.265	0.127	0.258	0.187	0.312	0.343	0.118	0.239	0.046	0.104	164.5
60	0.224	0.106	0.249	0.166	0.325	0.333	0.139	0.240	0.062	0.154	142.8
65	0.185	0.086	0.242	0.168	0.337	0.299	0.168	0.292	0.067	0.154	125.0
70	0.167	0.102	0.231	0.185	0.342	0.284	0.183	0.272	0.076	0.158	71.2

Note: Chi-squares indicate tests of the equality of distributions across racial groups.

Table 10.2   Fractions of People in Different (Nominal) Family Income Categories by Age, Race, and Sex

						Family Income							
	$0–$9,999		$10,000–$19,999		$20,000–$29,999		$30,000–$39,999		$40,000–$49,999		$50,000 or More		$\chi^2(5)$
Age	Whites	Blacks	Whites	Blacks	Whites	Blacks	Whites	Blacks	Whites	Blacks	Whites	Blacks	
							Male						
25 in 1983	0.176	0.221	0.296	0.351	0.260	0.322	0.157	0.057	0.065	0.037	0.046	0.013	11.2
35 in 1993	0.033	0.073	0.115	0.272	0.185	0.226	0.221	0.123	0.177	0.141	0.270	0.165	24.5
35 in 1983	0.070	0.259	0.190	0.292	0.289	0.236	0.244	0.101	0.108	0.094	0.099	0.018	31.6
45 in 1993	0.047	0.219	0.081	0.203	0.126	0.138	0.165	0.097	0.136	0.039	0.445	0.305	42.0
45 in 1983	0.068	0.191	0.174	0.367	0.243	0.295	0.219	0.048	0.131	0.040	0.165	0.060	26.5
55 in 1993	0.053	0.071	0.126	0.235	0.120	0.261	0.114	0.148	0.144	0.028	0.442	0.257	17.1
55 in 1983	0.102	0.237	0.190	0.349	0.240	0.171	0.196	0.133	0.127	0.071	0.145	0.040	7.6
65 in 1993	0.051	0.238	0.207	0.489	0.226	0.117	0.185	0.117	0.090	0.000	0.241	0.039	38.4
							Females						
25 in 1983	0.163	0.403	0.306	0.390	0.281	0.151	0.141	0.037	0.063	0.020	0.045	0.000	41.2
35 in 1993	0.074	0.214	0.113	0.188	0.186	0.185	0.180	0.131	0.182	0.082	0.265	0.200	44.4
35 in 1983	0.129	0.325	0.187	0.278	0.256	0.151	0.226	0.092	0.109	0.089	0.094	0.065	29.2
45 in 1993	0.041	0.216	0.108	0.200	0.127	0.169	0.127	0.101	0.154	0.088	0.443	0.225	57.7
45 in 1983	0.093	0.327	0.218	0.291	0.234	0.236	0.195	0.085	0.130	0.044	0.130	0.016	35.6
55 in 1993	0.039	0.209	0.154	0.206	0.171	0.145	0.179	0.143	0.121	0.132	0.337	0.165	44.6
55 in 1983	0.121	0.346	0.295	0.286	0.255	0.267	0.127	0.069	0.123	0.032	0.079	0.000	17.4
65 in 1993	0.110	0.221	0.266	0.417	0.206	0.139	0.166	0.123	0.103	0.012	0.150	0.089	12.3

Note: Chi-squares indicate tests of the equality of distributions across racial groups.

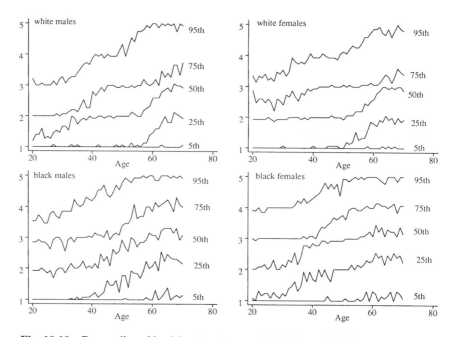

Fig. 10.10 Percentiles of health status by age for blacks and whites

Given that income and SRHS are negatively correlated, and given that blacks have lower incomes than whites, it is interesting to investigate how much of the differences in SRHS can be attributed to income, holding constant the distribution of health status conditional on income. To examine this question, we follow the analysis in DiNardo, Fortin, and Lemieux (1996) and reweight whites according to the black income distribution. The idea here is to recalculate what would have been the distribution of SRHS among whites using the actual conditional distribution of SRHS given income for whites, but with the black income distribution. Formally, if $p^w(h = i)$ is the proportion of whites whose SRHS (h) is in category i, we can write

$$(2) \qquad p^w(h = i) = \sum_j p^w_c(h = i \mid y = j) \pi^w(y = j),$$

where $\pi^w(y = j)$ is the fraction of whites in income (y) class j and $p^w_c(h \mid y)$ is the distribution of health among whites conditional on income. The counterfactual that we want to create uses the white conditional distribution and the black marginal to give

$$(3) \qquad \tilde{p}^w(h = i) = \sum_j p^w_c(h = i \mid y = j) \pi^b(y = j).$$

By comparing equations (2) and (3), we can rewrite equation (3) to give

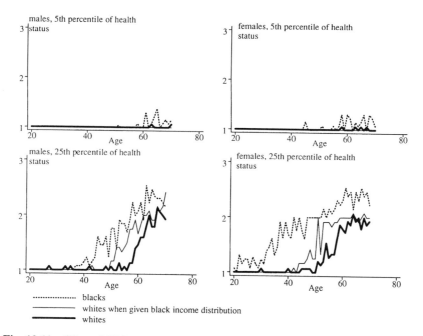

Fig. 10.11   5th and 25th percentiles of health status for blacks and whites, with and without adjusting for differences in income distributions

(4) $$\tilde{p}^{w}(h = i) = \sum_{j} p_{c}^{w}(h = i | y = j)\pi^{w}(y = j)\frac{\pi^{b}(y = j)}{\pi^{w}(y = j)},$$

so that, finally, we have

(5) $$\tilde{p}^{w}(h = i) = \sum_{j} p_{c}^{w}(h = i, y = j)\omega(j),$$

where $\omega(j)$ is a reweighting function equal to the ratio of the black to white marginal of income.

Figures 10.11, 10.12, and 10.13 show the age profiles of the 5th and 25th, 50th and 75th, and 95th percentiles of the distributions of whites, of blacks, and of whites with the counterfactual black income distribution. The general result is that income takes us a good deal of the way, but not all of the way, to explaining the difference between the two distributions of SRHS. Among those in good health—figure 10.11—the 25th percentile of the counterfactual white distribution is about half way between the 25th percentiles of the black and white distributions for men, but only a small way for women. Much the same is true for the 50th percentile in figure 10.12; a much larger fraction of the difference between blacks and white men is accounted for by income differences than is the case for women, particularly young women. At the 95th per-

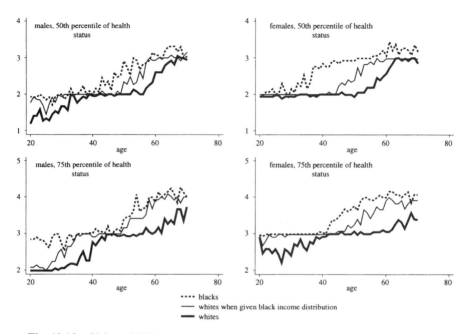

Fig. 10.12   50th and 75th percentiles of health status for blacks and whites, with and without adjusting for differences in income distributions

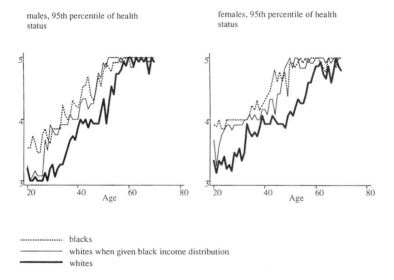

Fig. 10.13   95th percentile of health status for blacks and whites, with and without adjusting for differences in income distributions

centile, in figure 10.13, among those reporting poor health, the reweighting of the white age profile takes us most of the way to the black age profile.

The calculations for BMI are shown in figures 10.14 through 10.17. The age profiles of the percentiles of the BMI distribution are not very different between black and white men, except that the heaviest black men are a good deal heavier than the heaviest white men. In all cases, a substantial fraction of the difference vanishes when we reweight the whites to give them the black income distribution. For women, the situation is quite different. The percentiles of the black BMI distribution are at higher values of BMI at all ages for women, and only a small fraction of the difference is eliminated by conditioning on income.

10.4 Summary and Conclusions

We have presented evidence on life cycle patterns of two health-related indicators, self-reported health status and the body-mass index, as well on their relationship with income. We regard this work as exploratory; we have tried to generate stylized facts that are relevant to debates about health status, income, and inequality, even if, at this stage, there is no clear framework within which these facts should be fitted. We believe it is important to explore differences in health between people, even in the absence of an agreed methodology for thinking about inequality in health status, or even about health status itself. But by the same token, it is important to be cautious about attributing causality to any of our findings. Income and our measures of health status are linked in many different ways, through ability to pay for health, through education that is correlated with income, through lifestyle choices—such as whether to smoke and what to eat—that are conditioned by income, race, and sex.

From our findings, the following are worth highlighting:

- There is ample evidence for the proposition with which we began, that our two measures become more widely dispersed within any given birth cohort as that cohort ages. We view this as evidence in favor of a cumulative random model of health status.

- SRHS worsens with age, so that people do not report their health relative to the average health of their age group.

- The rate of dispersion with age of BMI, but not SRHS, is much more rapid for women than for men. BMI is more variable among women to start with. SRHS is more variable among young women than among young men, possibly reflecting pregnancy.

- Health status (positively measured) is positively correlated with income within cohort-year-sex cells. The correlation is lowest for the young, increases until ages 50–60, and then diminishes. BMI is uncorrelated with income for men but negatively correlated with income among women. This correlation is highest in middle age. These patterns are

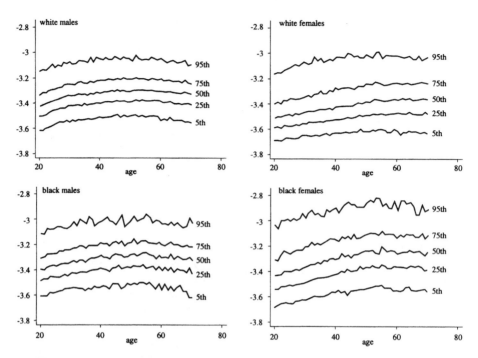

Fig. 10.14   Percentiles of log BMI by age for blacks and whites

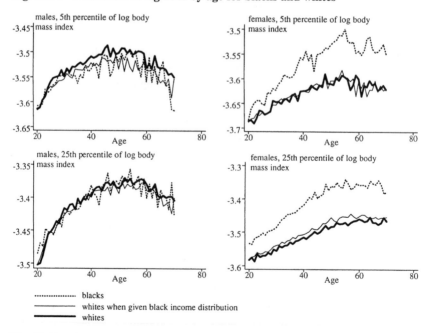

Fig. 10.15   5th and 25th percentiles of body mass for blacks and whites, with and without adjusting for differences in income distributions

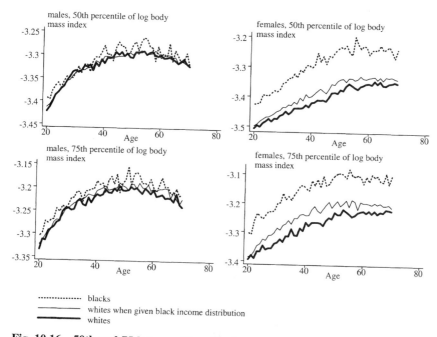

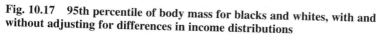

Fig. 10.16   50th and 75th percentiles of body mass for blacks and whites, with and without adjusting for differences in income distributions

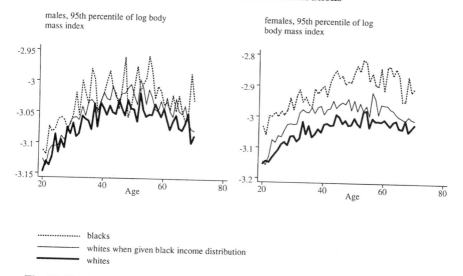

Fig. 10.17   95th percentile of body mass for blacks and whites, with and without adjusting for differences in income distributions

consistent with the hypothesis that those with lower health status earn less.

- The joint distribution of SRHS and income and the joint distribution of BMI and income "fan out" with age.
- Blacks consistently report lower health status than do whites. Some fraction—but not all—of this difference can be attributed to the lower income of blacks. Less of the difference is explained by income among women than among men, a result that is even more pronounced for BMI.

References

Adler, Nancy E., Thomas Boyce, et al. 1994. Socioeconomic status and health: The challenge of the gradient. *American Psychologist* 49:15–24.

Anand, Sudhir, and Amartya K. Sen. 1997. Draft report on broadening measures of inequality. Report prepared for the MacArthur Project on Inequality. Chicago: MacArthur Foundation.

Appels, A., H. Bosma, V. Grabauskas, A. Gostautas, and F. Sturmans. 1996. Self-rated health and mortality in a Lithuanian and a Dutch population. *Social Science and Medicine* 42:681–89.

Deaton, Angus S., and Christina H. Paxson. 1994. Intertemporal choice and inequality. *Journal of Political Economy* 102:437–67.

———. 1997. The effects of economic and population growth on national saving and inequality. *Demography* 34:97–114.

DiNardo, John, Nicole Fortin, and Thomas Lemieux. 1996. Labor market institutions and the distribution of wages, 1973–92: A semiparametric approach. *Econometrica* 64:1001–44.

Farber, Henry S., and Robert Gibbons. 1996. Learning and wage dynamics. *Quarterly Journal of Economics* 111:1007–47.

Grant, M. D., Z. H. Piotrowski, and R. Chappell. 1995. Self-reported health and survival in the Longitudinal Study of Aging, 1984–1986. *Journal of Clinical Epidemiology* 48:375–87.

Hall, Robert E. 1978. Stochastic implications of the life cycle–permanent income hypothesis: Theory and evidence. *Journal of Political Economy* 86:971–87.

Idler, E. L., and S. V. Kasl. 1995. Self-ratings of health: Do they also predict change in functional ability? *Journal of Gerontology* 50:S344–S353.

Kaplan, G. A., and T. Camacho. 1983. Perceived health and mortality: A 9-year follow-up of the Human Population Laboratory Cohort. *American Journal of Epidemiology* 177:292.

Lee, I. M., J. E. Manson, C. H. Hennekens, and R. S. Paffenbarger, Jr. 1993. Body weight and mortality: A 27-year follow-up of middle-aged men. *Journal of the American Medical Association* 271:1320–21.

Marmot, M., A. Feeney, M. Shipley, et al. 1995. Sickness absence as a measure of health status and functioning: From the UK Whitehall II study. *Journal of Epidemiology and Community Health* 49:124–30.

Mossey, J. M., and E. Shapiro. 1982. Self-rated health: A predictor of mortality among the elderly. *American Journal of Public Health* 71:800.

Seidell, J. C., W. M. Verschuren, E. M. van Leer, and D. Kromhout. 1996. Overweight, underweight, and mortality: A prospective study of 48,287 men and women. *Archives of Internal Medicine* 156:958–63.

Singer, Burton, and Carol D. Ryff. 1997. Racial and ethnic inequalities in health: Environmental, psychosocial and physiological pathways. In *Intelligence, genes, and success: Scientists respond to The Bell Curve*, ed. B. Devlin, S. E. Fienberg, D. P. Resnick, and K. Roeder. New York: Springer.

Smith, James P. 1995. Health and savings. Santa Monica, Calif.: RAND Corporation. Processed.

Stevens, J., J. E. Keil, P. F. Rust, et al. 1992a. Body mass index and body girths as predictors of mortality in black and white men. *American Journal of Epidemiology* 135:1137–46.

———. 1992b. Body mass index and body girths as predictors of mortality in black and white women. *Archives of Internal Medicine* 152:1257–62.

Troiano, R. P., E. A. Frongillo, Jr., J. Sobal, and D. A. Levitsky. 1996. The relationship between body weight and mortality: A quantitative analysis of combined information from existing studies. *International Journal of Obesity* 20:63–75.

Wilkinson, Richard G., ed. 1986. *Class and health: Research and longitudinal data.* London: Tavistock.

———. 1994. Health and wealth. *Daedalus* 123 (4):61–77.

Comment   David Meltzer

In earlier work, Deaton and Paxson (1994) used data from the United States, Great Britain, Taiwan, and Thailand to document that inequality in consumption, income, and earnings all increase with age. That work was of interest both because it provided a connection between demographic change and income inequality—a question that dates back at least to the work of Kuznets (1979)—and because it provided some evidence with which to test the predictions of alternative theories of resource allocation over the life cycle.

This paper extends their analysis to consider the distribution of two measures of health status: self-reported health status (SRHS) and the body-mass index (BMI). The paper begins with three justifications for examining this issue:

1. As a matter of curiosity, to investigate whether there is some general rule that dispersion increases with age—not just for income or earnings but more generally for other dimensions of human experience, for example, health status

2. Out of a particular interest in inequality in health status across age, because health is an important component of welfare (and perhaps implicitly also an indicator of welfare—income status, etc.—though this is not emphasized much in the paper

3. To a lesser extent than in the previous work, out of an interest in testing

David Meltzer is assistant professor in the Section of General Internal Medicine, Department of Economics, and Harris Graduate School of Public Policy at the University of Chicago and a research associate of the National Bureau of Economic Research.

a model of the evolution of health as a stochastic process of accumulated shocks over the life cycle analogous to the type of martingale process suggested by theories of life cycle consumption

Using data from the National Health Interview Survey (NHIS) from 1983–94, the authors decompose changes in SRHS and BMI into age and cohort effects, thereby permitting the analysis of changes in variation in these measures over the life cycle. These trends are examined by both gender and race, and their correlation with income is also examined. The paper has a tremendous number of results—and many are quite interesting—but I will focus my comments on some more general issues concerning variability in health with aging and the relationship of variability in health to welfare. I will organize my comments around the three motivations raised by the authors but will focus mainly on the first two.

I begin with the question of whether increases in variability in health status are a universal rule. It is in fact easy to determine that this cannot possibly be a general rule. Keynes knew the answer, "In the long run, we're all dead." Certainly, in this sense, variability in health status eventually goes to zero with age. Likewise the random walk idea, if taken literally, also falls away easily since presumably it should be two sided and we do not see people living forever or running 30-second miles at age 288. In fact we never see 90- or even 50-year-old competitive runners. Surely some components of aging are stochastic, but there are basic trajectories toward decline as well. Perhaps the relationship between age and variation in health status is best described by an inverted U.

But perhaps, even if increases in variability in health with age are not a universal rule, it is commonly the case that variability in health increases with age. In fact, this is just what one is taught in medical school. The classic example is how people respond to medications. Some older people are much like younger ones, while others are highly sensitive to medications. The possible reasons are many: changes in kidney function, liver function, lean body mass, or the sensitivity of receptors to the agent. The same lectures usually also refer to the idea of homeostasis—that the body has multiple approaches to trying to maintain equilibrium. As people age and some systems begin to deteriorate, there is at first ample reserve; then as reserves are depleted, other systems compensate. I am not sure whether biologists have articulated a model to explain increases in variability with age, but this seems to me a reasonable place to start—homeostasis and excess reserves, gradual deterioration, and then variability in observed function as weaknesses are revealed. Note that this would describe a stochastic process, but one with a powerful trajectory toward death.

There is already some evidence concerning changes in variability with age. I have not surveyed the literature concerning this; however, studies such as the Baltimore Longitudinal Study of Aging (BLSOA) (Shock et al. 1984) collected physiologic measurements—for example, of kidney function, pulmonary function, and liver function—on large numbers of people as they aged. The

BLSOA results are not consistently examined to assess variability, but it is interesting to note that one is not impressed by the increase in variability in any of these measures. Perhaps a closer look would identify further evidence of variability, and there may be questions about sample selection that may minimize variability in this study, but it would be interesting to examine these findings more fully. It would likely be valuable to review the biomedical literature to see what evidence there is for the common presumption that variability increases with age. Now I will turn to the evidence Deaton and Paxson have assembled to examine the idea that variability in health increases with age.

A first question is whether the measures of health they select—SRHS and BMI—are important measures of health. There is clear evidence that both are correlated with objective health outcomes such as mortality, and this is generally true even when a variety of other measures of health are held constant. While improvements in SRHS appear to be monotonically associated with improvements in objective health outcomes, there appears to be a U-shaped relationship between BMI and mortality, likely driven at the low end by the fact that poor health may result in low BMI. At high and even moderate BMIs, increased BMI is clearly associated with increased risk of diabetes and cardiovascular disease. The relationship at the low end of BMI aside, it seems difficult to argue that, for any individual, an improvement in SRHS or a reduction in BMI (anorexia and bulimia aside) is not generally a good thing.

Assuming that these are useful measures of health status, one question is whether the sample design of the NHIS is appropriate for looking at variability by age. Since the NHIS surveys only the living, it describes only part of the distribution of outcomes for people as they age, and of course not a random part. Likewise, the NHIS misses the institutionalized population. Presumably, the full population is more variable than the part that is responding to the NHIS. However, it seems to me that one could tell stories about the selection process into the NHIS sample that would increase or decrease variability in this sample compared to the full population over time. It is probably most likely that variability increases more over time than suggested by the NHIS due to selection out of the sample by death and by institutionalization. Another point worth remembering is that the relationships between income and health status may reflect causation in either direction. The effects may be largest at the middle ages and smaller at young and old ages because it is in the middle ages that a shock to health has the biggest effect on earnings. This could also explain why much more of the differences in SRHS between black and white men are accounted for by income. Likewise, it could explain why less of the differences in SRHS between black and white woman are explained by income, since women are less likely to be primary earners. Though this is suggestive, there is a long way to go to pin down such interpretations. Studies of specific diseases may offer creative ways to disentangle these two effects.

Since this is an exploratory paper I want to take advantage of the opportunity to throw out some ideas about expectations concerning health and health inequality more generally and try to make a further case for why we should all think hard about inequality. After this I want to come back to the central topic of the paper for a bit and think about SRHS again in the context of some of the ideas I will raise.

Let me begin with a postulate: that in health and medical care it is not only absolute levels but levels relative to some set of expectations that matter to people's welfare. The idea that expectations matter is surely not a new one; sociologists have argued this for years, and even economists such as Richard Easterlin have argued for the importance of such expectations in generational conceptions of welfare. But I think the case is ultimately more compelling in health care. In health care, the fact that life is at stake makes both the formation of expectations and the psychic penalties associated with deviation from expectations all the more salient. There is a powerful sense that we should do everything possible to preserve life, even at times when the quality of that life may be quite poor. The Bible tells us we should not kill. Perhaps this is why the doctor bringing news of a patient's death to the family reassures them that "we did all we could." There is no economic model to explain the solace in that remark other than a psychic return to knowing that an expectation about how life is to be valued was met—the patient is surely no less dead. The importance of expectations is also revealed by a similar phenomenon, that of "laying crepe" with the family of a sick patient: by preparing them for the possibility of their loved one's death, it is somehow made more tolerable.

I have been thinking recently about the implications of such a model of the role of expectations in health and in health care and think they are worth mentioning before discussing how they apply to this paper. The two most interesting implications relate to the welfare consequences of technological change and the policy implications of social determinants of expectations. It is in the latter that ideas of social determinants of health are perhaps most salient.

Let me start with the technical change idea. Though we are concerned about the costs associated with new technologies, the general presumption suggested by standard economic models is that they must be welfare enhancing. Presumably, free disposal ensures this. However, allowing expectations into the model changes this. Consider a model where expectations (H) shape people's utility from health (h), so that the goal is to minimize the gap (G) between expectations and health: $U(X, G) = U(X, H - h)$. What does technical change do in this case? The answer depends on the nature of the technical change—whether it is frontier enhancing or cost reducing. If it is frontier enhancing and this produces heightened expectations, it reduces welfare. In this case people will spend more yet be less satisfied. This is what Arthur Barsky has called the "paradox of health"—increasing dissatisfaction with health in the context of increasing capabilities (Barsky 1988). Only if technological change is cost reducing will it unambiguously increase welfare.

This result assumes that expectations are driven by technical change—that is, by the maximum technologically feasible. But let me begin to develop the link to this paper. Expectations are likely to be driven less by the extremes possible in theory than by the experiences one observes. If you have a cataract and your friends all had their cataracts removed, you expect to have yours removed. If people over age 55 do not get in vitro fertilization (IVF), you may not expect to get IVF if you are above that age. An interesting example of this is with respect to eligibility for organ transplantation. Often the rules are written more strictly than they are applied in practice. One possible reason is to lower expectations.

But if expectations are formed based on the actions and experiences of others, what does this mean for health care economics and policy? One key implication is that my personal decision about my health care affects your welfare. If I get a transplant—even by paying for it myself—you want one when you get sick. If I live to 90, you want to live to 90. As an older but still quite young friend of mine with a serious illness said recently: "It does not bother me so much that I am not completely healthy—but that it is at an age when all my peers are still so healthy." In the extreme, variability is the sole measure of aggregate welfare.

The economic implication is that with goods whose value is determined in such a social context, there is an externality associated with consumption. This implies that markets may not be efficient and that private interest may not serve the social good. I do not know if this is idle speculation or a truly important aspect of how we as humans perceive our welfare with respect to health. That seems to me an empirical question and one I do not know quite how to test. Perhaps studies such as this that examine inequality are a good place to start. But if it is true that expectations concerning health and health care are indeed important and socially determined, the implications are surely profound.

If we take seriously this idea of expectations and think about the meaning of SRHS, there are, in fact, multiple concepts of SRHS, differing in how they address the role of norms, that are important to consider. In the NHIS, respondents are simply asked to rate their health without specific reference to a comparison group; but in many other studies, respondents are explicitly asked to compare themselves to others of their age. In a recent review, Ellen Idler and Yael Benyamini conclude that it does not matter much whether people are *told* to make the comparison with people their own age: "It is possible that the comparisons with socially similar others are implicit in the cognitive process that produces these ratings; if so, directing the respondent's attention in this way would be redundant, which it appears to be" (1997, 30). A quote from a respondent helps illustrate: "My leg. That's the only thing that's holding me back. I feel good. And when I look around . . . I'm not sick. Believe me, some of these men and ladies around here . . . I'm not sick. I don't wanna brag, but I wouldn't wanta be the way some of these people here are that hafta be here." How a person defines the group in reference to which norms are formed is clearly complicated. This is illustrated by the response of one 85-year-old woman asked to compare herself to others her age:

Interviewer. Is it hard for you to compare your own health with that of other people your own age?
Respondent. Well most of them are dead, aren't they?

Thus it seems likely that SRHS may be age normed; however, we do not know for sure. Assume that SRHS is not at all normed by age. Then changes in SRHS reflect changes in health. In that case I begin to worry about floor and ceiling effects. Maybe young people vary a lot in health, but perhaps it is just in degrees of excellent health. This is an inherent problem with an ordinal and closed-end scale. On the other hand, if SRHS *is* age normed—and the cognitive psychologists studying it seem to think so—then it is not clear what variability means. The paper talks about the fact that second-order stochastic dominance—and therefore the meaning of standard measurements of variability—is not preserved under monotonic transformations, and in fact the evidence for SRHS is that we have exactly that sort of norming. This is the attraction of physiologic measurements, ranging from BMI to lung and kidney function, and more objective measures of functional status such as activities of daily living. I hope this paper will push us to probe more deeply into those issues.

References

Barsky, A. J. 1988. The paradox of health. *New England Journal of Medicine* 318 (7): 414–18.

Deaton, Angus, and Christina Paxson. 1994. Intertemporal choice and inequality. *Journal of Political Economy* 102:437–67.

Idler, Ellen, and Yael Benyamini. 1997. Self-rated health and mortality: A review of twenty-seven community studies. *Journal of Health and Social Behavior* 38:21–37.

Kuznets, Simon. 1979. *Growth, population, and income distribution: Selected essays,* 1st ed. New York: Norton.

Shock, Nathan, et al. 1984. Normal human aging: The Baltimore Longitudinal Study of Aging. NIH Publication no. 84-2450. Washington, D.C.: Government Printing Office, November.

11   Pensions and the Distribution of Wealth

Kathleen McGarry and Andrew Davenport

Over the past few decades, the financial status of the elderly improved dramatically. Poverty rates for those aged 65 or over fell from 25 percent in 1970 to 14 percent in 1994. These gains are attributed in large part to increases in the generosity of the social security program. Yet, despite the inclusiveness of the social security system and the progressivity of the benefit schedule, some subgroups of the elderly continue to face disproportionately high risks of poverty. Unmarried women, for example, had a poverty rate of 22 percent in 1994, while the poverty rate for married women was 5 percent. Similarly, the poverty rate for elderly blacks is close to three times that for elderly whites (31 vs. 12 percent).

Social security is just one component of retirement income, and given the structure of benefits, differences across individuals in the level of social security wealth are likely to be small in comparison to differences in the other components of total wealth. For example, despite large differences in lifetime income, the difference in mean social security benefits between retired blacks and retired whites is about $100 a month (Social Security Administration 1990). Given average life expectancies for the two groups at age 65 (for males), and a real interest rate of 3 percent, the difference in social security wealth is just $35,000. The large differences in economic well-being within the elderly population therefore stem from differences in the other modes of savings.

Recently, much has been written about differences in net worth and savings behavior between different groups of elderly individuals (Smith 1995).[1] Less

Kathleen McGarry is assistant professor of economics at the University of California, Los Angeles, and a faculty research fellow of the National Bureau of Economic Research. Andrew Davenport is a graduate student in economics at the University of California, Los Angeles.

The authors are grateful to Michael Hurd and James Smith for helpful comments. McGarry thanks the Brookdale Foundation for financial support.

1. Throughout the paper we will use the term "net worth" to denote nonpension, non–social security (and non–human capital) wealth.

well studied are differences in pension wealth and the interaction of pensions and individual wealth. In this paper we use data from the Health and Retirement Survey (HRS) to focus on differences in pension wealth for various subgroups of the retirement age population. We ask how pensions affect the distribution of wealth in the population. If individuals who have claims to pensions save less on their own as a result, then the inclusion of pension wealth with other assets may reduce inequality. Conversely, if a pension is just one component of a good job, then those with pensions will also have higher income and higher wealth than those without, and the inclusion of pension wealth may exacerbate wealth inequalities. We compare the distribution of net worth to the distribution of private wealth (net worth plus pension wealth). We find that the addition of pension wealth broadly reduces inequality but affects different subgroups of the population to different degrees: single men fare better with the inclusion of pension wealth, while single women fare worse. The differences by race are small.

Section 11.1 gives an overview of the pension data available in the HRS and discusses the assumptions we use to calculate pension wealth. Section 11.2 presents some broad descriptive characteristics of pension plans and patterns of ownership in our sample, section 11.3 analyzes the pension wealth of individuals, and section 11.4 focuses on the distribution of household pension wealth in comparison with net worth. Section 11.5 concludes.

11.1   Data

The Health and Retirement Survey is a nationally representative sample of the population born between 1931 and 1941 and their spouses or partners. At the time of the first interview in 1992, respondents were approximately aged 51–61. They were therefore approaching retirement age or recently retired. This sample is potentially more useful for analyzing the prevalence of pensions than random samples drawn from the entire population; older workers are more likely to be vested in a pension plan than are younger workers, they are more likely to be participating in an available plan, and they are more likely to be contemplating retirement. For these reasons they are also perhaps more knowledgeable about the characteristics of their pension plans.

The survey provides information on important economic measures such as the components of income and wealth, measures of health status, information about the current job, and details of pension plans. A more detailed description of the survey is contained in Juster and Suzman (1995). Here the aspects of the survey related to the calculation of pension wealth will be described. We devote much time to explaining the assumptions used in our calculations in the hope that they will attract attention to the rich data requirements and perhaps begin a discussion of the standard assumptions that should be used with these data.

The data on the value of pensions come from three sections in the survey.

The first section asks about up to three pension plans on the current job. The definition of pensions in the HRS is broad.

> Now I'd like to ask about pension or retirement plans on your job *sponsored by your employer or union*. This includes not only basic pension or retirement plans, but also tax-deferred plans like thrift, savings, 401k, deferred profit-sharing, or stock ownership plans. [Emphasis in original]

For each of these plans workers are asked whether the plan is a defined contribution (DC) plan, a defined benefit (DB) plan, or a plan that combines aspects of both DC and DB plans. The survey then branches to ask questions particular to the type of pension. DC plan holders are asked for the current balance in their accounts, the amount of money they contribute to the account, and the amount of their employers' contributions. The structure of DB plans results in more elaborate questioning schemes. Great care is taken in the survey to uncover the important nuances of the plans. Respondents with DB plans are asked first to report the age at which they expect to begin receiving a pension and the amount they expect to receive, either as a specific payment or as a percentage of final salary (expected final salary is also reported). In addition to benefits at this age, respondents are asked to report the earliest age at which they could receive full (unreduced) benefits and the amount of full benefits, as well as the age at which they can first receive any benefit and the reduction relative to full benefits.[2] As a first step to understanding the distribution of pension wealth, our analysis focuses on the value of pension wealth at the age at which respondents *expect* to receive benefits.[3]

For those not currently working, a subsequent section of the survey asks about pensions on the last job. In this section respondents are asked whether they had a DC or DB plan and, accordingly, the amount in a DC account when they left the employer, whether they are currently receiving benefits from a DB plan, or when they expect to receive benefits. For those currently receiving benefits the amount is obtained, as well as the date at which they started receiving the pension, and whether the pension was ever adjusted for inflation. For those who are not yet receiving benefits, the survey asks at what age they expect to receive benefits and how much their benefit will be. Questions about the earliest age at which pensions could be received are also asked, but neither the amount nor the age at which they qualify for full benefits was obtained.

A final section asks an identical set of questions for (up to three) past jobs

---

2. It is not clear in any of these questions whether the amount is in current or future dollars. We assume future income is reported in future dollars.

3. We choose to examine pension wealth based on the "expected age" in part to impose consistency between participants in DC plans, who were asked only about the age at which they expect to begin drawing benefits, and those in DB plans, and in part because this age provides the best approximation of the resources eventually available to the individual. Individuals may opt to collect benefits at ages that do not maximize pension wealth for a variety of reasons, such as the need to make the decision jointly with a spouse or because of health concerns. If pension wealth differs across sectors of the population for these reasons, that difference, in and of itself, is interesting.

that lasted five or more years. This section is asked both for those who are currently working and for those who are no longer employed.

From these three sections a complete pension history can be constructed. We calculate pension wealth for both DB and DC plans at the age at which the individual expects to begin receiving benefits and discount that value to current dollars. We therefore ignore any possibility that the worker separates from the firm before the expected retirement date or that the characteristics of the plan change during that time. We do not subtract a worker's own contributions from either DB or DC plans, although these amounts are known. Because we seek to analyze the portion of wealth "tied up" in pensions and not to comment on the relative compensation levels across individuals or firms, we believe this procedure is valid.

To convert the flow from a DB plan into a stock of wealth we use age-specific life tables.[4] We assume a 3 percent real rate of return and 4 percent inflation. Because we do not know whether pensions on the *current* job are indexed for inflation, we treat only government pensions as indexed. In calculating pension wealth from past jobs we treat a pension as being defined in real terms if the respondent answers yes to the question, "Are the benefits adjusted for changes in the cost of living?" By this method 46 percent of pensions from past jobs are indexed.[5] The large number of workers who claim that their pensions adjust for inflation contradicts results of past studies. Kotlikoff and Smith find that approximately 3 percent of pension recipients are in plans that provide automatic adjustments for inflation (1983, 274). Quinn (1982) reports data from Munnell and Connolly (1979) that only 6 percent of private pension plans contain built-in provisions for inflation adjustments.[6]

For DC plans we assume that wages grow with inflation but are flat in real terms.[7] We add employer and employee contributions in each year to the current balance and discount back to the current period.

An important omission in the HRS wave 1 data is the failure to determine

---

4. It is not obvious whether age-specific or age-, race-, and sex-specific life tables are preferred. Using separate life expectancies by sex implies that males and females with identical pension plans retiring at the same age will have different values of pension wealth. Because women live longer than men on average, ceteris paribus the value of pension wealth for women will be higher than that for men if detailed life tables are used. By a similar argument, the pension wealth of blacks will be lowered relative to whites if a life table that differs by race is used. Smith (1995) uses life tables by age, race, and sex, while Gustman et al. (1997) use those controlling for age alone. An earlier version of this paper (McGarry and Davenport 1996) used age-, race-, and sex-specific tables. We note the differences between the two calculations at several points in the paper.

5. A second question asks whether benefits had ever been adjusted for inflation. Of those who answered no to the first question, 13 percent said that their pensions had been adjusted at least once. We do not alter our calculations based on this second response.

6. We expect that the difference comes from the wording of the question. The HRS asks whether benefits are adjusted, not whether the adjustment is automatic. Pensions without cost-of-living adjustment clauses are often adjusted on an ad hoc basis (Allen, Clark, and Sumner 1986).

7. Wage regressions point to a flattening of the wage profile with age. Murphy and Welch (1990) show wages beginning to fall after about 25 years of experience, corresponding to an age similar to that of the HRS respondents.

whether the reported pension benefit would be paid to the worker's widow(er) should he or she die.[8] We expect that some reported benefits would be calculated based on single life, and some using joint survivorship.[9] Because we have no way to impute this information, we calculate two measures of pension wealth. Under the assumption that pensions are single life, we use the survival probabilities appropriate for the owner of the pension. For joint and survivor pensions, we use the survival probabilities of the couple. On average, for all married individuals, pension wealth is 20 percent greater if we assume that the reported benefits are from a joint life policy than if they are from a single life policy (benefits for unmarried individuals are unchanged). For the sake of brevity we report only the single life values in this paper. The conclusions are qualitatively unchanged if we use joint life values for couples, although the difference in pension wealth between married and single individuals is, of course, increased.

Much of our work in calculating pension wealth dealt with the handling of missing values. The HRS went to great effort to reduce the number of missing values. For many of the questions in the survey, including those used to calculate pension wealth, a respondent who could not report an exact answer was permitted to provide a categorical response based on a specified list of possible categories printed on a "range card." For example, a respondent who had a DC plan, but who did not know the exact balance, could report that it was between $2,501 and $10,000, or $10,001 and $50,000, and so forth. In cases where respondents used the range card we impute an exact value with the mean over the valid responses in that interval. If the datum was completely missing (i.e., no information on range was available), we used regression procedures to impute a value.[10]

The entire HRS sample consists of 12,652 individuals, including age-ineligible spouses. For our discussion of individual pension coverage and pension wealth, we eliminate those who were not born between 1931 and 1941 and who are therefore not part of the population representative sample. However, when comparing pension wealth and net worth on a household level, we include the pension wealth of age-ineligible spouses. In addition to imposing the age restriction, we eliminate those who are self-employed (446), because their behavior and choices with respect to pensions are likely to differ from

---

8. Wave 2 of the HRS will obtain this information for those currently receiving benefits. Hence, it will be possible to calculate accurately pension wealth for all but those currently employed.

9. Turner (1988) reports that in 1978 (post-ERISA, but pre-REACT) only about 40 percent of those with pensions had joint and survivor plans. More recent calculations, based on those first receiving benefits in 1989, place the percentage with survivorship benefits at 66 percent (Turner and Beller 1992).

10. For many of the pension variables there are a large number of missing values; in some cases close to half of the respondents were unable to report a value. Those with missing values on the pension variables are typically worse off than those who report values and have less generous pensions. Failure to impute values therefore leads to incorrect inference about the characteristics of pensions. The appendix provides details of the imputation methods, including a table of the number of observations with imputed values.

Table 11.1   **Distribution of Pension Holdings**

| Sample | Covered by Pension (%) (1) | Percentage of Each Type of Plan[a] | | |
		DB Only (2)	DC Only (3)	Both (4)
Entire sample (*n* = 8,330)	66	31	16	17
Ever worked[b] (*n* = 6,429)	78	36	18	22
Currently working (*n* = 5,438)	79	34	19	24
On current job (*n* = 5,438)	67	28	20	18
Males (*n* = 3,674)	82	39	16	26
Females (*n* = 4,656)	52	24	15	11
Whites (*n* = 5,826)	69	31	16	20
Nonwhites (*n* = 2,489)	54	28	14	10
All households (*n* = 7,122)	78	32	14	30

[a]Percentages in cols. (2), (3), and (4) do not sum to col. (1) due to missing values. Approximately 2 percent report that they do not know what type of plan they have.

[b]"Ever worked" is defined as either working currently or ever having held a job for five or more years.

those who work for someone else,[11] and those with missing information on pension status (48). With these restrictions our sample consists of 8,330 individuals.

11.2   Characteristics of Pensions

Differences in pension wealth across the population stem from differences in who is covered by pensions, in the generosity of pension plans as measured by the dollar value of benefits, and in the age at which benefits are payable. In this section we present summaries of these characteristics for the entire sample and then focus on differences between subgroups of the population.

Table 11.1 shows that in our sample of 8,330 individuals whose pension status is known, 66 percent report that they are covered by a pension. Our measure of pension holdings includes pensions from any job, not just on the current job. Individuals may therefore have two or more plans and may have plans from different employers. In fact, 25 percent of the sample have pensions that are not from their most recent jobs (current jobs if working). Many studies of pensions, in particular those based on firm-level data, miss this portion of pension wealth. Including all plans, 31 percent of the sample have DB plans only, 16 percent have DC plans only, and 17 percent are in plans that are a

11. The HRS specifically excluded Keogh plans in the question on pensions and asked about them in a later section of the survey. If we do not count Keoghs, only 7 percent of self-employed workers report having a pension.

combination of the two types or have at least one of each type of plan.[12] Among those who have ever worked, the rate of pension coverage increases to 78 percent. Current workers have the highest coverage rate at 79 percent. Some portion of the 79 percent may have pensions from previous jobs. Coverage falls when we look only at pensions from the current job, and there is a noticeable change in the proportion of DB plans relative to DC plans. This pattern is consistent with recent trends toward DC plans; older plans from past jobs are more likely to be DB plans than are plans on a current job.

These results show somewhat higher rates of coverage than do other studies. Bloom and Freeman (1992) use the 1992 Current Population Survey and determine that 57 percent of all workers are covered by pension plans on their jobs, a figure significantly lower than our 67 percent. Even and Macpherson (1990) report coverage rates of 53 and 36 percent among employed men and women. Our greater coverage can be explained by the age of the HRS sample. Individuals in their 50s are more likely to be participating in pensions than are younger workers, both because of vesting requirements and because of recent trends in pension availability. Even and Macpherson (1994b) calculate coverage rates of 49.2 percent for male workers aged 21–35 in 1988, but 69 percent for those aged 36–55. In a second paper that compares pension coverage for male and female workers in a 37–54-year-old cohort (Even and Macpherson 1994a), the authors find rates of pension coverage of 73 percent for men and 58 percent for women. Our sample is drawn from a somewhat older population, and we therefore expect higher rates for both male and female workers.

In our sample, men have coverage rates that are 30 percentage points higher than those for women. This difference is smaller than the gap of 41 percentage points found by Even and Macpherson (1994a) using the Newly Entitled Beneficiary Survey. In the distribution of types of plans, women are much less likely than men to have DB plans only, or to have two different types of plans. DB plans are typically thought of as accompanying blue-collar occupations, in which women are underrepresented. The difference in the percentages with both DB and DC plans can be similarly explained if these DC plans are supplements to a main DB plan. The difference in dual plans may also be due to the weaker attachment to the labor force of women, making it unlikely that they would qualify for pensions from two employers.[13] We do not explore the determinants of the difference here.

We also find that nonwhites are less likely than whites to have pension coverage, but the distribution of types of plans is more similar for whites and nonwhites than for men and women.

In the last row of the table we combine observations for spouses. A house-

12. For approximately 2 percent of the sample the type of plan is missing. We do not impute this variable.

13. Only 17 percent of women have pension coverage from a prior job, compared to 36 percent of men.

Table 11.2   Means of Selected Variables by Pension Status

| | | Covered by | Type of Plan[a] | | |
| | All | Pension | DB Only | DC Only | Both |
Variable	(1)	(2)	(3)	(4)	(5)
Age	55.9	55.80	56.02	55.68	55.51
	(0.035)	(0.044)	(0.064)	(0.089)	(0.085)
Sex (1 = male)	0.44	0.56	0.56	0.45	0.65
	(0.005)	(0.007)	(0.010)	(0.014)	(0.013)
Nonwhite	0.21	0.17	0.19	0.19	0.12
	(0.004)	(0.005)	(0.008)	(0.011)	(0.009)
Years of schooling	12.21	12.90	12.79	12.43	13.70
	(0.033)	(0.037)	(0.054)	(0.072)	(0.065)
Currently working	0.67	0.80	0.73	0.82	0.92
	(0.005)	(0.005)	(0.009)	(0.011)	(0.007)
Earnings (if > 0)	28,717	32,506	28,705	29,393	41,798
	(412)	(502)	(456)	(1,437)	(999)
Years on current job	16.84	17.60	17.40	17.04	18.61
(working)	(0.166)	(0.185)	(0.283)	(0.376)	(0.336)
Household wealth	200,913	211,281	206,225	203,360	231,087
	(4,409)	(5,559)	(8,071)	(12,181)	(10,026)
No. of observations	8,378	5,299	2,530	1,263	1,344

Note: Numbers in parentheses are standard errors.

[a]Numbers of observations in cols. (3), (4), and (5) do not sum to col. (2) due to missing values on type of pension. Observations in some cells differ due to missing values.

hold is considered to have a pension if either spouse reports pension coverage. "DB only" implies that at least one spouse has a DB plan and neither spouse has a DC plan; similarly, "DC only" implies that at least one has a DC plan and no one has a DB plan. "Both" means at least one of each type. The percentage of households with at least one pension (78 percent) is equal to the percentage of those who ever worked and have a pension.

Table 11.2 highlights the differences between those with pension plans and the entire population and compares the characteristics of pension holders across types of plans. Those with pensions are significantly more likely to be male than the overall survey population, 0.56 compared to 0.44. Pension eligibles have an additional 0.8 years of schooling relative to the population, higher earnings (among those with nonzero earnings), and longer tenure. Family wealth is slightly higher for those with pensions, likely as the result of a lifetime of higher earnings. This table provides a first indication that including pension wealth in the calculation of total wealth may not greatly reduce inequality.

There are also differences based on type of plan. Consistent with table 11.1, those with DB plans are more likely to be male than are DC holders. They also have lower earnings (conditional on working) than those with DC plans. Again consistent with the differences in table 11.1, individuals with DB plans are less

Table 11.3A   **Details of Defined Benefit Plans**

Characteristic	Mean	25th Percentile	Median	75th Percentile
Expected benefit				
Age[a]	61.6 (0.17)	60	62	65
Yearly benefit	14,146 (504)	5,400	12,000	20,400
Earnings	34,233 (787)	22,256	32,000	42,000
Earliest benefit				
Age[b]	58.1 (0.20)	55	59	62
Yearly benefit	10,650 (438)	3,108	7,800	16,000
Full benefit				
Age[c]	60.2 (0.19)	56	62	64
Yearly benefit	13,702 (533)	4,896	10,800	20,000

Note: The sample consists of only those individuals providing a value for each variable in the table. Characteristics are reported for primary plan on current job only.

[a]Expected benefit age is defined by the question "At what age do you expect to start receiving benefits from this plan?"

[b]Earliest benefit is defined by "What is the earliest age at which you could leave this employer and start receiving pension benefits?"

[c]Full benefit age is defined by "What is the earliest age at which you would be eligible to receive full or unreduced pension benefits from this job?"

Table 11.3B   **Details of Defined Contribution Plans**

Characteristic	Mean	25th Percentile	Median	75th Percentile
Expected age of receipt[a]	63.11 (0.13)	62	62	65
Earnings (if nonzero)	37,959 (2,941)	19,000	28,000	41,000
Balance in account	35,022 (3,231)	3,000	10,000	29,000
Employee contribution (% of salary)	5.5 (0.70)	1.8	3.6	6.3
Employer contribution (% of salary)	6.9 (1.00)	1.9	5.0	8.2
Employee contribution ($)	1,988 (181)	406	1,186	2,496
Employer contribution ($)	1,888 (206)	364	925	2,000

Note: Characteristics reported for primary plan on current job only.

[a]Expected age is defined by the question "At what age do you expect to start receiving *any* benefits from this plan?"

likely to be working than those with DC plans. Individuals with both plans appear to be the best off financially. They are the most likely to be male, have the greatest levels of schooling, wealth, earnings, and tenure, and are the most likely to be employed.

The generosity of pension plans depends not only on the benefit to which the worker is entitled but also on the age at which he can first collect any benefits, the age at which he can collect full benefits, and the magnitudes of the benefits. Table 11.3A summarizes these characteristics for individuals with DB plans, and table 11.3B presents similar descriptive characteristics for DC plans. The figures reported in both tables 11.3A and 11.3B are based on a sample of individuals with reported (nonimputed) values for each variable in the table.

The mean age at which individuals in DB plans *expect* to begin receiving benefits is 61.6, the median age is 62, and the 25th and 75th quartiles are ages 60 and 65. The expected yearly benefit is $14,146, compared to mean earnings of $34,233, implying a "replacement rate" of 41 percent of current earnings. On average, the *earliest* age at which individuals can collect benefits is 58.1. Benefits calculated with this retirement date are substantially reduced relative to benefits at the expected retirement age, averaging just $10,650, or 75 percent of the expected level. Median benefits fall somewhat more sharply.

The mean age at which an individual is first eligible for full benefits is *less* than the mean expected age of drawing benefits, 60.2 versus 61.6. Apparently many individuals expect to work longer than is necessary to qualify for unreduced benefits.

The distribution of retirement ages differs only slightly for men and women (not shown). The mean (median) expected age for men is 61.2 (62) compared to 62.2 (62) for women. A difference in ages at which men and women qualify for benefits is intuitive in that on average women have less tenure than men of the same age and may need to work to a slightly older age before becoming entitled to benefits. However, given the tendency for wives to retire with their husbands, and for husbands to be older than wives, the greater expected retirement age for women is somewhat surprising. Earnings, yearly benefits, and replacement rates for women are lower than for men. This difference may point to a future change in the retirement patterns of women as a greater number have sufficient commitment to the labor force to qualify for their own pensions. Expected earnings are $39,779 for men and $25,194 for women. Pension benefits average $17,194 and $9,181, respectively.

Racial differences are smaller than differences by sex. There are no significant differences in the age variables by race, although expected benefits and earnings do differ. The mean values for earnings are $34,869 for whites and $30,476 for nonwhites. Benefits for the two groups are $14,370 and $12,797, indicating similar replacement rates.

In DC plans (table 11.3B), the mean age at expected pension receipt is 63.1, slightly higher than for DB workers; the percentiles are also slightly higher. Contributions to DC accounts by firms, as a percentage of yearly earnings or as an absolute measure, are quite similar to individual contributions. The mean individual contribution is $1,988 per year (including zeros), compared to a mean salary of $37,959. The mean employer contribution is $1,888.

11.3   Individual Differences in Pension Wealth

A primary goal of this paper is to compare pension wealth across segments of the population and, in particular, to compare the pension holdings of males and females and of whites and nonwhites. In addition to sex differences, the literature on pensions has paid particular attention to differences between union and nonunion workers, and between public and private sector workers. Column (1) of table 11.4 presents the fraction of individuals with pension coverage by each of these characteristics, as well as by schooling level, health status, and income and wealth quartiles. Columns (2) through (4) report the distribution of pension wealth conditional on having a pension.

The first row of the table presents the statistics for the entire sample. Mean pension wealth for the 66 percent of the sample with a pension is $109,596. The median is just over half as large, indicating the skewness of the distribution.[14]

Subsequent rows divide the sample along observable characteristics. We look first at differences by marital status and sex. In the literature on wage determination, married men are consistently found to have higher wages than unmarried men. We see the same pattern with pensions; married men have pensions that are 50 percent higher at the mean than for the sample as a whole and 19 percent higher than for unmarried men.[15] Coverage rates are lower for women than for men, but even conditional on coverage, women have significantly lower pension wealth, less than half that held by married men.[16] Racial differences are as expected: nonwhites are 15 percentage points less likely to be covered by a pension than are whites and have pension wealth that is 83 percent that of whites.[17]

Those who are currently working are much more likely to have a pension than those who are not employed, but conditional on having a pension, the differences in pension wealth are small, with those who are not working having slightly richer plans. It is likely that those with generous plans are the ones who could most afford to retire by the survey date.

Differences by schooling also show the expected patterns. Those with schooling beyond a college degree are twice as likely to have pension coverage as those with fewer than 12 years of schooling, and they have over three times more pension wealth. Because more schooled individuals are likely to also have greater income and net worth, this large difference in pension wealth will add to the inequality of the income and wealth distributions.

---

14. We remind the reader that these calculations assume that all reported DB benefits are based on single life. Because some fraction of the sample will have joint and survivor plans, our results should be viewed as lower bounds on the amount of pension wealth. Reversing our assumption and calculating pension wealth as if all plans were joint survivorship plans leads to mean pension wealth of $123,134. All of this increase comes through increases in the pension wealth of married couples; the pension wealth of singles is assumed to be single life in both cases.

15. The relative advantage of men is reduced when sex- and race-specific life tables are used. In that case, married males have pension wealth that is 32 percent higher than the mean for the entire sample.

16. If sex- and race-specific life tables are used, pension wealth for men is lower and that for women greater. The mean values for married men and women are 140,326 and 71,792.

17. If race-specific life tables are used, nonwhites have pension wealth that is 78 percent that of whites.

Table 11.4   **Pension Ownership and Pension Wealth**

		Statistics over Positive Values		
Characteristic	Covered by Pension (%) (1)	Median (2)	Mean (3)	Standard Error (4)
All	66	62,889	109,596	2,295
Married*Sex				
Married male	86	94,301	148,366	3,724
Single male	69	79,137	124,719	6,975
Married female	51	40,418	68,327	3,839
Single female	55	42,784	63,674	3,035
Race				
White	69	67,061	114,437	2,782
Nonwhite	54	55,532	86,971	3,273
Work status				
Working	79	63,174	106,360	2,314
Not working	39	66,476	123,371	6,900
Schooling				
Less than high school	46	42,248	66,688	3,316
High school graduate	66	50,739	85,643	3,330
Some college	74	66,848	114,536	4,745
College graduate	80	95,844	150,790	8,667
Graduate school	90	147,656	199,892	8,374
Health status				
Poor	43	39,793	68,872	6,122
Fair	52	47,848	78,745	4,742
Good	66	57,120	101,022	4,771
Very good	71	71,605	113,261	3,794
Excellent	74	81,581	134,517	5,093
Household wealth				
Lowest quartile	44	31,301	56,532	3,670
2d quartile	68	52,643	82,078	4,178
3d quartile	74	76,206	115,746	3,604
4th quartile	72	95,947	153,936	5,466
Among those employed				
Union status				
Union	93	79,441	109,726	3,091
Nonunion	74	53,531	104,737	3,137
Sector				
Private	71	59,349	101,806	2,279
Public	91	139,245	159,456	10,430
Household income				
Lowest quartile	54	28,370	43,110	4,009
2d quartile	73	43,826	53,253	2,372
3d quartile	82	60,649	91,856	3,011
4th quartile	89	102,229	158,981	4,999

Much has been written about the correlation between health and wealth. Recently, the HRS has provided a good deal of information on the relationship; wealthier individuals are found to be in significantly better health than the less wealthy as measured by subjective health status (Smith 1995), by subjective probabilities of survival (Hurd and McGarry 1995), or by limitations with respect to activities of daily living (McGarry 1998). Here we see that the difference is also present for pension wealth. Seventy-four percent of those in excellent health have pensions, compared to 43 percent whose self-reported health is poor, a difference of 31 percentage points. Differences in the mean values are large, with healthier individuals having approximately twice the pension wealth of those in poor health.

Differences in pension wealth by wealth quartile are large. Moving from the lowest to the highest wealth quartile increases the probability of coverage by 28 percentage points and increases mean pension wealth by three times.

Among those currently employed, union workers have greater pension coverage than nonunion workers, and greater pension wealth than nonunion workers throughout most of the distribution, although the means for the two groups are similar. Government workers have more coverage and greater benefits than nongovernment employees. Pension wealth also increases sharply with total income.[18]

11.4 Distribution of Household Wealth

Inequalities in the distribution of net worth are well known. In this section we compare the distribution of pension wealth to the distribution of net worth and examine the fraction of private wealth comprised by pensions. The discussion thus far has used the individual as the unit of analysis. Because pensions "belong" to an individual this focus is appropriate. However, household net worth is not so easily assigned an owner. Therefore, in order to compare pension wealth to net worth, we aggregate pensions of husbands and wives to create a household total. This aggregation subsumes variation within the household. Comparing pension holdings of husbands and wives we find that in 48 percent of married households both spouses report having a pension, in 37 percent only the husband has pension wealth, in 10 percent neither spouse has a pension, and in just 6 percent of households only the wife has a pension.[19] There is also a positive and significant correlation (0.16) between pension wealth of spouses, although men are likely to have higher pensions. Seventy-eight percent of husbands have pension wealth greater than that of their wives. The median difference between pension wealth of the husband and that of the wife is $51,465.

18. To avoid contaminating the relationship with differences in retirement patterns, income quartiles are measured only for those currently working.

19. These numbers refer to married couples, not to all households as is reported in table 11.1. Married individuals are more likely to have pensions than nonmarried.

Table 11.5   **Comparison of Means of Household Pension Wealth and Net Worth**

Characteristic	Pension Wealth (1)	Net Worth (2)	Private Wealth (1) + (2)	Pension/ Private Wealth (1)/[(1) + (2)]
All households	92,691	159,796	252,486	0.34
Marital status*Sex				
Married couple	123,835	190,046	313,882	0.38
Single male	83,705	127,855	211,560	0.33
Single female	28,549	107,456	136,006	0.26
Race (male in couple)				
White	129,630	206,330	335,960	0.38
Nonwhite	68,420	75,663	144,083	0.34
Schooling (male in couple)				
Less than high school	40,945	74,257	115,202	0.25
High school graduate	79,977	152,059	232,037	0.35
Some college	110,123	173,062	283,186	0.42
College graduate	156,640	317,629	474,269	0.38
Graduate school	229,267	315,096	544,363	0.46
Health status				
Poor	31,152	58,806	89,958	0.21
Fair	50,069	102,650	152,719	0.26
Good	93,348	151,120	244,468	0.35
Very good	111,514	199,972	311,485	0.37
Excellent	133,776	219,167	352,943	0.43
Household income				
Lowest quartile	21,640	68,572	90,212	0.18
2d quartile	56,975	115,926	172,901	0.38
3d quartile	107,414	168,279	275,693	0.41
4th quartile	209,547	319,737	529,284	0.43
Household wealth				
Lowest quartile	23,458	738	24,196	0.36
2d quartile	68,670	51,662	120,332	0.38
3d quartile	125,807	138,446	264,253	0.36
4th quartile	171,982	533,629	705,611	0.24

Notes: Sample consists of households with nonmissing values in all columns and with neither spouse reporting being self-employed on the current job, or on the most recent job if not currently employed. $N = 4,938$. Note that pension wealth is calculated based on the assumption that no pensions are joint and survivorship. Assuming all pensions continue after the pension holder dies increases mean household pension wealth to $110,407.

Table 11.5 reports mean household pension wealth, mean net worth, the sum of the two components (private wealth), and the fraction of private wealth that is due to pensions. It has been observed that low savings rates among some segments of the population may be a result of individuals being "overannuitized" from social security. Low-income workers may be required by social security laws to "save" more than they would like during their lifetimes. The result of this forced savings is that they save little, if anything, elsewhere. Pensions provide a second annuity to most workers. We thus look to see whether low-income/wealth households hold a substantially greater fraction of wealth in pensions than in other assets relative to better-off households.

In the first row, household pension wealth for the entire sample is $92,691.[20] This number is fairly consistent with past studies.[21] The only other study we are aware of that calculates pension wealth using self-reports in the HRS is Smith (1995). He finds mean pension wealth of $104,000 over all households using slightly different assumptions about interest rates, inflation, and survivorship benefits and different life tables. If we assume that all pensions for married individuals are based on their joint life expectancy, our mean pension wealth for the sample increases to $110,407. Gustman et al. (1997) use employer reports of pension benefits for the HRS sample and calculate pension wealth of $116,012, surprisingly similar to our results with employee-reported information. Over nonzero values our household pension wealth values are $137,056 (single life) and $154,134 (joint life), which are similar to the McDermed, Clark, and Allen (1989) estimate from the 1983 Survey of Consumer Finances of $170,703 (converted to 1992 dollars).

The net worth reported in table 11.5 is lower than in some other studies using the HRS. The difference is due to the composition of our sample. We exclude the self-employed from this study of pension wealth. Including those who are self-employed (either currently or in a past job) increases average net worth to $238,336. The change in the medians is smaller, increasing from $72,900 to $81,200 with the inclusion of the self-employed. For comparison with private pensions, we also use reports on expected social security benefits in the HRS to make a rough calculation of social security wealth (not shown). Mean expected social security wealth for the sample is approximately $95,000.[22]

Differences in household pension wealth follow the differences illustrated in table 11.4. Married couples have far more pension wealth than singles, and single females lag greatly behind single men. Note that the difference in net worth between single males and single females is much smaller than the difference in pension wealth. The large fraction of private wealth for single women that is not from pensions may indicate a behavioral response on their part to save more in the absence of pension availability, or it may reflect a lump-sum award at the time of a spouse's death or divorce.[23]

Contrary to evidence of overannuitization presented elsewhere, the ratio of

20. This number is lower than the value for individual pension wealth reported in table 11.4 because table 11.5 includes those with zero pension wealth.

21. An exception is work done with the Retirement History Survey (RHS). Hurd and Shoven (1983) use the 1969 RHS and calculate household pension wealth of $25,403 (converted to 1992 dollars) for a sample with household heads aged 58–63.

22. Gustman et al. (1997) calculate average social security wealth of $116,000.

23. Pension wealth for widows is only $21,570, but their net worth is $104,786 (not shown).

pension wealth to total private wealth is similar for whites (38 percent) and nonwhites (34 percent), although the levels are much greater for whites.[24]

Both pension and nonpension wealth increase with schooling level, but pension wealth increases at a greater rate. Thus the fraction of wealth that is from pensions increases from 25 percent to 46 percent as one moves from the lowest to the highest schooling category.

We might expect unhealthy individuals to have high mortality rates and therefore to wish to have little wealth in an annuity based on average life expectancies. In fact, we see that for those in poor health the fraction of wealth coming from pensions is lower (21 percent) than for those in excellent health (43 percent), although it is also likely that the difference in pension wealth is due to a difference in the jobs held over the individuals' lives.[25]

As in table 11.4, pension wealth increases sharply with household income from $21,640 in the lowest quartile to $209,547 in the highest. Net worth also increases substantially with income quartiles, going from $68,572 to $319,737. Thus the lowest income quartile has only 17 percent of the private wealth (non–social security) of the highest. These patterns are repeated for wealth quartiles.

The differences in pension wealth by sex and marital status shown in table 11.5 are large. We would expect that much of the difference can be attributed to differences in observable characteristics such as occupation, schooling, or lifetime attachment to the labor force. In table 11.6 we control for a number of factors that are likely to be correlated with pension wealth and examine the difference in the probability of being covered by a pension and in the (log) amount of pension wealth conditional on having nonzero wealth.[26] In both cases, even with controls for industry and occupation we continue to see large and significant differences by sex. Men are 6 percentage points more likely to have a pension, and conditional on having a pension, their pension wealth is 42 percent greater than that of women. In table 11.4 the pension wealth of women was less than half that of men. The addition of the other explanatory variables has thus explained a large fraction of the difference. The differences by race are smaller but significantly different from zero. Nonwhites are only 2 percentage points less likely to have a pension than are whites, but the pension wealth of nonwhites is *higher* by 17 percent.

Education beyond a four-year college degree is correlated with a mean increase in pension wealth of 38 percent. Similarly, large differences hold between those in excellent health and those in poor health, although again the differences in the multivariate context are smaller than in the simple cross-

24. We note, however, there is a large difference in the ratio of social security wealth to private wealth for the two groups, with whites having social security wealth equal to 34 percent of private wealth and the figure for nonwhites being 54 percent.

25. Some annuity wealth may be in joint and survivorship plans or in DC accounts, which can be willed to be an heir. No such difference is observed in social security wealth, which is not voluntary.

26. The means of the regression variables are reported in appendix table 11A.2.

Table 11.6 **Probability of Pension Wealth and Amount**

Characteristic	Linear Probability of Pension		Log of Pension Wealth (over positive values)	
	Coefficient	Standard Error	Coefficient	Standard Error
Demographics				
Age	0.006	0.003	−0.013	0.015
Sex (1 = male)	0.062	0.023	0.416	0.092
Race (1 = nonwhite)	−0.019	0.011	0.170	0.045
Married	−0.062	0.015	−0.223	0.064
Number of children	0.005	0.003	−0.016	0.014
Number of children*Sex	−0.007	0.004	0.004	0.018
Schooling				
Less than high school	−0.078	0.013	0.013	0.055
High school graduate (omitted)				
Some college	0.017	0.013	0.093	0.051
College graduate	0.004	0.018	0.111	0.070
Graduate school	0.023	0.020	0.376	0.073
Health status				
Excellent (omitted)				
Very good	0.000	0.012	−0.060	0.048
Good	0.023	0.013	−0.164	0.050
Fair	0.030	0.016	−0.176	0.068
Poor	0.032	0.022	−0.360	0.096
Employment				
Working	0.381	0.199	−1.108	0.908
Part time	−0.081	0.018	0.000	0.081
Government	0.015	0.025	0.350	0.090
Union	0.139	0.011	0.108	0.042
Earnings ($10,000s)	0.003	0.002	0.072	0.011
Tenure (current)	0.000	0.000	0.007	0.002
Tenure (completed)	0.011	0.001	0.041	0.005
Large firm	0.137	0.019	0.359	0.079
Had previous job	−0.014	0.036	0.151	0.173
Hours (current)	0.001	0.001	0.006	0.003
Health insurance (current)	0.196	0.021	0.209	0.108
Health insurance (retiree)	0.016	0.018	0.124	0.068
Household income				
Lowest quartile	−0.073	0.018	−0.376	0.078
2d quartile	−0.013	0.015	−0.302	0.059
3d quartile	−0.010	0.013	−0.196	0.048
4th quartile (omitted)				
Household wealth				
Lowest quartile	−0.051	0.020	−0.433	0.082
2d quartile	0.005	0.014	−0.115	0.056
3d quartile	0.000	0.013	−0.010	0.049
4th quartile (omitted)				
No. of observations	6,212		3,362	
Mean of dependent variable	0.74		10.92 ($53,000)	
R^2	0.37		0.47	

Note: Also included are 12 industry and 16 occupation dummy variables, homeownership dummy, age and work status interactions, tenure on the previous job, and dummy variables for missing values on health insurance, prior tenure, earnings, and firm size.

tabulations in table 11.4. Large differences in pension wealth also persist by union status, government employment, firm size, and the presence of health insurance.

In table 11.7 we examine the entire distribution of household net worth, as well as the sum of net worth and pensions. We note how the distribution of resources changes when pension wealth is included. In row 1 of the top panel we report the fraction of the total net worth of the population that is held by each decile of the wealth distribution. If wealth were distributed equally, each decile would own 10 percent of the wealth. We see here a distribution that is far from equal; over 50 percent of the wealth is held by the top 10 percent of the distribution. The top 30 percent holds 80 percent of the wealth. Net worth is negative for the bottom 10 percent.

Rows 2, 3, and 4 show the distribution of households by sex and marital status. The numbers correspond to the percentage of each type of households in each decile (i.e., the rows sum to 100 percent). For example, 3.4 percent of all married couples have wealth that puts them in the lowest 10 percent of the wealth distribution. For single men the value is 13.4, and for single women, 16.9. Certainly, we would expect couples to have higher wealth than singles if we do not control for household size, but within the population of single individuals we see a substantial difference by sex as well.

Rows 5 and 6 report the distribution by race. A huge fraction, 17.7 percent, of the nonwhite population is in the lowest decile, compared to just 5.4 percent of whites. Only 3.4 percent of nonwhites are in the highest decile, compared to 14.0 percent of whites.

We now ask how pensions affect the distribution of wealth. In the second panel we repeat the same exercise but divide the population of households into deciles based on total private wealth (net worth plus pensions). The overall distribution of wealth holdings by decile is similar, although there is some shifting away from the highest decile. The wealth shifted out of the highest decile increases the portion held by the remaining deciles, thus mitigating an overall measure of inequality. The fraction of wealth held by the bottom 30 percent increases from 0.2 percent to 1.2 percent, while the fraction held by the top 30 percent decreases from 81.7 to 76.5 percent.

As is apparent from several of the tables, a single woman is much less likely to have a pension than either a single man or a couple, and conditional on having a pension, its value is much lower. Examining rows 2, 3, and 4 of each panel we see that pension wealth worsens the inequality faced by single women. The percentage of women in the highest decile falls from 5.3 percent in the first panel to 2.9 percent in the second, a fall of close to 50 percent. The percentage of couples in the highest category increases, and the percentage of single men slightly decreases. Comparing the top and bottom 30 percent, the portion of single women in the bottom 30 percent of the wealth distribution increases from 44.2 to 47.1 percent, while the percentage of single men in that portion of the distribution decreases from 44.3 to 40.9 percent. In the top 30

Table 11.7   Distribution of Household Net Worth and Net Worth Plus Pension Wealth (percentage of total in each decile)

					Decile					
	1	2	3	4	5	6	7	8	9	10
				Net Worth						
1. Net worth	−0.8	0.1	0.9	2.0	3.3	5.1	7.8	10.9	17.9	52.9
Household type										
2. Married	3.4	4.0	7.3	8.1	9.7	11.7	13.2	14.1	13.2	15.3
3. Single male	13.4	17.2	13.7	11.3	10.7	7.7	5.9	4.6	8.8	6.6
4. Single female	16.9	15.2	12.1	11.5	9.0	7.6	7.7	5.7	8.9	5.3
5. White	5.4	6.2	8.2	8.8	9.4	10.2	12.1	11.8	13.9	14.0
6. Nonwhite	17.7	16.6	13.2	11.5	10.5	10.0	6.7	6.8	3.6	3.4
				Net Worth + Pension Wealth						
1. Total net worth + pensions	−0.4	0.3	1.3	2.6	4.3	6.5	9.1	13.0	18.7	44.8
Household type										
2. Married	2.4	4.7	6.7	8.3	9.6	11.8	12.0	13.4	14.6	16.4
3. Single male	16.5	13.6	10.8	10.0	7.1	11.8	8.3	7.6	8.0	6.3
4. Single female	17.2	15.9	14.0	12.0	11.8	6.9	8.4	6.9	3.9	2.9
5. White	4.9	7.0	7.9	8.8	9.7	11.5	11.2	12.2	12.7	14.0
6. Nonwhite	18.9	14.9	13.5	12.0	10.4	7.2	8.2	6.8	4.9	3.3

percent, the fraction of women decreases from 19.9 to 13.7 percent, while the fraction of men increases from 20.0 to 21.9 percent.

Changes in the distribution by race are less dramatic. The portion of non-whites in the bottom 30 percent of the distribution is virtually unchanged, moving from 47.5 to 47.3, while the portion in the top 30 percent increases slightly from 13.8 to 15.0 percent.

11.5   Conclusion

As this paper demonstrates, there is a substantial amount of heterogeneity in pension holdings. Close to 40 percent of the population has no pension wealth, while those in the highest decile have average pension wealth of over $400,000. As the future of the social security system is brought into question, private pensions and wealth holdings become more important. Understanding the distributions of these assets will aid in determining appropriate policy options for the continued public support of the retired population.

Using the new HRS we find patterns of pension holdings that are consistent with earlier studies: Women have less pension wealth than men, and nonwhites have less pension wealth than whites—although the differences by race are slightly smaller than the differences by sex. In addition, workers in unionized jobs and government employees have greater pension coverage and pension wealth than other workers, and more educated workers have more pension wealth than the less educated. We then examine the ratio of pension wealth to total private wealth for subgroups of the population and find large differences between single women and either single men or married couples in the fraction of total wealth coming from pensions, but much smaller differences by race. We demonstrate the relationship between pension wealth and inequality directly and find that single women in particular fare much worse relative to couples when pension wealth is included in the calculation of total wealth, but there is little change in the relative well-being of whites and nonwhites. The paucity of pension holdings among women suggests that their eventual well-being as widows will depend heavily on the resources left after the death of a spouse. Thus the issue of survivorship benefits for pensions will have important consequences for the eventual poverty rates of widows. This will be investigated in future work.

Appendix

The construction of pension wealth for an individual required information on several components of the pension plan including, for example, age at which the individual expected to retire, expected benefit (in monetary terms or as a fraction of final salary), final salary, and so forth. In many cases information was available for most, but not all, of these items. Rather than discard any observation with even a single missing data point, we imputed missing values for these questions. The imputations were based on linear regression models with the following regressors: age, race, sex, marital status, tenure on current job (or completed tenure for past jobs), schooling, homeownership, income and wealth (in quartiles), 12 industry dummy variables, and 16 occupation dummy variables. There was also a set of regressors used in a subset of imputation equations. For example, in the equation used to predict firm contributions to DC plans, individual contributions (when known) were used. The R^2 for these regressions ranged from a low of 0.14 to a high of 0.76. Excluding observations with imputed values from the calculations in the paper did not alter any of the conclusions but did result in consistently higher estimates for pension wealth.

Table 11A.1 lists the more important variables for which we imputed values, the number of values imputed, and the number of valid responses that were used to estimate the imputation equation.

Table 11A.1   **Impution of Variables**

Variable Name	Number of Valid Responses	Number of Imputed Responses	R^2
Defined benefit plans			
Expected benefit	1,450	1,228	0.75
Age expect to receive benefits	2,455	241	0.40
Defined contribution plans			
Balance in account	1,061	427	0.22
Individual contribution	1,263	184	0.15
Firm contribution	886	553	0.14
Age expect to receive benefits	1,061	427	0.22

Table 11A.2   Means of Regression Variables ($n = 7,837$)

Characteristic	Mean	Standard Error
Demographics		
Age	55.88	0.036
Sex (1 = male)	0.45	0.006
Race (1 = nonwhite)	0.30	0.005
Married	0.73	0.005
Number of children	3.27	0.024
Number of children*Sex	1.41	0.024
Schooling		
Less than high school	0.29	0.005
High school graduate	0.36	0.005
Some college	0.18	0.004
College graduate	0.08	0.003
Graduate school	0.09	0.003
Health status		
Excellent	0.21	0.005
Very good	0.28	0.005
Good	0.28	0.005
Fair	0.14	0.004
Poor	0.08	0.003
Employment		
Working	0.70	0.005
Part time	0.41	0.005
Government	0.05	0.003
Union	0.25	0.005
Earnings	19,476	320
Tenure (current)	11.68	0.144
Tenure (completed)	2.42	0.082
Large firm	0.43	0.006
Had previous job	0.53	0.006
Hours (current)	40.10	0.134
Health insurance		
(current)	0.393	0.006
Health insurance (retiree)	0.277	0.005
Household finances		
Income in 1991	47,902	483
Wealth in 1991	184,748	4,389

References

Allen, Steven, Robert Clark, and Daniel Sumner. 1986. Postretirement adjustments of pension benefits. *Journal of Human Resources* 21:118–37.

Bloom, David E., and Richard B. Freeman. 1992. The fall in private pension coverage in the United States. *American Economic Review* 80:539–45.

Even, William E., and David A. Macpherson. 1990. The gender gap in pensions and wages. *Review of Economics and Statistics* 72:259–65.

————. 1994a. Gender differences in pensions. *Journal of Human Resources* 29: 555–87.

————. 1994b. Why did male pension coverage decline in the 1980s? *Industrial and Labor Relations Review* 47:439–53.

Grad, Susan. 1996. *Income of the population 55 or older, 1994.* Washington, D.C.: Government Printing Office.

Gustman, Alan, Olivia Mitchell, Andrew Samwick, and Thomas Steinmeier. 1997. Pension and social security wealth in the Health and Retirement Study. NBER Working Paper no. 5912. Cambridge, Mass.: National Bureau of Economic Research.

Hurd, Michael D., and Kathleen McGarry. 1995. Evaluation of the subjective probabilities of survival in the Health and Retirement Study. *Journal of Human Resources* 30 (Suppl.) S7–S56.

Hurd, Michael D., and John B. Shoven. 1983. The economic status of the elderly. In *Financial aspects of the United States pension system,* ed. Zvi Bodie and John Shoven, 359–93. Chicago: University of Chicago Press.

Juster, F. Thomas, and Richard Suzman. 1995. An overview of the Health and Retirement Study. *Journal of Human Resources* 30 (Suppl.) S7–S56.

Kotlikoff, Laurence J., and Daniel Smith. 1983. *Pensions in the American economy.* Chicago: University of Chicago Press.

McDermed, Ann A., Robert L. Clark, and Steven G. Allen. 1989. Pension wealth, age-wealth profiles, and the distribution of net worth. In *The measurement of saving, investment, and wealth,* ed. Robert E. Lipsey and Helen Stone Tice, 689–731. Chicago: University of Chicago Press.

McGarry, Kathleen. 1998. Caring for the elderly: Findings from the Asset and Health Dynamics Survey. In *Inquiries in the economics of aging,* ed. David A. Wise. Chicago: University of Chicago Press.

McGarry, Kathleen, and Andrew Davenport. 1996. Pensions and the distribution of wealth. Los Angeles: University of California. Mimeograph.

Munnell, Alicia H., and Ann M. Connolly. 1979. Comparability of public and private compensation: The issues of fringe benefits. *New England Economic Review,* July/August, 27–45.

Murphy, Kevin M., and Finis Welch. 1990. Empirical age-earnings profiles. *Journal of Labor Economics* 8:202–29.

Quinn, Joseph F. 1982. Pension wealth of government and private sector workers. *American Economic Review* 72:283–87.

Smith, James P. 1995. Racial and ethnic differences in wealth in the Health and Retirement Study. *Journal of Human Resources* 30 (Suppl.): S158–S183.

Social Security Administration. 1990. *Social security bulletin annual statistical supplement.* Washington, D.C.: U.S. Department of Health and Human Services.

Turner, John A. 1988. Pension survivors insurance for widows. *Economic Inquiry* 26:403–22.

Turner, John A., and Daniel Beller. 1992. *Trends in pensions 1992.* Washington, D.C.: U.S. Department of Labor.

Contributors

Alan J. Auerbach
Department of Economics
549 Evans Hall
University of California, Berkeley
Berkeley, CA 94720

Harish Chand
Department of Economics
549 Evans Hall #3880
University of California, Berkeley
Berkeley, CA 94720

David M. Cutler
NBER
1050 Massachusetts Avenue
Cambridge, MA 02138

Andrew Davenport
Department of Economics
University of California
Los Angeles, CA 90024

Angus Deaton
221 Bendheim Hall
Princeton University
Princeton, NJ 08544

Matthew J. Eichner
612 Uris Hall
Graduate School of Business
Columbia University
New York, NY 10027

Li Gan
Department of Economics
549 Evans Hall #3880
University of California, Berkeley
Berkeley, CA 94720

Alan M. Garber
NBER
204 Junipero Serra Boulevard
Stanford, CA 94305

Michael D. Hurd
RAND Corporation
1700 Main Street
Santa Monica, CA 90407

Thomas J. Kane
Kennedy School of Government
Harvard University
79 Kennedy Street
Cambridge, MA 02138

David Laibson
Department of Economics
Harvard University
Littauer M-14
Cambridge, MA 02138

Ronald Lee
Demography and Economics
2232 Piedmont Avenue
University of California, Berkeley
Berkeley, CA 94720

487

Thomas MaCurdy
Department of Economics
Stanford University
Stanford, CA 94305

Mark McClellan
Department of Economics
Stanford University
Stanford, CA 94305

Daniel McFadden
Department of Economics
549 Evans Hall #3880
University of California, Berkeley
Berkeley, CA 94707

Kathleen McGarry
Department of Economics
UCLA
405 Hilgard Avenue
Los Angeles, CA 90024

Ellen Meara
112 School Street
Somerville, MA 02143

David Meltzer
Section of General Internal Medicine
University of Chicago
5841 S. Maryland, MC 6098
Chicago, IL 60637

Angela Merrill
Health Services and Policy Analysis
140 Warren Hall #32
School of Public Health
Berkeley, CA 94720

Christina Paxson
219 Bendheim Hall
Princeton University
Princeton, NJ 08544

James M. Poterba
Department of Economics
MIT, E52-350
Cambridge, MA 02139

Michael Roberts
Department of Economics
549 Evans Hall #3880
University of California, Berkeley
Berkeley, CA 94720

Sylvester J. Schieber
Watson Wyatt & Company
Research and Information Center
6707 Democracy Blvd., Suite 800
Bethesda, MD 20817

John B. Shoven
Dean's Office of Humanities and
    Sciences
Building One
Stanford University
Stanford, CA 94305

James P. Smith
RAND Corporation
1700 Main Street, Box 2138
Santa Monica, CA 90406

Shripad Tuljapurkar
Mountain View Research
2251 Grant Road
Los Altos, CA 94024

Steven F. Venti
Department of Economics
6106 Rockefeller Center
Dartmouth College
Hanover, NH 03755

David A. Wise
NBER
1050 Massachusetts Avenue
Cambridge, MA 02138

Author Index

Subject Index

Accumulation. *See* Assets, accumulation for retirement; Estate tax; Excise tax; 401(k) plans; Income tax; Individual retirement accounts (IRAs); Pension accumulation; Tax Reform Act (1986)

Activities of daily living (ADLs): as measure of function, 433; relation of elderly problems to, 434–35

Advisory Council on Social Security (1994–96): Technical Panel on Assumptions and Methods, 420–21

Age schedules: payroll tax and benefits (1994), 402–4; with productivity growth, 405

AHEAD panel study. *See* Asset and Health Dynamics among the Oldest Old (AHEAD)

Anchoring: biases induced by, 14–15, 356–57, 387; model for, 363–65

Asset allocation: 401(k) plans, 168f, 171–72; taxation differences influence holdings inside and outside pension plans, 205–9

Asset and Health Dynamics among the Oldest Old (AHEAD), 15, 354, 358; anchoring experiment in, 365–68; nonresponse follow-up using unfolding brackets, 365–68, 372–79

Assets, accumulation for retirement: comparison among saver groups, 40–44; comparison within saver groups, 36–40; estate and excise tax on pension, 174–75; excess accumulation and distribution, 176–81; with or without 401(k) eligibility, 4–5, 44–50, 97t, 100–103t; inheritance from pension plan or conventional saving, 196–201; investment in bonds using pension plan or conventional saving, 187–91; investment in bonds with one-time contribution and withdrawal, 194–95; investment in stocks using pension plan or conventional saving, 191–94; investment in stocks with one-time contribution and withdrawal, 195–96; projected 401(k), 144–55, 170–72; in retirement plans of persons in different age cohorts, 50–55; taxation of assets inside and outside of pension plan, 205–9

Baltimore Longitudinal Study of Aging, 458

Behavior: effect of health events on, 302–3; influence of channel factors on, 110–11

Behavioral economics: behavioral principles, 109–10; insights related to IRA-401(k), 108–11; perspective of, 107

Beneficiaries: characteristics of Medicare, 251–52; liability related to pension accumulation, 180

Benefits (social security): age schedules of received, 401–4; with productivity growth, 405–8

Body-mass index (BMI): correlation between family income and, 445–47; correlation with health outcomes, 435–36; data for, 17–19, 433; percentiles by age of male and female, 440–41